In commemoration of

Alabama Power Company's Centennial

1906–2006

"Developed for the Service of Alabama"

THE CENTENNIAL HISTORY OF THE ALABAMA POWER COMPANY

1906–2006

Leah Rawls Atkins

Leah Rawls Atkins

1-31-2007

Alabama Power's first dam, William Patrick Lay Dam
at Lock 12 site on the Coosa River, constructed in 1913.

Published by
Alabama Power Company
600 Eighteenth Street North
Birmingham, Alabama 35291

Design and layout
Laura Borgman Pitts
Graphic Design Group, Alabama Power

Library of Congress Control Number: 2006932980

International Standard Book Number (ISBN)
0-9786753-0-4
978-0-9786753-0-1

Printed in the United States of America
1st printing

William Patrick Lay
(1853–1940)
President, 1906–1912

James Mitchell
(1866–1920)
President, 1912–1913
and 1915–1920

Thomas W. Martin
(1881–1964)
President, 1920–1949

I now commit to you the good name and destiny of Alabama Power Company. May it be developed for the service of Alabama.

WILLIAM PATRICK LAY

A new Alabama and a new South, no longer poor but proud; a South coming into its rightful place; a South that would retain all the finest traditions of its glorious past but which, through that mysterious force flowing silently through the thousands of miles of transmission lines, like life-blood to the human body, would grow richer and stronger industrially, and because of this would in turn grow stronger agriculturally. And the chain lengthens. Not only would ordinary creature comforts follow in the wake of electricity, but there would be better educational facilities, better roads, and better homes. To make money is all right. To build any industry is fine. To build an industry that saves mankind from toil that it can well be spared, that reduces the labor and drudgery of women and so provides leisure for education and culture, truly is a much finer thing.

JAMES MITCHELL
THOMAS W. MARTIN
May 1, 1912, Montgomery, Alabama

Construction crew
erecting a steel
transmission tower
in the Mobile River
Delta, 1926.

Contents

Artist's drawing of entrance
to 1925 corporate office
building, 1926.

Lay Dam powerhouse crew,
ca. 1920.

MORE THAN ELECTRICITY

*History is actually a bridge connecting the past with the present,
and pointing the road to the future.*

ALLAN NEVINS, *The Gateway to History*, 1962

Leading a company that is 100 years old is rather daunting. Realizing that
you have been part of the life of that company for half a century is downright
scary. I was two years old when my father went to work for Alabama Power,
so I do not know anything else. I grew up in an Alabama Power family. And I
am not alone.

Alabama Power families take pride in having generations work for the
company—grandfathers, uncles, fathers, mothers, brothers, sisters. We do not
call that nepotism; we call it a way of life. And it is an important way we pass
the culture of the company from one generation to another.

But even if you are not related by blood or marriage, there is still a kinship, a common bond, that exists between all Alabama Power employees. When you work for Alabama Power, it is understood that your job involves more than providing electricity. It is understood that you also have a responsibility to live up to certain standards and maintain a tremendous legacy.

The American historian Allan Nevins observed that when we think of history, we should not just think of the past, "for history is actually a bridge connecting the past with the present, and pointing the road to the future."

That is certainly the case with Alabama Power. When we asked Alabama historian Dr. Leah Rawls Atkins to write Alabama Power's history to commemorate our centennial, it was primarily to ensure that our employees understood the struggles and adversities the company has overcome, the contributions it has made to the state and its people, and, perhaps most importantly, the character and commitment of its founders.

Our founders, William Patrick Lay, James Mitchell, and Thomas W.

Martin, were men of vision and principle. Their basic values and philosophies continue to guide Alabama Power today.

We are enormously proud of our history and heritage, but I must confess that I initially wondered if anyone outside the Alabama Power family would have even the slightest interest in reading this book.

But as I have read Leah's words, I have realized that, just as all Alabama Power employees share a common bond, our company is forever linked with the people and the state it serves. Alabama Power's founders did not just build a company, they helped revolutionize Alabama's economy and changed the day-to-day lives of all its citizens. Although we take it for granted today, electricity isn't just another product. It is essential to our way of life. Alabama Power founders understood the responsibility that comes with providing such a service and truly believed that it is an honor and privilege to provide electricity to the people of Alabama. Those sentiments remain our focus at Alabama Power today.

It is a privilege to be able to share our history with you as we celebrate 100 years of service. We knew we had a good story to tell, but we could never have imagined what a remarkable experience telling it would be. Having Leah Atkins at our company for the past three years has been an honor and a pleasure. Leah has enlightened us, inspired us and, although she claims her work with us is through, she will forever be a beloved member of the Alabama Power family.

Charles D. McCrary
President and CEO
October 2006

Alabama Power crews on
the way to restore service.

Lake Martin, June 2006.

RUNNING WITH GOOD PEOPLE

There is nothing new in the world except the history you do not know.

HARRY S. TRUMAN, *Mr. President,* 1952

General histories of the twentieth-century American South pay little attention to hydroelectricity, steam generation, and an integrated transmission and distribution power system as factors in the economic development of the region, especially in the first two decades of the century. Histories of Alabama have also neglected to appreciate the connection between abundant and inexpensive hydroelectricity and industrial development in the state. When Alabama Power Company is mentioned at all in these studies, it is usually in the context of a Big Mule with powerful political influences, not in relation to electricity improving the quality of people's lives or to providing cheap and reliable hydroelectric and steam-generated central station power to spur economic development; not in relation to providing opportunities for average Alabamians to save for retirement years through stock purchases and dividends or to changing the geographical face of the state by creating lakes for recreational boating and fishing.

C. Vann Woodward's classic *Origins of the New South, 1877–1913*, volume nine in the Louisiana State University Press series *A History of the South*, ends its coverage of the development of the South with the year Alabama Power Company's first dam was completed. Woodward mentions cheap waterpower as one reason textile mills moved to the South in the last decades of the nineteenth century; but he fails to make note of William Church Whitner's two hydroelectric dams constructed in South Carolina in 1895 and 1897, Duke Power's 1904 hydroelectric dam on the Catawba River, or the importance of Alabama Power's 1913 Coosa River dam to the state's industrial development.[1] Alabama had an abundant supply of appropriate sites for the location of hydroelectric dams because of its many rivers and a fall line that cuts diagonally across the state. The recruitment of industries to Alabama in the early decades of the twentieth century was encouraged by the coming of central station power first offered by Alabama Traction, Light & Power Company, a Canadian holding company that funneled English investment capital into Alabama Power Company. Previously no one in the state had been able to attract Wall Street investors or capital from any other place to fund hydroelectric projects in Alabama. This may well have been one result of the regional economic competition prevalent in the period.

George Brown Tindall, who wrote the next volume in the *History of the South* series, *The Emergence of the New South, 1913–1945*, spends little time on the advance of electricity in the region and fails to appreciate the connections between the economic development of the South and the investments of private investor-owned power companies. Tindall did note that the southern states possessed "an estimated potential of 5,550,000 horsepower in their rivers, more than a third of the waterpower available 90 percent of the time east of the Rockies." He does briefly discuss James B. Duke and William S. Lee's organization of the electric industry in North Carolina, then moves to Alabama, where he confuses the development of the Alabama Power Company and neglects to cover Southeastern Power & Light and its significance.[2] The two most recent studies of Alabama, *Alabama: The History of a Deep South State* and *Alabama in the Twentieth Century*, ignore the development of the state's hydroelectric dams and transmission grids in analyzing the state's economic growth and development, although the latter does mention the Coosa dams as contributing to the extinction of some species that once lived in the free-flowing river and praises Alabama Power's leadership in establishing the Economic Development Partnership of Alabama in 1991.[3]

Perhaps the reason many historians of the twentieth-century South and of Alabama have not fully assessed the contributions of electrical companies like Alabama Power is because, as Texas Christian University history professor D. Clayton Brown wrote in his review of Duke Power Company's history, "academic historians generally shun official histories. They see them as biased and sterilized accounts devoid of critical analysis, puffed-up stories of little significance that feature recollections more appropriately confined to corporate annual reports."[4] No history of Alabama or of the economic development of the New Deal South would fail to cover the influence of the Tennessee Valley Authority, yet Alabama Power Company has had a more sustained impact upon Alabama and has improved the quality of the lives of more people in the state for a longer period of time than has TVA. In 1920, well before Franklin D. Roosevelt's New Deal formed a federally subsidized rural electrification program by executive order in 1935, Alabama Power completed construction of its first rural line, which was in northern Alabama in Madison County.

In 1987, when he was director of the Center for Southern History and Culture at the University of Alabama, historian Robert J. Norrell wrote that "I have come to believe from several years' research on the history of Alabama's industrialization that the Power Company's development is the single most important corporate history in twentieth-century Alabama."[5] I wholeheartedly agree with Professor Norrell, who now holds a distinguished chair in history at the University of Tennessee. In writing history, historians try to re-create the past as best they can, but even given the extensive corporate archives of Alabama Power, not all the documents survive to tell all the story and never are all the questions answered. Shelby Foote, the novelist known for his brilliant history of the American Civil War, was once quoted as saying that "narrative history is the kind that comes closest to telling the truth. You can never get to the truth, but that's your goal."[6] Recent history should be easy to re-create accurately, but documents are often scattered, have not been saved, or are sensitive, and the telephone and e-mail have replaced formal letters. The flow of events too often relies upon memory, and our memories of single events are not always alike. Then, too, there can be no interpretation of what happened, because no time has passed for us to analyze the effects, failures, and successes. Any history brought to the present changes its tone toward the end and becomes more a survey of current events than interpretative history.

This centennial history of the Alabama Power Company could not have been written without the help and assistance of many people. The commitment and support of Alabama Power Company's president and CEO Charles D. McCrary were essential, and his enthusiasm for the project gave me the energy to press onward. He read chapters as the manuscript progressed, corrected my errors, gave me subjects I had missed, and suggested people to interview. Former president Elmer Harris first asked me to write this book, but in 2001 I was occupied with another project, and by the time that was completed in the fall of 2002, the task seemed too daunting in the short time necessary to make the centennial date of 2006. But longtime friend Rod Mundy was the one who convinced me I needed to write this book. Rod was my contact person throughout the process. He read drafts of the manuscript, was always helpful in explaining complicated legal questions of federal and state regulation, and gave me good advice on content matters. As the project went forward, Elmer found time from his retirement activities to spend hours with me talking about Alabama Power, arranged interviews for me, and had his former assistant Doris Ingram help me search through his filing cabinets for historical materials. Glenda Harris explained the early development of the Alabama Power Service Organization.

As I began my research, I found the story of Alabama Power much richer than I had imagined. It is an important part of the history of the state of Alabama, and I am pleased I agreed to do it. I would not have undertaken this project without the commitment of Joe Farley to help me. I am especially indebted to him for all the time he spent going over the history of Alabama Power with me and talking about the company's people. He lived his life with Alabama Power and with Southern Company, and he willingly shared his knowledge, reading and correcting my drafts, making suggestions, and helping me interpret and find sources. He spent hours listening to my questions and helping me solve the riddles I found in the company's past. Scholars normally work alone, but Joe was very much part of my voyage of discovery into the corporate records and my struggle to interpret what they meant. He went to great lengths to find obscure documents and a few times during the research and writing of this manuscript, in an odd serendipity, files of pertinent Alabama Power historical materials simply appeared somewhere in the Balch & Bingham law firm and amazingly made their way to Joe Farley's desk, no doubt aided in their journey by his assistant Donna Collier.

Eason Balch Sr. and Jack Bingham have lived much of this Alabama Power history. Their keen minds and recall of events amazed me, and they were very kind to take my night and weekend calls to clarify a point or give me additional information on something about which I was writing. Jack's father is

Chester A. Bingham, who was one of the first attorneys Thomas W. Martin hired to research property titles to land that would be flooded behind the first Coosa River dam, now Lay Dam. The elder Bingham became a trusted officer of Southeastern Power & Light Company and lived for some time in New York representing Southeastern Power's and Alabama Power's interests. Eason went to work for Judge Logan Martin's law firm in 1948 and soon after became involved with Alabama Power's legal issues. I used Eason's old office next to the corporate archives, and he shared with me his collection of power company historical materials, once locating a valuable government document I needed. Without his help it would have taken me much longer to finish the manuscript. Eason and Jack spent hours with me sharing stories of people and events. Both reviewed the manuscript, for which I am very grateful. Walter Baker read drafts of chapters, did some editing, talked to me about the people of the company with whom he worked for over four decades, and he helped me understand his life's work in marketing. Samuel Heys of Southern Company did video interviews with Joe Farley, Bill Whitt, Eason Balch, and Jack Bingham in 1998 and 1999, and I appreciate his sharing copies of the transcriptions with me. Wilbur "Dub" Taft, who is writing a history of Southern Company, was kind to answer my queries.

Billy Ward, Harold Williams, Ollie Smith, and Judge John C. Tyson III told me about Thomas W. Martin and Alabama Power. My daily companion and guide to the company's records was corporate archivist Bill Tharpe, who amazed me with his knowledge and his ability to find the most trivial information I was seeking. He has a strong appreciation for the company's history and a proper sense of guardianship of its records. I am most grateful for his guidance and friendship and especially for his reading drafts of the manuscript, selecting the photographs and illustrations, and compiling the appendixes for this book. Mary S. Miller, a librarian in South Carolina, has been fascinated by the Muscle Shoals controversy for perhaps two decades, and I am grateful for her willingness to share her expertise and discuss her research with me. When her history of the Shoals is published, it will shed new light on our understanding of how this drama was part of the history of American chemical corporations and the larger picture of southern industrial development. She will surely think my treatment of Muscle Shoals is sketchy and incomplete and will no doubt disagree with some of my conclusions, but I leave to her to tell the definitive story of the Shoals.

Dorothy Green looked after me, explained who people were, found telephone numbers and addresses, helped me with copying drafts, kept my printer printing, mailed chapters to the editors, compiled the index, and was a dear friend, making me feel at home in the months after I arrived at the corporate office. I am grateful to Elaine Kwarcinski, who found the right people to give me the information I needed, especially when I moved into the more recent period. Vicki Grimsley took a special interest in this project, managed to slip me in to see a very busy CEO when I needed to ask a question, and helped me in many ways. Vicki and Jane Hawkins, on one glorious fall day, took me for my first ride in an Alabama-manufactured M-class Mercedes and on my first visit to Smith Lake and a tour of the dam. For one who has loved the Warrior River since 1939 when I learned to swim in its waters, the trip was especially meaningful. I am grateful for their friendship as well as the excellent interviews I had that day with retired company employees who were part of the early history of the dam. Debbie Self, Karen Bryant, Sandra Hight, Ellen Jenkins, Tabby Keahey, Kathey Washington, Bena Marino, Anita Baker, Myrtle Bell, and Kay Barrett helped me find material and arranged appointments. Sylvia Smith, Mike Wilkerson, Greg Anderson, Tracey Glover, Clara Hopper, and Terry Henderson at the Print Shop helped with duplicating drafts of the manuscript for readers to review. When I first arrived at Alabama Power, Reggie Eady set up my office; Ken Lee kept my computer working; and Wardell Morris made certain my little refrigerator was stocked with cold drinks for my guests. Anji Perrymon could answer any question I had and helped visitors find me. I appreciate their support.

Growing up on the Warrior River, I knew about Gorgas, but I had never visited it until Michael Sznajderman took me on a tour. Walking through the abandoned 1928 powerhouse with its ancient generators and rusting boilers was a powerful trip into history and spoke volumes about the technological revolution in generation. I could almost see the ghosts of men working in overalls and soft felt hats. Comparing in my mind the historical photographs I had so often seen in the archives to the sights I saw was overwhelming, especially my visit to the roof of the plant, looking at the river and the hills of Walker County where workers' cottages once stood and seeing the massive pollution control equipment recently installed. Buddy Eiland, a former undergraduate student of mine at Auburn more years ago than either of us care to recall, took me, Bill Tharpe, Chuck Chandler, and Michael Sznajderman on tours of the Coosa and Tallapoosa dams. I learned much about Alabama Power and its people on these long car rides over winding hill country roads and much about hydro generation on the dam tours.

Jerry Stewart and Jane Hawkins drove me one stormy day to Martin Dam, where Jerry had a meeting and Jane had arranged for me to meet with several people who shared their memories of growing up in the Martin Dam community and working at the dam. I am grateful to both of them for helping me understand the work of generation and the wonderful people who labor so hard—and so safely—to make it happen. Jeff Roper and William A. Tidwell took me to the Bessemer Angle where I could see and trace the transmission lines coming from Lay Dam to Magella substation and see the original lines over Red Mountain that supplied power to the Tennessee Coal, Iron and Railroad Company. The changes in pole and line technology were striking even to a historian. We rode over Red Mountain toward Brighton, and although the old Alabama Power Brighton substation had long since been replaced, we were able to locate the area where J. L. Vick's Alabama Power crew ran a line to the Tennessee Valley Authority substation in March 1960 to supply power to Bessemer after an ice storm took down TVA's transmission lines from Guntersville in a dozen places on Sand Mountain.

There are many people to whom I am grateful for sharing their Alabama Power experiences and their names are in the notes; however, I owe special gratitude to some who spoke with me many times—John Farley, Walter Baker, Walter Johnsey, Bruce Jones, Jim Miller, John Burks, Bill McDonough, Gibson Lanier, David Cooper, Zeke Smith, Banks Farris, Bruce Hutchins, Willard Bowers, and especially the division vice presidents, Ronnie Smith, Cheryl Thompson, Mike Saxon, Gerald Johnson, Gordon Martin, Marsha Johnson, Terry Waters, and Julia Segars. Jim Noles, who has a pictorial history of Alabama Power in the Arcadia series, took a special interest in the project, as did Mac Beale, Matt Bowden, Will Hill Tankersley, Mike Freeman, and Dan McCrary who shared special expertise. Doug McCrary gave me a copy of his long memoir, and I found his stories of Alabama Power interesting and very useful. For many years Jim Clements has spent Tuesday afternoons in the archives patiently clipping articles from *Powergrams* and creating biographical files on the company's people. I went to these files many times to clarify when someone began working at the company, was promoted, or retired. I especially appreciate Jack Minor, Chris Conway, and Steve Bradley for sharing their memories of the company's past and lending me their personal historical collections of the power company. Gibson Lanier opened his extensive archives of rate case files, and he read the rate case sections of the manuscript. Steve Spencer, Chris Bell, Robin Hurst, Mike Scott, Alan Martin, Art Beattie, Bill Johnson, Zeke Smith, and Bob Waters were just some of many who helped me understand Alabama Power. Robin served as my unofficial technical adviser. I appreciate Mark Crosswhite reading page proofs. There are many more names in the notes, and I thank them all and those I have neglected to mention for their help, too. I must confess, as with any recent corporate history, some of the best stories I heard remain part of the oral tradition of the company.

Sherie Mattox, Dawn Anderson, and Arnita Hines of Alabama Power's research services and library helped me find books, theses, and articles on interlibrary loan, searched data bases on the Web and newspaper indexes to which I had no access, purchased books for the library that I needed to read, and contacted other utility research specialists to find materials I wanted. I thank them for their support and interest. The research assistants at Balch & Bingham's library, Kathryn Kerchof, Martha Gabel, and Carolee Granquist, amazed me at what they were able to locate, especially Carolee, who found James Mitchell's grandchildren for me. After Tom Martin's death, Alabama Power lost touch with Mitchell's two children, who were both deceased when I began my research in 2003. I first spoke with Mitchell's great-granddaughter, Nadejda Stancioff Mishkovsky, who put me in touch with her father Peter and the rest of family.

I am most grateful to James Mitchell's grandchildren for their interest in this book. Ivan (Johnny) Stancioff sent me a copy of the autobiography of Carolyn Marion Mitchell Stancioff's husband. Peter mailed me copies of clippings and letters. Anne Stancioff Muheim and Nadia (Bamby) Stancioff and their brother Andrew retrieved all of their grandfather's surviving personal papers from Anne's home in Avignon, France, where they had been stored since the death of their mother in 1992. Andrew brought them back to his home in Washington, D.C., and shipped them to Birmingham for my use. James Mitchell's correspondence with his wife during the early years of his development of Alabama Power Company gives a personal side to his struggle to bring electricity to Alabama and keep his company solvent. I appreciate all the Stancioff family for their interest in and their support of this book and for their permission to use this material.

In early 2006 Joan Henderson Warbis went online from her home in Canada after promising her husband she would find a place for her grandfather's collection of papers relating to his work with James Mitchell, Alabama Traction, Light & Power Company, and Alabama Power Company beginning in 1912 when he was an accountant in Montreal. Warbis found a recent *Birmingham News* article about the company's centennial and her e-mail to the reporter was forwarded to Bill Tharpe. She mailed her Henderson collection to Alabama Power. Before her box of materials arrived, there was no photograph in the corporate archives of William J. Henderson, who was treasurer of Alabama Traction and a member of the board of directors of Alabama Power from 1917 to 1930. She also had copies of the two checks to the U.S. government that her grandfather had signed to pay for unit 2 at the Warrior Reserve Steam Plant (Gorgas). I am grateful to her for her contribution.

The University of Alabama Libraries were valuable for books and for their government documents collection, and Janet DeForest helped me locate those I needed. Clark Center, curator at the W. Stanley Hoole Special Collections Library, and his staff were very helpful in finding manuscripts, papers, and books. Elizabeth C. Wells located valuable materials in the Special Collections Department of Samford University's Davis Library. Joyce Hicks and Dwayne Cox at Auburn University's Special Collections and Yvonne Crumpler and Jim Baggett at Birmingham Public Library were most helpful. The staff at the Alabama Department of Archives and History, especially director Ed Bridges, Norwood Kerr, Rickie Brunner, Frazine Taylor, Mike Breedlove, Nancy Dupree, Willie Maryland, Mark Palmer, Cynthia Luckie, and Debbie Pendleton, were gracious and generous sharing their professional expertise on Alabama documents and manuscripts. Susan M. Catlett of Old Dominion University sent me copies of the George Wallace–Henry Howell correspondence. Judith Kirsch, researcher at the Benson Ford Research Center, mailed me copies of correspondence between Henry Ford's secretary E. G. Liebold and J. W. Worthington, and Saundra Taylor of the Lilly Library, Indiana University, Bloomington, had the Thomas W. Martin–Wendell Willkie letters duplicated for my use. I appreciate the help given me by the staff of the Manuscripts and Rare Books Library of Emory University, especially Anne Sinkey, Kathy Shoemaker, and Naomi Nelson.

The friends I made at Alabama Power's public relations department and the centennial committee were supportive in every way, especially Sheila Garrett, Carla Roberson, Carrie Kurlander, and Howard Torch. Bobbie Knight, Betsy Shearron, Robert Holmes, and Walter Heglar read all or parts of the manuscript. Shirley Gibbs found press releases, and Janice Guthrie did a lot of copying for me. I am grateful to Sharon Simmons for editing the index, copying, and helping with important last details before printing.

The beautiful design of the book is a result of the talents of Laura Borgman Pitts of the graphics department at Alabama Power. Laura did all the layouts and was patient with editorial corrections. Clyde Adams helped her scanning photographs, and Marjorie Strickland assisted in converting my copy to Laura's computer. I especially appreciate the work of Jay Lamar, who read the first draft, and Michael Sznajderman and Chuck Chandler, who so carefully read the page proofs and corrected my mistakes. Beverly Denbow did the final editorial work. Beverly has been a freelance editor for the University of Alabama Press for almost thirty years. She recalled that her first refrigerator was purchased from Alabama Power Company after she moved to Tuscaloosa from Pennsylvania. The book is edited using the University of Chicago Press's

Chicago Manual of Style, 14th edition, which has less capitalization and fewer commas than readers may be used to seeing. I am grateful to the many other people who read all or parts of the manuscript to weed out errors, but any mistakes that remain are my responsibility.

When I first began researching this centennial history of Alabama Power Company, I knew three things about electricity. When I flicked a switch, lights worked, I was happy, and my life was made easier. When I turned a switch and nothing happened, I was not happy. And from experience, I knew I did not like to be shocked, that electricity was dangerous, and that it should be treated with great respect. Today I have an appreciation of just how many people must do hundreds of jobs to make certain that I have electricity at my command. I have an understanding of the enormous amount of capital that is required to provide the capacity to generate enough electricity so I can turn on every electrical appliance, gadget, computer, business machine, and motor in my home and still have the electricity I require. And when it is raining, I now think not of a dreary day but of water flowing into rivers and the electricity that is being generated. Company engineers have patiently explained generation, transmission, and distribution to me. I have visited dams wearing my hard hat; and with earplugs in I have watched the turbines whirl. I have walked through hot steam plants in awe of those boilers and generators and read the WARNING! DANGER! signs that made me realize how hazardous this place really was and gave me great appreciation for the work of men and women who make certain the plants operate safely and efficiently.

On August 15, 2003, when I was driving through the hills of the Tallapoosa Valley where James Mitchell first had his dream of an integrated power system for Alabama, David Kestenbaum, the science correspondent of National Public Radio, was beginning an interview on the subject of the August 14 northeast power outage that sent Toronto, Detroit, New York, and places in between into a "cascading, uncontrollable outage."[7] The expert commented to Kestenbaum that "running an electrical transmission system was three parts knowledge and one part magic. You know how it works, but there is still the magic." For me, electricity will always be part magic.

In December 2003 the *Birmingham News* featured an Associated Press story about the problems of electrical supply in Changsha, China, the city of Mao Zedong's birth. The booming economy of southern China had outstripped the supply of electricity, and citizens endured the uncertainty of rolling blackouts. One woman avoided riding elevators lest a sudden power outage leave her trapped. Government planners admitted that "it could be years before supply catches up with demand."[8] This article gave me a greater appreciation of private enterprise capitalism and of Alabama Power Company's constant planning throughout the twentieth century to make certain it anticipated growth and that its capacity stayed ahead of demand so that Alabama's industry and its citizens would always have the reliable power they needed.

Eighteen months into this project, my husband and I celebrated our fiftieth wedding anniversary. At that point, I realized that for over half the years of this centennial history (except for a few months when we lived out of state), we had written a check each month to Alabama Power Company and that my family was part of this history, as were millions of other Alabama families over the past century and those living now in Alabama Power's service area. I learned through my study of the company that sometimes people believed their power bills were too high. There were times I thought that, too, but I always blamed it on the way we lived (cool in the summer, warm in winter), on the way we used and enjoyed electricity. I believed I had some control over the amount of electricity I used and thus had some personal responsibility for my own bill.

Throughout the process of researching and writing this book, personal memories of Alabama Power Company that had long been forgotten came to mind. Days without electricity after ice storms and snowstorms, hurricanes, and tornadoes threw my family back into the nineteenth century. Once at Lake Martin we were without electricity, had no telephone, were trapped by ice on the hill, and could not leave. With three children we broke ice on the shoreline and hauled buckets of water to flush toilets, warmed the house by only a fireplace, and slept in sleeping bags. We cooked over charcoal, ate peanut butter and jelly sandwiches, and drank canned juices and sodas for a day and a half until the Alabama Power truck came to the top of the hill, and men restored our power. Every family in the state has similar memories of times when their lifestyle reverted to a previous century when the lights went out. They remember watching power company men brave dangerous and icy conditions climbing poles and handling hot wires with long rubber gloves to restore their electricity, and they recall the feeling of ecstasy when the lights came on again. I will always remember the courage and skill, and the courtesy, of these men.

Another power company memory that came back to me was of a morning in the 1980s when I left Mobile driving north on I-65, trying to reach home before a storm came ashore somewhere on the Alabama-Mississippi gulf coast. Out of the early dawn mist, on one of those long stretches of the interstate south of Evergreen, I saw dozens of trucks of all sizes, all painted alike, coming toward me. Only when the first one passed did I recognize they were all Alabama Power Company trucks, moving into harm's way to help as I was fleeing from the storm.

The story of the Alabama Power Company begins with rivers—not street railways—and since the age of four, I have had a love affair with Alabama's rivers. I grew up on the Black Warrior River, and I know that river, twice traveling in our family boat from Camp Oliver on Bankhead Lake to Mobile and back, through the locks operated by the U.S. Army Corps of Engineers. I have been through every lock on the Tennessee River from Chattanooga, Tennessee, to Paducah, Kentucky, and can still recall the thrill of going through the high lock at Wilson Dam on the deck of the *Mississippi Queen*. Seven days after we married, George and I went to work for Toppy Hodnette at Kowaliga Beach on Lake Martin. Our children grew up on Lake Martin and now our grandchildren are learning to water ski on that lake, but only after reading the early correspondence and engineering reports in the files of Alabama Power did I fully appreciate why Lake Martin's water level must drop in late summer and fall, why this is so important, and how this reservoir was designed to fit into the overall plan of the state's hydroelectric generation system. These are my personal memories, but surely they have been shared by Alabamians over ten decades. I have been amazed that so much of my life prepared me to write this story.

For thirty-seven years I taught U.S. and Alabama history at several universities and public library settings, and I am embarrassed to confess that while I talked about TVA, I did not cover the history of Alabama Power and its contributions to the state and its people. I hope this centennial history will help teachers, students, citizens, public servants, and those who love Alabama understand the importance of electricity and the significant role Alabama Power, its men and women, have played in the history of our state. I hope readers will have a better understanding of the relationship between an adequate supply of electricity and Alabama Power; between electricity and the quality of life for Alabama citizens; between Alabama Power Company and the state's economic development.

This story of Alabama Power is also for the company's thousands of employees, past, present, and future, and their families. One of the first and most enduring things I learned in this project is how proud people are that their parents or grandparents worked for Alabama Power, how proud employees are to work for the power company today. In this history I hope that I have given tribute and voice (if not by individual name) to all the men and women who built Alabama Power Company and committed it to serve the people of Alabama. Many retirees and employees shared with me what they had heard longtime Alabama Power executive Banks Farris say many times:

My mama always told me to run with good people. I've been doing that all my life working with Alabama Power Company. My mama also told me, "Son, in the hierarchy of callings, if you are not preaching the gospel or tilling the soil, the calling next in line is to work for Alabama Power."[9]

I hope through these pages that young and new employees and children and grandchildren of company pioneers may feel part of the story, appreciate the men, and later women, who had dreams, worked together to overcome obstacles, fought to defend the company and its name and its property, and built a worthy enterprise. One purpose of reading history is, simply, to become part of a shared memory.

I take comfort in knowing that Thomas W. Martin understood history and recognized this book was going to be written. In his preface to *The Story of Electricity in Alabama Since the Turn of the Century, 1900–1952*, Martin wrote that "I fully realize that in the years to come, another may undertake the same task and perhaps come to other conclusions than those expressed. Such is the course of history."[10] I appreciate his giving me the freedom to interpret that history in my own way. So fifty-four years later, here is the history of the Alabama Power Company that Tom Martin prophesied.

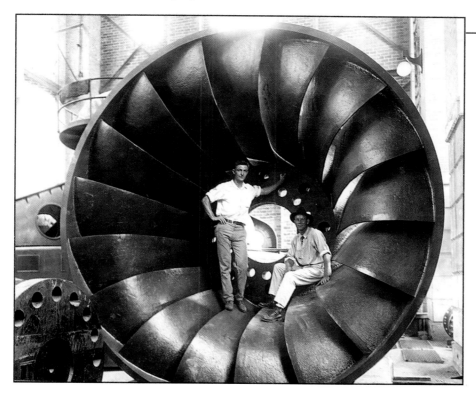

Water wheel of unit 1 Martin Dam, August 12, 1926.

Crossing the river at Selma. Alabama received its name from a wide river used by Indians for food and transportation and later by pioneers to ship cotton. This oil painting, ca. 1853/55, is attributed to William Frye. Courtesy of the Selma–Dallas County Library.

John Melish drew the first map of the Alabama Territory in 1818. The abundant water resources of Alabama are evident, and the early counties show the state's settlement patterns. Courtesy of the Alabama Department of Archives and History.

Chapter One

Nineteenth-century Alabama was an agricultural state, and cotton was the state's most significant commercial crop, which was produced without mechanization until late in the century.

Alabama: Before Alabama Power Company

I suppose I have put the motive power of these streams far below their capacity. With the facilities we would have for getting iron, coal, and building materials, we could build large machine shops, and all machinery cheaper than it could be obtained abroad.

DANIEL PRATT, *Southern Statesman*, May 26, 1855

The Alabama in which the Alabama Power Company was founded—the world of its culture, geology, geography, politics, and history—profoundly influenced what would become the state's largest stockholder-owned utility. This Alabama world significantly shaped the company's first one hundred years just as the company, in turn, shaped the state. The history of one reflects the history of the other, and their futures are still intertwined.

The Alabama men who worked one hundred years ago to bring Alabama an interconnected generating and transmission system that would provide dependable and inexpensive electricity were all born in the nineteenth century.

Their attitudes and values were formed by the history of their state and the culture around them. The men of northern and midwestern backgrounds who joined Alabamians in the endeavor were sometimes amazed and often puzzled at Alabama's culture, but their dreams of harnessing the energy of the state's rivers, of bringing electricity to drive the machines of industry that would push Alabama into an industrial revolution, were as genuine, if not as missionary-driven, as the state's native-born sons. And in the truest sense of American private-enterprise capitalism, both groups hoped to make the great adventure profitable. Without profit there could be no continued development.

ALABAMA IN THE NINETEENTH CENTURY

Agriculture, and specifically cotton production, dominated the economic life of Alabama in the nineteenth century. When the century opened in 1800, it had been only nine years since Secretary of the Treasury Alexander Hamilton presented his *Report on Manufacturers* to the nation. Hamilton summarized the state of American industry and advocated that "industrialization was the road from economic colonialism to world power." He believed that northern industries processing southern raw materials could create a strong and powerful nation and that the government should promote manufacturers.[1] But in 1800, Alabama was a long way from any industrial revolution. It was part of the Mississippi Territory, a frontier land with people tracing their ancestry to Native Americans, to French, British, and Spanish adventurers, to Scottish traders, and to African slaves. The clash of three cultures on the Alabama frontier—Native American, European, and African—caused a melding of stories, foods, legends, and tall tales, which created a rich Alabama culture that was nurtured in an agricultural society.[2]

The early settlement patterns were along the state's many rivers, rivers that are the key to the beginning of the story of Alabama Power Company. The histories of most electric utility corporations begin in an urban setting and grow from street railway systems or lighting companies. But Alabama Power begins with a high dam, its history closely tied to the state's abundant rivers and the construction of large hydroelectric dams on sites so isolated that Congress, afraid of high dam failure, was reassured that if a dam should fail only miles of vacant land would be inundated.

There are four main river systems in the state: the mighty Tennessee in the north; the Chattahoochee, which forms the state's boundary with Georgia to the southeast; the Tombigbee and Black Warrior to the west; and the main system, the Alabama, which gave the state its name and includes the Cahaba, Coosa,

The Tallapoosa River's Horseshoe Bend was the site of the historic 1814 battle between Andrew Jackson and the Creek Indians. Alabama Power Company owned much of this land and later gave it to the federal government to establish a military park near Dadeville.

and Tallapoosa Rivers. These rivers were navigable to the fall line that stretches west and south from the shoals called the Muscle Shoals on the Tennessee in a curve southward through Tuscaloosa and Wetumpka to Columbus, Georgia. The Tennessee was navigable on portions of the river above the shoals east of Florence, and the upper Coosa was navigable above the dangerous rapids and falls named the Devil's Staircase and the series of shoals that ran almost to Gadsden.[3]

As the century opened, Scottish-English traders from Charleston settled in the Coosa-Tallapoosa river valleys. A few families emigrated from the Broad River area of Georgia, settling in Huntsville and in the southern area of the territory near the Alabama River. Vast acres of rolling hills and valleys with springs, bubbling creeks, and fertile soil, vacant land for the taking, enticed pioneers. In 1812 the Tennessee militia, the famous Volunteers, came south with Andrew Jackson to fight the Indians. In 1814 the Creek nation was defeated near the banks of the Tallapoosa River at the Battle of Horseshoe Bend. The defeat of the Indians cleared the way for settlement in large areas of Alabama once controlled by the Creeks. Much of the Horseshoe Bend land was later given by Alabama Power Company to the federal government to form the state's first and only national military park.

The veterans of the Creek Indian War returned to Alabama with their families, buying land where they could and becoming squatters where land had not yet been surveyed for sale. These tough pioneers joined others in homesteads scattered from the mountains to the Gulf and in settlements such as

Florence and Montgomery. "Alabama fever" swept across the seaboard South. One North Carolinian wrote that the fever was "contagious," for as soon as a man met a neighbor returning from Alabama with stories of the beautiful land, he made plans to go see for himself.[4] The fertile Black Belt and bottomlands were perfect for cotton, and Alabama rivers provided the means to ship the white gold to market. The race was on to grab the best lands. The area's population exploded. This is why on the first page of her Pulitzer Prize–winning novel, To Kill a Mockingbird, Harper Lee has Scout explain that her family history in Alabama "really began with Andrew Jackson."[5]

A number of men who migrated to Alabama were well educated, wealthy, and had leadership experience in national and local governments in other states. Alabama was granted territorial status when Mississippi became a state (1817), and in two years Alabama itself was admitted to statehood. On the Alabama frontier, economic development was hampered by a lack of capital, yet there was deep and pervasive resentment against banks and a hostility toward wealth.[6] Historian Harvey H. Jackson III has noted, "When Alabama first became a state, Israel Pickens demonized the banks. He ran against them, and was elected governor."[7] But commerce needed banks and economic development needed capital, and so the state entered the banking business. Ultimately, this adventure was a disaster and proved that the state of Alabama was no more capable of running an untarnished and efficient banking operation than were private bankers.

Inadequate investment capital continued to be a problem that plagued Alabama throughout the nineteenth century and well into the twentieth. In the early period there simply was not enough surplus specie (gold) to invest and develop the infrastructure of the state, much less to diversify the economy from cotton production. In the nineteenth century the South was not part of the nation's capital market. Interest rates were high and the social and political climate discouraged capital from investing in industry in Alabama.[8] From 1820

Cotton was shipped to market on riverboats powered by steam engines. Later, where rapids and shoals prevented navigation, railroads carried cotton.

to 1860 a cotton culture dominated every aspect of life in Alabama. The soft white fibers in prickly bolls planted and picked by slave labor were the quickest way to make a fortune. But Alabama planters, operating through factors (cotton brokers) in Mobile or Liverpool, rarely accumulated the cash from their cotton that might have been invested in manufacturing. In the 1830s, the last Indian lands in Alabama were acquired by the federal government and opened for settlement and cotton planting; however, some Indian families remained on their farms as their tribes moved west.[9]

Demand for cotton to feed the spindles and looms of textile mills in New England and old England remained strong, and cotton prices were high on international markets. As cotton production increased, wealth in the state grew. Only a very few investors bothered with manufacturing and industrial ventures. Something of a bias against industries held sway, as though agriculture was the way a gentleman made his money. But Daniel Pratt had no such attitude. He was a New Englander by birth, and he became Alabama's most successful antebellum manufacturer. It helped that his first and main product was tied to cotton production. Pratt knew how to make cotton gins. This simple machine, patented by Eli Whitney in 1793, combed seeds from the fibers and made the Cotton Kingdom possible. Pratt went looking for falling water to power his factory and on Alabama's fall line found abundant places where flowing water would turn a wheel. Pratt tried to purchase a site on the falls of the Coosa River at Wetumpka, but the price was too high. He moved west, acquiring land at McNeil's Mill on Autauga Creek across the Alabama River from Montgomery. In 1851 Autauga Creek was described as "a large, fine, never failing stream."[10] There Pratt built Alabama's premier antebellum industrial complex.[11] Eventually he added a textile mill and a window, door, and carriage factory to his industrial village.

Agriculture so dominated the thinking of Alabama leaders that any other vision was obscured. The men who dreamed of manufacturing had problems raising capital.[12] The state's few entrepreneurs tried to diversify the state's economy, but the strong public prejudice against corporations and accumulations of capital made that difficult. Demagogues such as Williamson R. W. Cobb of Jackson County and Felix Grundy McConnell of Talladega County, both of whom served in the U.S. Congress, campaigned on common-man issues and railed against the domination of wealthy interests.[13] Historian Harvey Jackson explains the task Alabama candidates faced "of divining popular prejudices to discover what was feared or desired, then putting themselves forth as credible champions."[14]

The fundamental distrust of corporations in Alabama was a prejudice that retarded the state's economic development before the Civil War. One antebellum state legislator, expressing his opposition to corporate charters in 1848, charged that corporations were the way "a moneyed aristocracy proposed to govern a confiding people." Historian J. Mills Thornton III, in his study of antebellum Alabama, discusses the strong bias in the state against corporations, pointing out that the legislature was hesitant to charter companies and often rejected applications.[15] Historian Wayne Flynt notes the "resentment of the rich and fear of corporate wealth" and class division as major themes in antebellum Alabama history.[16] Hostility to railroad corporations was particularly common, influenced by the fact that Alabama's most valuable agricultural product was shipped mainly by steamboat. Some planters invested in railroads in order to ship cotton where there were no navigable streams, but there was still widespread distrust of railroads.[17] On February 14, 1855, the *Montgomery Advertiser* advised that railroads were unnecessary for Alabama and the "mania" for them would soon cease, thus protecting the state from being corrupted by combinations of talented men and money who would "debauch the public morals."[18]

The Alabama capitol, which was constructed at the top of Dexter Avenue in 1852 to replace the building that burned in 1849, was featured in a lithograph in *Harper's Weekly*, February 9, 1861, after Alabama voted for secession on January 11. Courtesy of the Alabama Department of Archives and History.

This attitude handicapped the development of the hill country and areas above the fall line not blessed with navigable waterways. The great English geologist Sir Charles Lyell, who traveled through Jefferson and Shelby Counties on his way to Selma in 1846, announced that the true wealth of Alabama was not in the Black Belt, the cotton-producing areas, but in the mineral belt of northern Alabama. Although the first coal was dug from the bed of the Warrior and floated down to Mobile as early as the late 1820s, the development of the region's iron ore was unexploited until Alabama seceded from the Union in 1861 and war came.[19] The nascent iron furnaces of northern Alabama and the industrial development around Selma blossomed with Confederate subsidies for war industries.

Defeat snuffed the life from these promising beginnings. The Civil War left Alabama prostrate and poor. Any specie was long gone. Confederate bonds were worthless. Land had no value, but taxes were higher than before the war. People were starving. Years of military occupation and reconstruction left the state exhausted. The relationship between former slaves and former masters was not solved by federal legislation of the period, and civil rights and social adjustments were another one hundred years in coming. Congress and the president soon tired of supervising the South. Discriminatory legislation called "Jim Crow laws" was enacted by southern states, and the black population, along with large numbers of white farmers who had once been independent, fell into tenancy and share-cropping. It was 1880 before the South equaled the cotton exports of 1860.[20]

With war and reconstruction over, the country turned its attention to winning the West and to spreading for peacetime pursuits the industrial might the North had amassed for war. In 1860 the United States ranked fourth in world manufacturing, but by 1894 the nation was in first place. Most of this manufacturing was located in eastern or midwestern states. New South promoter Henry Grady noted in 1889 that the South had abundant natural resources but limited capital for developing them.[21] Alabama was an excellent example of Grady's point, for there was little native capital to invest in manu-facturing or improving the infrastructure of the state. In an early survey of the Coosa River, Thomas Pearsall wrote about the river's great Staircase Falls and observed that "more than two-thirds of the real wealth of Alabama" was "in her water power, coal, and minerals," but Pearsall lamented that "of her water power, not one-thousandth part is used for propelling machinery."[22]

In agricultural areas of Alabama there were hostile attitudes against northern and foreign capital, but urban areas joined the South in adopting a New South philosophy based upon industry. This progressive economic creed was evident espe-cially in Birmingham. The "Magic City" and other industrial-based towns such as Gadsden, Anniston, and Fort Payne were examples of a New South that gave hope for the future even though the ownership of industries was likely to be absentee and northern.[23] In northern Alabama there was little interest in where the money came from, just the gratitude that it came, bringing jobs and good salaries. Railroad networks were finally built through the hill country, and technological advances spread across Alabama. Natural resources of coal and iron were developed.

As early as 1869 the state of Alabama gave tax exemptions to "infant industries" for one year. This included furnaces, mills, foundries, and tanner-ies. In 1897 Governor Joseph F. Johnston signed a bill to give tax exemptions to cotton textile mills for five years. During the legislative session of 1898–99, the question of tax exemptions was debated, and Governor Johnston vetoed a bill that would extend the tax exemption to ten years.[24] In 1880 Alabama

Tallassee Mills was one of the few antebellum textile mills in Alabama. It produced strong fabrics for the Confederate army utilizing waterpower at Tallassee Falls.

had $9.6 million invested in manufacturing. That figure rose to $46 million in 1890, to $70.3 million in 1900, and more than $173 million in 1909.[25] In 1900, the number of companies engaged in manufacturing in Alabama was almost triple the number in 1880.[26]

Before the Civil War, Alabama had a small cotton textile mill industry with only 36 active spindles. In the late nineteenth century, textile mills, once wedded to New England, began to move south to take advantage of low taxes, cheap labor, and proximity to raw materials. Between 1880 and 1900 the total number of spindles in Alabama, Georgia, North and South Carolina increased from 422,807 to 1,195,256. Alabama spindles rose to 886 active spindles in 1909 and by 1919 had reached 1,107.[27] Capital investment in cotton mills in the last decade of the century increased 131.4 percent in the South compared to only 12.1 percent in New England.[28] Yet at the turn of the century, Alabama had only 4,880 electric motors in its textile industry compared to 68,696 in South Carolina and 46,279 in North Carolina.[29]

But within the prosperous American nation, there were pockets of poverty. Many Americans were bypassed by the abundance exhibited in what is called the Gilded Age, and they resented the way that titans such as John D. Rockefeller, J. Pierpont Morgan, and Andrew Carnegie ran their empires. Southerners, and especially Alabamians, struggled to make a living and feed their families. Midwestern farmers were the first to organize because they were not sharing in the prosperity of industrial America. The grievances voiced by the nationwide Farmers Alliance were the fuel for the Populist Revolt. Common men of the Midwest and Plains joined to use the political process to take back their governments. In Alabama, farmers perceived that their state government was dominated by men with no concern for their problems. Poverty was the thread that tied poor black and white farmers together despite racial differences. By their political activities in the late 1880s and early '90s, this combination of black and white poor threatened the status quo of Jim Crow legislation that legalized segregation. Anti-Populist factions in Alabama united to follow Mississippi, which in 1890 adopted a new constitution that disfranchised black voters. For eleven years the move in Alabama was thwarted, but in 1901 it succeeded. A constitutional convention met and wrote a document that disfranchised the state's black voters and many, many poor white men as well. The election that ratified the document is generally recognized as fraudulent.[30]

In Alabama, the last decade of the nineteenth century was stormy both economically and politically. Not only were there political fights centered on economics and race, but a national depression struck hard at the nascent industries of the state. The Panic of 1893 shut down the new iron furnaces in Birmingham, sent hundreds of men into the ranks of the unemployed, and lengthened bread lines at charities and churches. Many families who had moved to the city for a better life returned to the farm to live with relatives.

The beginning of the Spanish-American War in 1898 finally sparked the economy, and as the century turned, prosperity was on the way back. In 1900, the population of Alabama was 1.8 million, and the percentage of people living in rural areas was just over 88 percent. Cotton was still king, the main and most valuable agricultural product. At the beginning of the twentieth century, the value of Alabama farms was almost twice the value of manufacturing capital, despite thirty years of development in the Birmingham mineral district.[31] Thomas W. Martin, who would serve as leader of Alabama Power Company for more than forty years, explained Alabama's lack of industrial development: "we southern people were too prone to be prisoners of our own past and were locked in it."[32]

ELECTRICITY COMES TO AMERICA AND TO ALABAMA

In the two decades following the end of the Civil War there was an explosion of inventions that changed the world. At the 1870 Centennial Exposition in Philadelphia, devices as diverse as a button-hole machine and a giant steam engine shared the stage with George Westinghouse's air brakes for trains. In 1876 Alexander Graham Bell introduced the telephone. Charles F. Brush had invented the arc lamp and an improved dynamo, and Thomas A. Edison perfected the incandescent electric lightbulb in 1879. Edison's biographer observed that these were exciting times and "America was on the threshold of an era of unrivaled material progress."[33] As these technological advancements began to reach the market, they changed American society and the way people lived their lives.[34] The one that most transformed the nation and Alabama was electricity.

Almost a century before Edison, the electrical experiments of Benjamin Franklin had stimulated interest in atmospheric electricity. Various scientists and inventors in the United States, Canada, and Europe began studying the phenomenon to determine how it might be harnessed and how it could be used. In America, Edison was the leader in discovering how to generate and deliver electricity. In 1878 he secured financing for experiments and the next year demonstrated his first incandescent lamp. He announced plans to generate electricity and transmit it underground to his laboratory at Menlo Park. This he did by the end of 1879. A flood of curious night visitors came to Menlo Park.[35] Orders followed from private individuals and cities that wanted electrical systems installed. In April 1881, the city of New York granted Edison the right to build an underground distribution system and a central station on Pearl Street to provide electricity to a small area of the city.[36] Edison's "goal was to make electricity so cheap that only the rich could afford candles."[37]

Before Edison was able to install lights in New York City, an Alabama mill community had electric lights. The Woodstock Iron Company in Anniston, Alabama, used one of its furnaces to power a dynamo to light its furnace operations and a few streetlights in its mill village. The *Selma Times Journal* reported on April 29, 1882, that the lights were "not dazzling nor brilliant, fitful nor glaring, but soft, gentle, harmonious."[38] Edison's system in New York began operations on September 4, 1882, when lights came on in J. Pierpont Morgan's office on Wall Street. The *New York Herald* reported there "was a strange glow last night" which was "a steady glare, bright and mellow" that "illuminated interiors and shone through windows fixed and unwavering." These "glowing incandescent lamps of Edison," which were being used for the first time, vindicated the scientist.[39] By January 1883 Montgomery had a Brush dynamo lighting thirty-one streetlights. Two years later, after Birmingham's city government refused to pay for an electric operation, the Elyton Land Company, which had founded the city in 1871, agreed to finance a plant and purchase equipment from Thomson Houston Electric Company.[40] In 1885 Capital City Railway Company petitioned Montgomery for permission to run its cars by electricity, and the next year electric lights came on in Selma.[41] For Alabama, it was the beginning of a new era.

Changes occurred beyond electric streetlights and industrial operations lighting as street railways moved from mule-drawn cars to steam "dummy lines" to electrification. Montgomery was the first city in the nation to electrify its street railway system, and on April 15, 1886, the cars first ran on what citizens of the capital city called the "Lightning Route."[42] The *Electrical World* deemed the Montgomery system "the largest electric railway plant in the world."[43] In Birmingham talk circulated in 1888 that the street railway cars might be electrified. The *Birmingham Evening News* wrote an editorial opposing

Montgomery, Alabama, had one of the first and largest electric street railway systems in the nation. When it began operation on April 15, 1886, citizens called it the "Lightning Route."

such a foolish step, writing that "overhead electrically charged wires to propel dummy trains are deemed more deadly and dangerous in a luckless city than yellow jack [yellow fever] in a town that opens trenches and graveyards in its midst in mid-summer." The company vehemently denied it was considering electricity, but at the same time it was quietly investigating the possibility. In the city rumors flew that the Montgomery mayor's horse had been electrocuted when it stepped on a track joint. The first electric cars in Birmingham finally came to the Highlands line on October 10, 1891.[44]

Through the last decade of the nineteenth century, many Alabama cities developed small municipal electric operations and financed them in different ways. Dynamos were very expensive, and many towns went without electricity because governing bodies could not afford the indebtedness. Fort Deposit probably had the most unique means of financing its electrical system: the city established its own whiskey store and used the profits to build its plant and transmission lines. Each municipality had its own problems with its electricity. Some operated on a "moonlight schedule," turning on the electricity only when the moon was not shining. Sometimes current would be off during the day, except on Fridays when women ironed clothes. Dadeville was served by a hydro plant on Big Sandy Creek, but heavy rains always filled the flume with sand and volunteers had to shovel it out. At Goodwater, spring rains brought hundreds of eels down Hatchett Creek, clogging the turbine and causing interruptions. Service, of course, depended upon the water flow in the creeks, and dry weather meant no electricity. These operations were isolated. There were no back-up systems and no interconnecting lines that would allow the transfer of power from one system to another, from one system working with surplus power to another system with a malfunctioning plant. Rates were high, and service was undependable. Electricity was a luxury available only for those few who could afford it.[45]

In Alabama, all of this would begin to change in 1912.

Shoals on the Coosa prevented
river traffic north of Wetumpka.
Wetumpka Bridge, Adrian E.
Thompson, 1847. Courtesy of the
Museum of Fine Arts, Boston.

U. S. Army Corps of Engineers
survey of the Coosa River shows
river obstructions and potential lock
locations from Wetumpka to Lock 4,
1889. Courtesy of Ed Tyberghein.

Chapter Two

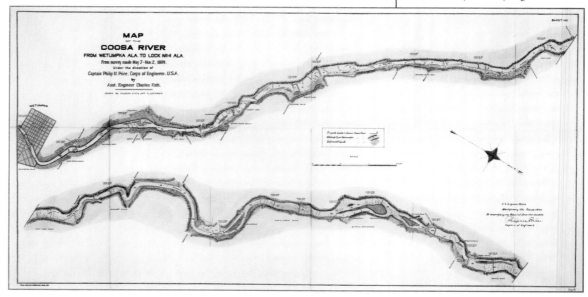

Shoals on the Coosa River, ca. 1912.

THE BEGINNING YEARS: THREE MITCHELLS, TOM MARTIN, AND CAPTAIN LAY

From the standpoint of conserving the natural resources of the state, the development and utilization of latent power now going to waste is of great importance.

JAMES MITCHELL, *Memorandum Relating to*
Water Power Developments of Alabama Power Company, May 4, 1914

The Civil War was raging on battlefields far away from Tallapoosa County when Sidney Zollicoffer Mitchell was born in Dadeville, Alabama, on March 17, 1862.[1] Mitchell would later become a powerful figure in the national electricity scene, an early investor in small generating plants in Alabama, a longtime member of the board of directors of Alabama Power Company, and at different times a threat to or a supporter of Alabama Power. His family's experiences were typical for many Alabamians of the period and give a glimpse into the lives of the state's people in the four decades before the founding of Alabama Power Company. Mitchell's experiences in the early years of the development of the electric industry illustrate how this new utility business began and how Mitchell earned his fortune.

Just four weeks before Sidney's birth, Union forces had occupied Huntsville, some two hundred miles north of Dadeville. It was planting season, and his father, Dr. William M. A. Mitchell, was supervising the cultivation of the family's garden. The U.S. agricultural census for 1850 and 1860 illustrates a limited farming operation with no cotton ginned in 1850 and only five bales ten years later.[2] The South was running short of volunteers and the Confederacy enacted conscription. The two Confederate generals for whom Sidney was named were both dead before he was one month old. The Civil War intruded directly into the Mitchell family's world only once. When young Sidney was two years old, Union raiders under Major General Lovell H. Rousseau came through Dadeville and stole silver, hams, and cattle from his parents on their way south to cut the railroad supplying Atlanta.[3]

In 1865, with the defeat of the South just a few months past, Sidney's mother, Elmira Sophia Jordan Mitchell, died. (Her name was to be remembered when it was given to Alabama Power Company's Jordan Dam.) Sidney and his older brother, Reuben Alexander, were sent to live with their grandmother, Ann Spivey Jordan, on her Coosa County farm.[4] The widowed grandmother was the daughter of a Presbyterian minister, a resilient woman sixty-six years of age who ran her large farm with the help of a few former slaves who had remained on the Jordan place. Sidney grew up working on the farm, plowing fields behind a mule, and hunting in the woods around the Tallapoosa River, in some ways an idyllic boyhood, yet one shaped by the South's defeat and the poverty of the Reconstruction period. Ann Jordan gave her grandsons discipline, a strong work ethic, and a good education, tutoring them herself to supplement the local school.[5] In later years, Sidney Mitchell told the story of his grandmother giving him "a large field of cleared land and a mule," explaining to him "that by my own efforts I must fight my way in the world and earn enough to clothe myself and pay my way through the country school."[6]

In 1879 Sidney was nominated to the U.S. Naval Academy. He passed his examinations and left his raccoon-hunting dogs, his horses, and his native Alabama behind. Although the land and the people remained always in his heart, except for short visits Sidney never returned to the state to live.[7] In 1883, after completing four years of academic courses at Annapolis, Sidney Mitchell went to sea aboard the USS Trenton. His assignment was to install an incandescent lighting system aboard ship, the first in the U.S. Navy. The technology was primitive and not dependable, but Sidney became fascinated by electricity, an interest that was to dominate the rest of his life. After he received his commission, he resigned from the navy and went to New York City. In Manhattan, Mitchell observed the new electric lights in a small part of the city and wanted to learn whether the new technology was more dependable than the system he had installed on board the *Trenton*. He sought out and took a job with Thomas A. Edison.[8]

Mitchell's work of only a few months must have pleased the great man. Edison made Mitchell the sole agent for Edison products in Washington and Oregon Territories. At the age of twenty-three, Sidney, now called S.Z., went west to seek his fortune. In 1885 at Seattle, he established a company and built a generation plant and distribution system, the first central station west of the Rocky Mountains.[9] For the next twenty years he sold and supervised the installation of Edison generators and helped towns, cities, and private companies find ways to pay for the new technology. The 1890s merger of General Electric and Thomson Houston by J. Pierpont Morgan and the problems GE faced with the acquisition of small underfinanced electric companies, especially after the Panic of 1893, caused GE president C. E. Coffin to ask Mitchell to return to New York to manage these companies and give them more direction, thus turning liabilities into assets. S. Z. Mitchell became president of Electric Bond & Share Company.[10] EBASCO, as it came to be known, provided engineering expertise and services to help these small public utilities operate their electrical plants efficiently. As an investment banking company, EBASCO helped finance these companies and served as a holding company. It became a giant player in the field of utilities, spawning controversy because of its power and size.

S. Z. Mitchell moved with ease among the Wall Street elite of banks, bonds, and utility stockholders while earning his fortune. He was a dapper man with a small moustache and was always sharply dressed. In one photograph taken in the field, S.Z. is wearing coveralls over a white shirt and tie, holding his shotgun and a string of birds over his shoulder. His Alabama rural upbringing and his navy years gave him an interesting collection of stories and

Left to right; Fern Wood Mitchell, Thomas W. Martin, S. Z. Mitchell, and Reuben Mitchell hunting the day after the dedication of Jordan Dam, November 22, 1927.

words. One Manhattan writer observed that perhaps Mitchell's "experience with mules laid the foundation of his now magnificent [sic] but unconventional vocabulary."[11] S. Z. Mitchell must have been an enigma to New Yorkers.

While S.Z. was establishing a life in electricity in the West and on Wall Street, his older brother, Reuben, stayed at home and tried to survive the hard times of post–Civil War Alabama. Reuben attended local schools, clerked in a family grocery store in Dadeville, worked in the cotton mill in Columbus, Georgia, and was the postmaster of Opelika. Perhaps encouraged by his brother, in 1888 he became the general manager of the electric street railway system in Montgomery. Two years later, Reuben moved to Gadsden where he was involved with land development, banking, and textile manufacturing. Governor Braxton Bragg Comer appointed him a colonel on his staff, and thereafter Reuben was known as Colonel Mitchell or simply "the Colonel." Later, as a vice president of Alabama Power Company and member of the board of directors from 1918 to 1937, he would push commercial sales and represent the company in various ways.

The two Mitchell brothers, most likely through S.Z.'s wealth and connections in New York, became pioneers in early utility development in Alabama. They held some ownership in companies in Decatur, Huntsville, Talladega, Anniston, and other communities. Years later Tom Martin, president of Alabama Power Company after 1919, observed that as president of EBASCO, S.Z. preserved some independent status. Sometimes he operated "jointly with his company, sometimes for the company, and sometimes for himself." Martin speculated that when S.Z. moved into electrical investments in Alabama it was "in the joint capacity."[12] The Mitchell brothers are credited with building the very first transmission line in the state, connecting Talladega, Anniston, and Gadsden.[13] The Mitchells' Alabama utility assets would eventually become part of Alabama Power. In fact, these operations would be the first income-producing assets for Alabama Power's holding company.

As the years passed, and as S.Z.'s fortune and reputation grew, he became a power to be reckoned with. In 1925, *Forbes* magazine praised S.Z. for his work with EBASCO, commenting that his idea of building strong investments in electric utilities and of financing small companies but leaving operational control to local companies had led to his financial success.[14] Both Mitchell brothers would eventually serve on the Alabama Power Company board of directors, but on several occasions S.Z. attempted to derail the company. Through the early years of the company's development, S.Z.'s powerful figure loomed large from New York City as his wealth grew and as the young Alabama utility company haltingly moved forward. S.Z.'s influence could be stabilizing, or it might foreshadow a takeover move. Management kept him close in order to watch him carefully. In 1930 *Business Week* called S. Z. Mitchell "the American reputed by many to be the world's wealthiest man" and claimed he was "practically unknown" outside his field.[15] He certainly was not well known in Alabama.

The Mitchell brothers, having grown up in the Tallapoosa and Coosa Valleys, knew those rivers. Everyone in Dadeville had picnicked at Cherokee Bluffs.[16] Reuben was working in the Coosa River city of Gadsden, when Alabama Power Company was incorporated. Judge C. J. Coley, local historian and former probate judge of Tallapoosa County, knew the Mitchells well. He recalled that S.Z. "always had a yen to return to his childhood haunts" and wanted to build a dam at Cherokee Bluffs.[17] Through his association with Alabama Power Company, S.Z. indirectly would accomplish this.

When the story of Alabama Power Company began in 1906, S.Z. was just getting settled on Wall Street with EBASCO, and Reuben was a banker in Gadsden. Soon S.Z. would no longer be obscure to the men struggling to bring electricity to Alabama, men who were fired by their mission to balance the agricultural economy of their state with industry and manufacturing fueled by electricity. Surely, in the process, they hoped—no, they expected, in the quintessential dream of American capitalism—to secure their own financial future, if any capital could be found. But in Alabama at this time, that was absolutely a gamble.

JAMES MITCHELL AND CHEROKEE BLUFFS

In November 1911, a tall distinguished-looking man appeared at the Montgomery law office of Tyson, Wilson & Martin to discuss dam sites in Alabama. His name was Mitchell, James Mitchell, but he was no kin to the Mitchell brothers of New York and Gadsden. Thomas W. Martin recalled from their first meeting that James Mitchell was a man in his early forties, "pleasant and agreeable" with "great personal charm" and both knowledge and experience in hydroelectric developments. Mitchell understood what it would take to develop the sites on the state's rivers. But much more important, he had the contacts with investment bankers who could finance the projects.[18] Mitchell was a Canadian by birth, born in Pembroke, Ontario, on June 19, 1866, to Charles Cameron Mitchell and his wife Mary Porteous. Mitchell's father, a farmworker and brick mason, was

James Mitchell, ca.1900. Courtesy of the Mitchell family.

born in Huntly, Scotland, and his mother was born in Canada. The young couple moved to the United States and settled in Swampscotts, Massachusetts, in April 1868, when James was still a toddler. His eight siblings were all born in the state. In 1878 the Mitchell family moved to Milton, Massachusetts, which became the family's hometown.[19]

The red-headed boy with clear blue eyes grew up on a small farm, spending time hiking through the woods, hunting rattlesnakes, and collecting birds' eggs and flowers. He was physically strong, bright with a "thirst for knowledge," and had an active mind.[20] Mitchell became interested in science in high school and in 1882 went to work for a Boston firm specializing in electrical experimentation and building electrical instruments. Two years later, in 1884, he joined the Thomson Houston Electric Company (later to become part of General Electric), which was building the first railway motors. Mitchell was soon in charge of the railway department and was later sent across the country to troubleshoot the electrical equipment of new street railways.[21] Mitchell's problem solving was ingenious and creative—and always effective. The company knew him as "an indefatigable worker, resourceful," and a "nothing ever stumped him" kind of a man who "had demonstrated an unusual engineering ability and adaptability in meeting unexpected situations and people."[22] He was to need all these talents in Alabama.

Thomson Houston sent Mitchell to Rio de Janeiro in 1890 to install an electric street railway system. Mitchell remained in Brazil, established his own business and worked with various electrical companies. He constructed the São Paulo tramways. He made several trips back to the United States, but he stayed in Brazil sixteen years.[23] Mitchell was highly successful, not only because of his electrical expertise and wide experience but also because of his reputation for fair dealing, his appreciation for Portuguese culture, and his quick mastery of both that language and Spanish. Late in 1906 he left South America and moved his family to Washington, D.C., seeking new business opportunities. After one summer at Royal Muskoka Lake in Canada, Mitchell moved his wife and daughter to London in 1907 and sent his son to boarding school in New York. Mitchell's last project in Brazil had been a hydroelectric dam on Rio don Larges financed by the London investment banking house of Sperling & Company.[24]

Sperling & Company, and especially Mitchell's friend E. Mackay Edgar who was associated with Sperling, convinced Mitchell to go with Sir Edward Stracey, an English consultant, at the invitation of the Japanese government to study possible power projects in Japan. British venture capital was financing electric developments all over the world, and Sperling was interested. Mitchell spent four months in Japan. His family resided in the resort towns of Kikko and Mianoshita, while Mitchell toured the remote mountains surveying possible sites for dams. He reported to London that the project put before Sperling by a Japanese syndicate was "not economically feasible."[25] On the return trip, his daughter Marion and her mother sailed home by way of Genoa, Italy, and Mitchell and his son Malcolm took the Trans-Siberian Railroad across Russia.[26] On this trip and in 1910, Mitchell checked out possible investments in Russian copper and gold mining, but these were never significant.[27] Mitchell's reports from various parts of the world earned the confidence of Sperling's directors, and in these years he mastered the details of corporate finance and securities.

Mitchell was living in London in 1911 when Sperling sent him to New York. He established an office on Broadway and listed his business as "engineering and manufacturing."[28] The British company was as interested as Mitchell was in developing power sites on southern waterways. Mitchell may have heard his friend George Westinghouse's address before the Southern Commercial Congress in Atlanta in March 1911, extolling the possibilities of southern industrial development with the use of the region's excellent hydro-electric sites.[29] Mitchell investigated the Clarks Hill site on the Savannah River but decided it was not economically feasible. Westinghouse and Paul T. Brady, an officer in the Westinghouse corporation, recommended that he go to Alabama. Mitchell later stated that he became interested in Alabama in September 1911. Charles Hinckley Baker, who had worked with railroads and was associated with a New York–based utilities company and a man Mitchell described in 1914 as a "concessionaire of water power sites," wrote Mitchell's wife after her husband's death that "It was I who brought the Alabama projects to Mr. Mitchell's attention in the first place."[30] Paul Brady had known about the Alabama sites for several years and had been in contact with a Gadsden man who needed financing for a dam on the Coosa River at Lock 12. William Patrick Lay, that Gadsden man, also claimed to have contacted Mitchell. (After 1929 the Lock 12 dam was known as Lay Dam.) But when Mitchell first came to Alabama, he went to the Cherokee Bluffs site on the Tallapoosa River.[31]

James Mitchell was told that Cherokee Bluffs south of Dadeville was the prime dam site in eastern Alabama. Years before, Henry Horne of Macon, Georgia, and James R. Hall and Nora E. Miller of Dadeville had explored and promoted dam sites in the area. Mrs. Miller, a Tallapoosa County land-owner and civic booster, was remembered for having the first automobile in Dadeville, a "Winton Six with a loud horn," in which she traveled the sand and chert roads of the county.[32] Cherokee Bluffs was a high ridge overlooking the Tallapoosa River and famous for its panoramic view of the surrounding countryside, a vista that stretched miles to the west and northwest and to the

Company surveyors at Cherokee Bluffs site, June 5, 1923.

south and southeast. Rocky cliffs on either side of the river rose high above the water, which rolled over and around boulders in a gorge. The terrain was rough and access difficult.

The early Cherokee Bluffs enthusiasts did attract some entrepreneurs. For instance, Henry C. Jones, J. S. Pinckard, and Jack Thorington became involved in 1896 when the group acquired the rights to the dam site. In 1900 they formed the Cherokee Development and Manufacturing Company with capital of $50,000 and a legislative charter that gave it extraordinary powers.[33] The company began constructing a small dam some miles below Cherokee Bluffs and three miles above Tallassee. When it began producing electricity on November 11, 1902, it was the first hydroelectric plant in Alabama. Its 33,000-volt transmission line, which provided service to Montgomery, was one of the nation's first long-distance transmission lines. Henry L. Doherty, a national utilities giant who formed Cities Service Company in 1910, succeeded the original owners, who then concentrated their efforts on building a dam at Cherokee Bluffs.[34]

Five years later, in 1907, Massey Wilson and Thomas W. Martin drew up the papers to change the Cherokee Development and Manufacturing Company's name to the Birmingham, Montgomery and Gulf Power Company and by charter amendment removed the 100-mile limit for transmission that would have restricted the company's growth. As Tom Martin once observed, it was the first suggestion of a regional power company. The vision of the Cherokee group was impressive, but it was beyond the members' ability to finance, even though by now they had attracted the interest and support of two well-connected entrepreneurs, Frank Sherman Washburn and Charles Hinckley Baker, and had the support of their two Montgomery attorneys, Wilson and Martin.[35]

Frank Washburn was an Illinois-born, Cornell University–trained civil engineer. He worked for railroads in the West, built water supply storage dams in New York, consulted with hydropower companies in California, and surveyed the Nicaragua route of a proposed canal.[36] He married a well-connected Georgia native, Irene Russell, whose sister was the wife of the president of the Nashville & Chattanooga Railroad, Edmund W. Cole. Washburn was once described as a conscientious engineer with a brilliant business imagination, "an adventurous pioneer, a sort of twentieth-century industrial Daniel Boone," a shy perfectionist who was always restless.[37] Irene encouraged her husband to settle down in the South, and they made Nashville their home in 1900. About this time, Washburn made a tour of the Southeast, exploring the fall line as he searched for hydroelectric dam sites. He believed that only when southern industry was set free from the use of soft coal and its black smoke and began to fuel its industries with the "white coal" of hydro-electric power would the region "deserve the appellation of the 'Sunny South.'" He also was interested in an abundant supply of cheap electricity to manufacture nitrates, and it would be this passion that dominated the last two decades of his life. In Alabama, Washburn was particularly impressed with Cherokee Bluffs on the Tallapoosa River and Muscle Shoals on the Tennessee.[38]

Charles Hinckley Baker was also born in Illinois and may have known Washburn at Cornell, for he graduated in engineering three years behind Washburn. Baker worked for railroads, too, but then he became involved with hydroelectric power development in the state of Washington, where he was president of the Snoqualmie Falls Power Company.[39] These were the same years during which S. Z. Mitchell was building central station electrical systems in Washington and Oregon. Three years before S.Z. arrived in New York, Baker moved east and was associated with the American Public Utilities Company at 100 Broadway in New York City, an address that a few years later he shared with James Mitchell and the holding company of the Alabama Power Company.[40]

Washburn and Baker were also involved with the Muscle Shoals Hydro-Electric Power Company. Montgomery attorney Massey Wilson drew up the incorporation papers for the Muscle Shoals Hydro-Electric Power Company on October 10, 1906. In this venture Baker and Washburn were associated with John Warren Worthington, a native of Birmingham, who at that time lived in Sheffield. In November the group incorporated the Alabama Interstate Power Company to consolidate the investments on the Tennessee and the Tallapoosa Rivers. Washburn and Worthington are almost absent from Alabama Power Company histories, and where Baker is mentioned, his name is incorrect. Baker's involvement with lawsuits over the Cherokee Bluffs site, Washburn's association with nitrate production and the Muscle Shoals dam site, and Worthington's duplicity against Alabama Power are story lines to come.[41]

Despite the addition of Washburn and Baker, the Cherokee group was not able to put together a financial package to build a dam. Investors were not willing to gamble big money on a large hydro dam in central Alabama. As investors saw it, there were no markets for the electricity that would be produced by the dam. Except for a few nearby small textile mills and crossroad communities, the nearest city was thirty miles away, and Montgomery was not an industrial or manufacturing center. In 1911 James Mitchell made contact with the Cherokee group, and he visited Dadeville, staying with Mrs. Miller in a house three blocks from the birthplace of the Mitchell brothers.[42] James Mitchell explored the region, traveling in Mrs. Miller's automobile, by horse and buggy, and on horseback through the rough terrain. Years later Cherokee Bluffs promoter Henry C. Jones recalled that he once asked James Mitchell how long it took him to decide to invest in Alabama "once the facts were made known." Mitchell's reply was "fifteen minutes."[43]

After his tour of Cherokee Bluffs, James Mitchell was advised to call on Massey Wilson at the Montgomery law firm of Tyson, Wilson & Martin, who together knew more about dam sites and riparian rights in Alabama than anyone. Probably unknown to the Cherokee people, attorney Massey Wilson had left the state. In 1909 he attended a stockholders meeting of the International Life Insurance Company of St. Louis, Missouri, to represent some clients who were involved in a dispute with the company's management. Massey Wilson so impressed everyone that he was elected president of the insurance company and remained in Missouri until he retired.[44] Although Wilson was not there in the firm's office in the First National Bank Building, Mitchell did find Tom Martin.

Attorneys Martin and Wilson and Alabama Law

In 1911 Tom Martin was a young man, thirty years old, and small of stature, born Thomas Wesley Martin on August 31, 1881, in Scottsboro, some seven miles northwest of the Tennessee River. His ancestors settled in Madison County when Alabama was still part of the Mississippi Territory, and his father moved to Jackson County soon after he graduated from the Cumberland Law School in 1873.[45] In the 1880s, the valley and mountainous region in the northeastern tip of the state was predominately an area of white farmers who were struggling to survive the hard times of post–Civil War Alabama, conditions that had pressed many into poverty. In 1880 nearly 50 percent of the county's farmers were renting their land or sharecropping.[46] Tom's father, William Logan Martin, was respected in the community. He served on the board of trustees of the local normal (teachers training) school and took a leadership role in getting a direct primary instituted for the nomination of candidates for county offices, one of the first county primaries in Alabama. This reform impulse put Martin in the camp with those younger interests opposed to older conservative Bourbon leadership. In 1889 Governor Thomas Seay appointed Martin to an unexpired term as attorney general, and the Martin family left Scottsboro for the state capital.[47]

Young Tom was eight years old, his brother William Logan Martin Jr. eighteen months younger, when the family arrived in Montgomery.[48] They both grew up in a political environment and enjoyed the excitement of the capital city. The Martin family was politically well connected, and from an early age Tom understood the value of maintaining that presence. His understanding of Alabama's political world, especially coming from a northern Alabama family and spending his formative years in the capital where southern Alabama politicians predominated, would be invaluable to him and to the company he would later lead. The Martin brothers attended the public schools and J. M. Starke's University School.

Young William Logan Jr. and Thomas Wesley Martin, April, 1887.

Professor Starke was a stern disciplinarian. He taught from a raised platform and lectured with an eighteen-inch mulberry stick in his hand that he used to apply sharp licks to the palms of the hands of students who performed poorly.[49] Years later, Professor Starke recalled the Martins as being "bright, diligent, ambitious boys."[50] Their father, meanwhile, had been appointed to codify Alabama laws and was working as a special judge of the circuit courts. In 1899 Tom entered the University of Alabama and studied in the academic and law departments. He was admitted to the Alabama bar on December 5, 1901, and began the practice of law with his father in the firm of Martin & Martin.

William Logan Martin Sr. "vigorously opposed" the Constitution of 1901 because he believed it would disfranchise many white voters, which it did. Before the election of 1902, rumors circulated in Montgomery that Martin was a possible candidate to oppose Governor William D. Jelks. One report noted that Martin somehow "has never managed to get into the spirit of Democracy as understood and practiced in the Black Belt, and while he has lived here [Montgomery] for more than twelve years, he is looked upon as a North Alabama man." Although the elder Martin was never "within the fold of the [Governor Joseph F.] Johnston [reform] wing" of the Democratic Party, he was considered a "good deal nearer" to this reformist faction.[51]

In 1903 an attorney friend of the Martins, Massey Wilson, who had been around Montgomery for years but was a native of Grove Hill, was elected attorney general. Wilson had served as an engrossing clerk in the Alabama House of Representatives for eleven years, was a delegate to the 1901 constitutional convention, and was a former state legislator from Clarke County. Wilson was considered one of the finest statutory lawyers in the state and one of the best in writing legislation. Wilson appointed young Tom Martin as his assistant. Martin served with Wilson for four years and then served another term under Wilson's successor as assistant attorney general after the position was created in 1907. All the while, Martin maintained a small law practice with his father.[52] In 1907 Martin's father was elected to the legislature representing Montgomery County. That the elder Martin was immediately elected speaker of the house of representatives proves the high regard in which he was held by his peers.[53] In his short time in the legislature, Martin supported the efforts of Wilson and his son to strengthen state laws involving dams on navigable streams. This support proved critical to the successes of investor-owned power companies.

Wilson and Martin first became interested in waterpower rights when they were in the attorney general's office and men approached them about Alabama laws and the right to build dams on the state's waterways. Wilson drew up incorporation papers for the Muscle Shoals Hydro-Electric Power Company and held a small interest in the company, probably given him in partial payment for his legal services. After studying Alabama law, Wilson and Martin determined that state laws were inadequate and actually discouraged waterpower development. Alabama was still operating under the 1812 mill dam statute enacted by the Mississippi territorial legislature. This law applied only to waterpower projects on nonnavigable streams. In 1903 the legislature amended the law to include hydroelectric dams. Wilson realized the unsettling nature of the state's dam laws, and he and Martin drafted changes that removed the restriction limiting these dams to nonnavigable waterways and included protection for the public and potential investors. Only two dams were built under this revised law—the 1903 dam on Big Will's Creek and the one constructed on Choccolocco Creek in 1905. In 1907 Wilson and Martin wrote two new bills to fine-tune state statutes after the passage of a federal act allowing the construction of a dam on the Coosa River. The federal act applied to the Gadsden group that had organized the Alabama Power Company in 1906. At this time, Wilson and Martin had no direct connection to the company. The two Wilson-Martin bills cleared both houses of the legislature and were signed by Governor Braxton Bragg Comer in 1907.[54] Later, these laws would become highly controversial.

The new laws aligned Alabama statutes with the current federal law, were tightly drawn, included many protective rights, and gave the power of condemnation to dam owners. The Alabama Code of 1907 included the acts and actually expanded the powers of hydro companies to condemn lands to be flooded behind a dam when acreage was held on both sides of the waterway. The laws also included a provision to exempt taxes for ten years on the hydroelectric investment, beginning when construction started.[55] Alabama offered these tax exemptions for investments in cotton mills, manufacturing plants, and steel mills. Fifty years later, Tom Martin looked back with pride on these statutes, noting that the laws "have been construed and upheld time and again by the courts of Alabama and the Supreme Court of the United States." Martin observed that, without these statutes, it would have been impossible "to develop the water power of Alabama."[56] The laws were, however, to become an issue in state politics in 1914.

Some two months after his father was elected speaker of the house and only days after the elder Martin helped push the new dam legislation through the house, William Logan Martin Sr. died unexpectedly from pneumonia on March 3, 1907, and was given a state funeral.[57] The next month the Montgomery newspaper announced that Massey Wilson had joined Tom Martin in the practice of law under the firm name of Wilson & Martin. Two years later, John R. Tyson, former chief justice of the Alabama Supreme Court, joined the firm as senior partner.

Mitchell and Martin—A Shared Vision

The Montgomery law firm of Tyson, Wilson & Martin had been recommended to James Mitchell by the Dadeville group that gave him a tour of the Tallapoosa River in 1911. Wilson and Martin had researched the titles, drawn up options, and knew the applicable Alabama law, and they also represented other people interested in dam construction in different places in the state. In later years, Tom Martin wrote many times about his first meeting with James Mitchell on November 11, 1911, but never with the emotion he must have felt as he came to understand and appreciate that here was the man who had the vision, the skills, and the venture capital contacts to bring his hydroelectric dreams to

Young Tom Martin in his Montgomery office in 1910.

fruition and to move the state toward economic change that would improve the lives of all Alabamians.[58] At some point Martin pulled out a map to show the world traveler the rivers and significant places for dams and hydroelectric power sites. Probably it was at this time that Mitchell realized the potential for one integrated electrical system based upon hydroelectric production backed up by steam generation. In long discussions Martin explained the tax exemptions that Alabama offered to new cotton mills, industries, and hydroelectric investments and convinced Mitchell that the Alabama statutes were tight enough to withstand court scrutiny.[59] Looking back on this day, Martin once observed that "I was lucky in the fact that I happened to be in the office that day Mitchell came in. I was lucky in that I happened to like him, and that he took a liking to me."[60] The two men departed Montgomery for Dadeville and another look at Cherokee Bluffs, as well as other sites along the Tallapoosa and Coosa Rivers.

As Martin sketched out the 1911 entrepreneurial power scene in Alabama, this is what Mitchell heard. There were basically six groups of investors with some overlapping—the Coosa River group, known also as the Alabama Power Company, directed by Captain William Patrick Lay of Gadsden; the Cherokee Bluffs–Tallapoosa River group of Jones, Pinckard, Baker, Washburn, Wilson, and Martin, which was allied with the Tennessee River group led by Washburn, Baker, and Worthington; a fourth faction, consisting of the two Mitchell brothers, Reuben of Gadsden and S.Z. of New York and EBASCO; a fifth group including Henry Horne, W. H. Taylor, W. B. Wadsworth, and S. W. Jackson, which owned the site at Duncan's Riffle (eventually the site of Mitchell Dam); and the Wetumpka group of Adolphe Hohenberg, J. M. Holley, Frank W. Lull, and Charles C. McMorris (who owned the site where Jordan Dam was constructed). James Mitchell envisioned a plan whereby the interests of these various groups could be combined by purchase and merger to create a system of efficient and economical electric production with dependable transmission and distribution across the state.[61] Mitchell knew that small scattered electric companies were inefficient and could not offer the cheap, dependable service that a larger company could provide. He planned to purchase and consolidate all the small interests and move forward with a large integrated system.

The information that intrigued Mitchell the most about the Gadsden group was that Captain Lay's Alabama Power Company held the right, by act of Congress, to build a dam across the Coosa River at Lock 12. The trouble was that the clock was ticking on the act: construction had to begin in three years and the dam was to be completed in seven. In fact, some construction had started, but despite frantic efforts, Lay could not find the money to build the dam. He once recalled that his strategy had been to seek funds in Alabama first, then across the South; failing that, he looked to New York and across the United States. Unsuccessful in all these places, Lay had prayed, "Anywhere, O Lord!"[62] James Mitchell proved to be the answer to his supplication.

William Patrick Lay was born in Cherokee County on June 11, 1853. His father and grandfather were local heroes, legendary river men who operated flatboats and then steamboats on the upper Coosa River.[63] A teenager during Reconstruction, Lay once offered that his most disturbing memory was coming upon a lynching scene. The reporter quickly moved to another question.[64] Lay grew up near a gristmill, and as a young boy during the Civil War he spent hours watching the wheel turn, dreaming

William Patrick Lay, ca. 1895.

about what else falling water might accomplish. Lay was far more a businessman than the title "Captain" implied, but he carried it with pride all his life. He was a bookkeeper, a lumberman, a steel man (among other occupations), and the owner of both a hotel and the first electric light plant in Gadsden. In 1902–03, he constructed a small dam and hydroplant at the old Wesson Mill on Big Will's Creek to supply electricity and water to the city of Attalla. In 1903 Lay sold the plant before it was completed, as he explained, "to devote my entire time to the Coosa."[65] Although it was three years later when Lay incorporated Alabama Power Company in Gadsden on December 4, 1906, Attalla has proudly claimed to be the birthplace of Alabama Power. Certainly, out of Lay's dream to harness the Coosa River came Alabama Power Company.[66]

In 1890 Lay helped organize the Coosa–Alabama River Improvement Association to convince the federal government to open the Coosa for navigation from Mobile to Gadsden. Dams would flood the miles of shoals above Wetumpka, covering the rocks and rapids with slack water, while locks would pass boats up and down the river. Precedent gave hope for federal investment to improve Coosa navigation. In the western part of Alabama on the Black Warrior River, the U.S. Army Corps of Engineers made studies in the 1870s and '80s and recommended a series of seventeen dams and eighteen locks. Construction began in 1895. This mammoth Warrior-Tombigee project was under way at the same time that Lay was lobbying for navigational improvements on the Coosa River. The Warrior system of locks and dams was completed in 1915, in time for iron and steel from the Birmingham

Board of Directors of the Coosa–Alabama River Improvement Association, 1895. Lay is front row, second from right. Courtesy of Coosa–Alabama River Improvement Association.

district to be shipped to support America's efforts in World War I.[67] But in the meantime, Lay and his friends pressed for Coosa navigation, admitting that Gadsden was no Birmingham, yet arguing it could be if the region had cheap water transportation to the Gulf. The Corps of Engineers had no plan to capture the falling water for hydro generation at the Warrior River's Lock 17. For decades, water spilled seventy-two feet over that dam, flowing to the sea unused. Cooperation was needed between private enterprise interested in hydro production and the federal government, which was constitutionally charged with improving navigation on the nation's rivers.[68]

At the turn of the century, Lay studied government surveys provided by Alabama senator John H. Bankhead Sr. Using his personal knowledge of the Coosa, Lay decided to focus on the site where the government proposed to build Lock 12. Lay pushed ahead with two challenges: obtaining the federal approval he needed to build a dam on a navigable stream and finding the funds to do so. He lobbied the Alabama congressional delegation, once hosting a meeting on the river aboard the *Leota*. Everyone he talked to favored the project, but no one came forth with any federal money, venture capital, or even a plan. Lay, with son Earl and friend and attorney O. R. Hood, incorporated the Alabama Power Company on December 4, 1906.[69] With Lay as the first president, this would become the company into which James Mitchell eventually consolidated all the smaller power companies and the one destined to serve the state's people into the twenty-first century.

The Gadsden group acquired titles and options on lands around Lock 12, and Captain Lay carefully crafted a bill that would give the company the right to construct a waterpower dam on the Coosa River at the location where Lock 12 appeared on the Corps of Engineers survey. The simple, short bill had strong support from Alabama's congressional delegation, especially John L. Burnett of Alabama's seventh district.[70] Lay avoided a debate over the merits of low versus high dams by not mentioning the dam's height. The law allowed the company "to build a dam of such height as the Chief of Engineers and the Secretary of War may approve." The great Johnstown, Pennsylvania, tragedy where a seventy-two-foot dam failed made Congress cautious about approving high dams.[71] Thirty minutes before Congress adjourned the 1906–07 session, the bill passed its final legislative hurdle and was signed by President Theodore Roosevelt on March 4, 1907. When it came time to secure approval for the dam plans, Lay had to reveal that his dam would be seventy-five feet high. The secretary of war and chief engineer balked until Lay pointed out that this dam was being built with private money and the government would lose nothing if the dam failed. Lay also noted that the site was in an isolated area where there were no people nearby if it should fail. Alabama Power Company's initial $5,000 capital was quickly depleted by legal fees and land purchases, but E. T. Schuler of Gadsden's local electric street railway system put up more money, and clearing of the construction site began in 1910.[72]

NATIONAL CONSERVATION MOVEMENT

To appreciate Captain Lay's struggle to receive his congressional act and to understand the world into which the Alabama Power Company was born, it is necessary to know something about the national political scene and the conservation movement that was sweeping through it. This philosophy retarded the development of a federal waterpower policy and delayed for years construction on Alabama Power Company's dam sites.

In the fall of 1901, President William McKinley was murdered by a deranged assassin, and his vice president, Theodore Roosevelt, became the youngest man to serve as president. Roosevelt shook up the establishment. He brought the zeal of a new century into the White House and unconventional decisions and policies to executive leadership.[73] Roosevelt is most recognized for ushering in the Progressive movement and for his fights against combinations of economic power. But the president's trust-busting hardly impacted Alabama, and some historians believe that the winds of the Progressive movement were but a rare breeze in the state. Ironically, in 1907, it was by Roosevelt's own acquiescence that J. Pierpont Morgan received permission for the United States Steel Corporation to purchase, for a fraction of its true worth, the assets of Birmingham's Tennessee, Coal, Iron and Railroad Company (known locally as TCI). The arrival of U.S. Steel in Alabama made the giant corporation a major player in Birmingham and in state politics.

The area of Roosevelt's program that most involved the Alabama Power Company story was the president's adoption of a policy of conservation, which in large measure came from the influence of U.S. Forestry Service director Gifford Pinchot. The first conservation mission was to preserve the nation's forests. Part of that goal included protecting the nation's rivers through erosion prevention and flood control, providing water for irrigation, domestic and commercial purposes, and protecting hydroelectric sites for governmental development. The latter became the most bitterly contested and heatedly debated aspect of the entire program.[74] This battle was fought in the halls of Congress and in the national press, political campaigns, and party conventions. All of the controversy had a profound effect upon Alabama's congressional delegation and state politics because the Muscle Shoals of Alabama's Tennessee River became the center of the dispute. The Muscle Shoals site came under James Mitchell's control soon after Mitchell began consolidating power interests in the state.

James Mitchell did not fully appreciate the conservation movement's potential threat to investor-owned utility companies that needed both hydropower and steam-generated electricity to serve customers cheaply and dependably. Hydro generation was less expensive but had to be backed up by coal-fired steam generation because hydropower depended upon the flow of water in the river, and that depended upon rain. In fact, rain was the subject of great interest in much of the early company correspondence between Birmingham and New York, London, and Nashville, and nearly every letter mentions or inquires whether or not it has rained. Mitchell was in South America when Teddy Roosevelt became president of the United States and when the early debates began. Encountering conservationist political opposition would puzzle, shake, and anger Mitchell.[75]

MONTGOMERY, MONTREAL, LONDON, AND NEW YORK

After November 1911 the days in Montgomery were busy ones following Mitchell's meeting with Tom Martin. While Mitchell began to put together an engineering team and make contacts for the financing he needed, the firm of Tyson, Wilson & Martin began checking land titles, debts, and incorporation papers and negotiating options on the companies, all mostly inactive, that Mitchell wished to purchase. As early as November 28, 1911, Martin was writing to Frank S. Washburn about legal strategy in Tallapoosa and Elmore Counties on behalf of the Birmingham, Montgomery and Gulf Power Company.[76]

Events in Montreal and London were moving even faster. Before Mitchell sailed for England, where his family was still living and where he intended to approach Sperling & Company for financing, he directed his Canadian bankers and attorneys in Montreal to draw up documents to create a holding company. The Alabama Traction, Light & Power Company, Ltd., created under the laws of Canada, was operational on January 5, 1912.[77] This would be the company that would funnel the funds to purchase the various hydro interests in Alabama, and it would sell stocks and bonds in London to finance the developments. Mitchell knew it would be easier to sell bonds on a Canadian company in England and more efficient to transfer funds from England to Canada than to shift them directly to banks in the United States. Mitchell was closely associated with Lawrence Macfarlane, an attorney who represented Sperling & Company in Canada, and Mitchell had a personal account with the Quebec Bank and an association with the Montreal Trust Company, which would hold the Sperling funds in trust. During this time, Mitchell was using his personal funds, and it would be many years before he was even reimbursed for his expenses.[78]

Mitchell arrived in London in late December carrying the prospectus for the Alabama projects and met with his old friend E. Mackay Edgar at Sperling & Company, which was located at Number 8 Moorgate in the financial district.[79] On January 10, 1912, Mitchell formally addressed Sperling with printed information on Alabama Traction, Light & Power Company, Ltd., and its options on waterpower sites on the Tallapoosa, Coosa, and Tennessee Rivers in Alabama. He shared detailed information on the dam to be built at Cherokee Bluffs on the Tallapoosa River. This was to be the first project for the company because it had the potential of providing the lowest cost per horsepower.[80]

By the end of January, Mitchell was back in New York when Edgar at Sperling & Company received a caller, the general manager of Bonbright's London office. Bonbright & Company was a venerable New York investment house, and its London man came with a cablegram from his home office. The New York office informed Edgar that an "Alabama Conference" had been held in New York City and that "S. Z. Mitchell [was] in our office today." The cable went on to say that Bonbright thought that "Sperling ought to be advised promptly that [the] Alabama prospectus contains important errors and that they would be regarded as deliberately butting-in against such interests as American Cities Company, EBASCO, General Electric of America, Standard Oil Co., H. M. Byllesby & Co., Chase National Bank, Central Trust Co., Guaranty Trust, Hallgarten & Co., Lehman Bros.," and other important financial interests.[81] All of these companies had been approached about investing in an Alabama venture, but as *Fortune* magazine pointed out in 1952, in 1912 "no northern capital would go into so wild a venture as electric power in Alabama."[82]

While James Mitchell did not see the contents of this telegram for four years, Edgar did send Mitchell a cable the same day, January 29, 1912, informing Mitchell that Sperling had received a threat from New York. Edgar's cable to Mitchell read: "Just been informed by Bonbright not advisable to enter Alabama situation because it is likely to cause trouble with strong interests such as Standard Oil, Halgerton [Edgar probably meant Hallgarten & Co.], S. Z. Mitchell, Chase National Bank. Have replied (cajones) lash the colours to mast. Edgar."[83] Tom Martin received copies of these cablegrams at the same time Mitchell did, in March 1916. By then Martin and Mitchell had personally experienced S.Z.'s lack of support for Alabama Power Company interests. In the years ahead, the EBASCO leader's motives constantly remained a puzzle and a concern for them.

CHEROKEE BLUFFS AND THE TALLAPOOSA

In the winter of 1912, oblivious of these attempts by Wall Street to block English capital from flowing into Alabama, Tom Martin busied himself in Montgomery communicating with stockholders of the various Alabama companies and dealing with landowners. He drafted all the legal documents, prepared options, and planned legal strategy. It is easy to imagine the excitement that must have been in the air at the small firm of Tyson, Wilson & Martin. Telegrams and cablegrams were coming and going, and figures were batted about that had more zeros than young Martin had ever dealt with before.

Mitchell's initial plan to build a dam at Cherokee Bluffs ran into trouble. First, Benjamin Russell of Alexander City, through his Industries Light & Power Company, was constructing a small dam at Buzzard Roost Shoals to supply power to his textile mill. Russell filed suit on January 22, 1912, attacking the charter of the Birmingham, Montgomery & Gulf Power Company.[84] His dam site north of the bluffs would be underwater with completion of the Cherokee Bluffs project. Initially, James Mitchell had options but had not acquired control of either the Birmingham, Montgomery & Gulf Power Company or its successor, the Alabama Interstate Power Company. In early January there was a flurry of activity led by Charles H. Baker working with Tom Martin to settle the legal contests so a merger could be completed.[85] Other landowners joined the Russell suit, scheduled to be tried in the Tallapoosa County Probate Court at Dadeville.[86] On January 24, Tom Martin was in Dadeville with resolutions transferring the dam site property and company interests from the Birmingham, Montgomery & Gulf Power to Alabama Interstate Power Company and filing a motion to transfer jurisdiction of a portion of the proceedings to federal court in Montgomery.[87] This Martin succeeded in doing.[88]

Ben Russell was difficult at first, but Mitchell held meetings with him in New York that lasted over six or seven days. Russell recalled that although he and Mitchell were on different sides, he was impressed with Mitchell's keen perception, his ability "to get to the core of things," his fairness and frankness, and what Russell called his "broad-gauged kindly manner." Mitchell won Ben Russell's "utmost confidence and respect." In the years ahead, the two men spent many days together traveling the hills and "rough, muddy roads" of Alabama, where Russell observed that Mitchell always had in mind "the other fellow, playing fair with him."[89] A settlement was made with Russell in February. In later years, Russell focused on his vision and his understanding about what the Cherokee Bluffs development would mean to his community. Certainly, the power from the Cherokee dam was many times greater than the little he might have generated at his Buzzard Roost site, which was closer to Alexander City.[90]

The second problem James Mitchell faced on the Tallapoosa River involved two downstream dams, one owned by Henry L. Doherty, owner of the Montgomery Light and Water Power Company, who settled quickly, and the other a dam site of the Mount Vernon–Woodberry Cotton Duck Company at Tallassee Falls. As early as January 11, 1912, Mitchell told Tom Martin to file a condemnation suit against Woodberry to test the Alabama law and receive the right to use the water not presently used or needed by the mill at Tallassee. They would also be testing the Birmingham, Montgomery & Gulf Power charter, which had succeeded to the Alabama Interstate Power Company, the name in which the suits were filed.[91] State law allowed a power company to capture the excess power that would occur downstream as a result of its upstream dam. A dam at Cherokee would increase the river's flow, and the Mitchell plan was eventually to build two more dams south of Cherokee Bluffs. Tom Martin prepared condemnation papers to be served on the textile mill, which used the water from a small dam to drive turbines for the mill shafting.

Interior of power-house at Mount Vernon–Woodberry Cotton Duck Company Tallassee Falls plant, June 1, 1924.

The Cherokee Bluffs reservoir would also flood lands that would have to be condemned. The first contests were in the probate court and then in the Tallapoosa circuit court. Tom Martin led a team of attorneys that included Ray Rushton, a well-known Democratic senatorial candidate with a brilliant legal mind who practiced in Montgomery; Lawrence Macfarlane of Montreal, an expert in utility laws; George A. Sorrell, a lawyer and civic leader in Alexander City; and James W. Strother, a native of Chambers County and the most prominent attorney in Dadeville.[92] There are occasional internal memorandums in the early files of the company complaining or questioning the expenses of Tom

Martin's legal department, but there is one thing for certain: he knew how to put together a strong team, and he never went into court without feeling he had a winning one. Eventually the Alabama Interstate Power Company won through appeals to the Alabama Supreme Court and the U.S. Supreme Court, but in spring 1912 the outcome was unknown and time was of the essence.[93] Mitchell tried compromise with the Tallassee mill, but failed. He believed he could not wait to build his first dam, so he looked to other properties he was purchasing as the case moved slowly through the courts.[94]

In fall 1911 Mitchell had discussed with Martin buying Captain William Patrick Lay's Alabama Power Company and its assets at Lock 12 on the Coosa, but a New York banking interest held an option on Lay's company. Mitchell went ahead and negotiated a contingency option with Lay, while trying not to signal Lay that he was really interested. He had to wait until the first option expired at noon February 1, 1912, before he could move forward.[95] In January an attorney for Leach and Company, which held the option, had called on Tom Martin; but Martin had refused to discuss Alabama's laws protecting dam development with the lawyer because he considered himself to be in a "confidential position" with James Mitchell.[96] The Alabama Power Company, a company that had almost no activity during its first five years, was about to be vitalized.

During March 1912, Mitchell's Alabama Traction, Light & Power acquired the Muscle Shoals Hydro-Electric Power Company and the Alabama Interstate Power Company (the Washburn, Baker, Worthington group), which meant Mitchell also acquired the Birmingham, Montgomery & Gulf Power Company and the Horne Alabama Railway Power Company, all owned by Alabama Interstate Power. Mitchell used Alabama Interstate Power as his operating umbrella for the first years. The Alabama Interstate Power Company's loans of $400,000, money used to acquire dam sites on the Tennessee and Tallapoosa Rivers, were paid by Alabama Traction to the First Savings Bank and Trust Company of Nashville.[97] These companies were really paper entities that owned power sites but had no other assets and no operational facilities. Not one produced a penny of income. All the companies were kept intact, but Mitchell's early correspondence was on the letterhead of the Alabama Interstate Power Company, which owned the Cherokee Bluffs site that Mitchell had targeted for the first dam construction and which gave the company interstate status. Frederick S. Ruth, Mitchell's administrative assistant, served as secretary-treasurer of the company and began running the one-room Montgomery office at 1116 Bell Building. James Mitchell was president and Tom Martin vice president.[98]

In April the Baltimore-based *Manufacturers Record* announced that James Mitchell, president of Alabama Traction, Light & Power Company and Alabama

Interstate Power Company—and backed by English money—intended to invest $55 million developing hydroelectric sites on Alabama rivers and had established an office in Montgomery. The paper, which focused on southern business and industrial news, noted that the parent company of Alabama Traction was the Southern States Securities Company, Ltd., of London, and that Lawrence Macfarlane of Montreal was president. The financial offering was handled through Parrs Bank, Ltd., "one of the greatest banking houses of London," and was "largely oversubscribed" through a syndicate headed by Sperling & Company. The paper also noted that Mitchell was associated with the American Cyanamid Company of Niagara Falls, Canada, which intended to build a nitrate plant on the Tennessee River at Muscle Shoals.[99] The *Manufacturers Record* was widely read in Alabama by businessmen, newspaper editors and reporters, bankers, and state and local government officials. The idea, later widely disseminated, that Alabama Power tried to keep its English money and foreign investors a secret was incorrect.

Mitchell returned to Montgomery in mid-April but only briefly, for ten days later he was back in New York in a meeting with Canadian bankers.[100] On April 30 and May 1, his administrative assistant Frederick Ruth was communicating with Mitchell, who remained in New York City.[101] On May 1, 1912, in Tom Martin's Montgomery law office, a ceremony took place that was often described by Martin. Captain William Patrick Lay turned over control of the Alabama Power Company to Mitchell and his associates, saying, according to Martin, "I now commit to you the good name and destiny of Alabama Power Company. May it be developed for the service of Alabama."[102] On May 1, Mitchell released a statement to the press:

> A new Alabama and a new South, no longer poor but proud; a South coming into its rightful place; a South that would retain all the finest traditions of its glorious past but which, through that mysterious force flowing silently through the thousands of miles of transmission lines, like life-blood to the human body, would grow richer and stronger industrially, and because of this would in turn grow stronger agriculturally. And the chain lengthens. Not only would ordinary creature comforts follow in the wake of electricity, but there would be better educational facilities, better roads, and better homes. To make money is all right. To build any industry is fine. To build an industry that saves mankind from toil that it can well be spared, that reduces the labor and drudgery of women and so provides leisure for education and culture, truly is a much finer thing.[103]

Over fifty years later, Tom Martin explained that the statement was intended "to express our own broad purpose to serve the ethical, moral and even cultural values of the people of Alabama."[104] By May 8, Mitchell was back in Montgomery, trying to find a business manager for his new company and checking his credit line with his Canadian bank.[105]

Mitchell remained, however, focused on building his dam at Cherokee Bluffs. During his visit to Alabama earlier in the spring, he wrote Frank Washburn on April 27, 1912, that he had "just returned from a trip up the valley of the Tallapoosa" to see what lands would be flooded by the dam at Cherokee. He went up Kowaliga Creek and found it to be "unquestionably the most thickly settled and best district that we shall invade." Mitchell wrote that he had visited with "both the Bensons" and "found them in a very receptive mood." He warned Washburn that "we will do a great deal of harm to their property and [we] must expect to pay them for it."[106] The Bensons were William E. Benson, who was a graduate of Howard University, and his father John, who had worked hard after receiving his freedom to purchase 160 acres on credit, acreage that was very near the plantation on which he had worked as a slave.[107]

In 1914, two years after Mitchell first visited the Bensons, the *Montgomery Advertiser* featured a two-page story on the Benson community and the Kowaliga Academic and Industrial Institute that Will Benson founded in 1897. Some 500 children and young people attended the school. In 1900, Benson established the Dixie Industrial Company, which eventually owned 10,000 acres and had 1,300 acres in productive fields. The company constructed the Dixie Railroad, primarily a logging railroad that hauled the boards from the community sawmill operation and carried people to Alexander City where they shopped or boarded the Central of Georgia to places north and south. A 1914 story in the *New York Times* claimed that this was the "first railroad in America to be conceived, promoted, built, and operated by negro people."[108]

Mitchell had Martin negotiate options on the Benson lands, and an agreement was signed in June 1913. Mitchell purchased the land from the Bensons, the Kowaliga Academic Institute, and the Dixie Industrial Company, but the right to cut and sell the timber on the land was maintained and the school remained open for several more years despite Will Benson's death in 1915, which was a heavy blow to the industrial school. In 1942 Alabama Power Company land manager B. R. Powell concluded that one obstacle to building the dam at Cherokee Bluffs was eliminated early because of the option and early purchase of "the flowage land of Kowaliga Academic Institute."[109]

In his 1912 letter to Frank Washburn, Mitchell expressed his concern over maintaining sanitary conditions while the dam was under construction, but he was pleased that there was so much pine timber on the company's land, most of it on higher elevations. This could be cut and sold to help with construction costs.[110] Mitchell also wrote that Eugene A. Yates had been hired as chief engineer and that he would begin work on Monday. Yates was a giant of a man, six feet, six inches tall. Tom Martin described Yates as physically powerful, yet a shy and modest man who was a superb engineer.[111] James F. Crist, who met Yates in 1923 on a Louisville & Nashville train, described him as a man with "presence," "distinguished in countenance, and seldom without a Homburg hat."[112]

Yates, a native of New Jersey, had graduated with a technical degree from Rutgers College in 1902. He worked for the Pennsylvania Railroad and was assistant engineer on the East River tunnels in New York City. After working on hydroelectric projects in Canada, he came to Birmingham to oversee some street railway work, known locally as the Tidewater line, and was then hired by Mitchell.[113] He was one of the best hires Mitchell made. Yates had a genius for design, construction, and

Eugene A. Yates, ca. 1924.

utility as well as talent as an administrator.[114] He immediately got busy going over all the studies and surveys of the Coosa and Tallapoosa Rivers and spent time in the field with survey crews so he could fully understand the engineering challenges he faced. He was somewhat taken aback by one survey that reported gold mining operations in the Tallapoosa basin.[115]

After weeks of investigating the Coosa and Tallapoosa Rivers, Yates informed Mitchell of problems on the Tallapoosa. He confirmed that at its proposed and proper height the dam would flood some roads, but more important, it would cover the Central of Georgia Railway bridge over the Tallapoosa River near Jackson's Gap and flood some of the tracks. Raising this bridge would lengthen the time allotted for preliminary construction and increase the cost of creating the reservoir. Yates believed that this problem should be solved before moving on and recommended that the Coosa dam be built first and that hydro development of the entire Coosa River be planned in advance of the first construction. Yates wrote that he was impressed by "the enormous amount of power which can be developed from Lock 12 to Wetumpka, if the whole river is controlled by one corporation, and if the separate developments are made so that on completion of all developments, they will work out as one big unit."[116] Mitchell made the decision to build first on the Coosa River. Yates was placed in charge of the engineering forces for Lock 12. He thought it advisable to invite MacArthur Brothers Company, Empire Engineering Corporation, and a number of other companies to send men to study the Lock 12 site. Then, he wrote, when "I am able to complete [the] form of contract, proposal, specifications and drawings for the gravity

Oscar G. Thurlow, ca. 1920.

William E. "Will" Mitchell, ca. 1920.

dam, they will be in a position to make us a bid in a short time."[117]

Two other men came to the company in early summer 1912 to work on the Lock 12 dam: Oscar G. Thurlow as design engineer and William E. "Will" Mitchell, James Mitchell's younger brother, as electrical engineer. Both would have a lifetime of association with hydroelectric development in Alabama and the Southeast. Thurlow was born in Massachusetts one year before James Mitchell graduated from high school. He earned a civil engineering degree at Massachusetts Institute of Technology and began his career building a bridge over the Connecticut River. After several jobs, Thurlow built two large dams in New York, then came south to construct the waterworks and dam on Village Creek for the Tennessee Coal, Iron and Railroad Company in Birmingham. James Mitchell brought him to Alabama Power Company as design engineer, and Thurlow designed the concrete spillway on the Lock 12 dam. Thurlow possessed fine organizational skills and was a good judge of character. He had a talent for building a workforce and inspiring men to work with him. He also had patience and perseverance.

Because of the age difference and his brother's long years in South America, Will Mitchell first remembers seeing his brother when he was fifteen years old. He did take James's advice to study engineering at Massachusetts Institute of Technology and with his degree joined the General Electric Company in New York. Will worked in Brazil for six years and then returned to the United States in 1911, the same year James came home from England. Will, now called W.E. by his associates, went back with GE, this time in the western states. In 1912 his brother James hired him to be the electrical engineer for the Alabama Interstate Power Company, working with Yates and Thurlow.[118]

In May, Mitchell held a meeting in Montgomery to sketch out a twenty-year plan "to develop 600,000 horsepower at a cost in excess of $100 million." Mitchell gathered Captain Lay, Eugene Yates, Oscar Thurlow, Will Mitchell, Reuben Mitchell, Frank Washburn, Armour C. Polk, and Wiley Alford together for the discussions, and plans were outlined.[119] By early summer, James Mitchell realized that he needed a general manager in Alabama with electrical and management skills, and he needed his administrative assistant, Frederick Ruth, who had been running the Montgomery office, back in New York City. After contacting several men in the East and putting the word out, Mitchell hired W. W. Freeman, who was vice president and general manager of an Edison company in Brooklyn. Freeman moved to Montgomery and began work on July 15, 1912.[120] Freeman's tenure with the company lasted just over a year, but it was the crucial first year of operations. He directed the move of the corporate offices from Montgomery to Birmingham, but his family never moved south and his wife had difficulty coping without her husband. Freeman handled myriad details for Mitchell and was candid and loyal in his confidential correspondence to his boss; however, the office was not operating smoothly.

THE FIRST YEAR

Throughout this first year, Tom Martin was busy securing good titles to lands that would be flooded by the company's dams and following up on the Woodberry lawsuit. In early years, Martin played no real role in company decisions beyond his legal sphere, but he was steady and dependable, on target with his legal advice, and he proved to be a master at understanding the politics of the local courthouse. For instance, he worked through a cadre

Chester A. Bingham, ca. 1912. Courtesy of Jack Bingham.

of county-seat lawyers, carefully picked for their legal experience and reputations as well as for their knowledge of local politics and canny ability to get things accomplished within the culture of the people. Knowing family relationships, feuds, and the details of local history was vital to dealing with people's land, including title verifications. Chester A. Bingham, a young Harvard law graduate who was a partner in an old prestigious law firm in Talladega, began his association with the company at this time. Bingham first worked out of his office examining titles and abstracts for lands to be flooded by the Lock 12 dam. Catching the eye of Martin and Mitchell for his abilities and high standards, Bingham was offered a position with the company and moved to corporate headquarters. He was known for his integrity and was a tireless worker and a meticulous lawyer. Bingham would work closely with Martin on preparations for various early lawsuits with which the company was involved, and he eventually handled much of the company's legal responsibilities dealing with finances. He traveled frequently to New York, and in the late 1920s Bingham moved his family to New Jersey and rode the train to Wall Street every weekday to work in the holding company's office there.[121]

Tom Martin's relationship with Frank W. Lull, an attorney and stockholder in a local power company at Wetumpka, typified his style of work. Lull was helping Martin with land titles along the Coosa and wrote Martin that some land he was working on for the company was tied up in chancery court. For some of this land Lull could not find the owners anywhere. On one parcel Lull reported that he was working through two friends who knew the landowner because "[I] wasn't on speaking terms with the gentleman we had to deal with." Lull was putting the lands in his and another attorney's names so it would not get out that a power company was purchasing the land. When Martin pressed him for closure, Lull responded that "all of the ingenuity of five of us lawyers in Wetumpka and the Bank officials and several hard-headed country-men have been taxed to the utmost for several months to get this matter closed." The local bank, interested in the economic development that would come with electricity, was putting up the front money.[122]

On June 6, 1912, James Mitchell wrote from Montgomery to Alabama Power director Frank Washburn in Nashville. After covering dam construction and engineering reports on the rivers, Mitchell informed Washburn that "while I am here on this trip, I intend going up through the small towns of the north and look over some of the properties belonging to the Electric Bond & Share Company, including Anniston, Talladega, and Little River as well. When I go back to New York, if my visit is satisfactory, I may then close up something with the Bond & Share Company."[123] The next month, on July 22, 1912, Mitchell did negotiate a deal with S.Z. and EBASCO and purchased the Alabama Power Development Company, in which Reuben Mitchell also held some interest.[124] The company had a small hydro plant on Choccolocco Creek at Jackson Shoals and transmission lines to Talladega.[125] The company also had a state-of-the-art steam plant under construction at Gadsden, a plant that Mitchell needed to provide reserve for the hydropower being planned. Following the sale, Webb W. Offutt, who had been serving as vice president and general manager of EBASCO's interests in northern Alabama, came to work with Alabama Power.

Years later, Will Mitchell recalled his brother's "trades" with S. Z. Mitchell: "Many interesting stories might be told of the negotiations of these two great pioneers in the electrical industry. Both keen, both of Scotch descent, one black-haired, the other red-headed! "[126] By the end of the summer, James Mitchell had also purchased the Anniston Electric and Gas Company, the Decatur Light, Power and Fuel Company, the Huntsville Railway, Light and Power Company, the Little River Power Company, and the Etowah Light and Power Company all from Electric Bond & Share. On September 26, 1912, the *Wall Street Journal* announced that James Mitchell had "purchased outright" all the Electric Bond & Share Company holdings in Alabama.[127] *Manufacturers Record* announced that the company was building a steam plant at Gadsden.[128] These companies produced the first cash income for Mitchell's holding company, a mere trickle compared to the funds that were being expended to purchase companies and land and to support the construction of the Lock 12 dam, which was under way at full speed by late summer.[129] The net earnings for the company's first year of operation was $26,268, while the amount being expended was millions of dollars.[130] It must have been painful for the young company to respond to firms inquiring about electricity and the possibility of building plants in Alabama by answering that the Alabama Interstate Power Company had no continuous power to sell.[131]

Just a few days after James Mitchell finalized his purchase of the northern Alabama properties from Electric Bond & Share, an event took place at the White House in Washington, D.C., that had an effect upon the story of Alabama Power Company and the history of economic development in central Alabama. On August 24, 1912, President William H. Taft vetoed an act sponsored by Alabama congressman Oscar W. Underwood that would have allowed Alabama Power Company to build a hydroelectric dam on the Coosa River at the Lock 18 site.[132] O. R. Hood, Lay's attorney in Gadsden, had warned Tom Martin in May that getting congressional permission to build the dam would be difficult. There was a concerted effort to have Alabamians pressure Congress for approval.[133] This was the first lobby effort James Mitchell sponsored. J. W. Worthington was the lobbyist in Washington, and the efforts were successful in getting the bill passed by both houses of Congress, despite considerable debate and opposition from the conservation advocates.[134]

Although the bill passed with Representative Oscar Underwood's strong support, the Alabama congressman was opposed by other Democrats and the issue was caught up in presidential politics. President Taft had the Republican nomination and was being opposed by former president Theodore Roosevelt, running as the Progressive Party nominee, and Woodrow Wilson, as the Democratic candidate.[135] Taft had little to gain by pleasing a solid Democratic state like Alabama. The president's veto caught everyone by surprise because it was thought the bill agreed with Taft's views on dam construction on navigable streams. The president stated in his veto that the federal government would not be paid enough for the waterpower site, funds that could assist the government in providing navigational improvements. Underwood vigorously objected to the veto, saying that the federal government was actually placing a tax on Alabama consumers for their use of a site that belonged to the state of Alabama, not the federal government.[136] Underwood even suggested that Alabama Power would go ahead and build the dam under the charter granted by the Alabama legislature.[137] The company had no intention of doing this, but Alabama Power eventually built that dam—Jordan Dam—and it was in service on December 31, 1928; however, the Taft veto precluded construction of the large nitrate plant being planned for central Alabama using electricity from the Lock 18 dam. The electricity from this dam and the construction of the nitrate plant were expected to spur huge investments in plants and manufacturing, bringing jobs to the area north of Montgomery and Wetumpka, economic development that never happened.[138]

Frank S. Washburn was the man behind the plan to manufacture nitrates. When Washburn was working in New York City on the Third Avenue Cable Railway, he was hired by William R. Grace Company to go to Chile to renovate a nitrate operation, which he did very successfully. He returned with considerable knowledge of the nitrate industry and an understanding of the American and British interest in nitrates as the prime ingredient in fertilizers and explosives. He believed that the United States needed a supply of nitrates that was not dependent upon foreign countries. When Washburn learned of two new European electronic-arc processes for nitrogen fixation, he went to investigate and returned convinced that the German cyanamide process was workable, though he needed a large supply of cheap electricity to make it profitable. This led Washburn to survey southern hydroelectric sites and into a partnership role in both the Tennessee River Muscle Shoals and the Tallapoosa River Cherokee Bluffs groups. His interest in waterpower and his knowledge of nitrates were behind his selection as a director on the first board of James Mitchell's Alabama Traction, Light & Power Company.[139]

Washburn was a brilliant, hard-working, and earnest engineer with a natural talent for business organization. He incorporated the American Cyanamid Company on July 22, 1907. Although Washburn was a well-to-do man with wealthy relatives and friends, he could not come close to putting together a financial package to build a dam at either Cherokee Bluffs or Muscle Shoals. In 1907, when he saw no possibility for hydroelectric development in Alabama, Washburn negotiated a deal for cheap electric rates from sources in Ontario at Niagara Falls; therefore, he located his first nitrate plant on the Canadian side of the river. The first carload of nitrates left the plant on December 4, 1909.[140] But Washburn did not lose interest in Alabama's hydroelectric potential. He planned to build his second nitrate plant in the United States and to locate it in central Alabama near Wetumpka. No historian of twentieth-century Alabama has pointed to President Taft's veto of Alabama Power Company's Lock 18 dam as an economic turning point for Alabama, but it clearly was a road not taken in the state's economic development.[141] Washburn located his first American plant in New Jersey. His plans for a nitrate plant in Alabama were revitalized when Mitchell arrived.[142]

Coosa River Reservoir and Lock 12 Dam

By June 6, 1912, Mitchell had decided to push forward with the dam at Lock 12. On August 1, 1912, three weeks before President Taft vetoed the bill for a dam at Lock 18, Alabama Power Company signed a cost plus

Left to right, James Mitchell, W.W. Freeman, O. G Thurlow and E. A. Yates inspect Lock 12 progress from a construction bucket suspended from an overhead crane, April 18, 1913.

Liner and shaft for unit 4 at Lock 12, January 23, 1914.

fixed fee contract with MacArthur Brothers Company of New York to build the Lock 12 dam.[143] *Manufacturers Record* reported on August 15, 1912, that the contract had been signed for a 1,500-foot long, 74-foot high gravity dam after the designs of Hugh L. Cooper. Harvey H. Jackson III, in his thorough study, *Putting "Loafing Streams" to Work: The Building of Lay, Mitchell, Martin, and Jordan Dams, 1910–1929,* has detailed, especially from the point of view of the engineers and workers, the building of the Alabama Power Company's first four dams.[144] The construction of the Lock 12 dam (later named Lay Dam) is well covered in Jackson's book. In 1912 the pressure was on the company and its engineers to meet the congressional deadline, and the construction contract carried a December 31, 1913, completion date. There was much work to do. Train tracks and trestles were needed to transport materials, supplies, and workers into the construction site. A camp with water, sanitation, and housing for workers and superintendents had to be built, along with dining halls, a commissary, a clinic, and a hospital where injured men could recover with good medical care. This was taking place while the lake bed was being cleared.[145]

The company spent much effort on determining how best to clean the reservoir floor. Mixed recommendations came from the state health department as well as from other power companies. Some wrote that trees left in the reservoir did not matter; others said to clear all the trees and brush. Yates advocated clear-cutting, with shoreline stumps cut low and trash trees and limbs burned to make the water clean and to destroy debris that might clog the turbines. The company was aware of potential problems and made plans to clear the reservoir correctly—whatever that was—and to work with the Alabama Health Department to follow state law. When hot weather came in 1913, sickness and malaria in the region were blamed on the waters collecting in the cleared reservoir behind the dam, and Alabama Power was widely criticized.[146] Protest meetings were held, and small-town lawyers who had done legal work for the company warned Martin of hostile feelings up and down the Coosa Valley. Tom Martin was particularly concerned. He understood the precarious financial condition of the company and knew that lawsuits were costly to defend.

Alabama Power had Yates, Thurlow, and W. E. Mitchell as well as Yates's assistant E. L. Sayers and resident engineer Armour C. Polk on site at Lock 12 most of the time during construction. It is significant to note that the young men who took leadership roles during the construction at Lock 12

Transmission line survey crew, Lock 12 line, September 16, 1913.

provided management leadership for the company in later years. To build the dam, expert engineers needed both skilled and unskilled labor, and many men in both these positions at Lock 12 worked their entire careers with Alabama Power, moving up the ladder of responsibilities in the decades ahead. The first laborers who were recruited by MacArthur were recent immigrants who came from the East, but southern heat and ten-hour shifts, around the clock, were too much. Soon native southern workers, black and white, were employed. Still it was hard to retain labor because the work was so hard.[147] There were some conflicts between the MacArthur people and the company during construction, a situation that convinced Martin and Yates and his engineers to form a separate Alabama Power construction company to build the next dam.[148]

While the dam was under construction, field engineers were poring over county soil and road maps and topographical sheets to determine the best route for transmission lines. Survey crews began walking the terrain, checking creeks and rivers, mapping out routes as straight as possible from Lock 12 north toward the industrial cities of Birmingham, Gadsden, and Anniston. B. R. Powell directed the land department and kept a good relationship with the landowners as the power company survey crews trooped through people's land without their permission (though under state law they had the right to do so). The names and addresses of landowners were gathered from tax records, and the legal department began securing the rights-of-way once a route was decided. Crews of the toughest men, directed by Captain J. S. White and led by P. O. Cotton, then began clear-cutting the path, setting poles and towers, and stringing lines. They moved slowly along this line, camping at night in tents and eating in tents or chuck wagons as they braved hot weather, snakes, and other Alabama pests.[149]

Corporate Office Moves to Birmingham

As the twentieth century opened, there was a significant difference on questions of business, industry, and capital between those prevalent in Montgomery and Birmingham (which was called the "Magic City" because of quick growth after its founding in 1871). Montgomery was an antebellum town of the Old South, a Confederate capital where "the Democracy" held sway. The population was mostly Montgomery- and southern-born. Cotton and the culture it fostered predominated and made Montgomery a merchant town. On the other hand, Birmingham was a booming industrial city of the New South, a city with no antebellum history where recent immigrants from Europe and the North rubbed shoulders with southern entrepreneurs and men on the make.[150]

The number of industrial customers who could use electricity was much greater in Birmingham than in Montgomery. As Tom Martin explained, "Markets within economical transmission distance must be developed by persuading industrial operators of the economy and efficiency of electric power."[151] The company planned its first triangle of transmission lines to connect Lock 12 with Birmingham and Anniston, then Gadsden.

One year before Mitchell arrived in Montgomery, the iron and steel town in northern Alabama had become a metropolis through annexation, making Birmingham the third largest city in the South. Its industries had many absentee owners and northern and foreign investors. In Birmingham, there was less concern over who you were or where you came from than there was interest that you came with money and you invested it. These were all reasons Alabama Power Company moved its headquarters from Montgomery to Birmingham's Brown-Marx Building in the fall of 1912.[152] Several other developments made this a fortuitous move. The Birmingham to Montgomery highway was finished in late summer 1913; the great cotton crop destroyer, the boll weevil, reached Montgomery in late fall 1913; the Panama Canal opened in 1914; and Lock 17 was completed in 1915, opening the Birmingham mineral district to the Gulf Coast by way of the Warrior-Tombigbee River system.[153]

In an interview with *Manufacturers Record* in October 1912, W. W. Freeman, Mitchell's general manager, announced the company's plans for industrial recruitment. He said that through exhaustive study, the company knew "the fields of consumption" were in Alabama, and it "can sell the power." Freeman explained that the company intended to bring new manufacturers into the area, that Alabama Power was "building properties that will last" and that were "designed to produce electric power on the cheapest scale possible." The company would have a tremendous amount of power to sell, he said, and it intended to put forth its best efforts to recruit industry into the state to use that power.[154]

In December 1912 the *Manufacturers Record* featured James Mitchell's activities in Alabama as president of Alabama Interstate Power Company and its construction of the Lock 12 dam. Mitchell announced that his company intended to bring new industries to Alabama and to fulfill a service to the people of the state. He wanted "the best possible relations with the people," for he said his company depended "upon their good will for life, and they will prosper if they will assist us in that way. Every place we have ever worked, we have been welcomed, and I am sure Birmingham will not prove an exception. The relation of people toward a public service corporation must be cordial, or that corporation cannot last long. Birmingham, I believe, will give us that encouragement."[155]

The construction of the dam and transmission lines from the Coosa River

occupied the company during 1913. In January, W. W. Freeman hosted a group of state dignitaries and newspapermen on a tour of the construction site. He stressed that the power company purchased supplies in Birmingham, had 700 workers at the dam, and employed 100 people in local offices. The *Birmingham Age-Herald* announced that the dam would produce enough electricity so that fifty-watt lights placed 100 feet apart would illuminate a highway around the world and the copper in the conductors would make 256,000,000 pennies. The *Birmingham News* praised Alabama Power Company and the corporation's recognition of its place as a public utility company serving the people with the lowest electrical rates possible. Soon after Freeman hosted state dignitaries, James Mitchell arrived with a party of London bankers and E. Mackay Edgar to inspect their public utility investments in North America, including Alabama.[156]

By January 1913 the entire Coosa River had been surveyed and mapped, and 50,000 acres of land had been surveyed in the valley of the Tallapoosa. The *Birmingham Age-Herald* reported that Alabama Power Company would flood 20,000 acres and had paid farmers "very liberal prices" for the land. The hydroelectric plant at Jackson Shoals on Choccolocco Creek was operating, and at the beginning of 1913 electricity flowed over transmission lines to Talladega, Anniston, and Gadsden. After one year of operation, Alabama Traction, Light & Power reported that the people of Alabama were "keenly interested" in all the company's activities and understood "their immense significance in the development and progress of this territory." Citizens and chambers of commerce were "lending the company encouragement of their approval and support."[157] In June 1913 the company hosted a tour of the Lock 12 construction site by state officials. Governor Emmet O'Neal headed the delegation and praised the move from the steam era to a new era of electricity. Freeman articulated the company's goal of selling electricity at a competitive price and its understanding of its place as a public service company.[158]

Problems Ahead: Not Enough Money and Too Many Mosquitoes

Alabama Power Company faced two serious threats to its future, one in 1913 and the other in 1914. In late spring 1913 the company was running out of money and funds were tight in England. This was followed in spring 1914 by the filing of hundreds of lawsuits that claimed that the reservoir waters of the Coosa were causing vaporous emanation, illness, and malaria in families who lived near the lake. The funds that James Mitchell had received from Sperling & Company were nearly depleted in eight months. Unfortunately, the first Balkan war broke out about this time in eastern Europe. Although not directly involving England, the two brief Balkan wars in 1912 and 1913 threatened to activate the European system of alliances and bring Britain into a general European war. That did happen after the 1914 assassination of the Austrian archduke in Serbia, an event that brought on World War I.

All three of these wars affected Alabama Power Company. The Balkan wars shook the financial markets of the world and sent European nations and the United States into a business recession in 1913. This occurred at a crucial time in the plans of the Alabama companies. The Lock 12 dam was still under construction, working against a congressionally mandated deadline, and money was running out. James Mitchell later explained to his wife Carolyn that many "well informed people" in American financial circles believed "the great drop in prices of the past year or so preceding the war was brought on by the constant liquidation [of assets] by big German industrialists who knew that the war was settled to come."[159]

James Mitchell went to London in the summer of 1913 to speak directly with Sperling leaders and was even more concerned over what he found when he arrived. He wrote W. W. Freeman that "it is useless to talk of placing any securities here at the present moment." Sperling was having trouble with other American and Canadian utilities investments, and Mitchell was "inclined to think that the Banks have put their foot down very strongly against further advances on American securities at the present time." Mitchell saw no way to get through the crisis without a loan in New York. He suggested that "every effort" be made to convince S. Z. Mitchell to take up the quota of securities to which he had agreed. He also advised Freeman that a visit to Birmingham financial interests might be needed. Mitchell told Freeman that only necessary expenditures should be made on the Gadsden Steam Plant until it was selling power and that he should work with manufacturers "to carry us until we can get this settled." Mitchell confessed that he did not know the Birmingham people "well enough to know whether it is feasible to have a frank talk with [W. P. G.] Harding [president of the First National Bank] on the present situation, but one thing is certain, that if we should be unsuccessful in the present juncture in getting the necessary money to keep things going at full swing, it is going to be a very unfortunate circumstance for Alabama." Mitchell observed that "Sperling & Company and their following raised every cent of the money for Alabama, and I have been guided entirely by their views."[160]

Freeman discussed the situation with S. Z. Mitchell and reported back to his boss in London that S.Z. was dragging his feet about coming up with money. Pressing S.Z. was touchy because at the time the Alabama Power Company was negotiating a contract to provide wholesale electricity to the Birmingham Railway, Light & Power Company, and S.Z.'s EBASCO was a principal stockholder in the Birmingham utility. American Cities Company also had a large interest and Sperling was heavily invested in both, which made the *Wall Street Journal* anticipate that the deal between Birmingham Railway, Light & Power and Alabama Traction, Light & Power would be successful.[161] On other matters, Freeman wrote that the dam at Lock 12 was progressing well, and contractor A. F. MacArthur anticipated it would be completed before the end of 1913. The Gadsden Steam Plant was "95% complete and steam will be on the plant on June 20th." Transmission towers between Lock 12 and Birmingham were finished, but all lines were yet to be strung. Freeman updated Mitchell on contracts for electricity being negotiated in the Birmingham area by both Frank Washburn and

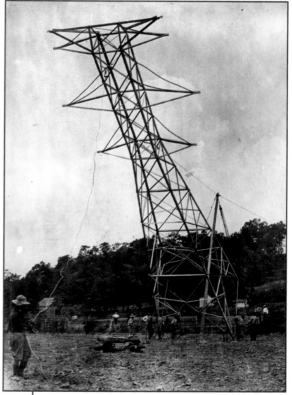

Erecting a steel tower on the Lock 12 transmission line, July 7, 1913.

J. W. Worthington and the company's commercial salesmen.[162] Mitchell had formally established a sales mission and hired Theodore Swann to head a new commercial department. Although Swann had many contracts pending with cities and industries, he was finding it difficult to close them.[163] Washburn wrote the *Birmingham Age-Herald* explaining that "the New Business Department" was "one of the largest and most important departments of this company."[164]

On October 13, 1913, Washburn addressed the Alabama Power directors explaining the company's financial situation. He noted that the company needed to generate $1 million gross income in order for Alabama Traction to be self-supporting and pay off the interest due on its bonds and to pay 6 percent dividends on its preferred stock on January 1, 1915, the date the stock became cumulative.[165] Company income was still a long way from covering the debt and expenses of operation and development. James Mitchell began piecing together enough capital to continue for another year despite the business recession in the United States and London. On November 13, 1913, Mitchell wired new general manager F. H. Chamberlain instructions not to pay anything except payroll until he heard from him. The final payment of $55,000 was due in December to MacArthur Brothers for completion of the dam at Lock 12. W. J. Henderson of Montreal, secretary-treasurer of Alabama Traction, Light & Power, recalled that throughout "the trade depression of 1913 . . . the stream of pounds and dollars continued to flow into Alabama." Often, Henderson wrote, Mitchell "pledged his personal resources" to ensure the work in Alabama would continue.[166] The New York construction company finished the dam on time, and James Mitchell was there to see the gates closed on December 28, 1913.[167] Heavy rains had water flowing over the dam crest by January 1, 1914. Tom Martin notified the Department of War that the dam was completed within the statutory requirement, although some clean-up work was being completed around the dam into 1914. By April 1, 1914, the powerhouse at Lock 12 was generating electricity from unit 1.[168]

Alabama Traction, Light & Power Company issued its first annual report, dated May 15, 1914, and covering the year 1913, to stockholders on July 28, 1914. The company had 160 miles of 110,000-volt transmission lines delivering current through three substations to a distribution system of 116 miles of 22,000 volts. Mitchell told the shareholders that although the earnings were insufficient to carry the company's fixed charges and operating expenses, the directors remained confident in the wisdom of their policy and nothing had changed their view about "the prosperity of the enterprise," which he believed "promises to become one of the largest and most important of its kind."[169]

The general European war that began in August 1914, later called World

War I, made it impossible to continue obtaining capital funds from England, yet the outstanding first-mortgage bonds prevented the Alabama Power Company from raising new funds in the United States. In a London meeting with bond-holders on October 21, James Mitchell was able to convince them to defer interest payments for three years and allow the sale of "new bonds and preferred stocks which would have priority over outstanding securities, including those of the British."[170] In his history of electricity in Alabama, Tom Martin called this decision "the magnificent gesture." The vote was unanimous, except that when the vote was taken, the EBASCO representative from New York, Niel A. Weathers, abstained from voting for those bondholders he represented. At this point in a draft of the manuscript of his biography, which was then being written by John Temple Graves II, Martin carefully marked out the lines: "The failure of Electric Bond & Share to vote its Alabama Power bonds with others in London in 1914, when generous forbearance by the majority of these bondholders had enabled the company to survive as a going and growing concern, was never fully understood."[171] In one draft of that manuscript, there is the handwritten suggestion that S. Z. Mitchell may have wanted the proposal defeated so that Alabama Traction and its subsidiary, Alabama Power, could be taken over more easily.[172]

Another view of this meeting appeared a decade later in a feature article about Alabama Traction. The *Wall Street Journal* explained the company's 1914 survival this way: "The average British investor has a lot of confidence in his broker, and from all that can be found out from this side of the ocean made no trouble for the company's management on account of the fact that property development was in abeyance and that bond interest may have been paid either out of principal or from the use of money borrowed in other ways." The *Journal* noted that in the United States "we might have had a receivership or a young panic so far as the company's securities were concerned," but "perhaps in accord with English custom, a meeting of the bondholders was called, held in London, [and] the position of the bonds placed squarely before those who owned them."[173] In any case, bankruptcy was avoided, and Alabama Power Company moved forward once more.

The second crisis the company faced involved the hundreds of lawsuits filed in 1913–14. The company was aware of potential problems in the area where malaria was endemic and had worked closely with local and state health officials. Historian Harvey H. Jackson III covers the details of the company's efforts to make certain the reservoir was clean. Most of these "mosquito suits" were scheduled for trial in February 1915. A dozen prominent attorneys had planned the power company's legal strategy for months. Tom Martin had requested that state health officer Dr. W. H. Sanders, Chilton County

Dr. William Crawford
Gorgas, ca 1914.

health officer J. T. Hunter, and local doctors C. J. S. Peterson, C. K. Maxwell, and Julius Jones inspect the farms, creeks, ditches, and backwaters of the lake. Their assessment was "that local conditions for terminating mosquitoes must be removed before attributing the present illness to the reservoir or lake."[174] There was also a study by J. A. Le Prince, sanitary engineer for the U.S. Public Health Service, which pointed to the breeding places of the anopheles mosquito being close by people's homes.[175]

When Tom Martin went to Washington to convince Dr. William Crawford Gorgas, surgeon general of the U.S. Army, to come to Alabama to investigate the conditions in the reservoir and the homes of the plaintiffs, he knew what Gorgas would find. Dr. Gorgas, an Alabama native and an expert on malaria, yellow fever, and the anopheles mosquito that carries malaria, toured the Lock 12 area for three days with Tom Martin, Oscar Thurlow, and Fred Hale, and he found exactly the same conditions the Alabama doctors had discovered earlier. Gorgas testified in the L. D. Hand trial, a case Thurlow described as "one of the worst suits which we had to contend with."[176] The army doctor explained simply in language the jury understood that the anopheles mosquito was able to fly only a short distance from its breeding ground, that the homes of the complainants were too far from the reservoir, and that the stagnant water in ditches, tin cans, and buckets around the homes were the places where these mosquitoes were bred.[177] The company won the case, and other suits were eventually dismissed.

Alabama Power Company, however, was concerned about malaria threats to people in the nearby counties and to its own workers at Lock 12 and initiated programs to improve the health of residents in central Alabama. The company worked with the state health department and supported educational efforts to encourage people not to allow water to collect near homes. Alabama Power encouraged and supported research into mosquito prevalence in Alabama and the mosquito breeding cycle. The company stocked its reservoirs with minnows that fed on mosquito larvae, and it took even greater care to clean the basins of future reservoirs.

TALLASSEE MILLS LAWSUIT

As the Alabama Interstate Power Company's suit against the Tallassee Falls–Mount Vernon–Woodberry Cotton Duck Company slowly worked its way through the court system, the textile mill attorneys attacked the Alabama law of 1907 that gave rights to builders of dams. They made much over the "foreign capital" and out-of-state men involved in Alabama Power Company. This tactic was ironic because the textile company itself was the result of mergers of mill interests from Maryland, Connecticut, and South Carolina with an Alabama mill. Alabama Power Company was criticized as being a foreign corporation, and much was made of the enormous combination of economic power Alabama Power possessed, charges so far from the truth they were ludicrous. Debt was what the company really had in abundance. One positive point in these charges was that the power company evidently had been successful in hiding the fact that it had been tottering on bankruptcy. Chester A. Bingham assisted Martin in preparing this suit, which involved the use of water and the excess waterpower that would result from an upstream dam at Cherokee Bluffs. After the court ruled, Bingham negotiated contracts involving the water flow in the Tallapoosa River at Tallassee.[178]

The Alabama Supreme Court ruled in the company's favor, something Mitchell called "epoch-making in the life of our company." But the Tallassee Falls company filed a rehearing brief through the textile mill attorneys, Goodwyn & McIntyre, listing the addition of Judge John McElderry Chilton and H. N. Randolph—two attorneys, Tom Martin wrote Mitchell, who had not been involved with the case before.[179] Martin sent Mitchell a copy of the document and warned him that the brief was not intended for the court but "for political uses." Mitchell replied that "it is certainly a most extraordinary document, and I cannot conceive that it will have anything but an adverse effect on any sane court." He wondered if it had been designed "to forward the campaign of those now electioneering in Alabama."[180] The brief attacked the power company, condemning it as a foreign corporation, calling the company an "octopus" and "a power trust" that wanted to steal the Tallapoosa River, as Ahab, the King of Samaria, in the biblical story stole the garden of Naboth.[181]

The octopus as a symbol representing hydroelectric companies appeared in Alabama at least as early as January 4, 1913, when *Southern Farming*, published by the Orange Judd Company of Springfield, Massachusetts, featured the "New Octopus Monster" of the "water power trust" on its cover. The octopus was stretched across a map from California to Maine, its tentacles controlling the nation's "white coal" of hydroelectricity, "one of the greatest discoveries of modern times." The weekly magazine told farmers that the "white coal" of the nation's rivers should be owned, controlled, developed, and operated by individual states.[182] Such control was not possible in Alabama because the Alabama Constitution of 1901 expressly prohibited state government from doing this,

THE ORANGE JUDD

SOUTHERN
FARMING

$1.00 a Year   JANUARY 4, 1913   WEEKLY

Do Not Let the New Octopus Mon[opoliz]e
the inexhaustible store of white coal in our Souther[n] [stat]es

White Coal Will Make Cheap Light, Heat and Power on Farms and in Factories—
Each State Should Own and Control, Develop and Operate, Its White Coal Supply

IF a vast deposit of oil or of natural gas or of anthracite coal were struck at different points in each of our coastal and inland states, what an excitement it would cause! But all the black coal, all the natural gas and all the oil that can be imagined would be of small importance relative to the inexhaustible supply of white coal that heretofore has run to waste, but which now is rapidly being monopolized by the hydro-electric trust.

What do we mean by white coal?

Dam a river, direct its waters into a canal or penstock so that its force shall revolve water wheels directly connected with electric generators. The product is electricity, which transmitted by wire, furnishes light, power and heat for any and all purposes. And be-

cause you can thus make the wheels go around without any of the filth, smoke, soot and dust of black coal, we thus transform flowing waters into "white coal."

This is one of the greatest discoveries of modern times. The apparatus and methods for utilising this discovery are being improved constantly. The loss of power between the dam and the consumer is being reduced. The efficiency of the method approaches perfection.

What is the first result of all this?

A few enterprising men form corporations, get control of water courses, and seek to monopolize the white coal supply. The so-called hydro-electric trust in its various manifestations has already

[To Page 8]

SPRINGFIELD, MASS   ORANGE JUDD COMPANY, Publishers   ATLANTA, GEORGIA
NEW YORK, Ashland Bldg   Business Established 1842   Candler Bldg

Southern Farming magazine opposing the "water power trust,"
the private ownership of hydroelectric sites, January 4, 1913.

even if it had the funds to do so (which it did not) and the will to do it.

In his reply to the court and in defense of the company, Tom Martin waxed eloquent, and with a suggestion from his legal assistant, Bernice Summers, turned the biblical argument around so that jealous King Ahab, who coveted the vineyard of Naboth, the commoner, was advised by his wife, Queen Jezebel, "Take and Pay Nothing," which was, Martin said, what the Tallassee Falls–Mount Vernon–Woodberry Cotton Duck Company sought to do. Mitchell wrote Martin that he "was immensely amused at the very clever manner in which you handled the very ancient question referred to by the counsel for the Tallassee Mills."[183] The brief of the Mount Vernon mills argued it was "a case of the Water Power Trust against the People of Alabama" and lamented that the "Power Trust" had powers "beyond the wildest dream of a Malay pirate."[184] Historian Harvey H. Jackson III described this rhetoric as populist, and indeed, attorney Goodwyn's father was a leading Populist politician of his day.[185]

Attorneys for the Tallassee Mills mailed briefs to the state's newspapers and to every legislator. One must wonder what James Mitchell, with no experience with Alabama demagoguery, thought about all this. His English and Canadian backers were pouring millions of dollars into Alabama, and he had invested much of his own fortune to bring electricity to the state. Yet at the time the suit began, all his combined Alabama companies were not producing one red cent and, when the suit ended, not much more. Mitchell addressed most of the points of the attacks on his company in a memorandum dated May 4, 1914, and issued it as a press release. He made clear that the 1907 Alabama law was passed before his group entered the state and was not enacted for its benefit; however, the ten-year tax exemption was a consideration encouraging investment in Alabama because for ten years his company would have difficulty meeting its fixed interest charges on capital funds. Mitchell reminded those who claimed the state of Alabama should be building dams that, in fact, the Constitution of 1901 expressly forbid the state from doing so. He noted that hydroelectric dams were actually a conservation measure because they reduced the amount of coal being burned. He wrote that "very few people of this state appreciate the true significance of the work which has been carried on for the past two years" at Lock 12: the thousands of men employed, the railroad freight rates, the supplies purchased from Alabama businesses, the 200,000 barrels of cement, and the thousands of dollars paid for land purchased at or far above fair and reasonable market prices. Alabama Power Company had much work still to accomplish. In closing, Mitchell wrote that he had confidence in the people of Alabama to understand that "the public at large will realize far more important results from those developments than will the stockholders of the company."[186]

After the Alabama Supreme Court ruled, Martin explained that the attorneys for the textile mill "sued out a writ of error to the Supreme Court of the United States." In 1916, Justice Oliver Wendell Holmes wrote the opinion siding with Alabama Power Company. The development of waterpower was for public use, and condemnation rights prevailed. Holmes included these often repeated words: "to gather the streams from waste and to draw from them energy, labor without brains, and so to save mankind from toil that it can be spared, is to supply what, next to intellect, is the very foundation of all our achievements and all our welfare."[187] The significance of the legal victory in the Tallassee Mills suit, beyond the right to develop the Tallapoosa, was the legal precedent Tom Martin considered of great importance. The trial marked the beginning of periodic demagogic attacks on Alabama Power Company, one reason why, from the very beginning, the company was constantly trying to get its own message before the people. Looking at the history of Alabama and its difficulty in securing capital investments before and after 1912, one might observe that the state's only hope in 1912 came from a Canadian-born, northern-raised man who had been away from his country for twenty years and from English investors who had confidence in what could be developed in Alabama. Both were willing to put their money behind their vision.

WASHBURN AND WORTHINGTON YEARS

On August 20, 1913, when the Alabama Power Company board of directors met in Birmingham, James Mitchell resigned as president, and the board elected Frank S. Washburn president and J. W. Worthington vice president. Both were on the original board of Alabama Traction, Light & Power and were elected to the Alabama Power Company board of directors at a New York meeting on August 5, 1913. The official company press release announcing Washburn's new position stressed his involvement with the production of nitrates through his American Cyanamid Company and the interest Alabama Power had in improving the industrial scene in the state by encouraging nitrate production as well as providing electricity for steel production through the new electric furnace. The release noted that James Mitchell was giving up active direction because his responsibilities in New York and London prevented him from an active management role that the Alabama company needed. The changes were, the release stated, "to secure closer and more nearly continuous direction of the company's management, affairs, and policies."[188]

All of this was true, but in the preceding summer Washburn and Worthington were writing Mitchell about serious management problems in the company. The leadership in the field and in the engineering department was excellent, but management and office support was not as strong or as organized. Mitchell's family still lived in London, and most of the Traction Company directors were in Canada, England, and New York. Washburn's home was in Nashville, and Worthington was living in Sheffield when he was not in Washington, D.C., or Tate Springs, Tennessee. Executive leadership merely passed in and out of the Alabama Power Company office in Birmingham, and the day-to-day direction depended upon a general manager. Mitchell's letters discussing these problems with Washburn and Worthington are insightful, and they illustrate Mitchell's personality and character. He did not like to deal with personnel problems, and he was most concerned about the careers and reputations of men who were failing him. Mitchell had many other business interests, such as Mexican Northern, a company constructing a dam in Mexico, and these investments kept him from being in Birmingham on a regular basis.

After August 1913 Washburn began to spend time in Birmingham, and by the end of October three top men in the office were gone. Washburn's correspondence was very detailed, and he was obviously a leader with hands-on experience, knowledgeable about engineering, chemicals, personnel issues, and especially legal matters involving hydroelectric statutes. One wonders how Tom Martin received Washburn's pages of advice on legal questions, especially involving the early suits. In his correspondence Washburn was direct, fair, and open, except in September 1913, just as men were being fired, when he initiated a new policy of no personal or offhand interviews with newspapers.[189] There was a real concern by Mitchell and the board of directors about the large amount of money flowing out of the company. For instance, on October 4, 1913, Washburn approved appropriations for transmission line construction ($24,140), circuit design and installation ($224,421), transmission lines from Jackson Shoals to Birmingham ($277,432), transmission lines from Sylacauga to Alexander City ($41,269), and a double circuit 110,000-volt line of towers from Lock 12 to Birmingham ($41,116).[190]

As president, Frank Washburn instituted the first uniform policies and procedures manual that stipulated job responsibilities and included an organizational chart that had a new business department as well as an industrial department charged with recruiting new industries to Alabama.[191] He put pressure on the commercial department to deliver signed contracts, and he required Theodore Swann to send him weekly letters report-ing what he had accomplished. Washburn himself began writing detailed letters to Mitchell every week.[192] He required all man-agers to submit weekly reports on sales calls and, later, reports on all power production and power outages.[193] In one of his executive memorandums he described the nature of a corporation and noted that "a feeling of antagonism is often created in the minds of those who do not thoroughly appreciate the advantages of the construction of a corporation." Washburn gave department heads the responsibility to make sure that subordinates understood the design and purpose of the company and that customers were the primary concern. Employees, he wrote in 1913, must feel "that they are being employed by individuals who are sensible to all human feelings and not by some great, intangible thing called a corporation. We want our officials, heads of depart-ments, and all our employees to feel that they are part of a great family rather than part of a great corporation."[194] By this time, Washburn was successful in his business career, had considerable wealth of his own, and was a trustee of Vanderbilt University. He was well connected with financial interests on the east and west coasts, and in 1913 he was sitting on the board of United Gas & Electric Corporation with Samuel Insull and S. Z. Mitchell.[195]

Frank S. Washburn. Courtesy of the Ayer Company Publisher, Manchester, New Hampshire.

John Warren Worthington was another matter. The son of a pioneer Jefferson County family, Worthington moved to Sheffield after a business association in Birmingham with Henry Fairchild DeBardeleben. Called Warren by his family and "J.W." or "Colonel" by his friends, he immediately became involved with various Sheffield civic and business interests and was president of the Sheffield Bank. He soon was associated with the Tennessee River Improvement Association, which campaigned for improved navigation on the river. Worthington was an engineer with experience as an industrialist and businessman but without the financial success he expected. His niece recalled that her uncle had traveled to Europe to study the German method of producing nitrates from the air, and this may be one reason he was associated so closely with Washburn. Worthington was described as "a man of exceptional vision, rhetorical ability, and intellectual faculties."[196] But he was also secretive, once described by an assistant as "having sneaking ways," a man his niece described as having "a passion for anonymity" and working "behind the scene," a man whose "ideas were very conservative" and who "had little use for what he called 'the people.'"[197]

Mitchell had trouble with Worthington, too. He objected to some changes that Worthington, as vice president of Alabama Power Company, made in accounting procedures, which resulted in the company's income showing up poorly. Mitchell was also displeased when he learned that Worthington had been informing S. Z. Mitchell about the company's business, and he sent orders that Worthington was not to discuss the company with S.Z. because S.Z. had "refused to abide by his written agreement to assist in the further financing of the Alabama Power Company, thus throwing the entire burden on Mr. Edgar and myself, and his interest in Alabama is becoming proportionately less as time goes by."[198]

Worthington has been labeled an American Talleyrand, a reference to the French minister who was able to serve Bourbon kings, revolutionaries, and Napoleon.[199] Unfortunately, Worthington left instructions to have all his papers and correspondence destroyed at his death lest "they might eventually reach other hands causing further misunderstanding," a task his secretary carried out.[200] However, letters to and from Worthington are found in various collections. While financially comfortable in 1913–14, Worthington did not move in the same circles Mitchell or Washburn did, and his investments soon suffered reverses. Worthington's arena was not business but politics. He was a polished and smooth operator whose letters flowed with the language of the nineteenth century, his effusive compliments and apologies blurring the meaning of his words. He often wrote indirectly, not really addressing his subject. He was not comfortable sitting at a desk in Birmingham but preferred the life of a lobbyist in Washington, where he made many friends and spent much of his time, especially when Congress was in session. Worthington was in his last years a recluse. Although other evidence backs up Worthington's opinion of inattentive company managers, his complaints might have been manipulative.

In his history of electricity in Alabama, Tom Martin totally ignores the brief tenures of Washburn and Worthington in Alabama Power Company's executive offices, no doubt because of controversies that later developed over Muscle Shoals and because to do so would require Martin to deal with problems and issues he preferred to ignore. And then, too, Worthington lived until 1942. Both Worthington and Washburn, certainly after 1915–16, had agendas not in the best interests of Alabama Power. Washburn wanted to produce nitrates with cheap electricity, and Worthington wanted dams and locks on the Tennessee River for navigation; he wanted cheap electricity for the Sheffield area; and he advocated cheap fertilizer for farmers. When each man determined that the Alabama Power Company was not going to be able to support these developments, they turned to other plans. Tom Martin was often unforgiving. He also probably omitted Worthington because the two had differences in 1914, once when Worthington went behind Martin's back to interfere in a legal matter Martin was handling.[201] Then there were some differences over Worthington's compensation, and Worthington once questioned the expenditures of Martin's legal department.[202] Tom Martin considered Worthington's later actions traitorous, and it is likely that Martin never trusted him from the beginning.

In the first months of the company's operation, Tom Martin was occupied with legal matters, and he was not involved with company business outside his legal responsibilities. But after the ascendancy of Washburn and problems surfaced in the Birmingham office, Washburn and Mitchell came to depend upon Martin. More and more Martin was consulting and advising Washburn, and especially Mitchell, on issues more operational and managerial than legal. It is no wonder that from his position as general counsel, Tom Martin becomes the most dependable, astute, and loyal follower James Mitchell had and certainly the most devoted to Alabama Power Company. These were critical years for the company. The problems that Washburn tackled and solved in his nineteen months as the president of Alabama Power Company, even if Tom Martin failed to recognize it in his history or his memoirs, gave Martin a stronger company when that title and responsibility passed to him a few years later.[203]

Warrior Reserve (Gorgas) Steam
Plant showing the original unit
and the U.S. government unit,
September 1923.

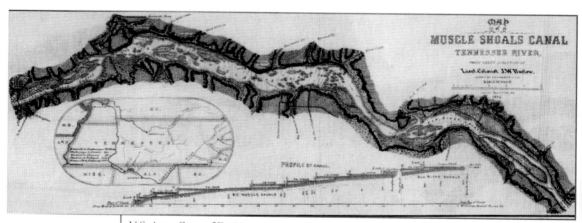

U.S. Army Corps of Engineers
map and profile of the Muscle
Shoals and canal design from
Harper's Weekly, 1890.

Chapter Three

Anniston street railway officials and employees
in front of the company car barn, 1919.
Courtesy of Lance Johnson Studios, Anniston.

INTRIGUE AT THE SHOALS
AND A WAR IN EUROPE

*The Alabama Power Company hopes and believes that its hydroelectric
developments in Alabama will bring to the production of iron and steel by
the use of the electric steel furnace, a new impulse.*

STATEMENT, ALABAMA POWER COMPANY BOARD OF DIRECTORS,

Birmingham Ledger, August 29, 1913

At the end of the nineteenth century, the mighty Tennessee was a wild
river, draining from a large watershed and flowing to the sea through northern
Alabama. Before dams tamed its floods and made still its waters, the river's
course was slowed by obstructions with colorful local names–the Suck, the
Boiling Pot, the Tumbling Shoals, the Skillet and the Pan. One historian of the
Tennessee described it as a "series of long pools, slanting and winding down
the slope of its mountain valleys, like some vast, crudely shaped stairway of
giants."[1] Close to the fall line, which ran a very irregular course in northwest
Alabama, the river was slowed by one group of shoals and rapids that ran for

thirty-seven miles and dropped 3.57 feet per mile over the course of seventeen miles. The water made a "terrible roaring sound," and the current ran in all directions. Named Little Muscle Shoals, Big Muscle Shoals, and Elk River Shoals, collectively these rocks and ledges were called simply the Muscle Shoals.[2] Before Europeans came, Indians lived near the shoals because it was an easy place to gather mussels. Stories differ about how the name came to be. Pioneers in small keelboats ran the shoals in high water, and it did take "muscle" to steer boats safely through the rocks and ledges.[3] In old records the name is spelled both ways.

This dangerous reach prevented navigation on the Tennessee River for generations. Alabama governors in their annual messages to the legislature often included plans to tame the shoals. None ever did.[4] The federal government appropriated funds from time to time to "improve navigation" or build canals, and though at least two were constructed, none ever operated effectively. The first railroad in Alabama connected one end of the shoals to the other.[5] Discussion in the nineteenth century about what to do with the Muscle Shoals pales when compared to the heated debates of the early twentieth century. And Alabama Power Company was right in the middle of the controversy because it owned the best two dam sites at the Muscle Shoals (where Wilson and Wheeler Dams were later constructed).

Florence, on the northern bank of the Tennessee, was an antebellum town; Sheffield, across on the south side of the river, was incorporated in 1885 in anticipation of becoming a great industrial city. Birmingham capitalists jumped into the development of Sheffield's brown ore deposits, proclaiming a great city would rise on the high cliffs above the Tennessee River just below the Muscle Shoals. In 1886 Colonel Edmund W. Cole, a Nashville railroad man, announced that he had invested more than $200,000 in Sheffield and predicted that in two years, "You would see the Tennessee alive with Sheffield shipping."[6] Cole's brother-in-law, Frank S. Washburn, became interested in the shoals area as a hydroelectric dam site and joined Sheffield banker, promoter, and hawker John Warren Worthington to push for the development of a dam at the Muscle Shoals that would provide navigation of the Tennessee as well as electricity.

In 1896 John A. Patten Sr. founded the Tennessee River Improvement Association to lobby for navigation of the Tennessee.[7] Part of the early arguments over hydro development involved the question of the federal government's power to control riverbeds versus a state's right to control nonnavigable streams. Alabama's congressional delegation generally took the states' rights position, and, encouraged by Worthington's lobby activities, the delegation pressed for funding to improve navigation on the Tennessee River. Alabama's Democratic delegation was hampered, however, because the Republican Party dominated the federal government and it was not interested in spending money in the South. Engineering studies of the Tennessee and appropriations for improvements had not been provided by Congress to the same extent as for rivers in other sections of the country. Federal money had been expended on the Muscle Shoals Canal, designed and constructed by the Army Corps of Engineers, so there was opposition to flooding the canal by a dam, even though the canal was totally inadequate and rarely used. As early as 1898, northern Alabama congressman Joe Wheeler was able to have an act passed for the private construction of a hydroelectric dam at Muscle Shoals, but funding could not be found and the statutory time limit expired.[8] Worthington began to speak to Alabama senator John Tyler Morgan about the Tennessee River as early as 1901, for at this time he saw government support as the only way to build the dam.[9] A bill for the Muscle Shoals was vetoed by President Theodore Roosevelt in 1903. The president favored having funds from the sale of electricity generated at the dam to go toward paying for navigational improvements, and this bill carried no such provision.[10] Worthington realized that a lack of engineering studies of the Tennessee River was one drawback to building a dam at the Shoals. In 1905 he convinced Senator Morgan to introduce a resolution calling for several engineering studies of the Tennessee River and the Muscle Shoals.[11]

The General Dam Act, passed by Congress in 1906, was expected to facilitate the development of the Shoals area.[12] The *Florence Times* reported that the Muscle Shoals Hydro-Electric Power Company, organized on October 10, 1906, planned to build two dams on the Tennessee River and sell water and electricity to public and municipal corporations. The newspaper verified that deeds to 106 acres had been recorded in probate court from Frank and Irene Washburn to the hydroelectric company.[13] Washburn was credited with an investment of $250,000.[14] The Tennessee River Improvement Association held its tenth annual meeting in Sheffield in November 1906, and a few days later Worthington gave a rousing speech to the Young Men's Commercial Club in which he painted a glowing picture of economic development that would come to the region after the Tennessee River was opened to navigation. The talk was enthusiastically reported by the *Manufacturers Record*.[15] Economic development, which Alabama so desperately needed, would come from navigation of the Tennessee and from electricity produced by a dam at the Shoals. On the very day Worthington spoke, November 14, the Muscle Shoals group joined the Tallapoosa River group and formed Alabama Interstate Power Company, which envisioned building dams on both the Tennessee and Tallapoosa Rivers.[16] The Rivers and Harbors Act of 1907 instructed the War Department to issue guidelines on what portion of the development should be for navigation and flood control, and thus was a federal expense, and what portion was hydro-electric and thus a cost to private enterprise. There was anticipation that a joint government-private investment might conquer the Muscle Shoals.

Oscar W. Underwood, ca. 1915.

In the campaign for the Tennessee River, Worthington became close friends with Oscar W. Underwood of Birmingham, floor leader in the House of Representatives from 1911 to 1915, an Alabama senator from 1915 to 1927, and a candidate for the Democratic presidential nomination in 1924. Underwood was known as a strong supporter of business, but he was also influenced by Worthington, who for years worked in Underwood's campaigns, raised money for him, and became somewhat his confidant.

John H. Bankhead Sr., ca. 1915.

When Worthington broke with Alabama Power Company, Underwood was influenced by Worthington's lead. The senator's biographer, Evans C. Johnson, explained that "Underwood's services to Birmingham industrial interests resulted not from venality, as his enemies argued, or laissez-faire convictions, as his friends claimed. Rather, he favored business interests as a result of the influence of personal friends to whom he owed political debts." Historian Johnson went on to give as an example J. W. Worthington, "a utility lobbyist who combined avarice with a vision for the development of Alabama" and through whose influence Underwood was pitted alternatively on the side of or against Alabama Power Company.[17]

Worthington also worked closely with John H. Bankhead Sr., the Jasper congressman and later U.S. senator and founder of perhaps the most prominent political dynasty in Alabama history. Both Bankhead's sons, John and Will, later served in Congress and provided powerful support for the New Deal. Worthington was probably never happier than when he was lobbying, moving about the Capitol and Senate and House office buildings and living at the New Willard Hotel, of course, on an expense account. James Mitchell invited Worthington and Frank Washburn to serve on the first board of Alabama Traction, Light & Power Company, and within a few months Mitchell had acquired the assets of both the Muscle Shoals Hydro-Electric Power Company and the Alabama Interstate Power Company for his holding company. In the next months, Mitchell financed a number of Worthington's trips to Washington to represent the interests of his Alabama companies. On September 12, 1912, the *Florence Times*, quoting Worthington, announced that the Alabama Interstate Power Company had "$55 million behind it" to spend on developing waterpower, and that the company had already let a contract on a dam at Lock 12 on the Coosa River in Chilton County and expected its largest dam would be built on the Tennessee River at the Muscle Shoals.[18]

In his early correspondence, James Mitchell recognized the enormous power potential of dams on the Tennessee River. He agreed with ideas first proposed by Washburn and Charles Baker that hydroelectric dams on the Tennessee and Tallapoosa Rivers needed to be operated together because the Tennessee, with a watershed of 28,000 square miles, had adequate flow for only ten months but not in the dry season of late summer and early fall. If a large storage reservoir could be built behind a dam at Cherokee Bluffs and transmission lines were connected into a system with the Muscle Shoals dam, the Tallapoosa waters could take up the slack when the Tennessee plant was idle due to low water.[19]

Eugene Yates asked Washburn for and received copies of the "mass of drawings" held by the Muscle Shoals Hydro-Electric Power Company as he began his study of the river and cost estimates for a dam for James Mitchell.[20] Mitchell knew enough about dam construction to realize before he received Yates's detailed engineering analysis and cost estimates that the dam at the Muscle Shoals would be extremely expensive to build. From the start, Mitchell believed the Tennessee was not the place for him to begin, and the extensive cost overruns, delays, and dangerous conditions encountered later when the federal government built Wilson Dam proved he was correct. Mitchell's plan was to begin his company on a solid footing, and he needed to generate and sell electricity as soon as possible. He thought, and Yates agreed, that three or four dams could be built on the Coosa and Tallapoosa for what one dam on the Tennessee would cost. Dams could be built on the Tennessee River in the future, after the Coosa-Tallapoosa dams were producing electricity, which was being sold and providing revenues so necessary to making Alabama Power Company a viable corporation.

Alabama Power and Alabama Politics

In January 1914 the people of Alabama were enjoying a heated Democratic primary, which was tantamount to election since the Republican Party was not strong enough to contest the Democratic Party in the general election. In February Dadeville civil engineer James R. Hall warned Alabama Power president Frank Washburn that there was trouble for the company in the Tallapoosa basin, which was to be flooded by the dam at Cherokee Bluffs. He wrote that landowners had initially paid little attention to the Cherokee development because some felt it was "preposterous and impossible," but since the Coosa River dam had been constructed, the community realized a dam on the Tallapoosa River was coming. There was dissatisfaction because the Alabama legislature had granted the company the right and power to condemn lands to be flooded, and Hall anticipated the issue would be "going into politics both local and state wide."[21] And indeed it did.

Judge William Logan Martin Jr., ca. 1923.

Alabama Power was brought into the attorney general's race between Tom Martin's brother, William Logan Martin, and D. H. Riddle of Talladega. Riddle had represented losing clients against Alabama Power in cases that were appealed to the Alabama Supreme Court, and he accused Martin of being "in the service" of the power company because his law firm, Martin & Martin, represented Alabama Power Company.[22] Despite the charges, Logan Martin defeated Riddle, was elected attorney general, and served until he resigned to volunteer as a West Point graduate for military service during World War I.[23] After Logan Martin returned from the army, he was appointed judge of the Alabama Fifteenth Judicial Circuit (Montgomery) and served until he moved to Birmingham in 1920.[24] After 1919, he was always called Judge Martin.

In the hard-fought gubernatorial campaign in the 1914 Democratic primary, former governor Braxton Bragg Comer and Charles Henderson were the leading candidates. Henderson was a major stockholder in the Pea River Power Company and was considered pro-business, but in almost every speech he attacked Alabama Power Company, and so did Comer.[25] To counter some of the bad press, James Mitchell sent a press release to all state newspapers on February 25 stating that the American Cyanamid Company, in conjunction with the Muscle Shoals Hydro-Electric Company, which was owned by Alabama Power, planned expenditures of $30 million to erect a dam and a large nitrate plant to produce fertilizer in northern Alabama.[26]

In the next weeks, the news coverage was more favorable to the company. Londoners E. Mackay Edgar and Edward Welton of Sperling & Company visited Alabama to inspect the dam at Lock 12. At that time the dam was finished, the generators were being installed, and electricity was due in Birmingham by April. Edgar called the construction on the Coosa "the finest he had seen at any hydro-electric plant," and on February 26, 1914, the *Birmingham Age-Herald* noted that Edgar had inspected many plants all over the world. This British group barely missed the visit of S. W. A. Eschaucier, a Dutch banker whom the *Age-Herald* called "one of the leading financiers of Europe."[27] He came to inspect the Alabama properties for possible investments. Frank Washburn went to London to explain the prospects to Sperling.[28] The newspaper reports pictured a flush company, a story good for enticing investors but fuel for populist orators and demagogues who had no access to the company's balance sheets, which showed the company was barely staying alive.

Governor Emmet O'Neal, who was not running for reelection because the constitution barred him from succeeding himself, was vigorously supporting Henderson against Comer. O'Neal also attacked the power company, charging it was a great power monopoly. He spoke with an entirely different tone than he had used after touring the Lock 12 dam in a speech where he praised the company's investments and contributions to the state. O'Neal also criticized Governor Comer for signing the 1907 dam law that gave companies investing in hydroelectric power the same ten-year tax exemption on that investment (but not on other assets) that the state granted to investments in coal mines, steel mills, and cotton mills.[29] The *Montgomery Advertiser* noted on April 26, 1914, that the *Abbeville News* defended the ten-year tax exemption on water-power development in the state and called attention to the fact that Charles Henderson started a power company in Elba and had "used the tax exemption structure" himself in the process.[30] Mitchell employed an Atlanta advertising company to direct a campaign to make Alabama voters understand the tax exemption issue.[31]

Despite all the hostile rhetoric against Alabama Power, and usually it was only called "the power company," it was not the main issue in the election. Prohibition was.[32] Political charges were made that the power company was on the side of Prohibition, but Worthington "hotly and effectively denied the existence of any coalition between Alabama Power and the prohibitionists."[33] Tom and Logan Martin were both in the prohibitionist camp and had a historical tie to former governor Comer because of Comer's friendship with their father.[34] The political race was so passionate and intense that former governor Comer pulled a knife on gubernatorial candidate Lieutenant Governor Walter D. Sneed at a rally in Dadeville, causing the *Montgomery Advertiser* to ask, "Has a political campaign ever reached the low level of this one?"[35] Henderson beat Comer in a primary runoff for the Democratic nomination. After the late summer general election, when all the Democratic candidates won (which was routine), Tom Martin learned that the attorneys for Tallassee Falls Mills (in the suit against Alabama Interstate Power Company) had sent a copy of their Alabama Supreme Court rehearing brief, with its demagogic charges, to every state legislator and most newspapers, despite the fact that Alabama Interstate Power Company/Alabama Power Company had won the case and the Tallassee company lost in the courts.[36] This brief, which Tom Martin called "a very remarkable document" intended "not so much for the court as for political uses," was probably where most of the trouble originated. Almost immediately, Alabama Power began working on an "attractive brochure," chiefly for use with legislators and prospective customers but also suitable as part of a report to stockholders.[37]

During O'Neal's gubernatorial term, despite pressure to regulate power and telegraph companies, the legislature had refused to extend the railroad commission's powers to regulate public utilities.[38] After Henderson was elected in 1914, Worthington was accused of working against Governor Henderson and helping the ultra-prohibitionists organize the legislature, a charge Worthington, then a vice president of Alabama Power, vigorously denied.[39] The Alabama Power Company leadership, especially Tom Martin, was very concerned.

WORLD WAR I AND MUSCLE SHOALS

In the World War I period, the development of the Muscle Shoals became inextricably connected to the idea of production of atmospheric nitrates by an electronic process. Frank Washburn's initial curiosity in the Shoals area and in hydroelectric generation came from his interest in the fixation of atmospheric nitrogen for use in fertilizers and in manufacturing explosives. In 1908, after Washburn lost hope that a dam would be built at the Shoals, he located his first American Cyanamid Company plant in Canada near the cheap power being generated by the Ontario government near Niagara Falls. By December 1909 that plant was manufacturing commercial nitrates.[40] Washburn lost some interest in the Muscle Shoals, but it remained a top priority with Worthington. In 1912 Washburn expected to locate his second plant north of Montgomery to take advantage of the Alabama Power Company dam planned for Lock 18 on the Coosa River near Wetumpka. In August 1912 after President Taft vetoed the bill that would have allowed Mitchell to build that dam, Washburn made plans to locate his first American facility in New Jersey. If Taft had not vetoed that bill and Alabama Power had been able to proceed with what later would be completed in 1928 as Jordan Dam, the United States would have had a nitrate supply when it entered World War I. But when war broke out in Europe in August 1914, nitrates were suddenly very much on the minds of the president and the generals in the War Department because the United States had no ample domestic source.[41]

By spring 1914 the American economy began to improve from the slight recession of the year before.[42] In March, Frank S. Washburn, James Mitchell, and E. Mackay Edgar sailed on the *Lusitania* for England to raise $30 million to develop a nitrate plant at Muscle Shoals.[43] In late March, the *Montgomery*

Advertiser published a story written by James's brother, W. E. "Will" Mitchell, on the "Remarkable Hydro-Electric Development in Alabama" detailing the developments of the company. In twenty-four months Alabama Power Company had built a dam on the Coosa River with a head of sixty-eight feet (the largest in the state), and furthermore, the power plant at the dam had the largest turbine ever installed in the United States up until that time. The steam plant at Gadsden had been completed, and five Alabama cities were receiving power. Transmission lines had been strung from Lock 12 to Sylacauga, Talladega, Anniston, and Gadsden. To the west, transmission lines ran from Lock 12 to Calera, Helena, Bessemer, Leeds, and Pell City and connected with the eastern loop at Jackson Shoals. A short line served Ben Russell's mills and Alexander City. The company also had small operations in Huntsville and Decatur. In this newspaper story, Will Mitchell pointed out the advantages of an interconnected system, which made it possible to electrify small industries where otherwise the cost of operating a separate power plant would be prohibitive.[44]

James and Carolyn Mitchell in Brazil, ca. 1906. Courtesy of the Mitchell family.

From New York, James Mitchell wrote his wife Carolyn in London on December 4, 1914, a few months after the war started, that "Alabama matters required me to put up some more money and take some additional responsibility pending the raising of new money." Two weeks later he told her: "I have been assured that we could get the extra money for Alabama, but I have not seen the color of it yet and will be on the anxious seat until it is really obtained." Mitchell had "not yet gotten down to Alabama as there has been so much to do in connection with legal and legislative matters." He warned Carolyn to "hold on to your cash" at least until "I get Alabama straightened out, which will, I hope, be soon."[45] On

Christmas night 1914, Mitchell wrote Carolyn from New York that he had "not yet found the necessary money for Alabama but hope to by March 1st when our next notes fall due."[46]

Alabama Power and World War I

British and French orders for American munitions and supplies after the European war began in August 1914 pulled the United States out of its business recession, but the British blockade of the German coast in November and the German announcement of a U-boat zone in February 1915 escalated the naval war. On the nineteenth of that month the Alabama Power Company board of directors met in New York to consider the financial condition of the company and to secure more loans. Edgar came over from London for the meeting. S. Z. Mitchell signed a letter that Electric Bond & Share would provide $2 million in funding. James Mitchell shared this news with his wife on February 13, writing Carolyn that he had been "leading the usual dog's life trying to get Alabama in shape. The next two weeks will tell definitely with what success. I think I have at last succeeded in getting the backing of one of the strongest concerns in this country [EBASCO], and we are now completing the arrangements for the sale of $2,000,000 of bonds which will put us in splendid shape."[47] In anticipation of this bond sale, in a very significant move, the board decided on February 19, 1915, to merge the assets of several small companies into Alabama Power Company. For practical purposes, the group of companies had worked as one from the beginning, but so many different names confused bondholders as well as the public.[48]

James Mitchell had a half-million dollars due on March 1 and nothing to pay it with until he sealed the deal with S. Z. Mitchell.[49] This increased EBASCO's equity in Alabama Traction/Alabama Power, but its interest remained a small percent.[50] After the 1915 merger, Alabama Power Company, represented by Francis E. Frothingham of Coffin & Burr and Harry M. Addinsell of Harris, Forbes & Company, sold a $2 million issue of three-year 6 percent bonds, its first in the American market.[51]

The board of directors also discussed plans to boost the power available to Anniston, Decatur, and Huntsville by building another steam plant.[52] But before anything could be accomplished, at the next board meeting on March 1, 1915, Frank Washburn resigned as president of Alabama Power Company to pursue his nitrate agenda, and James Mitchell again assumed the presidency. Brigadier General William Crozier, chief of ordnance, who was concerned about the supply of nitrates from Chile being cut off by German submarines, knew that Washburn was familiar with the German nitrate industry and held the American rights to the cyanamide nitrate process. Crozier made Washburn a consultant to the War Department, and Mitchell elevated Washburn to chairman of the board of Alabama Power, while Worthington remained as vice president. The board approved a payment to Washburn of $25,000 and reimbursed Mitchell $35,000 for his expenses incurred on behalf of the company from October 1911 through February 28, 1915. This was the first money James Mitchell received from Alabama Power Company, and it covered only his expenses for the first years.[53]

The consolidation of small companies into Alabama Power foreshadowed a general reorganization of the company.[54] About six years later, after Tom Martin became president, he received an updated list of companies owned by Alabama Power Company. In a strongly worded memo, he told the legal department that nearly all of those companies existed only on paper. He wanted the history and status of each one investigated and every company that could be terminated to be wiped off the books.

In April 1915 Mitchell booked passage to England on the *Lusitania*, a Cunard liner that he often used in his trans-Atlantic travels; however, when the ship sailed on May 1, Mitchell was not on board. Pressing matters kept him in New York City. Perhaps some of these matters dealt with the tragic death of his nephew, Nathaniel William Tileston, on April 7, 1915. Tileston, the son of Mitchell's sister Anna and her only support, had been working with Alabama Power for three years. As Mitchell explained it, Tileston was "killed by a shock and fell" while working at the Gadsden Steam Plant.[55] After the sleek *Lusitania* was torpedoed by a German submarine off the coast of Ireland on May 7, Mitchell's name appeared among the missing. His daughter Marion recalled that her mother "was telephoning and telegraphing and scanning newspaper lists with red eyes," and for twenty-four hours his family feared he was lost.[56] The sinking of passenger ships increased tensions between the United States and Germany. By December 1915, Congress was financing an American preparedness program.

For Alabama Power Company, preparedness meant being ready to supply the electricity war industries in the state needed. Months before war began in Europe, Alabama Power was producing electricity. The first generating unit of Lock 12 had gone into commercial service on April 12, 1914, and James Mitchell was there to see it. Electricity was being fed into the transmission system through the small Jackson Shoals hydroelectric facility.[57] From this point, the Gadsden plant operated only when hydropower was insufficient, but "full boiler pressure was maintained at all times and one turbine kept floating on the line," ready to be used when needed.[58] With electricity flowing, Alabama Power increased its push to sell electricity to distributors, to sell electricity directly by contract to large commercial users and to the small-town electric companies it owned, or directly to individual consumers. After July 1, Alabama Power was sending electricity to Birmingham through wholesale contracts to Birmingham Railway, Light & Power Company. The last paragraph of Alabama Power Company's report for 1914 noted that on "August 1, 1914, due to the European war, practically all new construction work was stopped. The construction organization disbanded September 1, and all unfinished work was turned over to the operating department to be completed."[59]

Warrior Reserve Steam Plant unit No. 1, June 27, 1917.

The next year, as war orders came in and demand for electricity increased, the company decided it urgently needed more generating capacity. To meet the wartime exigencies, in 1915 Alabama Power Company made plans to build another steam plant. The company wanted a location near coalfields with adequate water supply, and Tom Martin asked Abner Bell Aldridge, a longtime friend and a Walker County coal man, to find the perfect place. Aldridge recommended acreage where Bakers Creek flowed into the Mulberry Fork of the Black Warrior River. The company purchased coal lands nearby to provide its own source of fuel, and Aldridge organized the Winona Coal Company. Construction began in 1916 on what was called the Warrior Reserve Steam Plant (now named Gorgas). James Mitchell announced that the steam plant would be connected to the Coosa hydroelectric power grid and used as backup for that system.[60] In August 1917, the first unit at Warrior was completed, and the foundations and water intake systems for two more units were in place. The next year, Tom Martin and Senator John H. Bankhead Sr. visited with General William Crawford Gorgas in Washington and asked his permission to name the new post office at the plant community Gorgas after the general. Martin never forgot his friends or those who stood by him in adversity, and he always gave General Gorgas credit for saving the company with his testimony in the mosquito lawsuits. Besides that, Martin thought the Alabama native deserved the recognition of having a post office and a community in his home state named for him; however, the steam plant was not dedicated to Gorgas until 1944.[61]

COMPANY LEADERSHIP AND POLITICS

Mitchell and Martin both believed that a public utility needed to be a monopoly to serve the people in the most efficient manner with the cheapest electrical rates. They also understood and were committed to regulation by the state, but they wanted regulation that was fair and requirements that would protect investors and not hinder the raising of capital to build a strong company to serve the people of Alabama. For these reasons, Tom Martin kept a careful eye on bills introduced in the legislature. Governor O'Neal prepared a bill "to regulate public service companies," and Martin sent Washburn a copy of the bill on January 28, 1915. Alabama Power worked with other utilities to mold a bill that was fair to investor-owned companies, to their customers, and to the general public. As Tom Martin took a more active interest in the politics of Montgomery, Worthington began to feel, as Washburn reported to Martin, "very much distressed at what he feels to be a lack of appreciation and confidence in him."[62]

When Charles Henderson campaigned for governor in 1914, he had promised to extend the powers of the Alabama Railroad Commission to regulate power monopolies. As the founder and major stockholder in the Pea River Power Company and the Standard Telephone & Telegraph Company, he understood power companies and regulation. He had been elected to the Alabama Railroad Commission in 1906, was appointed president, and served until 1915 when he resigned after being elected governor. On September 25, 1915, Governor Henderson signed into law a reorganization of the old Railroad Commission, which then became the Public Service Commission.

Its powers were expanded to include the regulation of street railway, electric, gas, telephone, and waterpower companies. The commission was composed of three members elected to serve four-year terms.[63]

Colonel Reuben A. Mitchell, ca. 1920.

In October 1915 James Mitchell reported to his wife that "the Alabama project is now coming along splendidly and there is only one flaw, namely the securities of it are not readily saleable as no market exists outside of London, and naturally, nothing can be done there in these times. So my next big job will be to create a suitable market here for them."[64] James Mitchell sent Colonel Reuben A. Mitchell on a mission across the state to sell Alabama investors on purchasing the power company's stock. James Mitchell and Tom Martin decided that if Alabama citizens had a financial stake in their electric utility, they would be more supportive and perhaps the power company could foil the political attacks that kept coming from different directions.

Colonel Mitchell traveled to small towns in Alabama and visited with bankers and leading citizens. He learned and reported to Mitchell and Martin that the people of Alabama invested very little in state, county, or municipal securities. He quoted the vice president of Birmingham Trust & Savings Bank as saying that only about 14 percent of Alabama state bonds were held by citizens of the state, and even fewer held school, county road, or municipal bonds. Despite this, Alabama Power never backed away from trying to increase local ownership of its stocks and bonds. Tom Martin especially believed that customers and citizens of Alabama should own their public utility.[65]

In November 1915 Mitchell wrote Carolyn about his efforts to get the federal government to establish an arsenal in the Anniston district and his plans for a munition works. Mitchell had just received an order "for about a million dollars worth of 6" shells" and was unable to sail for England as he planned because Edgar was on his way to New York with some British interests who were coming to negotiate financing with New York banks.[66]

Meanwhile, in the fall a conflict was brewing within Alabama Power Company. At the November 2, 1915, board of directors meeting, J. W. Worthington presented the board with a large expense account. Many of the items, as James Mitchell was later to remind Worthington, "were incurred by you without the authority of the company and contrary to its declared policy." In his letter to Worthington, which was sent about other matters and written six months after the November 1915 board meeting, Mitchell explained, "I felt compelled to refuse your requests to subscribe to senatorial and congressional funds, [believing] that a public utility company cannot afford to have anything whatever to do with politics."[67] The contributions to political campaigns that

Mitchell thought unethical were not illegal at the time, although later they would be.

As a result of the board's refusal to accept his accounts, J. W. Worthington resigned from the board and as vice president of Alabama Power Company at this meeting. Although the minutes do not supply any details, Mitchell must have given Worthington a bit of a shove. However, Mitchell allowed Worthington to remain as president of Muscle Shoals Hydro-Electric Power Company, which was really only a paper company owned now by Alabama Power. The public word was that Worthington needed more time to concentrate on lobbying in Washington.[68] He was retained on a salary of $1,000 a month to continue lobbying on Alabama Power Company's behalf. Worthington requested that his resignation be kept confidential until December 1, but Worthington himself told several people, including Senator Bankhead when he met with him in Jasper in mid-November. The news was soon out.[69] A few years before he died, Tom Martin told his biographer that James Mitchell "had relieved" Worthington of his "duties as an officer and director of the company for personal reasons, which are not necessary to this story."[70]

Throughout 1915 it was evident that Tom Martin was assuming even more responsibilities. Frequently Mitchell turned to him for advice, especially on public relations and political matters, for although Mitchell had toured the world, he was uneasy because he knew so little about Alabama politics. Mitchell learned to trust Martin's judgment. Martin knew instinctively how things would play in local communities, and he took responsibility for drafting the company's press releases. Mitchell and Martin shared the same value system, one reason they worked well together. In many ways, the two were cut from the same cloth, with the same sense of ethics. They both wanted company matters handled expeditiously but with fairness and class. Martin initiated a practice of personally hand delivering Alabama Power Company property tax checks to each county's probate judge.[71] In rural counties where the power company owned dams, steam plants, and land, the company became the county's largest taxpayer. This brought Alabama Power status and some appreciation, but it was also fodder for demagogues.

Soon after World War I began, James Mitchell learned about the possibility of manufacturing shell casings for the British and French armies. With the encouragement of Birmingham steel man W. H. Hassinger, Mitchell devised a plan to start up the old Southern Car Company at Anniston. He organized the Southern Munitions Corporation in New York, then four months later he set up an Alabama corporation, the Anniston Ordnance Company. Mitchell also organized the Anniston Steel Company, which was solely owned by Alabama

Power Company.[72] Theodore Swann was sent to Anniston to manage the company. The power company insisted, to anyone who asked, that owning and operating industrial companies was not a pattern the company expected to repeat. But Mitchell wanted to experiment with the new electric furnace to produce steel, and he did not wish to compete with TCI, a valuable Alabama Power industrial customer. He went to Anniston, where Alabama Power was also the retail distributor of electricity. He believed the venture would be profitable and would prove the electric furnace economical. Mitchell's appreciation for English investors who backed his Alabama hydroelectric adventure and a home and family in London were other reasons he was ready to help the British war effort.[73]

On December 2, 1915, the *Anniston Star* praised James Mitchell for investing in Anniston. The next year Mitchell had an order from J. P. Morgan Jr.'s company for 100,000 steel casings. On March 19, 1916, the *Evening Star* reported that the first electric furnace in the South went into operation at Anniston under the supervision of Theodore Swann with Lieutenant Governor Thomas E. Kilby, Anniston native, watching. The initial run of steel shell casings was made.[74] But there were problems. The lack of skilled workers in the Anniston area made it difficult to produce casings fine enough to pass the rigorous inspection of the English government, and management soon learned that producing and selling electricity was their business, not making steel.[75] From this venture Swann formed his own Southern Manganese Company.

Company street railway car on Noble Street, Anniston, ca. 1916.

Mitchell spent considerable time in Anniston trying to make things work, and he became close to J. J. Willett, Anniston attorney and civic leader. Willett recalled that one day when nothing was going well, Mitchell suggested they go down to Lock 12 "and forget our troubles." They did and Willett saw a personal side of Mitchell relaxing on the lake that rounded out his view of the businessman.[76]

Because Mitchell was closely directing the Anniston industries, he came to Alabama more frequently and stories circulated through the power company and its crews about his willingness to do any job. Leonidas P. Sweatt Jr. recalled that during the war years the company once suffered a severe loss of power because of a complete failure at the steam plant in Gadsden. At the time Mitchell was on a regular inspection tour of the plant. Sweatt remembered that "pandemonium reigned; everyone was working under a severe nervous and physical strain, and at top speed to restore operating conditions to their normal state." All the men were working under one foreman. Just as soon as Mitchell realized the situation, "he shed his coat and position of authority, and became merely one of the boys, helping out in any place where it was needed most." This was hot, extremely physical, dirty work, but Mitchell never hesitated or faltered. Power was soon restored.[77]

Nitrates and Muscle Shoals

When the year 1916 opened, no one at Alabama Power Company realized what unpredictable pressures the European war and politics would force upon the company. The problem areas were, of course, nitrates and the Muscle Shoals. On January 22, 1916, the *State Sentinel*, a new and short-lived agricultural newspaper published in Birmingham, reported that the federal government intended to aid Frank Washburn's American Cyanamid Company by building an $18 million dam at the Muscle Shoals to provide electricity for the company to produce nitrates.[78] The next months were chaotic. Congress began a series of debates on several bills and amendments that covered the issues of nitrates and whether the capture of atmospheric nitrates was a viable process and whether these nitrates were suitable for fertilizer as well as for explosives. Senators and representatives debated issues of states' rights and whether the federal government constitutionally could, or politically should, generate and sell electric power. Then the question became if the government did support a nitrate plant and a dam with a hydroelectric plant, where and how would the electricity be used? The choice could put the government into competition with private enterprise. The debates were heated, and the sides crossed party and sectional lines, as well as political philosophies. Conservatives and progressives did not uniformly take one side or the other on each question in the arguments. It was, in essence, a culmination of the conservation movement, which one writer noted was a fight that "cost the nation hundreds of millions [of dollars] because of the delay."[79]

The details of these months deserve a book and have been treated elsewhere, but never fully.[80] Suffice to say, tensions increased between the Mitchell-Martin side and the Washburn-Worthington faction. Tom Martin, who always loved the political arena and who had for some time been uncomfortable with Worthington, began to spend more time working Capitol Hill in Washington and Goat Hill in Montgomery, and he assumed more responsibility for lobbying. In the political climate in both state and federal governments, it was absolutely essential for Alabama Power Company to stay informed so it would not be blindsided by opposing forces. On February 9, 1916, Frank Washburn testified before the House Committee on Agriculture as president of the American Cyanamid Company. Washburn resigned as a consultant for the War Department before he testified in order to avoid a conflict of interest. Washburn explained the cyanamide process and why he was interested in the Muscle Shoals as a source of cheap power. Alabama congressman Tom Heflin, who was on the committee, was concerned about southern farmers and elicited a response from Washburn that "60 percent of the fertilizer in this country is used in the seven Southern states." But the main interest of the committee seemed to be nitrates for explosives and the German development of its chemical industry, which had given that country an inexhaustible supply of nitrates.[81]

The key point was that Washburn proposed government construction of the dam with some type of cooperative partnership between the federal government and private enterprise. More and more it seemed to Mitchell that Washburn's nitrate corporation was his foremost concern, not Alabama Power Company. Mitchell noted that Washburn made these moves "without any discussion with me." Mitchell was personally heavily invested in the American Cyanamid Company, too, and served on Washburn's board, but he resented Washburn using the congressional groundwork for Muscle Shoals that had been prepared by Alabama Power "at such a great cost in time and money." On February 26, James Mitchell wrote Washburn advising him of his decision to abolish the salary of the chairman of the board of Alabama Power Company. Washburn sent Mitchell a letter dated March 1 including a letter of resignation as chairman of the board dated March 2, 1916. It was accepted at the Alabama Power Company board of director's meeting on March 10.[82]

On March 3, 1916, Mitchell wrote his wife in London that "I am again in trouble, and we have our backs to the wall fighting, if not for our lives, at least for our rights and Washburn has given me the 'double-cross.' While he was president and chairman of the Alabama Power Co., during the period I was so much in England and traveling in connection with finances, he took advantage of the opportunity to forward his own purposes by framing up a plan to get the Federal Govt. to take away our largest water power, develop it at the government expense to make cyanamid and from the latter, nitric acid for explosives." Mitchell explained to Carolyn that the plan "happens to be very opportune just now in connection with the government's plan of preparedness and consequently he finds much support for his plan which in ordinary times would be preposterous." He wrote that he had no idea how it would all come out. "It means the immediate improvement of navigation in Alabama and all the people naturally want it as it means spending some twenty-five or thirty millions of dollars in the state. So if we should come out openly and fight it, we would have the whole state against us; and if we fight in the dark, we are at a great disadvantage." He shared that he was again having trouble with financing. He thought he had it all arranged with Montreal Trust to redeem early bonds and reissue new ones in order eventually to raise $100 million capital, but the Canadian company had "pretty near upset the whole applecart." Mitchell was upset and wrote Carolyn that "I am about down and out."[83]

Washington and Muscle Shoals

In the Capitol, the Senate debates went on and on and were further complicated when the DuPont Power Company threw its hat in the ring and offered to build the dam at Muscle Shoals and to supply power for nitrates. By this time James Duke had invested in the American Cyanamid Company, and E. Mackay Edgar of Sperling & Company was on Washburn's American Cyanamid board; Sperling, at some point, was also investing in the nitrate company.[84] At about the same time that Worthington left the power company, Alabama senator Oscar W. Underwood, who had been close to Worthington for years, became publicly uneasy about the political weight of Alabama Power. Senator Underwood insisted that he was "not in any way tied . . . to the Alabama Power Company, but I do believe the development of this power is of great importance to our people. It is not only necessary to the development of the Tennessee River, but if this great power that is possible [because] of development at Muscle Shoals is utilized to its fullest extent, it means the greatest industrial development in the entire South." Underwood's biographer, Evans

C. Johnson, wrote that the political influence of Alabama Power was "probably exaggerated in the minds of Underwood's friends."[85]

The incentive in the Muscle Shoals issue for Underwood and other southern leaders was cheap fertilizer for farmers, many of whom were impoverished, trying to eke out a living on poor, eroded land. Underwood generally opposed the government entering the power business in competition with private capital, but he favored the construction of the Muscle Shoals dam by the federal government because of wartime necessity, and he was most interested in Alabama farmers having cheap fertilizer for their crops. The conservationists, who wanted to conserve the natural resources of the nation and who for years had been passionately advocating government production of electricity, used the wartime emergency to achieve the most significant step toward that goal. Unfortunately for southern farmers, the promise of cheap fertilizer proved to be just a political ploy.[86]

The National Defense Act, which became law on June 3, 1916, included a section written by South Carolina senator Ellison D. Smith that provided for the president to determine the most efficacious method for producing synthetic nitrates, selecting a location, and building a facility and a hydroelectric dam to operate the plant. The law clearly stated, in what was to become the infamous section 124, that the plant was to be constructed and operated by the government and not by private corporations and that the government could sell any surplus power under regulations the president determined.[87] The Muscle Shoals group now had to convince the president to select the Shoals area for the plant, and Washburn had to convince the government to select his cyanamide process. Various governmental executive committees began studying the issues.

Woodrow Wilson was only the second Democratic president elected since Abraham Lincoln in 1860, and southern Democratic congressmen immediately applied pressure on Wilson to select a site in the South.[88] A meeting to promote the Shoals was held in Nashville on July 14, 1916, and an elaborate oversized booklet was published and circulated to members of Congress and the press. The $25,000 color-production, *America's Gibraltar–Muscle Shoals–A Brief for the Establishment of Our National Nitrate Plant at Muscle Shoals on the Tennessee River*, was complete with maps, charts, graphs, and photo-

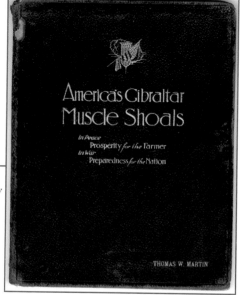

Thomas W. Martin's copy of America's Gibraltar.

graphs.[89] A large delegation of prominent industrialists led by Alfred M. Shook and Senator Underwood called on President Wilson. Months went by and still there was no decision from the White House, probably because Wilson was in the middle of a presidential reelection campaign and it was politically smart to keep up the hopes of voters that the nitrate plant might be located in their hometowns.[90]

Throughout the intense debates in Congress over whether and how a dam at the Shoals should be built, no one seemed to understand—probably many were not even aware and some cared nothing about the fact—that what they were arguing about was actually owned by Alabama Power Company. The company had title to the land on both sides of the river at two dam sites, where Wilson (Dam No. 2) and Wheeler (Dam No. 3) were eventually built. The company owned hundreds of acres in flowage lands and had plans for both dams that had been developed in cooperation with the Corps of Engineers. The company also had the results of extensive core borings in the river bottom, engineering reports, and river surveys. Mitchell, through Alabama Traction, had invested in this land and in all of these reports some half-million dollars in cash and two times that in Alabama Traction stock.[91]

In November 1916 Woodrow Wilson won a second term, breezing to victory on a promise to keep America out of the war in Europe. Soon after Wilson's inauguration, the German navy resumed torpedoing unarmed merchant ships and the damaging Zimmerman note became public, forcing the president's hand and sending him to Congress for a declaration of war. On April 6, 1917, Congress gave Wilson what he asked for. In the next months there was a severe shortage of munitions in Europe and pressure on the United States to provide explosives. While all of this was going on, the debate about whether to use the Haber technique for making nitrates, which was untried in the United States, or the proven cyanamide process that Washburn owned the rights to, continued to rage. German Fritz Haber established the conditions of combining nitrogen and hydrogen to produce ammonia for nitrates in 1909, and this technique was developed into an industrial process by Carl Bosch and was the method preferred in Germany; however, the cyanamide process was being used in both Canada and the United States.[92]

While the Haber versus the cyanamide process was being debated, President Wilson still made no decision about where the nitrate plant would be built. Senator John H. Bankhead Sr. "sardonically" remarked to the *Florence Herald* that he hoped the selection would be made "before the World comes to an end."[93] Finally, on September 28, 1917, fifteen months after the National Defense Act was signed into law, President Wilson announced that the Haber experimental nitrate plant would be built at Muscle Shoals. Decades later, long after he had left the Washington political scene, former Alabama congressman William B. Oliver gave "full credit" for the president's decision to J. W. Worthington.[94] One month after Wilson's selection of Muscle Shoals, Secretary of War Newton D. Baker announced that the cyanamide plant, called Plant No. 2, would also be constructed at the Muscle Shoals and would be built by Air Nitrates, a spinoff of Washburn's American Cyanamid Company. Although it was not announced for another five months, the government, through the Army Corps of Engineers, intended to construct Dam No. 2 (at a site still owned by Alabama Power) and a steam plant at Sheffield to serve as backup for the hydro generation.

The government faced the immediate problem of a lack of electricity at the Shoals. There was not enough power in the area to build one plant, much less two and a dam. At this moment, the government needed Alabama Power Company's electricity. The company's new Warrior Reserve Steam Plant at Gorgas had been operating with one 20,000-kilowatt unit since August 1917, and it also had underwater foundations in place with discharge canals for two other units. The Department of War approached Alabama Power Company and requested that it please help. James Mitchell wrote his wife from the New Willard Hotel that he was "in Washington where we are mixed up in interminable negotiations with the war department. The Government finds itself in great need of nitrates and are about to establish an enormous plant in Alabama, at Sheffield in the northwestern corner of the state. Electric power will be required, and so we are called upon to furnish it. Our present capacity being entirely sold out, we now have to face the erection of a steam plant of 100,000 horsepower in the coal fields near Birmingham and 82 miles of heavy transmission line, all of which has to be done in six months."[95]

Alabama Power agreed to build, at government expense, an additional 30,000-kilowatt turbo-generator at the Warrior Reserve plant at Gorgas. Colonel J. W. Joyes of the U.S. Army Ordnance Department was responsible for negotiating the agreement, which was not formally signed until after the construction was completed. He later defended his decisions, explaining that the department believed that "the probable cost and complication due to commandeering appeared prohibitive" and that it was best to work with the power company because "they had what we wanted" and "at that time . . . we were in the war."[96] Alabama Power Company had responsibility of securing rights-of-way and building ninety miles of transmission lines from Gorgas to Muscle Shoals. The government was also building a 60,000-kilowatt steam plant at Sheffield, but even after it was operating, there would not be enough electricity to supply the needs of the nitrate plants until the dam was completed. Since the government steam unit at Gorgas was on company property, the War Department contract included a provision that at the

Federal marshals stationed at the Warrior Reserve plant during World War I while unit No. 2 was under construction.

end of the war, or whenever the Tennessee dam was completed and its generators were operating, the government would sell its Gorgas unit to Alabama Power Company at "a reasonable price" to be determined by arbitration; there was a three-year time period after the war ended for this to occur.[97]

With patriotic fervor Alabama Power Company turned "its entire engineering and construction staff over to the United States."[98] Company survey crews operated from sunup to sundown, attorneys in every county between Gorgas and the Tennessee River began negotiating for rights-of-way, and line crews began setting poles and stringing 110,000-volt transmission cables. By May 1918 electric power from Gorgas was being delivered over this line, fully one year before the government steam plant at Sheffield was complete.[99] Tom Martin noted that, while during wartime cost of electricity was not a major concern, if all the steam plants being installed in Alabama for the government's use were operated continuously, they would "require some 3,000 tons of coal daily."[100] Overnight the Muscle Shoals area became one huge construction site. From a January 1918 population of 300, the town grew to 21,000 by the end of summer. Ten thousand men were on the construction sites. Prices on everything from land to rental units, from food to coal, shot upward in a price-gorging whirlwind.[101]

With Tom Martin leading the negotiating team, discussions between the Alabama Power Company and the government on the Muscle Shoals dam site continued through the fall and winter of 1917–18 but were stymied when the government refused to pay Alabama Power what the company had invested in its Muscle Shoals project. The Department of War insisted on appraising the dam site and riverfront land as farmland. The War Department also wanted, but refused to pay for, the engineering studies, surveys, maps, and plans for the dam that the company owned and had funded. The federal government threatened the company with using eminent domain to take the land at the appraised price of northern Alabama farmland. Disheartened by the caustic attacks on his company and on him personally, James Mitchell decided to just give the land for Dam No. 2 to the federal government. He instructed Tom Martin to prepare the legal papers for the donation.[102] At a special meeting of the Alabama Power Company board of directors in New York on February 18, 1918, a motion was approved that allowed the company's president or vice president to execute a proxy in the name of the company to vote the shares of capital stock of the Muscle Shoals Hydro-Electric Power Company, which was owned solely by Alabama Power Company. This proxy for executing "a conveyance donating to the United States the lands which it desires to acquire for the purpose" of building a dam and hydroelectric plant on lands owned by the Muscle Shoals Hydro-Electric Power Company was approved in Birmingham, at a special meeting of the stockholders of the Muscle Shoals Hydro-Electric Power Company.[103]

Martin was not present at the New York board meeting on February 18, and although he did not disagree with Mitchell's decision, one can gather from his correspondence that Tom Martin was ready for a good legal fight if Mitchell gave the word. However, the Alabama Power Company president thought the legal battle would be long, brutal, and in the end detrimental to his company, to Alabama, and to his nation at war. Mitchell may have been born in Canada, and in some accounts is called a Canadian, but there was never a doubt in his mind that he was an American.

Tom Martin and his legal consultants debated whether a deed of gift could have conditions that might bind the government to give priority to Alabama Power if it ever decided to divest the property. Such conditions were not included in the deed of gift, but Mitchell wrote a letter to the War Department on the day the Alabama Power Company board of directors approved his motion, February 18, 1918. In this famous and often reprinted letter, Mitchell offered to donate his company's Muscle Shoals site to the U.S. government, but Mitchell's only request was that his company "should receive consideration in the disposition of any surplus power not required for the needs of the government." Mitchell ended his letter with the comment, especially plaintive in light of developments on the Tennessee River in the 1930s, that "it is our understanding from you that the Government only desires to acquire the site at Dam No. 2 and adjacent properties, with flowage easement on such of our other properties as may be affected by this development. I need hardly assure you," Mitchell wrote, "of the desire of the Company to cooperate with the War Department to the fullest extent in placing at your disposition the benefit of all our engineering studies and records in relation to the projected development."[104]

The United States Treasury sent Alabama Power Company a check for the one dollar stated in the deed for assets for which Mitchell and his company had paid more than $1.5 million. The company never cashed the check. One of Tom Martin's favorite stories concerned a 1921 *Powergrams* article about the company's gift of the Shoals site to the federal government. The editor included a picture of the one-dollar check. Later, the government notified the company that it had violated a federal statute by printing a photograph of a government check. The company was fined $500, which was paid, and this check, unlike the one-dollar check, was cashed.[105]

At the end of February 1918 Tom Martin was in Washington, D.C., to negotiate the legal formalities of the gift of the Alabama Power Company/Muscle Shoals Hydro-Electric Power Company's dam site to the federal government and to make arrangements to turn over all its surveys, boring analyses, designs, and engineering plans for the dam at Muscle Shoals. On February 19, Alabama senator John H. Bankhead Sr. wired Worthington at Sheffield that "Alabama Power Company has unreservedly donated its lands at lock two [Muscle Shoals] to Government . . . Alabama Power Company is entitled to great credit for this patriotic and generous action and the press of the State should so regard it."[106]

Soon after this exchange, James Mitchell wrote Martin from New York that he had learned Frank Washburn had summoned Theodore Swann to consult on "the Southern power situation." Swann was then operating his own Southern Manganese Company in Anniston, but he maintained a close relationship with Alabama Power, which supplied his electricity.[107] Mitchell had heard that Washburn was trying to convince Colonel J. W. Joyes of the Ordnance Department to make a comprehensive study of electrical power in the South. Mitchell noted that this was exactly what the Alabama Power Company was doing. Mitchell worried about what Washburn had in mind and whether the government intended to go after Alabama Power's second Tennessee River site at Dam No. 3.[108]

In July 1918 there was no need for Alabama Power to pay a lobbyist to concentrate on the Tennessee River. James Mitchell and Tom Martin discussed discontinuing J. W. Worthington's salary. Harold S. Swan, the assistant secretary-treasurer of Alabama Traction and a close associate of Mitchell working in the Alabama Traction office in New York, wrote to Martin advising him that Mitchell thought it was "better for you to personally see [Worthington] and come to an understanding that his salary is to cease." Mitchell wanted to leave relations with Worthington on a cordial basis and wanted him to know that the company would "always be ready to cooperate in any matters that develop." Worthington was, Mitchell relayed, already "aware of the circumstances which no longer justify his receiving any remuneration from the Company."[109] Two weeks later Martin wrote Mitchell that Worthington had visited Birmingham on July 21. Worthington had volunteered that his salary should be cut because "he was not performing any active service for us."[110] Alabama Power faced continued problems trying to disassociate itself from the American Cyanamid Company and from Washburn and Worthington, an association that Mitchell believed was "very harmful" to the company's broad interests in Alabama. Mitchell advised general manager W. N. Walmsley to try to keep stories out of the newspapers that claimed any such connection.[111] Walmsley had been general manager of the company for only three weeks. He was a native of Indiana who had worked with Thomson Houston Company in Massachusetts, then with the Pearson companies in São Paulo, Brazil, where his work was so satisfactory he succeeded Mitchell as general manager when Mitchell retired in 1906 and left for England.[112]

The building frenzy at Muscle Shoals continued through the summer of 1918 while Bernard Baruch, head of the War Industries Board, coordinated the production of munitions and supplies. Americans responded to carefully orchestrated propaganda campaigns to save food and fuel to win the war, and, with their British and French allies, U.S. troops fought desperate battles to stop the German offensive drive on the western front. By September the Allied armies began their own assault on the German lines, and by late fall the war was winding down. The Muscle Shoals Nitrate Plant No. 1 cost the government almost $13 million to build, and it was never operational. American Cyanamid's Plant No. 2, built by its subsidiary Air Nitrates, cost $69 million to build, and it was ready for operation in October 1918.[113] This figure was far more than what was initially appropriated. Plant No. 2 ran one successful test, and then the war ended on November 11, 1918. The construction of the dam had hardly progressed at all. Very soon, the question became: what to do with the dam?[114]

POSTWAR CHALLENGES

Alabama Power Company had weathered the war despite many of its employees being drafted or volunteering for military service. The heaviest hit areas were in the field crews and sales force, which were composed of young men. Sons of many of the company's older employees went off to war. James Mitchell's son Malcolm, a student at Cornell, volunteered, and so did Lamar Aldridge, who had just joined the company's law department after graduating from the University of Alabama. He was an officer in the Eighty-second Division, fighting at St. Mihiel and the Argonne Forest.[115] Letters from all these servicemen were passed around the office. The great influenza epidemic of 1918 hit Birmingham in the fall, and in October the office had to operate at half staff. During this crisis company internal communications kept the office personnel aware of illnesses and the status of power company soldiers. Frederick L. Darlington, who was a manager in the Alabama Power office and a member of the company board, was working with the War Industries Board in Washington.[116] At war's end, Alabama Power employee David Cronheim wrote W. E. Mitchell from Camp Pike, Arkansas, that he would be discharged soon and was looking forward to returning to the company.[117]

Alabama Power Company survived the Great War and also the great Alabama flood of 1919. The Coosa River was off its banks into the trees, but the rushing waters had no effect on the dam at Lock 12. At the height of the flood, with water spilling through every floodgate, there was not even a small vibration in the dam. The Tallapoosa River ran so high that it washed out the Tallassee dam that provided electricity to Montgomery. This was the largest hydro plant in the state before Alabama Power Company built the Lock 12 dam, and after the dam's destruction Alabama Power Company purchased the Tallapoosa site. James Mitchell continued his routine of visiting Alabama every few weeks, and each time he arrived, the Birmingham newspapers made some announcement. Alabama Power Company staff assembled and presented him with reports that covered the company's operations since he had last visited, and plans were made for the future. With the war over, the Anniston Ordnance Company, which James Mitchell had organized to obtain British contracts, was shut down, but the mostly inactive Anniston Steel Company lumbered on into the 1920s, amid constant attempts to sell it.[118]

In the spring of 1919 Mrs. James Mitchell came with her husband and daughter Marion to visit Birmingham. They stayed at the Tutwiler Hotel. Carolyn Mitchell, described as a lady of "grace and charm," went to see the Lock 12 dam and was entertained at the Warrior Steam Plant at Gorgas. Her husband toured her through the beautiful homes on the South Highlands, and they discussed moving to Birmingham. But before any of this could be finalized, James Mitchell suffered a paralytic stroke in June.[119] Letters between James and Carolyn during World War I had occasionally mentioned his health. They both agreed he did not take care of himself.[120] Tensions from negotiations with the federal government over Muscle Shoals and from constantly blunting the attacks on his company had worn him down. He had been traveling too much, tending to his Alabama projects and other business interests.

There was the stress of war in Europe and pressures from the financial markets. The congressional Graham committee investigation was another strain. Soon after the war was over, this congressional inquiry began considering excessive spending during the war and keyed on Muscle Shoals, claiming waste and dishonesty in the construction of the two nitrate plants on the Tennessee River, none of which directly involved Alabama Power. All of these problems took a toll on the fifty-four-year-old Mitchell. When he fell ill shortly after his birthday, the Alabama Power Company board of directors gave Tom Martin executive authority of the company. At the time, the board of directors was composed of Mitchell; Tom Martin; Gerhard M. Dahl, who was vice president of Chase National Bank of New York; W. H. Hassinger, an influential entrepreneur, a large stockholder in the First National Bank of Birmingham, and a close friend of Martin; H. S. Swan, longtime treasurer of Alabama Traction, Light & Power Company; William H. Weatherly, president of the First National Bank of Anniston; Reuben A. Mitchell, S.Z.'s brother; C. E. Groesbeck, a vice president of EBASCO; and W. N. Walmsley, the power company's general manager.[121]

When the new year opened in 1920, Frank D. Mahoney, called "Mac," was the company's commercial manager. A University of Wisconsin–trained electrical engineer, Mahoney was a consultant with the Ordnance Department and assigned to the construction of Nitrate Plant No. 2 during the war. He came to Alabama Power in 1919. Mahoney wrote to Howard Duryea, the assistant general manager who was in New York with Tom Martin, that he firmly believed "the next two or three years are going to be momentous ones for the Alabama Power Company, and while it is possible that we all could make more money in other lines, I think that the enjoyment we are going to get out of watching this property grow is going to be eminently worthwhile." He was happy that Duryea had decided to stay on with the company and not return to United Electric.[122]

Replying from New York, Duryea reported to Mahoney that James Mitchell had recovered enough by the end of the year to walk several blocks without trouble, but Mitchell decided to resign as president of Alabama Power Company and did so on February 16, 1920. W. H. Weatherly of Anniston nominated Tom Martin, whose biographer suggests the board believed Martin had the same business philosophy as Mitchell and would continue the policies that Mitchell put in place at the beginning.[123] Martin recalled that "in the last days of his career" Mitchell had been concerned about his company having "a good corporate image." He wanted Alabama Power "to be an asset to the community," for he realized that "as Alabama grows, so will the Company." Martin was aware "of the moral and spiritual inspiration" with which Mitchell led the group who worked with him. It was this, Martin believed, "more than the

Company's material progress in his lifetime, [that] determined [the company's] destiny."[124] Martin agreed with Mitchell's ethics and was even more committed to the development of Alabama and the South than was Mitchell.[125]

After Martin was made president of Alabama Power Company, he added several men to the board of directors: Lawrence Macfarlane of Montreal, counsel for English investors; S. Z. Mitchell, president of Electric Bond & Share Company, which owned a large interest in Alabama Power Company securities; Richard M. Hobbie and Walter M. Hood of the company's legal department.[126] The addition of Macfarlane gave Martin quick entree to Sperling and London investors; S. Z. Mitchell brought clout, and the appointment put the EBASCO head in a position where Martin could keep close tabs on his movements. With Mitchell's health so precarious, Martin needed men with strength and influence on Wall Street. These selections were probably made with Mitchell's suggestion or concurrence.

Throughout the spring, the New York office remained hopeful for Mitchell's full recovery, and news of his progress was quickly shared. In May, Mitchell came into the New York office for a while and "seemed to take some interest in the progress of the Power Company," but he suffered a second stroke and died on July 22, 1920, at his summer home at St. James, Long Island.[127] Services were conducted at New York City's St. Thomas Church on Fifth Avenue on Sunday, July 25, with burial in the family plot in Milton, Massachusetts. His pallbearers all had connections to his Alabama Power Company: Charles H. Baker, Frederick S. Ruth, Harold S. Swan, S. Z. Mitchell, Frank Washburn, Colonel Hugh L. Cooper, and Frederick L. Darlington. A few days after the funeral, the New York Times published a short comment about Mitchell's estate, valued "at over $1,000,000 and all in personal property," mostly stocks and bonds. The newspaper reported the appraisal of the estate was $2,683,598.[128] On August 10, Howard Duryea reported from New York that 400 cards had been sent to friends and customers of the company notifying them of Mitchell's death.[129] On October 11, 1920, the final accounting of James Mitchell's estate showed his worth at $2,585,376.74. Among his vast stock portfolio he held 18,383 shares of common stock and 100 shares of preferred stock in Alabama Traction, Light & Power with a combined par value of $1,848,300. In the American Cyanamid Company, Mitchell held 256 shares of common stock and 1,000 shares of preferred stock with par value of $125,600.[130]

Martin Takes Over Alabama Power Company

Years later Tom Martin recalled that S. Z. Mitchell proposed that he, Martin, succeed James Mitchell.[131] Martin took over a company in deep financial trouble in the fall of 1920. The South was in a severe agricultural recession. The high selling prices of wartime had quickly faded. In New Orleans cotton was bringing 41.75 cents in April but fell to 13.5 cents by December 1920. Tobacco was selling for less than half what it sold for in 1919. Unemployment and unrest plagued the state's rural areas.[132] Massive out-migration of Alabama workers, especially black laborers taking advantage of war jobs in the North, had stressed the Birmingham labor market. Coal miners took advantage of the situation and increased demands for higher wages. The United Mine Workers promised a major drive to unionize the Alabama coalfields. Scattered strikes turned into a general coal strike by September 1920.[133] After rumors of a power company rate increase, Donald Comer, vice president of Avondale Mills, wrote Alabama Power Company on New Year's Eve 1920 that he was grateful power rates would "not be disturbed" for the next year because of the deflation and the difficult time cotton mills of the state were having staying in business.[134]

Thomas W. Martin, ca. 1920.

Under these circumstances, Alabama Power found it challenging to sign up new customers. Tom Martin observed that as more commercial and industrial customers were brought online, "there was a disturbing lack of future markets."[135] Many factories in such unsettled times refused to convert because of the cost of moving from steam to electricity. In fact, the company found it challenging to serve those customers it already had because typical Alabama storms played havoc with transmission and distribution lines. A cyclone destroyed portions of the Warrior-Sheffield line on April 19-20, 1920, and drought conditions during the summer and early fall reduced the flow of normal power from Lock 12, where Jake Benziger, a quiet and unassuming man, was superintendent. W. E. Mitchell observed that Jake had the "ability to keep the 'juice' on the lines under the most extremely difficult operating conditions."[136] The Warrior Reserve Steam Plant at Gorgas suffered a reduction of its output because of a batch of bad coal, and the plant's routine maintenance required that it be shut down for days while repairs were made. The federal government was not assuring the company that it would continue operating the steam plant at Sheffield, yet Alabama Power was guaranteeing electricity for the construction of Wilson Dam and needed to purchase this power. The New York securities market was in a lull, and a general uneasiness pervaded the utilities bond market over what the future might hold for southern utilities when the enormous potential of Muscle Shoals electricity was dumped on the market. In addition, the first mortgage of Alabama Power Company restricted the possibilities of raising new money.

Anticipating these problems, on December 12, 1919, Tom Martin addressed the board of the Alabama Traction, Light & Power Company. In a long memorandum on the financial policy of Alabama Power Company, he estimated that the company would need construction and improvements plus general operating funds of $38 million in the next decade, 1920–30. After giving detailed information about various options and the tax and business consequences of each one, he recommended that Alabama Power Company consider issuing preferred stock to enable the company to raise the funds it required. As these long-range plans were being finalized, there was a financial crisis in October 1920. Martin and the financial officers and staff scurried to make piecemeal payment of debts, to anticipate financial demands through March, and, optimistically, to plan for the construction of a second dam on the Coosa River, this one at Duncan's Riffle.[137]

Throughout November there was much communication between Tom Martin and investment brokers H. M. Addinsell of Harris, Forbes & Company, New York, and Francis E. Frothingham at Coffin & Burr of Boston. Under current conditions in the bond market, the company's first mortgage-bond would restrict the amount of new money that could be raised, new funding the company badly needed. On December 6, 1920, Martin advised Lawrence Macfarlane of the situation, and Macfarlane suggested that the existing mortgage of $10 million be closed and a new issue be made that could include "future developments." Macfarlane included a copy of a new trust deed that had been carefully written for another electric utility in the same circumstances as Alabama Power.[138] This is exactly what the company did. With approval of its stockholders, a new mortgage, dated June 1, 1921, was created. It allowed Alabama Power Company to issue $8 million par value First Mortgage Lien and Refunding Gold Bonds, 6 percent series, due in 1951. By the end of December 1921 the cumulative preferred stock sales that began in June 1920 had resulted in over 10,000 shares sold.[139]

Muscle Shoals and the Federal Water Power Act

Financial problems were not the only concern Martin had. The company still faced the Muscle Shoals controversy. The federal government's dilemma about what to do with its nitrate plants and the partially completed Wilson Dam at Muscle Shoals escalated when the European war ended and these questions became a central issue in Congress into the 1920s. Alabama Power Company was part of all these debates, many of them highly acrimonious. As the Department of War began to dismantle and dispose of war surplus materials, private proposals were sought for the Muscle Shoals projects—despite the provision of section 124 in the National Defense Act that specifically prohibited private involvement. No proposal was received. The War Department then decided to request authorization from Congress for completion of the dam and authority to operate the nitrate plants through a corporation established by the government. Needless to say, Frank Washburn opposed the idea, but it was incorporated into the Wadsworth-Kahn bill that some opponents charged would "deliver Wilson Dam to the Alabama Power Company."[140] Congressional debates centered on the merits of the cyanamide and Haber processes, the need for fertilizer, the issue of government ownership, and the ethics of the federal government being in competition with private capital.

In the middle of the debate, in January 1920, Congressman William J. Graham began his subcommittee investigation on waste and fraud in the Muscle Shoals project. The contracts and work of the American Cyanamid Company and Alabama Power Company were scrutinized. Much testimony was taken, some of it absurd. One man testified (incorrectly) that there were no bathing facilities in the construction camps, and much was made over a $4,000 order for prunes purchased for the dining halls, which at one time fed 10,000 men. When one man was asked if that was a lot of prunes, he replied, "maybe not if you like prunes."[141] In his majority report, Representative Graham excoriated Frank Washburn, J. W. Worthington, and the Muscle Shoals Hydro-Electric Power Company. Some of Graham's flack landed on Alabama Power Company, which still owned the Muscle Shoals company. Despite the extravagant charges, most against the American Cyanamid Company, historian Preston J. Hubbard concluded that the "committee failed to uncover any sensational scandals."[142] The minority report, written by Representative Finis J. Garrett, called the Graham majority report "reckless and biased" and vindicated Washburn, Worthington, and Alabama Power Company.[143] The War Department attributed the waste to the wartime emergency and the haste with which things were done.

While these debates on Muscle Shoals were ongoing, the long fight between the Theodore Roosevelt–Gifford Pinchot conservationists and private waterpower advocates was coming to a climax. Across the state of Alabama, Alabama Power Company had been criticized for not building dams on the other sites it owned. The company had a hard time getting local politicians and the people to understand that they could not build on these Coosa River and Tallapoosa River sites without federal permission, and Congress needed to establish a national waterpower policy to enable the company to build dams on its sites. James Mitchell had pressed Congress for such a law for years. Without a federal law to authorize and protect investments, it was impossible to borrow money for construction. The congressional fight over federal waterpower regulation and ownership that had started in Wilson's administration was ended by the passage of the Federal Water Power Act in 1920.[144] This act established the Federal Power Commission, composed of the secretaries of agriculture, interior, and war, which had the power to license use of water resources and public lands within federal jurisdiction.[145] Conservationists claimed that in preparing the bill the committee heard from only two witnesses: Colonel J. W. Worthington, who they claimed still represented Alabama Power Company, and Colonel Hugh L. Cooper, a friend of James Mitchell and an engineering consultant for private power companies, including Alabama Power Company. After amendments on the House floor that would fix charges for use of water, the bill was then opposed by investor-owned companies. The bill passed the House but failed in the Senate.[146] For several sessions the House and Senate deadlocked over wording. Everyone recognized the need for the law, especially power companies whose new investments in hydro had virtually ceased, while demand by customers for electricity was steadily increasing. The World War I economy had increased the use of electricity, but the only way to service this demand was by steam generation.

President Woodrow Wilson gave the matter his personal attention and had a model bill drafted. This bill passed the Senate but was again amended in the House. Tom Martin was quick to send a letter to Senator Bankhead congratulating and thanking him for his support and assuring him that the company planned work in Alabama under the bill. Martin just hoped that the final law would be "in such shape that we can raise money under it."[147] After a long conference committee examination, following a sensational filibuster led by Wisconsin's Robert M. La Follette, heated midterm congressional elections, and the election of a new Congress, the bill was finally reported back out of conference committee.[148] Although it did not include all the provisions each side wanted, it secured federal jurisdiction over waterpower on navigable rivers, now defined to cover almost any stream. The law also created a process for fifty-year leases on power sites with certain payments due to the government. Alabama senator Oscar W. Underwood was strongly in favor of the legislation and worked to get it passed. President Wilson signed the Federal Water Power Act on June 10, 1920, the same month that the Republican Party held its national convention in San Francisco.

The Republicans were looking for an issue for the fall 1920 presidential campaign, and the two nitrate plants standing idle and rusting at Muscle Shoals, representing federal investments of over $80 million, seemed like good symbols. Federal money would soon run out for the construction of Wilson

Dam, and that site, too, would be abandoned without additional appropriations. The government had already spent $17 million, and estimates by the Corps of Engineers for completing the dam ranged from $33 to $50 million. Meanwhile, independent engineer Charles G. Adsit, consulting for Alabama Power Company, determined that the dam could be completed for $20 million.[149] The Republicans attacked the Democratic project as a costly and embarrassing failure that contributed nothing to the war effort. The opposition party battered President Wilson for authorizing the construction of the dam so late in the war and criticized the connections between the government and Washburn and Worthington. In the summer a routine survey of state agricultural commissioners and experiment stations initiated by the Department of Agriculture asked about the supply of fertilizer. The responses indicated there was indeed a national shortage. The issue of cheap fertilizer for farmers became the passionate plea of the southern and midwestern farm block, while urban Republicans criticized the Muscle Shoals as a failed project. President Wilson was physically weak and politically emasculated. He had suffered a stroke and been rebuffed by the Republican-controlled Senate on the treaty he negotiated in Paris to settle postwar issues. The Republican platform was a masterpiece of ambiguity that helped Ohio senator Warren G. Harding and his vice-presidential running mate, Vermont governor Calvin Coolidge, get elected. President Harding took the view that "the Muscle Shoals project was a white elephant and had better be sold."[150]

After the election, the War Department and Corps of Engineers made a routine request for $10 million to continue work on Wilson Dam. Despite the

Wilson Dam under construction, looking south
across the Tennessee River, May 23, 1922.

army's hope of not becoming entangled with other Muscle Shoals issues, this bill headed into heated controversy. Colonel Hugh L. Cooper, recognized as one of the world's foremost hydraulic engineers, was the consulting engineer on Wilson Dam and testified that Muscle Shoals should be considered a power site and leased to a private power company. Since Alabama Power Company was the only company to have transmission lines into this area, Cooper was accused of trying to get the dam for Alabama Power. Cooper insisted that if the government went into distributing power it would drive private investment in utilities from the South. Considering the fear northeastern industries had of competition from uncontrolled southern industries, this was an interesting charge. The appropriations for Wilson Dam ran out in April 1921, and the construction site was shut down.[151]

In March 1921, Secretary of War John W. Weeks invited anyone to make an offer on the government properties at the Shoals, and on April 2, Major General Lansing H. Beach, who was chief of engineers, sent a letter to Alabama Power Company and to other southern power companies requesting ideas about what could be done with the properties. On May 20, 1921, the Georgia Railway & Power Company, Columbus Power Company, the Central Power Company, and the Tennessee Electric Power Company replied that because of the large capital expenses they could not send a proposal, but if the government finished the dam, they would be interested in purchasing power from the dam. On May 28, 1921, Tom Martin replied to Secretary Weeks assuring him that if the government was serious about wanting such a proposal, then Alabama Power Company would consider putting together an offer, but Martin wanted clarifications on several points, especially about a possible conflict with section 124 of the National Defense Act, a provision that required government opera- tion of the dam at Muscle Shoals.[152] Martin's letter was positive and encourag- ing. Years later Beach recalled that the power companies "replied to my invita- tion to the effect that neither the Government with its own capital, nor private capital could afford to complete the Wilson Dam and power development there."[153] This was absolutely not what Martin's letter said. Tom Martin, in this incident, believed that a cooperative program between private investment and the government could work and was the proper course.

MUSCLE SHOALS AND HENRY FORD

Major General Lansing H. Beach's recollection five years after the fact was that at this point he sent for Colonel Worthington, who was then with the Tennessee River Improvement Association. Beach recalled that on April 1,

1921, he told Worthington that "it seemed that I would get no offer for Muscle Shoals." If Beach was correct about his dates, then he talked to Worthington *before* he mailed the letter to Alabama Power Company and other private utilities in the South. Beach remembered Worthington saying to him, "Send Henry Ford an invitation." Beach sent Ford a letter the next day, and Ford's secretary responded that the Detroit automobile manufacturer was interested but wanted more information. Beach offered to send Worthington to Detroit to explain about the Shoals because Worthington was so well informed, but the lobbyist's poor health delayed his traveling. Martin's letter must have reached Beach only days before Worthington met with Henry Ford on June 6. A few weeks later Ford appeared in Muscle Shoals, causing rumors to fly across northern Alabama that Ford was interested in the Shoals.[154]

But Beach's letter to Henry Ford in April was not the first contact Ford had on the Muscle Shoals issue. Farm Bureau Federation leaders Gray Silver of Washington and Edward A. O'Neal III of Alabama had made an approach to Ford earlier.[155] Surely Worthington was aware of this. Two weeks after Ford made his proposal, the *Chicago Daily Tribune* published a story about Worthington's correspondence with Gray Silver and Claudius H. Huston, who had worked with Worthington in the Tennessee River Improvement Association and was now assistant secretary of commerce. Worthington intended to use Huston to help him "drive the Ford offer through Congress under the sponsorship of the farm organizations" whose support would be achieved by promises of cheap fertilizer.[156]

On June 21, 1921, Alabama senator Underwood received a "strictly confidential" letter from Worthington typed on letterhead of the Detroit Athletic Club. Worthington attached a copy of the "proposal Mr. Ford is now considering and at the present time he intends to make" for the Muscle Shoals. Since Ford knew nothing about the history of the Shoals and little about the issues, it was evident Worthington either wrote the entire proposal or greatly influenced the writing. For those who knew, it was similar to the one Worthington prepared for the Muscle Shoals Hydro-Electric Company several years before. Worthington wanted Senator Underwood's opinion of the proposal before Henry Ford sent it to the War Department. In his cover letter, Worthington also passed along information to Underwood that William Brown McKinley, Republican senator from Illinois, was "unalterably opposed to the government operating anything at Muscle Shoals."[157]

The draft that Worthington sent Underwood included much of the final Ford proposal, which Ford sent to the government on July 8, 1921. There were many reasons Alabama Power Company viewed Ford's entrance into the

Shoals quagmire a threat, but two provisions were particularly offensive: Ford asked for the "steam plant built and owned by the Government at Gorgas, Alabama, on the Warrior River" and the transmission line from Gorgas to Muscle Shoals. The government was to acquire title to the right-of-way lands of the transmission line and to the land of the steam plant at Gorgas before giving it to Ford. The Detroit automobile manufacturer also required the government to build Dam No. 3, a site (where Wheeler Dam was later built) still, at this time, owned by Alabama Power Company through its ownership of the Muscle Shoals Hydro-Electric Company.[158] Tom Martin was well connected, and he may have been warned of Worthington's involvement with Ford before the *Chicago Daily Tribune* publicly revealed this association in a series of stories in late July. An unknown party delivered copies of Worthington's correspondence to the *Tribune's* Washington correspondent, who confronted Worthington with copies for verification. The letters showed that the Muscle Shoals lobby group was behind Ford and proved that Worthington wrote the Ford proposal. The letters connected Worthington to commerce assistant secretary Claudius Huston, to Gray Silver of the American Farm Bureau, and to a campaign for cheap fertilizer as a way to get the Ford proposal approved by Congress.[159] In one letter to the farm bureau leader, Worthington warned him not to say anything about Ford wishing to manufacture aluminum, "for if that gets out and becomes known Mr. Mellon [the secretary of the treasury who was closely tied to the Aluminum Company of America] will be interested." He wrote that Ford absolutely was unwilling to sell any Muscle Shoals electricity to power companies like Alabama Power Company, Georgia Railway & Power Company, and Tennessee Power Company.[160]

Worthington corresponded with Ford's personal secretary, E. G. Liebold, telling him that the July 25 *New York Times* article on the Ford proposal, announcing that it was being rejected by the government, was hostile because the *Times* president and publisher was Adolph S. Ochs, a leading American Jew. Worthington insisted that the secretary of war "never told anybody that he had rejected the Ford offer." In August, Worthington wrote Liebold that the publication of "parts of my stolen correspondence has hurt me but nobody else." He thought the publicity of the scandal had "benefited Mr. Ford's case here."[161]

With the publication of these articles, there was no doubt where Worthington stood. For Tom Martin, Worthington's association with Ford and with this proposal was the ultimate betrayal. Martin believed that Ford's offer was a threat to Alabama Power Company and a bad deal for the state of Alabama and its people, for the U.S. government and the American people.

Henry Ford, left, and Thomas Edison at Muscle Shoals December 1921. Courtesy of the Tennessee Valley Authority.

For one thing, Martin was concerned that the power from Muscle Shoals would go to support one individual and his operations alone, whatever they might be, thus cutting off other potential industrial customers and munici-palities in northern Alabama and reducing opportunities for broad-based industrial recruitment and development. Martin fought the proposal in every way he could, accepting all allies. In this fight, Martin was on the same side as the conservationists and the liberals, including socialist-leaning Nebraska Senator George W. Norris, who wanted the federal government to produce and sell electricity and who was particularly hostile to private utilities. Norris would be Martin's best ally in the fight against Ford, and Alabama Power Company often cited Norris's accounting figures to show what a steal this scheme actually was.[162]

The main points of Ford's proposal were that the federal government was to finish construction and install the generating equipment of Wilson Dam and Dam No. 3 (later the site of Wheeler Dam). Ford was to hold a one-hundred-year lease on this property. The value of the Muscle Shoals assets, including those belonging to Alabama Power Company, were approximately $89 million but had cost the government some $103 million, for which Ford would pay a grand total of $5 million. Senator Norris estimated that Ford would pay only 2.79 percent interest on these assets beginning six years after both dams were completed.[163] The Ford letter set off a raging national contro-versy, nowhere more passionate and heated than in Alabama.

In early December 1921 Ford traveled to Muscle Shoals once more, this time with Thomas Edison in tow. The two were received as heroes. While visiting Florence a reporter asked Ford about a series of anti-Semitic articles that had been appearing in Ford's Dearborn newspaper. Ford wasted no time in responding with a diatribe against Wall Street, gold-standard capitalism, and Jews. He advocated his own rather quirky economic ideas, including the concept of eliminating the gold standard and using an "energy dollar" for currency. Ford assured Alabamians in the Tennessee Valley that his motivation was altruistic and he was thinking of their best interests. Ford's biographers believe he was.[164] Ford's anti-Semitic remarks were printed in the New York Times the next day, but Alabama remembered only Ford's promises of industrial development.[165] While prominent American Jewish leaders swore off driving Ford automobiles, Tom Martin demanded that the purchasing department never buy another Ford and as soon as possible to get rid of any the company owned. Management took the message to heart; company employees were rarely seen anywhere in Fords.[166]

Soon after the first of the year, Henry Ford issued a press release that made even more great promises to northern Alabama. He was going to create factories, bring jobs, and create a city and manufacturing center seventy-five miles long along the Tennessee River. The Detroit industrialist promised that the project would eventually be turned over to the residents of the region and suggested that this was "only the first of a whole series of such projects" that he planned to build across the nation.[167] Ford met with Secretary of War Weeks in mid-January 1922 and modified his proposal slightly, but it was essentially unchanged in the major provisions. On January 31, Weeks delivered the Ford agreement to President Warren G. Harding for his review and then submitted it to Congress.

On February 15, 1922, Alabama Power Company sent the War Department its own proposal. The Christian Science Monitor reported on February 21 that Sperling & Company of London was backing the power company in its proposal and that Secretary of War John W. Weeks stated it was "better in some respects than that of Henry Ford."[168] In the months that followed, the debate involved several major points. Henry Ford refused to be regulated by the federal government under the Federal Water Power Act or by the state of Alabama's Public Service Commission. Alabama Power Company would be regulated by both. Ford would pay no taxes to state and local governments nor any fees to the federal government under the Federal Water Power Act, while Alabama Power would do both. There was no recourse to the federal government if Ford did not do what he said he would. Ford, who turned fifty-eight a few weeks after he mailed his proposal, would never live to the end of his one-hundred-year lease. What would happen when the Tennessee properties and dams passed to his estate?

The most divisive issue was fertilizer. At times Ford implied he would operate Nitrate Plant No. 2 and produce fertilizers, but many times he said that he would not produce fertilizer if it were not *profitable* for him to do so. What would he really do? The American Farm Bureau Federation first supported government operation of the dam and government production of cheap nitrates, but when that seemed remote, it moved to support the Ford proposal and galvanized its members in an emotional and often irrational support for Henry Ford and in opposition to Alabama Power Company. The farm bureau vehemently attacked Alabama Power for opposing the Ford plan. There was no question that Alabama farmers and their supporters were smitten by the Ford mystique and trusted him to do things he publicly said he would do but that were not part of the actual proposal.[169] Worthington, who had never shown much interest in farmers, used the fertilizer issue to garner support for Tennessee River navigational improvements and hydro dams that he had worked for decades to bring about. Demagoguing became the order of the day, and passions ran high.

While all of these issues were important to Alabama Power, the threat to the Warrior Reserve Steam Plant at Gorgas was the most dangerous for the company. On many occasions Ford made it absolutely clear that without Gorgas he would not go forward with the rest of his offer. In his proposal and his talks, Ford did not differentiate between the portion of the Gorgas plant owned outright by Alabama Power and the additional unit that was constructed with government funds on power company property, a unit Alabama Power had a right to purchase. Congressional committees heard from War Department engineers, independent consultants, and neutral experts that Gorgas was not necessary to Ford's development. They found Ford's insistence upon Gorgas unreasonable and were puzzled why Gorgas was such an important issue to Ford. Perhaps it was really an important issue to Worthington.

The question of Gorgas threw the validity of Alabama Power Company's contract with the War Department on the table for national discussion.[170] Martin spent weeks in Washington, often testifying before various congressional committees discussing the Ford proposal. The company's legal department was churning out briefs and copying documents, while the public relations staff at the company directed the printing of pamphlets and materials to present the Alabama Power side to the public. Being bombarded with caustic attacks, most not substantiated by facts, Alabama Power was even criticized for daring to defend itself in what its opponents called a "massive propaganda campaign."[171] Tom Martin accepted speaking engagements when he could, but the need was so great that he put his brother, William Logan Martin, on the road, talking to whatever Alabama groups invited a power company spokesperson. Perhaps this was one reason why Logan Martin moved to Birmingham in 1922 and established a law firm that would eventually incorporate the company's legal department. The next year Logan Martin would be joined by J. Fritz Thompson and Perry Williams Turner. In 1923 Hobart A. McWhorter became an associate in the firm; two years later Arthur K. Foster joined the firm as a partner but left after three years to accept an appointment to the Alabama Supreme Court.[172]

In February 1922 the *Montgomery Advertiser* headlined, "Quick Action Expected on Ford Offer." Editorially the paper wrote that "Congress must approve the Ford plan" and blamed the Republicans for arbitrarily shutting down the project. The *Advertiser* predicted the "fight may be lively." This same day the paper reported that the boll weevil was coming closer to Montgomery County and cotton farmers in the area were desperate. The capital city paper reported each day on committee testimony in Washington, noting that the Alabama Farm Bureau, the local chamber of commerce, and former governor Emmet O'Neal opposed Alabama Power Company's proposal for use of the Shoals, an offer that was "in keeping with their diverse and sinister methods," and the goal of which was not to help farmers "but solely to swell the dividends of its Canadian and English Stockholders." The paper did note that Tom Martin had testified that Alabama Power would be operating under the Federal Water Power Act and the regulations of the Alabama Public Service Commission that protected the public and Mr. Ford would not.[173] The *Cordova Courier* favored Ford but wrote it would be better pleased if the work was done "under the guidance of an Alabama boy . . . a native of High Jackson [County] who probably dreamed of tremendous development on the Tennessee River before Mr. Ford ever heard of the stream."[174]

Mass meetings were organized all over the state. Governor Thomas E. Kilby was urged to make an offer to buy the Shoals for Alabama and to call a special meeting of the legislature to repeal "the Alabama Power Company's freedom from taxation."[175] This was a reference to the ten-year tax exemption on hydro plants, which the power company had taken advantage of in its investment at Lock 12 dam, an exemption that had only about seven months to run. The average citizen did not understand that these politically motivated charges related only to the hydroelectric plant, not to other property, ad valorem, and other taxes the company paid. Alabama law had provided these tax exemptions for many years to encourage investments in the state, particularly for cotton mills and other industrial plants locating in Alabama.

Alabama Farm Bureau president Edward A. O'Neal III was at almost every meeting, criticizing Alabama Power for interfering with Ford's offer, what he called "the greatest industrial project that was ever offered to Alabama." When congressmen came to visit Muscle Shoals, they were entertained at Chestnut Hill, the Ed O'Neal farm near Florence.[176] Often Logan Martin appeared on the same program with O'Neal and presented the power company's side and the facts, which must have been rather boring and legalistic to an audience when compared to the flamboyant and sensational charges of the pro-Ford speakers. Logan Martin countered every charge, regardless of how absurd and totally false it was. Perhaps the most ridiculous charge, seriously made and seriously believed, was that the Alabama Power Company (which had been incorporated in 1906 and was not controlled by James Mitchell until 1912) had influenced the drafting of provisions on corporations, sections 231–36, of the Constitution of 1901.[177]

Probably the most significant mass meeting was sponsored by the League of Women Voters and held in Montgomery on February 22, 1922, where former governor Emmet O'Neal and J. W. Worthington spoke. John Hornady wrote that this was where "the flames of fury were fanned afresh and the fight against Alabama Power Company was put on an organized basis." Committees were formed to investigate the power company; one committee was assigned the task of determining "when and where the Alabama Power Company was organized and who were the original stockholders."[178] When Captain William Patrick Lay read the proceedings of the meeting, he issued a lengthy statement, proudly saying that "I organized the Alabama Power Company in Gadsden, Alabama, my hometown, in 1906 under the laws of the State of Alabama." Lay put on record that in 1906 he owned 96 percent of the shares, that his son and his attorney owned the other 4 percent, and that the Alabama laws the convention attacked were good laws, written and passed by Alabamians. He was especially critical of someone he does not name but calls "Mr. Ford's chief propagandist," who, Lay charged, was one of the owners who sold the "English people" the Muscle Shoals property in the first place and who was behind getting the government to build the large nitrate plant there. This person was now the one trying "to have the government hand over all of this property" to Ford. Lay wrote that "certainly he is entitled to be called 'The Chief Propagandist.'" Lay's letter was printed and sent to newspapers all over the state. The convention called for an investigation of Alabama Power Company, none was conducted. This helps explain why Tom Martin did not discuss J. W. Worthington in his history of electricity in Alabama.[179]

GORGAS AND FORD

While the pro-Ford advocates were still fighting for the Detroit industrialist to be given the Shoals, Martin and Alabama Power won the fight for Gorgas. The Department of the Army, especially Colonel Joyes and General C. C. Williams, chief of ordnance, had insisted from the beginning that the contract was legal, that the army had initiated the joint project with the company, and that it was a good deal for the United States, especially when compared to other wartime government contracts, some of which had produced salvage rates as low as 1 or 2 percent. Furthermore, the War Department believed that the government had a moral responsibility to fulfill its obligations under the contract to sell its Gorgas unit to the power company at a figure determined by arbitration.[180]

On April 14, 1923, Tom Martin notified the chief of ordnance that Alabama Power Company was implementing the Gorgas contract provision that the federal government either had to sell its property to Alabama Power or remove it from the company's premises as required by the contract. The time set in the contract was ninety days. Martin explained that the growing demands for electricity in Alabama required that his company invest in additional steam generation to back up its hydro generation during the coming dry season so the company could serve its customers. Secretary Weeks asked the power company for and received several extensions while he was trying to get guidance from the Judge Advocate General's office and from the Department of Justice to work out something agreeable to Henry Ford. During this time, President Warren G. Harding died suddenly in California on August 2, 1923. A few weeks after Calvin Coolidge's inauguration, Attorney General Harry M. Daugherty reversed a previous opinion and determined the Alabama Power Company contract was valid. The company refused to grant the War Department a fourth thirty-day extension, and very quietly, on September 24, the government accepted two checks from Alabama Power Company totaling $3,472,487.25, and the company received a deed for all the government's property at Gorgas. For the federal government this represented a return of 72 percent of its value, while other government war surplus property had been sold for an *average* of 8.4 percent.[181]

As the year 1924 opened, Tom Martin prepared to present the government another proposal for operating the power plant at the Shoals. Alabama

Power would be joined by Tennessee Electric Power Company and Georgia Railway & Power Company. The *New York Times* suggested this plan would overshadow Ford's proposal, but the Ford proposal remained the center of attention in Congress.[182] Supporters of Ford claimed that Alabama Power Company was foreign-owned, and thus its control of the Shoals would jeopardize national defense. When the Ford offer was before the House of Representatives, Congressman Theodore Burton introduced an amendment that would have forced Ford to operate under the provisions of the Federal Water Power Act. It failed, and the Ford proposal, as contained in the bill written by Representative John C. McKenzie of Illinois, passed the House of Representatives on March 10, 1924, by a vote of 227 to 143. In the Senate, Senator George Norris insisted on holding new hearings, which began on April 16, 1924. An interesting exchange took place during Senator Norris's questioning of a representative of Ford. After the Nebraska senator had the Ford man agree to the sanctity of contracts in relation to the government's entering into an agreement with Ford, Norris then asked him, why then was Henry Ford asking the government to break its contract with Alabama Power Company on the Gorgas plant extension? The man's stumbling answer had little meaning.[183]

Alabama senator Oscar Underwood, who remained in constant contact with J. W. Worthington, urged the Senate to bring the McKenzie bill to a vote as soon as possible. The Nebraska senator gathered engineers and accountants who were not passionate on either side and had them analyze the complicated finances and dam construction estimates of the Ford proposal. Norris drafted a new bill that would provide for the creation of a federal power corporation to operate the Muscle Shoals facilities. The most damaging revelation for Ford advocates was a series of telegrams between Ford's representative in Washington and Ford's Michigan staff. A message was relayed from President Coolidge that the president wished someone to convey to Ford that "it is my hope that Mr. Ford will not do or say anything that will make it difficult for me to deliver Muscle Shoals to him, which I am trying to do."[184] There were rumors of Ford's political ambitions, and with party conventions scheduled for summer and a presidential election coming up in the fall, Coolidge intended to be the Republican nominee. Ford, realizing his Muscle Shoals proposal would now be defeated in the Senate, withdrew his offer on October 18, 1924, bringing this phase of the Muscle Shoals controversy to a close.

Senator Underwood drew up a bill that was a compromise between the Ford and Norris plans, but its provision to allow private power companies to lease and operate the hydro plant was attacked by many, including some southern senators.[185] The *New York Journal-American* published an editorial on December 13, 1924, attacking Senator Underwood as being in "the service of the railroads and other great corporations." The newspaper claimed that Underwood was working in the interest of General Electric Company because Electric Bond & Share Company (founded by GE but severed from GE in 1924) owned stock in Alabama Power Company and its own directors are "in Mr. Underwood's Alabama Power Company, to which the Senate of the United States is asked to give away the second most valuable property of the Nation, second only to the Panama Canal."[186] This "most valuable property," so described by the *New York Journal-American*, was the property Alabama Power Company had given to the nation for one dollar, the nominal amount stated in the deed of gift.

* * *

After the founding of the nation in 1776, the waters of the mighty Tennessee River roared through the rocks and ledges of this "most valuable property" at Muscle Shoals for almost 150 years, unnoticed except by the people of the area. The first pressing need for safe passage was for boats carrying cotton bales to New Orleans. The railroads came and provided another way to ship cotton. Then came electricity and the technology to harness falling water to improve the quality of people's lives and to make industry more productive. For many years no one could find the capital to invest in a dam for Muscle Shoals or for that matter capital to build a large dam and hydro facility anywhere in Alabama. Then James Mitchell arrived, had a dream, and made a plan. With Englishmen behind him who had more faith in Alabama than anyone before ever had, Mitchell started building. But a war intervened, then his life was cut short. Once when Abner Bell Aldridge was working with Mitchell on the Warrior Reserve Steam Plant that became Gorgas, he asked Mitchell how he "ever expected to get his money out of this great development." Mitchell replied that he "never expected to get it back." He just "wanted to build a monument" so that those who came after him "could say that his was a useful life."[187]

In 1924 the Muscle Shoals and the federal government were not yet finished with Alabama Power Company, nor the power company with the Shoals. In many respects, for the company the worst was yet to come. But the Shoals was not the only subject that occupied the company during the 1920s. Among other things, under the new Federal Water Power Act of 1920, there were a few more dams to build.

View of 1925 the Alabama Power corporate office
from Eighteenth Street looking north, 1926.

Chapter Four

Jordan Dam, constructed near the "Devil's Staircase" shoals on the Coosa River, was completed on December 31, 1928.

SOUTHEASTERN POWER & LIGHT: DAMS AND MORE ELECTRICITY

From the beginning, enlightened self-interest has told us that next to the manufacture of power itself our greatest manufacture must be customers, the upbuilding of industry, agriculture, commerce and whole civilization in order that there might be an outlet for the increasing production of electric power.

THOMAS W. MARTIN, *Story of Electricity in Alabama*, 1952

The decade of the 1920s is known as the Roaring Twenties, a time of prohibition, yet one could find illegal alcohol at a speakeasy or buy moonshine from bootleggers or gangsters. Blues and jazz found their way from Bourbon Street in New Orleans to Memphis and Chicago. Women cut their hair, shortened their skirts, danced the Charleston, and were called flappers. The Harlem and Southern Renaissances were influencing the nation's literature, Babe Ruth was a baseball hero, and at a frenetic pace, people escaped the realities of their lives through parties, sports, and entertainments. Disillusioned by the Great War and the politics of the peace, Americans retreated into isolationism and chose the conservative leadership of the Republican Party. And business boomed.[1]

As Americans enjoyed a rising standard of living, partly due to cheap electricity, speculation in real estate and stocks (much of it in utilities) soared.[2] The Florida land boom, which began in 1919 and crashed after the hurricane of 1926, was another real estate bubble that affected Alabama besides the Muscle Shoals boom.[3] In the 1920s, Alabama Power Company prospered, taking advantage of the Federal Water Power Act, the favorable economic climate, and the ease with which capital could be raised. During this period, Tom Martin kept tight control of the company and did not look favorably upon the antics of many Wall Street dealers, and he opposed the questionable stock practices that were pumping air into the bubble. Martin spent many days in New York City in the twenties, but he was never at ease among the ultrarich utility barons of the nation.

As the federal waterpower bill was being considered in Congress, Martin made certain that he was informed of its progress and the contents, amendments, and wording of the bill as it moved through committees in the House and Senate. Martin recognized that a federal waterpower policy was necessary to allow Alabama Power Company to complete the construction of its Coosa and Tallapoosa River dam sites, developments essential for the company to provide the electricity Alabama needed for its continued economic growth. Martin also knew that Alabama Power had to be able to raise money to build those dams and the new law must provide protection for that capital. He was active in educating Alabama's congressional delegation on the hydropower industry, and he cooperated with and supported the lobbyist hired by Electric Bond & Share. Martin himself lobbied for a law that would allow development of Alabama's resources.[4] Although the Federal Water Power Act of 1920 did not contain all the provisions Martin wanted, it was nonetheless a law Alabama Power could operate under and a law under which the state of Alabama and the company could grow and develop together.[5]

The deliberations of Congress were not Martin's only focus in 1920. The legislature in Montgomery also had his attention. Thomas E. Kilby, former Anniston City Council member and businessman successful in steel, banking, and cast-iron pipe manufacture, was elected governor in 1918 on a reform platform.[6] James Mitchell, Theodore Swann, and Martin knew Kilby well from the company's investments in Anniston during the war and were somewhat leery of him. In 1917 James Mitchell had written to W. N. Walmsley that "we must be very tactful as Kilby, who will doubtless be the next governor, is a particularly cranky individual and has already announced in his platform that he is in favor of no tax exemption [for hydro developments]."[7] While issues of prohibition, women's suffrage, education, child labor, convict lease, and legislative budgets dominated Kilby's agenda, he also pressed for strengthening the Public Service Commission in the 1919 legislative session. But Kilby met stiff opposition, and the effort failed. Then the governor launched an attack on commission chairman Sam Kennedy, who was running for reelection. Kilby claimed that the Public Service Commission had met only forty-eight days in five years and the members were not doing their jobs. Kennedy was defeated.[8]

Assistant General Counsel Walter M. Hood, a native of Birmingham who joined the company in 1913, wired Tom Martin, who was in Washington, D.C., that the governor was going to call a special session of the legislature "at once."[9] In that 1920 special session, antagonism toward the power company was especially evident. To placate some of the anti-utility feelings, the session enacted the Alabama Public Utility Act of 1920, patterned on a Wisconsin law. The statute was a far-reaching reform that greatly increased the Public Service Commission's budget and authority, including the authority to regulate utility rates.[10] The law addressed most of the weaknesses of the previous statutes, defined terms, and increased the commission's power to inspect facilities, books, and records. Utility companies could not issue bonds, stock, or debentures without the Public Service Commission's approval, nor could a utility construct new facilities without first applying to the commission for a certificate of convenience and necessity. With occasional fine-tuning, this extensive statute has provided the basis of Alabama's public utility regulation into the twenty-first century.[11]

The Kilby legislature also raised the question of ten-year tax exemptions for waterpower investments. Pressure to withdraw the exemptions contained in the 1907 act had been at issue since the Democratic primary of 1914 and when the company was attacked in the Alabama Supreme Court rehearing brief of the Tallassee Mills case. Governor Charles Henderson, in his 1915 message to the legislature, had recommended the repeal of tax exemptions from corporations developing waterpower, as well as the repeal of the 1907 statute that gave such corporations the right to the state's interest in the beds of streams.[12] None of this passed. In 1920 the only tax exemption in effect for Alabama Power was on Lock 12, as there had been no other hydro development in the state because Congress refused to grant permission. The two issues at stake in the 1920 debate in Alabama were whether the tax exemption on investments should be dropped for the future and/or whether tax exemptions should be revoked. Many interests feared the precedent of the legislature reneging on promises and were concerned about the violation of what was considered a contract and the effect of that action upon potential capital coming into the state. The proposal was defeated, although it was revisited three years later.[13] In December 1921, after the Alabama Supreme Court ruled the tax exemption did not apply to Alabama's franchise tax, Alabama Power Company paid the state $73,280.81.[14]

In 1922 William W. Brandon, a popular Tuscaloosa attorney, former state auditor, and once head of the state militia, was easily elected governor. During stump speeches, Brandon often said he would abolish tax exemptions on water-power investments.[15] The Henry Ford proposal for Muscle Shoals was before Congress, and Tom Martin was defending his company and opposing Ford's plan. Attacking the company was good campaign rhetoric. Brandon's platform had included economy in government and no new taxes. His campaign was so pro status quo that he even defended the convict lease system. As governor he initiated strict economy in state expenditures and supported the withdrawal of the ten-year tax exemption on hydroelectric investments.

Brandon's first legislature met in January 1923. On February 3, 1923, the *Montgomery Advertiser* warned that the "Legislature, we fear, is in a curious mood of antagonism to capital." The *Advertiser* quoted the *Selma Times-Journal* that the legislature was "hostile to capital, to constructive movements, to those substantial aids to enterprise and development without which to expect a bright future for the State would be an irridescent [sic] new dream." The Montgomery newspaper noted that anyone studying the state's economic problems "knows that nowhere on earth is there a more crying need for investing capital than in Alabama. The State is teeming with opportunities, bulging with advantages, such as God and Nature provide, but it must have the sinews of wealth, the fundamental prerequisites of industrial expansion before it can utilize these resources." The *Advertiser* feared New England cotton textile mills, which were moving to the South, were not coming to Alabama. The paper reasoned that if the tax exemption granted to waterpower developments was withdrawn then northern cotton mills would question whether the ten-year exemption Alabama was allotting them would hold through the decade.[16] Coming when it did, there is little question that the tax exempt drive was a fallout from Alabama Power Company's strong opposition to the Ford proposal for Muscle Shoals and the result of hostility against the company stirred by agrarian attacks and resentment that the Ford plan had not been accepted.

The general revenue bill that was introduced, debated, and enacted included a short provision that "subjects of taxation under this act and existing laws shall include all the property, real and personal, of hydroelectric power companies."[17] The ten-year tax exemption on Lock 12 dam had run out in October 1922, but the tax exemption on Mitchell Dam, which was claimed as the construction began in July 1921, still had eight years to go.[18] The first tax assessment on Lock 12 (and a few other properties associated with the dam) was made in 1923. That year Alabama Power paid a total of $527,169.32 in state, county, and city taxes and licenses. This compared with previous figures for 1922 of $158,940.62.[19] Looking back at the company's financial troubles over the ten-year exemption period on Lock 12, Alabama Power Company could not have survived the early years when it was spending so much borrowed money on capital expenditures with no income, and later inadequate income, if it also had been assessed taxes on Lock 12. Throughout the twentieth century, providing tax incentives for new industries was a common and acclaimed practice, if not a universally approved one. In Alabama the tax deferment offered to new industries began in 1869 with a one-year exemption. What made hydro investment different were the incessant attacks on "waterpower trusts" by agrarian demagogues, the aggressive actions of the pro–Henry Ford–cheap fertilizer dreamers, and the inability of a predominately agricultural state to understand the relationship between adequate electricity and industrial development. In 1924, when Mitchell Dam was first assessed and the company acquired new utility properties in Montgomery and Tuscaloosa, Alabama Power paid taxes of $673,813.13.[20]

Powergrams and Industry

As the number of employees, district offices, and generation units increased, Tom Martin became concerned about losing the small company feeling that had been such an important part of the office in the early years. A company publication could post announcements and news that needed to be communicated to employees. It could serve an educational function and pass the corporate culture to new hires. In April 1920 the first issue of Powergrams was delivered to Alabama Power Company employees and others who subscribed for $2 a year. The monthly magazine was written and edited by employees "devoting hours of overtime" to the project. In the inaugural issue Martin wrote that the purpose of the monthly bulletin was to make employees mindful of "our problems, our hopes and purposes" and to provide information and suggestions not only from the officers but also from the staff. Martin had

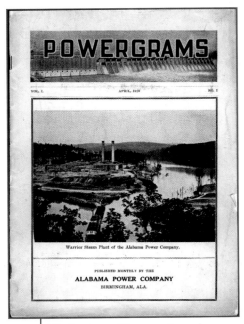

The first issue of Powergrams featured the Warrior Reserve (Gorgas) Steam Plant on the cover.

a keen sense of the importance of history, yet he did not mention that *grams* also meant record and that *Powergrams* would serve as a historical record of the company's people and its development. Frank D. Mahoney was the first managing editor of *Powergrams*. In 1923 the in-house publication was transferred to the new publicity department under management of W. J. Baldwin.

In a contest that attracted 135 entries, a cashier in the Birmingham office, A. H. Salter, suggested the name *Powergrams*, a combination of the Greek *grams* (meaning *writing*) with *power*. The first issue appeared three months before James Mitchell died, and he was well enough to write a short editorial endorsing the new magazine and thanking company officers and staff for their loyalty and hard work. He assured them that their support had been a source of comfort to him during his illness. Mitchell touched on the problems and difficulties the company had faced in the early years and how he believed that "these fundamental matters" had been decided wisely by the officers and directors. Now, he knew, the company was on a firm foundation, but "a great part of its permanent success depends upon the interest" of the staff. Mitchell looked forward to sending other messages to the employees. Unfortunately, he had only a few months to live.[21]

So much had been accomplished in the years since James Mitchell walked into Tom Martin's law office that November day in 1911 that it seemed much more than nine years to the men who lived it. When he wrote *The Story of Electricity in Alabama* four decades later, Martin paraphrased Mitchell's vision that electricity would create "a new Alabama and a new South, a South . . . which will grow richer and stronger industrially and because of this, in turn grow stronger agriculturally."[22] From the very beginning, Mitchell recognized that the industrial and commercial market for electricity was much less than Alabama's hydropower potential, and he knew his challenge was to increase the market for electricity.[23] One reason Captain William Patrick Lay had been unsuccessful in his capital quests was the concern investors had over the perception of a low demand for electricity in Alabama. Simply put, lightbulbs alone could not support a large electrical operation. To stimulate industrial sales Theodore Swann was brought in to head a commercial department. While this department concentrated on selling power to industries already in reach of Alabama Power electricity, there is no question from the correspondence in the files that Mitchell wanted and expected to attract new industry to the state and that this was also Swann's charge. Mitchell's investments in Anniston Steel and Anniston Ordnance, his experiments with the new electric furnaces, his encouragement of Swann's Southern Manganese Company, and his interest in Washburn's American Cyanamid Company all came from a commitment to Alabama's industrial development through attracting and recruiting new industries.

One of the constant themes in the history of Alabama Power Company is its steadfast commitment and dedication to the industrial development of the state. The company was the first, and for a very long time the only, entity in the state dedicated to convincing new industry to locate in Alabama and willing to spend the money and time to spread the message. Most of the state's large industrial employers were more concerned about protecting their cheap labor market from competition than in increasing job opportunities for the state's working people. Martin put it another way: "From the beginning, enlightened self-interest has told us that next to the manufacture of power itself our greatest manufacture must be customers, the upbuilding of industry, agriculture, commerce and whole civilization in order that there might be an outlet for the increasing production of electric power."[24]

Tom Martin recalled that in 1920–21 the company established a new industries division within the commercial department.[25] Vice President Reuben Mitchell supervised Thomas D. Johnson, who had responsibility for the first effort, which concentrated on attracting northern cotton textile mills.[26] In his "History of the New Industries Division," written in the early 1940s, Johnson stated that a separate new industries division was established in 1924. By that year, however, Johnson had already spent many weeks over the course of two years traveling throughout the East and New England. On his first trip, which was in 1922, Johnson spent six weeks in the Northeast and seldom met an executive who had been south of Washington, D.C., even though Henry M. Flagler's railroad had reached all the way to Key West by 1912. As a consequence, Alabama Power Company realized that a massive advertisement campaign was needed to educate northern executives about the advantages of locating a plant in Alabama. Trade journals and eastern newspapers were targeted, and exhibits were prepared for trade shows. Special flyers were printed and distributed. Even the relatively new medium of motion pictures was used, and a feature called "King Cotton" was produced. The Southern Exposition was one of the significant trade shows with a strong Alabama Power Company presence. It opened at Grand Central Palace in New York in May 1925.[27]

This new industries division exhibit in Boston, one of many on tour in the northeast in 1922, included the distribution of thousands of cotton bolls to eastern businessmen and industrialists.

The company spent large sums of money on these programs for several years without any sign of success.[28] First rewards finally came in 1924, when Tom Johnson was visiting in Boston and Russell Leonard, treasurer of Pepperell Manufacturing Company, told him that Pepperell would locate a plant in Opelika, provided Alabama Power could assist in finding a proper place. Johnson returned to Alabama and worked closely with the local people in an effort to find a suitable location for the plant. When the Pepperell party visited Opelika, they were unable to come to an agreement, however, and they left on the train to Birmingham without making a commitment. As soon as the textile mill officials arrived at their Birmingham hotel, I. J. Dorsey, a prominent civic and chamber of commerce leader in Opelika, called to say that "we are up at Will Davis' home—some forty of our leading citizens. We have had a prayer meeting. We are ready to go through with the Pepperell matter." Leonard returned to Opelika and finalized arrangements. Johnson wrote that the success with Pepperell, after discouraging years, "appeared to have broken the ice. It was as if this first major victory served as a green light for others to be on the move" to Alabama.[29]

One of the most remarkable documents in the Alabama Power Company Corporate Archives is a twenty-four-page accounting of the new industries located in the Alabama Power Company service area between 1925 and 1952. Pepperell Mills in Opelika begins the list. According to the data, Pepperell produced sheeting, spent approximately $1.7 million in capital investment, originally employed 600 people, and had an estimated annual payroll of $600,000. By 1953 the number of Pepperell employees had increased to 3,000.[30] In a list of plants by county location, between 1925 and 1952 plants were developed in sixty-two of the state's sixty-seven counties. Mobile led the list with ninety plants, followed by Calhoun County and Tuscaloosa County both with fifty-six new industries.[31] The Montgomery Chamber of Commerce credited Alabama Power Company with "aggressive cooperation" that convinced the West Boylston Company to construct a $2 million cotton mill in the city. The plant began operation on January 1, 1928.[32]

West Point Pepperell Mills in Opelika was the first industry to locate in Alabama after the organization of the "New Industries" division. Notice company housing surrounding the plant.

After targeting cotton mills, Alabama Power Company's new industries division went after paper mills. Gulf States Paper Corporation was the first success. It located in Tuscaloosa in 1927 and invested $5.25 million. Gulf States began its operations with a payroll of over half a million dollars and employed 550 Alabamians. The next year Alabama Power Company convinced International Paper Company to build a $6.5 million plant and Continental Bag Company to construct a $1 million facility, both in Mobile.[33] Direct revenue to Alabama Power from new industries rose from .025 percent of its total industrial revenue in 1925 to 42 percent of the company's entire industrial revenue for 1940.

Writing in 1941, Johnson looked back and noted "the bitter disappointments of those initial years, the failures, the seeming futility of our effort." The company had an unshakable resolve "during those early days" to deliver "our people from the hopeless character of their traditional means of livelihood."[34] Because of Tom Martin's leadership, the state of Alabama created the Alabama Industrial Development Commission. Governor Bibb Graves presided over the first meeting in May 1927. Martin served with George Gordon Crawford, Lindley Morton, Ben Russell, and Theodore Swann.[35]

Frank Mahoney directed the commercial department after the war until 1922. He reorganized it and stressed the importance of a utility's gaining the confidence of the public. Mahoney supervised a study on how the use of electrical appliances, specifically electric ranges, would affect the loads of the company in different locations. The company also wanted to know what the operational cost would be to the customer and how efficient the stove would be. The study was so satisfactory that the company formed a new section to concentrate on increasing domestic use of electricity through demonstrating electrical labor-saving appliances and machines. Later Alabama Power began selling electric ranges and refrigerators and pushing the new electric washing machines.[36] The front area of local power company offices displayed these products. For people living in small Alabama towns, these were the only sales outlets available to them beyond the Sears Roebuck catalog. Later the company would convince local furniture stores to add appliances to their merchandise. J. S. Sutherland was given responsibility for domestic appliance sales in 1922.[37] Scotty, as he was called, was an engineer who came to the company from the Tennessee Coal, Iron and Railroad Company. He was first hired as a concrete inspector working for Eugene Yates on Lock 12. Sutherland then worked with Mahoney and later with Francis P. Cummings on *Powergrams*.[38] When Mahoney left Alabama Power, he left behind a number of books on utility salesmanship. One, *Winning the Public*, he signed over to a company associate,

Earle R. Wald, who in 1925 passed it on to Alabama Power salesman Walker McCutchen.[39]

One of the longtime local managers, John F. Thompson, became a top salesman for Sutherland. Thompson began his work with Alabama Power Company before World War I, helped to build the power line from Lineville to Roanoke, and was one of the men who built the transmission line from Gorgas to Muscle Shoals. After serving in the war, he returned to the company and was given the duty of patrolling the transmission line between Lock 12 dam and the Clanton area and Leeds. Thompson rode a large red horse named Prince, furnished by the company. In 1926 he was assigned to head the Columbiana office, where he stayed until his retirement in 1960. In the twenties, Alabama Power Company featured the latest electric appliances in its offices. One day the owner of Davis Drug Store, who had a cow and sold milk at his store, told John that he had heard the "electric ice box" would keep milk from spoiling. He would like to test it. So Davis came down to the company's office, put his fresh milk in the refrigerator, and said he would be back at the end of the week. If the milk was still good, he would buy the appliance. The milk was still fresh, and the Davis Drug Store soon had one of the first refrigerators in Columbiana.[40]

Another use of electricity was introduced in the fall of 1927 when Montgomery County High School at Pike Road played Cloverdale High School of Montgomery. For the first time, the game was played at night in Cramton Bowl, where Alabama Power had turned the darkness into dawn with thirty 1,000-watt lights. Five thousand people were there, establishing an attendance record for an Alabama high school football game. Will Paterson, who refereed the game, noted that "the night football game solves the problem of early season games in the South" where intense heat during September and October make football games uncomfortable for fans and difficult for players. He predicted night games would be the future for southern football. Alabama Power's D. D. Black (lighting specialist), C. F. Voltz (general superintendent), J. R. Watson (electrical engineer), and G. A. Ralston (general foreman) directed the planning and installation of the lighting.[41]

Alabama Power's sales program was responsible for the creation of a character that became one of the most widely used—and beloved—symbols of the electric industry. "Reddy Kilowatt" was a cartoon character created by Ashton B. Collins Sr., a man Tom Martin described as a "brilliant commercial manager of the Company." Collins was a native of New Orleans who came to work at Alabama Power in January 1925 as assistant commercial manager. In 1926, after a meeting that discussed ways to sell appliances to a public still uneasy about the use of electricity, Collins watched a storm from his window. In a thunderbolt that paused before his eyes, Collins thought he saw a stick man in the intersection of the lightning bolts. He immediately took pen and paper and sketched out a spirited little man with bolts for arms and legs and a lightbulb for a nose and wearing funny little safety rubber boots and gloves. Reddy Kilowatt made his first appearance at the Alabama Electrical Exposition, where some 10,000 people were introduced to the sparky little guy. Eventually more than 200 power companies used Reddy in their advertisements. He appeared on billboards, stationery, advertisements, and giveaway merchandise like pins, earrings, lighters, and hats.[42]

Reddy Kilowatt, "Your electrical servant," from the October 1926 issue of *Powergrams*.

SAFETY AND HEALTH

A national movement for safety in industry and manufacturing began in 1907 and the National Safety Council was established in 1913 to fight carelessness and protect American workers. Alabama Power was involved in this movement because from its beginning the company wanted employees to have the knowledge needed to work safely and protect themselves.[43] Working with electricity is dangerous, and Alabama Power Company established standards of safety and safety training from the beginning. William Robert Loyd was employed by Alabama Power in 1913 as the manager of the casualty and tax department. Bill, as he was called, was a native of Georgia who moved as a child to Marshall County with his family and came to the power company after extensive work in Montgomery with the State Tax Commission. He began a program of education and training in safety that put Alabama Power in the forefront of the national safety movement. Loyd made certain that the most modern methods to prevent accidents and the best first aid practices were demonstrated to and understood by every employee.

Beginning with the first issue of *Powergrams* in April 1920, Loyd wrote a regular feature on safety that appeared in almost every issue during the early years. He made certain that an Alabama Power Company delegation attended the international safety congresses, where there were discussions of accident prevention, the use of rubber gloves, and the use of extension arms and other safety techniques. When there were accidents and fatalities, Loyd would detail the circumstances and tell what was done incorrectly and explain how the job should

Safety equipment and good judgment article from the November 1922 issue of *Powergrams*.

have been performed with proper safety precautions. Each year safety was a primary concern of the company's management.[44]

Alabama Power Company always offered the best medical treatment for any injuries that might occur on the job. Dr. Samuel R. Benedict, a Georgia native who received his medical degree from the University of Virginia College of Medicine and was the attending surgeon at St. Vincent's and Hillman Hospitals in Birmingham, was the company's chief surgeon. Benedict put together the company's medical program and wrote the handbook for procedures in case of accidents.[45] He recruited doctors across the state to join the company's list of surgeons, directed seminars on emergency medicine, and worked with the program presented at the annual meeting of the company's surgeons. Papers presented at these meetings were published, and their content was widely respected. Benedict, who was affectionately called "Doc" by everyone, was responsible for perfecting the "prone pressure method of resuscitation from electric shock or drowning," and his modifications were adopted and used across the southeastern states.[46]

WOMEN AT ALABAMA POWER COMPANY

The 1920s was a coming of age decade for American women. They had achieved the right to vote and assumed a greater independence. More women moved into the work place. Whether driven by choice or necessity, many found employment in the corporate and local offices of Alabama Power Company, which offered opportunities for women beyond secretarial, clerk, and telephone operator positions. Women participated in all the contests and activities of the company. For instance, in the third annual preferred stock sale, women sold one-tenth of the stock sold. Blanche Beall sold the most, 117 shares. Lucie Bouchelle earned second place in the contest by selling 103 shares.[47] Historian Harvey H. Jackson III uses Alabama Power Company as an example of the change in status for all Alabama women in the 1920s. He wrote that at Alabama Power "although men still handled things in the field and still held top positions in the company, the 'girls of the office' ran the office. Many were young women who had moved from the small towns where they had been raised to the big towns and the cities where there were jobs."[48]

Since Alabama Power Company had offices in most small towns, the company provided opportunities for women all across the state.

The number of women graduating from Auburn (then the Alabama Polytechnic Institute) and the University of Alabama in the 1920s provided a larger pool of professional women. The passage of the 1914 Smith-Lever Act increased funding for home demonstration agents, and Auburn's response was to create a Department of Home Economics in 1921. This department trained women to work with county agents in rural areas to improve the quality of farm life. Many of these women came to work for Alabama Power Company instead of the Agricultural Extension Service and began giving programs where they demonstrated electrical appliances for the home.

Adelia Gaboury was the first woman hired by Alabama Power Company to be a home economist. In 1922 she began to introduce electric appliances to women, often traveling to local offices where she held cooking schools. She recalled that "I used to take the train and had to carry a big trunk on board with me everywhere I went. It was filled with all kinds of pots and pans." She remembered that many women were cooking over open flames, but they were afraid to cook with electricity. Once she demonstrated "what electricity could do, they switched over without a backward glance." Gaboury convinced women that with electricity they could "cook scientifically using time and temperature."[49]

Home service advisors Mrs. A. D. Drake, Mrs. C. A. Kittredg and Miss Theresa Branch assisted in the Alabama Polytechnic Institute's "Better Farm & Home" demonstration, ca. 1923. Courtesy of Cooperative Extension Records, Special Collections and Archives, Auburn University Libraries.

In 1923 Alabama Power Company hired its first female engineer. She was Maria Rogan Whitson, who was Auburn's first female electrical engineering graduate and a Talladega native. Whitson had many job opportunities, but she selected Alabama Power over offers from both General Electric and Westinghouse.[50] One indication of the increasing significance of women to the company occurred when the 1925 *Annual Report* noted the existence of a women's committee. Alabama Power had "continued its policy of the education of women employees in utility principles and problems and in the dominant purpose of public utilities—service." The company's women had learned from this special training and were "better informed" and had "a keener sense of their responsibilities as citizen-employees and a deeper appreciation of their relationship to the industry and the public." Alabama Power's women addressed numerous civic organizations and schools across the state

Maria Rogan Whitson, Auburn and the power company's first female electrical engineer, 1923.

explaining how the company's service was connected to the advancement of industry and the prosperity of Alabama.[51]

CORPORATE ARCHIVES

On James Mitchell's death in 1920, W. E. "Will" Mitchell, Frederick S. Ruth, and Harold S. Swan were executors of Mitchell's estate, with Swan handling most of the administrative details. Swan had worked with the elder Mitchell, heading up his New York office (which was also the Alabama Traction, Light & Power and the Alabama Power Company office) and serving on the board of directors of Alabama Traction for many years. James Mitchell's vast holdings and extensive assets made this a complicated responsibility.[52] The company was in the process of moving its New York offices to another building when Swan wrote Tom Martin on September 5, 1920, asking for space in the Alabama Power Company suite to handle the Mitchell estate. The company rented five rooms in the Equitable Office Building in New York City's financial district, two for Alabama Power Company, two for Sperling & Company, and one now reserved for Mitchell's executor and staff.[53] In the process of moving, Swan supervised Stephen A. Dawley and the office staff in going through the files and boxing up Alabama Traction and Alabama Power Company records to be shipped to the Birmingham office.

In the spring of 1921 Tom Martin wrote from New York, telling general manager W. N. Walmsley to take care of these documents because of their historical value. Martin had in mind "collecting everything" into a "common library." About eight cases and six filing cabinets filled with Alabama Traction and Alabama Power Company correspondence and records arrived in Birmingham and were stored at the Magella substation vault in the western part of the city. Martin checked the documents before they left New York and saw that many of them related to the Muscle Shoals. He wrote that he wanted all these records safeguarded because the Muscle Shoals situation was "still developing so rapidly." This was the beginning of the Alabama Power Company's corporate archives.[54]

GORGAS

The Alabama Power Company's Warrior Reserve Steam Plant was in Walker County, a county with a reputation for tough, hard-working, and independent-minded people, some of them good moonshiners in the era of prohibition. Located twenty miles from Jasper, the steam plant was built in such an isolated location that it needed housing for its workers. A tent city for construction workers and then a company village were built around the steam plant and the coal mines. Its U.S. post office was named Gorgas, and soon the community gave its name to the steam plant. With its schools, dining hall, commissary, and churches, from the very beginning Gorgas held a special place in the culture of Alabama Power Company. For many years, James Mitchell's sister-in-law, Lena Mitchell, the widow of his brother Bob, operated the Gorgas dining hall. She first came to Alabama in 1913 to supervise the dining hall at the Lock 12 construction site. At Gorgas she developed a reputation for excellent food that spread far and wide, and she was especially noted for her mince pie, biscuits, and strawberry shortcake. James Mitchell and Tom Martin enjoyed escorting important people on visits to the Gorgas plant and always made certain they ate in the dining hall.[55]

Despite the Gorgas employees' commitment to work, they applauded the heavy sustained rains that kept Lock 12 generating the week of December 11, 1922, when they were able to shut down the steam plant; the "huge machines were idle" on December 17 for the first time after six months of continuous operation.[56] For plant operators, rain usually meant time for a little social life. In Gorgas, small houses in even rows were divided by sandy roads and nestled on two hillsides overlooking the Warrior River. The schools, one for white children and one for black children, were operated by Walker County, Alabama Power, and Winona Coal Company through a cooperative agreement. When times were hard in the 1929 depression and the county closed schools, the company kept its schools open. In perhaps James Mitchell's last trip to Birmingham, his wife Carolyn and daughter Marion accompanied him. During the visit Mrs. Mitchell toured Gorgas. She was impressed but said there needed to be "green spots" where children could play. She was assured that a playground was to be built.[57]

Gorgas was founded as a "mine-mouth" steam plant—the mine that provided coal for the plant was adjacent to the plant. The Winona Coal Company, owned by Alabama Power Company, mined coal at Gorgas for the steam plant during World War I and employed about 300 miners. In 1918 Winona used machines to mine the coal and mules to haul it to the tipple. E. P. Randle was the superintendent.[58] The United Mine Workers was defeated in 1908 in its attempt to organize Alabama coal miners but began a spirited campaign during and after the war. The Gorgas mine was probably little affected by the 1918–19 United Mine Workers strike, but some UMW miners went out against the Winona Coal Company during the strike of 1920–21, when some 12,000 to 15,000 of 26,000 coal miners in Alabama supported the UMW. Strikebreakers were employed by the Winona Coal Company, but Gorgas escaped much of the violence that swept though the Walker and Jefferson County mining camps.[59] Governor Thomas E. Kilby sent seven companies of the National Guard to the mines to maintain order. The strike was ended with arbitration by the governor that was favorable to management.[60] Drifton Coal Company purchased the assets of Winona Coal Company in November 1924, and the assets of both companies were folded into Southeastern Fuel Company, which was then owned by Southeastern Power & Light. In the first nine months of 1925, 238,302 tons of coal were mined.[61]

The International Brotherhood of Electrical Workers also worked to organize the steam plant employees. Royce Dean Northcutt Sr. in his delightful memoir, I Remember Gorgas, recalls riding with his father on day trips to Alabama Power Company locations. It was about 1928, and his father was representing the union, trying to enlist members. Northcutt notes that this was before the passage of the Wagner Act (National Labor Relations Act of 1935 that gave protection for labor union organization). When the company found out about his father's union activities, he was fired—for one day. After the Wagner Act passed, Northcutt's father became president of the union, but it was 1940 before Alabama Power Company recognized the IBEW as the bargaining agent. When Northcutt retired "some 30 odd years later, he received full pension credit for his employment prior to the firing."[62]

Charles Oglesby Lineberry, Gorgas plant superintendent, 1920–48.

The man who actually ruled Gorgas was the superintendent, and the most memorable superintendent was Charles Oglesby Lineberry, who was called "Chief" and who was the Gorgas plant superintendent from 1920 until his death in 1948. A Virginian, Lineberry began his work with Alabama Power Company in 1915 at Lock 12. He was employed at Gadsden in 1917, and then two years later at the age of twenty-nine he went to Gorgas as chief engineer. Lineberry was especially noted for his tight control, letters to employees, and memoranda to the village at large. His letter emphatically stating there was not a husband in Gorgas who would strike his wife, then warning that he was not going to let family fights "become a nuisance in Gorgas," is a classic in the lore of Gorgas and is part of the historical exhibit at the plant.[63] In 1924 Gorgas became the South's largest producer of steam power, providing 100,000 horsepower.[64]

WSY Radio

Electricity was not the only technological advancement changing America in the 1920s. Radio was another invention that altered the way Alabamians lived their lives, and it was the company's electrical engineers who initiated the first broadcast in the state. Radio grew out of an 1890s invention by Guglielmo Marconi and was perfected by the invention of the vacuum tube. International attention was riveted when on June 15, 1920, Nellie Melba's concert at Marconi's station was sent out over the airwaves from Chelmsford, England. In November 1920 Pittsburgh's KDKA broadcast the news of Warren G. Harding's landslide election. The world of radio arrived in Alabama when Alabama Power Company established WSY and began broadcasting on April 24, 1922.[65] The station, originally located on Powell Avenue in Birmingham, was first conceived by Alabama Power as a way to communicate with line crews working in isolated areas. Radio was so new that company engineers designed and built most of the transmitting equipment. Work on the station began in January, and public interest was so widespread that in April 1922 the company began broadcasting entertainment programs. WSY soon became the most popular radio station in the eastern United States. In February 1923 a severe ice storm across central Alabama pulled all the newspapers' press lines down, so WSY began broadcasting Associated Press and United Press news originating from Birmingham.[66]

The station was later moved to the radio shop in a popular city department store, Loveman, Joseph & Loeb, which allowed an antenna to be strung from towers on the roof. Alabama Power invited civic organizations to announce their activities on the radio and scheduled time for area churches to broadcast Sunday morning and evening services. Because agriculture was so important to the state and many farmers lived in rural areas without ready access to newspapers, the station began broadcasting market reports and special programs produced by state and federal agriculture departments. Music was often provided by the WSY orchestra, made up largely of Alabama Power employees.

The WSY station was recognized in the area for the way it signed off the air: three slow anvil strikes with the sound fading away. Within a few months the responsibilities of providing programming with free talent and no advertisements became expensive and time consuming. On November 6, 1923, the power company broadcast its last program from WSY, then dismantled and moved the equipment and gave it to the Alabama Polytechnic Institute at Auburn, which merged WSY with its own station,

WSY broadcast facilities located at the Loveman, Joseph & Loeb department store, ca. 1923.

WMAV, and the new call letters became WAPI.[67] The company was, after all, in the business of generating and selling electricity, but it had proved that radio could be a viable business and that people would listen.

Gas and Street Railways

Gas, water, and street railway franchises were sometimes included when James Mitchell purchased the small utility companies of several towns. Many of these early side operations were divested, but in the 1920s Alabama Power Company was still selling gas and operating street railways in some cities. In Anniston, Decatur, and Selma, Alabama Power operated the town gas plants, and in Anniston, Gadsden, and Huntsville it still ran the street railway systems. From time to time management had to deal with a variety of complaints—from impolite conductors to cars not operating on schedule to fares being increased. Despite much frustration behind the scenes, the company worked hard to deliver the same quality service in street railway operation that it did in the power business.[68] The Tuscaloosa electric, gas, and street railway utility was acquired in 1923.

The Montgomery operations were also acquired in 1923. This occurred because in December 1922 the city's utilities ran into financial difficulty. Alarmed at the prospect of no utility service, the chamber of commerce extended an invitation to Alabama Power Company to come into the city and buy the utility companies. Despite the demagogic attacks over the company's opposition to the Ford proposal for Muscle Shoals, Alabama Power's reputation was strong in the business community. Both the Montgomery Light and Water Power Company and the Montgomery Light and Traction Company were in bankruptcy. The two companies had competed with each other so fiercely that both were insolvent. The Montgomery Chamber of Commerce promised "hearty cooperation" to work with Alabama Power "to build up the industrial and commercial interests of this community."[69] At a chamber of commerce meeting in early 1923, "more than a hundred business executives" heard Tom Martin and Colonel Reuben Mitchell present a vision of the possibilities of Montgomery's future. At the end, men rose to their feet, applauded, and urged Alabama Power Company to come as soon as possible.[70]

How different this meeting was compared to the one in Montgomery the year before when the company was attacked for opposing the Ford proposal. Surely the irony made Martin's heart sing. The transfer of the Montgomery companies to a receiver took place in early February 1923, under order of Judge Henry D. Clayton. The Alabama Public Service Commission approved the transfer of the companies to Alabama Power Company a few weeks later.[71] The company assumed almost $2 million in debt from the Montgomery companies and immediately invested some $15,000 in new facilities and equipment.[72] Tom Martin sent the talented James M. Barry to the capital city as division manager. To Martin, having his company in the capital, the state's third largest city and the town where he had spent his youth, was especially meaningful.

ELECTRICITY FOR FARMERS

Tom Martin did not grow up on a farm, but he remembered an early childhood in Jackson County without electricity. Martin understood the importance of agriculture to the state's economy, and he realized that rural sections of Alabama were not benefiting from the revolution of electricity. The National Electric Light Association began to look at the rural market as early as 1911 and formed the Committee on Electricity in Rural Districts, but little was accomplished until 1923 when the Committee on the Relation of Electricity to Agriculture was formed.[73] The first Alabama Power Company distribution line that was classified as rural was built in 1920. The line ran down Whitesburg Pike in Madison County and served ten farms and one cotton gin. Only a rural line built in Minnesota the year before predates Alabama Power's service to isolated farmers.[74]

The power company's first rural distribution line ran down the Whitesburg Pike in Madison County and served one cotton gin and ten farms, one the dairy farm of Lily Flagg, the Jersey cow that set world records for milk and butter at the 1892 Chicago World's Fair.

While electricity was easy to adapt to industry and urban life with its concentration of customers and high demand, Martin knew that electricity could make a world of difference in the lives of Alabama farm families. Education was needed to show farmers the potential of electricity on the farm.[75] Electric motors could pump water from wells for indoor plumbing, and electric hot water heaters were much better than hot water poured from a kettle off a wood-burning stove into a No. 10 washtub in the kitchen. For women electric ranges were more convenient, and they were certainly cooler in the kitchen than the wood-burning black iron stoves common in rural areas. Refrigerators beat canning, smokehouses, and cellars. The washing machine was the choice of those who could afford it. But the less expensive electric "smoothing iron" proved to be popular with women whether they lived in cities or on farms and was usually the first household electric purchase.

Pole number 72,000 in the company's rural electric system, serving the Pittsview area.

Martin believed that electricity could also make the farmers' jobs easier and more profitable. It was the profitability part that had to be proved to Alabama farmers, who were notorious for refusing to change their ways. Martin often said that through electricity "we want to make agriculture a business rather than a mode of living."[76] From the company's point of view, the main challenges were to find economical methods of running rural lines, to locate cheaper or more efficient materials, and to reduce the cost of rights-of-way. More research was needed, especially on the applications of electricity to farms.[77] Demand had to increase. From a farmer's point of view, he could not understand why those huge transmission lines that passed overhead through his cow pasture could not drop off a little electricity for his farm on its way to the city.

The desperate economic condition of Alabama farmers, especially their need for cheap fertilizer, was highlighted during the Muscle Shoals controversy, and the Alabama Farm Bureau regularly attacked the company. This surely spurred Martin to move quickly and more decisively into rural electrification than did private utilities in other states. Sometime around 1922–23, the company began discussions on the possibilities of rural electrification with Alabama Polytechnic Institute professors Marion Jacob Funchess, who would become director of the Agricultural Experiment Station, M. L. Nichols, head of the Department of Agricultural Engineering, and C. D. Miller, associate agricultural engineer. On December 23, 1923, the company signed an agreement with API that it would provide $24,000 to fund research projects to determine the value of rural electrification to farmers.[78] Professor Funchess noted that the more prosperous farmers would be the first ones to change to new methods and that those farmers not totally dependent upon the cultivation of cotton would be the ones to have a wider use of electricity on their farms. Funchess could have been more explicit and said that the large number of tenants and sharecroppers on Alabama farms presented difficulties in bringing electricity to rural areas because the owners of the structures were not interested in upgrading tenant houses. Funchess believed much research was needed, and he saw a perfect partnership with Alabama Power.[79]

Professor E. C. Easter was the Auburn field representative who oversaw the Department of Agricultural Engineering and the research of the Agricultural Experiment Station. The university agreed to electrify its farm and to supervise the installation of electrical equipment and keep records of its use. In addition, certain farm communities would be jointly selected by API and the company for study. For its part, Alabama Power agreed to run at least three experimental lines into different agricultural areas of the state. In studying the use of electricity in these communities, Auburn was to give special consideration to community utilization by schools and churches and to applications such as refrigeration. Home demonstration agents would work closely with farm women to explain new electrical appliances, which were furnished by Alabama Power Company. Work began January 1, 1924.[80]

E. C. Easter

While research was ongoing at Auburn, Martin had Alabama Power Company's construction department studying methods that would reduce the cost of building lines. E. R. "Ned" Coulbourn, a young man with a recent mechanical engineering degree from the University of Alabama, made a significant contribution to rural electrification in Alabama and also in the United States. Coulbourn joined the company in 1924 and almost immediately was challenged to find a better way to build rural lines. Working closely with Westinghouse and other manufacturers, Coulbourn helped to develop steel-reinforced conductors, self-protecting pole type transformers, and unit substations, which made rural programs economically possible.[81]

E. R. "Ned" Coulbourn, Courtesy of Elizabeth Hanigan.

Alabama Power Company engineers came up with standard rural specifications that "resulted in material reduction in the cost per mile of line as compared with city lines" without reducing standards of safety or dependable service. In its history, Alabama Power Company has consistently supported research and quickly adopted the latest designs and inventions. Martin was always ready to invest money in equipment that represented cutting-edge technology or new ideas if the engineers he trusted recommended it. In 1924 he especially urged those men working with the company's rural construction program to seek "new devices and ideas" that would reduce the cost of rural line extensions.[82]

Martin sent a team into the Wiregrass, in the southeastern part of the state, to survey the possibilities of expanding rural and urban service there. A. C. Polk and W. E. Mitchell left Montgomery on April 30, 1924, and were joined in Ozark by James M. Barry. They reported to Eugene Yates that the area was agricultural and they saw no industrial load in any town they visited. All the hydro streams were small and all the distribution lines were "in poor condition measured by our standards," and they worried about some "hazardous conditions." Transmission lines were also "poor except for those of Alabama Power Company." Dothan, Polk noted, was the key town in the area.[83]

Alabama Power Company recognized that farm electrification could not be just a convenience; there had to be evidence that farm income could be increased by the use of electricity. While API was studying the application of electricity to farming operations, Alabama Power Company continued to expand its rural lines outside the project. From January 1924 to January 1926 the company increased rural lines from 40 to 350 and rural customers from 240 to 3,618. These lines served schools, churches, stores, and lodges as well as individual farmers. The company was already seeing that in short periods of time some of the lines originally constructed as rural lines were moving into the suburban line category as the growth of cities and towns spread outward. Peaks in electrical demands on rural lines were between six and ten o'clock in the morning and from six to ten o'clock in the evening, with a larger demand on Friday and Saturday nights.[84]

The Alabama Farm Bureau established its own Committee on the Relation of Electricity to Agriculture, which mirrored national Farm Bureau committees working with the National Electric Light Association. The committee was composed of T. J. Whatley, president of the Lee County Farm Bureau; Edward A. O'Neal III, president of the Alabama Farm Bureau Federation; and R. F. Croom, vice president of the Alabama Farm Bureau. In January 1925 the committee toured the research areas funded under the power company grant to API. They visited small cotton farmers in Five Points in Chambers County; dairymen, truckers, and poultrymen in Gardendale and Oak Grove in Jefferson County; and general farmers in southern Madison County along the Whitesburg and Meridianville Pikes. They also visited the Alabama Power Company dams.[85] In February 1926 Auburn presented a preliminary report to Alabama Power Company, and in April 1926 the city of Montgomery hosted the Southern Rural Electrification Conference where the results of the Auburn study were publicly released. Under the auspices of the Farm Bureau, Alabama Power Company and API distributed the report widely.

E. C. Easter's detailed research was spread nationwide, and after the work of the state Committee on the Relation of Electricity to Agriculture ended in Alabama, Tom Martin was able to convince Easter to join Alabama Power Company. In 1926 Alabama Farm Bureau president O'Neal, who only a few years before had been such a bitter critic of Alabama Power Company for opposing the Ford proposal, wrote an essay for *Powergrams*. He expressed his view of the power company's responsibility to the farm consumer and his own philosophy of rural electric development. O'Neal included the observation that "the Company must neither ride the economic hobby to the point where its service is not generally available in the community, nor on the other hand, can it ride the social hobby as some loud-speaking and visionary persons outside of the industry urge, to the point of financial bankruptcy."[86]

Meanwhile, the company expanded its sales department to include agricultural engineers to work with its farm customers in an effort to make electricity profitable to both the company and the farmers. The development of rural lines continued so that by the end of 1929 the Alabama Power Company had constructed 398 lines that ran 1,400 miles and served 7,155 customers who annually used 10.5 million kilowatt hours producing revenues of almost $500,000 a year.[87] In July 1929 the National Electric Light Association issued a special report from its Rural Electric Service Committee that featured Alabama Power Company's rural program. Tom Martin wrote in the introduction that his company had spent $2 million to bring electrical service to Alabama farmers, and that "while our revenue is not as yet making a satisfactory return on the investment, we are quite hopeful that the business will be built up to self-sustaining proportions within a reasonable time." Meanwhile, Martin viewed the project, from both "the economic and social standpoint," as "fully justified" and "an integral part of our program of service, confident that it is a contribution to the prosperity of Alabama."[88] Included were examples of the advertisement campaign in which the company targeted farmers: "Power Development and the Farmers," "What Factories Mean to Farmers," and "Kilowatt, The New Farm Hand."[89]

In its campaign to provide rural electricity to farmers, the power company featured stories about Alabama farmers such as Seth P. Storrs of Elmore County, who saw his property values go up when electricity came, and Mr. and Mrs. J. B. Hammond, also of Elmore, who were thankful for giving up "kerosene lamps, wood stove, ash can, andirons, and scrub board."[90] Alabama farmers who had electricity identified with the Tennessee farmer who, when giving witness in his church, said: "Brothers and sisters, I want to tell you this. The greatest thing on earth is to have the love of God in your heart, and the next greatest thing is to have electricity in your house."[91] Compared to other southern states, Alabama was far ahead in bringing electricity to rural areas. In his 1971 University of California dissertation on rural electrification in the South, Deward Brown concluded that Alabama's program of rural electrification was "the most significant attempt in the United States by private enterprise to promote the use of electricity on farms."[92] Which was what Tom Martin knew in 1929.

MITCHELL DAM

Alabama Power Company had many years to make plans for building its second dam using all the experiences of Lock 12. One early decision was that this dam would be built by its own people, and Dixie Construction Company was organized. As soon as possible after the Federal Water Power Act went into effect, Alabama Power Company petitioned for a license to build the dam long planned for Duncan's Riffle on the Coosa. Rumors circulated about these plans. Engineering consultants and supply firms wrote to inquire about the possibility of new business from the company. Cautiously, W. E. Mitchell would respond that "we are studying two or three [future developments] and . . . we hope to be able to work on at least one of these within the next six or eight months." He was not encouraging, writing that "we have always maintained an engineering staff of our own and have done all our own work."[93] The Federal Power Commission granted the license for the Duncan's Riffle dam on June 27, 1921, and Tom Martin announced that the dam would be named in memory of James Mitchell.[94] The dam at Lock 12 had not yet been dedicated to Captain William Patrick Lay.

Newspapers hailed the event, and Chilton County was enthusiastic about the company spending $8 million on the second dam in the county with no mention of mosquitoes. Most of the land had been surveyed, and owners knew where the reservoir waters would rise. The majority of owners were pleased with the compensation they received for their land, and few suits contested the condemnation.[95] One often repeated story about "Mr. Martin" and land value found its way into company lore and several histories. It involved the company land agent who told Tom Martin that certain land could be "had for $5 an acre." Martin asked him what the land was worth. He answered, "about $25." Martin quickly said, "then we should pay $25. Pay what it's worth but not a cent more. We must be fair if we expect others to be fair with us."[96] This story became the guidepost of the land department, in 1922 directed by Bowling R. Powell, as well as the company's people.[97]

As things geared up for construction, local farmers applied for jobs and Clanton store owners immediately enjoyed an increase in business. Verbena's economy boomed, especially at the new eating place called the Dam Cafe.[98] Lines were run fourteen miles downstream from Lock 12 to provide electricity. Land was cleared near the dam site and in the area where the village was to be built. Construction began on the roadbed the railroad would use to bring supplies and people to the dam site. Homes for supervisors and their families and bunkhouses for workers, dining halls, schools, and a hospital were soon under way, creating a village where 3,000 workers would soon live. There was running water, filtered and chlorinated from the Coosa, and a sewerage system for the camp. C. C. Davis, who was known for putting the safety of his men first, was the field superintendent for the construction of Mitchell Dam, as well as Martin and Jordan Dams. Cofferdams were started. After so long in the planning stages, Alabama Power Company was finally on the move again, building hydroelectric plants on the state's rivers.

On a chilly December 19, 1921, hundreds gathered for the first dedication of an Alabama Power Company dam. Lawrence Macfarlane came from Montreal to watch C. Malcolm Mitchell, James Mitchell's son, press the button to release the first bucket of concrete for the dam, which would eventually hold 340,569 cubic yards. The president of the Alabama Public Service Commission, A. G. Patterson, spoke and said that he was there in a dual capacity—protecting customers by ensuring fair rates and protecting the company's investors. Oscar W. Wells, president of the First National Bank of Birmingham, gave a rousing speech on the relation of electricity to industrial development. Tom Martin, in his remarks about James Mitchell, said Mitchell faced a task far "more difficult than any man could have foreseen." Governor Kilby was not present, but Attorney General Harwell G. Davis spoke briefly for him. The dam was to be "one of the largest in the South" and when finished would spread 1,200 feet across the Coosa.[99]

Through stories and photographs, *Powergrams* provided constant construction updates for employees.[100] The building of Mitchell Dam was documented more than the construction of the Lock 12 dam. The design of the downstream face of Mitchell Dam incorporated what became known as the Thurlow Backwater Suppressor, named after Oscar G. Thurlow. During floods, water rises at the bottom of the dam in a back roll and reduces the efficiency of the turbines. Thurlow designed the Mitchell spillway so that the energy of the falling water would sweep the backwater away from the draft tube discharge opening,

Workers lining up at the Mitchell Dam mess hall, 1923.

Mitchell Dam during construction in 1922.

Mitchell Dam went into service on August 15, 1923. The original powerhouse is in the middle of the dam.

thus maintaining a uniform head on the turbine.[101] The turbine runners at Mitchell were the largest ever constructed by Allis-Chalmers Manufacturing Company, and they were the largest that could possibly be shipped into the South because of railroad clearances.

The gates to Mitchell were closed on December 31, 1922, and water flowed over the spillway on January 3, 1923. Heavy rains continued, and in February the Coosa River flooded. Constant communication from upriver kept Lock 12 informed of the river's height, and word was sent downstream to Mitchell so men and equipment could be protected from the rising water. The flood sent an avalanche of logs and tree trunks against the Mitchell log boom. When it was over, the brush mat was so thick before the dam that men could walk on it. Lock 12 was able to draw down the river five feet so that Mitchell could be cleaned up and debris removed.[102] Following the completion of the dam, the construction camp at Mitchell was turned into a recreational area for company employees and their families. For years the cabins, lodge, and family houses were the scenes of company and employee day parties and weekend retreats. Tours of the lake were made on the company's gasoline engine–powered boat, *Old Maple*.[103]

Martin Dam

Cherokee Bluffs was the site that brought James Mitchell to Alabama, and his initial plan was for it to be the first dam he built in Alabama. Lawsuits and problems with the low level of the Central of Georgia railroad bridge made Mitchell turn to Lock 12 on the Coosa as the place for his first hydroelectric project. In 1922 the Federal Power Commission issued preliminary permits for the Alabama Interstate Power Company to build four dams on the Tallapoosa River. Alabama Interstate Power was the company and the letter-head that Mitchell first used for his operating company. It was still active on the company books and was the Alabama Power subsidiary that owned the Cherokee site. The license

First cofferdam being constructed at the Cherokee Bluffs (Martin) dam site, April 2, 1924.

for the dam at Cherokee Bluffs was granted on June 9, 1923, and construction began on July 24.

The winding sandy roads from Dadeville and from Tallassee and Eclectic handled the preliminary incursions into the Tallapoosa basin, with ferries providing river crossings. The nearest railroad to the Bluffs was William Blount's Birmingham & Southeastern Railroad, a line his family called the "Bump and Slide Easy."[104] In 1923 this line connected Eclectic and Tallassee, then ran south to intersect the Western Railway line at Milstead on its way to Blount's hometown of Union Springs. The line passed through Kent (or Asberry), and from there Alabama Power Company constructed a six-mile "tortuous spur track" with "tight curves and lofty trestles" into the Cherokee Bluffs construction site. The spur was built to a standard gauge sufficient for mainline traffic. The Birmingham & Southeastern Railroad's financial problems eased after dam construction began and 125 cars a day rolled over its tracks to supply the construction site. The small line even had to rent extra rolling stock and engines, especially dump bottom cars, from the Western Railway to handle the volume.[105]

The company's own Dixie Construction Company, which built Mitchell Dam, was in charge of the project. The construction village at Cherokee was similar to the Mitchell camp, but it had a larger commissary and more organized leisure activities and entertainment. Historian Harvey H. Jackson III points out that this was because the workers wanted it and the company hoped to prevent the unsavory influences that had come from the encampments of drummers and gamesters around the Mitchell construction site. Another reason was that Cherokee Bluffs was more isolated than was Mitchell, making it difficult for workers to leave and return to work.[106]

Because the reservoir was so extensive, covering 40,000 acres with a shoreline of over 700 miles, more land would be flooded and more people displaced than from either the Mitchell or Lock 12 dams. Susanna (or Sousanna), which was a small community just south of McCartys Ferry and Blue Creek, just north of Chimney Rock, had to be moved. Several churches, twelve cemeteries, and 900 graves had to be relocated. The farms and fields along Kowaliga Creek were flooded, but much of this land had been acquired by Alabama Power a decade before, and the families had already relocated.

A gala event to lay the cornerstone for the dam was held on November 7, 1925. The silver trowel, which James Mitchell had presented to Nora E. Miller in 1912 with instructions that the Dadeville woman was to shovel the first concrete into the dam at Cherokee Bluffs, was brought out. With both Mitchell and Miller deceased, Miller's nephew John Curtis Lovelace per-

Governor William W. Brandon speaking at the laying of the cornerstone exercises at Cherokee Bluffs, November 7, 1925.

formed the ceremony in memory of his aunt.[107] The guest list was a who's who of Alabama political and economic leadership. Governor William W. Brandon waxed eloquent, praising Alabama Power Company as "the greatest developer of Alabama's natural resources." Senator Tom Heflin, who had fought the company on the Ford proposal, now shared his pride in the dam that harnessed the stream where, as a boy, he had learned to swim.[108]

Three bridges were built across the reservoir. The Central of Georgia railroad bridge was relocated and elevated in an agreement with the railroad. A railroad bridge was built over the river below the dam site to provide an access to the eastern side of the river, and another bridge was constructed across Kowaliga Creek for the highway route connecting Alexander City and Eclectic. Foundations for the Kowaliga bridge were completed before the gates on the dam were closed, and the spans were shipped in on railroad cars, pulled on short railroad tracks up the slope beside the dam to the edge of the lake. Here the

Support pillars for the Kowaliga bridge spans were constructed before the reservoir was filled, April 16, 1926.

spans were loaded onto barges and pushed by a tug to the bridge.[109] There was some difficulty in completing the bridge because calculations were based upon a full pool, and the bridge had to be completed with the pool elevation down some ten feet. Because of dry weather, Lake Martin reached full pool much more slowly than anticipated, and it was years before the mud settled from the water and the lake ran clear.[110]

On June 8, A. C. Polk, construction manager, noted in his journal that the Cherokee Bluffs dam had stopped all flow of the river, and on June 16, 1926, the board of directors of Alabama Power Company passed a resolution introduced by Colonel Reuben Mitchell to name the dam at Cherokee Bluffs and the lake for Thomas W. Martin.[111] The lake finally was full for the first time on April 23, 1928, when seven floodgates were opened after a week of heavy rains.[112] The dedication of the dam was not scheduled for more than a decade; the usual reason given is that Martin, while pleased with the honor, was somewhat embarrassed at being the center of such attention. This was also just before changes in the company came and the 1929 depression began. Finally, on November 23, 1936, the dam at Cherokee Bluffs, then and now considered by many people the crowning star of all Alabama

Power Company dams, and the lake, the largest man-made lake in the world at the time, were dedicated to Tom Martin in a grand celebration.[113]

INTERCONNECTION

When Major Harry Burgess of the Army Corps of Engineers made his report on the Muscle Shoals in 1915, he pointed out that electric power connected to combinations of generation plants would prevent duplications of equipment and increase the efficiency of the plants. Consumers would have cheaper electricity if plants were interconnected.[114] An interconnected system would allow all waterpower to be used on first demand before expensive reserve steam systems had to be called upon. The supply would be larger and therefore more economical and more dependable.

Although James Mitchell had concentrated on developing the Alabama system, he realized from the beginning that a southern regional system would be more efficient. As early as 1913, Mitchell had a report compiled on the use of central station power in the southern states through 1911. Mitchell also had his engineers draw maps of the generation plants of the South and the transmission systems from Jackson, Mississippi, to North Carolina and including Tennessee and northern Florida.[115] Because of the large hydropower potential in Alabama and the company's intention to build other dams, new markets were needed, especially until the Alabama residential and industrial load increased. There were times when waterpower was spilling over the Lock 12 dam unused, and connections to other states would provide a market for the electricity that could have been generated if the water was put to use. This was viewed as an important way to provide additional cash flow for the company.[116] Still some newspaper editors and politicians never understood the economies involved and often opposed interconnection. A few even advocated that power generated in Alabama should stay in Alabama.

In 1917, with the possibility of the United States entering the European war, James Mitchell asked Oscar G. Thurlow to begin surveying power systems in states adjoining Alabama. Specifically, Mitchell wanted information on the populations of towns served by electrical systems. He wanted to know the location of each town, the capacity and the load of the town power plant, data on undeveloped power, and the number of industries served.[117] Thurlow checked with Westinghouse and GE for turbine units in the South and suggested that

Martin Dam went into service on December 31, 1926 and was dedicated to Thomas W. Martin on November 23, 1936.

the logical place to tie into the Georgia system would be with a 110,000-volt line from Alabama Power's Anniston substation. This would require no extra transformer apparatus, only an extra switching structure in each station, which Thurlow estimated would cost about $15,000 each. The transmission line would run forty-one miles to the Georgia state line and then would be only thirteen miles to a Georgia substation at Lindale. For its part, the transmission line would cost Alabama Power Company $307,500. W. E. Mitchell proposed that Alabama Power Company also tie in with the Columbus Electric & Power Company at Lanett.[118] Interconnections were delayed until after the war for several reasons. Alabama Power was focused on the Muscle Shoals development, which had a high military priority, and there was not one strong utility company in Georgia to negotiate with but several smaller companies with divided territory.

Following World War I, the Army Corps of Engineers published a report detailing the problems caused by shortages of electricity during the war. Industries and manufacturing had placed heavy demands on electrical supplies, and shortages of electricity resulted. In the section devoted to the southern states, resources of each state were listed and the report recommended "interconnecting these to make a unified and balanced system, utilizing in each instance the most available sources of power without regard to existing individual ownership or state lines." This 1921 study stated that such interconnection would provide the most economical and reliable service and estimated that the area's electrical needs would increase to over one million kilowatts in the next few years. To supply these demands, the engineers recommended that power sites on the Tallapoosa at Cherokee Bluffs (with a large storage reservoir) and on the Coosa River be interconnected with Muscle Shoals and with central stations in Georgia and the Carolinas.[119]

An agreement was reached with the Georgia Railway & Power Company on May 4, 1920, to send surplus power not needed in one system to the other state. The interchange of power was to be transferred through a Gadsden-Lindale line. This was the first important step in integrating the power systems of Deep South states, and it came none too soon, for the severe drought the next year diminished the hydropower available in

The first interconnection of power lines between Alabama Power and the Georgia Railway & Power Company was accomplished through the Gadsden-Lindale transmission line in May 1921.

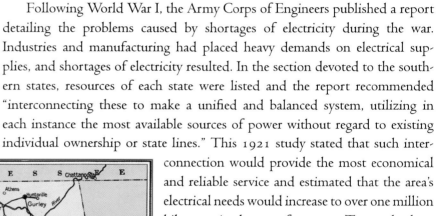

DISTRIBUTING SYSTEM
of
ALABAMA POWER CO.
FURNISHING POWER TO ALL CLASSES
OF INDUSTRIES & MUNICIPALITIES
PRESENT TRANSMISSION LINES
PROPOSED " "
HYDRO-ELECTRIC PLANT
STEAM " "
PRIMARY SUBSTATION

Georgia and North and South Carolina. Although Alabama Power could not supply its own needs and make up all the power that was needed in the three states in 1921, it was able to send considerable waste power of its own and to lease the government's Sheffield steam plant and forward this 60,000-kilowatt capacity to Georgia and north some 600 miles into the Carolinas.[120]

In the fall of 1924 Alabama suffered the most severe drought in the state's history to that time. Except for one slight rainfall, no rain fell between September 29 and December 4.[121] Power from Georgia, however, was able to flow into Alabama. Anyone who doubted the value of an interconnected southern power system was convinced after droughts in 1921 and 1924. On July 10, 1923, Alabama Power Company negotiated a second interchange agreement, this one with the Columbus (Georgia) Electric & Power Company.[122] In November 1923 Tom Martin met with Secretary of War John W. Weeks and briefed him on the possibilities of interlocking electric power companies and sending power from Muscle Shoals a long distance from Tennessee. Alabama Power also renewed its lease on the government steam plant at Sheffield near the Shoals.[123]

In 1924, *Manufacturers Record* of Baltimore, Maryland, produced a special issue on the South. Entitled *Blue Book of Southern Progress*, the small book gave detailed statistics and information about southern states. The development of "the Southern Super-Power Zone" of electrical transmission across the southeastern states was featured. Alabama, with "potential maximum horse-power" at 943,000, led the region, and the map illustrated how much of the state was developed with transmission lines and generation, especially in contrast to Georgia and South Carolina. Alabama Power Company advertised the state and its economic development on the back cover of the book and ordered a quantity of books to be used for the state's industrial recruitment.[124]

Southeastern Power & Light Company

In April 1924 Tom Martin gave a major address before the American Institute of Electrical Engineers meeting in Birmingham. He briefly traced the economic development of the South from an 1880 total manufactured products value of $500 million to a 1922 total value of $10 billion. Property values in the southern states rose from $6.5 billion in 1900 to $30 billion in 1922. He believed that the "progressive movement toward power development in Alabama" and other states was partly responsible for this dramatic advance. Martin praised the interconnection agreements of southeastern power companies, which gave them the combined power of almost three billion kilowatt hours. He noted that this development had decreased the cost of electricity 70 percent from 1914 to 1924. Martin took an opportunity to criticize Henry Ford's plan for Muscle Shoals, which at the time was still before the Senate. He explained in detail the financial subsidies that the federal government would be giving one individual and the economic power one man would have over other manufacturers. In conclusion, Martin warned about the withdrawal of Muscle Shoals power from the interconnection of southern power resources, and he recommended the Federal Water Power Act of 1920 and the Federal Power Commission as the best means to "conserve and utilize in the public interest" the navigation and water resources of the Tennessee Valley.[125]

The fight over the Muscle Shoals and the Ford proposal was generating such hostile feelings in the state toward the company that Tom Martin was deeply concerned. For years much had been made of a so-called foreign ownership of Alabama Power, although more ownership of the company was American and Alabama-based than ever before. In 1921, after Alabama Power paid the state treasury its taxes due, the Birmingham News pointed out that those who prated about "the evils of trusts and corporations and the iniquity of 'foreign capital' should pause a while. These so-called foreign moneys when they are invested in Alabama industry and development become Alabama moneys." The newspaper noted that "There are two kinds of capital—the sort that takes all and gives nothing, and the capital that practices reciprocity. A fool should be able to discriminate. The capital that creates new payrolls and that develops a State's natural resources and that pays substantial taxes into municipal and county and State treasuries, is benevolent capital. There is nothing foreign about it." The News concluded that "It makes no matter whether its stockholders live in New England or old England, whether in Chicago or Zanzibar. They have cast in their lot with us for better or for worse."[126]

In the spring of 1922 the Christian Science Monitor ran a story about control of Alabama Power Company being "in the hands of foreign investors" but countered that Boston bankers stated the securities were so widely owned that "anything other than American control is next to impossible."[127] The interest in and fear of foreign investors reflected the national scene where anti-foreignism was running rampant, fueled by the "Big Red Scare" of 1919–20. The Sacco-Vanzetti case in Massachusetts, the True American movement, and the rise of the new Ku Klux Klan, which enrolled some five million members by the mid-1920s, were other examples of anti-foreignism. One result of this hostility to foreigners was the enactment of tighter immigration laws. In 1923 Martin stressed Alabama Power's local ownership, countering that "a large majority of the shares of preferred stock are held by more than 7,000 stockholders" who were living in Alabama. Martin had pushed the sale of stock in Alabama, running stock sales contests for employees. In addition to preferred stock, Martin noted that "a large volume" of Alabama Power bonds and the common stock of Alabama Traction was also owned by Alabamians. Martin estimated that more than $12 million of Alabama Power securities were owned by Alabama residents, some no doubt purchased in the summer of 1923 when Alabama Traction sold more utility bonds.[128]

During 1923 and 1924, the Alabama Power Company board of directors discussed its financing and its relationship to Sperling & Company and the original stock and bondholders. The board agreed that a new American holding company should be formed, and this company could hold the stock of Alabama Power Company as well as the stock of other southern power companies that might be acquired. Both the issue of foreign ownership and the initiative of southern power company cooperation could be addressed. With the idea approved by the board, Tom Martin prepared to go to London to discuss the plan with Sperling & Company and British investors in Alabama Traction. Most of the stocks and bonds of the Alabama Traction, Light & Power Company, Ltd., had been acquired by Americans during World War I as British investors liquidated assets under the stress of the wartime economy in Great Britain, but major holders still remained in England. Martin was convinced that this move would strengthen Alabama Power Company financially, allowing it quick access to American investors and ultimately allowing the company to serve its customers more efficiently.

As Martin was making plans to sail for England, the Democratic convention opened in New York City's Madison Square Garden on June 24, 1924. Alabama's U.S. senator, Oscar W. Underwood, was a favorite-son candidate for the presidential nomination, and surely Martin would have closely watched these proceedings, a "fourteen-day donnybrook" where 16,000 delegates voted over nine days, the longest American political convention on record. The American Bar Association was also meeting in New York in early July, and 800 members sailed together on July 12 aboard the Cunard liner RMS *Berengaria* for a bar association meeting that opened in London on July 20. Tom Martin was registered to attend the convention in England, which was a good cover story (if he felt he needed one) for his trip to London.[129] Ten years earlier, James Mitchell had traveled to London during World War I to request that English investors defer interest for three years on Alabama Traction, Light & Power bonds, cancel some provisions of the trust deed, and authorize Alabama Power to issue and sell bonds and preferred stock in order to raise funds in the United States. Approval of this prevented the bankruptcy of the company. Now a new

Sir E. Mackay Edgar at a visit to the Jordan Dam site, February 15, 1928.

Alabama Power Company president was going to England with a new plan. As the Martins left New York, Alabama Traction stock was selling for $46.[130]

Tom Martin arrived in London on July 18 and first consulted with Sir E. Mackay Edgar. In 1920 Edgar had been made a baronet by King George V to recognize his activities in support of Great Britain during World War I.[131] Martin knew the financier from Edgar's visits to Alabama to inspect the properties of the company and from attending board and financial meetings in New York City. Over more than a decade, Edgar had secured nearly $11 million for Alabama Power Company developments, and he had been Mitchell's friend and adviser. Sperling had recently suffered some reversals and was involved in litigation in American courts over its Cities Service Company investments. The situation was favorable to Martin's proposal.[132]

In July 1924 Sir Edgar was the head of Sperling & Company, which also included Sir Edward Baulet Stracey and Eric Stephen Astley Sperling. During meetings with Martin and in the general shareholders meeting, the English firm and the remaining British investors approved the plan to swap stock in the new American holding company for the stocks and bonds of Alabama Traction, Light & Power. To sweeten the deal, Alabama Traction bondholders were given a bonus. In any year when a dividend was paid on the common stock of the new American holding company, Southeastern Power & Light, a 1 percent additional interest on Alabama Traction, Light & Power 5 percent bonds would be distributed.[133] Years later, Martin simply noted that the "English investors had always shown a liberal attitude toward the Alabama development." With his business finished in London, Martin decided to return home earlier than he planned, regrettable for a man so devoted to history to leave early on what was to be his only trip to Europe.[134] He and Mrs. Martin sailed for New York on July 23 on the *Olympic* of the White Star Line, thus missing the queen's July 24 garden party to which they had been invited.[135]

The years after Tom Martin left London were not kind to Sir E. Mackay Edgar. During the boom period the English financier had made a considerable personal fortune by organizing and financing large hydroelectric companies all over the world. In London Sir Edgar was known as the "Man with a Load of Millions" because of his reputation for investing a million pounds "if the amount was needed." In the high stakes world of British finance, Edgar became the darling of the city until his luck ran out one year after Martin visited him in London. Edgar's first mistake was selling his holdings in hydroelectric companies, which probably included some of his Alabama Traction, Light & Power stock and bonds. These holdings eventually were worth more than £4 million. Instead of keeping these assets, Edgar gambled with debentures for an Irish cotton mill and became involved in a scheme to purchase a British company. His luck left him, and Sir Edgar declared bankruptcy in 1925 and dissolved his partnership with Sperling. It was after this that Sir Edgar made his last trip to Alabama and was photographed at the construction site of Jordan Dam. Tom Martin kept Sir Edgar on the board of directors of the holding company that replaced Alabama Traction and probably financed Sir Edgar's trip to a board meeting and the inspection tour of Alabama Power's new construction. Sir Edgar died almost penniless in 1934 in the village of Chalfont St. Giles.[136]

Tom Martin returned to Alabama and set in motion plans already made to incorporate the Southeastern Power & Light Company as a holding company under the corporation-friendly laws of Maine. Articles of agreement were signed on September 2, 1924, in Augusta, Maine, with a certificate of organization and bylaws properly filed. A special meeting of the board of directors followed in New York City where the board considered and approved the proposed offer to be made by Southeastern Power & Light to Alabama Traction, Light & Power. Martin's press statement stressed that the ownership of Alabama Power Company would be vested in "an American Corporation."[137] On October 6, the Southeastern Power & Light board met in Augusta, Maine, and voted to increase the board to twelve members (from the five required for charter). Thomas W. Martin, Niel A. Weathers, Lawrence Macfarlane, W. J. Henderson, Chester A. Bingham, J. C. Cartwright, and Douglass Clark were approved; Tom Martin was elected president.[138] Chester Bingham was a Talladega attorney who began working with land condemnations on the Coosa River, then became important in guiding the financial and securities operations of Alabama Power and the new holding company. Bingham moved to New York in 1927 to better direct the operations of Southeastern Power & Light. Douglass Clark was Martin's administrative assistant; he joined the company in 1920 as Martin's secretary and often accompanied Martin on trips to Washington and New York, bringing along his portable typewriter so their work could continue.[139]

Shareholders of Alabama Traction, Light & Power had been notified on September 24 of the general meeting on October 10 to approve the transfer of assets and liabilities to Southeastern.[140] In a printed notice, W. J. Henderson, secretary-treasurer of Alabama Traction,

W. J. Henderson, August 1928.

announced that Martin had addressed a general meeting of the company and explained that "the arrangement provided that holders of the preferred stock of the Alabama Traction, Light & Power would receive preferred stock in the Southeastern Company, share for share: two shares of the non-par common stock of the Southeastern Company for each share of common stock of Alabama Traction; and unsecured 6 percent, 100-year debentures for the outstanding bonds of Alabama Traction."[141]

Henderson, who was a Montreal accountant and associate of Lawrence Macfarlane, had served as secretary of Alabama Traction since its inception. He was respected for his keen foresight, his integrity, his sound judgment, and for establishing the company's "banking and investment connections along safe and sound lines."[142] For several years, just before and during World War I, the Henderson family lived in Birmingham, then returned to Canada. But Henderson continued to work with Alabama Traction, Mitchell, and Martin. In 1924 Henderson helped Martin make the financial arrangements for the transfer of assets from Alabama Traction to Southeastern Power & Light, for which he now served as vice president and treasurer. Under Henderson's direction, arrangements were made for Coffin & Burr of Boston and Harris, Forbes & Company of New York to mail printed flyers on November 1 announcing the sale of $7.5 million in gold notes, 6 percent series, and detailing the assets of Southeastern Power & Light, which held 187,510 shares of common stock and acquired all the assets of Alabama Traction, Light & Power, a Canadian corporation.[143] Through the years, Henderson frequently visited Alabama, consulted with Martin, and knew the Alabama situation well. Mitchell had placed him on the Alabama Power Company board of directors in 1917, and Henderson remained a board member until he resigned in 1930. He was a resource for Martin and the company until his death in Montreal in 1952.[144]

Alabama Power Company's New York office became the headquarters of Southeastern Power & Light. Martin had watched the movements of Wall Street bankers and investors, the wheeling and dealing of takeovers and mergers, and he was aware that problems could develop. He had guided the company through the dangerous times following the death of James Mitchell, and as Joseph M. Farley noted in his story of Alabama Power Company presented as a Newcomen Society address in 1988, "Mr. Martin was able to ward off predators who undertook to acquire the company."[145] Now, in 1924, Martin was especially leery of S. Z. Mitchell and EBASCO. Joe Farley, Eason Balch, and Chris Conway wrote in their manuscript history of the company that "Martin never described in his book any outright efforts by others to take over the company during this transaction, although in 1924 the possibility existed."[146] Martin himself only wrote in his *Story of Electricity in Alabama* that a ten-year voting trust agreement was signed on October 15, 1924, to provide "a continuity of management." A large block of common stock was deposited with W. H. Hassinger and Martin, who were together designated voting trustees.[147]

Members of the company's management team had purchased stock in Alabama Power as well as in the Canadian holding company, and some of this stock was included in the voting trust.[148] Insider trading was not illegal in these years, and certainly management knew what was transpiring. For instance, in the summer of 1923 Will Mitchell wrote Howard Duryea asking about purchasing Alabama Traction stock. Duryea replied that W. J. Henderson said he could get 200, possibly 500, shares of Alabama Traction common stock "at about $20.50 per share cash terms."[149] A list of holders of 10,000 shares or more in Southeastern Power & Light showed that Hassinger and Martin controlled 523,740 shares or 24.735 percent of Southeastern stock.[150] The *Mobile Register* reported that sometime before the creation of Southeastern Power & Light Company, "a small group of insiders" purchased 50,000 shares of Alabama Traction stock from James Mitchell's widow for $8 a share soon after Mitchell's death in July 1920. At the time of Mitchell's death, this stock in his estate was appraised for $7.60 a share. The 50,000 shares must have included all the stock from his estate plus additional stock from her own holdings.[151] The deal between Alabama Traction and Southeastern Power called for a swap of two shares for one (which would have made the Mitchell stock 100,000 shares) and a year or so later a five-share-for-one stock dividend from Southeastern Power would have increased this stock to 500,000 shares, which would account for the bulk of the 523,740 shares controlled by Hassinger and Martin in 1924.[152] At that time, 1924, Electric Bond & Share held 198,400 shares, or 9.571 percent.[153] According to the historian of Electric Bond & Share, three years later, in 1927, EBASCO held 15 percent of the ownership of Southeastern Power & Light Company.[154]

W. H. Hassinger was the man who put up the money for the stock. Hassinger was a close associate of Martin and a native of Louisiana. He had been educated at Rensselaer Polytechnic Institute and worked with iron and steel companies in Pittsburgh before he appeared in Birmingham after the Great Iron Boom to start the Alabama Rolling Mill Company, which began operating on February 27, 1888. Hassinger was on the board of the Henderson Steel & Manufacturing Company, and he was involved with Henderson in the first successful production of steel in Birmingham. Hassinger was

W. H. Hassinger, 1921.

one of the founders of Republic Steel and earned a fortune in iron and steel. He retired in 1910 but remained on the board of the First National Bank of Birmingham and on the Alabama Power Company board from September 1917 until his death on March 28, 1935. Tom Martin trusted him without reservation. In later years Martin often recognized Hassinger for the leading role the steel entrepreneur played in protecting the company from predators.[155] In their treatment of this episode, Farley, Balch, and Conway explained the trust deal succinctly: "Hassinger put enough of his own money into the common stock of the company to discourage a hostile takeover."[156] And it worked—but only for five years.

By the end of 1924, Southeastern Power & Light was making news. Its annual report showed favorable returns, and its securities were selling at par. By midsummer rumors of additional acquisitions sent its stock up sharply, and the Wall Street Journal reported that the holding company was considering a five to one stock split. Two weeks later Southeastern did exactly this in order to facilitate a refinancing plan that would allow it to retire by conversion all the Alabama Traction, Light & Power stock. Part of this financing included issuing 473,378 option warrants to purchase stock at $50 a share and debenture bonds carrying option warrants in the ratio of twenty warrants to each $1,000 debenture.[157] Tom Martin explained that he wanted the stock split to reduce the price of Southeastern common stock and place it "more readily within the reach of the individual investors."[158]

The Wall Street Journal headlined the Southeastern Power bond prospects and the debentures with warrants as a "chance for speculative profit," explaining that the option warrants fueled the speculation because "as the new stock is selling around $30 and the option price of the warrants is $50, many investors and traders expected to pick them up at around a dollar or two."[159] According to the Wall Street Journal, by December 1925 Southeastern Power & Light had approximately 1,700,000 shares of common stock outstanding and 473,378 option warrants.[160]

GEORGIA POWER COMPANY AND MISSISSIPPI POWER COMPANY

Meanwhile, Alabama Power Company was expanding in the state. In 1925 it acquired the Mobile Electric Company through Alabama Power subsidiary Gulf Electric Company. Mobile presented a problem for Alabama Power because in 1926 the downtown area was served by direct current and the decision to change to alternating current was costly for Alabama Power. A new transmission line from Jordan Dam was completed, and this provided for the city's growth.[161] Tom Martin also had his eye on Georgia. He was aware that in the early 1920s the two largest Georgia utility companies were teetering on the edge of bankruptcy. The Georgia Railway & Electric Company had leased its assets to the Georgia Railway & Power Company, and by December 1924 both companies had exhausted their borrowing capacity and needed new financing of about $13 million to continue to serve the public. With drought conditions and a decreased interest by investors in financing street railways, the companies found it impossible to secure new capital.

Martin had always thought it logical that the Georgia system be connected to the Alabama Power system in a more formal way than the agreements on shared power. In the fall of 1925 he contacted Randal Morgan, who represented the largest stockholder in the Georgia Railway & Electric Company, and C. Elmer Smith, whose family was the largest stockholder in the Georgia Railway & Power Company, to explore possibilities. They discussed the problems and opportunities with H. M. Atkinson, chairman of the board and a large stockholder in the Georgia Railway & Power Company. Atkinson, according to Georgia Power Company historian W. Hubert Joiner, "was quick to see the advantages of such an affiliation, not only for the stockholders of the two companies but also for the eventual development of the state."[162] These men and others held a series of meetings with Martin, culminating with a conference in New York in January 1926 in which a deal was reached.[163] Atkinson wrote a letter to stockholders revealing the financial problems of the Georgia companies, detailing the needs for future capital, and explaining the benefits that would come to the stockholders, the company, and the state of Georgia from joining with the Southeastern Power & Light Company.[164]

By April 1, 1926, the legal paperwork was completed for the Georgia companies to join Southeastern Power. On that same day, Eugene Yates reported to W. J. Henderson the operation figures for Southeastern Power & Light and compared March 1926 to the previous March. In 1926 the operating companies produced 158,586,325 kilowatt hours, a 23 percent increase over March 1925. Yates wrote that while some of the increase was due to the extension of lines by various companies, principally it was "the result of the industrial development in sections served by these companies."[165] On June 24, 1926, W. E. Mitchell wrote Yates that there was a need for the creation of a service company, perhaps named Southeastern Engineering Company, because there were problems; examples were the Georgia easement form, which did not satisfy Alabama Power, and the lack of records of voltages over certain lines. On July 1, 1927, Southeastern Engineering Company was incorporated to act in a management capacity for the operating companies.[166]

Atlanta was concerned in the spring of 1926 about the drought in northern Georgia, but Preston S. Arkwright, longtime Atlanta utilities leader, assured the city there would be enough electricity coming from Alabama through the power interchanges.[167] Chester A. Bingham worked on the consolidation of the two Georgia companies, Georgia Railway & Power Company and Georgia Railway & Electric Company, into the Georgia Power Company, which was completed on February 25, 1927, when a number of other smaller power companies were acquired and folded into Georgia Power. Arkwright, who became president of the Georgia Railway & Electric Company in 1902, became the first president of Georgia Power. H. M. Atkinson was chairman of the board.[168] Tom Martin sent several people from Alabama Power Company to operate Georgia Power. W. E. Mitchell, who was then vice president and manager of operations for Alabama Power Company, left in April 1927 to become vice president and general manager of Georgia Power Company. C. B. McManus and J. M. Oliver went with him.[169]

As early as 1914, James Mitchell had Mississippi on his mind, and he sent Alabama Power people to the Magnolia State to check out the utility situation. They returned uneasy over the Mississippi political climate, which was even more populist and anticorporation than Alabama, and they were discouraged because the state had no adequate utility legislation. Under the leadership of Governor Theodore G. Bilbo, a noted southern demagogue, tax assessments for railroads and public service corporations rose $40 million.[170] When Bilbo was defeated in 1923 by Henry L. Whitfield, the new governor was able to get the legislature to pass laws protecting investment capital, creating tax incentives for investments, and giving eminent domain powers to hydroelectric companies. The next year Harvey Couch came out of Arkansas to create the Mississippi Power & Light Company and begin expanding in the state.[171]

To counter Couch's move, Tom Martin immediately sent James M. Barry to organize the Mississippi Power Company in southern Mississippi and acquire and consolidate small, single-town utilities.[172] Barry first set his sights on the Gulfport & Mississippi Coast Traction Company and met its general counsel, Barney E. Eaton. Barry sent Eaton to meet with Martin in Birmingham. The two made plans together, and Eaton was tapped to be president of the new Mississippi Power Company, owned by Southeastern Power & Light. Alabama Power Company intended to reach Gulfport through transmission lines from Mobile and to reach Meridian and points south from Demopolis. Martin sent an outstanding team to Mississippi to help Eaton. L. P. "Lonnie" Sweatt Jr. became the general manager, with help from Ernest L. McLean. Lamar Aldridge served as secretary, and Robert M. MacLetchie was treasurer.

A number of prominent Mississippi businessmen accepted positions on the Mississippi Power Company board of directors.[173]

GULF POWER AND SOUTH CAROLINA POWER

Martin and the Alabama Power management team for some years had studied an expansion into the Florida Panhandle. They anticipated purchasing a number of small isolated systems in the towns between Flomaton and Pensacola and planned to move west along the Gulf Coast to Mississippi. Martin's initial contact in the area was Judge Francis B. Carter, a native of Marianna, a former Florida Supreme Court judge, and a prominent Pensacola attorney. On February 10, 1925, Southeastern Power & Light added the properties of the Pensacola Electric Company to its holdings. In October, Southeastern merged it with several other small electric companies to form Gulf Power Company, which became an operating public utility on February 6, 1926, after acquiring the Chipley Light and Power Company.[174] Judge Carter was tapped to be the first president of Gulf Power, and he served until 1928.[175]

As Martin usually did, he sent proven people to Gulf Power, men who understood how he wanted a public service utility to be managed. On January 1, 1925, he assigned Wells M. Stanley to Gulf Power with the title of general manager, to be assisted by Robert W. Williamson, a former division manager.[176] Stanley had started his utility work as a meter reader in Huntsville in 1909. He came to the company from the Attalla electric properties, was transferred by Alabama Power to Huntsville to manage local operations, and in 1917 became manager of Alabama Power's northern operations. Eighteen months after arriving in Pensacola, Stanley was elected vice president and general manager of Gulf Power.[177]

By 1927, a 110,000-volt transmission line ran from Union Springs to DeFuniak Springs, Florida, and connected the Alabama Power system with the Gulf Power system.[178] In 1928 Martin assumed the presidency of Gulf Power.[179] Southeastern Power incurred a large increase in expenses for the year as a result of the Gulf Coast extension of operations and the long drought that reduced the amount of water available for hydro generation. Despite this increase in expenses, gross revenue for Southeastern Power & Light almost doubled. The year 1925 was notable for Southeastern Power because it was the first year that steam generation, at 57 percent, exceeded hydroelectric production.[180]

South Carolina was the next logical expansion for Southeastern Power & Light. The state was covered with small utility companies that also offered trolley services, their main market for electricity. Sometimes the companies also

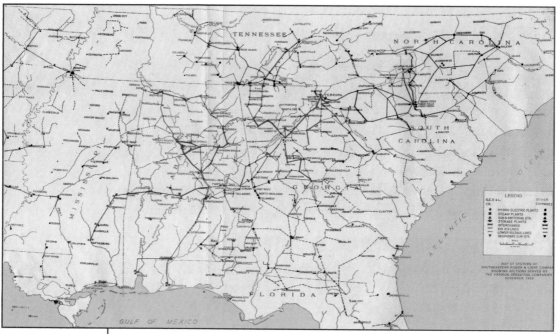

Transmission system of the Southeastern Power & Light Company in red, 1926. Green indicates other companies.

sold gas. On December 17, 1926, Southeastern Power & Light through the consolidation of several companies in the Charleston area organized the South Carolina Power Company. In the following year, Southeastern Power poured more than $1 million into improvements in the South Carolina properties. Martin sent James F. Crist to South Carolina, where he established a rural electrification department, built the first lines to rural areas, and established the first industrial development department in South Carolina.[181]

Electricity cannot be saved or stored. It exists for a fraction of a second, is used or wasted. The Southeastern Power & Light system allowed for electricity not being used in one area to flow to another. The interconnected system brought continuous and reliable power at cheap rates. The Southeastern Power & Light holding company was able to call on the resources and talents of all its companies to provide legal services, effect operating economies, standardize account procedures, and provide purchases in bulk. Pooled resources made the latest technology affordable. With the changes in time zones, peak demands occurred at different hours in different areas. The large holding company was able to pool the financial assets of all the companies to make certain there was adequate capital available for new developments and improvements in the system.

FORBES AWARD

In 1923 Tom Martin began a concerted effort to advertise what his company was doing to improve Alabama. He highlighted the company's national advertisement campaign to convince new industries to come to the state. He tried to educate newspaper editors on the need for capital and the importance of investments in Alabama. The company used reprints, press releases, motion pictures, exhibits at regional, national, and international expositions and fairs, radio broadcasting, and personal visits to influence industries to locate in Alabama. The company purchased a dozen prize thoroughbred Herefords and six Jersey bulls to improve the cattle and dairy industry in the state. When it was discovered that calcium arsenate could kill boll weevils, but scarcity and high prices prevented many Alabama farmers from using it, the company assigned its "ablest engineer" to the job and discovered an improved and cheaper process to produce calcium arsenate. All of these and other such programs resulted in the company winning the national *Forbes* Public Service Cup for 1924, a recognition given by *Forbes* magazine for the best overall public relations campaign by a light and power company.[182]

A New Corporate Building

Offices in the Brown-Marx Building had well served Alabama Power Company since it moved its headquarters from Montgomery in the fall of 1912. The sixteen-story building was located in the very heart of the Birmingham financial district, on the northeast corner of First Avenue and Twentieth Street. Locally, this intersection was known as the "heaviest corner on earth" because of the tall buildings that dominated each corner. After twelve years, however, space was cramped for the company on the ninth floor, and various departments of Alabama Power were housed around the city in four separate locations. With the lease on the Brown-Marx floor coming up for renewal in October 1925, the board of directors decided to build a corporate headquarters large enough to house all its operations. In 1924 the company purchased land on the northwest corner of Sixth Avenue and Eighteenth Street, an area six blocks north of the main business district but only one block from the new post office and the federal courthouse. The Federal Reserve Bank Building, designed by the Birmingham architectural firm of Warren, Knight & Davis, had just been completed on the corner of Fifth Avenue and Eighteenth Street, one block south of the company site.[183] In 1924 this location on Sixth Avenue and Eighteenth Street seemed off the beaten path of banks and businesses and still had residential houses to the north and west. By the end of the twentieth century, however, the financial and business district had left the First Avenue area and moved north to Fifth and Sixth Avenues, joining Alabama Power Company.

Tom Martin envisioned a building of design and structure that would represent the company well to the Birmingham community, but time was of the essence. The company's own Dixie Construction Company, which had the Cherokee Bluffs dam under way, would construct the building. Eugene Yates, recently made general manager of the company, suggested bringing in creative designer and draftsman Sigmund Nesselroth, with whom he had worked in New York. The Hungarian immigrant had studied architecture at Harvard for two years and apprenticed with New York City firms for some time. Nesselroth moved to Birmingham with his family and began preliminary designs and drawings. He probably helped select the building site, which was on the crest of a small knoll. But, as University of Alabama at Birmingham architect and art professor James Alexander noted in 1988, it was obvious that Nesselroth had "neither the architectural registration nor the drafting staff necessary to produce the required documents and specifications for such an important structure."[184] Warren, Knight & Davis was hired as the architects. Nesselroth was then employed by the architectural firm and served as draftsman and supervisor of construction. Controversy surrounds the role Nesselroth played in the design of the building, with both Warren, Knight & Davis and Nesselroth claiming primary credit.[185] John M. Schnorrenberg, former UAB art professor who has done extensive research on the controversy, has concluded that the design of Warren, Knight & Davis completely transformed the preliminary work of Nesselroth and nothing in Nesselroth's career, both before and after his employment by Alabama Power, suggests that he was an architect of great distinction.[186] The young designer was always on a salary, earning $500 a month while Alabama Power Company rendered a $30,000 architectural fee to Warren, Knight & Davis.[187]

The building, according to Birmingham architectural historian Marjorie White, broke new ground in southern architecture because it departed from the commercial skyscrapers of the Chicago style common in Birmingham. Alabama Historical Commission architectural historian Robert Gamble has noted that the setbacks and angular profiles of the power company building achieved a dramatic silhouette, by which the architects of the 1920s sought to catch the spirit of the modern age. The building was the earliest and one of the finest examples of art deco design in Birmingham. Professor Alexander describes the building as "Neo-Gothic Art Moderne." The building was constructed of Alabama materials. As Martin proudly proclaimed, "in line with the Company's policy on all its construction work, the materials, labor, and supplies for the new building are being obtained within the State of Alabama as far as is economically possible to do so." This included the structural steel, limestone, marble, brick, colored tile, cast-iron pipe, cement, lime, and pine lumber.[188] The building won numerous awards, attracted international attention, and was honored at the Southern Architecture and Industrial Arts Exposition in 1929 with a gold medal and first prize for best commercial building.

For the decorative outside of the building, New York sculptor Edward Field Sanford Jr., recognized for his work on the California capitol, designed three figures as symbols of power, light, and heat. Carved in the stonework of the frieze above the impressive Sixth Street doors, the figures stand eight feet tall over the main entrance.[189] Sculptor Sanford also designed a female statue holding lightning bolts with lightning bolts coming from her head. The twenty-three-foot statue was placed on the peak of the building's sloped roof. The sculptor explained that he wanted to create a symbol "of the State of Alabama rising triumphantly in her electrical progress." The 4,000-pound statue, soon called Electra, was cast in bronze and covered with gold leaf. Occasionally the beautiful naked female figure high in the sky sparked controversy, but since 1925 the city has accepted her as one of the art symbols of Birmingham.[190] The company occupied the building in September 1925 and almost immediately noted an efficiency from having all departments under one roof.

A few months after Electra was placed on top of the Alabama Power Company building, a local caricaturist, whose regular column was a front-page feature for the *Birmingham Post*, wrote about Electra. Under the pen name of Dr. B. U. L. Conner, he began a love story about Vulcan, the cast-iron god, and Electra, the gold-leafed goddess. Birmingham's famous statue of Vulcan had not yet been placed on top of Red Mountain but was standing at the state fairgrounds. It seems that under the spell of a springtime Jones Valley moon, Vulcan decided to check out the rumors of a new girl in town, and he "raced down 18th st.,

Edward Field Sanford in his New York studio with Electra just before the statue was sent to Alabama to be erected atop the newly constructed corporate office building.

Steeplejacks posing with Electra after securing her to the summit of the 1925 corporate office building, May 10, 1926.

his iron heels hitting the pavement with an abandon that sunk great holes in the asphalt." After a few moonlight visits, Vulcan managed to help Electra climb down from her perch. The two fell in love, and at night while the city slept, the pair moved about Birmingham sharing high adventures. There was much poking fun at the relationships of men and women and the dating protocols of the day. Rest assured Electra was able to take care of herself with her lightning bolts. One romantic contact sent Vulcan reeling into the doors of the Sixth Avenue Presbyterian Church (then located across the street from the power building) because Electra had "forgotten to shut off her current." The popular story, billed as "a New Romance in the World of Literature," ran serially for weeks on the front page, complete with drawings of the "man and the maid" that were surprisingly racy for the times.[191] And so Electra took her place in the art and the lore of the city, in the hearts of its people, as well as being the symbol of Alabama Power Company.

Jordan Dam

Tom Martin reported that the 1927 construction and operating budgets for Alabama Power Company were $17 million, with most of the money going to fund a hydroelectric dam at Lock 18 on the Coosa River above Wetumpka and a dam at the upper Tallassee site on the Tallapoosa River. Wetumpka is a city divided by the Coosa River and located at the end of the fall line shoals known as the "Devil's Staircase." The city's name is an Indian variation of "rumbling water." The one thing travelers and early settlers recorded about the falls, other than the impossibility of passage and the dangerous nature of the swirling waters, was the "roar that was heard for miles."[192]

In 1912 James Mitchell received congressional approval to build a dam at what was shown as Lock 18 on Army Corps of Engineers' maps of the Coosa River; however, the bill was vetoed by President William H. Taft on August 24, 1912. Under the Federal Water Power Act, the company requested permission to build a dam at Lock 18, and it was approved. In the spring of 1926 the company announced that its next dam would be at Lock 18. As soon as crews completed their responsibilities at the Martin Dam construction, they were shifted to Lock 18. The dam above Wetumpka was to be 125 feet high and 2,066 feet long, lower but much longer

Tom Martin in the cab of a Dixie Construction Company locomotive at the Jordan Dam construction site, August 8, 1927.

than Martin Dam. While Martin was designed as a reservoir, Lock 18 was to be a run-of-the-river dam.[193] The company built the construction camp on the eastern side of the Coosa and the railroad terminus on the western side. The village was similar to the ones built at Mitchell and Martin, a complete community with houses, a hospital, mess hall, and commissary; however, there was one difference. Wetumpka, a trade center for three counties, was only a few miles down the road, and one could walk there from the construction camp. Some workers took housing in town, and Wetumpka immediately began to enjoy a business boom.

The Alabama Power board of directors voted to name the dam in honor of the Mitchell brothers—Colonel Reuben A. Mitchell and Sidney Z. Mitchell—to recognize their work to support the electrical development of their home state. The Colonel had worked tirelessly, traveling the state to increase support for Alabama Power Company. S.Z., as head of Electric Bond & Share Company, had provided both financing and counsel. Since there already was a Mitchell Dam, the brothers suggested that the dam be named for their mother—Elmira Sophia Jordan. The Jordan family, going back to their grandfather, Reuben Jordan, who had fought with General Andrew Jackson in the Creek Indian War, had lived near the Coosa River.[194]

Reuben (left) and S. Z. Mitchell were both honored at the dedication of Jordan Dam, November 21, 1927.

A large crowd turned out for the dedication ceremony on November 21, 1927. Owen D. Young, board chairman of General Electric Company, spoke, along with Governor Bibb Graves. Governor Graves said that the "trustees for the investments of other people's money" look not to today or tomorrow but to a hundred years from now. Graves hoped that "by instilling in our children's children" the right values, "there will never be a soil where the Soviet seed of socialism can ever find a fruiting place." For the last few years, and, the governor said, "I suspect for the future, the Alabama Power Company is doing more to develop and build up our state than any other force there is in our community."[195]

During the ceremony, Dr. George H. Denny, president of the University of Alabama, awarded S.Z. an honorary doctor of laws degree, which had been secretly approved at the board of trustees meeting in September.[196] The day after the dedication, the Mitchells took Tom Martin hunting on the Coosa County land where they both grew up under the guidance of their grandmother, Ann Spivey Jordan. It was this trip that convinced S.Z. to re-create and expand his grandmother's farm and make it a hunting preserve. He began purchasing land that had left the family and developed the Ann Jordan Farm at Kellyton.[197] Jordan Dam was finished in January 1929 with an installed capacity of 144,000 horsepower, which ultimately would be increased to 216,000 horsepower.[198]

The Upper Tallassee Dam

The upper Tallassee project was located at the historical site of Alabama's first hydroelectric dam, which was built in 1902 by Henry C. Jones and his associates. Jones was an Auburn electrical engineer with an interest in high tension transmission.[199] The facility was later acquired by Henry L. Doherty and the Montgomery Light & Water Power Company. The transmission line from that dam to Montgomery was the first long distance line in the state. The great flood of 1919 washed the dam away, leaving Montgomery without a source of central station power. When Alabama Power Company obtained the site, the company replaced the dam in 1924, but the second dam was little more than a rebuilding of the original low dam with some improvements to the powerhouse. A higher dam was needed to take full advantage of the water coming through the Martin Dam generators, and the upper Tallassee project started on January 18, 1927. The third dam was eighty-seven feet high, and its reservoir impounded 2,000 acres, backing the Tallapoosa waters up to the foot of Martin Dam. The dam was in service

The original upper Tallassee hydro plant (above) was replaced by a new dam in 1928 which was renamed in honor of Eugene A. Yates on June 28, 1947.

on July 1, 1928.[200] Almost twenty years later, on June 28, 1947, it was renamed and dedicated to Eugene A. Yates.

Lower Tallassee Dam

Alabama Power Company had long planned to replace the dam at Tallassee, a site the Indians called "the Great Falls." A small dam here had provided waterpower to run the antebellum mill that had manufactured important textiles during the Civil War. On April 5, 1928, Dixie Construction Company began work on the sixty-two-foot dam, which was called the lower Tallassee hydroelectric development. The construction leadership team was composed of Armour C. Polk, Fernand C. Weiss, C. D. Riddle, and P. M. Bedette; the design team included Carl James, F. E. Hale, J. A. Sirnit, and H. J. Scholz. Dixie Construction Company faced unique challenges in the construction of the dam because it was built directly over the older dam but was longer and higher with a wider foundation. The power plant on the eastern side of the river, which operated the textile mill, had to remain in service to run the plant until the power facility on the western bank could be operational. During construction, floods were more devastating than any the company had faced in the construction of its other dams. During the great flood of April 1928, when Lake Martin was full for the first time and the dam had seven floodgates open, at the construction site at Tallassee the floodwaters washed away tracks, bridges, and cribs, leaving the site covered in debris.[201]

The lower Tallassee dam was in service by the end of 1930 and on October 28, 1939, was named for Oscar G. Thurlow, the company's longtime chief engineer who had designed the dam. In introducing Thurlow at the dedication service, Tom Martin recalled a May day in 1912 when he stood on the bridge over the Tallapoosa at Tallassee with Thurlow and James Mitchell, and they looked at the spot where the old dam stood. Sometimes, Martin said, the Tallapoosa River "stream flow was so reduced that it could not operate the power machinery which was installed." He remembered Mitchell saying that if the seasonal floodwaters could be impounded above Cherokee Bluffs, a large amount of power, far beyond what was then available, could be created

The lower Tallassee hydro plant at Tallassee Falls was finished in 1930 and was renamed in 1939 in honor of chief engineer Oscar G. Thurlow.

for public use at Tallassee. In his response to the honor and the occasion, Thurlow was the consummate engineer, reminiscing over his years in Alabama, remembering his associates in the company, and explaining the technological advances in hydro generation since the Lock 12 dam had been built twenty-seven years before.[202]

Public Relations Problems

In 1928 Alabama Power Company had two serious public relations crises that were tied to the Federal Trade Commission's investigation of utilities. One involved a University of Alabama professor who was working for the company, and the other came from circumstances surrounding the organization of a second newspaper in Mobile. In September during the Federal Trade Commission's investigation of power utilities, Professor James S. Thomas, head of the University of Alabama extension program, testified that part of his salary came from Alabama Power Company. The company donated money to the university, which compensated Thomas for working with the Alabama Power publicity committees, compiling information and statistics on rural development, and giving speeches. Thomas toured the state talking to Rotary, Kiwanis, and Civitan Clubs advocating industrial expansion in Alabama and sharing his research into the advances that result from economic development in rural areas. The sticky point was that Professor Thomas was billed as a representative of the university, and his connections with the company were not publicized.[203] However, Thomas's relationship to Alabama Power was hardly a secret. The administration at the university knew about it, and Thomas had an office in room 405 of the company building. His name appeared on the lobby directory as "James S. Thomas, Director Extension U. Of Ala 405."[204]

Martin issued a statement that Thomas had been surveying the economic conditions of the state "with a view of interesting the citizens of the agricultural counties in bringing manufacturing plants to absorb surplus labor and consume farm products." He explained that the chief purpose of the surveys was "to bring about a balance between agriculture and industry in the poorer counties" and urged concerned individuals to read Thomas's speeches and judge for themselves. The speeches were published. Martin insisted that the professor was promoting the state of Alabama, not spouting utility propaganda as some newspapers claimed.[205] Newspaper coverage pressured the University of Alabama board of trustees to fire Thomas. The board met at Homecoming on October 20. President George H. Denny had written a long letter to the trustees on October 16 outlining his position on the Thomas affair. While

Denny admitted that the university was not completely aware of Thomas's financial arrangements with the utility company, he opposed firing the professor because there was no university policy against Thomas using his expertise to do research and speak for the industrial development of the state. On the contrary, Denny believed that the faculty of the university should "legitimately use their expert knowledge for the benefit of industry" in the state and should be compensated for it, a practice that was common at the University of Alabama and at universities across the nation. President Denny recommended that a board committee study the question and adopt some policy that would prevent any misunderstanding in the future. The board approved the president's recommendation.[206]

The newspapers that were the most vocal against Professor Thomas and Alabama Power Company were the *Mobile Register*, the Montgomery *Alabama Journal*, the *Florence Times-News*, and the *Sheffield Tri-Cities Daily*, all of which were owned by publishing giant Frederick I. Thompson, who edited the *Register*. Thompson, a progressive who opposed investor-owned utilities, had been attacking private power utilities for years. His *Mobile Register* was particularly the nemesis of Alabama Power Company. The newspaper regularly referred to the company as the "Alabama arm of the power trust." Through editorials, political cartoons, news stories, and headlines, the oldest newspaper in Alabama constantly badgered Alabama Power Company over one thing and then another. Under the tight control of Thompson, the paper criticized the company on everything from rates and policies to the company's opposition to the Ford proposal for Muscle Shoals. When Alabama Power first brought power to Mobile, the city was not initially connected to the system's hydropower, which was cheaper to produce. The previous Mobile distribution system was direct current, which caused the power company an additional expense; therefore, rates were higher in Mobile than Montgomery and Birmingham. Much was made of this rate discrepancy until the line from Jordan Dam was completed to Mobile, and the discrepancy ended.

According to writer Ralph E. Poore Jr., who has researched the history of the Mobile newspapers, a group of Mobile engineers and businessmen with power company connections were having lunch one day during a conference when the conversation turned to Thompson. Tom and Logan Martin were there. The problem was, the group determined, the *Mobile Register* had no competition. Thompson had managed in some fashion to offend most of the people in the city, and the Mobile businessmen thought the answer was to give Mobilians a choice for reading and advertising. They agreed that it would not be difficult to find financial backing for a second newspaper to compete with

Thompson's *Register*.[207]

Mobile attorney Thomas M. Stevens asked Tom Martin to see if Victor C. Hanson, publisher of the *Birmingham News*, might be willing to take on Thompson in Mobile. Hanson had fought Thompson in Birmingham for years until he purchased Thompson's newspaper, the *Birmingham Age-Herald*, in 1927.[208] Hanson declined but recommended Ralph B. Chandler, who had been founder and president of the *Birmingham Post* but had sold out and started a business in the East. Chandler agreed to go to Mobile. As Auburn University journalism professor Judith Sheppard writes in her *Alabama Heritage* essay on Chandler, the editor "roared into Mobile, Alabama, in early 1929 with a bankroll of cool and mostly borrowed cash, a roster of fifty powerful friends, and a preposterous idea" of establishing a new afternoon paper to drive the *Register* out of business.[209] As Sheppard calls it, the list of investors was "a veritable roll call of the city's oldest and richest families." The deal was, Sheppard writes, for these businessmen to come up with $100,000, and Chandler was to find the rest. Chandler used some of his own money and borrowed some from Joseph F. McGowin, wealthy Mobile financier and partner and brother of James Greeley McGowin, lumber baron of Chapman and president of the W. T. Smith Lumber Company. Both Joseph and Greeley invested in Chandler's great adventure, a newspaper called the *Mobile Press*.[210]

Thompson branded the *Press* as a "power trust newspaper," and when he either heard the story or surmised it, the *Register* editor immediately contacted Senator George W. Norris of Nebraska, who was closely associated with the Public Ownership League of America and was opposed to private utilities. For years Norris had been fighting against private "power trust monopolies."[211] Norris brought the Federal Trade Commission's attention to the financial dealings, claiming that Alabama Power Company financed the *Mobile Press* as a way to control the media. The FTC was already investigating whether the newspaper holdings of the International Paper Company related to a market for newsprint or control of the media to support its power company holdings.[212] The *Mobile Press* published its first issue April 15, 1929.[213]

The FTC held hearings in Washington, D.C., and issued subpoenas to Chandler, several investors, Victor Hanson, and eventually to Abner Bell Aldridge and Logan and Tom Martin. Chandler denied that Alabama Power had any ownership in the *Mobile Press*. D. Paul Bestor Jr., president of the First National Bank of Mobile, said he was a stockholder in the *Press* not an officer, and he was a director of Alabama Power Company, but Alabama Power had no money in the *Press*. What came out in the sworn testimony was that Aldridge, who felt that Thompson had once tried to "ruin him," borrowed $50,000 from Logan Martin, then loaned it to McGowin, who loaned it to Chandler, who testified he had no idea it did not come from McGowin. Tom Martin testified that if Logan lent the money it had nothing to do with the Alabama Power Company. Logan testified it was his own money.[214]

All this was played out on the front pages of state newspapers during the late spring and summer of 1929. In June, the *Press* and editor Chandler began headlining the biographies of its fifty investors, identifying them as some of Mobile's most active and committed community and business leaders. The paper made fun of the FTC hearings, once asking, "what prominent business man or financial leader [would] be chosen next to travel to Washington at government expense in the Thompson-Norris personally conducted vacation tours?" Although it was evident that many of the Mobile investors had some connection to Alabama Power, no direct link was ever proved, and the FTC took no action.[215] However, Senator Norris used the occasion to condemn the power company for setting out "to start a new paper in Mobile" to "publish its propaganda."[216] In this contest between public and private power, each side called its information "educational materials" and the opposition's information "propaganda."[217]

Bernard Capen Cobb

Once while discussing the history of Alabama Power Company and the man he always calls "Mr. Martin," Joe Farley observed that "Mr. Martin never wrote about his failures." The best example of this was Tom Martin's encounter with B. C. Cobb and Martin's loss of Southeastern Power & Light, a story not told in *The Story of Electricity in Alabama*. Bernard Capen Cobb, the son of a minister, was raised and educated in genteel modesty in Boston, Massachusetts. He moved to Michigan with his parents after he graduated from Phillips-Andover Academy in 1891. Cobb began his career as a cashier and a clerk, but his impressive appearance and good manners convinced people that he "was to the manor born." He was once called "the impeccable Beau Brummel of the utilities business who was always dressed as if he were going to an exclusive party." The historian of Michigan's Consumers Power Company observed that "no Hollywood casting director could have found a better actor to play the role of a Wall Street tycoon."[218]

Mergers, acquisitions, expansion, consolidation, holding companies, and the creation of superpowers dominated the American utilities industry in the late 1920s. The man most associated in the public's mind with the power industry of this era, and more widely known than B. C. Cobb, was Samuel

Insull, who as a young English immigrant began his career in 1881 as Thomas Edison's private secretary. Insull rose to be one of the wealthiest men in America, earning his fortune by developing the electrical systems around Chicago and in the Midwest through Chicago Edison and Commonwealth Electric. Building electrical plants, constructing transmission and distribution lines, and acquiring smaller isolated companies required large amounts of capital. As electric utilities expanded, so did the earnings of the investment bankers who marketed the bonds. In fact, as Insull's biographer Forrest McDonald has noted, in the mid-1920s "financing utilities was many times as profitable as running them."[219] Insull's hostility to New York financiers, his distrust of J. P. Morgan, and some strategic mistakes caused his downfall after the 1929 depression, but in the 1920s he was at the top of his game.

The center of B. C. Cobb's kingdom was in Michigan, east of Insull's Chicago-based empire. Cobb's Commonwealth Power Corporation merger in the spring of 1928 set Wall Street talking.[220] Tom Martin had met both Insull and Cobb through professional associations and was somewhat familiar with their utility holdings. However, Cobb knew far more about Martin. The New York newspapers covered the formation of Southeastern Power & Light in 1924 as well as the details of the stock dividends and stock option warrants of the 1925 refinancing plan. In August 1925, Southeastern Power & Light stock reached 155¾; but in May 1926 the stock had fallen to a high of 46¾.[221] In March 1927 the *New York Evening Post*'s columnist Paul Willard Garrett wrote of Martin's optimism about his holding company, which had gross revenues of $36 million, a 20 percent increase over the previous twelve months. Martin was in New York to push a $45 million bond issue for Georgia Power, and writer Garrett noted that Wall Street bankers were emphasizing the growth potential of the South, which was to Garrett evidence that "American investors are ready to send their funds to sections of the country that once were considered backwards."[222] In August 1927, Southeastern Power stock was at 38½ and rose to a high of 57¼ in 1928. On May 24, 1928, the *Wall Street Journal* published a feature on Southeastern Power & Light, noting that it owned one of the largest hydroelectric systems in the nation, and its profits were soaring.[223] On January 13, 1929, Southeastern Power & Light stock was selling at a high of 82⅝.[224]

Cobb recognized the potential of the South and the income produced by Martin's operating companies.[225] In January 1929 the utilities group of investment bankers linked to J. P. Morgan—that is, Morgan, Drexel & Company, and Bonbright & Company—organized the United Corporation, a huge utilities holding company.[226] Bonbright had been acquired by Alfred Lee Loomis and

Landon Ketchum Thorne in 1920, and between 1924 and 1929 Bonbright, alone or with associates, had underwritten some $1.6 billion in utility financing.[227] According to the *Wall Street Journal*, this marked the first interest of J. P. Morgan in the utilities field.[228]

Throughout the spring of 1929, Cobb strengthened his position on Wall Street, and in May the *New York Times* featured the successes of Southeastern Power & Light.[229] Cobb surely read the newspapers, but there is a possibility Cobb even obtained a copy of the confidential report on Southeastern Power & Light compiled for Tom Martin by Coverdale & Colpitts Consulting Engineers in November 1927. After completing an extensive evaluation of the properties and operation of Southeastern Power & Light, the engineers concluded that the company was "soundly organized, effectively operated, and aggressively managed." They noted that Southeastern Power & Light "has been aggressive in securing additional business" and its "earnings will grow substantially" in the years to come.[230] Cobb had no doubt spent considerable time in 1927 and 1928 studying Martin and his companies, and he had developed great respect for the Alabama utility executive. The Michigan businessman appreciated the way Martin managed his companies, so much so that Cobb and his group, which included backing from J. P. Morgan, Bonbright & Company, and Drexel & Company, began buying shares of Southeastern Power & Light on the open market and acquiring option warrants. At one time Cobb controlled 238,884 shares of Southeastern stock.[231] These were the days before the Securities and Exchange Commission, and there was no Southeastern stock transfer agent in New York. Martin did not hear of any volume of transactions that would have warned him of a raid.[232]

The story presented in the history of Michigan's Consumers Power Company is based upon an interview with longtime Cobb associate Lyman Robinson, who worked in Georgia for a while and recalled hearing the story in Birmingham. One day, probably early in 1929, Cobb placed a call from his New York City office to Thomas W. Martin in Birmingham. When Martin answered, Cobb identified himself and said: "Mr. Martin, I just acquired control of your company. I want you in my office Friday morning at eight."[233] In the published account, Martin is portrayed as keeping his cool, quickly reviewing the railroad schedules in his mind, and replying, "Let's make it nine-thirty." To which Cobb responded, "That's fine. See you then. Goodbye." The author of the Consumers Power history confesses that the conversation, while not fictitious, "is an extrapolation based on the characters of the two men involved"; however, Cobb did spring "the news on Martin without any preliminaries" and the conversation was brief.[234]

On May 23, 1929, Cobb incorporated the Commonwealth & Southern Corporation with the financial assistance of Bonbright's Alfred Lee Loomis and Landon Ketchum Thorne, who took seats on the C&S board of directors.[235] The next day the *Christian Science Monitor* reported that Commonwealth & Southern "will shortly own more than 40 percent of Southeastern Power & Light."[236] When Logan Martin testified before the Federal Trade Commission the next month and was asked under oath about the organization of Commonwealth & Southern, he replied that Southeastern Power & Light Company "had nothing to do with forming C&S" and that his Southeastern Power stock had already been exchanged for Commonwealth & Southern stock.[237] On May 30, Southeastern Power & Light's stock added to a six-point gain and advanced to a new high on news that it was being exchanged for 4½ shares of Commonwealth & Southern stock and 2¼ option warrants.[238] As soon as Commonwealth & Southern stock hit the market there was aggressive demand, although on June 7, 1929, it closed lower than it opened. Southeastern Power stock continued to rise.[239] On June 12, Commonwealth & Southern extended a stock trade offer for Southeastern Power & Light stock, with J. P. Morgan & Company serving as depositary. What was surprising Wall Street was that Southeastern stock was selling at a record high, while C&S, which owned 40 percent of Southeastern Power, was selling so low. On the next day, after heavy buying by J. P. Morgan & Company, C&S established a sales record for a single stock with 586,800 shares sold. In July, J. P. Morgan announced his company held 925,000 common shares and 580,000 option warrants in the Commonwealth & Southern Corporation.[240]

In February and March 1930, Southeastern Power & Light was folded in with Cobb's other utility assets. This gave the Commonwealth & Southern Corporation, on March 6, 1931, consolidated assets worth $1.162 billion, making it one of the largest of the utility holding companies, yet its share of the nation's electrical market was only 15.1 percent.[241] In his history of Alabama Power Company, Tom Martin wrote that "in 1929 when the growth of so-called holding companies throughout the nation was reaching its peak," there were certain groups that conceived the idea of bringing together "a new and massive holding company."[242] Cobb offered Martin the presidency of C&S, and Martin accepted in June 1929, but Martin also kept the presidency of Alabama Power Company and never really moved to New York City. Local and state newspapers hailed a native Alabamian heading a billion-dollar Wall Street corporation, but B. C. Cobb held the power and was chairman of the board.[243] Martin's influence made Eugene A. Yates vice president and put Yates on the Commonwealth & Southern board. Martin also placed Stephen A. Dawley as assistant secretary. Dawley had labored loyally and long for the company in the New York office since beginning his work with James Mitchell.

James F. Crist knew both Martin and Cobb well. At the time Crist was with South Carolina Power, a part of Southeastern Power & Light. He wrote in his book, *They Electrified the South*, that the two "were about as congenial as two unacquainted junkyard dogs," that "Martin was proud of his image as a prominent and public-spirited builder of the South and its institutions," and that "Cobb's interest was strictly in earnings-per-share." Crist did not believe Cobb cared "about his public image."[244] This agrees with Lyman Robinson's portrayal of Cobb "as probably one of the best utility organizing men in the country" but a fellow who had a "bad personality" for employee and public relations and a man who would not "brook any interference."[245] Thus began the three-year period that Tom Martin's biographer refers to as "that strange interlude in New York."[246]

This photograph reflects the uncomfortable partnership between Thomas W. Martin (left) and B. C. Cobb.

THE END OF THE TWENTIES

Despite constant attacks from politicians and newspaper editors, Alabama Power Company made great strides in the decade of the 1920s. Men such as Lonnie Sweatt Jr., Francis P. Cummings, Jim Barry, Bill Loyd, Milo Long, Tom Bragg, Stephen A. Dawley, B. R. Powell, Chester A. Bingham, Robert MacLetchie, and George H. Middlemiss provided strong leadership that took Alabama Power into Southeastern Power and into a regional interconnected system. In 1939 Oscar Thurlow looked back on his years with the company and remarked that "Our map of a projected transmission system made in 1912 compares favorably with what we have today," although at the time, Thurlow laughed, "it was passed over with the facetious comment that we had neglected to show a line to Mexico City." Thurlow, praising the company for its lead in technology, noted that Alabama Power Company had used a hydraulic laboratory, very unusual for that day, to test certain design features of intakes and draft tubes for large turbines. The company "played an important part in the design of the simple water passages which are standard today," and "Alabama Power Company's methods are described in detail in textbooks on hydraulic laboratory practices published not only in this country but in Europe as well." Thurlow pointed out that the power company "made the first studies of comprehensive development of the Tennessee River, studied the lignite fields of south Alabama and the gas fields of Mississippi as competitive sources of power."[247]

The prosperity of the 1920s was real, a genuine boom based on increased consumption, but its foundation was soft.[248] Stockholders, corporations, and the government ignored warnings as the dizzy market flew upward. Americans escaped reality and the bubble grew.[249] Employment and production were high, and as economist John Kenneth Galbraith concluded, "American capitalism was undoubtedly in a lively phase."[250] In the roaring bull market, stock prices had no relation to value, and Americans purchased them with borrowed funds. Overextension of credit was everywhere. There were unsound banking practices, questionable financing, and a "greed born of fantasy," a bull market "at its best . . . a house of cards."[251] The weaknesses in agriculture, unemployment from technological advances, problems in coal mining and cotton textile manufacturing, Prohibition, European problems, and a stock boom that had no relation to value eventually undermined the prosperity of the 1920s and brought the nation's economy to a sudden halt.[252]

When the crash came in October 1929, Tom and Evelyn Martin had been in their new home on Stratford Road atop Red Mountain in Birmingham for three years. Since their marriage in 1919, they had lived at the Richmond Apartments on Highland Avenue. Now that Tom Martin was president and on the board of directors of Commonwealth & Southern, the couple had an apartment at the Plaza Hotel in New York City.[253] On Sunday, October 20, the stock market made the headlines on the front page of the *New York Times*: "STOCKS DRIVEN DOWN AS WAVE OF SELLING ENGULFS THE MARKET." The story went on to relate that the "bear party," which was the largest and most impressive that Wall Street had known in recent years, "rode rough-shod over the frightened bull faction."[254] On October 21, Tom Martin was in Dearborn, Michigan, to attend the dedication of the Edison Institute of Technology at Greenfield Village and to celebrate the Golden Jubilee of the Invention of Edison's Incandescent Electric Light. It was quite a gala. President Herbert Hoover came from Washington, D.C.; Albert Einstein spoke from Germany by radio; and Edison received special greetings from Germany's President von Hindenburg and Italy's inventor Guglielmo Marconi. For Tom Martin, who enjoyed such an occasion more than most, it was a memory for a lifetime. His hosts were Henry and Edsel Ford. Sometime during the festivities, Martin discussed the Muscle Shoals situation with Henry Ford, who confided to Martin that he had been misled, admitting that "the logical plan would have been to work with your group."[255] History often turns on little things.

While the great inventor was being honored in Michigan, market sales were the third largest in history. Three days later, on October 24, the *New York Times* headline was "Prices of Stocks Crash in Heavy Liquidation, Total Drop of Billions." There were 12,894,650 shares sold amid "disorder, fright, and confusion," an "avalanche of selling to bring about one of the widest declines in history." In the next few days valiant attempts to stabilize the market failed, and by week's end 37,502,180 shares sold.[256] On Tuesday, October 29, the great crash came.[257] That day the Alabama Power Company board of directors had convened in a special meeting in Birmingham. Tom Martin was not present, so Eugene A. Yates presided. The main item of business was to approve a recommendation from the executive committee to name the Lock 12 dam in honor of Captain William P. Lay.[258] A dedication service was held at the dam on November 23. State leaders, friends and relatives of Captain Lay, and Alabama Power Company people gathered, 2,500 strong, to honor the founder and first president of Alabama Power Company. Governor Bibb Graves was not there.[259]

The Wall Street debacle saw 240 stock issues losing $15.8 billion in one month.[260] The crash of the New York stock market closed one era in American history and marked the beginning of another. The economic developments that followed were baffling to many, and "what had happened and what was happening was not always clear" at the time. As noted by one historian of the utility industry, Forrest McDonald, the basic problem for the U.S. electric industry "was thus not so much that production and consumption declined, but that the machinery, the thinking, the techniques of the industry were geared to rapid expansion, and consumption suddenly ceased to expand." McDonald went on to observe that "the high ratio of fixed to variable costs which characterized [the electric industry's] economies made its institutions relatively inflexible in times of sudden changes in economic conditions."[261]

Martin watched the stock market debacle from his New York office at Commonwealth & Southern. He probably knew R. M. Searle, a Rochester, New York, utility executive who committed suicide on November 13 after losing over a million dollars from his stock portfolio. The *New York Times* account of his death noted that Searle had favored Commonwealth & Southern stock, but his holdings in that corporation at the time of his death were unknown.[262] In Tom Martin's biography, a version of which Martin himself carefully read and edited before his death, there is nothing about how Martin viewed this intense economic calamity in his country. But on the question of Commonwealth & Southern, the author does observe that Tom Martin "was troubled."[263] Before too long—within twenty-four months—he was back in Birmingham.

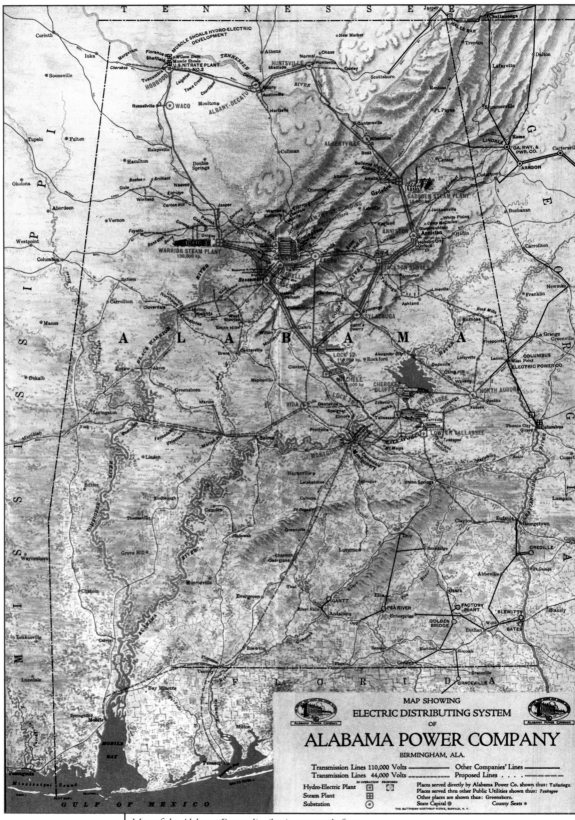

Map of the Alabama Power distribution system before
the loss of its Northern Division to TVA, ca. 1930.

Chapter Five

Crew unloading the oldest pole
in the Northern Division at the
Decatur salvage yard in 1940.

Depression and New Deal: The Tennessee River Again

*It is difficult to believe . . . that the Tennessee Valley Authority will build lines,
particularly in view of the fact that this Corporation and its subsidiaries have
offered to purchase surplus power generated by the Government as rapidly as it
can be absorbed and redistribute it to its consumers at rates which will give full
recognition to any savings made by the Government in the cost of generation.*

REPORT TO STOCKHOLDERS FOR 1932,

THE COMMONWEALTH & SOUTHERN CORPORATION, May 27, 1933

Recessions and economic panics have come and gone throughout U.S.
history, but people have managed to survive the hard times. What made the
depression that began in 1929 different was its duration and the fact that for
twenty-four months it grew progressively worse. In urban areas of the nation
and in Alabama, widespread unemployment strained the social welfare fabric.[1]
Under these conditions, electricity became a luxury. Its use was rationed by
families and businesses, and utility bills sometimes went unpaid. Many factories shortened their workweek and slowed production, thus reducing industrial use of electricity. When S. Z. Mitchell was asked how the country could

"overcome the present trade depression," he replied, "the remedy is more work and less talk."[2] Meanwhile, stock values continued to decline. United States Steel stock, which reached a high in 1929 of 261¾, fell to 134⅜ in 1930, to 36 the next year, and by 1932 was selling for 21¼. In the same time period, the price of General Motors stock declined from 91¾ to 7⅝. Commonwealth & Southern's common stock dropped from 23¾ to 1⅝. There could not have been a worse time for B. C. Cobb, Tom Martin, or anyone else to begin a new holding company than in the spring of 1929.[3]

Life was hard even before the depression for this Chilton County family living near Higgins Ferry in the Mitchell Dam reservoir area.

Alabama was a poor state even before the stock market crashed, and for many of its people, especially those who lived on small farms and raised their own food, life was little harder than before the deflation of stocks on the New York market. Willie Bass was typical of the state's rural poor. He was a Coosa County moonshiner who fished the power company's Coosa River lakes and worked his crop on shares with the man he called "Ol' Man Mac." But Mac did not own Bass's house or the land. Bass was proud that he built his "shack" on "Alabama Power Company lan'," and although the company was supposed to charge three dollars a year for rent, Bass recalled they "never come 'round to git any money" but only asked him to watch out for forest fires.[4]

As the Great Depression deepened, Alabama Power Company's load dropped. The business office had many delinquent accounts, which the company handled with as much compassion as possible while managing to pay its own bills. Budgets were cut and trimmed, new hires ceased, the number of employees declined. The new industries division, now called a department, which had grown from a staff of one in 1924 to a staff of four by 1929, went back to one person in 1930. *Powergrams* had adopted a newspaper format in 1928 but now was thinner and leaner. Economies were instituted in every place where safety, efficiency, and customer service would not be affected. After adjustments were made for the sale of gas properties and the acquisition of new properties that were not part of operations the full year, gross earnings of Alabama Power decreased $613,402, a loss that continued for a few more years before earnings turned upward again.[5]

In Columbiana, John F. Thompson, who had been the company's local manager since 1926, struggled to make sure his customers did not lose their electricity even when they missed paying a month's bill. The local managers, who were Alabama Power Company's strong foundation in towns around the state, were given considerable leeway from the corporate office in decisions not to cut off electricity for nonpayment if the manager, knowing the family, vouched for them. John's son, Ed, who himself worked for the company for forty-three years, looked back on his father's forty-three years with Alabama Power (mostly served in Columbiana) and observed that "local managers were an important key to the power company's success." For the community, they *were* Alabama Power Company. Thompson recalled that his father would go out many times at night and during storms and climb a pole to get someone's lights back on while his mother answered the telephone in the office. John Thompson, like dozens of other local managers, took care of his customers, especially during the depression.[6]

COMMONWEALTH & SOUTHERN

Meanwhile in New York, the earnings of Commonwealth & Southern dropped, too. On December 19, 1929, the board of directors discussed the general business situation, dividends, and the revenue forecasts for the next year.[7] The *New York Times* listed the major stockholders of Commonwealth & Southern as American Superpower Corporation, Electric Bond & Share, the United Corporation, and the United Gas Improvement Company, which together held approximately 50 percent of C&S's outstanding stock warrants.[8] United Gas had swapped its block of Southeastern Power & Light stock for C&S stock. The board of Southeastern Power & Light made the official vote to merge with C&S on February 11. The *Christian Science Monitor* reported on February 15, 1930, that Commonwealth & Southern, "the youngest of the corporate giants," which was "organized less than a year ago under the sponsorship of some of the most powerful banking interests in the country such as J. P. Morgan & Company and Bonbright & Company, was the third largest utility holding company with assets of $1 billion." Later the newspaper noted that Drexel & Company was also associated with C&S.[9]

Commonwealth & Southern took several steps to strengthen the corporation and protect its growth. Stock dividends were eliminated and only cash dividends were made, and the intermediate holding companies were abolished.[10] In April C&S established a new engineering firm, Allied Engineers, Inc., to provide technical and construction expertise to C&S operating companies. Eugene Yates was chairman of the board of Allied Engineers. In May

C&S organized a service company, Commonwealth & Southern Corporation of New York, to provide management, financial, and supervisory services at cost.[11] By midsummer the *Wall Street Journal* reported that Commonwealth & Southern was efficiently run, had $45 million in cash, held assets 2½ times its current liabilities, and had 107,000 holders of common stock and 18,000 holders of preferred stock.[12] In November 1930, during the Federal Trade Commission investigation of public utilities, FTC engineer Judson C. Dickerman testified that Southeastern Power & Light's "properties formed the most intricate system of interstate and inter-company connections" yet studied by the commission and that Southeastern had been "taken over in January" by Commonwealth & Southern.[13]

Despite the favorable FTC report for Alabama Power's holding company, the economic depression caused income to drop. A 1931 comparative statement of gross income of C&S subsidiary companies for the full year 1929 listed over $147 million in earnings, which decreased to just over $141 million in 1930. In 1932 total earnings fell to $114.5 million.[14] B. C. Cobb and Tom Martin, whose salaries had been $75,000 in 1928–29, had their pay cut to $60,000 in 1931–32.[15] As C&S president, Tom Martin kept a heavy hand on the expenses of his subsidiary companies and encouraged reductions in expenditures, including salaries and expenses.[16] Within Commonwealth & Southern, the relationships between the northern and southern operating companies were as dismal as the corporate earnings and the economy. The southern companies were not happy in their union with the northern companies and believed they were not respected nor were they receiving fair attention to their needs. Joe Farley remembers horror stories told to him by southern power company executives who had to deal with the Commonwealth & Southern office in New York City. James F. Crist dreaded taking the South Carolina Power budget to New York to receive B. C. Cobb's approval, because Cobb "would let us cool our heels in his outer office, sometimes for three days before granting us an audience." Then, Crist observed, "perhaps because we were such a small segment of his operations, or maybe because of a touch of indigestion, he would give us a cursory and curt review."[17] Lyman Robinson, who was an assistant controller, recalled that in the early years the New York office of Commonwealth & Southern "was like two armed camps," with Cobb at one end of the hall and Tom Martin and Eugene Yates at the other. Robinson remembered that this hostility did not end until Martin and Cobb left and Wendell Willkie came in and "cracked enough heads so that they quit their fighting."[18]

New York City was a familiar place to Tom Martin, but he still did not

B. C. Cobb

like the Big Apple.[19] He spent many hours riding the train from Birmingham to New York after James Mitchell established the first Alabama Traction office there in 1912. With the organization of Southeastern Power & Light, Martin was in New York even more frequently. On these visits, he always read the *New York Times*, but he probably paid only cursory attention to Albany politics. However, in 1928, when B. C. Cobb took over Southeastern Power & Light and began organizing a superpower holding company and Martin became the first president of Commonwealth & Southern, the national spotlight shone on New York State. Its governor, Alfred E. Smith, was the Democratic nominee for president of the United States. Franklin Delano Roosevelt had recovered from polio enough to respond to Smith's plea and accept the nomination to succeed Smith as New York governor.[20] Although Al Smith lost the presidency in 1928 to Herbert Hoover, Roosevelt bucked the national Republican tide and became governor of New York in January 1929.

Tom Martin surely knew Roosevelt because Roosevelt's office at Fidelity and Deposit Company in the 1920s was in the Equitable Office Building at 120 Broadway, the same building where Alabama Power Company and later Southeastern Power & Light had their New York offices.[21] Roosevelt had also corresponded with Tom Martin. After contracting polio in 1921, the New York politician searched for cures and treatment. In 1926 he discovered the hot pools at Warm Springs, Georgia, and believed exercise and swimming in the warm water helped improve his condition. Roosevelt invested in the facilities, built a house on a mountain top, and bought a farm but discovered that his electrical bills were high and his service undependable. On November 5, 1926, Roosevelt wrote "my dear Mr. Martin," explaining that he had purchased the old Warm Springs resort and intended to begin "an extensive development. We, in this and the neighboring communities, are suffering from the usual high cost and inefficient service of small local power plants." Roosevelt noted that "recently a new high tension power line has been put through within 6 or 8 miles of this place and running to Thomaston, Georgia." The New Yorker had found it difficult "to learn the company which is the real owner of this new line, whether it be the Georgia Central Power and Light Co., or the Georgia and Alabama Co." He reported that "the latest information is that it is at least a company controlled by the Alabama Power Co., or by the Southeastern Power and Light." Roosevelt inquired of Martin if Warm Springs and the communities around it could be added to this service.

The letter was quoted by Wendell Willkie on January 21, 1935, in a speech to a joint meeting of the Economic Club of New York and the Harvard Business School Club. The Georgia Power Company soon included Warm

Springs in the new interconnected system and Roosevelt's rates decreased. Roosevelt, Willkie recounted, often praised the power company for quick reaction to his letter.[22] A few years before, in a 1931 speech before a conference of governors in French Lick, Indiana, Governor Roosevelt had himself drawn attention to the 1929 Alabama Public Service Commission ruling and Alabama Power Company's policy not to penalize a man "because he happened to live a fairly long distance from a main transmission line."[23]

While Tom Martin was president of Commonwealth & Southern and living at the Plaza Hotel, Governor Roosevelt began his fight with the private utility industry in New York. Roosevelt, as his gubernatorial career opened, had no underlying philosophy other than a general progressive sense from his days in Woodrow Wilson's administration and a devotion to pragmatism.[24] Roosevelt surrounded himself with a number of men and women who pushed the left wing of his party, and they certainly influenced him. But his philosophy and most of his political policies—on all issues—were being formed and fleshed out. In New York the issues with private power companies were rates, regulation, and power development on the St. Lawrence River. Governor Roosevelt wanted the state of New York to generate and transmit power and private enterprise to distribute and sell it.[25] He believed that state regulation of rates was not working, and at that time he advocated that the state generate power and contract with utilities to deliver it over their transmission and distribution systems. Roosevelt began a correspondence with prominent socialist Norman Thomas, who favored state ownership of hydropower sites and state generation and transmission. By 1933 FDR "would agree with much that Thomas said on water power."[26] After a bitter battle with the New York legislature, Roosevelt won. However, in the end, the project failed because any development of the St. Lawrence River required an agreement with Canada. Constitutionally, only the federal government had the power to negotiate treaties. President Hoover, sensitive to the opinion of private utilities, which were vehemently opposed to Roosevelt's policy, did nothing to initiate a treaty.[27]

Governor Roosevelt's dispute with New York's private power companies caused consternation on Wall Street, where most of the utility companies' securities and bonds were sold and held. The business of finance was actually more lucrative than the production and sale of power. This was why there were so many connections between major investment banking firms and utility companies—the companies needed the capital to develop additional generation and to expand and the securities firms made profits by purchasing and selling stocks and bonds. In 1932, two Columbia University professors, James C. Bonbright and Gardiner C. Means, published *The Holding Company: Its Public*

Significance and Its Regulation and explained the interrelationships between the major holding companies in the nation.[28] Coming on the heels of the Insull failure and the Federal Trade Commission investigations, the book was widely discussed among those who favored stricter regulation as well as those who opposed it.

As early as 1929, Roosevelt used the term "yardstick" in a speech in Syracuse. In 1930 he mentioned the idea of government competing with private utilities to create "a yardstick" on rates, but the concept did not originate with Roosevelt.[29] H. S. Raushenbush's articles in the socialist *New Leader* and Carl D. Thompson and Judson King's work with the socialist-progressive Public Ownership League of America had earlier suggested that public power could serve as a yardstick for private companies.[30] Thompson was the one who advocated a public superpower system for utilities in 1924 as a way to bring costs down for consumers.[31] In response, private utilities noted that government power paid no taxes, spent free tax dollars, borrowed money at low interest rates, and thus could never serve as a fair yardstick for the cost of power production. Tom Martin was surely mindful of the issues and knew all the players as the New York drama unfolded. No doubt, he had Muscle Shoals on his mind, that contentious problem for the nation and for Alabama Power Company. Even after Henry Ford pulled his proposal for the Shoals in the fall of 1924, the issue found no permanent solution.

MUSCLE SHOALS AGAIN

Ford's opponents claimed victory when the automobile manufacturer withdrew his bid for Muscle Shoals, but Tom Martin announced in 1924 that the offer for the Shoals made by several power companies "still stood." Senator George Norris abandoned his temporary alliance with Alabama Power Company and went on the attack.[32] Alabama senator Oscar Underwood believed the sale of government-generated power to private companies was the answer to the Shoals issue. Senator Norris adamantly opposed the sale of Wilson Dam. Months of parliamentary maneuvers, amendments, and conference committees dominated the legislative process, and Tom Martin was in Washington much of the time when Congress was in session.

During the debates, Underwood was attacked by a Hearst newspaper editorial that portrayed the Alabama senator as "a servant of special interests" who had initiated a "steal" of Muscle Shoals for the "power trust." Among other things, the paper falsely claimed that Alabama Power Company was controlled by the General Electric Company and Electric Bond & Share—exactly the scenario that Mitchell, and then Martin, had worked diligently to avoid.[33] In the 1920s anti-private power factions who claimed that the presence of men on the power company's board associated with EBASCO proved that EBASCO controlled Alabama Power neglected to analyze the company or to study the history of the company.[34] Martin certainly stayed close to S.Z., and after the formation of Commonwealth & Southern, by 1930 J. P. Morgan controlled EBASCO. Martin was able to convince S. Z. Mitchell and C. E. Groesbeck, both executives of EBASCO, along with Lawrence Macfarlane of Montreal to resign from the Alabama Power board of directors, effective December 29, 1932, in order to make places for Alabama residents to join the board. S.Z. retired from EBASCO before the end of 1932. Taking his cue from James Mitchell, Martin maintained close control of his board until late in his life.[35]

Wilson Dam was completed in 1925.

Meanwhile on the question of Muscle Shoals, in 1924 Congress deadlocked again. Unable to reach any agreement, it passed a resolution establishing a commission to make recommendations for Muscle Shoals.[36] Wilson Dam was finally completed in 1925. When the commission recommended leasing the facilities, President Calvin Coolidge quietly allowed the secretary of war to seek bids on selling the power. Once Coolidge remarked that if anything was "needed to demonstrate the almost utter incapacity of the national government to deal with an industrial and commercial property, it has been provided by this [Muscle Shoals] experience."[37] The agrarian faction continued to oppose private power development. Kansas journalist William Allen White bitterly wrote that on the Shoals issue Coolidge was not able to tame the progressive farm bloc, which "sought trouble" and thrived on turmoil.[38]

Alabama Power Company responded to the secretary of war's request for bids to purchase Wilson Dam power. By this time the company was under the control of Southeastern Power & Light holding company. Alabama Power was easily the highest bidder for government power because it was the only company to have transmission lines into Muscle Shoals. The company began purchasing electricity on short-term contracts and transmitting it to five states on Southeastern Power & Light's interconnected system. The sale of Tennessee

River power was a profitable arrangement for the government and also for Alabama Power. Wilson Dam provided electricity when drought conditions prevailed on other river systems in the Southeast. Unfortunately, the power supply from Wilson Dam could not be depended upon by Alabama Power Company or the southeastern states because the U.S. government could stop the flow of electricity whenever any short-term contract expired; therefore, the company had to continue making investments in generation to increase its capacity to meet and anticipate future needs of Alabama's industry and the people of the state.[39]

When talks in Washington once again moved to leasing power from Wilson Dam on a long-term basis, only two proposals were seriously considered. One came from a combined offer from the Muscle Shoals Power Distributing Company (with Tom Martin as president) and the Muscle Shoals Fertilizer Company (with Oscar G. Thurlow as president).[40] The other proposal was presented by American Cyanamid (Frank Washburn had been dead for some years). Farm Bureau leaders and J. W. Worthington appeared before a congressional committee to testify for the cyanamide company's bid. Senator Underwood endorsed American Cyanamid's proposal because he believed it had a stronger commitment to manufacturing fertilizer.[41] At one point Union Carbide, which earlier had made an independent proposal, joined with American Cyanamid. Former Alabama governor Thomas E. Kilby, who at the time was running for the U.S. Senate, urged opposition to the Muscle Shoals companies' bid because he believed it would be the creation "in Alabama of a monopoly so gigantic and so powerful that in time to come the very life blood of the state and its people could be squeezed out at will."[42]

If the congressional Muscle Shoals debates were not confused enough, in January 1927 Alabama governor Bibb Graves went to Washington and muddied the waters even more. He testified before the Senate Agriculture Committee that Alabama was claiming ownership of the Tennessee River "within the State of Alabama, its waters, banks, beds, and soils," and that the state expected some compensation for power generated at Wilson Dam. Senator Underwood, because he faced strong opposition in Alabama due to his attack on the Ku Klux Klan, announced that he would not seek reelection. Underwood retired from Congress on March 4, 1927. Alabama voters selected Birmingham attorney Hugo L. Black to replace him. Although at the time Black's attitude on the Muscle Shoals issue was not yet fully understood, in the long run he was to be less opposed to government operation of power plants than was Underwood, and he was more hostile to Alabama Power.[43]

In the summer of 1930, Alabama Power's short-term contract to purchase some power from Wilson Dam was attacked by Senator Black. The secretary of war refused to sell Wilson Dam power to the town of Muscle Shoals, and the dispute involved whether the contract with Alabama Power was an exclusive agreement.[44] The *New York Times* published a feature article on "The Great Dam Controversy" by Anne O'Hare McCormick, who wrote that Muscle Shoals had become "a political issue rather than a power site." She called the dam "a colossal demonstration of unemployment. Waiting, it is groomed and kept in the pink of condition by the army and civilian engineers in charge. If Uncle Sam could work the giant as well as he maintains it in idleness—for something like $216,000 a year—he could easily disarm opposition to governmental operation." Russians who visited the site marveled "that only one of the eight generators was at work, developing but a fraction of the horsepower already installed." McCormick noted that "the power station does generate and sell to the Alabama Power Company a little of its electric energy." McCormick explained that opposition to government in business was strong "in regions like this, where government does not fulfill even the humblest citizen's ideal of efficiency or honesty."[45]

Power Company Is Investigated

Meanwhile, politics in Illinois and Pennsylvania were exploding over revelations of big money spent by power utilities to elect or defeat senatorial candidates. It began in Chicago in the summer of 1926, when Democratic senator James Reed of Missouri and Progressive senator Robert M. La Follette Jr. of Wisconsin held hearings that revealed influence peddling and large contributions to candidates. The star witness was Samuel Insull. Under oath, the Chicago utility executive was frank about some of his large political contributions but refused to answer questions about others, which sent the Reed committee and newspapers into a frenzy. Insull's name was even more sullied in the public's mind, and scandalous and lurid stories of the "power trust" filled the nation's newspapers.[46]

In Congress, a proposal for the federal government to build a dam on the Colorado River in Boulder Canyon was coming before the Senate and House, and once more the debate was gearing up over leasing the Muscle Shoals to Alabama Power Company. Norris supporter Thomas J. Walsh of Montana introduced a resolution in December 1927 for Congress to investigate "the alleged power trust" and its influence on politics.[47] Tom Martin carefully followed Walsh's statements.[48] The investigation was triggered not only by the Insull matter but also by a Federal Trade Commission investigation of the

General Electric Company.[49] The proposed congressional investigation was eventually delegated to the Federal Trade Commission, which began taking testimony on "the power trust," an inquiry briefly mentioned in the previous chapter. This in-depth investigation lasted four years and by 1934 had produced seventy-two volumes of testimony.

Early in the investigation, Kenneth G. Harlan from the municipal plant of the city of Tacoma, Washington, compared Tacoma's favorable rates to Alabama Power's higher rates. Tom Martin wrote a letter to Senator Heflin to set the record straight and provided additional information on the rates of Alabama Power Company. Martin's chart showed that his company's average rates were 1.24 cents per kilowatt hour compared to Tacoma's 1.04 cents. Alabama Power's rates compared more favorably to some other cities with municipal plants, such as Jacksonville, Florida, which charged 4.00 cents and Cleveland, Ohio, which charged 2.32 cents. Martin noted that the material published in the *Congressional Record* some ten days before failed to deduct the $1.3 million in taxes paid by Alabama Power Company (and not paid by the municipal operation). Eliminating taxes paid would make the figures even closer.[50] Judson King, who was providing information for the congressional committee, charged that Martin's statistician included wholesale electricity in the figures and Tacoma's did not. In his book Carl D. Thompson made his own fervent indictment of private utilities and included a chart of Alabama Power Company's operations for 1929. Thompson listed the overall gross revenue of the company as $17.3 million, but he failed to deduct the company's $15.1 million in expenses, also given on his chart. He gave the company a misleading bottom-line profit of $17.3 million rather than $2.2 million.[51] The fight over Muscle Shoals had thrown Alabama Power Company onto the national stage and subjected it to the scrutiny and criticism other companies were spared.

Private utilities were in a fight for their very existence. They were criticized and attacked when they defended themselves, and their side of any story, including educational literature and press releases, was called propaganda by public power proponents. Neither side liked or trusted the other, and passions ran high. Statistics and figures presented by both sides were selected to prove a point. There was no doubt the Federal Trade Commission probe uncovered unsavory and pernicious practices on the part of private utilities. However, after three years of scrutiny, with federal examiners poring over the books and records of Alabama Power Company, in January 1931 the commission's chief engineer-examiner, Judson C. Dickerman, testified that there were no unsavory practices at Alabama Power. The company made available all information and documentation Dickerman requested. He noted that Alabama Power

Company produced about 95 percent of all electric energy sold to the public in Alabama and was a major wholesale supplier to the Birmingham Electric Company and small municipal systems in the state.

Engineer Dickerman concluded in the report, which was released by the Federal Trade Commission on February 17, 1931, that Alabama Power Company was well organized with competent staff, its plants were economically constructed with "high-class engineering," and the company was strategically located, well maintained, and efficiently operated. Dickerman stated that after intense study he concluded that "the whole organization reflects painstaking ability." The commission investigation revealed that the company's operations were controlled by local officials and not dominated by the holding company, and that rates and stock issues had been carefully supervised by the Alabama Public Service Commission. The Federal Trade Commission publicly stated that the company had given its full cooperation in the investigation.[52]

As soon as the Federal Trade Commission's report exonerating Alabama Power was released, an attack on the company was made in the Alabama legislature. On February 18, 1931, Richard Bledsole Kelly Jr., a representative of Talladega County, claimed that there was a persistent belief across the state that electrical rates were unfair in Alabama. He introduced a joint resolution in the Alabama House of Representatives for the legislature to "investigate rates charged for power and light by public utility companies in Alabama." He wanted an inquiry on how rates were established and upon what basis the company's taxes were assessed.[53] There followed an old-fashioned demagogic foray against Alabama Power Company. Kelly said that the company listed its value as $174,423,037 for rate purposes and reduced it to $56,055,078 for paying taxes. It was up to the legislature, he insisted, to correct "these manifest injustices to the people of this state." Representative Charles E. Carmichael of Tuscumbia in Colbert County (Muscle Shoals country) claimed the federal probe had shown "a lot of rotten facts about the Alabama Power Company" and "The time has come for the legislature to rise in its might and smash the widespread political machine of this giant corporation." Representative John Henry Lovelace of Tallapoosa County attacked the *Montgomery Advertiser* for suggesting that anyone was trying to make political capital out of the investigation. John Milton Snodgrass of Scottsboro, Jackson County, said the newspaper was "trying to bring politics into this matter in efforts to muddy up the water." He claimed that everyone knew the rates were too high, and he seemed unaware that anyone could purchase Alabama Power stock, because he added that "their stock manipulations need the light of day. Why I know men in Alabama who have got rich off of Alabama Power Company stock who couldn't even make a living any other way."[54]

Although there was arduous debate in the house and an attempt to defeat the resolution, it passed, and a legislative panel of eight members was established.[55] Representative Finis E. St. John, an attorney from Cullman, was made chairman. Although St. John had voted against the resolution, he promised a fair investigation in a "thorough-going manner."[56] Other members of the committee were Richard Kelly Jr. (who had made the original charges); Hubert T. Davis of Fort Davis in Macon County; Gilbert E. Davis of Gordo, Pickens County; Senator Amasa Coleman Lee (who was known as "A.C." and was the father of Nelle Harper Lee and the man she used as a pattern for her fictional lawyer, Atticus Finch, in To Kill A Mockingbird) of Monroeville, Monroe County; Lee Edmundson of Jefferson County, who was president of the Standard Casket Manufacturing Company; Emmett F. Hildreth of Eutaw, Greene County, who fought in France during World War I and studied at the Sorbonne in Paris; and Senator Charles S. McDowell of Barbour County, who was the former mayor of Eufaula and lieutenant governor in 1923–27.[57] The committee was given the power to summon witnesses, papers, records, and books and had a reporter to take down and transcribe all testimony. The investigation began on April 23, 1931. Throughout the spring and into the summer, the committee heard witnesses and traveled to Alabama Power generation facilities.[58]

The Public Service Commission was somewhat miffed about the whole investigation, because it suggested that the commission was not doing its duty. During testimony, the commission went to great lengths to educate the committee members on how rates were structured, to explain accounting procedures and depreciation, and to help them understand why some items included in a company's value for rate purposes were not included in its valuation for taxes because those particular items were not subject to taxation. As an example: if the company had to relocate a county bridge and several miles of road because the reservoir would flood these structures, the commission explained, that expense was part of the cost of the dam project and part of the book value of the dam. In no way were these items taxable, but they could and should be items included for rate-making purposes.[59]

Tom Martin appeared before the committee and delivered one of his strongest speeches in defense of Alabama Power. He gave his usual rundown of the company's history. It was a tight presentation and to the point. Martin noted how difficult it had been to obtain the initial $100 million capital, which the company had invested in Alabama, and that it was 1927 before Alabama Power Company was able to secure loans in New York with the same interest and terms as companies from other states. He stressed Alabama Power's investments in research, in industrial development, and in rural electrification programs. He noted the company's support of new technology and new industry recruitment, as well as its records of Alabama weather patterns and river flows. He explained why Alabama Power already paid more than its fair share of taxes compared to what other state utility companies were paying, and he observed that "capital is liquid and seeks the section [of the country] which offers the fairest treatment."[60]

The questions some legislators asked witnesses showed an embarrassing ignorance of the work of the Public Service Commission and the Alabama Tax Commission. Explanations were an educational process, not only for these legislators but also for newspaper reporters and others who sat in on committee sessions. On July 25, 1931, the legislative investigative committee presented its report to the legislature and traced the work of the committee. The report stated that the committee gave wide publicity to its first meeting, which was held in the Alabama Public Service Commission's hearing room. Pleas were made for *anyone* who had *any* grievance against the company about rates or service or any other matter to come forth and present it. Several other meetings were held, and the same public invitations to present grievances were announced in state newspapers. Not one person ever appeared before the committee, at any meeting, to complain about Alabama Power Company. In its report, the investigative committee concluded "that the so-called 'persistent belief in the minds of many Alabamians' is the product of those seeking selfish ends and that this 'persistent belief' does not exist in the minds of the customers of the utility companies." The report detailed the committee's methods of operation and summarized testimony from the Public Service Commission and the Alabama Tax Commission. The committee concluded, among other positive things, that Alabama Power cooperated with state regulation and that the Alabama Public Service Commission was doing its job; that Alabama Power Company was actually paying a higher percent tax than any other state utility company; that delinquent charges were a normal method of covering expenses for collecting bills; and that the monthly minimum charge (called a room tax because it was based upon the size of a house) was fair.[61] Richard Kelly, who had initiated the investigation, remained unconvinced. He issued a minority report that, while more tempered than his earlier stand, still called for higher taxes on the company and stricter regulation.[62]

While Alabama Power was defending itself before the Federal Trade Commission in Washington and before the Alabama legislative committee in Montgomery, the question of Muscle Shoals was again before the Senate. U.S.

senator George Norris wrote another Muscle Shoals bill that was labeled by its supporters as ambitious and by its opponents as socialistic. An exhausted Congress passed it, hoping to be rid once and for all of the Shoals issue, but President Calvin Coolidge used a pocket veto to kill the measure just months before he left office.[63] With a pocket veto, the president had no obligation to state why he refused to sign the bill.

NATIONAL POLITICAL EVENTS

Herbert Hoover was elected president in 1928. He was supported by business interests and the utilities industry, and initially he believed that state regulation of private utilities was sufficient. In December 1929, however, Hoover recommended creating a stronger Federal Power Commission. The long transmission lines with interconnections and the volume of power being moved across state lines, as well as some of the revelations being made before the Federal Trade Commission, convinced Hoover that more federal involvement was needed.[64] The Democrats who controlled Congress refused to act on the president's request, and in 1931 Norris again secured congressional approval for yet another Muscle Shoals bill. Hoover vetoed that bill on March 3, 1931. In his message to Congress, the president stated that he was "firmly opposed to the Government entering into any business, the major purpose of which is competition with our citizens."[65] Hoover believed that the government could do certain things when there was a national emergency, but he was against "the Federal Government deliberately" starting out "to build up and expand" a major initiative to produce power. This was, he thought, against "the ideals upon which our civilization had been based."[66]

Ironically, in 1930 the giant dam on the Colorado River was started as a public works project to provide jobs and stimulate the depressed economy. Hoover agreed to this program, which would provide for water storage for irrigation and flood control and, only incidentally, power production. Congress had appropriated $2.25 billion for public works programs, one of which was a lock at the Wheeler Dam site on the Tennessee River, a construction project directed by the Army Corps of Engineers and contracted to private engineering companies on November 12, 1932, after the presidential election. The Wheeler lock would have a thirty-seven-foot lift.[67] Alabama Power owned property at this site, and the transfer of ownership to the federal government would occur later.

Between 1921 and 1933, 138 Muscle Shoals bills were introduced in Congress. The debates often deadlocked the legislative process, and a weary public wondered when it all might end.[68] This was the situation with the government properties at Muscle Shoals as Hoover's last presidential year came to an end. Meanwhile, the Great Depression lingered—and lingered. Despite optimism at various times during 1930–32 that the economy was turning around, the nation—and President Hoover—could not get men back to work and the unemployment crisis was not solved. The length and severity of economic distress was unmatched in American history. With Hoover's reputation weakened by the harsh conditions in the country, Roosevelt's political advisers were ecstatic. They began traveling across the nation to organize support for an FDR bid for the Democratic nomination. Political pilgrimages to Albany began in earnest, and Martin watched from the corporate headquarters of Commonwealth & Southern.

MARTIN LEAVES COMMONWEALTH & SOUTHERN, RETURNS TO ALABAMA POWER COMPANY FULL TIME

Tom and Evelyn Martin in front of their Birmingham apartment on Highland Avenue, ca. 1922.

Perhaps it was coincidental that Tom Martin resigned as president of Commonwealth & Southern in June 1932, which was the same month both political parties met in Chicago. The Republicans had little choice but to renominate President Hoover, which they did in early June with little enthusiasm. Tom Martin must have been concerned about what a Roosevelt administration might mean to private utilities, especially his company, should the New Yorker win the Democratic nomination. He may have been anxious enough to feel his full-time presence was needed in Alabama. It was true that he and Mrs. Martin never enjoyed living in New York. Southerners and Alabama Power employees and customers certainly understood a man's desire to "come home" as enough of a reason for doing that. Home folks also appreciated Martin wanting to "devote full time" to his company. Then, too, although he was very respected and well known in national utility circles, Tom Martin was not as prominent and influential in New York as he was in Alabama.

All of these reasons were valid, but there was obviously something else. The Commonwealth & Southern *Annual Report* for 1931 was released the end of May 1932, over the signatures of both Cobb and Martin. Tom Martin's personal copy has notations by his own hand in the margins that leaves one wondering what he meant.[69] Perhaps he was concerned about an overvaluation of stock carried on C&S's books, something that was adjusted the next year.[70] Still, he was leaving the holding company in good shape. James C. Bonbright and Gardiner C. Means, Columbia University professors who published a study of holding companies in 1932, called Commonwealth & Southern the "best managed of the utility holding companies." The professors praised C&S for abandoning "the principle of the profit-making management service contracts" and organizing a company that provided services to its operating companies for cost.[71]

In explaining Martin's departure from C&S, his biographer wrote that Martin "began to see himself as merely a front man for operations he was not to control" and that "he was troubled by the artificialities of what he saw and was supposed to be a part of." The author speculated that Martin "must have brooded more and more over the strange situation, irked by the lack of real power and the presumption that he would put up with it."[72] Years later, Martin himself gave an explanation of his departure. He said in a speech before a joint session of the Alabama legislature on August 11, 1961, that he "resigned [as president of C&S] after two years, unable to agree with some of the policies and methods employed and their economic and social implications."[73] Clearly, Martin was concerned over Cobb's methods of operation. If one thinks of the Tom Martin of Jackson County, the young man in Professor Starke's Montgomery classroom, and the son of William Logan Martin Sr., the situation from Martin's point of view was understandable. In one early version of the manuscript of his biography, a comment was included that Cobb and Martin "separated with no shedding of tears." Reference was made to a June 2, 1932, letter from B. C. Cobb to Martin, a story omitted from the published biography. Cobb was evidently replying to a letter Martin wrote to him. In what Martin's biographer calls a "carefully worded letter," Cobb was quoted as writing, "Some of the matters you mention I would prefer to discuss with you in person rather than write about them. So far as I know our records here in New York and also in Alabama are clean . . . that is as it should be."[74]

Although New York matters weighed heavily on Martin's mind, there may have been another more important reason he decided to come home. A confidential memo to the files dated May 11, 1932, Birmingham, over the typed signatures of Martin and Perry Turner, relates the details of a long informal meeting the two company leaders had with the members of the Alabama Public Service Commission on May 10, 1932, in Montgomery. Martin had brought Turner over from the law firm when he went to New

Perry Turner, ca. 1928.

York in 1928 and placed Turner in an administrative position to run Alabama Power Company while Martin was spending so much time in New York. Turner was a skillful administrator, a kind man who carried stress well, and a solid attorney who was well liked within the company and the law firm.

Martin and Turner sat down with public service commissioners at their invitation. Commissioners present were Hugh Hamilton White of Montgomery, Henry F. Lee of Eufaula, and Frank Perryman Morgan of Randolph County.[75] In essence, chairman White expressed the commission's concern over rumors across the state that the management of Alabama Power Company did not have sufficient executive authority to deal with the commission and that the holding company and B. C. Cobb were making all the decisions from New York, even over such petty matters as how automobiles should be painted. Various rumors had come to the attention of the commissioners while they were campaigning across the state in the Democratic primary. The memo stated that "The Commission had reached the conclusion to exercise its powers to see that officials of the Power Company were stationed in Alabama with authority to discuss its affairs and give prompt decision on matters arising with the Commission" because "the large investment of the Company in Alabama and its gross revenue of over seventeen million dollars required officials with experience and authority to manage it."

Martin asked if the commission was concerned over the reduction of personnel and salaries because of the depression, and the commissioners said no, they were especially concerned about "management and public policy" issues. The commissioners told Martin and Turner they had "for years been able to deal with the Alabama Power Company through its executives in Alabama and felt that this relationship had been of value to the public and the company as well and that it was very necessary that it continue." Martin asked if something particular had happened; the commissioners replied no. Martin gave the commission a copy of the Commonwealth & Southern report for 1931 and discussed the debt of the holding company and its relationship to Alabama Power. Chairman White noted "that the Commission was particularly interested in seeing that the Company should continue to have competent management of its policies and its business by officers living in the State."[76] These discussions may have been the main reason Tom Martin decided to leave the presidency of Commonwealth & Southern and return to working and living full time in Alabama.

For all of these reasons, Martin made his decision. On June 28, 1932, the Birmingham News featured a front-page story headlined "MARTIN QUITS AS HEAD OF UTILITIES HOLDING COMPANY." Tom Martin had resigned the presidency of Commonwealth & Southern to "give his entire time to Alabama Power Company." The press release noted that B. C. Cobb, who was chairman of the board of Commonwealth & Southern, temporarily assumed both responsibilities.[77] Martin's resignation shared the front page of the city's afternoon newspaper with reports from Chicago Stadium where Senator Alben W. Barkley of Kentucky had delivered the keynote address to open the Democratic convention. Roosevelt's men had given up their attempt to abolish the party's two-thirds majority rule, which had allowed the South to dominate the selection of candidates since long before the Civil War. They were forced to gamble that Roosevelt could make the coveted majority. The Democratic platform advocated "stringent regulation" of private power companies and "conservation, development and use of the nation's water power in the public interest," but it was the party's support for the repeal of the Eighteenth Amendment and a possible end to Prohibition that grabbed the headlines in the *Birmingham News*.[78]

Roosevelt's opponents for the Democratic nomination were his old friend Al Smith, House Speaker John Nance Garner, and Wilson's secretary of war, Newton D. Baker, whose assistant floor manager was Wendell Willkie, a lead attorney for Commonwealth & Southern and one of the few Democrats in his New York law firm. The front page of the next day's *Birmingham News* announced that the "Tide of the Convention turns to Roosevelt," while the editorial page complimented Tom Martin on his accomplishments, especially on bringing new industry to Alabama. The newspaper welcomed him back into the community, full time.[79]

Perhaps Tom and Evelyn Martin were packing their belongings and boarding a train for Birmingham at the same time that the New York governor was flying to Chicago to break tradition by appearing before the Democratic convention. In his acceptance speech, Roosevelt pledged "a policy of rigid regulation of public utility holding companies" and a "new deal for the American people."[80] With Martin back in Birmingham, Perry Turner returned to the law firm.[81] Joe Farley recalled that if this end to Turner's Alabama Power executive career ever bothered him, "Perry Turner never mentioned it."[82]

The law firm founded by Logan Martin in 1922 was called Martin, Thompson & McWhorter in 1932, and Logan was called "Judge Martin" by his contemporaries. The firm served Alabama Power Company well, and for decades many lawyers from time to time moved from the law firm to take various leadership roles in Alabama Power Company and its affiliated companies. Jack Bingham, whose father Chester worked with Tom and Logan Martin and who himself joined the law firm in 1948, recalled that "Judge Martin had a broader legal experience" than the legal department of the company and "his services to the public, the bar, and the Alabama Power Company were very significant." Judge Martin selected quality people who could fit well with the firm's major client.[83] The experiences of the 1920s and 1930s proved how wise Tom Martin's decision was to ally closely with an independent law firm rather than depend upon an in-house legal department, which he himself had directed in the early years. Tom Martin recognized that it was more prestigious to be represented by such a firm, and he believed the legal support from a firm was somewhat more independent and therefore stronger and more professional. Until his death, Tom Martin held the title of general counsel of Alabama Power Company, and attorneys, especially young ones, could count on Martin carefully reviewing their work. Outsiders with little knowledge of the company and its operations often question the close association with a law firm and so many attorneys. The volume of legal work required of a large statewide power company is staggering. Writing deeds and reviewing abstracts, land records, tax records; filing condemnation papers and guiding litigation; negotiating franchises and rights-of-way, and reviewing contracts, stock and bond sales all keep attorneys busy. The paperwork and regulations required by the state and federal regulatory commissions are endless, and volumes are filled with the testimony of Alabama Power Company experts on every phase of the company's engineering and financial operations.

PRESIDENTIAL ELECTION OF 1932

The 1932 presidential campaign moved into high gear by midsummer. In August, Roosevelt invited Judson King to his home at Hyde Park, even though five months earlier Roosevelt had refused to answer King's National Popular Government League's query to candidates about their views on private versus public power.[84] King, a socialist, was hostile to private power and an unyielding supporter of government power development everywhere in the nation, especially at Muscle Shoals. King had been a thorn in Tom Martin's side and his perennial opponent in the Washington lobby arena.

On September 15, 1932, almost on cue, the Cook County, Illinois, prosecutor announced an investigation into the financial dealings and the collapse of Samuel Insull's utilities empire. Insull had failed to interpret the 1929 economic crisis correctly. The Chicago utilities giant believed the depression would be over rather quickly, and he kept expanding, merging, and acquiring. This meant he had to keep borrowing capital. Insull, who intensely disliked and distrusted eastern investment bankers, was eventually caught in a web slowly and deliberately spun for him by New York banker J. P. Morgan, and in April 1933 Insull was simply unable to come up with the money necessary to continue.[85] The Insull scandals made headlines, and Roosevelt took advantage of the opportunity to attack the utilities industry.[86] What was not fully recognized at the time, by Roosevelt or the nation, was the sinister role played by Morgan in Insull's fall. That information came later and would set in motion demands for stringent regulations on investment bankers and holding companies.

On September 21, 1932, the Democratic candidate made a major campaign speech in Portland, Oregon, before 8,000 cheering advocates of public power who wanted the federal government to build dams on the Columbia River. Roosevelt outlined his power program, which resonated with King's influence. "The Insull failure has opened our eyes," Roosevelt said, calling Insull's empire a fraudulent monstrosity. If elected, Roosevelt would use public power projects such as Muscle Shoals to create yardsticks, which could then be used to regulate power rates. He wanted rigid regulation of the power industry by the Federal Power Commission, regulation of the issue of stocks and bonds by utilities, and sound investment principles in rate making.[87] In his memoirs, Hoover wrote that when Roosevelt cited the Insull crash in his speeches, the New York governor never mentioned that "we had Insull under indictment" or that Insull built most of "his fantastic empire after I urged regulation" and Congress failed to act. Hoover saw a distinction between the federal government producing power as a by-product of dams designed for flood control, irrigation, and navigation and the government building dams "to develop power for power purposes," which he thought pushed the federal government "into the socialistic area."[88] With Hoover reeling and unpopular because of the frustrations of the depression, Roosevelt put together a winning coalition of voters from the solid Democratic South, northern urban areas, new immigrants, blacks, and labor. The New York governor swept to a landslide victory in the November elections.

Three weeks after the election, Alabama congressman Lister Hill of Montgomery, who had introduced a Muscle Shoals bill in the previous Congress, arranged to visit the president-elect at nearby Warm Springs, Georgia. On November 29, Hill and Roosevelt talked about Wilson Dam and the government producing electricity. Earlier, Hill had asked for and received information from Tom Martin about the details of the Alabama Power Company contract to purchase power from Wilson Dam. Alabama Power had paid the federal government at least $2,220,000 each year for 1931, 1932, and 1933. The day after seeing Roosevelt, Hill wrote W. M. Richardson, a director of the Florence Chamber of Commerce. While the young congressman believed it inappropriate to quote the president-elect, Hill confided to Richardson that he was most "gratified" in Roosevelt's opinion on Muscle Shoals and that the president would come to northern Alabama in January.[89]

On January 2, 1933, the Birmingham News reported that President-elect Roosevelt had announced from his home in Hyde Park, New York, that he would visit Alabama on January 21. During the campaign, Roosevelt had promised to see Muscle Shoals, and he planned the trip as a brief detour on his annual winter journey to Warm Springs. His special train would stop in Muscle Shoals for two hours, then travel to Montgomery, where he would have dinner with Governor Benjamin M. Miller. The train would continue southeast to take Roosevelt to his small white house on the hill that overlooked the pools of warm water where for years he had taken therapy for his paralyzed legs. Roosevelt invited the Tennessee and Alabama congressional delegations to join him for the Muscle Shoals tour, and he had with him a number of public power administrators from the West. The office of progressive Republican senator George Norris announced that he also had been invited.[90]

A week later the Birmingham News featured a story on Muscle Shoals and how renewed government activity would bring 10,000 jobs to Alabama, but in the state there was concern expressed about how much influence Norris would have over the president and what type of bill Norris might write and the president might support.[91] J. W. Worthington was deeply concerned over the bill that was emerging, because Norris had omitted provisions vital to Alabama, especially on taxation and revenue for the state. Worthington wrote Lister Hill that "5 percent on the gross is an insufferable injustice and staggering wrong to the State of Alabama—he [Norris] offers the state a mess of tax potage for the state's sovereign and property rights at Muscle Shoals—he confiscates these rights by his own wish to do so, but with no moral or constitutional right of law to support him."[92] An elderly woman wrote Hill from Montgomery, concerned about the effect a government takeover of Muscle Shoals might have on her Alabama Power Company stock, which she invested in "little by little just as I would put money in the savings department of a reliable bank to have something in my declining years." Hill dodged the issue, noting only that "if the stock is well secure then you have no cause for worry."[93]

On the early morning of January 21, the president-elect's special six-car train rolled over the Southern Railway tracks into Sheffield. Roosevelt made brief remarks from the train, then left by car for a tour of the area, visiting the steam plant and Nitrate Plant No. 2. At Wilson Dam, Roosevelt "was struck by the sight and sound of the foaming waters roaring unused over its massive spillways."[94] State politicians all had remarks for the reporters. Senator John

Bankhead Jr. stressed electricity to make cheap fertilizer. Congressman Lister Hill stayed close to the president's side and made almost every photograph. Senator Norris stood in the background, beaming.[95] On the Nebraska senator's return to Washington, reporters asked him about the prospects for his bill. The white-haired Norris replied, "He is more than with me because he plans to go even farther than I did." Norris was concerned only with Wilson Dam. Roosevelt envisioned the Tennessee River as a regional development program based on government-produced hydroelectricity, navigation, and soil conservation. A new Norris bill was being drafted.[96]

President Roosevelt touring in Alabama with Governor Frank Dixon, Lister Hill, who was elected to the Senate in 1938, and Congressman Henry Steagall, 1939. Courtesy of the Henry J. Stern Collection.

Tom Martin must have realized that events had been set in motion that would bring his company into serious confrontation with the president of the United States and the federal government. Martin may not have anticipated how close the government would push Alabama Power to the brink of disaster, but surely he knew that he had the fight of his life before him. At the present, however, there was little he could do but wait for the president to be inaugurated in March 1933. Of course, Congress would still have to approve the president's program, and perhaps Martin hoped that there were still enough supporters of private enterprise in the Senate to prevent the adoption of a socialist program without protection for the investments of holders of stocks and bonds.

A New Leader for Commonwealth & Southern

Seven months after Martin left New York and the presidency of Commonwealth & Southern, on January 24, 1933, a farm-raised Indiana attorney was tapped to be president of the large holding company. Thirty-seven-year-old Wendell Willkie had arrived in New York four weeks before the stock market crashed in October 1929. The solidly built young man with brilliant eyes and tousled dark hair came from an Akron, Ohio, utilities law firm. He had been recruited by Judge John C. Weadock, a real power behind Commonwealth & Southern, to be the junior partner in Weadock's law firm, which did legal work for C&S.[97] Willkie soon had a reputation for being perceptive, bright,

Wendell Willkie reading an issue of *Powergrams*, November 1935.

articulate, and resourceful. Tom Martin worked with Willkie in 1929–30 to fold the operating companies into Commonwealth & Southern, and Willkie later gave Martin equal credit with B. C. Cobb in creating C&S. There is no doubt that Martin and Willkie worked well together, liked each other, and shared mutual respect.[98] As for Cobb, he retired before the end of the year, broken in health and spirit, leaving young Willkie to lead alone. In 1940 Alfred Lee Loomis, a partner in Bonbright & Company, was asked his opinion of Willkie. He replied, "I guess I'll have to say I approve of him, because I appointed him head of Commonwealth and Southern."[99]

One of Willkie's biographers, Ellsworth Barnard, dismissed Martin's critical tenure at Commonwealth & Southern with one sentence. Ignoring Martin, Barnard offers that "Cobb was primarily a production man, not a financier, and although Willkie was later given credit for many reforms, most of them were initiated by Cobb."[100] This conclusion ignores Tom Martin and shows little understanding of the history of Alabama Power Company and Southeastern Power & Light. Numerous reforms for which Barnard gives Willkie credit were actually part of the programs of Southeastern Power & Light before it became part of Commonwealth & Southern. Martin is the one who probably implemented the reforms at C&S. For instance, the creation of a service and management company, which Martin had initiated at Southeastern Power, Barnard credits to Cobb. The increase in sales programs to push the use of electrical appliances that Martin had developed for years at Alabama Power Company and at Southeastern Power & Light, Barnard credits to Cobb as well. Steve Neal, in his biography of Willkie, credited both to Willkie.[101] All these programs had Tom Martin stamped all over them.

Willkie's biographers also give Willkie credit for the Commonwealth & Southern rate reform called the "Objective Rate Plan." But this was first suggested in a report by W. R. Waggoner, who had joined Alabama Power in 1923 from the Montgomery Light and Water Power Company.[102] Alabama Power was constantly looking for ways to lower rates without threatening the solvency of the company. Back in the 1920s, Alabama Power Company received Public Service Commission approval for a promotional residential rate plan that would lower rates to consumers as their use of electricity increased. With the onset of the Great Depression and the fall of commodity prices, Waggoner began working with other company engineers in October 1931 to come up with some way to reduce rates.

The severe economic conditions decreased the use of electricity so there was abundant supply for growth and increased use. The concept was to reduce rates if customers increased use of electricity. The idea was first proposed in a memorandum from Waggoner to Frank A. Newton, Commonwealth & Southern's New York rate expert, on October 21, 1931. The plan was complicated, and Tom Martin and Waggoner gave engineer J. A. Zobel credit for working out the problems and coming up with a practical application and workable plan. The first draft of the objective rate plan was sent to Martin and James M. Barry in early 1933.[103] (The Tennessee Valley Authority bill was not introduced until April and not passed until May 18, 1933.) Alabama Power informally discussed the idea in June with I. F. McDonnell, the chief engineer of the Alabama Public Service Commission, and in August submitted a formal request to the commission to do experimental applications. The commission granted this request on September 2, 1933, which was the first public announcement of the objective rate policy.[104]

Although Tennessee Valley Authority leadership later claimed that TVA was responsible for forcing Commonwealth & Southern's southeastern companies to reduce their rates, it must be noted here that TVA did not publish its wholesale and residential rates until it did so for Tupelo, Mississippi, on September 15; and that four days *after* the September 2, 1933, Alabama Public Service Commission announcement of Alabama Power's objective rate, I. F. McDonnell at the commission received a personal letter from Llewellyn Evans, TVA rate expert, who commented favorably on the objective rate plan.[105] Even Thomas K. McCraw in his study of TVA gets the sequence wrong, saying that Alabama Power Company put the objective rate in place two weeks after TVA director David E. Lilienthal announced the TVA rates.[106] The time line shows that Alabama Power Company may have influenced TVA rates more than the other way around.[107] The TVA contract for Tupelo, which had been part of the Mississippi Power Company–Southeastern Power system since 1926, was signed on October 27 for implementation on February 7, 1934.[108] The objective rate plan was gradually adopted by all the southern C&S companies and by 1937 was being used across the nation by eighty-two companies and two municipal plants.[109]

Before moving to the conflicts between TVA and Alabama Power, the story of Samuel Insull should be concluded and his fate noted. Anti–private utility forces had made Insull a true villain, characterizing him as the best example of the abuses of utilities and the corporate excesses of the 1920s. Insull continued to expand and borrow money after 1930, and ultimately, the New York bankers, under the influence of J. P. Morgan, gained control of Insull's debts and refused to extend and secure his loans. As his biographer noted, "for want of ten million dollars, a billion and a half dollar corporation went under," taking with it the savings of thousands. Stockholders lost everything. When

Insull could not find the money to continue, he resigned from all boards and signed away corporate responsibilities, leaving his lawyers and accountants to make sense from the chaos. Insull left the country.

Meanwhile, Roosevelt, who was then campaigning across the Midwest in the fall of 1932, made political hay by blasting Insull in every campaign speech. A Cook County grand jury indicted Insull on fraud and related charges, and Insull, fearing a lynch mob trial, decided to move from France to Athens, Greece, which had no extradition treaty with the United States. Thus began, as one historian has written, "one of the most bizarre international legal fiascoes in history."[110] Insull was taken into custody in Instanbul, returned to the United States, jailed, and brought before a court in Chicago. The trial began October 2, 1934, with talented prosecutors and investigators drawn from state and federal agencies assigned to the case. No stone was left unturned by the prosecution. All the questionable business practices of the 1920s were exposed. The defense put Insull's entire life on trial, his rags-to-riches story, his drive to make electric power "universally cheap and abundant," his concern for his stockholders, and his generous philanthropy. The role of J. P. Morgan's manipulations was irrefutably exposed. The jury withdrew to deliberate at 2:30 P.M. on November 24, 1934. In five minutes they determined that Insull was *not guilty* on all charges, but the sheriff suggested they wait a while before returning to the courtroom so no one would think the judgment was fixed. Later, Insull was also acquitted of two more federal and state indictments.[111]

WENDELL WILLKIE, COMMONWEALTH & SOUTHERN, AND TVA's DAVID LILIENTHAL

Alabama Power Company and Tennessee Electric Power Company were the Commonwealth & Southern subsidiaries that were most endangered by Roosevelt's regional development and production of hydropower on the Tennessee River. By 1931 both companies had transmission lines connecting with Muscle Shoals generation plants and were distributing power, and Alabama Power Company had its entire Northern Division, the strongest division in the company, threatened.[112] After Roosevelt was inaugurated on March 4, 1933, the new Congress began passing legislation at such a frenetic pace that it became known as the Hundred Days Congress. The first major New Deal programs were enacted in this time frame. On April 10, Roosevelt sent a message to Congress asking for a broad plan for regional development of the Tennessee Valley. The next day Senator George Norris introduced a bill in the Senate.

Hearings on this bill and others were held April 11–15, with the most riveting session involving the appearance of Willkie on April 14. The C&S president testified that the bill threatened $400 million in Commonwealth & Southern securities. He said he was not opposed to government power production if the government built no transmission lines to market the power, but he did "feel a great urge as a trustee for these securities holders." Willkie was able to influence the House of Representatives to restrict government construction of transmission lines and prohibit duplication of services, but these restrictions were eliminated in the Senate.[113]

Alabama congressman Lister Hill had also introduced a Muscle Shoals bill in the House. The Hill bill was not as extensive as the Norris bill, and when Hill and Norris conferred with the president, Roosevelt insisted on the Norris bill. They did agree on a name—the Tennessee Valley Authority. Senator John Bankhead introduced an amendment that would have provided some protection for private power companies in the area and inserted into the record Governor Roosevelt's speeches and writings on the 1931 New York State Power Authority, which were more favorable to private power investments. But Bankhead did not prevail.[114] The Norris bill passed overwhelmingly.[115] On May 18, 1933, the president signed the Tennessee Valley Authority Act at his desk with a crowd of supporters gathered around him. He asked George Norris, "Are the transmission lines in here?" When the Nebraska progressive with strong socialist ideas said they were, Roosevelt looked about the room, "made a mock inquiry for the representative of the Alabama Power Company," and then signed the bill.[116]

On this very day, the office of Secretary of the Interior Harold L. Ickes issued a statement charging that Alabama Power Company and Tennessee Electric Power Company were buying power at Muscle Shoals, transferring it between private companies in violation of the contract. When the story was reported on the front page of newspapers, some papers "made it appear that the companies had been stealing the power." Thomas W. Martin and the president of Tennessee Electric Power quickly wired Roosevelt that the story was "unqualifiedly false" and demanded an immediate investigation, which never happened. Months later the charge was proved wrong, but there was little media coverage. Willkie believed the story was "invented in retaliation" against him for testifying against the bill.[117]

TVA was an experiment in regional planning that included constructing dams and producing and selling electricity in competition with private companies, flood control, the manufacture of fertilizer, navigation improvements, reforestation, and elimination of erosion, and general improvement of "the

The three original TVA commissioners. From left, Dr. Arthur E. Morgan, Dr. Harcourt A. Morgan, and David E. Lilienthal, ca. 1933. Courtesy of TVA.

economic and social well-being of the people living in the said river basin."[118] Of all the New Deal measures, the Tennessee Valley Authority was the most revolutionary and the most socialistic.[119] Roosevelt appointed as TVA directors flood control engineer Dr. Arthur E. Morgan (as chairman), agricultural educator Dr. Harcourt A. Morgan, and Wisconsin utilities regulator David E. Lilienthal.[120] Lilienthal had experience with power regulation and was hostile to private utilities. He envisioned public operation of production, transmission, and distribution. A. E. Morgan and Lilienthal differed on the subject of how to treat private utilities, with Lilienthal taking a harder, more hostile line. After an initial meeting with A. E. Morgan resulted in conciliations favorable to Commonwealth & Southern, on August 9, 1933, the TVA board gave Lilienthal responsibility for negotiating with C&S. There are indications Willkie went into the talks not fully appreciating what he was up against in dealing with Lilienthal.[121] From the standpoint of Alabama Power, however, it is interesting that Tom Martin was very quiet on the national scene during this period. He had no role in any direct negotiations with TVA—that was C&S's responsibility—but he was in constant contact with Willkie and had much influence on the younger man.[122]

Willkie and Lilienthal met for the first time in early October when they had lunch at the Cosmos Club in Washington. The TVA director recalled that Willkie took out a piece of paper and offered to buy all the power from Wilson Dam for the next six years (until Norris Dam was completed) for $500,000, telling him that "reaction against government spending was bound to occur." Lilienthal interpreted some of Willkie's conversation as "threats" and the TVA director "was pretty badly scared" when he left. There were other meetings between the two men, and they both felt pressure because the Alabama Power contract for purchasing electricity from Wilson Dam expired on January 1, 1934. Willkie was shocked at Lilienthal's overall ideas about public power and his goals for TVA.[123] Meanwhile, the market value of Alabama Power Company's preferred stocks and bonds continued to fall.[124] Willkie and Lilienthal finally hammered out a deal in December, and Commonwealth & Southern and TVA signed an agreement on January 4, 1934. C&S would purchase power from Wilson Dam until Norris Dam was completed, and it agreed to sell specific properties in Alabama, Tennessee, and Mississippi to TVA for $2.9 million. Included was the site of Wheeler Dam, owned by

Alabama Power Company. The financial situation stabilized for a while, but the fight was not over.[125]

ALABAMA POWER AND TVA

On August 11, 1934, R. H. Woodrow, representing a group of holders of Alabama Power perferred stock, sent a letter to Tom Martin and the board of directors of Alabama Power Company stating that the Tennessee Valley Authority was proceeding with its yardstick program in a manner that "clearly involves the destruction of equity values of the Alabama Power Company." Woodrow's group opposed TVA's forced sale of transmission lines and the Wheeler Dam site and flowage lands in the January 4, 1934 contract and claimed that if the sale was approved by the Alabama Public Service Commission, it would cause the preferred stock of the company to be liquidated on a nominal basis. The stockholders requested that the board oppose the contract and the sale. Tom Martin replied to Woodrow that the company board of directors discussed but "declined to take the action requested by you" and sent him a copy of the minutes of the board meeting.[126]

The next month the Birmingham law firm of Cabaniss and Johnston filed suit for the stockholders against Alabama Power and TVA.[127] Cabaniss was an old and prestigious firm established in Birmingham in 1887 that merged with Forney Johnston's firm in 1920 and specialized in corporate and civil law. Johnston was the son of an Alabama governor and U.S. senator, and he was a longtime activist in state politics, which meant Democratic Party politics. Johnston, however, had become adamantly opposed to the New Deal and specifically to TVA.[128] The names of the thirteen stockholders and the Tutwiler Investment Company were listed in alphabetical order on the initial filing in the Eighth Judicial Circuit Court of Alabama. George Ashwander was first, so the case went into history as *Ashwander v. Tennessee Valley Authority*.[129] Tom Martin and Willkie insisted they had nothing to do with the case, that they believed the C&S contract with TVA was legal. Later when it came out that the Edison Electric Institute (of which Willkie was a director) paid Cabaniss and Johnston $50,000, sworn testimony and the minutes of the Edison board of directors showed that Willkie was not present when the action was approved.[130] Everything was put on hold while this case slowly made its way through the court system, except that TVA was building dams as fast as it could. TVA's general counsel observed that while "Forney Johnston is writing briefs . . . we are pouring concrete and the Supreme Court of the United States will never declare $300 million of concrete unconstitutional."[131] The district court upheld the stockholders in January 1935 and issued an injunction preventing eighteen municipalities from purchasing power from TVA. This was a "devastating defeat" for TVA.[132] But only a temporary one.

Throughout 1935 open war raged in the valleys and the hills of Tennessee, Georgia, and northern Alabama. There were pockets of genuine distrust of government and especially the federal government, even in an area that was strongly unionist in 1860. There was opposition to flooding homes, farms, churches, and burial grounds.[133] Some citizens distrusted the investor-owned power companies more. Others were excited about cheap electricity and the promises of jobs and new lives to come. One woman chased a Georgia Power Company representative off her property with a shotgun until the TVA pole setters could arrive. Lilienthal accused Alabama Power Company of sending swarms of men in "their little red buggies" soliciting rural folks for electrical customers. The company, he said, was building a "Hindenburg Line across the northern part of the state to prevent TVA from getting a further foothold south." Lilienthal's reference was to the system of trenches German general Paul von Hindenburg built in 1917 during World War I to prevent the Allies from moving into Germany. TVA crews were placing their poles two feet from Alabama Power Company poles, some that had been there for decades, while Alabama Power was setting new poles and stringing new lines into new areas. TVA lines sometimes almost touched Alabama Power lines. Lilienthal believed opposition to TVA was stronger in Alabama than elsewhere.[134]

Tupelo, Mississippi, was the first city to vote for TVA power, but it was in Mississippi Power Company's area. In Alabama, Florence, Sheffield, and Muscle Shoals went for TVA power quickly because the power from Wilson Dam was right there. These cities were Alabama Power customers. James Crist, in his book *They Electrified the South*, included a long quotation written by an Alabama Power Company lineman that Crist found attached to a scrapbook of photographs taken as the linemen were removing the distribution lines during the company's retreat from Scottsboro. The lineman wrote:

> In Scottsboro our company, the Alabama Power Company, used to provide electrical service, but the Tennessee Valley Authority offered to sell electricity to the City, and the Public Works Administration undertook to finance the construction of a city-owned electrical distribution system. So a new system was built. And it was necessary for us to make arrangements to move away. These are the men who removed our electrical distribution. First we took down the transformers. We took them to the warehouse, washed them with oil and filtered the

Dismantling the Northern Division. Top left, removing Alabama Power Company service from a customer's house. Bottom, taping salvaged wire. Right, Paul Hardeman, general foreman of dismantling crews, scraping the company's sign off the Decatur office window.

oil. At the same time we reeled in our service wires and some short run of secondary wire on hand reels. We used the truck to reel all the rest of the wire, putting wire of sizes up to # 2 on metal reels and larger sizes of wire on wooden reels. We tried to do the work neatly, so that our second-hand wire would be just as convenient as new wire for those who might get it to use. When all the wire was in, we retired the poles and the crossarms and racks and other equipment that the poles were still supporting. We sent linemen and groundmen ahead of the truck. The linemen removed crossarms and racks with the equipment that was on them, and the groundmen reduced these to their component items on the ground below. These were picked up and taken to the warehouse on the small truck. Next behind these two men, two men with pile poles loosened the poles in the ground; then the larger truck, with its derrick and winch, was used to pull up the poles and place them at the side of the street. Behind the truck with the derrick came the truck belonging to the contractor who had agreed to fill up the holes which were left when the poles were pulled up. The poles were loaded on the truck and trailer. . . . The winch on the truck did most of the work. The poles were taken to the pole yard beside the railway and loaded on flat cars. The last work we did on the retirement of our distribution system at Scottsboro was to load the last carload of poles. And now we are gone.[135]

When the twentieth century ended few people were still living who were involved in the TVA fight, but stories shared long ago were still told by those who were children then and by old-timers who heard about the struggle to save the northern properties of Alabama Power. Many of the men and women who were on the front line in that battle had been associated with the company from the very beginning, had seen its rise from a dream to the reality of serving the people of Alabama and been part of the development. The northern properties and the people employed there were considered part of the family. Nearly all of the employees were also stockholders. This commitment to Alabama Power Company was something that Lilienthal and the government power advocates could not comprehend, nor were they able to understand how emotional it was for the company's employees. The company's local managers were at the center of the fight, and because elections were the key to which way a community might go, they worked day and night getting the Alabama Power Company message out. Stockholders pressured their friends and neighbors, explaining that their retirement savings would be wiped out if the company went under.

William O. "Bill" Whitt, who retired from the company in 1988, was born and raised in an Alabama Power family. His father, W. W. Whitt, came to Alabama Power in 1925, worked in Courtland, and then was named local manager in the northern Alabama town of Haleyville, where he stayed until his retirement in 1965. W.W. had little help in the office "during the days of the

Great Depression," and young Bill often assisted him. Whitt recalls fondly the "hassle we had with the TVA." When TVA came and began spreading south, Bill remembered that his father thought "we had a good chance of stopping it at the top of Russellville Mountain," but "Mr. Thomas Martin did not think it could be done and told Daddy that." Franklin and Winston Counties were Republican strongholds with independent-minded people. Martin met with local political

W. O. "Bill" Whitt, ca. 1988.

leaders, and they made a commitment to work together against TVA.[136]

Every Sunday Bill would go to Birmingham with his dad. He would ride the elevators in the corporate office while his father met with Tom Martin, Thomas Bragg, and M. E. Wiggins. The company, Bill remembered, "gave Dad everything he needed. We didn't even see him at home for three or four months. I can recall one time that Mom wrote a letter to Dad in *Powergrams* telling him the children were just fine." His father worked with county politicians and the Haleyville mayor, and, as Bill observed, "It just boiled down to a Democrat-Republican fight, and you don't get into that kind of fight in Winston County without it getting pretty bad." The city of Red Bay in Franklin County voted to stay with Alabama Power in the 1930s, but by 1946 the Franklin County Rural Electric Cooperative was having such financial trouble that Red Bay agreed to join. In 1937, Alabama Power supporters defeated TVA's attempt to take Haleyville. The Alabama Power line at the top of the mountain held, as W. W. Whitt said it would, and eventually became the boundary line in the TVA Financing Act of 1959. In 1999 Bill Whitt observed that "there are still hard feelings" about TVA.[137]

Thomas Bragg, ca. 1943.

BIRMINGHAM, BESSEMER, AND TARRANT CITY

While the fight was going on in the northern part of the state, the company was directing battles in areas it could see from the top floor of its building—fights for Birmingham, Bessemer, and Tarrant City. The contest in Birmingham against a municipal power system with electricity provided by TVA was long and bitter. Alabama Power Company and Birmingham Electric Company stood with businessmen who were opposed to the government operating businesses and who were against socialism. Birmingham city government was in poor financial condition in 1933, and the prospects of revenue from operating a municipal power system were attractive.[138] The election was not just on the issue of municipal versus private ownership and operation. The municipal power campaign began against a background of Birmingham voters mistrusting city government, which had been dominated by the Ku Klux Klan in the 1920s, reeked with suspect deals, and operated on a corrupt patronage system. The Democratic primary campaigns for city commission seats were bitter and resulted in the renomination of Jimmie Jones and nominations for newcomers W. O. Downs and Lewey Robinson, two cohorts of Governor Bibb Graves's Birmingham supporter Horace Wilkinson.[139] This group fought for the New Deal and against the Birmingham Big Mules, including Alabama Power Company.[140]

The election had two parts—officially electing the Democratic nominees for city commission, which was not contested, and deciding on municipal ownership of electricity, water, streetcars, and steam heating in the city, which was divisive.[141] Lewey Robinson was leader of the public ownership campaign, which promised federal dollars and cheap Muscle Shoals electricity.[142] Opponents organized under the Citizens Protective Committee with Holt McDowell as secretary. This group stressed that the city already had a lower electrical rate than most municipal plants in Alabama, because Alabama Power was selling power to Birmingham Electric Company at a wholesale rate of 6.53 mills, while TVA was selling Muscle Shoals power to northern Alabama cities at a wholesale rate of 7 mills.[143] They pointed out that Birmingham did not have the money, was already deeply in debt and could not issue any more bonds, and that the federal Public Works Administration (PWA) would not lend money to acquire an existing system but only to build a new system.[144] The Birmingham Parent–Teacher Association council opposed municipal ownership because of the loss of tax dollars for public schools. Opponents also pointed out that county government would lose $141,075 in taxes that had been used to build roads.[145]

On October 3, Mervin H. Sterne, respected Birmingham investment banker, gave a powerful speech before a group of Alabama Power Company stockholders gathered at the Thomas Jefferson Hotel. Sterne traced the "sad history of public ownership" in Alabama. There were, he said, too many unanswered questions on the current issue, and he recommended that the Birmingham municipal proposal be voted down.[146] In the end more Birmingham voters had more confidence in Alabama Power and Birmingham Electric to deliver cheap dependable electricity to their homes and industries than they did in the city commission. The vote on October 9 was 6,923 for municipal ownership and 9,696 against. The vote on water, streetcars, and steam was even more overwhelmingly opposed to city operation.[147]

Bessemer and Tarrant City decided differently. Both these small towns had a larger percentage of blue-collar voters, a lower property tax base, and a higher union membership than did Birmingham. Bessemer mayor Jap Bryant favored TVA power and campaigned strongly for it. On October 20, 1933, by a vote of 485 to 395, Bessemer voters approved establishing a municipal power system. The city hired an engineering firm to prepare a loan application to the Public Works Administration and in November 1934 made application; however, by this time all PWA funds were depleted and the Ashwander suit had stopped appropriations. Eventually the city received $1,238,000 ($557,000 as a grant with the rest a loan) from the PWA. The city of Bessemer cooperated with Tarrant City, which had also voted to establish a municipal system, and both cities finally received their TVA power from a transmission line from Guntersville with a substation in Fulton Springs.[148] Operating within the shadow of the Alabama Power Company general office building on Eighteenth Street, this was as far south as TVA power intruded.

Meanwhile, the Ashwander case was moving through the courts. Publicly, Tom Martin knew nothing in advance of the filing of the Ashwander case. But such ignorance would be totally out of character for him. Martin was opposed to TVA, yet he was concerned about receiving enough money to liquidate the debts of these properties, and he feared the government might just take them without any compensation. He believed in the legal system, and he would not have been passive while he believed there was a remedy in the law. On the other hand, Willkie was the head of the holding company, and Martin could not openly differ with his boss. Power companies across the nation were stunned after President Roosevelt said he would build other regional river and power developments, and they saw TVA as an important experiment to challenge. Martin knew Forney Johnston, but they had been on opposite sides of various issues and personally did not care for each other.[149] Martin would never have approached Johnston or the Edison Electric Institute himself, but surely he knew who did. It is interesting to note that the stockholders who sued were not well-known stockholders, not the wealthy Birmingham businessmen with power company connections one might expect to find listed on such a suit. As the legal fight developed, Martin certainly followed every legal move very carefully, because the company and Martin were being sued along with TVA.[150]

David Lilienthal and Wendell Willkie both knew that transmission and distribution lines were at the heart of the conflict. Without transmission and distribution, TVA was merely a producer selling at the switchboard and no danger to C&S or Alabama Power. From the beginning, however, TVA had adopted the policy to generate, transmit, and sell to municipalities and cooperatives that would distribute the electricity. These towns had no money to build distribution systems. Alabama Power Company was already serving northern Alabama and had hundreds of miles of distribution lines. The real threat came when the New Deal Public Works Administration offered outright grants (gifts) to municipalities and farmers' electric cooperatives for 30 percent of the cost of constructing distribution lines and 3 percent loans for the remaining 70 percent. The Ashwander injunction kept these grants and loans from happening until the U.S. Supreme Court upheld the TVA position on February 17, 1936. Although the court failed to rule on the constitutionality of the unique independent gov-

ernment corporation established in the act and its production of power in competition with private companies, Alabama Power Company transferred fourteen
municipal properties and the Wheeler Dam site to TVA on May 1, 1936.[151]

Neither Tom Martin nor Willkie was happy with the outcome. They
wanted to force the Supreme Court to rule on the constitutionality of the
TVA Act, which set up a powerful government corporation with almost no
congressional or presidential oversight. Willkie and Martin did not believe it
was constitutional for the government to use taxpayer monies to take over their
customers and destroy their company, especially without fair compensation.
They believed it was unfair to establish a "yardstick" on power production
that was subsidized by taxpayer money and where large costs of power production were charged to "navigation and flood control," expenses Alabama Power
assumed as part of its routine hydro costs. On May 29, 1936, nineteen area
electric utility companies filed suit against the Tennessee Valley Authority in
the eastern district of Tennessee. They challenged TVA on "broad constitutional grounds" to prevent it from "generating, distributing, and selling electric
power in the area served by the complainants."[152] After the federal district
court dismissed the suit, it was appealed to the U.S. Supreme Court. Once
more the high court evaded the constitutional issue and used a technicality
to rule against the private companies. Alabama's Hugo Black, who had been
appointed by President Roosevelt in 1937 and had only recently arrived to the
bench, did not participate in the Supreme Court's 5–2 decision.[153]

The Public Utility Holding Company Act of 1935

By this time President Roosevelt had played his second card against
the utilities. During a "fireside chat" on April 28, the president blamed the
"unfair practices of selfish minorities" for the "recent collapse of industries"
and stressed the need to eliminate holding companies in public utilities.[154]
Roosevelt had forced the division of commercial and investment banking in
the Glass-Steagall Banking Act. He delivered the regulation of securities issues
(one of his campaign promises) with the 1933 Securities Act, which required
financial statements to be submitted and approved before any stocks and bonds
could be issued. Roosevelt and his advisers, reacting to the revelations about
J. P. Morgan in the testimony in the Insull trial, did not believe that this act
regulated the utilities holding companies enough, so the president had Tommy
Corcoran and Ben Cohen, young protégés of Harvard law professor Felix
Frankfurter, draft a utilities holding company bill. Frankfurter, a controversial
adviser to the president, despised Wall Street lawyers and "denounced busi-

nesspeople—especially bankers and public utilities" men.[155]

The president talked Burton K. Wheeler into sponsoring the administration's bill instead of the one the Montana senator had written himself. Texas congressman Sam Rayburn would sponsor the bill in the House. Wheeler, who was beginning his third six-year term in January 1935, recalled that "the lobby that fought this bill was the biggest, bitterest, and most extravagant during my time in the Senate." Wheeler opposed holding companies, claiming that they extracted unreasonable sums from their operating companies, and he once said that "the only difference between Jesse James and some of these utility men is that Jesse James had a horse."[156]

Testimony and evidence presented in the hearings on this bill proved that Commonwealth & Southern was not guilty of the abuses that Senator Wheeler opposed or that the bill specifically addressed. Commonwealth & Southern's 1933 write-off and adjustment of some $563,123,255 in stock value and Willkie's removal of bankers from the C&S board the previous year strengthened Willkie's position.[157] Willkie testified against the Wheeler-Rayburn bill before the House Committee on Interstate and Foreign Commerce on March 14, 1935. He had no problem with regulations to stop abuses of some holding companies and suggested amendments to the bill, but he fought the bill because of its inclusion of the "death sentence" would have meant the end of holding companies, including Commonwealth & Southern. Willkie read to the committee a 1929 quotation from a Wisconsin public utility commissioner: "The spread of rural electrification, the amazing advances in telephony, the rise of superpower systems—these and many other technological developments so intimately related to the public welfare are directly attributable to the efforts of the holding company. Perhaps most important of all, to the holding company must go the credit for the unprecedented flow of capital into the public utility industry making possible extension and improvements of services." Wendell Willkie was quoting David Lilienthal.[158]

The requirements of the Public Utility Holding Company Act of 1935 would also add an extensive level of administrative oversight and legal expense for holding companies.[159] Willkie used his opportunity to testify under oath to defend C&S. He wanted to destroy what he called myths about the excessive influence on C&S by financiers and bankers, such as "the House of Morgan" and "utility giants like Electric Bond & Share and the United Corporation,"— all of which were minority stockholders in Commonwealth & Southern.[160] Willkie was particularly worried about financial difficulties the operating companies would face should they have to function without the financial security that a holding company offered.[161]

The Wheeler-Rayburn bill was extremely complicated, so much so that when Senator Wheeler asked Senator William E. Borah if it were true that the utility people had convinced him to attack the bill, Borah replied: "How the hell can I make a speech about it? There isn't anyone on the Senate floor who understands it but you." The only reason Wheeler understood the bill was because the administration men who wrote it, Corcoran and Cohen, spent every night for a week drilling Wheeler at his home.[162]

Willkie testified against the utilities bill before the Senate Committee on Interstate Commerce on April 25, 1935. During questioning, the chairman, Senator Wheeler, who was particularly hostile to Willkie, made a statement that Tom Martin, as president of Alabama Power Company, had "spent, off and on, about a year with the House of Morgan trying to get the Commonwealth & Southern set-up." Willkie immediately responded, "Oh, I do not believe so, Senator Wheeler." The committee was stunned to learn that the average kilowatt hours used in Georgia was 900, while the national average was only 625–650. They were surprised that C&S rates were so low and had been falling for the past ten years. Senator Wheeler tried to get Willkie to agree that "the reason you lowered your rates was because of the Tennessee Valley Authority." But Willkie responded, "Oh, sir, those rates were in effect in Alabama prior to the operations of the T.V.A." When questions were asked about using competitive bids for construction and one senator implied that it had been done differently before, Willkie refused to take any credit, responding that "my predecessor [Tom Martin] was one of the finest men who ever lived, and one of the cleanest and most honorable men who ever lived."[163]

In 1935 the pressure against the bill from utility lobbies was so great that Alabama senator Hugo Black began an investigation into the expenditures and activities of companies trying to defeat the bill. Black elicited testimony about mass telegrams that were fraudulently produced, huge amounts of money spent, and influences on editorials. Black's work galvanized public opinion against holding companies, helped the bill pass, and had something to do with Black winning a Supreme Court appointment. Southern senators were leery about the Wheeler-Rayburn bill, especially the death sentence in Section 11 that required the elimination of holding companies that served "no demonstrably useful and necessary purpose." Roosevelt refused to back off. In the end, the Securities and Exchange Commission was given some flexibility about allowing holding companies to continue that had contiguous and linked properties and that were determined by the SEC to be operating within the public interest.[164] The president signed the bill on August 26, 1935, and a whole new set of problems was created for C&S and Alabama Power Company and their attorneys. The issues in the Commonwealth

& Southern struggle to survive were not finalized until the period 1947–49, when the northern and southern properties of C&S were separated (with some divestment) and the Southern Company was created, a story for another chapter.

GENERATION, TAXES, AND FINANCE

Severely depressed economic conditions and an inability to secure capital had prevented Alabama Power Company from increasing its capacity in the 1930s. The possibility of having the contract at Wilson Dam cancelled by the government would have put the power company in a bind except that reduction in the use of electricity had leveled out the load. Unit No. 4 at the Gorgas Steam Plant went into operation on August 15, 1920, and was used only when hydropower was not available.[165] In the 1930s Alabama Power Company reservoirs, especially Lake Martin, faced problems of serious silting in their headwaters, the reason Lake Martin remained muddy for a decade. Silting reduced the size of the reservoir, and the loss of top soil damaged area farms and decreased property values. The company worked with the Tallapoosa County Soil Conservation Service to remedy this situation by terracing and by planting slash pine trees. In 1934 the company created seed beds near Jordan Dam to propagate slash pine. The experimental work resulted in 70,000 trees being planted on company lands adjacent to hydro plants and around the reservoirs the first year and even more the next year.[166]

Trees planted on company lands helped reduce erosion and silting in Alabama Power reservoirs and provided poles for use on company lines.

The falling market value for Alabama Power's securities as a result of TVA's presence in Alabama was cause for great concern, but the more serious repercussion of having TVA in its backyard was its inability to take advantage of prevailing low interest rates to refinance its senior securities. The northern companies in Commonwealth & Southern refinanced more than $250 million during 1934–36, but having "the continuing threat of government competition" made it impossible for Alabama Power to refinance,

thus it lost savings in interest and preferred dividend charges that amounted to more than $2 million a year.[167]

The Alabama tax burden that TVA was exempt from and that the company shouldered was a particular thorn in Martin's side. Granted, the Tennessee Valley Authority did make payments to state and local governments in lieu of taxes, but the amount was far less than Alabama Power was paying in taxes. For Martin, it had always been a source of pride that Alabama Power Company had grown to become the largest taxpayer in Alabama, though he worried and often complained that taxes restricted the company's progress and that the percentage rate the company paid was higher than for other utilities in the state. In 1935 the company paid taxes in sixty-six of the state's sixty-seven counties and paid "twenty-one different kinds of direct taxes," fourteen to the state and seven to the federal government. The total was $2,565,976. While Alabama Power was paying taxes on its land, the Tennessee Valley Authority, according to a University of Alabama study, had withdrawn thousands of acres of prime farmland in the Tennessee Valley from the tax assessment roles. Estimates were that Limestone County lost 52,000 acres, which had been producing $1 million in taxes each year to the county and state; Morgan County lost $70,000 in taxes a year; Lauderdale County lost taxes on land and farm equipment that had previously sent $1 million into state and local government budgets.[168] The Alabama Power Company's *Annual Report* for these years showed a restrained anger at the federal government for the unfair way the company was being treated.

ALABAMA POWER IN THE 1930S

After his resignation from the presidency of Commonwealth & Southern in 1932, Tom Martin committed himself to strengthening his company in every way. He encouraged the sale of appliances in Alabama as he had promoted appliance sales by the operating companies of Southeastern Power & Light long before he went to New York to lead Commonwealth & Southern. After Willkie began a major appliance sales program, Martin pushed it at Alabama Power, making it a huge competition among divisions and departments with rewards and honors for the winners. Willkie worked out a C&S program whereby customers could add appliance purchases to their electrical bills and pay for the appliances over several months with only a little interest charged. This program of installment sales went on for several years until other companies and banks realized that it was good business and began to approve installment loans for appliance purchases. In 1934, C&S subsidiaries sold $10.5 million in appliances, 80 percent on Willkie's deferred payment plan.[169]

When he was in Wisconsin, David Lilienthal recognized that appliance sales and cheaper rates would increase the use of electricity. In the fall of 1933 he developed a plan, approved by Roosevelt in December, to provide federal financing of appliance purchases. The TVA director set up the Electric Home and Farm Authority (EHFA) to loan money for installment purchases of electric appliances in the TVA area, but he always planned for the program to go nationwide. He hoped to hold "this out as a kind of bait for cooperation on a yardstick program," but Willkie did not take it.[170] Lilienthal worked with General Electric and Westinghouse to have them design and produce cheaper appliances that would be approved by EHFA for the finance program. Some designs were successful, but not GE's four-cubic-foot chest-style refrigerator— it was too small and too inconvenient to use. Even so, the Electric Home and Farm Authority still pushed its sale. In the long run, the EHFA proved to be insignificant: its installment loans were less than 2 percent of credit for electrical purchases and less than 0.1 percent of total national consumer credit between 1932 and 1935. Alabama Power Company continued to encourage its own sales programs, but the company benefited from some spinoff from the EHFA in appliance design and from mass consumption and production of electrical appliances.[171]

Alabama Power Company's rural electrification program slowed with the depression. Some farm families who had signed up for service withdrew their applications as the economy worsened. The company had hoped that eventually heavy farm equipment would make rural routes profitable, but farmers typically added lights first, then an iron, a washing machine, and perhaps a radio. Expensive refrigerators and ranges came next. Then the choice was electric pumps to provide running water and flush toilets, then hot water heaters, important quality-of-life improvements. The design and production of affordable electric farm equipment, which would provide the heavy loads Martin envisioned in the 1920s, had still not materialized.[172]

The company had large increases in gross dollar revenue from electrical appliance sales in 1934 and again in 1935. In December 1935 *Powergrams* announced a record 57 percent increase in sales. In 1936 sales of electrical appliances reached $1,753,124.[173] Reduced rates, installment purchases, and an improved economy helped. In August 1937 the company began a "Silver Anniversary Sales Event" that lasted for two months. There were other ways the company found to sell and increase the use of electricity. It supported more outdoor lighting and encouraged lighted displays at Christmastime. The company ran demonstrations of improved lighting in industrial plants, such as the one R. B. Wickham and Harold Howard designed for the West Point Manufacturing Company. It hired twenty-three lighting specialists to help people design new lighting for their homes and businesses.[174] Company salespeople pushed for better lighting in schools, on streets, and in public buildings and encouraged towns to increase lighting at parks and to light ball fields for night games.

Alabama Power's home service department increased its programs. Its home economists ran cooking schools so homemakers would know how to operate the latest electrical appliances, and they offered special programs for chefs and cooks. Local offices increased the number of home demonstration agents and presented programs to encourage the purchase of electrical appliances, especially stoves, refrigerators, and washing machines. Alabama Power home economists even made house calls after a purchase to explain how products worked. These women would demonstrate the new appliances and, on their travels, also check the distribution lines down rural roads and suburban streets. They stopped at houses not connected to explain what electrical appliances could do for a household. With the success of such programs, the home service department was strengthened and the number of women employees increased.[175] The company also worked with local furniture companies to display and sell appliances, and in July 1935 *Powergrams* reported that eighty-seven Alabama furniture stores featured displays of appliances.[176]

Alabama Power Company also encouraged the development of air conditioning technology and the installation of equipment. In April 1935 *Powergrams*

In September 1935 Constantine's in Mobile became the first restaurant on the company's system to be air conditioned.

announced that a whole block on Dexter Avenue in Montgomery was adding air conditioning and would join the city's Empire Theatre, which was the first theater in the nation to be air conditioned.[177] In July 1935 air conditioning came to Gadsden when Frigidaire equipment was installed at Usry Drug Store. In September, Constantine's in Mobile became the first restaurant on the company's system to be air conditioned; the installation was with Carrier equipment.[178] During the Senate hearings on the 1935 holding company bill, Willkie was asked whether the high use of electricity in the South was related to the high use of air conditioning, and he replied, "No." By the end of the decade, however, nearly all Alabama theaters and large department stores in southern cities were air conditioned. Cool temperatures gave a boom to daytime shopping during summer months, and theaters were a comfortable retreat on hot July nights in Alabama. Residential cooling developed largely after World War II.

Because national events and the fight for survival against TVA produced uncertainty and poor publicity for the company, Tom Martin sent letters to stockholders and customers more frequently, explaining the company's side of news reports. He tried to reassure them that although the company was in a difficult dispute, he had confidence it would survive. Martin stressed that the ownership of Alabama Power Company was not on Wall Street in New York but on main streets across Alabama.[179]

In 1935 Tom Martin had another battle closer to home. On May 11, 1935, President Roosevelt signed an executive order establishing the Rural Electrification Administration (REA), which was to operate under and with funds from the Emergency Relief Appropriation Act of 1935 with the goal of electrifying the nation. As soon as possible, Alabama Power filed with the agency a list of 4,000 rural projects that would serve people living in fifty-three counties in the state. The cost of these lines was estimated at $1.4 million. Without waiting for any reply from the government, the company began working on portions of these lines, authorizing $800,000 for the project. In September 1935 the REA wrote Alabama Power that "it is our desire that rural electrification shall go forward with the utmost speed. The more the companies do through their own financing, the greater will be the total of miles built with their funds and ours combined."[180]

Gordon Persons, chairman of the Rural Electrification Authority for Alabama, disagreed. In October, Persons, owner of radio station WSFA in Montgomery and appointed chairman of the state Rural Electrification Authority by Governor Bibb Graves, advised farmers who wanted electricity not to sign any agreement or contract with a private utility.[181] Persons encouraged farmers to seek grants and borrow federal dollars to create cooperatives. Some did, and Alabama Power Company cooperated with the effort by providing wholesale electricity for those cooperatives within the company's service area. During the three years from 1936 to 1938, the company built 3,900 miles of rural lines to serve 18,758 new customers. Progress continued at a rapid pace each year until 1941, when it dropped off during the war years because of the impossibility of obtaining supplies, especially copper, which were going into the war effort.[182]

Franklin D. Roosevelt was, of course, renominated by the Democrats in 1936. His opponents had little hope the popular president could be defeated, but the American Liberty League, which was founded in 1934 to fight social-ism and the New Deal, tried. The Republicans only could come up with a rather colorless and mild, yet honest and sincere nominee, Kansas governor Alfred Landon. Roosevelt pictured the Liberty League as "Economic Royalists" and enjoyed attacking them. With many people now employed, some working on government projects, and with an improved economy, the president swept to victory. The electoral count was 523 to 8.[183]

During the decade of the 1930s, Alabama Power lost several steadfast friends and longtime employees. W. H. Hassinger died in March 1935 at the age of seventy-three. He had gone off the board of Commonwealth & Southern when Tom Martin left the holding company, but he remained on the board of Alabama Power. Martin always gave Hassinger credit for protecting Alabama Power from predators. Lamar Aldridge, who came to the company in 1915 fresh from college, died on July 10, 1939. As longtime treasurer, Aldridge was a sound-thinking and steady leader who was praised by Tom Martin for his loyalty, cordial personality, and "true sense of honor."[184]

The company lost Colonel Reuben Mitchell in January 1937. James Mitchell and Martin may well have brought the Colonel into the company initially because of his powerful and wealthy brother, S.Z. of EBASCO, but through his hard work, commitment to the welfare of the Alabama Power Company, and loyalty to Martin, he became senior vice president in 1921 and earned his own place in the history and the heart of the company.[185] S.Z. had visited his brother in Birmingham before Christmas and knew he was not well. The retired EBASCO leader wrote Tom Martin that Reuben's death was a "grievous shock to me. You know my father and mother both died when I was quite small and the Colonel was really father to me."[186]

Reuben, left, and
S. Z. Mitchell at
Lay Dam,
August 18, 1923.

The End of a Terrible Decade

In late 1933, longtime spokesman for the Duke Power Company, William S. Lee, gave a major address to the American Engineering Council as its seventh president. After tracing the history of electricity in the United States and the South, he ended with a warning. The power industry was facing, he said, "destructive governmental regulation, destructive governmental competition, and destructive taxation. Unless saner judgment prevails, this great industry will see its handiwork sacrificed to political ambition, political oppression, and political aggression—to the lasting benefit of none and to the detriment of all."[187] Tom Martin could not have summarized his own apprehension better.

The 1930s were difficult years for the power industry and Alabama Power Company in particular. In 1935 the *Montgomery Advertiser* carried an account of Tom Martin's visit to his hometown of Scottsboro, writing that Alabama Power had "performed two worthy functions" for the state. First, the company had invested $100 million in the state. The newspaper noted that "the second function of the Alabama Power Company is to make reform newspapers unspeakably dull and uninteresting because of their preoccupation with Tom Martin's 'octopus' or whatever it is they call it when trying to 'Arouse the People' and to give otherwise useless politicians an issue."[188] In a speech in Selma in 1939, Martin closed his remarks on electricity in Alabama with the comment: "It lies within the power of the state by its public policies, to meet the electric power question, upon which the growth and progress of the state so much depends. . . . Regulate the industry, yes, but at the same time, by laws and public policies . . . invite those who have capital to invest [and] give that investment reasonable security."[189]

Despite a sharp recession in 1937 that bottomed out quickly in 1938, the economy turned around by the end of the decade, primarily because of arms orders from Europe and U.S. government defense spending. A secret document compiled by the Federal Power Commission in 1938 detailed the shortages of electricity the nation would face in case of war. The secret survey estimated that Birmingham would need an additional 222,000 kilowatt hours and that the investment capital needed to build this additional generation capacity in peacetime would be only $1.8 million but in wartime would cost $33.3 million. The document recommended reallocating war orders to industrial plants that were less suitable for production but were located in areas with plenty of electricity and recommended interconnecting the government's Tennessee Valley electricity with existing private investment systems. The report also recommended that utilities be "induced to go ahead with their expansion programs" and means be found to assist them with financing. The report estimated the costs necessary to increase capacity in sixteen cities. Birmingham's estimated cost, $1.8 million, was the lowest of any except Bridgeport, Connecticut.[190] At this time, Alabama Power was serving 635 communities directly, 74 others with wholesale power, with a total population of over two million. Yet, by 1939, Alabama Power had still not reached the revenue level it had achieved in 1929.[191]

No one seemed sorry for the 1930s to be gone. Alabama Power Company had endured through the most severe depression in the nation's history, surviving attacks from demagogues, public power advocates, socialists, and the federal government. Martin had deferred to Wendell Willkie's national leadership during this period, but he remained at the center of resistance in Alabama.

The continued success of the company during the 1930s was a testament to the management group, many of whom had provided leadership for the company since the days of James Mitchell: men such as Marvin P. Randall, who had worked with the finances of the company since 1912; Walter M. Hood, who had served as attorney and then secretary for close to twenty-five years; Thomas Bragg, an Auburn professor and faculty director of athletics who came to the company in 1920 as manager of the company's investment department; James M. Barry, division manager, engineer, and general manager, who was destined to follow Martin as president; Stephen A. Dawley, who had been so dependable and such a trusted manager in the New York office.[192]

There were also the division managers, engineers, local office managers, plant managers, salespeople, shop crews, line crews, home economists, accountants, clerks, secretaries—statewide some 2,000 strong—for whom working for Alabama Power Company was far more than just a job and a paycheck. There were men such as P. P. "Pass" Means, a line crewman since the company first began operations; J. O. "Buddy" Jowers, who started work on April 1, 1912, on the first survey crew at the Lock 12 (Lay Dam) site; and Temple Sanders McGehee, who began in 1919 stringing 44,000-volt line in Huntsville and Decatur and was local manager at Boaz in 1935.[193]

By 1940 Alabama Power had for the moment settled its differences with TVA. The two giant power corporations began to live, if not cordially, at least as cooperative neighbors. From Alabama Power's point of view, however, a threat remained. From time to time there were disagreements, litigation, and congressional action to clearly define the relationship. On July 18, 1940, after years of negotiations, Alabama Power Company sold properties in eleven north Alabama counties to TVA and was compensated $4,268,648.13, "substantially less than the Company's investment in the properties." Other Alabama Power Company facilities were sold to the cities of Scottsboro, Decatur, Hartselle, Fort Payne, Russellville, and Albertville.[194]

Alabama Power Company had been dealing with the Tennessee River and the Shoals area since 1912 when it acquired the Muscle Shoals Hydro-Electric Company. The battle for Muscle Shoals had thrust Alabama Power Company into the national spotlight at a time when there was widespread criticism of investor-owned private utilities. But after almost thirty years, the specter of the Muscle Shoals quit stalking the company, and the Tennessee River ceased consuming a disproportionate amount of time and energy for the leaders and people of the power company. But within Alabama Power deep-seated feelings of resentment remained, and old-timers grieved, as one might for lost family. Some of the company employees went with TVA and some stayed with the new municipal systems. Those men and women who moved to TVA employment were required to sign an oath of loyalty to the Tennessee Valley Authority and to profess support for the concept and aims of public power. Bill Brownlee, who was working for the Tennessee Electric Power Company out of Chattanooga, was one of many Commonwealth & Southern employees who refused to sign. Brownlee took a job with Commonwealth Associates in Jackson, Michigan.[195]

Many Northern Division employees did not wish to leave Alabama Power, and Tom Martin found a new place for them in the company, although Alabama Power had not been hiring because of the depression and at the time these transfers were somewhat of a burden on the company. Alabama Power retiree Ken Winnette's father Rube was in a Northern Division line crew at Huntsville when Ken was born in 1933, then the family moved to Fort Payne. Winnette recalled that "Mr. Martin invited every family to come to the power company building, and he told the employees they could stay with the power company or go with the co-ops or TVA, and Daddy chose to stay with the power company. We moved to Pell City." Over two decades later, after he left the military, Winnette asked his uncle Walter R. Winnette what he should do with his life. His uncle replied, "Just like me and your daddy, go with the power company."[196]

Looking back, irreconcilable philosophical differences, politics, personalities, sectionalism, a deep-seated hostility to investor-supported private utilities, campaigns with demagoguery that took advantage of weaknesses in the system, and unethical practices in other companies in other areas prevented cooperative programs between private enterprise and the federal government in northern Alabama and the Tennessee Valley. Cooperative programs between the federal government and private utilities, particularly Alabama Power Company, projects that would have included navigation and flood control and could also have included soil conservation and education, would have resulted in savings for customers, stockholders, and taxpayers. And the Tennessee River would have been conquered perhaps more than two decades earlier.

Joe Farley recalls a train trip he made one winter afternoon traveling home from Knoxville to Birmingham. As a young attorney in the 1950s, Farley had accompanied "Mr. Martin to a meeting with the directors of TVA." Farley remembered Martin being talkative that evening and reminiscing about the early days of Alabama Power and the fight to defend the company from TVA encroachment. Farley has forever regretted that he took no notes, but he will always remember one surprising thing Martin shared. Looking out the window at the rapidly passing southern countryside he loved so much, Martin said: "No private company alone could have found the capital to develop the entire Tennessee River."[197]

Map of the Alabama Power transmission and distribution system in 1942.
TVA had taken over most of Alabama Power's Northern Division by 1940.

Chapter Six

Mitchell Dam crew, ca. 1940.
Courtesy of O. J. McGriff.

DEFENSE, WAR INDUSTRIES, AND THE FORMATION OF THE SOUTHERN COMPANY

In the economics of electric power there is wise company and there is unwise. This history includes both.

THOMAS W. MARTIN, *The Story of Electricity in Alabama*, 1952

Tom Martin once said that as soon as the Tennessee Valley Authority developed customers for its electricity, things would be better. In September 1939, world events determined that point would come sooner than it might have. America was so preoccupied with its own economic problems in the 1930s that little attention was paid to the rise of Italy's Benito Mussolini or to the more dangerous dictatorship of Adolph Hitler, who began to rearm Germany in violation of the treaty that ended World War I. To Alabamians, the expansion of the Japanese in Asia seemed a world away. Isolationist sentiment was strong, but the Roosevelt administration quietly began to increase the size of the U.S. military, improve its facilities and equipment, and generally strengthen the nation's defense, projects that needed lots of electricity. Some of the dollars for defense flowed into Alabama through the Works Progress Administration (WPA) and later the Public Works Administration (PWA). In August 1939, with Europe on the brink of war, Alabama Power Company was indirectly part of a PWA controversy that involved the governor and the state legislature.

Governor Bibb Graves, a strong supporter of the New Deal, had given Alabama Power grief during his two nonconsecutive terms. Constitutionally, Graves was barred from being a candidate for reelection, but he intended to make his last year difficult for the power company. In February 1938 the media reported that Governor Graves was "repeatedly [conferring] with Alabama Power Company's Tom Martin." Rumors, mostly tongue-in-cheek, circulated that Graves was "figuring on taking over the Alabama Power Company and putting the state into the kilowatt business," except no one could see where Graves could get the money.[1] During his two administrations, conservatives attacked Graves because of the large number of state jobs he promised and delivered to friends and supporters, a situation that moved Jefferson County senator James A. Simpson to write the state's first merit law. The governor's cronies were called the "pie men" or "the pie eaters."[2] Major Squirm, author of a humorous political column for the pro-business news magazine *Alabama,* reported that his wife thought that under Graves's power plan "the pie eaters would be put in charge of the power plants and transmission lines." In that event, the major responded, he was heading "to Camden to borrow one of [former governor] Benjamin Meek Miller's kerosene lamps."[3] By February 14 it was revealed what the governor really wanted from Tom Martin: Alabama Power Company to reduce its rates "to the TVA 'yardstick' level without a reduction in its taxes—[the] highest in the state."[4]

In 1939 Frank Dixon, a Birmingham attorney who was allied with business interests, became governor and was more understanding of the power company's tenuous financial position. The company's securities were depressed because of the surrounding competition from PWA-financed municipal systems, from REA-financed cooperative systems, and the uncertainty of whether the company would be compensated when municipal or cooperative operations duplicated its distribution lines.[5] During Dixon's first legislative session, Henry H. Booth, a petroleum distributor from Anniston, introduced a senate bill that required municipal electric systems to acquire existing systems by fair compensation and detailed how value was to be determined. The legislature passed and Governor Dixon approved the law, which went into effect on August 18, 1939. The bill was clearly written to protect Alabama Power Company "from duplication of its facilities by cities and TVA without the equivalent of condemnation proceedings which [meant] compensation for the dispossession." By this law, municipal systems were required "to follow certain procedures before the Alabama Public Service Commission."[6]

On August 24, PWA administrator John M. Carmody, who had come to his position the month before from the Rural Electrification Administration, wired Governor Dixon from Washington and demanded that the "Booth law" be immediately repealed. Carmody was not unknown to Dixon, for in February and March the REA administrator had tangled with the governor over the legislature's postponement of an electric cooperative bill.[7] This time, Governor Dixon sent Attorney General T. S. "Buster" Lawson to the capital to explain to Carmody that the Booth law related only to businesses engaged in distribution of electricity and no other programs, and it exempted all municipal systems approved by voters before August 18. On September 2, Carmody told the governor that Alabama's PWA total was $14.5 million in 118 projects, including the Jefferson Hospital in Birmingham, the "marine tunnel" (later named the Bankhead Tunnel) in Mobile, and several dormitories on college campuses. He threatened that if the law was not amended, he would cut off all PWA funds to the state. Although Carmody wrote Dixon that he would be convinced of the state's position should a court of competent jurisdiction rule that other PWA projects were exempt, the federal administrator's attitude failed to change when the circuit court in Mobile ruled exactly that way.[8] Carmody admitted his main concerns were Bessemer and Tarrant City, which would be served by TVA's line. Their PWA loans had been based on extending their distribution lines and taking over Alabama Power Company's industrial customers outside the city limits of these towns.[9]

Grover Hall, the award-winning editor of the *Montgomery Advertiser*, attacked Carmody in an editorial claiming that a "grotesque bureaucrat" was trying to "blackmail the legislature and the governor of Alabama" on a law that was "an honest, fair and decent measure by any test." Hall called Carmody "fanatical," "a left-wing zealot with reference to the subject of public ownership of electric power plants," and an "unreasoning extreme radical," who, Hall wrote, "looks like a catfish wearing specs."[10] A student of Hall's journalism career called the editor a "long-time Alabama Power Company partisan," which was a huge turnaround from the editorial attacks the company had suffered in the 1920s. President Roosevelt intervened and invited Hall to Washington to discuss the issues, but Hall insisted that his displeasure was "more on Carmody's uninvited, flagrant interference in state affairs than against the substance of Carmody's proposal."[11]

The Carmody amendments, which the state legislature hurriedly wrote into a new law, excluded "all projects on which federal loans, grants or commitments have been made." The wording satisfied the Alabama League of Municipalities, the Public Service Commission, and Alabama Power Company.[12] Carmody did not achieve a victory because the main protection for the power company's investments, which the Booth law provided, remained, and the law was good for Alabama Power. The company's financial position improved, and it was able to secure funding for expansion. On the day the law went into effect, Alabama Power announced it would build a new $4 million steam plant at Chickasaw to serve the Mobile area. This would be the first of three 40,000-kilowatt units planned, a plant that would back up the $1.8 million high-tension line from Jordan Dam to Mobile. The Chickasaw plant filled, for a while, the city's critical need for electricity.[13]

The Carmody conflict shared the front pages of Alabama newspapers with unsettling reports and photographs from Europe. German tanks rolled into Poland on September 1, while Nazi planes bombed Warsaw. World War II had begun. The U.S. stock market surged higher on September 5, with cotton prices soaring on wartime demands. Nazi troops moved into Warsaw on the seventh, and President Roosevelt announced a national emergency on September 8. On September 10, the Seaboard Railroad announced that it had placed a rail order with Tennessee Coal, Iron and Railroad Company, which was TCI's largest rail order to that time. TCI was an Alabama Power industrial customer.[14] The amount of electricity used in the Birmingham district for the last six months of 1939 reached record kilowatts. All seventeen blast furnaces were operating at 90 percent capacity and all steel mills at 95 percent capacity.[15]

World War II was a global conflict that in many ways affected the South more than the Civil War had. The war was a twentieth-century watershed event that changed the lives of the state's people and set in motion economic, political, and social changes that drastically altered the history of Alabama.[16] In explaining the effect of World War II on the South, *Fortune* magazine waxed eloquent, explaining that the military needs of the war "burst over the walls of regional protectionism and poured in fertilizing rivers of money such as the South had never seen before."[17] Over the course of the war, almost a billion dollars of federal and private money were pumped into Alabama, and full employment was reached.[18] The enormous commitment of federal funds in Alabama boosted

War increased the demand for steel and electricity as Alabama industries began to convert to arms production.

economic development, and the demands for electricity soared in the company's service area. Furthermore, Alabama Power Company, as well as its employees and their families, made inordinate contributions to the American war effort. Ironically, the numerous in-house accounts of the development of electricity in the state and the testimonies and histories of Alabama Power Company pass over the World War II years with a few sentences.

The state of Alabama was in an excellent position to benefit from spending on defense. The state had a strong Democratic congressional delegation that was influential at the White House and knowledgeable about parliamentary procedures to make sure Alabama received its fair share of federal expenditures. The state's mild climate and its flat Black Belt cotton lands were perfect for air-bases and touch-and-go flight training fields. Alabama had rivers for transportation and industry, minerals and steel mills in Birmingham, a port on the Gulf coast, and a shipbuilding industry in Mobile. The state had people who needed jobs, and Alabama had plenty of electricity. Alabama Power Company put its industrial development program into high gear and began internal planning for various contingencies. Thomas D. Johnson, head of new industries recruitment, encouraged Alabamians to push for defense industries because agriculture was so depressed. He noted that in 1927 the South harvested cotton from 40 million acres to sell at 20 cents a pound, but in 1939 just 25 million acres had been planted and cotton was selling at only 10 cents a pound.[19]

For the twenty-four months before war broke out, the state had benefited from national spending on defense and private investments. In 1937 the Tennessee Coal, Iron and Railroad Company invested $29 million in its Fairfield facilities, and the Aluminum Ore Company built a $5 million plant in Mobile. In 1940 Hollingsworth & Whitney constructed a $6 million plant and Gulf Shipbuilding Corporation a $3 million facility, both in Mobile. The federal government spent $4.5 million on a flight training school in Montgomery. In 1941 Alabama Drydocks invested $2 million to improve its shipbuilding capability, and Landsdowns Steel & Iron Company in Gadsden put $7 million in a plant to produce steel shells. The U.S. Army expended $8 million at Anniston Ordnance Depot, $3 million in a flight school in Selma, and $15 million in Brookley

Drydocks in Mobile during wartime, ca. 1942. Courtesy of the ADDSCO Collection, University of South Alabama Archives.

Field in Mobile, the only army air depot with a port for ocean shipping. The Army Air Corps spent several million dollars constructing flying schools in Dothan and Tuskegee. The Alabama Ordnance Works in Childersburg started manufacturing smokeless powder and TNT in facilities that cost $75 million. The federal Office of Production Management reported on October 20, 1941, that between June 1940 and September 1941, $485,906,000 was invested in defense contracts and awards in the state of Alabama and that Alabama was seventeenth in the nation in total defense spending.[20] Most of this investment was in Alabama Power Company's service area.[21]

During these years there were other new Alabama industries that manufactured or produced various products—shirts, socks, tung oil, textiles, coal, gravel, veneers, creosote, furniture, manganese, ribbons—as well as various food processing plants.[22] When Governor Bibb Graves took credit for the location of the Hollingsworth & Whitney plant in Mobile, *Alabama* magazine quickly gave the credit to "the two tenacious Thomases of Alabama's heaviest-taxed utility," referring to Tom Martin and Thomas D. Johnson, Alabama Power's industrial recruiter.[23]

The high esteem in which the company's industrial development program was held is illustrated by a letter Mobile district congressman Frank W. Boykin wrote to a man named Edward J. Harding on July 3, 1940, regarding the possible location of unnamed but important defense "projects" in Alabama. Boykin had met with Harding and several of his friends the night before to discuss locating this new industry in Alabama. Boykin sent a copy of his Harding letter to Governor Dixon and wrote on it "No publicity yet." In his letter, the congressman wrote that after the visit he "wired one of the livest wires in Alabama, Mr. T. D. Johnson, head of the New Industries Division of the Alabama Power Company, and told him what you and I talked about. In my judgment, the Alabama Power Company, and especially Mr. Johnson, has done more to bring new industries to Alabama than any other concern, and they have more information at their disposal relating to the possibilities of the various sites for every type of project in Alabama than any other organization." Boykin told Harding that while he was dictating the letter, Johnson called him long distance from Birmingham and said he was willing to come to Washington, D.C., immediately or whenever Harding wished to speak with him.[24]

INTERNATIONAL BROTHERHOOD OF ELECTRICAL WORKERS

In October 1940 Alabama Power Company recognized the International Brotherhood of Electrical Workers as the collective bargaining agent and negotiated a contract for those "covered employees" at the generating plants. This action came after the passage of the Wagner National Labor Relations Act of 1935 and a negative vote against the IBEW in late fall of 1937. The National Labor Relations Board conducted the 1937 election in the Alabama Power Company generating plants to determine whether or not the "field employees engaged in operation, maintenance, and construction" desired to be represented by the IBEW. Operating vice president E. W. Robinson reminded supervisors that the decision was "strictly up to the employees" and that the company and its "principal supervisors are forbidden to do anything to influence the outcome of the elections." Robinson wrote that the company intended "to be scrupulously careful in this respect" and expected its department heads and supervisors to do likewise and "avoid even the appearance of attempting to influence the result."[25]

The election, under the supervision of the National Labor Relations Board, was held over three days—November 29, 30, and December 1, 1937—to determine if employees of Alabama Power wanted the International Brotherhood of Electrical Workers as their representative for the purpose of collective bargaining.[26] The tabulation was certified by Charles H. Logan, regional director, National Labor Relations Board. The vote was 635 against the union and 551 for the IBEW.[27] Although two new groups, the Alabama Power Employees' Association and the Independent Union of Alabama Power Employees, were organized to represent company employees, by the fall of 1940 it was evident from company surveys that about 70 percent of the employees of the generating plants were members of the IBEW. At this point, Alabama Power recognized the IBEW as the bargaining agent, refused to recognize the two company groups, and on October 25, 1940, began negotiations on a working agreement with the IBEW.[28]

James M. Barry presided at these meetings, welcomed the representatives of the IBEW, and expressed hope that the discussions would reach an early agreement. J. R. May represented the IBEW in the talks. Many of the issues submitted by the union were completely acceptable to the company, some items needed modification, and a few points the company could not accept. The closed shop and certain overtime provisions were two concepts the company opposed. The talks went well and were amicable. Union leader May observed that "It seems we are closer together than we may have realized." Agreements were reached on seniority, holidays, company-funded group life insurance for employees who were with the company for six months, and the provision that no employees would be forced to live in company housing, but if they did, rental rates were established in the agreement.[29]

In the nation, the pro-union New Deal political climate, the passage of the Wagner Act, and the coming of World War II strengthened union organizing drives and altered the balance of power between capital and labor. When Alabama Power began the 1940 negotiations with the IBEW, it was decades after the IBEW had negotiated with other companies, which later formed Georgia Power, and it was after Mississippi Power, Gulf Power, and South Carolina Power all had contracts with the IBEW.[30] One of the driving forces of union support was adequate safety programs. Working with electricity is dangerous without safety precautions. From the beginning, Alabama Power had stressed safety programs, but James Mitchell gave more attention to safety after his nephew, Nathaniel William Tileston, was killed after coming into contact with a live wire. Anna Mitchell Tileston's son was twenty years old and a "finished electrician" who had been working with Alabama Power at the Gadsden Steam Plant for three years.[31]

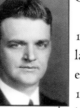

Hobart McWhorter, ca. 1940.
Courtesy of Harold Williams.

Attorney Hobart McWhorter played an important role in the 1940 labor negotiations. He was the company's expert on federal laws regarding unions, wages, and hours, and he was so fair that he earned the praise and respect of the IBEW and its members.[32] The 1940 agreement was renegotiated in 1942, when issues of seniority, job descriptions, and titles were updated and more jobs were covered under the contract.[33]

Alabama in 1939–1940

When World War II began in 1939, Alabama agriculture was much weaker than industry. The summer had been too wet and many crops were ruined. A farmer, E. C. Boswell, complained to Governor Dixon on September 30 that the yield of cotton, peanuts, food, and feed stuff would not allow farmers to pay bankers and merchants for fertilizer or their furnishings. He asked the governor to find jobs for farmers driving trucks or working on roads, anything for wages. Greensboro gin owner Madison Jones complained about his minimum electrical charge, writing that he was "not a fanatic against the Alabama Power Company," but with the cotton crop lost, he could not pay his base electrical bill because he had so little cotton to gin.[34] Alabama Power Company had revived its 1916 cotton gin rate, Schedule "L," in the summer of 1933 because of poor crops and depression conditions. The Alabama Public Service Commission approved the rate reduction on August 29, 1933, in time for the ginning season, but the monthly charge of $1.75 per horsepower installed and three cents per kilowatt hour was still too much for some gin companies with the crop so devastated in 1939.[35]

While Alabama agriculture tried to recover, war raged in Europe in 1940. Germany invaded the Low Countries in May, France fell in June, and the Battle of Britain began in August. That year Electric Bond & Share Company compiled a report on the significant role that electric utilities would play in national defense. Everyone used the term "national defense" because the nation's attitude was one of neutrality but preparedness in case of attack. Even so, the more knowledgeable and realistic appraisals indicated the United States would eventually become involved in the war. The EBASCO report pointed out that "utility electric power generating capacity of all kinds in the United States at the end of 1939 was 53,750,000 horsepower, 87 percent of which was owned by private power companies." Germany had 11,150,000 horsepower and the British Isles had 11,880,000 horsepower. EBASCO expected 2,650,000 horsepower to come online in the United States during 1940 and anticipated another 5 million horsepower being added by 1942. In 1939, when the war began in Europe, Commonwealth & Southern accelerated its increase in generating capacity to meet wartime production needs.[36] Private utility companies assured the public that through interconnection, decentralization of generating stations, and the pooling of electrical resources, they absolutely could provide for the nation's need for electricity to run defense industries and military bases.

Willkie and the Presidential Campaign of 1940

As early as the fall of 1939, Commonwealth & Southern president Wendell Willkie was being mentioned as a possible presidential candidate. Willkie's "success in 'hardball' negotiation with Ickes, Lilienthal, and Roosevelt gave him a national name and was the foundation for his presidential nomination."[37] Willkie quietly changed his party registration to Republican and gathered a group of dedicated supporters who planned his campaign for the Republican nomination. When the Republican convention opened in Philadelphia on June 24, which was two days after the fall of France, it was uncertain whether Roosevelt would go against tradition and run for a third term. The events in Europe hurt Republican isolationists, and in a crowded field of nine candidates and several favorite sons, Willkie won the Republican nomination, a feat columnist H. L. Mencken thought a miracle. The selection of a Wall Street public utilities man at the top of the ticket was balanced by the vice-presidential selection, progressive farm advocate Charles L. McNary, who had sided with public power as a senator. Roosevelt assessed Willkie as the strongest possible opponent but was relieved that Willkie's foreign policy views eliminated the European war as a campaign issue.[38]

Former Commonwealth
& Southern president,
now Republican
candidate Wendell
Willkie in hometown
Elwood, Indiana, as
he opens his campaign
against President
Roosevelt on August
17, 1940. Courtesy of
the Associated Press.

In July the Democrats nominated Roosevelt on the first ballot after a care-fully managed "spontaneous surge." On July 8 Willkie resigned as president of Commonwealth & Southern. The C&S board of directors met on July 17 and selected Justin R. Whiting to replace him. Whiting was an attorney who had been associated with B. C. Cobb in Michigan and was brought to New York in 1933 when Willkie moved into the executive position.[39] Cobb and his attorney, John C. Weadock, had watched Whiting, a "methodical intro-vert," for some time. Whiting would preside over the eventual dissolution of Commonwealth & Southern, an event that neither Cobb, Weadock, nor Willkie would live to see.[40]

In the election Willkie was strongly supported by investor-owned utili-ties and business interests and by old-line isolationists, who found him less objectionable than Roosevelt. After Willkie succeeded Tom Martin as C&S president, *Powergrams* frequently reprinted Willkie's speeches and reported on his honors and activities, but there was no endorsement in the 1940 election. Willkie ran a good race, but in his bid for a third term Roosevelt handily defeated him; however, Willkie generated 22.3 million votes, the largest ever for a Republican candidate and a total not matched until Dwight Eisenhower's 1952 campaign.[41]

There is every reason to believe that Tom Martin strongly supported Willkie's 1940 race with campaign contributions and personal activities, but he would have been very discreet. In Alabama only Democrats held state and local offices, and Martin had to deal with them. In 1944, when his former C&S boss again ran for the Republican nomination before withdrawing in late spring, Martin's correspondence with Willkie illustrates their comfortable friendship as well as Martin's close communication with Claude O. Vardaman, Alabama's Republican State Committee chairman, who worked for Birmingham Electric Company. On April 7, 1944, Martin wrote "Dear Wendell" expressing his hope that Willkie would join with others and help "elect a Republican President."[42] Willkie replied, thanking him for his "constant support throughout the years."[43] In August after Willkie suffered a heart attack, Martin sent his friend get well wishes but chided him for not taking a stronger domestic stand against the Democrats in a recent article in *Collier's* magazine. On October 2, Willkie's secretary acknowledged the receipt of Martin's letter, which she promised to bring to Willkie's "attention within the next few days." She never had the opportunity. Following three more massive heart attacks, in the early morning hours of October 8, 1944, Willkie died at the age of fifty-two.[44]

Willkie's last act as Commonwealth & Southern chief executive officer had occurred on May 31, 1940, when he filed a thirty-six-page brief with the Securities and Exchange Commission questioning the constitutionality of the Wheeler-Rayburn Public Utility Holding Company Act.[45] The act had been challenged in the courts by a number of holding companies, but the one filed by Electric Bond & Share became the test case. The Supreme Court ruled in 1938 by sustaining a lower court ruling that holding companies had to register with the Securities and Exchange Commission, but the Supreme Court failed to rule on the constitutionality of the "death sentence."[46] As the SEC and utilities holding companies debated the meaning of various portions of the law and the SEC took testimony, time moved inexorably on.

At the far end of the table, Wendell Willkie presides at his last board meeting as president of Commonwealth & Southern, July 1, 1940. Tom Martin, fifth from the right, has pushed back from the table and is the only man not looking at the camera, as if to distance himself from the board. Eugene Yates is second from the right on the left side of the table.

After war began in Europe, someone woke up to the fact that the United States was making preparations to defend itself, that defense industries were being built all over the country, and that they needed a lot of reliable electricity. The nation very likely would soon be involved in war. Perhaps it was not a good idea *right now* to move into the unknown and break up the nation's smoothly functioning investor-owned power systems. The events at Pearl Harbor at the end of 1941 reinforced the point. Although testimony was taken and investigations conducted by the Securities and Exchange Commission throughout the war years and C&S court filings delayed action, the division of Commonwealth & Southern would come some years after the war was over.[47]

MITCHELL DAM—ORIGINAL COST BY THE FEDERAL POWER COMMISSION

One provision, Section 4 (a), of the Federal Power Act that established the Federal Power Commission allowed the commission to determine the original construction cost of a dam in order to determine if the returns on investment were in line with that cost. Mitchell Dam was the first Alabama Power dam constructed under the Federal Water Power Act of 1920 and one of the first in the nation to come under this act. Alabama Power filed an itemized statement that the cost of Mitchell Dam (known as Project No. 82) was $10,646,056.76. The Federal Power Commission took testimony and investigated the items and figures that Alabama Power had detailed as the cost of construction of Mitchell, as well as Martin and Jordan Dams. R. E. Howard Jr., Alabama Power auditor, testified to the company's costs in 1920–29, and George D. Woods of First Boston, earlier vice president of Harris, Forbes & Company when he was working with Alabama Power on bond sales, testified to the cost of money in the 1920s. On March 29, 1930, the Federal Power Commission disallowed almost $4 million from Alabama Power's cost.[48]

The company protested and appealed. Alabama Power's case was presented by Perry W. Turner, Walter Bouldin, W. M. Moloney, and W. D. Lavender to the U.S. District Court of the District of Columbia. Figures at controversy were a $3.5 million fixed capital item, a general administrative cost to Alabama Power of $171,028.98, a $375 expense charge by W. J. Henderson (who was then the secretary-treasurer of Alabama Traction, Light & Power Company), and a bill for $750 from a consulting firm. The questioning of a $375 expense in a $10 million project illustrates the detail with which the Federal Power Commission accountants went into each item. The appeal was heard first in the U.S. District Court, then that decision on the original cost of construction of Mitchell Dam was appealed to the U.S. Court of Appeals of the District of Columbia. In the decision on *Alabama Power Company v. McNinch et al., Federal Power Commission*, which was rendered September 27, 1937, Alabama Power won some of its arguments, and the case was sent back to the Federal Power Commission, which issued an order on November 26, 1940, with Mitchell cost assessed at $7,098,512.51. Another appeal resulted in an original cost of $7,209,363,99.[49]

World War II

On December 29, 1940, in a fireside chat, President Roosevelt called the American nation "the great arsenal of Democracy" and recommended that the United States send aid to Great Britain. In March 1941 the Lend-Lease Act, which eventually funneled $14 billion in aid to the Allies, began to stimulate the economy in Alabama.[50] In the two years before the Japanese attack on the United States territory of Hawaii, Alabama Power suffered increases in its operational expenses because severe drought reduced the use of hydro production and forced the company to generate more electricity at its coal-fired steam plants. In 1940 there was an 18.5 percent increase in operational expenses, which was one of the causes of a decrease in net income of 26.7 percent. In 1941 there was a 24.85 percent increase in operational expenses, but increased sales produced a net income increase of 17.2 percent.[51]

The great drought of 1941 almost stopped hydro generation at Lake Martin. Courtesy of the National Archives and Records Administration, College Park, Maryland. [Record 114-P ALA -D2 -93"]

The two years of drought and the demands of expanding defense industries depleted the Lake Martin reservoir. Bill Crouch, then the superintendent at Martin Dam, recalled that the water was so low you could walk out to the twelfth and thirteenth gates.[52] All state rivers were running low. In 1941 hydro plants had decreased production 5.57 percent, and steam and purchased energy increased

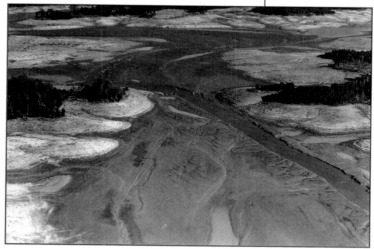

50.02 percent. Kilowatt-hour sales were up 17.46 percent. Because electricity was needed by defense industries, in May 1941 customers were requested to voluntarily reduce their use of electricity so "that larger amounts of energy might be supplied for certain essential war purposes." In the summer the state went on daylight saving time in order to conserve electricity; however, the shortage of electricity escalated, especially since Alabama Power was sending "substantial quantities of off-peak power to TVA to manufacture aluminum."[53]

Germany attacked Russia in June 1941, and during the autumn the U.S. relationship with Japan continued to deteriorate. On October 30, 1941, the Priorities Division of the Office of Production Management "announced a power conservation program designed to assure full and uninterrupted operation of defense plants in the Southeast." Pooling of power became mandatory to avoid a real crisis. General rains in November delayed the implementation of the order, but the government imposed conservation of electricity until all reservoirs were filled.[54] Demand for power kept gross sales high, but return on investment was not as good as it should have been because of the cost of coal-fired steam generation.

The drought conditions and electrical shortages in the spring of 1941 gave a sense of urgency to hearings before the Corps of Engineers on possible hydroelectric and navigational development of the Coosa-Alabama Rivers. In 1939 Senator Lister Hill proposed that the U.S. Army Corps of Engineers try to negotiate some cooperative program with Alabama Power and Georgia Power for the Coosa. If the companies refused, Hill suggested that the federal government and the state of Alabama develop the Coosa alone.[55] The *Alabama Journal* favored adding locks to Alabama Power Company dams and building other dams and locks on the upper Coosa to provide a nine-foot channel from Rome, Georgia, to Mobile.[56] During the spring and fall of 1941, development of the Coosa was again discussed in Washington. J. W. Worthington, the former vice president of Alabama Power who wrote the Ford proposal for Muscle Shoals, was now eighty-five years old and living in a rustic cabin at Tate Springs, Tennessee. He was in constant communication with Alabama senator Lister Hill. Worthington was unsure of Hill's views, but he was determined to influence him. When Senator George Norris introduced legislation to expand TVA to the Cumberland River, Worthington advised Hill to use this move as a threat "to shock the Alabama and Georgia Power Companies into real cooperation on the Alabama-Coosa." Worthington recommended that Hill "at the most appropriate moment . . . let slip . . . [that] you propose to add the Alabama-Coosa to the TVA also."[57] Hill did suggest the idea to David Lilienthal, but the TVA director wired the senator that it would require an amendment to the TVA basic act, "and [I] believe you will agree this [is] not feasible to secure at this time."[58]

Hill wrote J. R. Hornaday, the chairman of the Coosa-Alabama River Improvement Association, who was pressing the Alabama senator for action.

On May 29, 1941, Hill suggested that "if we could get the Coosa-Alabama River embraced in the plans of the Tennessee Valley Authority for immediate construction of dams and production of power to meet the needs of the national defense, it would not be long before we would have the development of the River which we so devoutly wish for."[59] Hill arranged for Worthington to check out a copy of the Corps of Engineers' Review of Reports on the Coosa, and Worthington sent Hill an exhaustive analysis that formed the basis of Hill's inquiry into the matter. Worthington had doubts that Alabama Power would cooperate, despite the testimony of the company's vice president for public relations and advertising, Thomas Bragg, before the engineering board of review that the company would.[60]

In one letter, Worthington criticized TVA for not paying attention to "the Dry Season Records on the Tennessee and Coosa" that showed "during the extreme low water years even the normal demand for power can not be supplied by hydro-power." He wrote that "all this sad situation on the Tennessee is due to the neglect of the TVA in not building the reservoirs which must be built in order to operate the mainstream power stations in very dry weather." Worthington went on to write that "you will not disagree with me that there is very reproachful irony in the TVA showing motion pictures of its national defense contributions when the only contribution it is making or can make is power and these power stations so boastfully shown in the motion picture are idle because of the absence of reserve reservoir capacity."[61] These comments are particularly interesting because the studies made by Washburn, Worthington, and Mitchell in the period 1906–16 had reached these same conclusions about the low water problems of the Tennessee watershed and were exactly why they planned to connect the Muscle Shoals and Cherokee Bluffs dams to the same system.

Worthington was adamant that the dams on the Coosa were as important to national defense as the two reservoirs above the Hiwassee Dam in western North Carolina, and he believed Hill could get the Coosa dams approved under some sort of "emergency authority."[62] In May and June, Worthington pressed Hill to come to Tate Springs, Tennessee, for a conference. Hill wrote Worthington that the Federal Power Commission had gone over the engineering reports and believed that the Coosa could produce not one billion kilowatt hours but two. Hill promised Worthington that "we are going to build this Coosa yet and we are going to put a Worthington Dam on it."[63] Alabama Power was unaware of the contents of the correspondence between Hill and Worthington.

The National Rivers and Harbors Congress met in Miami in mid-November 1941. One topic of discussion was the development of the Coosa River. The convention endorsed improvements to the Coosa River and the addition of more hydro facilities, which were given emergency status by the group. The chairman of the Gadsden City Commission, J. Herbert Meighan, attended as the representative of Governor Frank Dixon and presented a resolution for federal funding for the Coosa, noting that five defense plants were being constructed on its banks. All of Alabama Power Company's dams on the Coosa had been designed so the federal government could add locks, but locks had not been added because the demand for industrial shipping on the Coosa never reached a level to justify the expenditure. No development of the Coosa came during the war, but in March 1945, a month before he died, President Roosevelt signed a Rivers and Harbors bill that promised $500 million after the war for improvement of the nation's rivers, including $60 million allotted to Alabama's Coosa River development. This 1945 act included a clause that prohibited the Federal Power Commission from licensing any private enterprise dams on the Coosa. Senator Hill's commitment to federal development and the expansion of TVA was behind the provision, which would have to be repealed before Alabama Power could develop its original Coosa plan.[64]

The entrance of the United States into the war after the attack on Pearl Harbor in December 1941 put the Coosa River development on hold, and defense plants in the Coosa Valley had to rely on railroads for shipping. Additional Coosa dams would have to wait until after the war was over.[65] J. W. Worthington, who had such an active role in the early development of hydroelectric power in Alabama and later turned against the Alabama Power Company, never lived to see the completion of the Coosa River hydroelectric development. Worthington died at Tate Springs on April 4, 1942. The urn containing his ashes was "deposited in the Tennessee River above Wilson Dam."[66] A few days after his death, his friend E. A. de Funiak noted that "It is somewhat startling how closely the TVA development followed Worthington's plan."[67]

As the company geared up to respond to the war crisis, it also mourned the passing of three of its early leaders. The founder and first president of Alabama Power Company, Captain William Patrick Lay, died on November 21, 1940. Lay had been involved with Coosa River improvements long before others were interested, and his lifetime had spanned decades of remarkable economic advancement in his native state.[68] Richard Martin Hobbie, Montgomery businessman, onetime manager of the Alabama State Docks, and a director of the company since February 1920, passed away on December 24, 1940. On February 16, 1941, the company lost Frank M. Moody, who had served as a director for more than twenty years. Martin praised Moody's wide experience and "calm, deliberate, unselfish judgment" as contributions to the company's growth and development.[69]

Before the war was over, on October 30, 1943, Thomas Bragg died in Houston, Texas, following an emergency operation. He had served the company in many positions since 1920 and was at the time of his death vice president in charge of public relations and advertising. Martin noted that Bragg "was known and respected by men and women in every part of Alabama" and his loss would be "keenly felt."[70] In 1946 the company lost George H. Middlemiss, who had come to work for Alabama Power in 1916 and created much of the organizational structure of the company, including establishing the Eastern and Western Divisions. Middlemiss selected and trained the men who held divisional responsibilities and later was manager of production and transmission for the Commonwealth & Southern system. C&S president Justin Whiting noted that Middlemiss "exercised the greatest skill and judgment in the handling of intricate problems arising from the coordination of the integrated power system of the southeast."[71]

For some years, Alabama Power wanted to take advantage of the current very low interest rates and refinance its entire debt. Jacob Hekma, Commonwealth & Southern vice president, advised Tom Martin on June 14, 1940, not to try it. Alabama Power Company bonds were selling too low and had been "stricken from the list of investments legal for savings in New York State because they did not meet the requirements as to times earnings." Under the circumstances, Hekma recommended refinancing steps should be deferred until the bond market generally improved, the TVA sale was completed, and the investment community appreciated that the TVA threat to Alabama Power had been eliminated. He also suggested that the company needed to go through "a period of rising earnings month by month, so that the earnings applicable to interest charges are stabilized to show the requisite times earned." Hekma warned that it was "not a question of one of these factors but of all, if the Alabama Power Company, and I think the time will come when it can, is to refinance on as favorable basis as the northern companies." He advised that at "the present time any refunding is completely out of question if the object is to make a real saving."[72]

As the company moved into 1941, Martin became convinced that refinancing was absolutely essential and some of Hekma's 1940 concerns had disappeared. Alabama Power began "informal discussions" with the Alabama Public Service Commission and the Securities and Exchange Commission on refinancing. The Public Service Commission gave approval after hearings and some adjustment to the plans, and the company proceeded to make a formal application before the Securities and Exchange Commission. Plans moved forward for refinancing to occur sometime at the end of the year. Several Alabama Power Company attorneys, including Walter Bouldin and Chester

A. Bingham, who was then treasurer of the company, were in New York City on Sunday, December 7, 1941, with all the paperwork ready to be passed out Monday morning to the investment syndicates that planned to bid.[73]

Then in the afternoon radios flashed news around the world that the Japanese had attacked Pearl Harbor and the United States was at war. The financial markets were closed on Monday so things could settle down, and the company refinancing was delayed until after the new year. The trust indenture dated January 1, 1942, remained the basic mortgage indenture under which the company's bonds were issued until it was defeased in May 2006.[74] All transactions were completed on January 23, 1942, in New York at the Chemical Bank & Trust Company, and the board of directors meeting in Birmingham adopted the final resolution "calling in all outstanding bonds." The mortgage indenture covered "298 closely printed pages" and the refinancing saved the company $1.4 million a year in interest payments. The *Annual Report* for 1941 expressed appreciation to the Commonwealth & Southern Corporation "for its generosity in contributing the Southeastern Fuel Company securities and 11,302 shares of the Company's preferred stock as additional investment by it in the Company's common stock without the issue of additional shares."[75]

The refinancing depleted the company's surplus. To protect preferred stockholders, the company agreed not to pay any dividend on its common stock except out of earned surplus.[76] The refinancing now enabled Alabama Power Company to acquire the capital it needed for construction of new facilities. For eleven years, poor economic conditions eased the normal growth demands on the company and gave it somewhat of a reprieve from increasing its capacity. From the completion of Thurlow Dam in 1930 to the opening of the Chickasaw 40,000-kilowatt steam plant near Mobile in 1941, the company did not have to build new generation to service increased demands. The reduced load of the depression years and the loss of its customers to TVA in northern Alabama left the company with some surplus generation, but the rapid industrialization for war and military mobilization quickly took up this excess. Eugene Yates remarked that the increased loads "came into existence almost over night."[77] Alabama Power Company was faced with demands for electricity by a defense industry that was rapidly expanding and given service priority by the defense production policies of the United States government. Rural line extensions and nonessential expansions were put on hold. Requests for electricity without a sufficiently high priority were refused.[78]

Mobile was especially a challenge for Alabama Power. The city's population doubled between 1941 and 1944, as thousands of men and women seeking defense production jobs moved to the area. In 1939 the city was furnished with electricity from Jordan Dam and the old downtown steam plant on Royal and St. Louis Streets. In order to meet the anticipated load, Alabama Power built a line from Mitchell Dam on a different route than the line from Jordan. Demands for electricity in Mobile increased 48 percent between 1940 and 1942. The new Alabama Power steam plant at Chickasaw went online in 1941, but longtime company employee Frank S. Keeler, who wrote a brief history of electric service in Mobile, recalled that the load kept increasing. The docks and shipyards, Brookley Field, Alcoa's power-hungry bauxite refining plant at the state docks, and the families that poured into the area placed ever increasing demands on Alabama Power. Another demand came from the new Bankhead Tunnel that connected the Eastern Shore with Mobile and used electricity to operate lights and the large ventilating fans that pulled carbon monoxide from the tunnel. As a result, the company was given priority for supplies to construct another 40,000-kilowatt coal-fired unit at Chickasaw, which doubled the kilowatts at Mobile. This generator went online in 1943.[79]

Birmingham boomed, too, and full employment was reached by 1943. At the beginning of the war, the company was in a strong position in the district because of Gorgas and the hydro facilities. But even these reserves were strained by 1943, because 85 percent of the city's industrial plants had converted to wartime production and many operated three shifts a day. A new blast furnace at TCI increased production 17 percent.[80] Childersburg, before the war a sleepy little town of 500 people and two policemen, suddenly had 600 troops from Fort McClellan guarding its ordnance plants, where some 25,000 men then worked. Few could find accommodations in the community and many commuted down the new Florida Short Route (Highway 280) from Birmingham.[81]

In 1941 the company received a certificate of convenience and necessity from the Public Service Commission to add a unit to the Gorgas Steam Plant, but this unit could not be installed until 1944, partly due to financing. The original Gorgas unit (No. 1) was 20,000 kilowatts; the U.S. government generator built during World War I was 30,000 kilowatts (No. 2). In 1924 a 20,000-kilowatt unit (No. 3) went into service. Four years later the company built a plant across Bakers Creek and installed a 60,000-kilowatt generator (No. 4); and in 1941 a second 60,000-kilowatt generator (No. 5) was added. On September 16, 1944, the new steam plant was formally dedicated to

Unit No. 4 and No. 5 at the 1928 building at Gorgas Steam Plant provided electricity for war industries.

William Crawford Gorgas, whose name was the official name of the post office and had been commonly used for the plant for over two decades. Tom Martin enjoyed a ceremony, but he also used dedications and celebrations to promote and showcase the company's accomplishments and to invite political leaders to speak and participate. The dedication at Gorgas was one of those grand occasions.[82]

The Commonwealth & Southern operating companies were able, because of the close integration and a construction program, to increase their electric output after the outbreak of war. In the twelve months ending on August 31, 1942, the companies produced 5.879 billion kilowatt hours, which was a 30 percent increase over the preceding two years. Between 1941 and 1944, 345,000 kilowatts of additional generating capacity were placed in service. Commonwealth & Southern's CEO Justin Whiting wrote in *Southern Agriculture* that the economic activities in the southern states during the war would "continue to strengthen and develop this section in time of peace" and that the basic ingredient would be electricity.[83] Alabama Power had paid dividends of $2.3 million in 1942 and 1943. Gross and net income had increased.[84]

Alabama Power used many innovations to help increase the supply of electricity. One was a floating power plant on a barge. The barge could be towed where it was needed. The Defense Plant Corporation operated a 30,000-kilowatt generating plant on a barge tied up in Pensacola on the Escambia River, and both Gulf Power and Alabama Power distributed electricity from it. The operation of the generator was directed by R. B. Cowan, who had worked under Rother L. Harris in the Alabama Power production department and who joined the Army Corps of Engineers early in 1943. The idea was to ship these units where extra electricity was needed and eventually to use the barges overseas.[85] With no spare parts and no new electrical supplies, the company's engineers were creative in making do. In Anniston, a twenty-two-unit apartment building, which was needed for military personnel and workers and their families, could not be completed because the meter troughs were designed for socket meters and no socket meters were available. The Anniston district superintendent figured out a way to adapt the existing meter troughs to accept a conventional meter, a solution that was safe and efficient—and used materials worth just fifteen cents.[86]

The Alabama Power Family Goes to War

Beginning in 1940 *Powergrams* became not only a company publication of articles and notices but a way the power company family could stay in touch and informed about the military service of its members. The company printed some copies of *Powergrams* on lightweight paper to mail overseas.[87] Photographs of soldiers and sailors dotted the pages with announcements of who was joining which military branch and where they were going. A large number of the enlistments were from the women of the company. Sara Dickinson, former home economist, became a WAVE, and Mary E. Smith, a Prattville cashier, joined the WAAC (Women's Army Auxiliary Corps). In October 1942 Lillian Brandon from the promotional department was a WAC (Women's Army Corps) on her way to Fort Des Moines, Iowa, for six weeks of training. The daughter of Mobile general foreman J. T. Dill, Evelyn Dill, was a private first class in the WAC, and Louise Powell, an accounting machine operator, learned to fly in the Civilian Pilot Training program at Howard College. Kathleen Landis, who had worked for years in the purchasing department, had one son in Sicily and the other in the Pacific. She enlisted in the military to use her skill at speaking four languages.[88] There were many others from the company who served.

After the attack on Pearl Harbor, enlistments increased. The company's people had skills needed by the military—engineers, linemen, supply personnel, generator experts, and secretaries. Many of its employees went into the Seabees and constructed bases in jungles and deserts, and during battles Alabama Power people often ran telephone lines to connect the front with base commanders. The company established a "separation allowance of two weeks regular pay" for employees with one year of service and one week extra pay for those with more than six months of service with the company.[89] Photographs of servicemen and women in *Powergrams* were numerous, spaced between letters posted from military bases and censored letters mailed from stations close to battlefields and from ships at sea.

Alabama Power's C. C. Teague family had five sons of their seven children in the military. All four sons of the E. C. Miltons of Tallassee were in the service. William Charles Martin Sr., who worked in the meter reading department of the Mobile Division, had three sons, William, Percy, and Fred, and a daughter, Mary Elizabeth, in the military. David C. Akins, the assistant storekeeper at Gorgas, had five sons in the army and navy.[90] Ed Thompson was thrown into the Battle of the Bulge in January 1945.[91] Clarence H. Wilson, once an Alabama Power serviceman at Greensboro, was now in charge of three refrigerator plants in the Fiji Islands. Mel Pratt of Fairfield brought in a photograph of his nephew standing in front of a tent with a large sign that read "ALABAMA POWER COMPANY, NEW GUINEA SUB-STATION, DIVISION MGR., R. S. WHITE, JR." Captain J. R. Watson called his generation unit at an unknown site in the Pacific "The Off-and-On-Power Company."[92]

Alabama Power Company, "New Guinea Sub-Station," ca. 1944.

Lieutenant Colonel H. Neely Henry, who left for military service from the industrial development office, was awarded the croix de guerre with palm and the Bronze Star for his leadership during the invasion of France and thirty-seven months overseas. Lieutenant Raphael Elmore Kearns, who was with the Mobile and Atmore district line crews, won the Silver and Bronze Stars fighting at Iwo Jima, Saipan, and Tinian in the Marine Corps. Lieutenant Colonel Thomas H. Vaden, formerly superintendent of the Southern Division, won his medals for "meritorious service" during the Battle of the Bulge. Sergeant Owen W. "Woody" Hocutt wrote to the company from "somewhere in France" and told about his adventures in the war, ending with "and I used to think tree trimming was dangerous!"[93] Some 800 Alabama Power Company employees and others from company families left to serve in World War II. Some did not come home. Bobby Dawkins, son of Martin Dam superintendent R. D. Dawkins, was one of those. Young Dawkins, who was serving in the Army Air Corps, was killed in the South Pacific.[94] The experience of the company family during the war years was a microcosm of the experience of the American people.[95]

A number of things changed at the company during the war. The government ordered that no photographs were to be taken around plants.[96] Military personnel and armed guards watched over steam and hydro plants, waters were restricted around the company's dams, and the rivers and lakes were patrolled by the U.S. Navy or Coast Guard. Jack Minor, who was born at Gorgas and delivered newspapers as a teenager, recalled the guards and the pass he needed to move from one side of Bakers Creek to the other.[97] Employees were issued passes, and all plants were closed to visitors. Locks were changed and key access limited, and thousands of feet of "cyclone fencing" were installed around plants. Special lights were put up at substations and regular floodlights were replaced. There were instructions about air raids, and each office had emergency plans and a general defense organization. The man in charge at the corporate office was E. C. Easter, designated the "police chief." Because Alabama Power had long required its people to be trained in first aid and emergency management, company personnel took leadership roles in their communities across the state. A major test blackout occurred in Birmingham on March 17, 1942, to see how the people could cope in case of enemy attack, and the company studied the effects of the blackout on its load.[98]

The state of Alabama enacted a speed limit of thirty-five miles per hour in order to conserve gasoline, and the company made sure drivers of all trucks and cars understood this restriction. The company collected spare parts and scrap metal and conserved rubber and all supplies. In 1942 it furnished Thomas Bragg as the state chairman of the scrap metal drives and fought a "war on waste," urging ·

workers to work safely and carefully. Some employees began to ride bicycles to work. The company urged its employees to buy war bonds and invested its own reserves in government bonds. Company personnel supported the Red Cross with donations of money and blood. Alabama Power provided fruits, donuts, cookies, and small gifts for soldiers coming through Birmingham's Terminal Station during the Christmas holidays in 1944.[99] The company provided personnel for many civilian volunteer jobs, such as serving on local Selective Service boards and on USO committees and heading up Red Cross drives.

J. F. Hixon, Southern Division agricultural engineer, directed the victory garden activities of the company. Suitable land was located near the company's generating plants, and gardens were planted. Alabama Power sponsored ads in state newspapers that included instructions about raising food, and the company worked closely with the Agricultural Extension Service at Auburn to write the copy for the advertisements. Some of these stories featured the J. S. Sharp family, who moved to a forty-acre farm near Mitchell Dam. Only four of their eleven children were still at home, but they managed to raise chickens, hogs, and cattle and produce oats, peanuts, sweet and Irish potatoes, and fruit from seventy-five trees.[100]

The company constantly was relied upon in emergencies. For instance, the L&N Railroad called with an urgent need for floodlights so its employees could load a large group of troops at night. Lights were installed before dark. Maxwell Field needed a quick rerouting of power lines adjacent to the field without a power loss. Mission accomplished.[101] Soon after the attack on Pearl Harbor, the War Department wrote the company requesting articles, pictures, or materials the company might have on Japan. Margaret F. Johnston, Alabama Power librarian, sent a list of books, and the Military Intelligence Service wrote back requesting the copy of *Fifty Years History of Tokyo Electric Light Company*, which was checked out and mailed. After the war, the book was returned, but no one ever knew whether the dams in the photographs were bombed.[102]

Employment of women increased during the war years to replace men and women who enlisted. Women read meters, assumed more responsibility in the office and in sales, and made more repairs on appliances, a real challenge with no new spare parts available. Georgia Hilliard spent her time at the warehouse, repairing meters. Christine Sorrell was the first woman telephone operator at Magella.[103] On March 16, 1945, Mary Cochran, who had been with the company since 1928 and had served for eleven years as secretary to Walter M. Hood, was elected by the Alabama Power Company board of directors to the position of assistant secretary. She was the first woman elected an officer of the company.[104]

One of the most tragic accidents in the history of Alabama Power Company occurred at Lay Dam at 9:50 A.M. on February 14, 1944, when the No. 4 generator went out of control. Despite safeguards, centrifugal force sent the spinning rotor or flywheel, which weighed 100,000 pounds, reeling through the downstream wall of the powerhouse, tearing a gaping hole and killing three men, Tommy Thomason, William Jerome Vinson, and Macie Jones, and mortally injuring John Jackson. James M. Barry, vice president and general manager, immediately praised the men who died "devoting their best efforts and skill to protecting the property and service of the company" and those who immediately assessed the dangerous situation, took action, and began rendering aid. The rotor was cast in 1913 and a report suggested that "internal flaws in the metal led to disintegration."[105]

Long before the war was over, Alabama Power began to plan for the postwar period. In the fall of 1943 Tom Martin made major addresses across the state. In these speeches he warned that the South must rely on itself to fulfill its goals. He challenged private enterprise to provide the jobs needed to absorb the seven million men and women of the armed forces and the twenty million persons employed in war industries back into the peacetime economy. Martin, who was serving as regional vice chairman for the Committee for Economic Development, urged those present to make plans for the reconversion of plants and factories to peacetime uses.[106] Fernand C. Weiss, an Alabama Power vice president, was chairman of the company's postwar planning committee, which solicited suggestions from every employee.[107] Unfortunately, one tower of strength in the company's industrial development was not around for the challenge. After twenty-seven years of service, Tom Johnson left the industrial development office in the spring of 1943 to take a position with Vanity Fair Mills in Reading, Pennsylvania. He was replaced by John Rush "Pete" Lester, who had been with the company since 1921.[108]

In April 1945, with the war winding down in Europe, Tom Martin sent a letter and questionnaire to each former employee still in the military. He thanked them for their service to the country, saying that "we, at home, have been carrying on in your absence, trying to keep our service ample and up to its usual high standards so that the many war plants we serve will keep on producing the things you need." Martin wrote that as their thoughts turned to peace, he wanted them to know: "We want you back with us; with the plans which we have ahead, and the opportunities for the future which Alabama offers, it seems clear to us that there will be a place for all our former regular employees." Martin thought they might want their old jobs back, but he also recognized that through military service they might have learned new technical skills and developed qualifications more valuable to the company in a "more advanced job." He enclosed a questionnaire he wanted returned to him personally so the company could make plans for the future.[109]

By 1945 *Powergrams* began reporting the return of the company's people and announcing where they were "back on the job." Gorgas especially celebrated the return of First Lieutenant Gladys Ann Mealer, sister of Gorgas locomotive and crane operator R. L. Mealer. A Birmingham native and St. Vincent–trained nurse, Lieutenant Mealer had been captured by the Japanese after the fall of Corregidor and spent the war years in a prison camp in Manila.[110] Returning people noticed one change at the company—the new cafeteria that opened for lunch in December 1944. Employees could select a meat and two vegetables for thirty-five cents, add a piece of pie for another dime and coffee for a nickel. Alabama Power was now providing a group life insurance policy for all full-time employees at no cost to the employee. Benefits were based on length of service and ranged from $500 to a maximum of $2,500. (These benefits, in 1944 dollars, seem small, but by the twenty-first century life insurance benefits had increased twenty-fold.) There was a new retirement plan. Initial discussion began in the fall of 1942, and the plan was approved by the stockholders in August 1944, announced on December 4, 1944, and was made retroactive to July 1.[111] The company would pay the entire cost of the plan, but *Powergrams* warned that it should not be "a substitute for individual thrift."[112] Susie Baxter, who began work in home demonstration in the Northern Division in 1928 and then transferred to the Southeast Division, was the first person to receive a check from the employee pension plan.[113]

Another change returning company employees would notice was the new bill for electric service that was generated on a postcard by mechanical masterminds, machines and people working together on the seventh floor. Holes were punched onto cards and machines read the information and printed it on cards that were addressed and mailed to customers. A series of machines—sorting machines, printing machines, multiplying machines—whizzed cards through at amazing speeds. Systems of double checks made certain the amount of electricity used was moved correctly from the meter reader's card to the machine. It was an amazing process, and employees from other departments came to watch the masterminds at work.[114]

Rural Development

By 1943 the war was going well enough for Tom Martin to predict its end. He wanted to have a jumpstart on his favorite project—rural electrification, a program ended with the start of war and the wartime restrictions on electrical

Walter Baker, center, demonstrates electric farrowing of baby pigs at the Alabama Power Company state fair exhibit in 1947 to S. J. Morris, president of the Alabama Landrace Association, left, and G. B. Phillips from the Alabama Extension Service.

equipment. The company received permission from the War Production Board to cut trees from its own timberlands and set poles in anticipation of the war's end. When materials were available, the company would be ready to string wire and deliver service. The manager of the company's rural and towns divisions, E. C. Easter, called "Pap" by his friends, was given responsibility for developing the program to sign up new customers. Easter recruited Walter Baker and W. A. "Bill" Cochran to implement the project.

Baker, a Birmingham native with a marketing degree from the University of Alabama, came to Alabama Power after briefly working with the U.S. Army on the construction of Redstone Arsenal. He worked in the Eastern Division and moved to Birmingham in 1946. Baker was to spend the rest of his career with the company in a variety of positions but mostly in rural development, sales, and marketing. He was a talented writer and was often called upon to write for *Powergrams*. In 1989 Baker wrote the history of the marketing department, which was published as *Milestones in Marketing*. He recalled spending the World War II years "battling rural cooperatives at home" and surveying and signing up new customers. Bill Cochran grew up in Bessemer, left Auburn with an engineering degree, and was recruited by Easter to develop rural sales. He worked in the engineering department for several years during the war before he and Baker began the rural program.[115]

Baker was assigned Blount County to solicit applications for electric service from prospective customers, J. C. Waller had Etowah County, and Bill Cochran was given Fayette County. These three men worked all week soliciting applications, marked the customers on a large county map, and gave that information to Leon Murray in the engineering department. Murray would then send out crews to lay out the lines for the construction people to set the poles. The program was moved to other counties, where teachers were employed to survey areas during the summer months. In the last two years of the war, some "20,000 poles were cut, treated, and set, enabling thousands of farmers and other rural customers to obtain electric service much earlier than would otherwise have been possible." Tom Martin noted that in developing rural lines the company made its "greatest progress" in any one year in 1947. That year Alabama Power completed 3,078 miles of rural lines and connected 18,043 new customers.[116]

In the twenty-four months following the war's end, Alabama Power had 31,930 new customers being served by 5,591 miles of rural lines. In 1946 Baker and M. B. Penn, manager of rural sales, compiled the company's entry in the Edison Electric Institute's 1947 contest for the Thomas W. Martin Rural Electrification Award. In 1932 Martin had provided funds for the award that honored the utility that accomplished the most for rural electrification and agriculture in its area during the year. In 1947 Alabama Power won the award for the second time.[117] Thereafter the company waived its right to compete for this recognition but continued to participate in other contests that focused on accomplishments in farm electrification, winning several national awards in the ensuing years.[118]

One of the problems Alabama Power faced in bringing electricity to the state's farms was that so many of the farmers were tenants or sharecroppers. In 1946, company surveys reported that a high percentage of farm dwellings along existing lines had not been wired and therefore could not be connected for service because neither the landlord nor the tenant was willing to wire the house. In many cases competent electricians were unavailable in rural areas and the company's rural engineers had to assume responsibility. To address this problem, Bill Cochran wrote an instructive handbook, *Electricity for the Farm*, that explained wiring in simple language. This handbook became a text for agricultural extension agents and vocational teachers. The book also included practical and profitable applications of electricity on the farm, because as Cochran recalled, most of the rural people wanted electricity but had no idea what they could do with it besides lighting.[119]

Home economists under home service department director Edith Hitchcock taught rural women how to use electricity in the home. The company's massive educational effort was "eminently successful, both in establishing firm customer relationships and in rapidly expanding the uses of electricity on Alabama farms."[120] To help educate farmers, Alabama Power distributed copies of General Electric's pamphlets on farm wiring and residential wiring design and each month began mailing the magazine *Electricity on the Farm* to 7,000 farmers,

Home service director Edith Hitchcock, standing, with home service advisers, left to right, Wilma Bond, Jean Deason, Olga Ellis, Mildred Hodge, Lillian Jenkins, and Ruth Leigh, ca. 1948.

Below, cover of Bill Cochran's handbook, *Electricity for the Farm.*

to agricultural extension home demonstration and county agents, and to vocational teachers.[121]

In the spring of 1947 the head of the Alabama Electric Cooperatives, Maury A. McWilliams, spread information contained in REA administrator Claude R. Wickard's survey of rural electricity completed for the Rural Electrification Administration. Wickard commented on the low percentage of Alabama farms with electricity and the high charges of Alabama Power Company. Congressman Frank Boykin asked for the rates and found that Alabama Power's wholesale rate to Alabama Electric Cooperatives (.007) was lower than the rate currently being charged by TVA (.0075) per kilowatt hour. Chester Gause, manager of industrial power sales for the company, wrote the congressman that Alabama Power was ready to supply the needs of all the cooperatives in its service area. (Boykin insisted that Alabama needed more farmers' distribution co-ops, not generating cooperatives.)[122] This controversy may have sparked E. C. Easter's survey of Alabama Power's rural development program. Within the next few years, when the ongoing building program was completed, the survey showed that 98 percent of the 83,000 farms in the service area of the company would have electricity.[123]

Toward the end of the war Alabama Power Company joined Southern Bell Telephone Company in experiments to see if it would be possible for electric and telephone service lines to be strung on the same set of poles in rural areas. There was concern for safety and whether the high voltage would cause noise on the phone lines.[124] This combined use of poles was successfully worked out and enabled both Alabama Power and the telephone company to provide service in isolated areas at more reasonable costs.[125]

RECONVERSION AND SOUTHERN RESEARCH INSTITUTE

As part of Alabama's reconversion planning efforts, Tom Martin served as chairman of the Talladega County War Plants Conversion Committee, which grew out of a state chamber of commerce committee planning the conversion of Talladega County's war plants to peace purposes. Alabama Power had worked closely with the state's congressional delegation to locate the huge smokeless powder plant at Childersburg. The committee met on July 21, 1944, and arranged for an engineering study of how the Alabama Ordnance Works at Childersburg and the Brecon Ordnance Plant at Talladega could be used in peacetime. Alabama Power provided 25 percent of the cost of the engineering report. The committee organized the Coosa Valley Development Corporation to promote the Talladega-Childersburg sites to new industries.[126]

The conversion committee's engineering study reported that the manufacture of newsprint was a logical use for plant No. 1 at Childersburg. Tom Martin had long been interested in developing Alabama yellow pine as a raw material for newsprint. This engineering study led to the formation of the Coosa River Newsprint Company, organized March 18, 1946. Alabama Power Company agreed to provide 25,000 kilowatts of electrical power and gave the company the exclusive right (under certain conditions) to cut pulpwood on the company's 50,500 acres. Plant No. 2 was leased by Beaunit Mills, Inc., a textile firm that planned to produce rayon yarns.[127] In December 1950 Alabama Power published a thirty-four-page booklet entitled *Forward March* that detailed industrial development in the state since World War II. There were essays on the history of the state's industries and on its agricultural products and natural resources. The booklet was meant to educate potential industrial development prospects as well as the state's citizens.[128]

Tom Martin wanted new industries to use Alabama's raw materials in new ways, especially the state's underused resources. He was inspired by a speech in March 1940 by a University of Alabama chemistry professor who called for more scientific research in the South. Martin had long recognized the importance of research, and he immediately began to study the possibility of establishing and funding a research center in Alabama. In the fall of 1941 the Alabama Research Institute was created to promote utilization of the mineral and agricultural resources of Alabama.[129] Tom Martin pledged that Alabama Power would match individual contributions; however, the Japanese attack on Pearl Harbor in December put all efforts on hold. By the spring of 1944, with the war in Europe pressing toward conclusion, the research center became a reality with a new name to reflect a broader mission.

The Southern Research Institute began operations in a large house on Twentieth Street South in Birmingham on property purchased by Tom Martin, who was able to convince the state's corporate leadership to support the research and become involved in its direction. Thus began the history of the Southern Research Institute, which would make contributions to medical research in cancer and diabetes and improve the safety of blood transfusions. Southern Research also found methods to improve sterilization in the food industry. In 1999 the institute became part of the research programs of the University of Alabama at Birmingham.[130]

The original home of the Southern Research Institute on Twentieth Street South in Birmingham.

For Alabama Power Company, Tom Martin's active involvement in the health research field brought him closer to a former adversary of private power, Alabama's powerful U.S. senator Lister Hill. In the 1950s this connection with Southern Research and their friendship would help enable the company to develop its properties on the upper Coosa River.

POSTWAR BOOM: ALABAMA POWER COMPANY'S FORTIETH ANNIVERSARY

The Gadsden Chamber of Commerce honored Alabama Power Company on its fortieth anniversary with an elaborate luncheon on December 4, 1946.

The day before, the *Gadsden Times* featured front-page stories about the company's founding in the city and its progress and developments over the course of forty years. On hand to receive commendations were Tom Martin and Massey Wilson, three sons of Captain William Patrick Lay—Carl, Orville, and Everett—and Colonel O. R. Hood, one of the original incorporators. During the year the company also celebrated serving 230,185 customers, including 45,000 customers who were classified as rural. Alabama Power was proud of making a substantial contribution to the nation's efforts to win World War II and was anticipating several new projects that were intended to increase and improve residential and industrial service in postwar Alabama.[131]

Thomas W. Martin and Massey Wilson, right, at Gadsden Chamber of Commerce luncheon honoring Alabama Power on its fortieth anniversary, December 4, 1946.

As soon as the war was over, Americans began demanding consumer products that had not been manufactured during the conflict. People wanted to buy new cars, new kitchen appliances, washing machines, and radios. Patriotic citizens had invested in war bonds and saved money during the war, a savings estimated at $100 million, and now they were ready to spend it. Planners hoped that this sudden increase in purchasing power would offset the disappearance of markets caused by peace and ease the return of the eight or nine million men and women of the armed forces who would be seeking jobs in the private sector. Tom Martin believed that research into new products and medicines and capital invested in infrastructure would help the economy.[132]

The conversion to a peacetime economy was gradual and not completed until the end of the decade. Cities, impressed with the first highway lighting in Alabama, a 2.25-mile stretch between Gadsden and Attalla completed in July 1940, began to order new street and highway lights. Veterans who went to war from rural homes with no electricity came home with an appreciation of how electricity could improve the quality of life. A few weeks after the war was over, the Alabama Power sales department staff began meeting to plan for the economic boom they knew was coming. Postwar sales plans were reviewed and a meeting scheduled later for the sales supervisors in all five divisions— J. H. Brown (Southeast), S. G. Kimbrough (Southern), D. C. LaGrave (Mobile), J. W. Holland (Eastern), and W. S. Seale (Western).[133]

The mid-1946 economic boom was accelerated by federal programs to provide housing for returning veterans. The Veterans Administration and Federal Housing Administration loans fueled a construction explosion that required distribution lines to new houses and new subdivisions and kept Alabama Power scrambling to provide service. Industries in Mobile were dislocated as the shipyards decreased employment, but other sectors of the Alabama economy, such as textile mills, did well.[134]

New Technology: Heat Pumps and Air Conditioning

As early as 1946, Alabama Power Company was interested in determining if the technology of a new piece of equipment called a "heat pump" and used for cooling might be reversed and used for heating. The company cosponsored several grants to Southern Research Institute to test heat pumps.[135] On August 5–6, 1947, Alabama Power engineers and salesmen were part of a conference held in Birmingham under the auspices of the Southeastern Electric Exchange to discuss the heat pump. Some seventeen southern and southwestern electric companies were represented. The use of the heat pump for heating during the winter months would be of "great importance to the electric utilities" in balancing the impact of the rapid growth of residential air conditioning.[136] Alabama Power had invested heavily in the research that developed the heat pump, with the Southern Research Institute testing the engineering data. A companywide campaign was initiated to name the new equipment, and J. O. Summers won the $25 prize with the suggestion of "Airomat." However, it never replaced the original working name of "heat pump."[137]

By 1950 heat pump equipment was being manufactured, and Alabama Power was ready to embark on a large advertising campaign to promote sales. Mobile was selected as the first market because of the availability of water, which was used as a transfer agent in the early designs, and because its muggy, hot summer weather would be a perfect selling point. Alabama Power would cooperate with Air Engineers of Birmingham, which would sell and service the equipment. E. C. Easter, C. W. Cheatham, Charles T. Brasfield Jr., and C. M. Kilian, along with many other company employees, were all involved in the promotional effort. Colonel Cheatham, a former employee who had just returned from the war, was given responsibility for spearheading the program.[138]

Alabama Power Company planned a $73 million construction program for 1948–51. New generating units would add 282,000 kilowatts and boost the company's generation capacity by 40 percent, an additional load needed to provide for the increased industrial and residential demands of postwar Alabama. On April 7, 1949, the first of two new 60,000-kilowatt units were online at the Gadsden Steam Plant. These units were designed to burn either coal or natural gas.[139] That same month preliminary work started on a new 100,000-kilowatt unit at Gorgas and a third 40,000-kilowatt unit for Chickasaw. A 22,000-hydro unit was being installed at Mitchell Dam.

Alabama Power Company began using two-way radio telephones in trucks on a trial basis in 1947 to determine if this system would provide quicker, more efficient service. The program was so successful that in 1948 the service was increased to six communication stations—in Gadsden, Anniston, Tuscaloosa, Clanton, Montgomery, and Mobile. Service communications in the Birmingham area were still handled through Southern Bell facilities. On June 1, 1949, the company began using light aircraft to patrol approximately 1,000 miles of transmission lines in the Western Division to see if inspection by air was sufficient. Flying certainly was easier than walking the line or riding a horse. The flights were made once a month with emergency inspection flights made when needed.[140] This system proved to be so successful that it was gradually expanded to cover all transmission lines.

The Organization of the Southern Company

The most significant event of the late 1940s for Alabama Power was the formation of the Southern Company, which began full operations in October 1949. For years, utility holding companies argued in court and before the Securities and Exchange Commission over the meaning of the Public Utility Holding Company Act of 1935. In March 1940 the SEC ruled that Commonwealth & Southern was not in compliance with the law because it "was not confined to a single integrated public utility system as defined in the Act." Eason Balch, who began working for Judge Martin's law firm in 1948, recalled that the activities of the SEC were in a sense "deferred during the war years."[141] The SEC report of March 10, 1941, showed that the largest stockholder of C&S was American Superpower, which owned 9.96 percent.[142] On March 19, 1941, the SEC declared that C&S would have to divest itself of certain properties. Several options were discussed. It could retain the Alabama system, and perhaps Mississippi and Florida; it could select the Georgia system and perhaps retain South Carolina. Or C&S could keep the Consumers Power base in Michigan as the focal system of the corporation.[143] Commonwealth & Southern was the first electric utility dismembered by the government under the 1935 act. Across the nation, while the C&S case was before the SEC, other utility holding companies closely watched what was happening.

Tom Martin noted in November 1941 that the divestment would be complicated for "there were many conflicting interests to be reconciled, local ambitions to be satisfied, legal difficulties to be resolved, and hundreds of incidental transactions to be consummated."[144] Commonwealth & Southern CEO Justin Whiting's testimony before the SEC about "the holding company's efficiency, not only in customer service but also as a national power resource, must have given the Commission at least some pause" as America came closer to becoming involved in World War II. Whiting stressed that the

Commonwealth & Southern CEO Justin Whiting, 1940.

locations of C&S systems, including Michigan, Alabama, and Florida, were in areas of high national defense activity where industrial and military installations were concentrated. Throughout the war years, issues were thrown into court and testimony taken by the SEC to determine which division of operating companies was the most viable, with C&S reluctant to support any division at all.[145] In June 1943 the *New York Times* noted that Whiting's "defensive tone" at the SEC hearing foretold of a stiff defensive posture for the company, while Tom Martin was not at all displeased at the prospect of divestment of the southern properties as a whole, which would be a re-creation of his old Southeastern Power group.[146] To him, it was the only logical plan.

Herbert J. "Hub" Scholz, who had worked alongside Eugene Yates, Oscar Thurlow, George Middlemiss, and Will Mitchell to create this power integration in the Southeast, testified at length before the SEC. Scholz, a brilliant Alabama Power engineer who was at this time with the C&S service company, presented system studies, charts, maps, and diagrams that had not been created for the commission but were generated in the course of ordinary business and then pulled from the files of the service company and operating companies. Scholz testified about the long-range plans southern engineers had drawn up years before and the common rules and technical engineering standards used in all the C&S operating companies in the South.[147] In his book on southern electrical leaders, James Crist credits Winthrop, Stimson, Putnam & Roberts attorney Hayden N. Smith for keeping the southern properties intact. Smith used testimony from southern engineers to show "that the operating companies had achieved substantial economies from coordinated management, planning, and operation over many years." Crist noted that Smith was able "to establish conclusive proof that these economies came about through the working of operating and economic forces and not merely as a product of financial legerdemain."[148]

Martin testified before the SEC in 1942 about the history of Alabama Traction, Light & Power Company, Alabama Power Company, and Southeastern Power & Light, and he detailed the integration of the systems. His testimony was carefully prepared by attorneys in Logan Martin's law firm, but Hayden Smith read over Martin's outline and made numerous suggestions, which were incorporated. Smith particularly advised Martin to stay away from any mention of "financing" because that was not relevant to the subject of his testimony, which was the question of "integrated system." Smith noted, "We are not trying to show the benefits or desirability of holding companies."[149]

By the mid-1940s the southern system had been integrated for more than twenty-five years, and many of the system's leaders had grown up under Martin's leadership at Alabama Power. Looking back to the 1940s, Martin wrote in 1952 that "in the economics of electric power, there is wise company and there is unwise." Martin considered "the organization of the nation-wide group known as Commonwealth & Southern" *unwise*.[150] By 1945 there were obvious disagreements over the vision for the future of the company that would hold the southern properties. Tom Martin was determined that it would truly be a *southern* company, and in the years leading up to SEC approval, he spent many hours arguing with and defending his position to Justin Whiting and the Commonwealth & Southern leadership. There were four major points of contention. Martin refused to accept a service company controlled from New York; he was adamant that the headquarters of the new holding company would be in the South; he wanted only southerners as directors; and he insisted on a southern man being president. Later, there were such other issues as legal representation and connections with banks and investment houses.[151]

Initially, Whiting suggested the new company be named Commonwealth Southern (Inc.), but the first document in Southern Company's corporate minute book is a certificate of incorporation for the Southeastern Power Holding Corporation that was filed on November 9, 1945. On January 21, 1946, an amended certificate changed the name to The Southern Company.[152] (For some years, "The" in the company name was capitalized, but later it was not.) Organizational meetings of the incorporators were held in January and February 1946. Temporary officers and board members were elected, and Edwardo Andrade, an attorney for the law firm of Winthrop, Stimson, Putnam & Roberts, was elected president.[153]

Years later Martin recalled to John Temple Graves, who was writing a book about the power company leader, that there were meetings in Atlanta at the Henry Grady Hotel and meetings in Birmingham between the northern and southern leadership of Commonwealth & Southern, and compromise was difficult. C&S executive Granville H. Bourne came to Birmingham for a two-day meeting to explain "just how the New York office could function with the Southern program."[154] Whiting "was opposed to having a majority of directors from the South; was opposed to having board meetings in the South; thought it would be to the best advantage of the company to continue its principal place of business in New York." Tom Martin remembered that he left the Atlanta meeting thinking he had won his arguments with Whiting but later realized that Whiting had not changed his position.[155]

William H. Brantley Jr. joined the Southern board in October 1946. Brantley married a daughter of W. H. Hassinger, who financed the purchase of stock in Alabama Traction from James Mitchell's estate and his widow, stock that was placed in a voting trust on the creation of Southeastern Power & Light. Hassinger's large stock holdings were converted into Commonwealth & Southern stock and passed through his estate to a trust for his children. His son-in-law, Bill Brantley, had drawn up the family trust and was the executor of Hassinger's estate. Brantley represented this stock interest on the Southern board. Brantley was not as close to Tom Martin as his father-in-law was, but he was a brilliant attorney, was devoted to the South, and tried to do the best he could for the Southern Company. He was far more important in securing an independent southern company than the records show.[156]

William H. Brantley Jr.
Courtesy of the Birmingham Public Library.

Brantley once witnessed a confrontation between Martin and Whiting. In a letter dated January 13, 1959, Brantley recalled that it was necessary for the Southern Company board to meet, organize, and "take certain necessary actions preliminary to the actual severance from Commonwealth & Southern." Whiting, he noted, had "tremendous power in arranging the details of Southern Company's organization and personnel." Since the Southern Company was a Delaware company, the first meetings were held in Wilmington "so there could be no doubt about their validity." The board members met in New York City, discussed various issues, then together rode the train to Wilmington, where all formal decisions of record were made.

On one trip (but he gives no date), Brantley remembered when he was in a compartment with Tom Martin, Justin Whiting, Jacob Hekma, and Georgia Power leader Preston S. Arkwright. Brantley suddenly noticed that Tom Martin's voice had changed, indicating he had his "dander up," and he started listening to Martin's conversation with Whiting. Brantley noted that he was new to the group and was trying to learn the politics of the board. Martin and Whiting were arguing over a draft of bylaws, and Martin said they were not what had been previously agreed upon. Brantley remembered Whiting saying "with some heat that no final agreements had been made and that his proposals would be put into effect" and Martin replying that "this Southern Company is going to be a Southern company in fact as well as in name and it's time you understood it." Whiting told Martin that what he (Whiting) wanted would be. Martin would not back down, and Brantley recalled Martin saying, "We will not accept anything that takes away our freedom. This company is going to be a true Southern company, and I will never yield on that."[157]

Brantley observed that Martin and Whiting stopped talking, but he later learned the issues were "offices in New York, power and choice of general counsel, who would be the top officers of Southern Company, and banking connections." Brantley concluded that "the strange thing to me was that neither Mr. Hekma nor Mr. Arkwright said a single word. Hekma I'm sure was on Mr. Martin's side but he did not support him. Mr. Martin stood alone and asked no help. I would have stood with him if I had known enough to make a sound decision, or if he had asked me. But he did not. He fought Whiting all by himself."[158]

Brantley related that the new bylaws that Martin read placed all of the executive power in the hands of the chairman, not the president of Southern Company. Martin saw this arrangement as an end run attempt around his candidate to head Southern Company, Eugene Yates. Whiting and the New York group were backing Granville H. Bourne to lead the new company. Bourne was a Michigan man, an officer in Consumers Power, and the controller of Commonwealth & Southern.[159] The original bylaws of the Southern Company provided only for a president but were amended on October 9, 1946, at the meeting when Whiting, Bourne, Martin, Yates, and Brantley, along with Arkwright, Percy H. Clark, E. L. Godshalk, Beauchamp E. Smith, and Pearson Winslow, were elected to the board of directors. This was the significant first meeting where the attorneys who had incorporated the company stepped aside and the real corporate leadership was selected. The new bylaws called for "an office in Atlanta, Georgia," increased the number of directors from six to eleven, and added the position of chairman of the board, where corporate power resided. Eugene Yates was elected chairman of the board, and Granville Bourne was elected president.[160] This was a victory for the southern properties, but the war was far from over.

John Temple Graves became involved in recollecting the story of the founding of the Southern Company in the late 1950s after Tom Martin approached him about writing his biography. Graves was a well-known southern writer and *Birmingham Post* syndicated newspaper columnist. In 1955 Graves had written the *History of the Southern Research Institute*. Martin gave Graves much material on himself and on Alabama Power, as well as extensive interviews. During the months and years that followed this arrangement, several drafts were produced. In one of those drafts, Graves, who had spoken with both Brantley and Martin about the organization of Southern Company, wrote that Martin was "mightily concerned" after one early meeting, and when he returned to Birmingham, Martin went directly from the train station to his office and wrote a long handwritten letter to Whiting, marking it confidential. In his letter, Martin questioned the need for a chairman and a president with two high salaries. He praised Bourne's qualifications as an accountant, but he did not feel the controller had enough experience in public relations "and the immeasurable things that are involved in the development of good will of our business so essential to our enterprises." Martin thought it essential to keep Yates involved in the new company and feared he might otherwise leave or retire.[161]

Perhaps Martin thought his fight was over, but when the 1946 *Annual Report* for Commonwealth & Southern came out in late April 1947, it included the comment that the "local executive officers of the operating companies being divested have expressed the desire in these proceedings for their companies to continue to avail themselves of the services of the staff of the Service Company."[162] This was the exact *opposite* of what representatives of the southern operating companies had expressed, and now Martin had to press for a southern service company as well. Martin clearly did not stand alone in this fight. At one Atlanta meeting C&S northern leaders met with Martin and Arkwright, president of Georgia Power; former Georgia governor E. D. Rivers; Clyde Williams, president of the First National Bank of Atlanta; John C. Persons of Birmingham's First National Bank; Gordon D. Palmer of the First National Bank of Tuscaloosa; and J. B. Converse of Mobile, as well as southern power leaders James M. Barry and Yates.[163]

Sometime during these months, Martin accomplished a successful maneuver around Whiting, the details of which are not fully recorded and the time sequence unclear. Tom Martin went to see Eugene W. Stetson, a southern man and an investment banker who had enjoyed great success on Wall Street. The Georgia-born and Mercer-educated banker had arrived in the Big Apple in 1916 to be vice president of the Guaranty Trust Company and rose to be chief executive officer in January 1941.[164] Martin knew Stetson from the 1920s.

In 1926 Stetson had been part of a bankers group that toured the properties and operating subsidiaries of Southeastern Power & Light Company, and at a dinner in Birmingham, Stetson addressed the group with a talk entitled "A Southerner in New York." Stetson was passionate about his native South and supported economic development of the South, as Martin did. Stetson was involved with a number of high-profile financial arrangements, probably the most successful being the financial package for the purchase of the Coca-Cola Company from the Asa Candler family on behalf of the Woodruff group. Stetson was also close to John A. Sibley, who became president of the Trust Company of Georgia in 1946. Although Stetson had recently retired (on December 31, 1946), he remained on the Guaranty Trust board, and he retained all his New York financial connections.[165]

Martin explained the situation to Stetson, saying he believed the Southern Company would be much stronger "if we could have less domination from a New York group." Martin invited Stetson to associate with the new company in some way and help "work out the policy problems." Graves writes that Martin and Yates met with Stetson on October 22 and 23, 1947, and the banker agreed it was essential for Southern Company "to detach" itself from the "dominating influence of the New York office." They agreed on a program, and, according to Martin, Stetson "undertook to discuss this with one of the officers of Bankers Trust Company, which had become the voting trustee of a large block of Commonwealth & Southern stock (eventually to become Southern Company stock), and obtained in effect, a concurrence on their part in our program."[166]

Martin, Yates, and the southern operating companies of C&S eventually won the battle in moving for an independent Southern Company.[167] Although Eugene Yates was "northern born," he had spent most of his life living in the South. More important, Tom Martin had known and worked with him since 1912 and considered him the best leader for the southern group of companies.[168] To recognize Yates's importance to Alabama Power Company's history, as well as to the history of integrated southeastern power grids, and no doubt to elevate Yates's standing with this tribute, Martin had the Alabama Power board rename the Tallassee plant in Yates's honor, a delayed but well-deserved recognition.[169] On June 28, 1947, Martin hosted a ceremony at Alabama Power's upper Tallassee dam to dedicate it as the Eugene A. Yates Dam. W. J. Henderson came from Montreal to honor his old friend. Most members of the new Southern Company board of directors came also. Afterwards the group traveled to Birmingham, where Martin and the company entertained them.[170] At the dedication, Yates shared his early experiences in the Tallapoosa Valley and with Alabama Power. He talked about the economy of "mass production and distribution of electricity," the growth of the power company's load, the creation of Southern Company, and his vision of the economic progress to come in the South.[171]

On August 1, 1947, the Securities and Exchange Commission approved the organization of the Southern Company, which would be allowed to acquire and hold the stocks of Alabama Power, Georgia Power, Mississippi Power, and Gulf Power but would not be permitted to hold South Carolina Power. Harllee Branch Jr., in his Newcomen Society address, gives Southern Company's birthday as August 1, but its corporate organization was not completed until the next month.[172] Throughout the fall of 1947 and through 1948, the struggle for control between northern and southern factions continued as financial arrangements of the separation of the companies were argued. Eugene Stetson advised John A. Sibley that the valuation of Southern Company stock at $10 a share was too high, that some New York buyers were only willing to pay $5, and that if they waited until the stock hit the market, the price would be cheaper.[173]

Bill Brantley did not believe that the common stockholders were getting a fair break in the division, and although Martin agreed with him, the Alabama Power president had to remain neutral.[174] Brantley was allied with attorney Al Snyder, who was representing the C&S common stockholders and was trying to keep the bankers from scooping "$14,000,000 more out of the common stockholders. Believe me," Brantley recorded in his diary on May 20, 1948, "the richer they are, the greedier they are." A month later, Tom Martin called Brantley to his office and "outlined a still more recent plan for dissolution of C. & S." Brantley's objection continued to be "that the preferred gets too much."[175]

During this time, Stetson was involved in helping guide Yates. Gradually, the board of the Southern Company became more southern. Jacob Hekma left the board on February 17, 1949.[176] On June 1, Stetson wrote Sibley explaining that the officers of both the northern and southern operating companies had requested that he "sit in the center of the picture" in order to prevent an "undesirable group" from securing proxies. Stetson was committed to "what might be termed definitely a southern control of policies," to which, Stetson wrote, there was "so far no opposition."[177] On June 29, 1949, Stetson's Guaranty Trust was named transfer agent for Southern Company, with Sibley's Trust Company of Georgia as a co-transfer agent in Georgia. On July 19, Southern Company stock was traded over the counter for the first time, and on the twenty-third, Tom Martin hosted fifteen investment bankers on a tour of Alabama Power Company's hydroelectric dams. The *Birmingham Age-Herald* headlined its story "NATION'S BIG MONEY TAKES A LOOK AT THE SOUTH'S FUTURE."[178] On September 23, 1949, the Securities and Exchange Commission ruled that a common service company for Southern Company and the northern companies of Commonwealth "would obviously constitute a violation of the [holding company] Act and a failure to comply with our order."[179]

On September 30, 1949, "pursuant to Commonwealth's plan for compliance with Section 1" and under orders of the Securities and Exchange Commission, Commonwealth & Southern delivered the common stock of the four operating companies to Southern Company in exchange for its own stock. Commonwealth & Southern Corporation ceased to exist on October 1, 1949. The author of the history of Michigan's Consumers Power wrote that "after fourteen years on death row, Commonwealth & Southern was executed," but "by then, even the condemned almost welcomed the release."[180] The Southern Company was now on its own. John Sibley and Eugene Stetson had been promoting the Southern Company as a good investment in various meetings around the South, including one set up by Tom Martin in Birmingham, and the company received a warm welcome from investors.[181] The last compliance with the SEC order occurred on October 28, when South Carolina Power was sold to South Carolina Electric & Gas Company.[182]

When it was clear that the Southern Company would have its own service company, Herbert J. Scholz, James Crist, Carl James, and Bill Ketchum holed up in a Tutwiler Hotel suite for two weeks "outlining the functions" this company would perform for the operating companies. Although much of the organization was patterned on the old Southeastern Power & Light and C&S service companies, Crist recalled that "we made a number of changes designed to make the new company more responsive to the needs of the operating companies."[183] A nonprofit company, Southern Services, Inc., was organized under Alabama law, with the four operating companies owning the common stock.[184] Headquarters were established in Birmingham. Bill Ketchum and Ernest C. Gaston served under Scholz with Oak Charlton, E. D. Early, Norman Williams, and Bill Brownlee. In the early years, Homer Tickle and Rudolph Freese handled the books.[185]

James Crist, in his story of the founding of Southern Company, noted that the southern group "had engineers, lawyers, and accountants, but no one who knew much about holding company finance." He probably was not aware of Tom Martin's long years working with the finances of Alabama Traction and his holding company, Southeastern Power & Light. Martin spent months on Wall Street watching, if not helping, B. C. Cobb put together Commonwealth & Southern. Maybe Crist meant those people who were working directly in the Southern Company office in Atlanta. There is no indication that Martin himself ever wanted to be president of the new company. Age could have been a factor—he was sixty-six years old in 1947—but Yates was a year older. Perhaps Martin realized he could fight harder for Yates than he could honorably fight for himself, which would look self-serving. Martin's notes and his biographer shed no light on this question. Martin simply may have had enough of Wall Street financiers, enough of holding company management, although he would remain on the Southern Company board of directors until his death.[186]

To assist Southern Company with finances, James Crist noted that James A. Lyles of First Boston Corporation helped outline the first security presentations; that Hayden Smith "told us what we could not say"; and that Eugene Stetson's "advice was of great value."[187] When Stetson died on July 20, 1959, the Southern Company board of directors expressed its sorrow, noting that he "was financial advisor to our companies from the time the Southern Company was organized in 1947."[188] The important role Stetson played in garnering support from major New York banking houses and trustees of large blocks of Commonwealth & Southern stock for a southern company free of old C&S control, which was also what the SEC wanted, is not fully documented.

At the October 27, 1949, Southern Company board of directors meeting, Justin Whiting and Granville H. Bourne resigned. Whiting had been president of Consumers Power Company of Michigan since 1941, and this was now his only position.[189] The exit of Whiting and Bourne from Southern Company's board of directors signaled the final victory for Martin and Yates. When the Alabama Power Company board of directors next met, on November 1, 1949, Tom Martin resigned as president of Alabama Power Company after almost forty years, but he retained the position of chairman of the board. The timing was good because Southern Company was off and flying on its own. The Alabama Power board elected James M. Barry president and appointed Lewis M. Smith as general manager. In addition to being chairman of the board, Martin held the title of general counsel, which may have meant more to him than any other title. Martin continued to keep a heavy hand in all things—indeed, perhaps too heavy.[190]

The new Alabama Power leader, James M. Barry, was born in San Francisco and graduated from the University of California in 1910. He worked on a number of western hydroelectric projects and was employed by several electric companies. Barry was encouraged to come south by his college friend George Middlemiss, and in 1918 he accepted an Alabama Power position as local manager in Anniston. James Crist described what a mess Barry faced at Anniston and how well he straightened it out, success recognized

James M. Barry

when Barry was moved up to manager of the Eastern Division. Barry, a brilliant engineer, was involved with the construction of Mitchell Dam, then he was sent to Montgomery in 1923 where he worked with Lonnie Sweatt,

Southern Division manager, to modernize the city's streetlights. When this "long and tedious" project was finally completed with great success, the two engineers "retired to Lonnie's office to congratulate each other over a bottle of Old Overholt." As the glasses were raised, "the door opened and in walked Tom (teetotaller) Martin." As James Crist tells the story, "Whiskey was not tolerated on company premises; indeed, it was not tolerated, period. Martin looked at the ceiling. 'Good job boys,' he said and walked out."[191] Jack Bingham, whose father Chester was a lead attorney with Alabama Power and later lived in New York while representing Southeastern Power & Light, recalled the summer of 1937 when he was Barry's office boy. Young Jack was about sixteen, and he found "Mr. Barry very businesslike, very serious, very professional, yet kind and considerate of me."[192]

One of the first challenges Barry faced as president of Alabama Power was working through the purchase of Birmingham Electric Company, some-

Architect's drawing of the BECO building on Twenty-first Street and First Avenue North.

thing that had been talked about for thirty years. BECO, as it was commonly known, was a profitable property of Electric Bond & Share's holding company, National Power & Light, and it was a wholesale customer of Alabama Power. For years EBASCO had recognized that the Securities and Exchange Commission would probably force it to sell Birmingham Electric, so the holding company invested no capital in infrastructure in Birmingham. The company's run-down equipment and poor line conditions presented challenges to Alabama Power. Just as EBASCO thought, the SEC broke up National Power & Light and ordered EBASCO to sell its major interest in Birmingham Electric. After long negotiations, Eugene Yates, as chairman of the board of Southern Company, announced on June 21, 1950, that EBASCO and Southern Company had reached agreement, subject to government approval, for BECO to operate as part of Alabama Power Company.[193]

Back in 1925, the Public Service Commission had established definite retail service areas in Jefferson County for BECO and Alabama Power, and their business relationship had worked well for both companies. For months before June 1950, EBASCO and Alabama Power Company worked to negotiate an equitable purchase that would satisfy the SEC. During 1950, 96 percent of the common stock of BECO was acquired. On September 14, 1950, Tom Martin, as chairman of the board of Alabama Power, James M. Barry as president, and Lewis M. Smith as vice president and general manager wrote the BECO employees a letter of welcome, stating that for the present, Birmingham Electric would continue to operate under its own name.[194] Since SEC regulations would not allow an electric utility to hold transportation properties, the streetcar, electric bus, and bus portion of BECO had to be sold. Alabama Power had difficulty selling the transit properties but finally did so on June 30, 1951. On November 26, 1952, the federal district court issued an order enforcing the merger, and it was filed with the Alabama secretary of state on December 1, 1952.[195]

COAL MINES

When Southeastern Power & Light was absorbed into the Commonwealth & Southern Corporation, C&S also acquired Southeastern's subsidiary, Southeastern Fuel Company, which had developed from the original coal operations of Alabama Power around the mine-mouth steam plant at Gorgas. Southeastern Fuel owned approximately 18,000 acres of Walker County coal lands, including some 16,000 acres purchased from the Sloss Sheffield Steel & Iron Company on April 5, 1924. While these coal lands were valuable to Alabama Power Company, they were worthless to C&S or even Georgia Power because western Kentucky and West Virginia coal could be purchased and shipped at a lower cost. These coal mines had not been in operation since 1931. Most of the lands were located between the Mulberry Fork of the Warrior River and Lost Creek, and an appraisal established their value to Alabama Power as $2,639,403. As part of Alabama Power's refinancing plan, on September 10, 1941, the Securities and Exchange Commission issued an order allowing the transfer of the securities of Southeastern Fuel Company from C&S to Alabama Power. The property was recorded as a $1.6 million asset, and Southeastern Fuel Company was dissolved.[196]

These coal lands included three workable seams of coal: Pratt, America, and Mary Lee. The estimated recoverable coal in the Pratt and America seams was 36.5 million tons, and in the Mary Lee seam diamond-bit drilling resulted in an estimated tonnage of 89 million. After the ownership transfer, Alabama Power reopened the mines, and in the first full year of operation, 1942, the mines produced 246,447 tons of coal. By 1947 production had increased to 485,585 tons. The coal that was used by the Gorgas steam units was charged to the operating expense of Alabama Power at cost, which was "substantially less than the market price of commercial coal from that field." This large coal reserve assured power supply and was particularly valuable because the coal was easily mined and was located near the Gorgas Steam Plant and the Warrior River. The coal could be sent down the river by barge to the steam plant at Chickasaw.[197]

Harry M. Johnstone, who came to the company in 1942, managed the mines until 1954. George Nason was his superintendent, and his foremen were Thomas W. Wood and Grady Latham. The most efficient machinery and technology were used to mine the coal, and little handwork was required. In January 1950 Gorgas mines began using a new machine, only the second one in the state that mined and loaded the coal. The machine represented the most advanced technology, and the company kept it in almost continuous operation.[198] Before the coal could be used by the steam plants, rocks, slate, and debris had to be removed, and the coal had to be washed and then pulverized and milled into a fine powder. To ensure continuous supply, huge coal piles were maintained near the steam plants. Mine safety was always stressed just as safety was emphasized in all areas of the company's operations. Safety programs were held once a month, and during the war, posters urged safety with slogans such as "Accidents help the Axis" and "Maximum tonnage with minimum accidents is the way to whip the Japs and the Axis."[199]

In 1943 Alabama Power began a program to improve the living conditions of the miners. Existing roads were improved, and a new road was cut through to the village of High Level to end its isolation. Studies were made and surveys conducted to determine what was needed and what the miners and their families wanted. Hugh Sherer was put in charge of Gorgas housing, and soon he was called "Mayor." The improvement program stretched over several years. Construction involved new communities in Goodsprings and Key Village, as well as renovation of older houses built at Gorgas in the 1920s. Closets, bathrooms, modern kitchens, and windows and doors with screens were added. Some older houses were simply demolished and new houses constructed. In 1946 thirty-five new houses were built with modern facilities. The company's improvements included a more complete water system and modern sanitary sewage disposal system. The United Mine Workers Journal reported favorably on UMW International representative John J. Hanratty's inspection of the company's mining communities.[200]

Gorgas was the site of an extensive underground gasification project conducted by Alabama Power Company with the cooperation of the U.S. Bureau of Mines. The Gorgas experiments were the pioneer work in this field in the United States.[201] For many years there was an interest in determining whether coal could be burned underground and gas collected and used. Milton H. Fries was the consulting engineer and manager of coal operations for Alabama Power, and W. C. Schroeder represented the U.S. Bureau of Mines. Preparations began in October 1946, and the first experiment was conducted at 2:00 P.M. January 21, 1947. The engineers were able to select a location where fire could not spread and to provide pumped air for oxygen

Tom Boykin of Gorgas mines seals up crevices in one of the coal gasification access holes before firing.

and a piping mechanism to capture the gas. On March 18 a thermite bomb was dropped to ignite an underground field. One hundred people were there to observe the experiment. Other tests were conducted over a period of several years. In October 1950 gas from underground burning coal actually propelled a gas turbine. The experiments attracted international attention, and the 1950 experiments were observed by Dr. Albert DeSmaele of Brussels, Belgium, who was involved with financing similar tests in Europe. Experiments went on for some years with much favorable national publicity. Ultimately, however, the experiments had limited success, and the technique was never economically viable.[202]

As the last half of the twentieth century began, Gorgas was as special as it had been three decades before. The opening of the Thomas W. Martin High School in 1950 allowed Gorgas children to complete their education in Gorgas, and the athletic and social activities of the high school added to the culture of the community. The nearby coal mines gave Gorgas a unique personality, and its feeling was different because families lived in the village and children grew up there. There were so many workers at the plant and in the mines who were relatives, second and third generations, that any new worker was warned to be careful what he said about anyone. Ray Olive, longtime Alabama Power employee at Gorgas, observed in June 2003 that the people of Gorgas "have a good work ethic, do what it takes to get the job done, and have a loyalty to the company." He then smiled and said, "We know how to pull off miracles. Like having a boiler out and turning it around in twenty-four hours."[203]

THE END OF THE FORTIES

Before the story of Alabama Power Company closes on the postwar era and moves into the 1950s, one observation needs to be made about the company's personnel. Because of the hard times of the 1930s, almost no new people were employed. The loss of the northern properties to TVA resulted in the company absorbing Northern Division employees who wished to remain with Alabama Power, causing the company to be almost overstaffed. Then came the war years when young men and women went into military service, and there was a labor shortage, and the postwar years when the company made sure that employees returning from the military had jobs waiting for them. Almost no new hires were made and the effect of not hiring young people in the 1930s and 1940s and moving them into responsible positions was felt two decades later when the group from which company leadership was drawn was unusually small. It took another decade for this situation to wash out.[204]

Company leadership was also affected at the end of the decade when Hobart A. McWhorter died on December 13, 1950, from injuries suffered in a tragic automobile accident. McWhorter, a partner in Martin, Turner and McWhorter, was a Harvard law graduate who joined the firm in 1923. He went to New York in 1927 to work on legal issues for Southeastern Power & Light and returned to Birmingham in 1929 after Southeastern was folded into Commonwealth & Southern.[205] McWhorter, who was very close to Thomas W. Martin, named his first son Martin (born in Birmingham in September 1929). His granddaughter wrote over fifty years after his death that he "was the heir apparent to the presidency of Alabama Power." Members of the law firm agreed that McWhorter was being groomed for a leadership position at the power company. The McWhorter family story is that sometime in 1949 McWhorter was approached about leaving the law firm for Alabama Power, but he declined, preferring to continue his law career.[206] Nonetheless, McWhorter's death was a great loss to the company.

The 1940s were years of growth for Alabama Power Company. Its operating revenue more than doubled from $22.3 million in 1940 to $50 million in 1950. Its net income climbed from $3 million to almost $9.5 million. The value of utility plants increased from $185.3 million to $282.8 million. Customers served directly by Alabama Power Company more than doubled from 150,407 in 1940 to 355,282 in 1950.[207] This growth came despite the loss of its large Northern Division service area and customers to TVA. As 1949 came to a close, the company had outgrown its historic 1925 building. In February 1950 Alabama Power began construction on a twelve-story annex to the corporate headquarters, a building that would be air conditioned and equipped with the latest in fluorescent lighting.[208] But even this new addition could not hold all the company's operations. After the acquisition of the Birmingham Electric Company, many of the company's departments moved to the old BECO building on First Avenue. The round neon Birmingham Electric Company sign on top of the building was replaced by an Alabama Power Company neon sign, but it was many years before all the city's residents stopped calling the northeast corner of First Avenue North and Twenty-first Street its common name since 1921—"BECO Corner."

On March 31, 1950, Lewis M. Smith gave a speech to the Southeast Division employees at Ozark. He told them a company that operated in the public interest had increased responsibilities. To him, the real story of Alabama Power Company was the "exciting story of the men and women in it," the human dimension that was the organization's most valuable asset. Smith pointed out that the company expected its employees to be valuable members of their communities, which were "the grass roots" of Alabama "where our customers live."[209]

After Birmingham Electric Company was acquired by Alabama Power Company, the old neon BECO sign atop the building was replaced with an Alabama Power Company neon sign. Courtesy of the Alvin W. (Bill) Hudson collection.

In May 1950 Alabama Power hosted the board of directors of the General Electric Company, took them on a tour of the industrial areas of Birmingham, and treated them to lunch at the Mountain Brook Country Club. In his remarks to the group, Tom Martin predicted great industrial development in the South and a rapidly increasing load in the future for his company. One of Martin's favorite sayings was that "The last half of the twentieth century belongs to the South." Certainly, the South and the state of Alabama had contributed inordinately to the nation's defense and war activities in World War II. Alabama had benefited from tremendous industrial development because of the war. The commitment and service of the power company's people to the nation's war effort were exemplary, and the company provided leadership in the conversion to a peacetime economy. As the decade ended, national and international events once more came to play a vital role in shaping the history of Alabama Power Company.

The Lewis Smith Dam is one of
the largest earth- and rock-filled
dams in the eastern United States.
It is 300 feet high and its reservoir
covers more than 21,200 acres.

Chapter Seven

Downstream view of Lay Dam
showing the redevelopment
completed in February 1967.

COLD WAR WORLD,
THE COOSA, AND THE WARRIOR

There is something about a river that stirs the imagination of men. You can build a half-million-kilowatt steam generating plant and it stirs only a passing interest, but an undertaking to build a dam on a major stream becomes very properly a matter of almost proprietary interest to thousands of people.

WALTER BOULDIN, at Southeastern Electric Exchange, March 1959

In the late 1940s and early 1950s world events once more intruded upon the history of Alabama Power Company. The cold war between the United States and the Soviet Union following World War II made the peace an uneasy one. The testing of an atomic bomb by the USSR and the fall of China to communism in 1949 kept defense spending up, Alabama military bases active, and the demand for electricity high. The confrontation between capitalism and communism dominated U.S. foreign policy, and Alabama Power, which was the essence of private enterprise, supported and benefited from the anti-socialism that was an important part of American culture in these years. Yet the company also recognized the irony of the federal government's "war on communism" and its continued support for policies that weakened private enterprise and especially investor-owned utility companies.[1]

Alabama Power Company had always stressed patriotism, and in these years the company supported such programs and institutes as the Freedom Forum of Harding College, where selected employees attended short courses on American citizenship, leadership, socialism, and communism.[2] On January 22, 1950, the *Selma Times-Journal* praised the company as a "symbol of progress and development" for Alabama, commenting that "despite the fulminations of socialists and demagogues, the power company, an outstanding example of private enterprise, has been the foremost factor in Alabama development for the past thirty years."[3]

After North Korean troops moved across the 38th parallel into South Korea on June 25, 1950, the United States was pulled into another war in Asia. Democratic president Harry S. Truman reacted swiftly to the North Korean invasion, and for several years a hard-fought war raged on the Korean peninsula. The need for war materials escalated. The demand for electricity in the Montgomery area increased so rapidly that by 1947 it had reached the company's estimate for 1950, and Alabama Power added a 110,000-volt transmission line from Jordan Dam to Montgomery and had a new transmission substation under construction. Alabama Power also made plans to increase the company's generation in the Mobile area. A large steam plant was designed with an initial capacity of 250,000 kilowatts and an expansion potential of one million kilowatts. Ground was broken at Salco on July 20, 1951, and the James M. Barry Steam Plant was operating in July 1954.[4]

With the outbreak of the Korean War, for the second time in less than a decade Alabama Power Company sent members of its family off to war. Lieutenant Ellis E. Stanley, the son of Mitchell Dam electrician A. B. Stanley, was assigned with the Fifth Air Force in Japan and Korea. Luther Chesnut III, son of Southern Division auditor L. T. Chestnut Jr., was in the navy, and Captain Eugene A. Yates Jr. flew one hundred combat missions in Korea and was awarded the Distinguished Flying Cross for leading four F-51s through heavy anti-aircraft fire to attack the Sang-ne airfield.[5] Three company employees, John A. Bryant Jr., Richard C. Cory, and Robert S. Taylor, were activated from the National Guard and served with the Thirty-first Division. Horace W. Milton died while serving with the merchant marines, and James R. Carroll, a lineman in the construction department, was killed in Korea on May 18, 1951.[6] For the two wars, World War II and the Korean War combined, Alabama Power granted leaves of absence for military service for 1,294 employees.[7]

As the Korean War grew unpopular in the nation, Republican hopes soared for electing a president for the first time since 1928. Following an exciting primary campaign and convention maneuvering that left Senator Robert A. Taft and the conservatives defeated, World War II hero General Dwight D. Eisenhower was nominated by the Republican Party. One of Eisenhower's philosophies, identified with him even before entering politics, was leaving much in the social-economic field to private enterprise rather than government.[8] In Alabama the fight continued between loyalists and those who had bolted from the Democratic Party to the Dixiecrat Party in 1948. The Alabama Supreme Court upheld a loyalty oath for Democratic electors, and the slate was pledged to the national party's candidate, Adlai Stevenson. To balance the ticket, the Democratic convention tapped Alabama senator John Sparkman as the Illinois governor's vice-presidential running mate. This native son gave the Democrats strength in the state.[9]

The Republicans wrote a 6,000-word platform charging Roosevelt and Truman with attempting to establish socialism and Democrats with working "unceasingly to achieve their goal of national socialism."[10] The Republican platform offered support for private, investor-owned utilities, and in a press conference Eisenhower referred to TVA as "creeping socialism."[11] Therefore, it was not surprising that Judge Logan Martin was, as attorney Eason Balch recalls, "a great supporter of Eisenhower."[12] Judge Martin quietly encouraged the state Republicans and Citizens for Eisenhower, who began working to carry Alabama for the Republican ticket.

One morning in September Judge Martin called one of his firm's newest attorneys, who began his first day at the law office on the Tuesday after Labor Day in 1952. Logan Martin knew the young man's parents, often lunched with his father, and had followed his education with interest. Joseph M. Farley's Harvard law degree came on top of pre-engineering at Birmingham-Southern College, an undergraduate degree in mechanical engineering from Princeton, and graduate work in business administration at the University of Alabama.[13] Harold Williams, who joined Judge Martin's firm the same day Farley did, later commented that "Joe Farley was educated to be president of the power company."[14] Farley had degrees that suited Alabama Power Company leadership well, but only time would tell where they might carry him. Judge Martin, who started Farley down this path, was not around to see the result, but he did live long enough to appreciate the talent he had recruited.

On that fall day, with the presidential campaign dominating the news, Judge Martin told Farley he knew he was interested in politics and asked if he wanted to work for the Eisenhower campaign. Farley was delighted. He spent six hard weeks traveling, meeting people, and organizing. In later years this experience and the contacts he made proved valuable to both the law firm and the company.[15] The Eisenhower people reported the general had "a fair chance to carry Alabama," and the candidate visited Birmingham, the first time a Republican presidential candidate had ever campaigned in the state.[16] Eisenhower, however, polled only 35 percent of the Alabama vote. Nationwide, the World War II hero lost only Alabama and eight southern and border states as he swept to victory.[17]

On August 22, 1952, while the presidential campaign was in full swing, James M. Barry resigned as president of Alabama Power to become chairman of the executive committee of Southern Company. Barry had worked closely with Tom Martin since 1918. He was the consummate engineer, a comple-ment to Martin's legal training, and after he became president of Alabama Power in October 1949, he rarely opposed his chairman of the board. Attorney Jack Bingham, who was so much involved with the Securities and Exchange Commission and company financing, observed that although "Mr. Martin did not give up the executive power very much, there were plenty of things for Mr. Barry to do" as president because Barry was essentially an operating man. Yet there must have been some eagerness on Barry's part to be more on his own and perhaps, after thirty-four years, to be in a position where the day-to-day crises were not so numerous or so pressing.[18] Eugene Yates, Southern Company board chairman, noted in announcing Barry's new position that with the expanding business of Alabama Power Company "the system's operations in Alabama are an increasingly important portion of the [Southern] Company's business as a whole." Southern Company established an office in Birmingham in the summer of 1952, and it was from this office that Barry operated.[19]

Lewis M. Smith

After Barry resigned, Lewis M. Smith, with Martin's support, was elected president. Some were surprised at the selection. Smith was a loyal and methodical company man, a gentleman and an engineer who came to work for the company in 1923 as a draftsman. By 1939 he was chief electrical engineer. Smith was elected a vice president in 1945 and general manager in 1949. He held responsible civic and church positions and represented the company well before civic groups. Walter Baker remembered that Smith was a stickler for dress and had once admonished him for not wearing a hat to work. Smith was respected in the company and the community, but his manner seemed too mild to lead aggressively.[20] Perhaps he was exactly what Tom Martin wanted. Smith was competent, but he was not one to challenge Martin, and ill health limited his energy. At the dedication of Smith Dam several years after Lewis Smith died, Martin observed that "Lewis was possessed of humility, candor, tact. He was one of the most useful and trusted citizens of our time."[21] The five years Smith served as president of Alabama Power Company were critical years, but the leadership roles were taken by young men in the company and the law firm. Smith's greatest contribution to the company might well be that he gave new leaders, who would serve Alabama Power and the Southern Company into another generation, the opportunity to grow.

INTEGRATION OF BIRMINGHAM ELECTRIC COMPANY INTO ALABAMA POWER COMPANY

Alabama Power Company faced several challenges integrating the employees and equipment of Birmingham Electric Company into its own operations. After all the necessary approvals, the merger was effective on December 1, 1952, but it would be years before workers from the two companies were molded into one workforce. The level of training and professional development that employees of Birmingham Electric had received was not up to the higher standards of Alabama Power. Some of the practices common at Birmingham Electric were against the safety regulations of Alabama Power, and a massive training program had to be instituted. Alabama Power gave David D. Wendel the responsibility for implementing the engineering educational programs for Birmingham Electric's engineers, linesmen, and support personnel.

Dave Wendel came to Alabama Power in 1927 after earning two Auburn electrical engineering degrees and briefly left to serve as an officer in World War II. He was a tall man with prematurely gray hair, a meticulous dresser who moved up in company ranks from district superintendent to manager of transmission.[22] Lee Styslinger Jr., who was the young president of Altec Industries, Inc., worked closely with Wendel. Styslinger recalled that "he was a very sophisticated individual, and when he spoke you knew that you'd better listen."[23] Wendel understood the engineering standards and safety regulations of the company probably better than anyone. He spent time on the road checking operations, using his keen eye for finding mistakes in procedures or seeing when something was not being done correctly. Company people often feared his visits, and they made certain he never found an error twice.[24]

In 1959 Wendel assigned Bill Whitt to direct a new training program out of the Birmingham District and assigned Walter Johnsey to help him. Whitt came from an Alabama Power family. His father had been the Haleyville local manager who saved the area for Alabama Power Company in the TVA struggle. Johnsey grew up in a Walker County coal mining community. He spent time in the military until a second physical examination uncovered that he had sight in only one eye (the result of a youthful mining accident), and he was sent back to Alabama. Johnsey earned an engineering degree at Auburn and was interviewed for a job with Alabama Power and hired by Wendel in 1951. Johnsey was placed in a training program and over a few years was based in various towns in central Alabama until he was assigned to help Whitt with standardizing the practices of former BECO employees.[25]

The main problem of the merger with BECO was that Alabama Power was operating on a grounded system while Birmingham Electric was using the 13-kV Delta system. Whitt recalled that "the delta system leads you into taking some approaches to doing work that you would not take on the grounded system. In other words, you take chances." As the two systems were being tied together, Alabama Power was rebuilding, upgrading, and strengthening the Birmingham Electric system and converting it to the grounded system. Whitt remembered that this was "one of the more difficult things we had to deal with first. We had to develop work habits that would protect our employees and make them accept those work practices." Whitt divided and relocated the employees so there was "a pretty good mixture in each of the crew headquarters around Birmingham— from both Alabama Power and Birmingham Electric. We brought these employees together, and they developed into an outstanding workforce."[26]

The workers of the two companies had their own contracts with the International Brotherhood of Electrical Workers, and each company was represented by a different local union. Smoothing out the differences in the two contracts was another challenge that had to be addressed to integrate the workforces. Covered employees of BECO were represented by IBEW No. 1322, and Alabama Power's covered employees were members of local No. 930. There were differences in pay, job titles, and job descriptions. Generally, Alabama Power's employees were paid more, except for the lowest job classification of helper, which was the same.[27] Alabama Power and the IBEW began negotiations in February 1953 and in March initiated a study of the two contracts that would highlight the differences and make recommendations for combining the two in one contract.[28] Neely Henry's August 18 memorandum to the officers of the company gave a list of the concessions that the company made to the union, including adding Christmas Eve as an additional paid holiday, increasing pay for substitutions, granting time off with pay for voting, and increasing vacation time after fifteen years of service to fifteen working days per year. A new agreement was signed on October 19, 1953.[29]

Alabama Power was also faced with servicing and maintaining on BECO's 128 cars and trucks. BECO had no service facility included in the merger, and Alabama Power Company decided to expand its own Birmingham general garage. Property was purchased on Sixth Avenue and all company personnel who had worked at the general garage were shifted to the newly created Birmingham Division, which was headed by Charles T. Hunter, who came to Alabama Power in 1924.[30] The merger with BECO increased the number of customers and brought about the separation of the residential and commercial division. J. Paul Brown, who came to the company in 1924 as a salesman in the Western Division, headed residential, and Luther T. Cale, who had been with Birmingham Electric since 1926 and with Alabama Power since the merger on December 1, 1952, was appointed the first manager of commercial sales.[31] Folding Birmingham Electric's operation into Alabama Power increased the size of the company in terms of customers, employees, and service area and meant that operations were scattered in several buildings around the city.

Eisenhower, TVA, and the Upper Coosa

When Eisenhower became president, liberals still wanted to expand federal hydroelectric developments on other rivers, while conservatives were against more government projects. The president was opposed to government power production. He told his cabinet that "TVA taxes Massachusetts to provide cheap power in the TVA area to lure Massachusetts industry away."[32] At a cabinet meeting on July 31, 1953, Eisenhower used the Tennessee Valley Authority as an example of federal violation of free enterprise, saying, "By God, if ever we could do it, before we leave here, I'd like to see us *sell* the whole thing, but I suppose we can't go that far."[33] Eisenhower's political philosophy was important to Alabama Power Company because it gave the company hope that it might be able to complete its original plans to develop the upper Coosa.

The original Coosa River plan was conceived by James Mitchell and developed by Eugene Yates in 1912. The entire river was to be developed as one coordinated program for maximum hydro production, economy, and efficiency.[34] Just as Yates and Thurlow Dams on the Tallapoosa were being completed, the 1929 depression came, and the demand for electricity fell while investment capital dried up. The creation of TVA in northern Alabama and the beginning of World War II prevented Alabama Power from completing its original plans. The 1945 Rivers and Harbors Act reserved development of the Coosa River for the federal government and denied the right of the Federal Power Commission to license any dams on the Coosa. There was talk from public power people of expanding TVA south to the Coosa River.[35] The federal government made no appropriations for the river in the presidential years of Harry S. Truman.

With a change in the political philosophy in Washington, Martin was hopeful. He doubted the Eisenhower administration would approve funds for the federal government to build dams on the Coosa, and there was simply not enough demand for commercial river traffic to justify the construction of government locks. The company's downstream dams and reservoirs were already controlling the worst of the river's flooding, so there was no reason for a cooperative federal-private development for flood control. Soon after Eisenhower's election, Martin began to push the company's plans for more Coosa dams. The first obstacle Martin and the company faced was the state's two strong Democratic U.S. senators who were public power supporters. Alabama Power Company would have to win the approval of Lister Hill and John Sparkman to get legislation through the Congress, beginning with the repeal of the suspension of authorization for the Coosa River. On the other hand, both senators were advocates of the industrial development of Alabama and were political realists. The contest for the upper Coosa was to be Tom Martin's last fight, and in this battle he had a few good men who would help him win. From the holding company, Barry would support Martin and Alabama Power, but younger men would carry the responsibility for getting approval for the Coosa River projects and for convincing Hill and Sparkman of the benefits of these projects for Alabama and its people.

DIXON-YATES

The Dixon-Yates controversy in Eisenhower's first administration involved an offer by private power to provide electricity that was needed in TVA's service area. The affair was strictly related to Southern Company, not Alabama Power, but it illustrates the Eisenhower administration's utility philosophy and the president's determination not to expand TVA. More important, while the Dixon-Yates contract was being debated in Congress and by the media and the public, Alabama Power Company was seeking approval for its programs on the Coosa and Warrior Rivers. The most bitter aspects of the Dixon-Yates brouhaha came after Alabama Power Company's legislation was signed by the president, but it influenced the climate of public opinion in the nation, affected the political pulse in the capital, and rekindled the issue of public versus private power, making Alabama Power's task more difficult.[36]

The Dixon-Yates controversy began when Governor Frank Clement of Tennessee led a delegation to meet with President Eisenhower in October 1953. The group wanted the federal government to construct a steam plant so TVA could be assured of enough power to supply the city of Memphis. The new

Atomic Energy Commission (AEC) facility at Paducah, Kentucky, was using so much electricity that TVA could not guarantee the Tennessee city's future needs for electricity. Eisenhower defended AEC's use of TVA electricity, telling Clement "that since the federal government had paid the costs of developing the TVA power plants, it was ethical and proper for the federal government to use a reasonable portion of the output."[37] The president opposed putting the burden of providing electricity for Memphis on the nation's taxpayers. Governor Clement contended that TVA's monopoly obligated it and the federal government to supply the needs of the area. Eisenhower disagreed and said he opposed investing more federal dollars in public power.[38]

President Eisenhower then asked members of his staff to study the problem and seek another solution. In his budget message, the president announced that some demand in western Tennessee and Kentucky for electrical power would be met by private companies. This encouraged Eugene Yates to write TVA commissioner Gordon R. Clapp on February 9, 1954, with an offer to sell power to TVA from a Georgia Power steam plant being planned for the Tennessee River near Guntersville. Clapp responded that Yates misunderstood the president's budget message and should contact the Atomic Energy Commission, which was committed to taking private power to relieve the demand on TVA.[39] After many meetings, studies, and surveys, Middle South Utilities, under Edgar H. Dixon, and the Southern Company, under Eugene Yates, submitted a contract whereby a new company, the Mississippi Valley Generating Company, would build a steam plant with private investment capital of some $107 million. The plant would supply the electrical needs of the city of Memphis and the Atomic Energy Commission beyond what TVA could supply.[40] After this contract was accepted by the government, a full-scale battle began in Congress that revived the public versus private power controversy of past years.[41]

E. A. Yates

The Dixon-Yates contract became one of the most heated controversies of the first Eisenhower administration. As the contract made its way through the final approval process, it became an issue in the congressional elections of 1954. In Birmingham, Bill Brantley watched all of this unfold from his seats on the Southern Company and the Alabama Power Company boards of directors. He believed he knew the facts. He fumed in his diary against the Democrats, "who have told the biggest lies" about the contract and misrepresented the background that led up to the contract.[42] Democrats portrayed Dixon-Yates as a scheme to destroy TVA and criticized the contract because it was not competitively bid, "a misconception," Brantley wrote, "that the Government can buy electric power just as it buys coal, pig iron, or apples."[43]

Alabama senator Lister Hill, speaking on the floor of the Senate in February 1955, was the one who gave the coup de grace to Dixon-Yates, charging in a dramatic speech that there was a conflict of interest because the banker who had arranged financing for Dixon and Yates had also consulted on TVA for the Bureau of the Budget, which had opposed more funding for TVA.[44] Democrats also charged that President Eisenhower's Augusta National golfing buddy, Bobby Jones, who was a director of Southern Company, had unduly influenced the president.[45] The result of the furor was that the city of Memphis was convinced to build its own steam plant, the Eisenhower administration bailed out of the contract in July 1955, the federal courts refused to force the government to pay damages for expenses incurred as the project went forward, and Southern Company was stuck for about $1 million in expenses.[46]

When Eugene A. Yates died at his New York home on October 5, 1957, at the age of seventy-six, the last name of the chairman of the board of Southern Company had entered U.S. history unfairly in connection with a political controversy. Yates's early engineering work in Alabama, his design of Alabama Power Company's generation and transmission systems, and his leadership role in Southeastern Power & Light and later in the formation of Southern Company should justly be remembered instead. Harllee Branch Jr., who followed Yates as president of Southern Company, credited Yates with the company's financial prestige and observed that "Mr. Yates bestrides two periods in the company's history, the era of the builders and the era of the statesmen, and it is appropriate that his additional contributions should be recognized."[47] Yates Dam stands as a monument to those endeavors. On Yates's death, Tom Martin released a statement that "because of his modest and retiring nature, Mr. Yates' genius as an engineer and progressive-minded executive was known more in utility, financial and engineering circles than by the public generally." Martin said that in his career of more than forty-five years Yates had made "notable contributions" to the southern electric utilities industry.[48]

The Dixon-Yates story ended with the city of Memphis borrowing money to build its own steam plant. When it was finished, the city announced a "big jump" in rates, some 20 percent, which was shouldered by residential customers. In 1959 the Memphis mayor-elect noted that the rate increase was "the result of the failure of engineers employed to take certain factors into consideration in computing costs for operating the $121,000,000 new plant built for Memphis."[49] That same year the Chattanooga News–Free Press summarized that Dixon-Yates was "just a faintly remembered term to most citizens. To the fanatic electric power Socialists it is the equivalent of profanity. To the citizens of Memphis it may well become a symbol of what might have been a happy and economical solution for them." The editorial concluded: "The soundness of the Dixon-Yates arrangement was clear from the beginning, and there is cause for deeper appreciation of it as the results of the alternative begin to come to bear."[50]

THE COOSA RIVER ONCE MORE

The same month the Tennessee delegation visited President Eisenhower requesting more electricity for Memphis and thus setting in motion the Dixon-Yates controversy, the Coosa-Alabama River Improvement Association requested that Alabama Power consider further development on the Coosa River. Alabama Power Company filed an application to the Federal Power Commission on November 12, 1953, requesting permission to build five power plants on the Coosa River. These extensive projects caused a doubling of the company's engineering and construction staff as many young engineers were hired. Alabama Power also used consultants George F. Sowers, James P. Growden, and Byram W. Steele, and the company worked closely with the officers and staff of the Corps of Engineers.[51]

The company's engineering staff took the older river surveys, forty years of company records of water flow and floods, and began extensive new geological studies and borings to determine exactly where the dams should be located. New dams were planned for the general area of Centre, for the area of old Lock 2, and for one close to Howell Mills Shoals, which was not far from Pell City. Other developments were expected near Columbiana and Wetumpka. All were locations that somewhat followed the 1953 Corps of Engineers report. As Alabama Power engineers worked, management began planning how such extensive construction projects could be financed, and the governmental relations group and attorneys began discussions on exactly how the company might obtain the necessary federal legislation to permit the developments.[52]

The sticky point was the 1945 Rivers and Harbors Act, enacted, as Representative Armistead Selden explained, "at the height of the federal 'multi-purpose dam' fever." This law staked out the upper Coosa for public power projects and suspended the authority of the Federal Power Commission to authorize any private power construction. Before the commission could issue any permits, Congress had to restore the FPC's authority to license the Coosa.[53] Since 1945 the Corps of Engineers had produced plans for Coosa development, but there had been no congressional appropriations to fund them. As Alabama Power engineer Fernand C. Weiss noted, "for twenty years through the era of the so-called 'New Deal' and 'Fair Deal,' in spite of all local efforts, not a dime of federal money was appropriated for the construction of a single dam on the Coosa."[54] Following the election of Eisenhower, Alabama Power Company began lobbying the Alabama congressional delegation to support legislation to allow the company to finish its own plans for the river by completing the Corps of Engineers design for a coordinated development of the entire river. Tom Martin, Walter Bouldin, Edwin I. Hatch, and Alvin W. Vogtle Jr. took the lead in this lobby and educational effort. Bouldin was an experienced attorney, and Hatch and Vogtle were young lawyers with Judge Logan Martin's firm. All three would eventually become executives with Alabama Power Company. Together they provided a formidable new leadership in governmental relations.

Walter Bouldin speaking at the Weiss Dam groundbreaking ceremony, April 26, 1958.

Walter Bouldin was a native of Scottsboro and a University of Alabama graduate who came to the law firm in 1928 following graduation from Harvard Law School. For the next twenty-four years Bouldin earned a reputation as "a brilliant and distinguished attorney."[55] John Temple Graves described Bouldin as "deep-voiced, graceful, with a photographic memory."[56] James Crist recalls Bouldin as "tall and distinguished looking, with a shock of white hair and a flair for compelling rhetoric," a man who could quote the classics in Greek or Latin and Dante's *Inferno* when he missed a putt on the golf course.[57]

Walter Jr. remembers his father spending "the first years of his career with the Martin law firm trying to protect Alabama Power Company from the Tennessee Valley Authority," a "struggle with government power that continued in one form or another through his career." Bouldin was an avid Crimson Tide football fan and a good storyteller, and he was accomplished at hunting and fishing, but his son knew that he worked "long hours and put himself under great stress" because he "cared deeply about Alabama Power Company and what he conceived as its mission to serve the citizens of the state of Alabama with reliable power at the lowest possible cost."[58]

In 1952 Bouldin left the Martin, Turner, Blakey & Bouldin firm (which changed its name many times over the years until it became Balch & Bingham in 1985) to fill the new position of financial vice president for Alabama Power.

Within the law firm and Alabama Power he had a reputation for choosing the right path, no matter how much more difficult that path might be. In whatever situation Bouldin found himself, he was "uncompromising in the face of principle." He gave the Coosa lobby effort energy, a sincerity of purpose, and a commitment to the state of Alabama.[59] Bouldin was elected executive vice president of the company effective January 1955 and president of the company in 1957.

Ed Hatch brought to the Coosa River lobby effort a great personality and a keen ability to win friends and influence people. Hatch was born in Uniontown and graduated from Sewanee and the University of Alabama School of Law. He began his law practice in 1936 by opening a Montgomery office of Judge Martin's firm. Hatch was a hail-fellow-well-met, an able man good at socializing. He soon became the most recognized and well-liked, as well as the most successful, lobbyist in Montgomery. Tom

Ed Hatch

Martin had always enjoyed the political arena and believed, as president of the state's largest utility company, he had a responsibility to stay involved. By 1952, however, Hatch had assumed most of the Montgomery and Washington lobby duties for Alabama Power and was a partner in Martin, Blakey & Hatch.[60]

Alvin Vogtle, a Birmingham native and Auburn graduate, was a pilot and World War II hero. After his plane ran out of gas and he crash-landed in North Africa, Vogtle was captured by the Germans. His first daring attempt to escape from a Nazi prison became the basis of a Hollywood movie, The Great Escape.[61] Just before the war, Vogtle received his law degree from the University of Alabama and joined Judge Martin's law firm. He became a partner in 1950. Vogtle was an extremely bright attorney who

Alvin Vogtle

had striking leadership characteristics. He would eventually leave the law firm for an executive position with Alabama Power, but in the 1950s he was closely involved with the expansion plans for developing the upper Coosa and the Warrior.

Another young attorney, S. Eason Balch, was destined to play a significant role in protecting Alabama Power from unfair encroachments by public power and the cooperatives. He was the company's point man in hearings before the Federal Power Commission. Balch became an expert on federal regulations and public utilities and was a close adviser to Walter Bouldin. Balch was born in Madison, Alabama, and graduated in commerce and business administration from the University of Alabama in 1940.

S. Eason Balch

He served in World War II, received his L.L.B. degree from the University of Virginia, and joined Martin, Turner & McWhorter in March 1948.

For the first years, Eason Balch worked with Hobart McWhorter, whom Balch believed was at that time the "best corporate lawyer in the state of Alabama." McWhorter was an expert on federal regulations—wage and hour, labor relations, and securities law—many of them recently enacted New Deal laws that were being constantly interpreted and changed. Perry Turner once said he would leave it to McWhorter to be the company's "loose leaf" lawyer, and McWhorter was a brilliant one. Looking back, Balch laughed that somebody had "to carry McWhorter's briefcase and run errands for him," and while doing so he "learned a lot from him." After McWhorter died, the labor work fell to Balch. He spent most of 1953 in labor negotiations and became familiar with the company in the process. Balch was a meticulous lawyer with a keen memory for the fine details of legislation and the history of the company. He was always well prepared for hearings and had a reputation for defending his legal position and Alabama Power with determination and passion. Balch was especially involved in defending the company against the Rural Electrification Administration and state cooperatives, activity that will be discussed later.[62]

Tom Martin's new team of Bouldin, Vogtle, and Hatch had the challenge of getting Congress to approve new legislation to de-authorize the Coosa and then obtain a Federal Power Commission license for Alabama Power. Joe Farley recalled that Hatch and Vogtle were constantly in Washington calling on Alabama congressmen, and especially Senators Hill and Sparkman, who "were noncommittal at best." Both were opposed but reluctant to say so. Farley's role was to receive Ed Hatch's telephone calls and write up a memorandum for Judge Martin to take downstairs to Tom Martin.[63] Civic and governmental bodies in the state, especially those in the Coosa Valley, were enthusiastic about the new dams and recreational lakes, and civic, political, and labor interests flooded the Alabama congressional delegation with resolutions and appeals. Senator Lister Hill had a standard form letter to respond to the hundreds of letters he received advocating the development.[64] Congressman Albert M. Rains of Gadsden was the driving force behind the legislation, and eventually it had the support of the entire Alabama delegation in the House except for Representative Bob Jones of Scottsboro. Jones was a strong supporter of TVA and public power, but at this time there was no possibility of public funding. Former lieutenant governor Clarence Inzer of Gadsden, who was close to Lister Hill and served as an Alabama Power Company consultant, was very helpful. Governor Gordon Persons, who had been associated with both rural electrification and the Alabama Public Service Commission, was philosophically and politically opposed to Alabama Power, but gaining the governor's approval was crucial. Local chambers of commerce, civic clubs, and political leaders interested in economic recruitment helped convince reluctant politicians to support development of the Coosa River by Alabama Power.[65]

The Alabama Electric Cooperative, an association of rural co-ops then headed by Maury A. McWilliams of Prattville as president and John Ford as executive manager, led the fight against Alabama Power's proposal. The association's position was that only one dam site on the Coosa was protected by the 1945 Rivers and Harbors Act, and Alabama Power should just build its dams on other sites on the river. But this position was destroyed by a legal opinion written for Alabama Power by Judge Martin's partner, James C. Blakey, who insisted that the 1945 act effectively froze the entire upper Coosa from private development.[66] Blakey, a Kentucky native who was affectionately called "Colonel," came to Judge Martin's firm after his graduation in law from Harvard University in 1927. Known for his personal integrity, Blakey was a sagacious attorney with a broad understanding of history and the law. After the death of Hobart McWhorter in 1950, Blakey became the chief trial lawyer and negotiator for the law firm. Often in the background, he was nevertheless responsible for handling many of the company's more difficult legal matters.[67]

The campaign to convince the governor to support and Congress to approve Coosa River development by Alabama Power filled the spring months of 1954 with activity. Farley recalled this was his "first experience with Washington and Capitol Hill problems," and he was surprised how "a relatively simple piece of legislation" was so complicated. There were strong discussions behind closed doors between Tom Martin and the governor, conversations with Alabama's two U.S. senators who were delaying action in the Senate, and communication with the Public Service Commission. These interests applied pressure on Alabama Power Company to reduce the wholesale rate it charged to the state's cooperatives. Joe Farley wrote in his Newcomen address that the rate reduction was "made as the *quid pro quo* for support from Hill and Sparkman."[68] On April 2, 1954, the Colbert County *Standard and Times* reported that the Alabama Power Company dam proposal lacked the approval of Representative Bob Jones, and that John Ford, representative of the cooperatives, was on Capitol Hill urging Congress to restrict the company's plans. One Alabama congressman was quoted as saying the issue was not private versus public power but "private power or no power."[69]

The details of the negotiated agreement are found in a letter Tom Martin wrote to Governor Persons on April 8 "confirming our discussions." Martin stated that "Upon the enactment of legislation by the United States Congress

restoring jurisdiction to the Federal Power Commission to grant a license to the Company for its proposed Coosa River Development, and upon the granting of such license by the Federal Power Commission to the Power Company, the Company will enter into new contracts with each of the twelve distributing cooperatives, which we now serve, for power supply to each delivery point." The new contracts would incorporate a reduced rate to go into effect when approved by the Alabama Public Service Commission for bills dated May 1, 1954, and thereafter, which meant that the reduced rate, known within the company as "the Coosa rate," actually went into effect before construction started on the new Coosa dams. Based on 1953 purchases of electricity by the cooperatives, Martin predicted that the new rate would cost the company $117,476 a year.[70] Although not part of the agreement, Martin extended the new lower wholesale rate to municipalities because he believed it would be unfair and unethical if the company had different wholesale rates for cooperative and municipal systems.[71] The lower rate also allowed a cooperative to purchase power cheaper than it would cost the cooperative to generate it.

Charles R. Lowman, who was associated with the Alabama Electric Cooperative and who wrote the history of the cooperative in 1991, either never knew the full story and the political pressure that was applied to Alabama Power to offer the reduced rate to cooperatives or he elected to omit it from his story. He does write that it was a serious mistake for the cooperatives to accept the lower rate because it reduced their ability to prove need while they were trying to move into generation and transmission, even if that generation was not needed and that transmission duplicated Alabama Power systems.[72]

As soon as word of the arrangement leaked out, Albert M. Redd of Robertsdale, who was manager of the Baldwin County Electric Membership Corporation, which was a member of the Alabama Electric Cooperative, wrote Governor Persons. Redd asked the governor for "a letter telling in detail your part in effecting this last proposed rate reduction by the Alabama Power Company to the REA distribution cooperatives and to municipalities." Redd wanted "a summary" of the governor's "personal participation and your telephone calls to and from Mr. Martin, Mr. Hill, Maury McWilliams, etc., first proposals, counter proposals, your suggestions to both parties, and the final result." The governor thanked Redd for the letter but replied that he would "rather just forget it" because he didn't "like publicity," and he recommended that if Redd discussed the matter with his board to "please do so verbally."[73] After mid-April Governor Persons joined the campaign for congressional approval of the legislation Alabama Power needed, and the tone of his correspondence was enthusiastic. Senator Hill assured the governor of his effort to obtain congressional approval for the Coosa River development.[74]

Tom Martin, Lewis M. Smith, and Fernand C. Weiss appeared before the House Committee on Public Works on May 18, 1954, and presented Alabama Power's plan for Coosa development. The chairman of the committee, George A. Dondero of Michigan, told *Birmingham News* correspondent James Free that it was "the first private enterprise suggestion" of a partnership to provide flood control and navigation that he recalled in his twenty-two years on the House committee. In essence, Alabama Power was assuming responsibility for the Corps of Engineers 1953 plan for the river's development. Free pointed out that the remarkable event, which might "have important influence in many areas of the United States," received only "scant attention" in the news because it came one day after the U.S. Supreme Court rendered its decision on May 17, in the landmark school desegregation case, *Brown v. Board of Education*, which was controversial in the South and dominated the media's attention.[75]

President Eisenhower signed the Coosa River development act on June 28, 1954. The Alabama Public Service Commission granted a certificate of convenience and necessity for the project on February 16, 1956, and on September 4, 1957, the Federal Power Commission issued a license for Alabama Power to build five dams on the Coosa. The application was amended several times. The original Corps of Engineers study included a low dam at Fort Williams Shoals to provide a navigational channel to the base of what became Logan Martin Dam. Alabama Power engineers, however, determined that if the height of Lay Dam was increased sixteen feet, it could accomplish the same purpose with far less cost. Redeveloping Lay Dam would also give the company the opportunity to replace the older turbines at Lay with more efficient modern equipment, but there was a problem. Lay Dam was completed under a congressional act and therefore was not subject to regulation by the Federal Power Commission. The question the company and its attorneys debated was: would the redevelopment of Lay Dam mean any modifications to Lay would have to be approved by the FPC, in which case, would that mean Lay Dam would have to be relicensed by the FPC every fifty years? Southern Company CEO Eugene Yates was opposed to endangering Lay Dam's independent status, but Tom Martin, realizing it was the key to the entire development, insisted, and the request was made and approved by the FPC.[76]

Another modification of the application to the Federal Power Commission was the decision not to build a dam at Wetumpka but to excavate a channel from the Coosa above Jordan Dam and create a lake behind a new dam with a channel wide and deep enough for barge traffic should the federal government decide to build locks in the company's dams. Creating a new lake and dam was far less expensive than constructing a new dam on the river at Wetumpka and would avoid flooding lands close to the city. This modification was also approved by the FPC.[77]

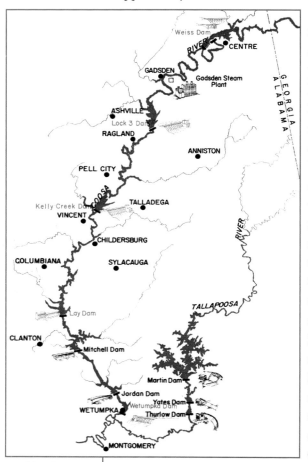

Map showing existing and proposed dams on the Coosa River, 1957.

Some ten days after the power commission issued the license, Eugene Yates sent a memorandum to his top operating people announcing that Alabama Power had been granted a license to build Coosa River dams with an estimated cost of $121 million and two dams on the Warrior "at a cost probably of $35 million or more." Yates was deeply troubled by the large amount of money that Southern Company would have to invest in Alabama Power to fund these projects. Already, he wrote in his memorandum to Alabama Power executives, Southern had "an investment of some $120 million in Alabama," capital raised by the sale of Southern stock. Yates believed the matter was "of such concern to the Southern Company that prior to acceptance of the license the entire program should be presented to the board of directors of the Southern Company for approval." He suggested a joint meeting of the boards of directors of Alabama Power and Southern Company to discuss the issues.[78]

James Crist recalled that Yates thought that the extensive hydro development was too costly and that there would not be enough customers for the electricity generated. But Martin wanted the dams, and Martin prevailed.[79] As expenditures increased, it became evident that the cost estimates of the Coosa projects had been far too low. Yates discussed with Alvin Vogtle the possibility of Alabama Power Company backing out of the projects and surrendering its FPC license. Vogtle advised Yates that in that case Lay Dam could not be withdrawn from FPC authority. Company folklore, but most likely true, relates that Martin threatened Yates that if Southern Company did not back Alabama Power's development on the Coosa River, he would go to the SEC and fight to withdraw Alabama Power from Southern Company. Yates backed down.[80]

Crist wrote that Martin had been correct in his long-term analysis.[81]

The 1954 federal legislation placed a time constraint on the company by requiring that all dams be completed within ten years.[82] Alabama Power had not constructed a dam in almost twenty-five years, not since the completion of Thurlow in 1930. In the depression and wartime years under Commonwealth & Southern, that holding company was in no position to spend money on developing the Coosa and was more interested in growth outside the South; furthermore, Alabama Power had difficulties with its 1941–42 refinancing. The company's engineering leadership was, however, intact and experienced. Fernand C. Weiss, chief engineer and vice president, had been involved with all previous Alabama Power projects. A Texas native, Weiss had joined Alabama Power in 1913 after graduation from Massachusetts Institute of Technology and began as an assistant engineer on transmission construction. In 1926 he became vice president of Dixie Construction. He worked on Martin, Jordan, Yates, and Thurlow Dams and served as the chief engineer on the construction of the Chickasaw Steam Plant. In 1929 Weiss was construction manager of Commonwealth & Southern's Allied Engineers. Later he became construction manager for Alabama Power, but during the depression the company was not

Fernand C. Weiss, ca. 1957.

doing much construction. Mary Cochran, who came to work for Alabama Power in 1928 and retired in 1974, remembered that during the depression whole floors in the office building were vacant, and the construction department had only a skeleton crew. Weiss held that group together. In August 1941 he was elected a vice president of the company. Martin praised Weiss for his "wise and prudent administration of the company's construction work."[83]

Douglas F. Elliott and E. R. "Ned" Coulbourn were two of Weiss's popular and talented assistants. Elliott worked under Weiss in construction and was responsible for building the coal-fired plants and the first dams on the upper Coosa. He was a New Orleans native with an engineering degree from Massachusetts Institute of Technology who joined Dixie Construction Company in 1924 while Martin Dam was being built. He transferred to Alabama Power in 1931 and by 1959 was vice president in charge of construction.[84]

Coulbourn also came to Alabama Power in 1924. He was assigned to Allied Engineers in the Commonwealth & Southern period and returned to Alabama Power in 1932. He was a short man, not forceful, but he had a quiet strength about him. Doug

E. R. Coulbourn. Courtesy of Elizabeth Hanigan.

McCrary, who worked with him for years, observed that Coulbourn "helped me more than anyone." Sometimes, when McCrary "wanted a snap decision," Coulbourn would "let it sit there working in his mind. We always knew he wanted to do the right thing."[85]

THE SIPSEY FORK OF THE BLACK WARRIOR RIVER: LEWIS M. SMITH DAM AND LOCK 17 GENERATION

On July 27, 1954, Alabama Power filed an application before the Federal Power Commission for a preliminary permit for developments on the Warrior River. This permit was issued December 27, 1954. The Black Warrior River rises from the last hills of the Appalachian Plateau, called the Cumberland Plateau in northwestern Alabama, and flows south through an area of rocky soils. The Warrior flows through a different geological terrain than the Coosa, drains a smaller area, and never has had the volume of water or consistent flow of the Coosa. Historically an important river for transportation in Alabama, shoals and shallow areas prevented navigation in the nineteenth century above the falls at Tuscaloosa. The opening of mines and mills in the Birmingham mineral district put pressure on the federal government to provide navigation to an area west of the city. Low water in dry seasons had been a problem on the Warrior since the appearance of steamboats on the river.

In 1889 Congress made its first appropriation for a series of dams and locks to facilitate interstate commerce on the Tombigbee–Black Warrior Rivers. In 1913, while the Corps of Engineers had the last and highest of the dams, Lock 17, under construction, Alabama Power was interested in placing a hydro plant there. But when the dam was completed in 1914–15, the company decided that hydro generation would not be profitable because of the low water flow.[86] In 1923 Alabama Power changed its mind and petitioned the Federal Power Commission for generation facilities at Lock 17 but was refused.[87] In 1915, after the completion of Lock 17, the Black Warrior River (called Bankhead Lake above Lock 17) was made navigable on the Mulberry Fork to barge traffic north of Cordova. Birmingport on the Locust Fork became the loading point for coal shipped south and iron ore imported to enrich the region's native ore.[88] The Warrior and the people of rural western Jefferson County were celebrated by Alabama writer Howell Vines in his 1930 novel, A River Goes with Heaven.

Except for the new lock at Tuscaloosa, which was constructed in 1939, few improvements had been made by the Corps of Engineers. In dry seasons, river traffic in the area between Tuscaloosa and Demopolis was still impeded, and above Tuscaloosa sometimes there was not enough water to work the locks. By 1950 the Warrior locks and dams were in various stages of deterioration. On April 3, 1950, the Alabama State Planning Board released a study of the Warrior-Tombigbee River system that pointed out the need for deeper channels and larger locks and the dangers of the shallow pools in the river. In May 1949 three vessels of the Warrior and Gulf Navigational Company towing twenty-five loaded barges were stuck below Lock 3 for six days because they were grounded.[89] Alabama Power's Gorgas Steam Plant below Cordova used river water for steam and for cooling, but in dry weather the river was so low the heated discharge started circulating into the intake structure.[90]

When Alabama Power Company announced plans to build a dam and reservoir on the Sipsey Fork of the Warrior River and applied to the Federal Power Commission for a license, there was little objection to these plans.[91] On August 27, 1954, Congressman Carl Elliott of Jasper wrote Governor Gordon Persons that "the unemployment in this area [of northwestern Alabama] is so unbelievable" that he was dedicating his time to pushing the project and asked the governor to reply "promptly and positively" to the notice coming from the Federal Power Commission. Elliott urged "the matter be speeded to the utmost through the administrative machinery."[92]

The new dam would be located just north of Parker Bridge on Highway 69, fifteen miles east of Jasper at a site known as Upper New Hope. This was the general area where the 1953 Black Warrior River survey by the Corps of Engineers had recommended a storage reservoir to increase the flow of water downstream in dry weather. The Sipsey Fork of the Warrior drains 944 square miles and flows from valleys in Winston, Cullman, and Walker Counties through coalfields into the Mulberry Fork and then south through Gorgas. A high dam would impound water in the rainy season, helping to control floods, and would release this water in the dry season, improving navigation downstream. The lake would provide another supply of industrial water for Birmingham, and water through the turbines would refresh the slack water pools near Tuscaloosa, increase water flow at Gorgas, improve conditions for fish in the river, and make the area more attractive for new industries. The more forceful downstream flow would also help keep saltwater from moving up the Mobile River and thus would increase the riverbank areas available for industry needing freshwater supplies. This would also help the water flow at Alabama Power's Barry Steam Plant on the Mobile River at Salco, which in 1953 was almost ready for service. In addition, the Warrior dam would create a deep and clear lake for recreation and fishing.[93]

Alabama Power began extensive research and geological testing under senior engineer Richard S. Woodruff to determine the best place to site the dam and where to find rocks suitable for construction. Company structural engineers—Woodruff, D. F. Elliott, and E. R. Coulbourn among them—met with consultants, including internationally known expert Silas H. Woodard, over many months. The most important decision to make was the best type of dam to build for maximum efficiency and economy.[94] The company used both aerial and ground surveys and set up a soil testing laboratory on-site to examine the extensive boring samples. The decision was to construct an earth and rock-fill slope dam some 300 feet high with a crest 2,200 feet long and wide enough for a service road. The base would be one-quarter mile wide, and the impounded lake would cover 21,200 acres. A high-water emergency spillway would be cut through the mountain on the west bank to serve during heavy floods that were predicted once every fifty years, although as of 2006 water had never been high enough to flow over the spillway. Excess water would flow into Mills Creek, releasing any flood pressure on the dam. Water reached the powerhouse through two tunnels, which were 26 feet in diameter and 1,925 feet long. An 80,000-kilowatt generator was planned, with a second to be installed later. The plant was generating electricity in 1961. The board of directors voted to name the Warrior dam for Alabama Power Company president Lewis M. Smith, who had been closely involved in its planning and design.[95] The dam was formally dedicated on May 23, 1961.

Construction view of Smith Dam looking southwest, January 18, 1961, showing to the center right the emergency spillway to Mills Creek.

The redeveloped Bankhead Lock and Dam. One wall of the old lock remains near the dam. The powerhouse went into operation on July 12, 1963.

With its enormous amount of reserve water, Smith Lake now made hydro generation at Bankhead Lock and Dam economical, and the company moved forward with plans to build a power plant on the western side of the dam in Tuscaloosa County. Meanwhile, the Corps of Engineers made major improvements to the 85-foot dam and to the lock. It excavated a canal from the eastern side of the river, built a new single-chamber lock, which replaced the original two locks, and increased the dam's height by several feet. Alabama Power constructed a powerhouse carved from the bottom of a 220-foot-high rock bluff. The company's Bankhead plant went into operation on July 12, 1963, with 45,125 kilowatts.[96]

When the Corps of Engineers determined to replace the low dams of Locks 13, 14, 15, and 16 between Tuscaloosa and Lock 17, Alabama Power Company filed an application before the Federal Power Commission on November 10, 1959, requesting a license to install two 20,000-kilowatt units at the proposed Holt Lock and Dam. A hearing was held in Tuscaloosa on December 5, 1962, to address whether there should be a power plant at Holt and, if so, whether it should be operated by the federal government or Alabama Power. Cooperatives were now objecting to Alabama Power Company's operation of the Holt plant and favored federal construction. However, they were outnumbered in the crowd, which was virtually a Who's Who in western Alabama businesses and governments, all advocating private power for a variety of reasons. Since generation was made possible by the construction of the company's Smith Dam, it seemed fair to allow Alabama Power to benefit from the generation of power at Holt. For maximum efficiency, there needed to be communication and cooperation between the operations at Smith and the plants at Bankhead and Holt. Some people at the meeting were opposed to their federal taxes being spent for construction when private capital was available. The benefits to local governments and the school systems from taxes paid by Alabama Power influenced many citizens to support the company's position.[97] The Army Corps of Engineers recommended that power development be included in the Holt Lock plans but did not recommend who should generate it. The decision was delayed for a while.

LAND ACQUISITIONS FOR COOSA AND WARRIOR LAKES

In the early years, Alabama Power had acquired some land in the upper Coosa area near possible dam sites, but the new developments there and on the Warrior required extensive additional land acquisitions. The company had to gear up its land department to handle the acquisitions because of the short time frame in which to build all the dams. The land along the Warrior in Walker, Winston, and Cullman Counties was steep, rocky, covered with timber, and mostly uninhabited. Few owners were unwilling to sell; however, the Weiss and Logan Martin reservoirs were a different story. Weiss particularly would flood rich bottomlands, including the most valuable and productive Cherokee County farms, land that had been cultivated for many years and perhaps for centuries before that by Indians who lived in villages along the Coosa. Prosperous farmers opposed a lake and initially tried to prevent the Federal Power Commission from granting a license to Alabama Power. When that effort failed, some joined a landowners association organized primarily by Birmingham attorneys who would oppose the Alabama Power Company on a contingency fee basis.[98]

As soon as company engineers decided on exact locations, the company's land department began working with surveys and ownership plats. All of Alabama Power's early hydro developments (1913–30) covered about 70,000 acres. The reservoirs being projected in the 1950s would cover more than 95,000 acres. Ollie Smith, a Mobile native who had been with the FBI before taking his University of Alabama law degree and joining Judge Martin's law firm in 1947, was in charge of purchasing the land. He moved to the Alabama Power Company in 1951 and four years later was head of the land department. Smith remembered clearly "Mr. Perry Turner's admonition that the company is not well served by driving too hard a bargain," and Smith's goal was to offer fair prices. Roughly 95 percent of the land for these developments was acquired by purchase. When owners refused to sell, Smith turned the files over to the law firm for condemnation proceedings and the law firm was inundated with title examinations. Joe Farley and James

H. Hancock (later a federal district judge) handled the condemnations for the Warrior lands, and Harold Williams handled the Coosa lands. Tom Bevill represented many of the landowners in Walker, Winston, and Cullman Counties.

Williams grew up in Avondale and Pell City, served in the India-Burma theater in World War II, and joined Judge Martin's firm in 1952 after graduating from Columbia University with a law degree.[99] A quiet-spoken gentleman who never lost his cool, he was a master at dealing with both clients and adversarial attorneys. Maurice Bishop, an experienced attorney in eminent domain and condemnation preceedings, was the main attorney for the landowners association. Harold Williams smiled, remembering back to this time when as a rather young lawyer he was concerned about going up against Bishop and decided to take a special short course in condemnation law in St. Louis. Williams arrived in the classroom to find that his instructor was Maurice Bishop.[100]

When Alabama Power was acquiring land in 1912–13 for the Lock 12 reservoir and the other dams constructed in the 1920s on the Coosa and Tallapoosa Rivers, landowners often insisted that their entire parcel be purchased. This left Alabama Power with large acreage away from the lakes. In the 1950s the Federal Power Commission required that the company take only the land it needed, so the company confined its purchases to land to the shoreline plus easements for rights to a fifty-year flood line. This was satisfactory for landowners because they now understood that lakefront property was very valuable.

Doug McCrary, a young Auburn engineer, became a hydrology expert and was given the task of determining flood levels for Weiss Lake. He came to the company in 1953 after graduating from API with two mechanical engineering degrees. He interviewed with Warren Turner in the Alabama Power Company engineering department and went to work for $360 a month, including a $10-a-month bonus for having a master's degree. McCrary was to have a long career with Alabama Power and other companies

Douglas L. McCrary

in the Southern Company system. C. J. Coley Jr., who worked with McCrary at the company, described him as smart and unassuming. McCrary developed a reputation as a meticulous engineer with a strong work ethic who found creative ways to solve problems.[101] McCrary spent the first months modifying steam plant pipe drawings. Then he started poring over Coosa River maps, checking possible dam sites and flood records to determine where the water would back up at each given site. Using historical stream flow records, he did calculations on a Friden calculator to determine capacity at each possible site and recalled that "in about 1954 or 1955, we would sometimes use the big computer upstairs in the accounting department. We would have to put jumper wires on a plug-in board to make the computer do the calculations for us. It was a major operation, and it took about as long to set up the problem as it did to make the calculations by hand."[102] Once a month engineers and consultants met to discuss the river development; attending were Fernand Weiss, E. R. Coulbourn, George Sowers from Law Engineering, E. C. Gaston and Dick Randolph from Southern Services, and Silas H. Woodard, an elderly engineer who had helped design the Panama Canal. McCrary was assigned responsibility for attending the meetings and writing up minutes, and he remembered that the sixth-floor conference room was so full of cigar smoke that one "could hardly see across the room."

McCrary was often called upon to be an expert witness for the company because the question of land value made it necessary to determine what lands would be underwater in floods and for how long. He remembers testifying in probably "a hundred cases involving the Coosa and Warrior Rivers," and although it "was no fun," McCrary thought the experience helped him.[103] The flood level was particularly important in the condemnation suits in Floyd County, Georgia, where Rome attorney John Maddox, whom Harold Williams called "perhaps the greatest trial lawyer that I have ever worked with," put McCrary on the stand to testify in numerous cases. Proceedings were in state probate court, but Georgia juries were fair to Alabama Power. Georgia landowners wanted damages based on the acquisition of the flood easement, but the company countered their claims with expert testimony by McCrary. Maps of each parcel of land with prior floods noted showed that flooding would actually be reduced by the construction of the dam. For land appraisals, the company used a large national agricultural appraisal firm out of St. Louis, Doan Agricultural Service.[104]

Alvin Vogtle hired attorney Hugh Reed of Centre to represent Alabama Power in Cherokee County. Harold Williams recalled that Reed was an "unreconstructed southerner," a man "who had great loyalty to his clients, and his clients loved him." The decision to take Alabama Power Company's position against some of his longtime clients and friends was difficult, but Reed based it on his love for Cherokee County and his conviction that the lake would be good for his county and in the long run a more significant asset for landowners. When the time came for filing lawsuits, Reed knew everyone, all the large and small landowners, and, as Williams recalled, he was able "to keep friendships going."[105]

Alabama Power decided on the Coosa River lands to proceed not under state law but under federal law, which allowed an estimate of just compensation to be deposited with the court while the company began construction. The court's decision on land value was affected by the increased value of property that fronted on the lake. In some cases Alabama Power paid about 20 percent more than the company had offered but much less than landowners wanted.

Other landowners, who had contested the compensation offered by Alabama Power, had to return money to the court because the price Alabama Power had estimated as the value of the land was much higher than the amount the court actually awarded. These events encouraged other landowners to settle without legal expenses.[106] Reed was so successful in handling the Weiss lands that he was hired to work with the company on lands needed for Logan Martin and Henry reservoirs, where the protective association organized by Birmingham attorneys, including Maurice Bishop, Frank Bainbridge, and his son Frank Jr., again represented landowners. In general, the association did not prove to be the windfall the Birmingham attorneys had envisioned, and one of these disappointed men, Bishop, would rekindle his opposition to Alabama Power in the critical years of the 1970s.

WEISS, LOGAN MARTIN, AND NEELY HENRY DAMS

On April 26, 1958, there was a special groundbreaking at the location of Weiss Dam celebrating the company's resumption of its construction on the Coosa River. It was a Martin-type celebration. Four regional high school bands played, the Gadsden post of the Veterans of Foreign Wars raised the flag, former lieutenant governor J. Clarence Inzer presided, and Governor Jim Folsom and all Alabama congressmen except Bob Jones of the Eighth District were introduced, as well as Georgia congressman Erwin Mitchell from the Rome area. John Temple Graves wrote that "rarely has so much of rank and so much of file, of state and of federal, of private and of public, been represented."[107] There were speeches by many men followed by a barbecue lunch served to 10,214 people. The company placed orders for turbines, generators, and transformers and began building a $30 million dam, which was completed in 1961.[108] The scenic lake was named for Alabama Power engineer Fernand C. Weiss but was sometimes referred to as the Pearl of Cherokee.

Hugh Reed was correct about the economic impact of the 30,200-acre lake on Cherokee County. In 1968 Zipp Newman, longtime *Birmingham News* sports editor, wrote that in 1967, only six years after completion of the dam, $15 million was spent in Cherokee County by lake visitors; that the value of homes and recreational facilities on the lake was about $20.4 million; and that Bill Coffey, who owned Yellow Creek Fish Camp, bragged that people from all over the nation came to the lake to fish, especially for crappie.[109]

In the company's plans for the upper Coosa, a dam was planned for the area where Kelly Creek flows into the Coosa. Engineers were concerned about the underground limestone stratum that runs beneath the area and the jointed and faulted bedrock that allowed for substantial groundwater movement. The riverbed was extensively drilled, and the results were studied to determine the best site for the dam along a three-mile stretch. A site north of Kelly Creek was determined to offer the best location. Construction started in July 1960 and proceeded uneventfully under the watchful eyes of Richard S. Woodruff and S. R. Hart. The dam was completed in August 1964, and the 15,263-acre reservoir began filling. With three units, the generating capacity was 128,250 kilowatts. On June 24, 1967, the dam was dedicated in honor of Tom Martin's brother Logan, and it was always called Logan Martin to separate it from the lake on the Tallapoosa.[110] Logan Martin Lake, which was less than one hour from Birmingham, was soon a popular place for homes and cottages and for fishing and recreational boating.[111]

After the reservoir was filled, leaking started below the dam from the cavities or voids in the limestone bedrock and appeared as large boils in the tailrace. Doug McCrary, Clayton Gore, David Holland, and John Winefordner worked on weekends looking for sinkholes and testing to see if they could discover how much water was leaking and where it was coming from. Red dye was pumped into the sinkholes through a pipe from a barge, and water downstream was monitored and tested to see how long it took the dye to appear downstream. Holland remembered the times there were three of them balancing a fourteen-foot aluminum boat trying to keep the boat steady while one dropped a flow meter in a sinkhole. Winefordner could not swim, and he was always happy to finish and get off the water. McCrary estimated they dumped enough sand and gravel in sinkholes to fill a football field twelve feet high. They stopped that and began sealing the lake bottom with chert and clay. The lake, dam, and tailrace were closely monitored, and remedial grouting, filling sinkholes, and constructing a French drain bolster were procedures used to mitigate the seepage.[112]

In 1962 work began on the dam planned for the Coosa River near Ohatchee. When completed in 1966 the reservoir covered 11,235 acres and backed water to the edge of Gadsden. The dam had three generators with a capacity of 72,900 kilowatts and was dedicated to H. Neely Henry, Alabama Power's senior executive vice president. The lake was soon a popular fishing spot, especially around Canoe Creek.[113]

Environmental Affairs

In 1958 John Farley, who was working under E. R. Coulbourn, was having coffee in the company cafeteria when Coulbourn came over and asked him, "What in the world is limnology?" Farley replied, "I don't have a clue, but I'll find out." Farley went to the library, looked up limnology, discovered it was the science of the physical, chemical, and biological properties and features of fresh waters, lakes and ponds, wrote it up, and brought it back to Coulbourn. Coulbourn read the paper, then told Farley, "You are now the company's limnologist." With Farley's new appointment, the company's environmental affairs department was created under the supervision of Doug McCrary. This was the beginning of Alabama Power Company's formal ecological and environmental programs. They began four years before Rachel Carson published her 1962 book *Silent Spring*, which is usually considered the beginning of the modern environmental movement. Because of the early work done by such organizations as the Audubon Society and the Izaak Walton League and the concern of health departments to protect drinking water, most states had antipollution water laws long before the 1950s. Alabama's law was passed in 1949. After 1965 the federal government became increasingly involved, and even more so after passage of the 1969 National Environmental Policy Act, the establishment of the Environmental Protection Agency, and water pollution control acts and amendments in 1972 and 1977.[114]

John Farley, the company's new limnologist, attended Princeton and then Cornell as part of the navy's V-12 program and served three years as an officer during World War II. He worked a few years with Alabama Power, then was called back by the navy when the Korean War started. After the war, John, who is Joe Farley's older brother, worked for Southern Research for a few years, then found his way back to Alabama Power and was working under Coulbourn.[115] John Farley recalled that litigation had been started in Virginia involving hydroelectric dams and downstream paper mills. The issue was whether the hydroelectric plant owners were responsible for keeping high levels of dissolved oxygen in their discharge so the downstream paper mill could continue to discharge high volumes of untreated waste. This issue raised the level of concern among utility executives and prompted the beginnings of studies to address dissolved oxygen issues.

The Izaak Walton League wrote Governor Persons in 1954 and raised questions about Alabama Power Company's conservation policies on its Coosa River projects. Tom Martin responded to Governor Persons's queries with a vigorous defense. He wrote that "Our record and policy over the years is perhaps the best evidence of our interest in and support of sound conservation policies and practices." He gave illustrations of the company's fish hatchery program, its conservation practices on its timber and coal lands, its mosquito control programs, and its recreational and wildlife programs.[116]

As Alabama Power went about constructing dams on the upper Coosa,

John Farley recalled they became aware that there were "all kinds of problems on that river." He was given three college students for the summer of 1958, and the four of them made a survey, taking water samples and testing the entire Coosa, concentrating on temperature and oxygen content. The samples went to Ted Jaffe, professor of civil engineering at Auburn, who identified serious problems. A paper mill was dumping untreated waste into the river in Georgia, and when Alabama Power Company complained, the paper company sued Alabama Power for impounding the Coosa and thus destroying the assimilative capacity of the river. Cities that dumped raw sewage into the river wanted Alabama Power to pay for sewage treatment plants. The paper mill at Childersburg that Tom Martin had worked so hard to acquire for Talladega County wanted to solve the problems without litigation. It built settling ponds and worked closely with Alabama Power to improve the quality of the river's water.

Company Leadership in the 1950s

H. Neely Henry

A number of engineers, representing a new leadership generation, were important to the operation of the company in the 1950s. H. Neely Henry, whom many credit with actually running the day-to-day operations of Alabama Power for years, began his career with Alabama Power Company in 1924. He was a brilliant Virginia Military Institute electrical engineer who left for World War II and returned a full colonel with a chest full of medals. A robust, big man with a voice that resonated, Henry served as an office manager, district manager, and manager of the company's industrial development efforts. He gained a reputation as an excellent judge of character and an efficient manager who ran a tight ship and was willing to delegate responsibility. John Temple Graves once described Neely Henry after a company presentation as "all dignity, competence and friendliness." By the 1950s Henry probably knew the company better than anyone. He was named vice president, then executive vice president on January 1, 1955. Walter Johnsey, who worked under Henry for four years, remembered him as a man who had a way with people and who was able to get things done.

Rother L. "Judge" Harris

Henry's relationship with the company's attorneys was sometimes strained because he saw things from an engineer's point of view.[117]

For twenty years Rother L. Harris was Neely's right-hand man. Called "Judge" because of the way he viewed problems, his ability as an expert witness, and tall tales of his once running a kangaroo court at Gorgas for construction workers, Harris was a Chilton County native. He was a University of Alabama engineering graduate who came to

Alabama Power Company in 1924 from Dixie Construction Company. A superb engineer, Harris was involved with company operations and engineering assignments, rising to manager of production in 1951 and vice president in charge of operations in 1956. Doug McCrary credits Harris with teaching him "how to operate the hydro reservoirs to obtain the most energy from stream flows while maintaining the capacity of the units to meet loads during the peak periods."[118] Harris grew up with the company's generation plants. Joe Farley once wrote that Harris's "knowledge of the company's system and of its generating requirements and the quirks and personalities of each of the generating units gave him a working knowledge unparalleled at the time when the sophisticated computers of today were not available."[119]

Harris was a tough guy who demanded perfection. All the construction, engineering, and operational people had to come before him for a budget review, and they all dreaded it because nothing got by him. He brought discipline to operations and kept close control of the budget. Harris literally ran the company, and, as Elmer Harris observed, "no one got things done unless Judge said grace over it."[120] Stories about Judge Harris have become part of company lore. He had a reputation of being prudent with a nickel, not only with the company's money but his own as well. He was never one to be concerned about having new suits, and wearing out was not a reason to purchase anything new, though falling apart and not repairable might be. One of the reasons Alabama Power was able to operate with no rate increases in this period was Harris's tight budget control.[121] Occasionally, he did support something innovative, especially if it would bring economies in operations. Joe Farley remembered that Harris did not even approve of having heaters in company cars.[122] Walter Johnsey recalled the time when Neely Henry told him to add air conditioners to one large order for plain Chevrolet fleet cars. Somehow, it slipped past Harris the first time, but he found it later and came to Johnsey roaring, "Who did this?" Harris struck it out, but Henry put it back in. Harris was a dedicated man who worked six or seven days a week and knew more about the company's electrical operations than almost anyone. Johnsey credits Harris's close supervision with the budget and Henry's management as reasons Alabama Power moved into the 1960s on such a strong foundation despite having no rate increases.[123]

Walter F. Johnsey

NUCLEAR ENERGY

From the late summer of 1945, when the United States dropped two atomic bombs on Japan and thus brought World War II to an end, there was interest in peacetime uses for nuclear energy. The nature of nuclear technology was classified, and atomic research was controlled by the government. A year after the war was over, President Harry S. Truman signed the Atomic Energy Act of 1946, which established the Atomic Energy Commission to supervise nuclear research. The half-century-old conflict between government ownership and private enterprise rose once more over the question of private access to nuclear technology. In 1947 the Industrial Advisory Commission was established by private utilities to push for security clearances for industrial researchers to determine how nuclear energy might be used in the production of electricity. Along with propulsion of submarines, this was its most obvious commercial use.[124] Nuclear energy could not directly produce electricity, but the heat it produced could possibly heat water and create steam to drive a generator. Executives at Detroit Edison led the initiative, but private industry's access was limited by the Atomic Energy Commission.

The first successful experimental reactor to produce electricity was constructed by Enrico Fermi and Walter Zinn at the Argonne National Laboratory in December 1951. Four 200-watt lightbulbs glowed brightly. Alabama Power Company mentioned the possibilities of nuclear power in its 1952 *Annual Report*, suggesting that nuclear generation would be "more nearly competitive in high cost fuel areas" and predicting that the first plants would be constructed outside the South, which had cheap coal. On December 8, 1953, President Eisenhower gave his famous "Atoms for Peace" speech before the United Nations. He promised that nuclear energy technology would be developed for peaceful use. Eisenhower signed the Atomic Energy Act of 1954, which allowed private development of nuclear technology and gave the Atomic Energy Commission the job of both promoting and regulating the nuclear power industry.[125]

In 1953, in preparation for moving into nuclear generation, Southern Services, Inc., the engineering and service company of Southern Company, hired Ruble Thomas, a young Georgia Tech engineer, and sent him to the Oak Ridge School of Reactor Technology. Alabama Power Company joined twelve other electric utilities and eight manufacturing companies to form a nonprofit entity, the Power Reactor Development Company, to design, construct, and operate a demonstration atomic energy plant to test the commercial application of nuclear power. H. J. Scholz of Southern Services was elected vice president, a trustee, and chairman of the technical and engineering committee. Walter Bouldin of Alabama Power was elected a trustee and member of the finance committee of the Power Reactor Development Company. The plant was built on Detroit Edison property southwest of Detroit.[126]

Ruble Thomas was sent to Detroit following his nuclear engineering experience at Oak Ridge, and for four years he worked on the breeder. The initial cost estimate of the nuclear plant was $40 million, and Alabama Power agreed to contribute $800,000 over five years. The announcement was included in the company's 1955 *Annual Report* with the observation that because Alabama had abundant cheap coal resources the company was able "to proceed more deliberately in the field of atomic power."[127] Alabama Power sponsored, along with Southern Research Institute and other groups, a major three-day conference in Atlanta in April

Ruble Thomas. Courtesy of the Georgia Power Company Archives.

1956 that brought together the national leadership of nuclear power experts to discuss the status of the research and the future of atomic energy in the South.[128] Thomas served as manager of nuclear power for Southern Services from 1959 to 1964, when he became manager of nuclear management planning and research. Alabama Power continued its support for the Fermi Plant near Detroit and for nuclear power development. The company stayed on the cutting edge of nuclear research, but it would be more than ten years before Alabama Power moved toward nuclear generation.[129]

Industrial Development

The 1950s continued to show outstanding progress in industrial development in Alabama. In 1951, forty-five plants located in the company's service area. Tom Martin was especially pleased when Beaunit Mills and North American Rayons came to Childersburg and invested more than $20 million and provided jobs for 400 Alabamians.[130] Congressman Frank W. Boykin of Mobile was committed to working with Alabama Power Company to recruit industry, and Boykin pressured Governor Persons to promote a tax exemption law for new industries. When the governor finally approved the legislation that Barbour County legislator George C. Wallace had sponsored, Persons wired Boykin that he had signed the act. The Mobile congressman waxed eloquent in his thanks to the governor, writing that he could see from his room at the Washington Hotel a display window at Garfinkel's filled with "the most beautiful nightgowns and all sorts of women's apparel" made in Alabama by Vanity Fair. Boykin wrote that the new law put Alabama on an even plane with other southern states, and he told the

governor he had sent a copy of the act to Thomas W. Nichols, the president of Olin Matheson Chemical Company, which was planning a $60 million plant at McIntosh. A few months before Boykin wrote the letter, on March 13, 1951, Alabama Power had signed a contract with Matheson to supply 25,000-kilowatt electrical capacity for the new plant, a significant event for the new industries and marketing departments and another reason the company pushed forward with plans for Barry Steam Plant.[131]

Olin Matheson Chemical Company under construction, ca. 1952.

Barry Steam Plant under construction, October 5, 1953.

"Live Better Electrically": Marketing and Sales Programs

Alabama Power's sales department remained strong into the 1950s and flourished under the presidency of James M. Barry, whom Walter Baker described as being "imbued with a marketing spirit."[132] Division vice presidents—Otto K. Seyforth, Anniston (Eastern), Charles S. Thorn (Birmingham), Frank S. Keeler (Mobile), A. Sidney Coleman, Montgomery (Southern), W. Marvin Wade, Eufaula (Southeast), and Henry Maulshagen, Tuscaloosa (Western)—met with general manager E. W. Robinson in January 1953 to discuss the year's sales program and accept the challenge of increasing sales by 13 percent.[133] The division vice presidents were real powers in the company and, as one company man joked, ruled their own kingdoms. It was unheard of for anyone representing corporate headquarters to visit a division without first notifying the division vice president.

In April 1953 Alabama Power signed its largest single industrial power contract to that time. The company agreed to provide a capacity of 130,000 kilovolt-amperes to the Tennessee Coal, Iron and Railroad Division of the United States Steel Corporation. In 1956 Southern Electric Steel Company built a new plant using an electric steel furnace to produce steel bars for concrete reinforcement. It was important to the management of the steel company that Alabama Power Company give them an off-peak electrical rate, so the company only operated the plant at night.[134]

Heat pump sales increased as the efficiency of the equipment improved and costs decreased and as more manufacturers entered the market. In 1953 General Electric began making its Weathertron heat pump, and by 1957 nine companies were manufacturing heat pumps. The next year Carrier joined the group. Air Engineers handled sales, installation, and service out of offices in Mobile and Birmingham.[135] Alabama Power began using heat pumps in all new company complexes, including offices in Tuscaloosa and Phenix City and in new facilities built at Gorgas. In 1958 the Edison Electric Institute introduced a new program that used signs placed in front of new homes to announce that they were ALL ELECTRIC and GOLD MEDALLION HOMES. When Walter Bouldin removed his gas furnace and installed heat pumps, he was one of the first home owners in Birmingham to receive the Gold Medallion recognition.[136] The sales success of heat pumps (with air conditioning) and electric air conditioning units in the 1950s caused the company's summer load to increase so much that more sales of electric heating were needed to balance the seasonal load.

Edward A. Wilson, who started his company career in 1917 as a draftsman and worked in industrial sales, was made general sales manager in 1954. The next year the corporate sales department moved to the former building of Birmingham Electric at 2100 First Avenue North.[137] Despite this extra space in the corporate office building, the company was still cramped for space because more employees were needed to handle the new construction on the Coosa and Warrior Rivers. In 1957 construction began on an addition to the building's northern face. The eight-story building, which had a distinctive bright blue steel exterior that many people, including Tom Martin, thought was an affront to the 1925 building, was completed in February 1959. Although it was connected to each floor of the original building, it had its own elevators and heating and air conditioning systems.[138]

In 1955 Harllee Branch Jr., Southern Company CEO, became president of the Edison Electric Institute. On February 8, 1956, in a nationwide closed-circuit television program, Branch announced an advertising campaign called

General Electric spokesman Ronald Reagan speaking with Tom Martin and Walter Bouldin during a visit to the corporate headquarters in October 1960.

LIVE BETTER ELECTRICALLY, which became the common slogan for the country's utilities. Alabama Power sponsored the program at the Tutwiler Hotel, and 450 company people attended. The advertising campaign was aimed at the millions of young people who were marrying and establishing new homes and at the owners of older homes with inadequate service and outdated wiring. Advertisements appeared in leading women's magazines and in *Look, Life,* and the *Saturday Evening Post.* J. Paul Brown, manager of residential sales, supervised Alabama Power's participation.

This program followed by one month the national advertising campaign of Southern Company and its four operating companies, a campaign that stressed the "economic, industrial, cultural, [and] recreational" advantages of the South.[139] In 1964 the Edison Electric Institute sponsored the All-Electric Building Award and began pushing all-electric commercial buildings. Alabama Power played a major role in the kickoff for this campaign. M. B. Penn, Luther T. Cale, and Richard A. Peacock all made presentations. Samuel H. Booker became general manager of marketing in 1962 and began his marketing accomplishments, which became legendary. Alan Martin, who worked with Booker, remembers Booker's marketing philosophy as "Shoot at everything that flies, and count everything that falls."[140]

Other new programs helped increase company sales in the late 1950s and early years of the 1960s. Dusk-to-dawn lighting service was introduced. These lights were inexpensive to operate at a flat price of $3 a month and automatically came on each evening and went off in the morning. They were particularly popular in rural areas where there were no streetlights. The lights were installed on high poles to light areas between barns and houses and around churches and schools.[141] Another sales boost came from radiant heated concrete-

Oneonta district employee Jean Blackmon helps promote "Dusk to Dawn" lighting. ca. 1960.

slab brooders that were used to keep baby chicks warm and from peanut driers developed by the agricultural engineers at Auburn. More farms were using electric pumps to provide running water. Farmers raising sweet potatoes used electrically heated hotbeds to force seeds to germinate early.[142]

One problem that hampered the sale of electrical appliances, and thus the sale of electricity, was that homes built before 1930 had been wired for only a few lights, an iron, and maybe a fan. The typical 30-ampere service entrance (power box) was inadequate to carry additional appliances, and even newer homes were not wired adequately for stoves, clothes dryers, room air conditioners, and hot water heaters. In 1954 Alabama Power introduced a plan that allowed home owners to finance rewiring of their homes through the company. The plan was very popular. In 1960 Alabama Power initiated a program that would help customers improve the outside service entrance facilities to enable home owners to receive more electricity.[143] All of these programs increased the residential use of electricity. Alabama Power was also helped by the General Electric Company's extensive television advertising, which encouraged appliance sales. The GE spokesman was Hollywood movie star Ronald Reagan, who visited Birmingham in October 1960 to open the new GE appliance distribution center. Reagan spoke to 250 people at the company auditorium and talked about the dangers of communist infiltration and his experiences in the film industry.[144]

SOUTHERN ELECTRIC GENERATING COMPANY

For some years Southern Company had encouraged Georgia Power and Alabama Power to establish a cooperative generating plant near Alabama coalfields. This was particularly advocated by Eugene Yates, and James F. Crist helped develop the idea. The Alabama Public Service Commission granted Alabama Power permission to proceed, and the Southern Electric Generating Company was organized in May 1956 with H. J. Scholz as president. He was followed by Crist. The plant needed to be centrally located to the loads of both companies, so land was selected on the Coosa River in Shelby County near Wilsonville. The Southern Company financed some $50 million by making additional investments in the common stocks of both companies. Another $100 million was raised by Southern Electric Generating Company's sale of debt securities to the public.[145]

The SEGCO plant was expected to use three million tons of coal a year. Before construction began, coal land surveys were made using the latest technology, including an auger drill mounted on a caterpillar tractor, a machine that was assembled in the Gorgas shop. Alabama Power sold some of its coal

lands to the new company, and SEGCO acquired additional coal lands in the nearby Shelby and Warrior fields. New coal mines were planned for Maylene in the Montevallo seam of the Cahaba field, with another one south of Parrish in Walker County, which was the first mine to open. Southern Railroad agreed to ship the coal on a train that would be dedicated to this shipment and would run a load every day, arriving each morning full and returning empty each evening to the mine.[146]

The management complications were worked out between Georgia Power and Alabama Power, but in a few years it seemed that expenses for legal and accounting fees and overhead were unduly high. After Alabama Power Company located an 880-megawatt unit next to the units that were jointly owned, an arrangement was made for Alabama Power to manage the joint enterprise through a management contract.[147] Andrew E. Burnett, called "Strut," was the first operating manager at the Wilsonville plant. A Bessemer native and Auburn engineering graduate, Burnett received a Sloan Fellowship to study economics and industrial management at Massachusetts Institute of Technology. Construction on the Wilsonville plant began in the fall of 1958, and the first two SEGCO 250,000-kilowatt generators went online the summer of 1960. The other two were operating in 1961 and 1962, respectively.[148]

Fiftieth
anniversary
seal.

FIFTIETH ANNIVERSARY OF ALABAMA POWER COMPANY

The fiftieth anniversary of Alabama Power came in the middle of a decade that saw tremendous growth in generation, transmission, and demand. The golden anniversary was celebrated at Gadsden, where Captain Lay founded the company in

December 1906. The chamber of commerce hosted a luncheon and the mayor proclaimed "Alabama Power Company Day." Three sons of Captain Lay were present.

Tom Martin spoke and reiterated part of the company's published statement of policy: "We recognize a triple responsibility—to the public, to our employees and to our security holders—and our obligation to try to maintain a just balance among these three groups. The company and every man and woman in our organization should take constructive interest in community affairs, contributing time and effort to worthy civic undertakings and supporting them financially; and we will continue to encourage among our employees a realization that citizenship carries with it duties as well as privileges."[149] In 1956 Alabama Power Company was serving 583,559 customers and had connected 150,000 rural customers to its lines. There were 5,300 employees working in 638 job classifications.[150]

ALABAMA POWER COMPANY INNOVATIONS AND TECHNOLOGY

Throughout its history, Alabama Power tried to stay on the cutting edge of technology, and its engineers were always innovative. E. R. Coulbourn's designs for conductors, transformers, and substations, which were used by Westinghouse and other manufacturers, made rural electrification economically feasible. F. H. Britton Jr., commercial lighting engineer at the corporate office, was able to solve the lighting problem in coal mines. Because of coal gas and dust, the U.S. Bureau of Mines allowed only battery-powered portable lights. Britton designed portable lights from explosive-proof materials. Men at Alabama Power's North Birmingham shop took Britton's designs and built the lights, which were used at Gorgas.[151] Royce Murray developed a transformer field dry-out process that was adopted by major transformer manufacturers, and he improved equipment for testing rubber gloves in the laboratory. C. M. Pettus, Mobile Division, worked with Dr. Raymond Self of the Alabama Ornamental Horticultural Experiment Station at Spring Hill to devise a way to treat seeds and bulbs with a thermostatically controlled bath to eliminate fungus parasites.[152]

E. D. Early, manager of the Southern Company power pool, created the "Early Bird," the world's first computer to determine incremental cost for delivered power. Teletypewriters were used in system operations to make certain there were no mistakes in understanding instructions about system operations. In 1958 Alabama Power had the largest and most modern telephone system supplied by Southern Bell Telephone Company. It took four months to install and cost $150,000. Teletypewriters were installed at Magella for instant communication. The latest system for keeping track of materials and supplies and for accounting and inventory was installed in 1963.[153] Alabama Power began using helicopters to spray chemicals on the dense swamp portions of the Barry-Pinckard 230-kV transmission line right-of-way. In August 1960 the appearance of a helicopter in rural Alabama caused excitement. A story was told of one farmer who rushed a mile through dense woods when the chopper landed because he thought it had crashed.[154]

Bucket trucks revolutionized line repairs.

By 1960 Alabama Power Company had introduced aerial lift bucket trucks, sometimes called cherry pickers, into all divisions.[155] There is an interesting connection between Alabama Power Company and Birmingham's Altec Industries, Inc., which in 2006 was the world's largest manufacturer of utility industry equipment. In 1929 Lee Styslinger Sr. was a thirty-three-year-old engineering graduate of the University of Pittsburgh. He purchased the Alabama Truck Equipment Company on Vanderbilt Road and moved his family from Pennsylvania to Birmingham that year. Styslinger introduced a number of innovations—aluminum in truck bodies and all-steel truck bodies—but his health was poor and he died in 1952, leaving his company in the hands of his family. His son, Lee Jr., reorganized the company into Altec Industries, Inc., in 1956 and began to specialize in utility equipment, partly because, he recalled, "I felt they would pay their bills."

Although Altec started off as a distributor and did not invent the cherry picker, it helped design, assemble, and customize what Alabama Power Company wanted. In the early 1970s Altec decided to go into manufacturing and with talented designers and engineers was able to patent a number of significant improvements in utility trucks and equipment. Altec worked closely with Alabama Power and Southern Company to supply the trucks and equipment the operating companies needed. Styslinger recalled his early years of working with Alabama Power's Jeff Wells, who was head of transportation. "There was once a time when Jeff would call and tell us to build four units, and we would do that with no paperwork." Looking back over his company's history, Styslinger observed, "if one company helped build Altec, it was Alabama Power Company."[156]

Storms of the 1950s, Safety and Health

Thunderstorms, tornadoes, hurricanes, and ice storms play havoc with an electrical system, and it is costly to repair damage and restore power. Alabama Power has always had emergency plans, which can be implemented as soon as severe weather is reported. On February 11, 1958, an ice storm hit Mobile and temperatures fell to fifteen degrees. On February 14 a massive snowstorm moved into the Western, Birmingham, and Eastern Divisions, causing heavy damage. Haleyville had sixteen to eighteen inches of snow. But the ice storm of March 2, 1960, in northern Alabama created the most destruction to the company's system to that date. Lines on Lookout and Chandler Mountains "were literally torn to shreds," and almost all rural customers north of Gadsden were without electricity. Distribution and construction crews from all over the state were sent to help.[157]

Periodically, tornadoes skipped and hopped through the state, but as soon as the weather cleared enough for planes to fly, Alabama Power sent air patrol pilots up to locate potential sources of trouble. By the 1950s, radio communication was widely used. This included communications between crews, with headquarters, and between the ground and pilots. On the night of April 18, 1953, two pilots, D. J. Faulkner and E. S. Weaver, were checking tornado damage in the Lay Dam area. On their return trip to Tuscaloosa their instrument lights went out; heavy winds had blown them off course, visibility was zero, and their commercial long-wave radio was not working. All they had was their portable short-wave FM radio on the Alabama Power Company frequency. They had no idea where they were. They flew below the clouds and radioed, asking for all company people to see if they could spot a plane flying low with its landing lights blinking. Headquarters cleared everyone off the frequency. Paul Anderson, foreman at Demopolis, located them first, then J. D. Berry, local manager at Greensboro, spotted the plane. Meanwhile, J. B. Carl and Bobby Cardinal of Dixie Air took off from Tuscaloosa, found Weaver and Faulkner, and led them back to the Tuscaloosa airport.[158]

To react quickly and correctly in any emergency and to work safely in dangerous conditions have always been important goals of the company's safety program. First aid, artificial respiration, and water safety have been part of these programs. J. L. Shores, who had come to the company in 1925 as safety engineer and first aid instructor, rose to be manager of safety by 1953 and was called "Daddy Shores" by everyone because he was responsible for making all employees safety conscious.[159] Banquets and awards were regularly used to recognize the safety records of various divisions and departments in the company. In 1957 Alabama Power won the National Safety Council's first-place award for the fourth time in seven years, an unheard of feat. Tribute was paid to Shores and to the company's safety creed, which James M. Barry had written many years before: "There can be no operating condition which justifies our employees taking the slightest chance in performing their work. We want them always to take the safe way, even though our service may suffer thereby, or our costs be increased." In 1956 the Western, Mobile, and Southeast Divisions had no lost-time accidents. In 1957 Gorgas construction employees marked forty-six months without a lost-time accident. In 1963 the North Birmingham shop employees won an Edison Electric Institute award for working one million man-hours without a disabling injury.[160]

The company's medical department, organized under the direction of Dr. Samuel R. Benedict, had developed under guidance of Doctors E. M. Mason and J. M. Mason. In 1957 the department was headed by Dr. J. M. Mason III with the assistance of Dr. E. B. Glenn. Prospective employees were given

Nurse Mary Martin, Dr. E. M. Mason, Ferdnand C. Weiss and J. L. "Daddy" Shores at the first aid tent at the Weiss Dam groundbreaking ceremony, April 26, 1958.

physical examinations, and all employees received "birthday examinations" without charge. Emergency injuries were treated. Mary Martin was one of two registered nurses who gave eye exams, doctored those in need, and became somewhat of a company legend in the process. Mrs. Martin was a St. Vincent's School of Nursing graduate who came to Alabama Power Company in 1949. Her son Alan, who in 2006 was the executive vice president of Alabama Power, noted that his mother "always looked like a nurse was supposed to look. She wore a starched white dress and cap, white hose and white shoes." Mary Martin recalled that linemen were always getting splinters in their arms from sliding down poles, and once it took her hours to pull wood slivers from a young man's arms. The lineman joked to her that she must be good at plucking a chicken, and the next day he showed up with a fat hen for Mrs. Martin. The medical department also supervised the mosquito eradication program. Inspectors made certain that company sanitation systems and water systems operated effectively and nurses administered inoculations, such as typhoid fever shots.[161]

COMPANY PROGRAMS AND SOUTHERN RESEARCH INSTITUTE

Throughout the 1950s Alabama Power supported a number of community programs. Its work with 4-H Clubs and Future Farmers of America was widely recognized and constantly strengthened. One of the company's programs, Junior Achievement, taught selected high school seniors about business, finance, production, and sales.[162] Alabama Power worked closely with Auburn's agricultural education programs to teach the application of electricity to farms. Tom Martin chaired the fund-raising drive to raise $850,000 to establish an engineering program at the University of Alabama's extension program in Birmingham. The drive was successful, and eventually the enlarged university offerings, combined with the medical and dental schools, led to the creation of a separate campus, the University of Alabama at Birmingham, and a separate degree offering. Martin wanted engineers in the Birmingham area to have the opportunity of earning or completing their degrees, and many Alabama Power employees took advantage of the new program.[163]

Alabama Power Company held its first "Old Timers Reunion" on September 19, 1950, at Martin Dam. Several hundred former employees attended, including black employees. Photographs in *Powergrams* indicate it was an integrated function. Tom Martin gave a long speech reminiscing about the past and thanking everyone for their part in the company's success. On November 2, 1951, the Old Timers met at Jordan Dam. The cold, inclement weather hardly dampened the spirits of the 500 people who attended, men in

The popular "Old Timers Reunions" were one of Alabama Power Company's first integrated social functions.

coats and ties and women wearing hats. On September 23, 1955, the reunion returned to Martin Dam with a crowd of 646. Reunions were held for the next four years, but the crowds outgrew the company's facilities.[164]

As the years passed, Tom Martin was pleased with the successes of Southern Research Institute, which had been responsible among other things for fine-tuning the heat pump. Southern Research gained international recognition for two conferences in Birmingham: the Age of Space in May 1957 and the Economic Future of the South in May 1958. In 1961 the institute held a coal technology conference. Leading scholars and researchers from all over the world attended these meetings and shared their research. Alabama Power supported all these activities, especially research on burning coal with less environmental impact. When he organized the institute, Martin had envisioned the mission of Southern Research as developing products to make southern industry more competitive and successful and as creating more jobs. Southern Research expanded to medical and space research as the University of Alabama medical school began to focus attention on medical research in the city. Southern Research made significant contributions in cancer research and other medical fields.

Recreational Lakes and Lake Shore Cottages

After the construction of Lay Dam in 1913, Alabama Power Company encouraged private landowners to utilize the lake for recreational purposes, and the program expanded with the lakes behind Mitchell, Martin, and Jordan Dams. In the early years, private landowners subdivided their property and built fish camps and rough cabins. Since the land owned by Alabama Power Company was considered part of a project, the Federal Power Commission would not allow Alabama Power to sell its land, so the company began to lease it. For a while, the fact that they did not own the land was not an important matter to those who were building on the lots because the houses were mostly small and inexpensive cabins. After World War II, the economic boom increased demands for recreational homes, and people wanted to construct more substantial houses. Alabama Power worked with banks to help them understand the situation so that people could borrow money to construct houses on leased land. In the 1970s the Federal Power Commission changed its policy and allowed the company to subdivide its land and sell it.

Alabama Power Company realized that with its plans to develop more lakes on the Coosa and Warrior Rivers, it would have to expand its recreational services. Richard Scott, the supervisor of recreational development, noted in 1955 that "this recreational program is not a source of potential profit to Alabama Power Company. It is not approached with any idea of profit, but as a service to the people of Alabama who enjoy wholesome outdoor sports." In the 1950s and 1960s lakeshore lots were being leased from the company almost as quickly as the land department could survey and build chert roads to the property. Some of the houses were simple cabins or weekend cottages, while others were substantial permanent homes. Alabama Power Company also reached agreements with the State Conservation Department to construct picnic areas and boat launching sites for the public. In 1962 two projects had been completed, one on Lake Jordan at Bonner's Fishing Camp and one on Lake Martin at Young's Island.[165]

Economic prosperity along with improved boat and motor designs and manufacturing techniques increased boat sales, and fishing became more popular after the company expanded its program of improving the fish population. Company-sponsored fishing contests drew thousands of fishermen. Inboard racing courses were established for official speed checks, and regattas were held for both inboard and outboard boats. Water skiing became common on the lakes.[166] The company worked to control the mosquito population on Lake Martin, first by spraying an oil solution from boats, then in 1953 by spraying from airplanes. Mosquito control on other lakes was achieved by fluctuating the water level eighteen to twenty-four inches each week.[167]

Horseshoe Bend National Military Park

In the 1950s Tom Martin joined with Tallapoosa County probate judge C. J. "Jack" Coley and Tom Russell to push for a national military park at Horseshoe Bend, where Andrew Jackson and the Tennessee Volunteers defeated the Creek Indians in 1814. Alabama Power had owned the site for a long time. In

Cherokee Indian Richard Crowe presents Tom Martin with a peace pipe and a certificate making him an honorary member of the Oconaluftee Village at Cherokee, North Carolina, for his efforts in establishing the Horseshoe Bend Military Park.

the early years two dams were once considered for the Tallapoosa River. The second dam planned for north of Cherokee Bluffs would have inundated the site of the battle, but Tom Martin recommended to James Mitchell that the historic site never be flooded. In 1923, when the final plans were being made for the Cherokee Bluffs dam, the dam's height was made high enough so one dam would be sufficient; however, the company retained the right to construct the second dam.

In the early part of the century, supporters of Horseshoe Bend petitioned the government, but the Department of the Interior rejected the petition for a military park at Horseshoe Bend because the battle did not have national significance. With the 150th anniversary of the battle approaching, Martin and his Tallapoosa County friends, Judge Coley and Tom Russell, were determined to be successful with a second request. Martin recalled an obscure biography of Jackson that claimed the victory at Horseshoe Bend affected the Treaty of Ghent, which ended the War of 1812 between Great Britain and the United States. Martin hired London researchers to comb the British archives, and with the material they uncovered and other data claiming that the victory led to Jackson being elected president, he presented his case to a congressional committee. The committee approved, and Congress passed an act stating that the defeat of the Creek Indian nation at the Battle of Horseshoe Bend had a part in bringing about the Treaty of Ghent. Bill Brantley, a noted Alabama historian and longtime board member of Alabama Power and Southern Company, was fond of saying that Tom Martin was the only person who ever got history changed by a congressional act.[168] In any case, President Eisenhower signed the proclamation in 1959 on the day before Martin's seventy-eighth birthday.[169] Horseshoe Bend National Military Park was established, and Tom Martin delivered a gift deed from Alabama Power Company to the secretary of the interior for 560.66 acres.[170] On March 27, 1964, the sesquicentennial of the Battle of Horseshoe Bend, 5,000 people gathered to dedicate Alabama's first military park.[171]

RATES AND THE PUBLIC SERVICE COMMISSION

In 1957 Alabama Power established a statewide standard urban residential service, Rate A-13, for all customers except for service rendered from rural lines. The rate was revised the next year to give a discount for high summer usage.[172] On August 18, 1959, the Montgomery Junior Chamber of Commerce invited Edward A. Wilson to address the question of electric utility rates. Wilson, who came to Alabama Power as a draftsman in 1917, rose through the industrial power sales department to be general sales manager in 1954 and vice president in 1958. He recalled that being asked to discuss rates was indeed a first. After explaining the need for "huge amounts of capital funds" and stating that rates "must be sufficient to cover all operating costs and provide a fair return on the capital invested in plant facilities necessary to supply dependable service," Wilson pointed out that Alabama Power Company was "one of the very few, if any, utilities which in its entire history has never had what is known as a general increase in its rates." By this, Wilson meant an "increase of some percentage applicable to all customers." Operating for such a long time without a rate increase was accomplished despite increases in wages, taxes, materials, and equipment. When adjusted to price indexes comparing 1939 and 1959 prices, electricity was the only commodity that had decreased in cost. Wilson cautioned that in the future economies of scale and "improvement in operating efficiencies may not keep pace with inflation."[173] Within ten years, this is exactly what happened.

THE END OF THE MARTIN ERA

In April 1964 the original Gadsden Steam Plant units constructed in 1912 were demolished. James Mitchell had acquired the partially completed plant when he purchased the Alabama Power Development Company from EBASCO and S. Z. and Reuben Mitchell. When the units began operation on August 1, 1913, they represented state of the art technology and produced the first major electricity James Mitchell's holding company, Alabama Traction, Light & Power, had to sell. The only other power came from the small hydro plant at Jackson Shoals. The new Gadsden plant was operational in 1949, and the old Gadsden units were last operated in November 1952. The two silent turbines once had a capacity of 5,000 kilowatts each and produced steam pressure to 185 pounds per square inch at temperatures of 350 degrees Fahrenheit. To compare, the new turbines that Alabama Power was then installing at the Greene County plant provided 2,400 pounds per square inch, reached 1,000 degrees Fahrenheit, and produced 250,000 kilowatts.[174] The demolition of the old Gadsden plant's obsolete units represented the end of a bygone era.

As Tom Martin moved into his late seventies and his health gradually declined, everyone realized that the Martin era was drawing to a close, too. Martin did not have the energy he once had. After a company board of directors meeting sometime in the early 1960s, he returned to his office to meet with his personal attorney and friend, William J. Ward, who recalled that "Mr. Martin sat down sadly and said, 'I go to meetings and all I do is kick dust in the air.'"[175] The death of his brother, Logan Martin, on June 19, 1959, was a great personal loss to him. The brothers were close, even though company files show that Judge Martin always addressed his correspondence to "Mr. Martin." Years later, on June 24, 1967, after both the Martin brothers were dead, the Kelly Creek Dam on the Coosa River was dedicated to Logan Martin.[176]

In his last years, honors and awards came to Tom Martin from every quarter. To the older honorary degrees awarded from Cumberland University (1931) and the University of Alabama (1943) were added honorary degrees from Alabama Polytechnic Institute at Auburn (1956), Birmingham-Southern College (1957), and Spring Hill College (1958). In the summer of 1961 Martin was honored by the Alabama legislature on his eightieth birthday and was invited to address a joint session on August 11, with the 13th, which fell on a Sunday, being declared "Thomas W. Martin Day" in Alabama. In his remarks, Martin spoke lightly about his own role in the company's success. He noted that the capital accumulation of Alabama Power Company had reached $500 million in the fifty years since James Mitchell came to the state, and he anticipated that the construction program under way and the construction planned would double the company's capital account to $1 billion by 1970. Massey Wilson was present in the Alabama House chamber to listen to Martin—two old warriors who had been there together at the beginning of electrical development in Alabama. In 1962 the state honored the three founders of Alabama Power Company—Lay, Mitchell, and Martin—with Industry and Science Awards at the Department of Archives and History.[177] Bronze plaques with images of the three leaders were unveiled. In 2006 these plaques were placed in the foyer of the Alabama Power Auditorium in the Alabama Department of Archives and History's new west wing.[178]

In February 1963 Martin, who refused to fly, boarded a train for Los

Angeles to attend the celebration of Thomas Edison's birthday. The three-day trip left him so exhausted he was unable to participate actively in the meeting. After he returned home, he never really recovered his strength. In April, Alabama Power's bylaws were amended to allow President Walter Bouldin to assume the responsibilities of chief executive officer with Martin remaining as chairman of the board and general counsel. Martin was encouraged to do this by Harllee Branch Jr., president of Southern Company, who sent Martin's old friend and longtime member of the company's board of directors, Colonel William J. Rushton, to talk to him. In his last years Tom Martin was somewhat unhappy that he had lost control and that the company was moving on without him. He spent more time with Southern Research Institute affairs, where the staff absolutely doted on him.

One thousand Alabama Power employees signed letters in the fall seconding the nomination of the Birmingham Business and Professional Women's Club for Tom Martin to receive the Humanitarian Award of the Morris Karpeles B'nai B'rith Lodge No. 368. Martin received that award on November 11. He was especially touched by the support of the employees. In December 1964 Tom Martin was recognized for his fifty-two years of service to Alabama Power Company with the first wristwatch ever presented by the company for extended service. On December 7, 1964, Richard A. Peacock, Alabama Power's advertising manager, notified the *Birmingham News* that the regilding of Miss Electra had been completed and that this symbol of electricity in Alabama on top of the Alabama Power building stood out now more than ever.[179] That same day Tom Martin was admitted to St. Vincent's Hospital with an acute heart attack. He died December 8, 1964, at the age of eighty-three, just as he was making plans to leave the hospital to attend a Southern Research Institute dinner.[180]

Tom Martin had spent his life building Alabama Power Company, a life he led with dignity and a strong sense of ethics. He played a leadership role in bringing electricity to the Southeast and had developed engineers and lawyers who carried his management and leadership style to utility companies in five states. Martin had been the dominant force in the creation of Southern Company. Ollie Smith's favorite memory of him occurred when a management team was seated around a conference table discussing the case of a man who had defrauded the company. As their turn came, each person spoke in anger and used strong language. Judge Logan Martin wanted to see the man prosecuted. When it was Tom Martin's time to make the decision, he said, "I agree with everything that has been said. The man is a scoundrel. He has disparaged the good name of the Alabama Power Company. But, having said all of that, what is the *wise* thing to do?"[181]

Friends and associates had honored Tom Martin on his seventy-fifth birthday on August 13, 1956. At the luncheon, speakers gave comparisons between Alabama Power Company in 1915, its second full year of operation after the completion of Lay Dam, and the company in 1956. In 1915 Alabama Power employed 350 people, had an annual payroll of $312,734, served 18 communities and 5,305 customers with plants valued at $10 million. In 1956 Alabama Power Company employed 5,300 people, had an annual payroll of $27 million, served 620 communities and 583,559 customers with plants valued at $430 million.[182] The testimonials at this gala birthday luncheon are interesting appraisals of the man. Company president at the time, Lewis M. Smith, paid tribute to Martin, detailing his many successes in building Alabama Power. In praising Martin the man, Smith observed that Martin never commanded, called employees his associates, and always said they worked *with* him, never *for* him. Smith said Martin worked long hours, had an unpretentious desk in a modest office, and was courteous—except, Smith could have added, when Martin was riding the elevator, which he expected to go directly to the floor he needed.[183]

Although Tom Martin was often criticized by his opponents, Alabama Power people did not find faults—at least not openly. With so many accomplishments to praise, rarely did friends leave to history candid assessments of Tom Martin. One of the most insightful analyses of the Alabama Power executive in his last years came from longtime friend Bill Brantley, who wrote in his diary after attending Martin's 1956 birthday celebration. Brantley recorded that journalist and writer John Temple Graves, who was working on a biography of Martin, spoke about the utilities executive. Graves "praised [Martin] in a very good talk," Brantley wrote, "except he made two errors. He referred to Mr. Martin being a 'little man.' This always is a tender spot with Tom. Then he spoke of Tom's love of praise and again Tom winced." Bill Brantley noted that "John was dead right and truthful about both, but you just can't mention those two things to Tom with[out] his resenting it—what he knows is the truth."[184]

Brantley went on to observe that "no doubt he is a great man. A marvelous achiever, a hard worker and a ruthless opponent. But he is not modest and he is expedient. Perhaps one has to be to win the point in this competitive world. No sons—no child, he seems to be struggling to be forever remembered. He will have laid plenty of foundations for praise & high tribute, busts, memorials, oratory, an achiever but he is also a lonesome, unhappy man."[185] For some time, Mrs. Martin had been virtually a recluse. She and her husband spent most of their time at Martinwood, their home on Shades Mountain, where

Martin kept horses he rode until February 1964, when he sent them to Judge Coley in Tallapoosa County. Several huge Great Danes lived at Martinwood and were loved as part of their family.[186]

If Martin ever pondered his demise or reflected on his legacy, no account has survived. He loved the saying, "The second half of the twentieth century belongs to the South," and he worked hard to make it true. Called a "human dynamo" and "a regular powerhouse," he was praised as "one of the builders of Alabama."[187] Tom Martin devoted his entire life to Alabama Power Company and its people and through electricity, economic development, research, rural electrification, and hundreds of other causes to improving the quality of life for the people of his beloved South and his home, Alabama. Former governor John Patterson, reminiscing about his friendship with "Mr. Martin" and his numerous trips with him to recruit industry to Alabama, said that Martin was small in stature, but "he commanded respect and attention," and when he called, "it didn't matter what I was doing, I answered the phone. That's how influential he was in the state of Alabama."[188] With Martin's death in December 1964, a significant era in the history of Alabama Power Company ended and a new one began.

Tom Martin presents an Alabama Power hard hat to Governor John Patterson, ca. 1961. Walter Bouldin is seated at left.

Joseph M. Farley speaking at a press conference at the Corporate Headquarters on June 14, 1972 regarding the company's request to the Public Service Commission to increase retail service rates.

Chapter Eight

Alabama Power's service
awards ceremony in 1965.

A New Era Dawning:
Hard Years in Wallace Country

*We have a pressing need to communicate to Alabamians the fact that the
increased rates customers pay for electric service help insure reliable service
by permitting us to maintain a strong financial position, thus encouraging
outside investment.*

Joseph M. Farley to Stockholders, March 29, 1976

The passing of the Thomas W. Martin era in the history of Alabama
Power Company happened just before the climax of a social and political revolution that changed Alabama, the South, and Alabama Power Company.[1] The
modern civil rights movement was born on a cold day, December 1, 1955,
when a tired seamstress, Rosa Parks, was arrested for violating the bus segregation laws of the city of Montgomery. The final stage in Alabama began
in Selma on January 2, 1965, one month after Tom Martin's death, when
the Reverend Martin Luther King Jr. announced from the pulpit of Brown's
Chapel that he would assist Selma's qualified black citizens in registering to

vote.[2] In the last ten years of Tom Martin's life, the racial barriers that had been enacted as Jim Crow legislation in the years before and after his birth in 1881 tumbled one by one, ended by court orders and federal statutes. The demise was encouraged by demonstrations and marches and accompanied by resistance and too often by violence.[3] The civil rights movement of the 1960s changed America, and it changed Alabama Power Company. Alabama and Birmingham were center stage for much of the civil rights movement, and the most despicable scenes were played out at Kelly Ingram Park and the Sixteenth Street Baptist Church, both of which were neighbors and could be viewed from the windows of Alabama Power corporate offices.

Alabama Power Company followed laws and customs when it built separate black worker villages during the construction of its first dam at Lock 12, a pattern repeated in the construction of other dams in the 1920s.[4] On transmission line crews, which nearly always had an integrated labor force, the rough living conditions were in closely pitched camping tents as the crews moved together through unchartered and often rough and wild terrain. The experiences at Lock 12 convinced the company of the superiority of black and white southern labor over imported northern immigrant labor, and this, too, was repeated in the labor selections on company construction projects.[5] In these years, almost all black employees of Dixie Construction Company and Alabama Power were in unskilled jobs, but their photographs and their individual contributions to the company were applauded in promotion, service, and retirement notices or obituaries in *Powergrams* from its inception in 1920.

In the 1920s the Ku Klux Klan was at the peak of its power in the state, and Alabama Power was once the target of Klan wrath because the company sent integrated workforces out in the same trucks and allowed whites and blacks to ride together on Montgomery streetcars, which at the time were operated by the company.[6] The second Alabama Power Company president, James Mitchell, grew up in the Northeast and was tolerant of racial and cultural differences, but Captain Lay's and Tom Martin's racial attitudes were typical of Alabama white prejudices. Martin was paternalistic but once fired his long-time gardener, Robert Porter, after Porter's teenage son, John Thomas (who was named for Tom Martin and had been working for the Martins), dared to question why he was not paid for his overtime. Although the Porters never again worked for the Martins, Mrs. Martin kept up with the Porters through her other servants. When young John received his Ph.D. degree in theology from Morehouse College, Mrs. Martin sent him as a graduation gift a very fine and expensive pastor's robe.[7] In 1962, young John was the Reverend John

Thomas Porter, who was installed as minister of the Sixth Avenue Baptist Church with his friend the Reverend Martin Luther King Jr. in attendance. Reverend Porter would join the Birmingham protest marches the following spring. Three decades later, on October 22, 1993, Reverend Porter would become a member of the Alabama Power Company board of directors as the second African American to serve on the board.[8]

Reverend John Thomas Porter.
Courtesy of Mrs. John T. Porter.

In 1949, soon after the Porters left the employment of Tom and Evelyn Martin, the Ku Klux Klan made a resurgence in Birmingham, and Avondale Mills textile leader Donald Comer organized a Committee of 500 to oppose it. Tom Martin was on his steering committee.[9] In the 1950s and 1960s the Birmingham Chamber of Commerce was dominated by conservative businessmen. Robert G. Corley, in his study of the quest for racial harmony in Birmingham beginning in 1947, noted that the elite business leadership of Birmingham had differences but generally was committed to business progressivism and the view that economic growth could cure social ills. Corley's view was that the silence of the "critical moderate voices" in the Birmingham business community was one reason the crisis came to Birmingham in 1962. He places Alabama Power Company within the city's "elite businesses," and there is no question the company was quietly involved in trying to solve the city's racial problems.[10]

As a regulated public utility, Alabama Power had kept a low profile, but company leadership was actively engaged. James M. Barry worked with retired Independent Presbyterian minister Dr. Henry M. Edmonds, who was involved with social programs, to support the Urban League's projects.[11] Walter Bouldin served on a study committee to recommend appropriate action by the chamber of commerce, and in 1961 Tom Martin was on the chamber's Committee of 100 to plan for the city's future. Alabama Power management was concerned about the deleterious effect racial demonstrations, conflict, and violence would have on economic development in the city and the state. The nation was still enjoying a postwar boom, and Alabama had passed two acts, the Cater Act of 1949 and the Wallace Act of 1951 (sponsored by then state legislator George C. Wallace), both of which encouraged economic development by allowing municipalities to issue tax-free bonds to build factories and support industrial recruitment.[12] Prosperity was everywhere, and Alabama Power Company encouraged economic development for the state and for Birmingham.

Historian J. Mills Thornton III, in his study of the civil rights era in Birmingham, agreed with Corley that the city's white economic elite wanted commercial and industrial growth and programs to attract northern industry. They pursued these goals, Thornton noted, with a "zeal in the cause . . .

very nearly obsessive," even though some of the old industrial giants did not support development that might bring new industries in competition with the local labor market and drive wages up. Not all advocates of economic development were racial moderates, but Thornton contends that many of them were, especially utilities such as Alabama Power.[13]

Alabama Power encouraged its young employees to take an active role in civic organizations, and company individuals were involved in moderate leadership roles in civic and church groups in the 1960s.[14] Virgil Rice and Guy Cofield both served terms as president of the Jaycees. Some, like Wylie Johnson, who was in transmission and distribution, were members of the Young Men's Business Club, a progressive alternative to the chamber of commerce. The YMBC was sometimes characterized as being downright radical, especially after it became the first civic club in Birmingham to invite a black speaker. W. Cooper Green, executive vice president of Alabama Power and a former mayor of Birmingham, chaired the chamber of commerce's secret Senior Citizens Committee. Green, as an industrial recruiter, insisted that businesses considering the location of new plants wanted a peaceful community without violence, whether violence came from "the malfeasant [who] wraps himself in the Confederate flag," from a picket line, or from demonstrations. The Senior Citizens Committee was formed to find solutions to the demands of black citizens, and Walter Bouldin served on it. The committee's subcommittee on race, which was chaired by realtor Sid Smyer, was the liaison between the white businessmen and the leadership in the Birmingham black community.[15]

W. Cooper Green

In the spring of 1962, George C. Wallace won the Democratic nomination for governor. Part of his platform was a promise to emphasize industrial recruitment for Alabama. At that time, the Democratic nomination was tantamount to election. As a state legislator, Wallace had been a floor leader for liberal governor James E. Folsom, and he had been responsible for the Wallace Act. In 1948 Wallace had opposed the Dixiecrats and their states' rights position and remained a supporter of the national Democratic Party. But in 1962 there was a heated primary contest in which Wallace made race the main issue. He defeated more moderate candidates, including former governor Folsom and a newcomer to Alabama politics, Ryan deGraffenried. Wallace's fiery language played well at the branchheads, the grassroots of the state.[16]

By summer of 1962, demonstrations began in Birmingham led by African-American citizens who were boycotting downtown merchants. They had moderate demands—integrated fitting rooms, rest rooms, and water fountains and the hiring of black salespeople. The demonstrations gave Wallace material for

George and Lurleen Wallace on the campaign trail in 1962. Courtesy of the Alabama Department of Archives and History.

his gubernatorial campaign. The Ku Klux Klan met in Tuscaloosa to plan a response, causing tensions to increase in Birmingham. The president of the chamber of commerce, Richard A. Puryear, who was also president of Alabama Gas Corporation, drafted a statement on September 19 requesting that chamber members issue a warning to all employees to avoid demonstrations and warning that employees who participated in public protests and violence would be fired.[17] Walter Bouldin and Tom Martin published a watered-down version of the statement in the October 1962 issue of *Powergrams*. They urged company employees to stay away from demonstrations, but Bouldin and Martin did not threaten to fire those who did become involved in the protests.[18]

Besides using race as an issue in his campaign, George Wallace occasionally made populist attacks on big business. Chambers of commerce and economic conservatives were uneasy about him. Still, Wallace was formally elected in the general election in November 1962. He had promised in his campaign more aggressive industrial recruitment by the state, and after he became governor his program of industrial development was supported by Alabama Power. Worded another way, the Alabama Power Company's existing industrial development program for Alabama turned out to be the governor's program because Alabama Power's department was staffed with experienced people, was well organized, was adequately funded, and was the longest running effort in the state. As Alabama Power's chief industrial recruiter, Cooper Green always gave all the credit to the governor and stayed in the background, which had been the company's policy since its successful recruitment of Pepperell Mills in 1924.[19]

In Wallace's later administrations, when he became involved in national politics, his economic development travels across the country became political forays as well as industrial recruitment trips. Historian Jeff Frederick, who has studied the Wallace administrations, notes that these trips and the scheduling of prospects were sometimes arranged by Alabama Power people and that Wallace "was quick to brag to prospects that other states could never supply energy as cheaply as Alabama Power."[20] Joe Farley insists that Alabama Power never paid for the governor to take any of these trips. Although not recognized at the time, Wallace and Alabama Power were on a collision course. In 1962, race dominated politics. Eight years down the road, politics changed, and Wallace shifted his emphasis from race to rates.

The Birmingham civil rights protests continued through the fall of 1962 but without much support or success. Meanwhile, efforts were being made to change the form of Birmingham's city government, a plan instituted to bring a more moderate leadership to the city and give citizens a stronger voice at city hall. The plan was also conceived as a way to rid the city of its police commissioner Bull Connor and his reactionary rule. Individually, a number of power company employees supported the drive to change the form of city government, which was being spearheaded by the Young Men's Business Club. When the change from a commission to city council structure was successful and the challenge to it settled, M. Edwin Wiggins, retired Alabama Power executive,

M. Edwin Wiggins

was elected to the city council and the council elected him its president. Historian Mills Thornton identifies Wiggins as being on the moderate side, a key leader on measures to alter the direction of the city.[21] Despite the change in city government and the defeat of Bull Connor, who was contesting the election and was still in power, massive demonstrations began in Kelly Ingram Park in the spring of 1963, a few months after Wallace was inaugurated in January for his first gubernatorial administration. The Reverend Martin Luther King Jr. was arrested on Good Friday for defying a court order. On May 2, children began to march, and Connor arrested 959 and took them to jail in school buses. The next day hundreds of children gathered at Sixteenth Street Baptist Church. When they marched, they were met by Connor's police dogs and water from fire hoses. The infamous scene will always be part of the city's burden of history and was seared into the memories of the company's people who watched horrified from office windows. Banks Farris can never forget what he saw, and as a young boy of eleven, Charles McCrary was forever changed by the scenes.[22]

In June 1963 Wallace made his famous and carefully choreographed stand in the schoolhouse door in Tuscaloosa to prevent African Americans Vivian Malone and James Hood from enrolling at the University of Alabama.[23] In August 1963 the Student Non-violent Coordinating Committee delivered a petition to Selma mayor Chris B. Heinz with a list of demands, including the mandate that Alabama Power hire blacks on line crews.[24] In Birmingham, schools were scheduled to be integrated in September, and the city was uneasy. On Sunday morning, September 15, 1963, Walter Baker's First Methodist Church Sunday school class had gathered at the Alabama Power building for its lesson. Baker had received special permission from the company to meet there because First Methodist's new Sunday school building was under construction at the church site just a half block away. Suddenly, a huge explosion shook the Alabama Power building. The members of the class had no idea what had happened, but they decided to leave. Four ushers escorted them across the street and back to the Methodist church. It was some time before they learned that the Sixteenth Street Baptist Church had been bombed and four young girls killed.[25]

Civil rights demonstrations in Kelly Ingram Park, May 2, 1963. Courtesy of the Birmingham Public Library Archives.

Cynthia Wesley died in that explosion. In the late 1970s her father Claude Wesley looked back to the '60s and said, "I think everyone knew the South couldn't stay the way it was."[26] When the civil rights movement came, Tom Martin knew what was right, and he knew what had to be done, even though his personal prejudices and his paternalistic philosophy were at odds with these actions. Martin recognized that the economic development he advocated for Alabama needed a peaceful society and a positive press. In the 1960s he accepted that change had to come, and before he died in 1964 he understood that a new era was dawning.[27]

The 1960s were turbulent times for the nation. In 1962 a Supreme Court decision required state legislatures to follow their constitutions and reapportion their legislatures, which ended rural domination of Alabama's legislative process and shifted power to urban areas, causing a sea change in the state's politics. President John F. Kennedy was assassinated on November 22, 1963. His vice-presidential successor, Lyndon B. Johnson, pushed through a number of social programs he called the Great Society and escalated an unpopular war in Vietnam. Two more political assassinations occurred in 1968—in April, Rev. Martin Luther King Jr., and in June, New York senator Robert Kennedy. The Civil Rights Act of 1964 and the Voting Rights Act of 1965 were the climax of the civil rights movement in Alabama, and both had an impact on the nation. The resulting diversification of the company by race and gender has been one of the success stories of Alabama Power. It was a long time coming, and the full story will be told later, but the company started down that road in 1965.

CHANGES IN COMPANY LEADERSHIP

G. Thornton Nelson

Joseph M. Farley, ca. 1952.

Cooper Green, who was tapped by Tom Martin to head the company's industrial development department, retired from the company as executive vice president on April 1, 1965.[28] He was replaced by G. Thornton Nelson. That same month, Alvin W. Vogtle Jr. left Alabama Power to become vice president of both Southern Company and Southern Services. Vogtle was replaced by Joseph M. Farley, who left his partnership in Martin, Balch, Bingham, & Hawthorne to become executive vice president of Alabama Power. Farley had been deeply involved in the company's legal work since his arrival at the law firm. He had worked closely with Walter Bouldin, who, Farley recalled, had left the law firm to become Alabama Power's vice president for finance on the same day Farley arrived at the law firm in 1952. Farley had always been influenced by Bouldin's impeccable judgment, his excellent assessment of situations, his ability to keep his cool, and his talents as a writer and speech maker who could, as Farley recalled, say more in a ten-minute talk than most people could in an hour presentation.[29]

Troy and Luverne

In 1964, Troy and Luverne, two towns south of Montgomery, decided to end their contracts with the Alabama Electric Cooperative, which was providing wholesale power to the cities' municipal distribution systems. Troy had tried to leave the cooperative once before in the late 1940s, but the Public Service Commission rejected Alabama Power's proposed contract. The two towns studied their contracts and determined that they could obtain electricity at wholesale rates cheaper from Alabama Power than from the co-op. They decided the power supply would be more reliable and Alabama Power's industrial development department could better assist the towns in recruiting industrial plants and jobs. Both cities gave notice to the cooperative that they were terminating their contracts. This potential loss was a blow to the Alabama Electric Cooperative, which estimated it would lose 15 percent of its annual sales. When Alabama Power presented the Troy and Luverne contracts to the Alabama Public Service Commission, the cooperative opposed the contracts.[30]

In the hearing on Troy's contract, Alvin Vogtle, who was in his last year as executive vice president, explained that the city had approached the company several months before, concerned that the co-op (with its 44,000-volt system) did not have enough existing power to supply the city's future needs. He testified that Alabama Power would be supplying Troy from a 110,000-volt transmission system. Vogtle also refuted a newspaper story accusing Alabama Power of not servicing rural areas. He traced the history of the company's support for rural electrification and stated that the company "now serves more rural families in the fifty-five counties in which it operates than all the rural electric cooperatives combined in that area."[31] Wylie Johnson, superintendent of transmission, testified that the company would build a 26-mile transmission line to Troy and that the company had 230 men within a 100-mile radius to service the line. H. S. St. John, manager of Troy's utilities department, explained that service had not been satisfactory from Alabama Electric Cooperative and interruptions in service were "frequent." W. L. Garlington, an engineering consultant, estimated that over the ten-year contract, Troy would have net savings of $736,400. The Public Service Commission approved the Alabama Power contract with Troy on October 26, 1964.[32]

The Luverne case came before the commission the following month. Experts estimated that Luverne would save $244,038 over the first ten years of the contract with Alabama Power. After three days of hearings, the Public Service Commission approved the company's contract with Luverne on November 25. Alabama Power began serving both cities on June 1, 1965. The Alabama Electric Cooperative then filed a petition with the Federal Power Commission. There was a jurisdictional question, which the company lost. The FPC continued to hear the wholesale rate case involving the terms of the contracts. The

James H. Miller Jr.

hearings in Washington, D.C., on what was called Case E7183 lasted for months. Jim Miller recalled the rented suite, Philly cheese steak sandwiches, smoke-filled rooms, and long nights poring over transcripts and planning the next day's testimony. Eason Balch and Jack Bingham were the lawyers on this case, while at various times Doug McCrary, Bill Guthrie, and Jim Miller were there to testify. Bingham remembered E7183 as "the Tale of Two Cities."[33]

One phase of the testimony began on November 8. Eason Balch recalls the exchange in Washington on Tuesday, November 9, 1965, when the manager of Alabama Electric Cooperative, Charles R. Lowman, was on the stand explaining how unfair Alabama Power's ratchet provision was. This pricing was established by the high load capacity and then became the capacity charge for the next eleven months. Balch recalls Lowman testifying that the co-op had designed its system so it could avoid the application of the ratchet by putting half the system in blackout before the high load point was ever reached. When questioned by the shocked FPC attorney, Lowman replied that they would indeed throw traffic lights out and hospitals into darkness rather than incur the ratchet. While Balch and the Alabama Power group were in a cab heading back to the hotel, the radio reported that the northeast power grid had failed and New York, Boston, and Philadelphia had been thrown into the dark by a cascading blackout of the entire East Coast.[34]

The Federal Power Commission ruled in Alabama Power's favor, stating that Alabama Power's wholesale rates in contracts with Troy and Luverne were just and reasonable. The co-op then requested a rehearing and asked the Federal Power Commission to eliminate the wording in its ruling that said the Alabama Electric Cooperative "was operating its system in such a manner as to provide unreliable service to its customers." The Federal Power Commission refused to grant a rehearing or change its wording. It did, however, order its staff to work with the cooperative, Alabama Power, and the Southeastern Power Administration to assist the co-op in finding ways "to improve the reliability of its service."[35] In his history of the Alabama Electric Cooperative, co-op executive Lowman noted that Troy and Luverne were expelled from the co-op on March 17, 1967.[36]

The controversy over electrical service to Troy and Luverne was one outgrowth of a long-standing dispute between Alabama Power and the Alabama Electric Cooperative over the co-op's duplication of generation and transmission facilities. In fact, some of the rate information that Troy and Luverne used in making their decisions came from public testimony and exhibits presented in this dispute. At the time the Troy-Luverne issue was being settled, a case had been before the state finance director, state courts, and federal courts for some years involving a $20,213,293 loan to enable Alabama Electric Cooperative to build a steam generating plant and over 700 miles of transmission lines. The cooperative had applied for the loan in the fall of 1959.[37] This loan, filed with the state finance director on February 5, 1962, and called the "H" loan, would come from the U.S. Treasury through the REA and carry a 2 percent interest rate. Alabama Power opposed the loan because it duplicated Alabama Power generation and transmission facilities already in place and the company considered it a violation of the original REA Act because the proposed project would provide no new electrical service to any rural customer that was not already receiving electricity. Alabama Power also opposed the loan because the interest on the loan was less than half the rate the government was paying to borrow the money to lend to the cooperative, because AEC paid no federal or state income taxes, and because Alabama Power was supplying all of its additional electrical needs at wholesale rates cheaper than the cooperative could produce electricity.[38]

One of the most disturbing aspects for private power companies about REA loans was that while investor-owned companies were required to justify all actions in open hearings, the REA hearings on loans were never public. To secure documents to see what information the co-op presented to the REA, power companies had to use the legal system. In congressional testimony in 1962, Walter Bouldin said that Alabama Power "found that the co-op's application to the REA was loaded with accusations against our company. We were able in open hearings to refute these accusations. But the important point is that REA had accepted these charges and evidently based its finding upon them. Our company was accused, tried, and convicted with no opportunity on our part to confront the witnesses against us."[39] In a speech before the New York Society of Security Analysts, Southern Company president Harllee Branch Jr. detailed the problems with the loan, especially the secret nature of the REA application. Branch noted that the proposed plant "would not bring electricity to anyone to whom it is not now available."[40]

Alabama Power fought the "H" loan's acceptance when it was presented to the state finance director for approval (a process required by the REA Act). After the loan was approved by finance director Maurice Patterson on December 9, 1962, Alabama Power opposed the loan through state and federal courts.[41] Alabama Power had won a previous case in 1948 involving a $5,516,600 loan to AEC to build a steam plant at Gantt, because it proved Alabama Power had an adequate supply of wholesale power to sell and was providing it to cooperatives in south Alabama at 7.2 mills, which was below the 11.4 mills that it cost AEC to generate the power.[42] In 1961 President John F. Kennedy appointed Norman M. Clapp, a relative of Gordon Clapp, chairman of TVA, as administrator of the REA. Clapp issued Bulletin 20-6, which changed the regulation to enable REA to finance generation and transmission projects not previously authorized. With vague wording Clapp encouraged cooperatives to establish their own generation and transmission capability. Eason Balch, who was the lead counsel for Alabama Power in opposing this policy, believed that Clapp generally opposed private power companies. Alabama Power lost in the Alabama Supreme Court.[43]

Alabama Power then contested, as an anti-trust violation, the long contracts AEC used to secure the loans. A federal court dismissed the case for want of jurisdiction. The company appealed to the Fifth U.S. Circuit Court. After several hearings directed by Balch, Jack Bingham, Frank H. Hawthorne, and James H. Hancock, circuit court judges Richard Rives and Walter Gewin supported the lower court and ruled against Alabama Power on April 2, 1968. Judge John Godbold in a split decision gave a long, spirited dissent upholding Alabama Power's standing to sue and insisting among other points that the district court did not determine the question of fact. Judge Godbold was particularly concerned with the conflict between the REA administrator's statements that some customers of member cooperatives would be "supplied with electric energy for the first time," while affidavits filed by Alabama Power stated that "the major portion of the proposed expanded project of Alabama Electric Cooperative is to furnish electric service to persons who have been, were at the time the loan was approved and are now being supplied by central-station electric power generated in central stations of Alabama Power Company and Gulf Power Company." The dissent was Eason Balch Sr.'s favorite opinion.[44]

Two Strikes in 1966

In 1966, Alabama Power Company's earnings were affected by two strikes, one by the United Mine Workers and the other by the International Brotherhood of Electrical Workers. The United Mine Workers called a strike at the Gorgas coal mine and the two mines that serviced Gaston, the Southern Electric Generating Company plant at Wilsonville. During the strike, the company incurred increased fuel costs. After seven weeks, a contract renewal was signed that matched the wage and fringe benefits of other non-commercial coal producers.[45]

The second strike began after Alabama Power could not reach an agreement with the International Brotherhood of Electrical Workers. E. Davis Long, manager of human resources, was the senior negotiator, along with Charles Brasfield and Hugh P. Foreman. Bill Whitt, who was then vice president of the Birmingham Division and a member of the negotiating committee, recalled that the talks went on for a long time. At one point company negotiators reached a tentative agreement with William L. Hopper Jr., the IBEW's state business agent, but final approval to pay two-tenths of one percent of the wage settlement was not forthcoming. On August 12 Walter Bouldin wrote all employees notifying them that they needed "to be prepared, on short notice, to help maintain electrical service to the public."[46] The strike by 2,400 employees covered by the union contract began on August 16, 1966. The workers who went on strike operated the steam plants and hydro units, kept the transmission and distribution lines in repair, and read meters. Nonunion employees would have to do these jobs to keep electricity flowing to customers.[47]

Alabama Power had a short-term plan to secure facilities and a long-term plan to operate the system and serve its customers. Foremen and plant managers knew how to operate the plants, but supervisors, clerks, marketing people, assistant engineers, and others had to help. People were given special training to do their new assignments and were sent all over the state. Beds were set up inside plants and food and refrigeration were provided. When the strike began, everyone thought it would be a short strike. No one believed that it would

Birmingham Division vice president Bill Whitt and senior general clerk George Lucas work to restore service during the strike, November 1966.

be one of the longest strikes in utility history, the longest strike against an Alabama utility, or that the noncovered employees and executives of Alabama Power would be required to put in so many hours to keep the system operating. However, they worked for 141 days, almost five months, which then and in memories seemed to all an eternity.[48] In the words of one IBEW member who was on strike, "the company liked to have worked their people to death."[49]

Doug McCrary, a senior engineer II, was sent to Barry Steam Plant, where the plant superintendent was Clyde Fowler. During the strike, McCrary was able to come home only twice. Because of the picket lines at the gate, the salesmen and engineers who were now plant workers lived inside the plant. Cots were scattered around the buildings, and McCrary slept in the switch house. Many of the sales and marketing managers were put to work cooking for those staffing a plant. Day and night shifts were determined. McCrary recalled that supervisors who had once been operators were actually running the units, while others were given duties that required less specialized expertise. Safety was constantly stressed. McCrary "was assigned to read gauges, check temperatures, and things like that throughout the plant." Like most of the other managers, he did not fully understand what he was doing but was intrigued about learning it. The superintendents knew what needed to be done, and it was their turn to boss managers and vice presidents.

Three days into the strike, a boiler tube at Barry leaked in unit 3 and shut it down. About the time the smoke should have cleared from the stack above the plant, McCrary heard cheers from the picket line outside. Superintendent Fowler tapped McCrary as the guy to weld the leak in the boiler tubes because he had done welding before. At the maintenance shop Hunter Sellers and Frank Davis helped him select the proper welding rod. McCrary practiced, then he and Davis, who did not know how to do it but had seen it done, went into the boiler through a two-foot manhole. In tight quarters, through tedious maneuvers, McCrary and Davis finished the job. To McCrary's surprise, the welding held and the unit was operational again.[50]

Bill McDonough, who was assistant to Walter Bouldin, worked on a line crew in Greene County as a laborer. John Farley read meters and did duty in the powerhouse at Mitchell Dam. Jim Miller Jr. spent Christmas Day at Greene County Steam Plant working as a cook and repairing equipment. Jim Clements read meters at Hamilton, then went to Haleyville to work on a line crew. Howell Dulaney, a senior engineer, performed as a lineman. Walter Johnsey, who four years later became a vice president of the company, acted as the assistant plant manager at Gorgas and elected to work on Christmas Day so someone else could go home.[51] Twenty-nine-year-old Jabo Waggoner Jr., who had business and law degrees, was first assigned to the Greene County Steam Plant. He drove to Demopolis and with a load of groceries was flown under the cover of darkness by helicopter into the plant. He remembers engineer Jimmy Long giving him a jackhammer and putting him to work breaking up a huge clinker in the boiler (fire pit). Waggoner stayed at the plant six weeks, then was sent to Montevallo to serve on a line crew. After that, he went to Oneonta to read meters. During this time he was campaigning for a seat in the state house of representatives, which he won. Having the same name as his father, who was popular and well known to voters, certainly helped him.[52]

There was some violence and more than sixty cases of suspected sabotage. The *Mobile Register* reported on October 31, 1966, that lines had been sabotaged, guy wires holding up a transmission tower were cut, and a pole had been sawed in half. In other areas of the state, wires were cut, substations were shot up, and tacks covered the roads from the plants so that if a vehicle left the plant, it would have four flats before it reached the main road. Jack Bingham recalled that Harold Bowron was "in the thick of the fight, rushing around the state getting affidavits and injunctions to protect the company's property and the safety of its people." Bowron worked out of what was called the "war room" on the thirteenth floor of corporate headquarters where events were monitored so response to violence could be quick for the safety of employees and the public.[53]

There were nighttime harassing telephone calls to families whose fathers were confined in generating plants. Steve Spencer, who was a young boy then, remembered that his family received "lots of calls" during the strike. His father Roy, who was a district superintendent in Birmingham, borrowed a .22-caliber rifle that he left with Steve's mother when he was away from home.[54] There were a few personal confrontations, some of them between noncovered employees suffering from exhaustion and the stress of seventeen-hour days. On December 8 the *Montgomery Advertiser* ran a story about power being cut to the Prattville area because "an axe-wielding saboteur" under the cover of darkness had destroyed a line that served the local hospital. The newspaper story noted that the "white collar workers" were able to restore power after forty-five minutes. On the front page next to the strike story, the paper reported that Alabama Public Service Commission president Eugene "Bull" Connor had suffered a stroke.[55]

As the strike wore on, it became extremely difficult for strikers who were doing without paychecks. Brad Sandlin, an IBEW member who was working at Gorgas, recalled that the strikers "liked to have starved to death." His wife earned lunch money for the children and essentials by picking cotton. He took a part-time job with a local well driller. David Shaw, who was working at the

Because of its isolation, the long strike in 1966 made it difficult for IBEW workers at Greene County Steam Plant to find temporary work.

Greene County Steam Plant when the IBEW went on strike, left town to get a job and paid someone to walk his picket duty.[56] Historian Jeff Frederick observed that the governor "typically responded to strikes by touting his pro-labor records, but staying as clear of the disputes as possible." The official Wallace policy was not to get involved; however, the governor did become involved in the Alabama Power strike after pressure from the IBEW.[57] Wallace had a strong labor base, with one poll in 1965 showing 72 percent of union labor supporting him.[58] He could hardly refuse trying to help settle the strike.

The strike occurred during the fall gubernatorial election, but since the 1901 Alabama constitution prevented a governor from serving two consecutive terms, George Wallace convinced his wife Lurleen to run, and she was elected in November. With the Wallace family succession secure and as state government and the city of Montgomery were anticipating Lurleen's inauguration, Wallace invited Alabama Power representatives and the IBEW to his office in early January 1967.[59] There were two marathon arbitration sessions. The first one lasted twelve hours, from 2:30 in the afternoon until 2:30 A.M. The second began the following day at 4:30 P.M. and adjourned after an agreement was reached at 9:00 P.M.[60] The governor never said much about his role in this settlement, although he announced it when the arbitration was over. IBEW representative Bill Hopper praised the governor, and Joe Farley noted that Wallace's influence was critical in ending the strike. Later Farley observed that the governor "never bragged about it." The governor wrote Walter Bouldin about the personal satisfaction he felt because "the issues involved were of a concern to the public generally." Wallace praised the company's negotiators, stating that he was pleased that the discussions were "very amenable" and "conducted with a high degree of professional skill."[61]

On January 12, 1967, the IBEW signed a new labor agreement with Alabama Power. The contract called for a wage increase of 3.9 percent effective August 15, 1966, and 4.4 percent effective August 15, 1967. Holiday work was paid at time and a half; four weeks vacation was granted after twenty years of service instead of twenty-five years; and the company agreed to increase its contributions to each employee's hospital and surgical insurance programs. Union representative Hopper said "We're glad to be getting back to work."[62] Southern Company president Harllee Branch immediately wrote a letter to Walter Bouldin congratulating him on his "magnificent leadership" of an organization that conducted itself "with so high [a] degree of courage and devotion as you and your people."[63]

The problem was that Bouldin's people were also those who went on strike, and now there had to be healing and coming back together so everyone could work closely once more. As Bill Whitt observed, the striking workforce "were good people." For the company and the union members, it was difficult getting through the discipline procedures for those who had committed violence against the property of the company and dismissing or reassimilating those workers, but Alabama Power made every effort to maintain a good relationship through the process. Whitt's actions were typical. As division vice president, he visited every area, never mentioned there had been a strike, but was available in case anyone wished to talk to him. He told his workers "to low-key it, try to put it behind them, heal the wounds and get back to work." For his division and for the company, Whitt recalled, it worked well.[64]

The 1966 IBEW strike was one of those benchmark events for Alabama Power that everyone who was there remembered and never forgot what part they played. For months, people shared their stories with each other, almost playing "can you top this?" Both management and the union decided they really did not want to go through such a long strike again, and in the future concerted efforts were made to avoid one. The company learned lessons, sometimes the hard way, about how to prepare for a strike and how to develop a strike plan. New plants included a kitchen, baths, and living quarters, and some old plants were retrofitted. Management had a greater appreciation of what it took to run the system and came to know their system and their people in ways they never had before. Noncovered employees were glad they survived and proud of the new skills they learned, although they never cared to do these jobs again. Covered employees were somewhat amazed that the company struggled through without them for so long. There was a great deal of bonding and camaraderie, friendships made, hard times shared—on both sides of the picket lines. Everyone learned from the experience, and Alabama Power came out stronger in the end.[65]

SOUTHERN SERVICES, NEW DAMS AND MORE GENERATION ON THE COOSA

In the early history of Alabama Power Company, the people of the subsidiary companies and service companies moved back and forth between the affiliated companies and Alabama Power, and their roles in the history of Alabama Power were easily integrated into the story of the company. Most of the employees who worked for Dixie Construction Company and Allied Engineers either began or ended or spent some of their careers with Alabama Power. This was not true of Ernest C. Gaston, who began his work with Dixie Construction Company in 1923 and stayed with the affiliated service companies. In 1940, H. J. Scholz gave Gaston the responsibility of the design department for the southern companies in Commonwealth & Southern. In 1949 Gaston went with Southern Services, and when Scholz retired in 1957 he became president.

Ernest C. Gaston

Ernie Gaston, who held a mechanical engineering degree from the University of Alabama, was a distinguished gentleman with great patience and a fine talent as a designing engineer. He is important to the story of Alabama Power because he was involved with so much of the design work on the company's generation, both steam and hydroelectric plants, in the 1950s and 1960s. He was responsible for the dam designs on the Warrior and upper Coosa Rivers and for the large generating plant on the Coosa River at Wilsonville, which was named the Ernest C. Gaston Steam Plant.[66] An important part of Alabama Power culture is to master the correct company pronunciation of the Gads-*den* and Gas-*ton* steam plants, to prevent anyone from misunderstanding which plant is being discussed.

Between 1964 and 1967 Birmingham's Harbert Corporation was awarded five contracts for the redevelopment of Lay Dam. This construction involved building a cofferdam, raising the dam height fourteen feet, removing the old turbines and generators, and preparing the powerhouse foundation to carry the new and much heavier generators and turbines. Raising Lay Dam eliminated the necessity of building a dam at the Fort Williams site in order to have a navigable channel to the foot of Logan Martin Dam.[67]

On October 3, 1967, Alabama Power accepted bids on the sale of $28 million first-mortgage bonds to finance the construction program of the company. These funds would provide for the completion of Lay Dam's redevelopment, finishing the Holt hydroelectric unit, and the installation of a 350,000-kilowatt unit at Barry Steam Plant. Four of the six new generating units at Lay went into service in 1967 and the other two in mid-1968. In 1969 additional construction money came from $54.4 million in internally generated cash and from $36 million from sales of securities and interim short-term bank loans. The next year, Alabama Power sold $90.6 million in securities to help finance this construction.[68]

Workers at Neely Henry Dam lower the unit 1 turbine runner into place, November 2, 1965.

Construction had started on the Lock 3 Dam at Ohatchee near Ragland on the Coosa River in 1962, and hydroelectric generation there went into service in 1966. This reservoir covered 11,235 acres and the dam's rated installed generating capacity was 72,900 kilowatts. Both were named for longtime company leader and senior executive vice president H. Neely Henry. At the dedication ceremonies on September 14, 1968, Senator John Sparkman gave the major address and praised Alabama Power for its vision and leadership in developing the Coosa River.[69]

As part of the complete development of the Coosa River, a dam was originally planned for Wetumpka, south of Jordan Dam, but after careful study this low-head dam was determined to be very expensive for the amount of electricity it would generate. Alabama Power engineers who studied the river and the terrain were challenged to find a plan that would produce enough income to make the investment worthwhile and that

The redevelopment of Lay Dam raised the height of the dam fourteen feet and doubled the size of the reservoir.

would also incorporate opening the river for navigation if the federal government ever determined to appropriate the money for locks. The study resulted in a new project requiring more investment but generating far more electricity. A redevelopment of Jordan Dam would raise the dam height seven feet. Additional spillway gates would be installed at Jordan, along with a forebay lake impounded by earth embankments and located a few miles away. The lake would be connected to the Coosa riverbed one mile north of Jordan by an intake canal large enough for navigation. This new reservoir was built, and the last of the dam's three generating units went into service on August 26, 1967.

For several years the project was called Jordan No. 2 Development, but on a sunny September day in 1969, 1,800 people gathered to dedicate the dam to Alabama Power's former president and then chairman of the board, Walter Bouldin. Because of its modern generators, Bouldin was Alabama Power's largest capacity hydroelectic generating plant with 225,000 kilowatts of installed capacity. In his remarks that day,

Bouldin Dam has the largest generating capacity of all Alabama Power's hydroelectric plants.

Congressman Bill Nichols from Alabama's Fourth Congressional District predicted that one day tugs would push barges from Mobile to Rome, Georgia. Governor Albert Brewer praised Alabama Power for having the courage to invest $194 million on the Coosa River, saying that it exemplified "the strength of free enterprise, the ability of capitalism to work quickly, economically, and effectively for the good of the entire populace."[70]

This dedication was one of those gala events that Tom Martin would have been proud of, and he would have been prouder still because it also celebrated the completion of the Coosa River project originally conceived by James Mitchell and Eugene Yates in 1912 and pushed so hard by Martin in the mid-1950s. Politicians from the capital and from the county seats along the river from Cedar Bluff and Centre to Montgomery mingled with the company's retirees and young junior engineers to enjoy the celebration. Alvin Vogtle was there, no doubt reminiscing about his years working in Washington to make the Coosa project possible. Now president of Southern Company, Vogtle led the delegation of holding company leadership, which came to celebrate a new dam that carried the name of a friend, a man recognized as a national leader of the industry, president of the Edison Electric Institute, and consultant to three U.S. presidents, Walter Bouldin.[71]

HOLT AND THE BLACK WARRIOR RIVER

When George Wallace began his first year as governor, the question of who would build and operate the generation at the new Corps of Engineers Holt Lock and Dam on the Warrior was undetermined. Wallace had blasted the federal government and opposed the Rural Electrification Administration in his campaign speeches, making it difficult for him to support the federal government

instead of an investor-owned power company. He was keenly aware of the flow of tax dollars that would come from Alabama Power's operation. Wallace aide Cecil Jackson recommended that Wallace support generation at Holt on principle but not take sides on who would operate it. Wallace, however, eventually supported Alabama Power.[72]

The completion of Holt Dam on August 15, 1968, marked the final phase of Alabama Power's hydroelectric development of the Black Warrior River.

The Federal Power Commission issued a license to Alabama Power on October 7, 1965. In the years prior to this license, there was extensive discussion on whether the Holt generators would reduce the oxygen content of the water below the dam by pulling water from the bottom above the dam and whether this would have a detrimental effect on fish. Because of the discharge of industrial waste from the Birmingham area into creeks that flowed into the Warrior above Bankhead Lock and Dam, it was suggested that the company install an upstream skimming weir to draw off top water, which was usually higher in oxygen. The Federal Power Commission did not initially include this provision in its license but did require a five-year study of the water quality in the Black Warrior River. The study was to be made by the Alabama Water

Improvement Commission and the U.S. Public Health Service to see if a skimming weir was necessary. By its license, Alabama Power would provide electricity free of charge for the operation of the lock, provide support for fish and wildlife resources, and maintain recreational support—beaches, picnic and camping areas, boat launching ramps, and access roads.[73]

RECREATION

Alabama Power had acquired extensive acreage along Little River in DeKalb and Cherokee Counties with the acquisition of the Little River Power Company, part of the S. Z. and Reuben Mitchell–EBASCO purchase in 1912. In 1967 the company signed a twenty-year lease with the Alabama State Department of Conservation that would open up these 10,000 acres of virgin timberland to hunting for the first time. Years before, Alabama Power had donated a large tract of acreage north of the new hunting preserve for the state to create a twelve-mile parkway along the rim of Little River Canyon. This scenic drive on top of Lookout Mountain opened in 1954.[74]

As the years passed, more Alabama citizens depended upon the company's reservoirs and forested lands for recreation. The state's artificial lakes provided 145,000 acres of water playgrounds. Zipp Newman, longtime sports editor of the *Birmingham News*, wrote a series of articles about the state's lakes, calling them "enchanting" and claiming that "no electric power company has made possible more recreational centers for fishing, hunting, swimming, boating, skiing, and camping than the Alabama Power Company."[75] Newman discussed

Alabama Power's lakes provide 145,000 acres of recreational opportunities for Alabamians and are a tourist destination for the state.

all the lakes, evaluating fishing opportunities at Weiss, Mitchell, Yates, and Lay. He reminisced about the special place Lake Martin held in the college football world because the presidents and football coaches of Auburn and the University of Alabama all had lakeside summer homes at Lake Martin and entertained guests there.

The First Rate Case: 1968

Following the assassination of President John F. Kennedy in 1963 and the election of President Lyndon B. Johnson in 1964, American participation in the conflict in Vietnam escalated. By 1968 President Johnson had poured half a million men and $30 billion a year into the war. One result for the country was a war-bred inflation that ushered in a new historical period with stressful and challenging economic conditions.[76] Partly offsetting these circumstances, the electrical industry, including Alabama Power, had taken advantage of technological advances and economies of scale to reduce the cost of electricity even as the industry encouraged its use with campaigns and advertising. Investor-owned utilities provided electricity for the vast majority of Americans. Low rates and continued growth of the industry pleased both customers and investors, resulting in little concern for state and federal regulators. Inflation, escalating costs, and high interest rates would change this dynamic.

From the beginning, Alabama Power had maintained a construction program to serve the state's ever-increasing demands for electricity. By the end of the 1960s, however, national events and economic pressures over which the company had no control bore heavily on its financial position and additional revenues were necessary. As Joe Farley recalled, "Money was getting more costly and interest rates were beginning to rise. The pressure was developing on the company's earnings."[77] The company's 1967 rates allowed the average Alabama Power customer to purchase electricity well below the national average, and even with the proposed rate increase, costs to customers would remain low compared to other regions. On March 29, 1968, president Walter Bouldin wrote in his annual report that "pressures of inflation significantly affected 1967 expenses as the cost of wages, fuel, supplies, materials, and virtually all other elements necessary to provide our customers with electric service, including the cost of investment capital, continued to rise." Bouldin had announced in February that the company had filed for a rate increase with the Alabama Public Service Commission in order to cover the cost of providing electrical service and the cost of investment capital. The company also requested that increases in certain taxes be reflected in billings.[78] This was the first time in its history that Alabama Power Company had ever filed for a general rate increase.

John Burks

Rate design has always been a meticulous challenge involving many considerations, and Alabama Power has always had some of the best rate experts in the country. Stalwarts in this area, such as Chandler Murton and Norman Mandy, were recognized authorities. John Burks was another one, and he was followed by Oscar Walker. Considerations that affect rates include customer cost (fixed costs to provide and maintain service, such as billing and distribution), energy costs (the cost of fuel and operating expenses), and capacity demand (the cost of generating plants, transmission lines, and other facilities). Burks once explained that while no customer is exactly alike in demand for electricity, residential customers are more similar than commercial and industrial customers who might vary widely in the times when they need electricity and the amount of electricity they demand. Some industrial customers might have a relatively steady demand over the course of a twenty-four-hour period, while others might need more electricity at different times. Burks explained that Alabama Power attempts to design for each class of customer rates that are fair, competitive, and equitable while still covering the costs of serving that class of customer.[79]

The year 1968 marked the beginning of fifteen years of serious financial problems for Alabama Power and was a watershed year in the history of the company. In past years, economies of scale, the large percentage of hydro generation, new generating capacity constructed at reasonable costs, financing arranged at sensible interest, and efficient management had allowed the company to serve its customers with decreasing rates, which were always below the national average. As recently as four years before the 1968 crisis, the company had a substantial rate *reduction*, partly the result of an adjustment in the corporate federal income tax laws. In 1964 the schedules for residential customers and large industries were reduced. The lower rates were also applied to commercial customers who previously had been served on rate schedules of Birmingham Electric Company, which made Alabama Power's rates more nearly uniform. The 1964 refunds and rate reductions cost the company approximately $1.5 million a year in lost revenue but were implemented to promote growth and development in the company's service area.[80] One significant addition in the 1964 case order was a fuel clause adjustment provision that allowed increases as well as decreases in the rates to compensate for changes in the cost of fuel for generation. As Jack Bingham noted, when this clause was added fuel costs were stable and not an issue. The extension of the fuel clause was providential, however, for within eight or nine years the cost of fuel escalated dramatically, and this provision saved the company from even greater distress.[81] In the 1964 refund rate case, the public service commissioners were president C. C. "Jack" Owen, Sibyl Pool, and Ed Pepper.

Jack Bingham well remembered the historical February 1968 filing. From Atlanta, Harllee Branch was pressuring Alabama Power to increase its rate of return on investment. With support from its attorneys, the company planned carefully for its presentation before the Public Service Commission, with Eason Balch as the lead attorney. It was not a simple matter. Alabama Power had to explain and prove its need, detail its financial records, and prepare testimony from engineers and the financial staff. Putting together

Jack Bingham

such interrogatory testimony, charts, graphs, and exhibits took an inordinate amount of time. George B. Campbell, vice president for finance and accounting, began the preparations before going to Southern Company, and after that the responsibility went to Liston Cook, vice president of accounting, and Walter Johnsey. Alabama Power engaged New York attorney Cameron MacRae, a specialist in rate cases for utility companies, to assist with testimony preparation.

On the day the rate case was to be filed in Montgomery, Harllee Branch assembled a number of Southern Company directors and important financiers in New York for a carefully planned joint announcement of Alabama Power's rate case filing. In Montgomery, company attorneys took their stack of papers to the Public Service Commission. Jack Bingham, looking back to this day, smiled in the telling and noted that at the time it was dead serious business. Walter Bouldin never saw the humor, because when the attorneys arrived at the Public Service Commission office, they discovered that it was closed for the state holiday of Mardi Gras. The public relations coup was lost, but the filing took place as the attorneys went out to PSC secretary Wallace Tidmore's house, and he stamped the filing for the following day.[82]

When the 1968 rate case was presented in hearings that stretched for several months, the personalities of the Public Service Commission had changed. Bull Connor, the Birmingham police commissioner who had lost his position when the form of city government changed, ran for the Public Service Commission in the spring of 1964 and defeated Owen, a Bibb County native, former extension service county agent, and World War II hero who had been elected to the commission in 1946. Years later Sid Smyer revealed to Howell Raines, a Birmingham native and New York Times journalist, that "he and other white leaders" had promised Connor the support of the Birmingham business community for his campaign for the Public Service Commission in return for his promise to never again run for a Birmingham office.[83] When Joe Farley first heard this story, he shook his head and said, "Mr. Martin and Mr.

Bouldin would have had a fit. Not so much because of Bull, but because Owen was a good commissioner. Sometimes he voted against Alabama Power, but he was always fair."[84] Connor's campaign manager thought his victory came from name recognition and his identification as a strong segregationist and as a Wallace supporter. In December 1966 Connor suffered a paralytic stroke and was impaired the rest of his life, confined to a wheelchair, and in considerable pain. He often presided over commission meetings without much of a clue as to the business being transacted and sometimes fell asleep during testimony. He depended upon his assistant, longtime friend James T. "Jabo" Waggoner Sr., to guide him, although he did not always act as Waggoner suggested.[85]

Commissioner Pepper, who was a former state finance director and key member of Governor James E. Folsom's cabinet, was soon enmeshed in an FBI sting operation stemming from three trucking requests before the commission. On February 6, 1967, the forty-one-year-old Pepper was indicted by a grand jury on two counts of extortion, but on the night of February 7, he and his wife died in a tragic fire at Dale's Penthouse Restaurant on the eleventh floor of the Walter Bragg Smith apartment hotel in Montgomery.[86] Owen ran for Pepper's vacant seat and was elected once more to the Public Service Commission.[87] Except for the two years after Connor defeated him, Owen had served on the PSC since his first term began in 1947.[88] Pool was a Marengo County music teacher who worked with the Farm Bureau and the Linden Chamber of Commerce before serving in the Alabama House of Representatives. In 1946 Pool was elected secretary of state and became the first woman in Alabama to win a statewide race. She was elected to the Public Service Commission in 1954.[89]

When Alabama Power's first ever general rate increase request came before the Public Service Commission in 1968, the only opposition came from the Alabama Textile Manufacturers Association and the Alabama Gas Association. These groups claimed that Alabama Power made a mistake in building expensive dams when it was cheaper to build coal-fired steam plants. At that time, coal was selling for $5 to $6 a ton, but eight years later coal prices soared to $20 to $25 a ton. No residential customers appeared as intervenors. One interesting conflict came when Joseph L. Lanier Sr., who was associated with the Pepperell Manufacturing Company, a large textile mill in eastern Alabama, opposed the increase. Lanier was a member of Southern Company's board of directors, and he appeared to support the Alabama Textile Manufacturers Association's opposition to Alabama Power's rate increase. Harllee Branch was insistent that Alabama Power had to get its rates up, and Lanier had not been able to persuade Branch to stop Alabama Power from asking for the increase.[90]

The public hearings went on all spring in what Eason Balch characterized as "a hard, tiresome proceeding."[91]

At the last hearing on June 14, 1968, Rucker Agee was one of the most important witnesses for Alabama Power. Agee, a widely known and well-respected Birmingham investment banker, whom Connor knew and respected, testified to the appropriate rate of return for Alabama Power's common stock equity, a return that was clearly not being achieved. In closing arguments Eason Balch described the arduous hearings and observed that there is "little wonder that Alabama Power Company has put off 45 years coming down here to undertake to get a rate increase." Without any discussion, Commissioner Pool suddenly moved to deny the rate increase. Owen objected, saying no one in their right mind would agree to that because the courts would overrule the commission since it had not considered and studied all the exhibits and testimony.

The hour was approaching five o'clock, and there was much confusion. Pool again said she was voting to deny. Owen cautioned that the courts would overrule the commission because adequate deliberation had not taken place. Connor called for Owen's vote. Owen moved to take up the motion in executive session. Pool said, "My vote still stands." Bull Connor responded with: "I vote with the lady." Owen again complained. Attorney Henry Simpson, who was also representing the power company, asked the commission for a reconsideration of the vote. That failed, and just before the PSC adjourned, Connor said, "Goodbye. All of you who want to, come back tomorrow." Since tomorrow was a Saturday, Connor was certainly muddled. The rate increase had been rejected. After the meeting one of Alabama Power's attorneys asked Connor, who was being pushed in his wheelchair down the hall, if he realized what he had done. The commission president replied, "Well, whatever it is, we'll fix it on Monday."[92]

Fixing it on Monday was quite involved and took eighteen months and an appeal to the Montgomery circuit court. During the next regular commission meeting, Public Service Commission examiner C. C. "Chris" Whatley referred to Docket No. 16044 order, which had been placed on the commissioners' desks earlier in the week. Connor asked if that was a nineteen-page document, and when Whatley replied it was, Connor boomed, "That's the first thing I've got against it—it's too durn long." Pool was still hostile to Alabama Power, and she introduced her own order (which she admitted she did not write but refused to say who wrote it), that was very punitive to the company. Owen and Connor voted against it.[93]

Judge Richard Emmet of the Circuit Court of Montgomery County issued an order on August 26, 1968, that the company could place under bond the proposed rate increase in effect pending review. The new rate schedule began on September 19, 1968. The court remanded the case to the commission. The commission's order on April 28, 1969, addressed the merits of the rate case and approved the company's retail rate increase, following the principles of an Alabama Supreme Court case involving Southern Bell. Pool still opposed, but Connor and Owen voted for the increase. The Alabama Textile Manufacturers Association appealed back to the circuit court as an intervenor, and Judge Richard Emmet dismissed the appeal. Additional earnings for 1968 were some $2.2 million and for 1969 approximately $6.3 million. With increased rates finally permitted, the company's 1969 *Annual Report* explained that the increased income was partly accounted for "by recoveries of the federal income tax surcharge permitted under the fuel-and-tax clause in the revised rates. This provision adjusted rates to consumers to reflect tax decreases as well as increases and, therefore, reduced rates with the reduction of the federal surcharge effective in 1970."[94]

Alabama Power continued to shoulder a higher tax burden than other utilities in the state, a burden that represented almost 19 percent of its operating revenues. The company still resented the unfairness of some 20 percent of the nation's electricity customers purchasing power from government production that paid no taxes. Alabama Power was the largest taxpayer in Alabama, and while proud of its contributions to education and state government, the company felt increasing rancor at being pressured by politicians and customers for even lower rates while legislative bodies kept increasing its tax burden and enacting laws that required it to compete with non–tax paying, government-supported generation and distribution. In 1967 Bouldin reminded stockholders that the "group of consumers of federally owned and sponsored power developments and rural electric cooperatives is not sharing equally in the federal tax burden with the 80 percent of the nation's electricity consumers that are served by investor-owned utilities such as Alabama Power."[95]

The year 1968 not only marked the start of fifteen years of rate cases, it also marked a renewed period of political attacks on the company. Since the spring of 1914 when Alabama Power unfortunately found itself injected into the Democratic primary, the company had carefully monitored the Alabama political scene, closely watched bills being introduced into the legislature, and cautiously tried to protect the assets of its stockholders and its financial interests. During his second gubernatorial campaign in 1934, Bibb Graves coined the term "Big Mules" for his Birmingham big-business opponents, painting the imagery of a farmer hitching a small mule to a wagon loaded with corn and tying a large mule to the back of the wagon. The large mule ate the corn while the little mule pulled the wagon.[96] At midcentury, political candidates and historians often lumped Alabama Power as a Big Mule with TCI and the Alabama Farm Bureau, two entities with which it had little in common except perhaps for a general opposition to the New Deal and excessive taxation.

Often the Big Mules disagreed on issues. Historian Wayne Flynt in his account of Alabama in the twentieth century points out that the planter–Big Mule alliance forged early in the century at first gained strength from racial polarization. But "later it came unglued due to the civil rights movement, the Voting Rights Act, urban-rural clashes, the metropolitanization of Alabama (especially the migration into the state of new high-skill, well-educated populations), clashes over demands for improved infrastructures, and a slow but steady modernization that accompanied Sunbelt growth." Flynt contends that the Black Belt wing of the old Bourbon coalition was gone by the 1960s. This itself meant that a new age was dawning in Alabama.[97]

New Leadership

In December 1968, H. Neely Henry and R. L. Harris both retired. Alan R. Barton replaced Henry as senior vice president of transmission and distribution, and James H. Miller Jr. replaced Harris as senior vice president of electric operations. Both Barton and Miller were elected to the board of directors. Barton, a native of Connecticut and a fine engineer, served in the navy during World War II and came to the company in 1948

Alan R. Barton

with an Auburn electrical engineering degree. He was assigned to Mobile as a junior engineer. Later, Barton moved to Birmingham and became part of the transmission and distribution engineering area, then became vice president of the Western Division. In 1968 he was elevated to senior vice president.

Jim Miller also began his work with the company in the Mobile Division as a junior engineer after graduation from Tulane University and a tour of duty in World War II in the navy. He moved to Birmingham in 1958 and became an assistant to Walter Bouldin before assuming responsibilities under R. L. Harris as assistant manager of electric operations.[98] Miller was a tall, distinguished-looking man with a ready smile and a good story to tell. He was an excellent engineer, a tough but fair boss who emphasized training and education for his plant people and insisted on top maintenance for equipment. He understood budgets and ran a tight ship. Once when working on budgets an assistant used the phrase "lean and mean." Miller responded that "it was O.K. to be lean, but you can't be mean." At a PSC rate case hearing when a woman went on and on about the poor electrical service she had, Miller asked her exactly where she lived. When she told him, he responded with delight, "Lady, we don't supply your electricity."[99]

When the Alabama Power stockholders and directors met in Eufaula on April 18, 1969, they elevated Walter Bouldin to chairman of the board and selected the company's talented young executive vice president, Joseph M. "Joe" Farley, as president. Just a few months earlier, on February 1, 1969, Alvin Vogtle had succeeded Harllee Branch as president of the Southern Company when Branch was elevated to chairman of the board. Alabama Power anticipated a close working relationship with Vogtle, who was well known in Birmingham and had spent many years with Alabama Power.[100]

While Joe Farley had been with Alabama Power management and a director of the company for only four years, he had been directly involved with Alabama Power's legal and regulatory matters for seventeen years. His education in engineering, law, and business provided excellent training for a utilities executive. His keen mind, recall of facts and numbers, and understanding of the legal process made him an impressive witness in regulatory or other cases. In fact, Eason Balch, who was responsible for many of those proceedings, considered Farley the strongest witness he ever put on the stand.[101] Farley was a good judge of character and had the ability to select the best people and place them with responsibilities that strengthened the company. Once described as "young, serious, and committed," Farley had intense powers of concentration and often walked the halls with a determined focus. He was a strong and inspired leader, and as an executive he was accessible to his people.[102]

Joseph M. Farley

Farley was a kind, almost shy, gentleman with a sense of modesty and impeccable southern manners and the highest priciples. But he did not suffer fools gladly, and he was sometimes impatient. His irritation at unanswered telephones became legendary as well as his passionate defense of Alabama Power and his own integrity.[103] Walter Johnsey recalls a time when a witness at a Public Service Commission hearing assailed the company and called into question Farley's character and honesty. Farley followed the man out as he left after his testimony. Johnsey and Jack Minor exited also and found Farley engaging the man in a spirited conversation in the hallway.[104] In his leadership of the company through difficult times, Farley was resolute and tenacious. He faced the challenges with fortitude and perseverance. And, as Eason Balch noted, often with a sense of humor.[105]

Farley was to serve the company longer as chief executive officer than any man other than Tom Martin. His devotion to the company's mission of service to the state of Alabama and its people ran as deeply as Martin's did. Joe Farley came to the power company presidency at the end of a decade that changed the nation and at the beginning of an inflationary spiral that challenged previously held concepts of utility financing and administration. He had to deal with continued hostile encroachments from federally funded cooperatives, attacks from state politicians and regulatory commissions, complicated federal legislation, and new untested, contradictory, and often bewildering agency regulations. But he had a strong leadership team to help him. The new company management included Barton and Miller as senior vice presidents and vice presidents Sam Booker (marketing), Liston H. Cook (accounting), S. R. Hart Jr. (engineering), Charles P. Jackson (treasurer), Walter Johnsey (administration and finance), E. Davis Long (employee relations), G. Thornton Nelson (industrial development), and Jesse S. Vogtle (public affairs). Richard Bowron was secretary. Division officers were William O. Whitt (Birmingham), A. Clayton Rogers Jr. (Tuscaloosa), William L. McDonough (Mobile), Hugh P. Foreman (Montgomery), Raymond T. Garlington (Eufaula), and F. Otto Miller (Anniston).[106]

Nuclear Plant on the Chattahoochee

Alabama Power Company had started its preparation for nuclear development, beginning with Southern Company's hiring of Ruble Thomas some fifteen years before the company was ready to move forward with a nuclear generation plant. Georgia Power began its construction of Plant Hatch in 1967. On May 13, 1969, Walter Bouldin, chairman of the board of Alabama Power, announced that the company would be building its first nuclear-fueled generating plant. Thomas was to be very much involved in the site selection of the plant as he had been for the two plants being constructed by Georgia Power, Plant Hatch and Plant Vogtle. State and local leaders praised the company for its planned investment of $165 million for the plant and called it a milestone in Alabama history. If Alabama Power had really known what the eventual cost of the plant would be and what dire financial times were lurking down the road, the decision to build may not have been made. But history has proved the decision a good one for Alabama Power and its customers, for the state, and especially for the Wiregrass area. With great ceremony at a Dothan luncheon on June 2, 1969, the company announced that the plant's location would be on the west bank of the Chattahoochee River between Columbia and Gordon. The decision was greeted enthusiastically by the chambers of commerce, mayors, and county commissioners in the Wiregrass. Bouldin stressed that the construction of the plant in Houston County would give Alabama

Power its first generating plant in the southeastern part of the state. The *Eufaula Tribune* predicted that more industry would locate in the region because of the availability of power, a prediction that has certainly come true.[107]

On August 21, 1969, the company requested a certificate of convenience and necessity from the PSC to build the plant (the certificate was granted on August 27), and also filed its Preliminary Safety Analysis Report and application for a construction permit with the U.S. Atomic Energy Commission. Initially, the plant was called SEALA for southeast Alabama, but at the October 29, 1969, board meeting at the insistence of Colonel W. J. Rushton, the board of directors voted to name the nuclear plant for Farley.[108] Proud of the honor but modest, Farley seemed somewhat uneasy with the recognition in the next few years, and Don Thornburgh, who was then manager of fuels, recalled that sometimes Farley seemed to shy away from calling the plant by his own name.[109]

Because the public had questions about nuclear power, the company established a special committee to formulate and administer a public information plan for the plant. Walter Johnsey was made head of the company's nuclear public information committee; Richard A. Peacock, advertising manager, and T. L. Longshore, assistant to the president, worked with Johnsey. Peacock coordinated a speakers bureau and released information about the plant. Longshore was responsible for community programs and regulatory information. Within a few months, the speakers bureau was presenting programs around the state on "Alabama Power and the Nuclear Age."[110]

After long study, Walter Bouldin concluded that the nuclear plant required special construction expertise, and although he had great confidence in the company's construction department, he believed a national company with broader experience should undertake the task for a number of reasons. In the end, he decided to go with Daniel Construction Company, a well-known and widely esteemed company with offices in Birmingham. In evaluating Bouldin's leadership of Alabama Power Company, two important decisions that he made on the nuclear program stand above many in the minds of those who worked with him. First, Bouldin decided to build the nuclear plant, which with hindsight, despite the enormous trouble and cost overruns, was absolutely the right thing to do. Then he picked Daniel Construction to build it, even though it had never built a nuclear plant before. Daniel was founded in South Carolina in 1934 by Charles E. Daniel, and three years later his brother Hugh opened a Birmingham office. By 1955 Hugh was president of Daniel. Bouldin knew the company and was confident that it could be trusted with the responsibility and that Alabama Power could work with Daniel.[111]

Alabama Power selected Westinghouse Electric Corporation's pressurized water reactor steam supply system and turbine generators for the Farley Nuclear Plant. Left: Construction work on unit 1 containment structure in 1972.

Below: The reactor for Farley unit 1 arrives by barge.

Joseph M. Farley

NUCLEAR ELECTRIC GENERATING PLANT
● UNIT No.1 SCHEDULED FOR 1975...829,000 kw
● UNIT No.2 SCHEDULED FOR 1977...829,000 kw

Alabama Power Company

TEMPORARY
JOSEPH M. FARLEY NUCLEAR VISITORS CENTER
VISITING HOURS 1 TO 5 PM - WEDNESDAY THRU SUNDAY

In June the company announced that it would build a second unit at Farley. Grading and excavation started for unit 1 in September 1970 under a permit waiver. After a number of bids were received, the company decided to select low bidder Westinghouse Electric Corporation and its pressurized water reactor steam supply system and turbine generators. Southern Company Services did some design work, but Bechtel Power Corporation of Gaithersburg, Maryland, designed the plant's nuclear components. Bechtel's designers visited the site before beginning their designs. Construction was delayed

The Farley plant became a popular attraction in the Wiregrass area.

a few months until the U.S. Atomic Energy Commission issued permits, but in August 1972 permits were granted and construction was accelerated with a goal of having, an 860,000-kilowatt unit 1, operating by late spring of 1975.[112]

Early in the planning stages, Jim Miller (power generation), Alan Barton (construction), and E. Davis Long (employee relations) determined that a nuclear power generation plant was not like any other steam plant, and special expertise was needed. The Alabama Power team to oversee the work was put together by Herman Thrash under Jim Young of the company's production department. Six engineers with no nuclear experience were selected to go back to school at Georgia Tech for master's degrees in nuclear engineering. They were George Hairston, Bob Berryhill, Don Cain, John Dorsett, Hugh Thompson, and Bill Mintz. After earning their degrees, they were sent to the Westinghouse Training Center at Zion, Illinois, to be certified. In the next few years, some fourteen other Alabama power engineers received the same nuclear education and training.[113] Ruble Thomas, who had developed a reputation as one of the nation's foremost experts on nuclear power, was very much involved in Plant Farley as vice president of nuclear power, advance planning, and research at Southern Services, which became Southern Company Services in 1976. Thomas had a depth of knowledge beyond concrete details, the flexibility and foresight to ensure safety at all times, personal integrity, and the ability to lead and inspire.[114]

Doug McCrary was promoted to vice president of construction on January 15, 1971, and closely supervised the construction of Farley. McCrary observed that there was not much opposition to the nuclear plant from Dothan residents, but he remembered one time when he went to Dothan to talk to a man who had been complaining about the plant. McCrary explained how Dothan would grow, workers would come into the area, and the tax base would increase and bring prosperity to the area. The man looked at McCrary for a moment then said, "Listen, mister, we've got two Sears stores and a K-Mart in Dothan, and I can get to work in five minutes. I don't want this place to grow."[115]

Bill Lindstrom was the construction superintendent for Alabama Power for the first years the plant was under construction, then Jimmy Mooney took over; Dick Fox was Daniel's project manager and was later replaced by Ralph Williams. The construction of offices, a warehouse, and other needed facilities began first. McCrary recalled the paperwork "establishing procedures for construction and handling the documentation was a major undertaking." The nuclear plant was a union job with about thirty-two different crafts involved. McCrary worked closely with unions on the state and local levels and turned to the national pipefitters union when problems came up locating expert welders in the area. Daniel eventually employed some 4,000 workers in three eight-hour shifts each day. Effort was made not to disturb the labor market in the Wiregrass, fearing that after the completion of the project, local men would be left unemployed. By January 1974 the first of two 860,000-kilowatt generating units was 60 percent complete, the 322-ton reactor vessel had arrived by barge from Chattanooga, and work continued on the cooling towers. When complete, they would cool about 635,000 gallons of water per minute "to prevent the release of any significant amount of heated water into the Chattahoochee River."[116]

Alabama Power Company's nuclear leadership had a decidedly naval tone. Robert P. "Pat" McDonald, a good example, joined the company in 1974 after twenty-two years in the navy, all but three served in the nuclear program. A graduate of the U.S. Naval Academy and the Naval War College, he retired as captain commanding the U.S. Atlantic Fleet of nuclear submarines. In his first years at the company, he was manager of operations quality assurance and in 1977 was promoted to vice president of power supply.[117]

Robert P. "Pat" McDonald

Problems with permits from the Atomic Energy Commission delayed construction and increased costs. The regulatory process was a nightmare. A U.S. Supreme Court decision caused a different type of environmental impact statement to be required. Alabama Power's Plant Farley was the first to compile one, and as Joe Farley noted, "No one knew how to write one." The application developed by Southern Company Services and Bechtel "became the model for others to follow." After these delays and lost time, the Atomic Energy Commission determined that a lake should be constructed to provide a thirty-day supply of cooling water if the Chattahoochee River should ever run dry.[118] Complying with government regulations in an industry so new that the rules and the requirements of construction were constantly changing caused delays in finishing Plant Farley.

SALES AND MARKETING

Samuel H. Booker, longtime leader of the company's sales program and vice president of marketing since 1967, led the company when Alabama Power reorganized its sales efforts in 1968. Booker had come to the company after World War II as an agricultural engineer working with rural electrification programs. Terry Waters, who worked in market and research planning, remembered Booker as one of the most respected and deeply loved company officers. He was widely known in the state and served on a number of committees and boards, such as the Judson College trustees and the Baptist Hospital Foundation. Walter Baker described

Samuel H. Booker

Walter Baker

Booker as a friend to everyone and "a great delegator" who seldom interfered once he assigned responsibility for a project. He cared deeply for people, a trait that flowed from his background and his Baptist faith. His philosophy of marketing was based on personal contact and carefully conceived promotional programs.[119]

The newly reorganized marketing department would have broad functions, primarily aimed at promoting those electrical loads in all markets that were economically beneficial to both the company and its customers. The company had already introduced a new rate, the AE for all-electric dwellings, and had adopted Edison Electric Institute's "All-Electric Building Awards" program, which was directed toward the commercial market. Alabama Power's new programs were designed to give emphasis to these concepts. Incentives were established for company sales employees, home builders, developers, and others participating in these programs. A new high-load factor rate (HLF) was introduced to reward industrial customers who required high electrical loads. By the end of 1971 Alabama Power was serving 65,364 electrically heated dwellings, which was up 90 percent over 1968, and the number of off-peak dusk-to-dawn lights had increased to 60,161.[120] Even so, system loads were becoming a problem. This problem was occurring nationally as well as on Alabama Power's system. The answer was to increase winter demand by heat pumps to balance the summer air conditioning demand.

The marketing department used the theme "Narrow the Gap" to push winter electric heating. Joe Farley addressed the company's annual sales conference in 1972 and, as Walter Baker suggested, gave the company "a clearly stated marketing policy" that would serve it well in future years. Farley said:

> We serve the public best when we market electricity vigorously, but selectively. In doing so, we seek to utilize our enormously expensive facilities efficiently and thereby provide our customers with reliable, full-value electric service; our investors with a reasonable return on their money; and our employees with stable employment at fair wages. To do less is to fail in our basic responsibility as an investor-owned electric utility.[121]

The marketing department continued the promotion of off-peak loads and promoting high load factors for industrial customers. The marketing department's promotional campaigns during 1969–71 were responsible for additional off-peak loads, increased sales of dusk-to-dawn lights, more underground distribution lines, and $5 million in electric appliance sales.

THE SECOND RATE CASE: 1970

The national scene at the end of the 1960s was important to Alabama Power Company for at least two reasons: the economy went into an insidious inflationary spiral that increased the cost of money and the cost of doing business, a problem faced by all utilities and businesses in the nation, and the former Alabama governor was encouraged by the unsettled political times to run for president on the American Independent ticket.[122] George Wallace had no chance to win the presidency in 1968, but he added color and some confusion to the campaign by adding a third party and racial issues. Wallace's focus on the presidential contest diluted his interest in state politics so long as his base of support remained strong and unchallenged and he was in control. He had never relished overseeing the day-to-day details of running the state, and after his wife, Governor Lurleen Wallace, died on May 7, 1968, and Lieutenant Governor Albert P. Brewer succeeded her as governor, George Wallace was freed of even his advisory duties. In the November 4, 1968, presidential election, Richard Nixon won by just half a million votes over Hubert Humphrey in a tight contest. George Wallace, running on his American Independent ticket, received forty-six electoral votes from the Deep South and almost ten million votes nationwide, the largest third-party vote in American history. But Wallace folks believed that 1972 would be the real contest for Wallace's presidential aspirations.[123]

Meanwhile, the increasing demands for electricity coupled with inflation simply meant it cost Alabama Power more money to borrow capital for construction and more funds to operate. Another rate increase was required. Adding to the seriousness of the situation was the fact that in applying for a rate increase, the company had to produce statistics based on a previous eleven-month period. Since inflation was rampant and the rate process took so long, before one increase could be fully implemented, another one was needed. On November 6, 1970, the company filed schedules requesting a second rate increase, this one for residential, commercial, and industrial customers.[124]

Months later, Joe Farley, in his 1970 annual report, stated that the 1968 increase was "more than offset during the ensuing two years by increases in but two of the company's expenses: interest on long-term debt and wage costs." He pointed out that the price of almost everything the company needed to "supply reliable electric service also has continued to rise, and in some instances, by very substantial amounts." Additional revenue was critical because the company had a long-range construction program that envisioned spending $693 million over the following three years. This program included expensive additional generating units at steam plants Barry, Gorgas, and Gaston; new high voltage transmission lines, especially in northwest and southeast Alabama; the construction of two units at Farley Nuclear Plant; a dam at Crooked Creek on the Tallapoosa River above Martin Dam; and extensive investment in electrostatic precipitators to help remove fly ash from stack discharges of coal-burning steam plants.[125]

When the 1970 rate case was filed on November 6, 1970, the Alabama political scene had changed. Albert Brewer was now a lame duck governor. The previous June, George Wallace had fought Governor Brewer into a Democratic primary runoff. Wallace had not lost his magic when denouncing "the rich and powerful." The campaign was nasty, and Brewer came close to winning. Although hundreds of Alabama African Americans had registered to vote, Wallace still made busing and freedom of choice issues in his campaign, and in the runoff he harped on the "bloc vote" (a code for black vote) that was going for Brewer.

Wallace also took a page out of Huey Long's 1930s Louisiana political career, more recently adopted by Virginia attorney and state senator Henry E. Howell Jr., with whom Wallace was in contact. Howell, known as "Howlin' Henry," was a brassy populist firebrand who championed the little man. Howell insisted automobile insurance rates were too costly and that electrical rates were too high. He excoriated the Virginia Electric and Power Company in his campaigns for office. Wallace and Howell both attracted the labor vote, but the difference was that Howell tried to keep the race issue out of his campaigns. He opposed segregation and was popular among black voters. Howell's attacks on Virginia Electric were successful in his candidacy for lieutenant governor as an independent in 1971, and he used them in three unsuccessful campaigns for governor, the last being in 1977.[126] Wallace specifically added utilities to his list of Big Mules. Stewart Alsop, writing for *Newsweek* after traveling Alabama with the Wallace campaign, came to understand Wallace's "almost mystical hold" on the state's people, writing, "you could feel the electric current generated by a great demagogue pass[ing] through the crowd as Wallace denounced banks and utilities, and the rich on Wall Street who don't pay their taxes." Alsop observed that Wallace's "attacks on the big newspapers, the banks, and the utilities account for that electric current in his shirt-sleeved crowds at least as much as the race issue."[127]

The first warning came to Alabama Power Company when Joe Farley received a telephone call from board member and Chapman lumberman Earl McGowin, who had been in touch with Grover Hall Jr., former editor of the *Montgomery Advertiser*. Hall was then the editorial page editor for the *Richmond*

(Virginia) *News Leader* and a close Wallace confidant. Hall told McGowin that Wallace seemed upset with Alabama Power. It was soon evident that the Alabama governor was adapting Howell's populist strategies to Alabama. Wallace may also have thought that the Alabama Power leadership was not enthusiastic enough about his national campaign in 1968. Wallace attacked all utilities—gas, telephone, and electric—claiming their rates were too high, a good political strategy since everyone paid at least one utility bill. These attacks were only the beginning of what was to come. When Alabama Power filed for its second rate increase in November 1970, Brewer was still in the governor's office but was packing up to move in January before Wallace's second inauguration.[128]

Joe Farley reminisced about this year and recalled that after the rate increase request was filed, Eason Balch and Schuyler A. Baker, who had been friends with Wallace when they were students at the University of Alabama, went with him to see the governor to explain why Alabama Power needed a rate increase. Baker had recently joined the law firm, which at this time was called Balch, Bingham, Baker, Hawthorne & Williams. His addition was significant because he brought his client Central Bank with him, which gave the firm a much broader practice. Baker, who had helped found Central Bank in 1963 as its organizing president, was Wallace's Jefferson County campaign manager in his first gubernatorial race.[129] But this visit by old friends had no influence on Wallace. Joe Farley recalled that the governor "was polite, cordial, and friendly but said that the public did not want these increases, that we needed to do something to avoid having them." The governor would not consider that the power company had any legitimate business need for rate increases at all.[130] Soon after his inauguration, Wallace sent a strong message to utilities by hiring Birmingham attorney Maurice Bishop to represent the governor's office as an intervenor in proceedings on rates before the Public Service Commission. Bishop, a partner in Bishop, Sweeney & Colvin, was an expert in regulatory proceedings and condemnation law and had opposed Alabama Power Company in representing landowners in condemnations along the upper Coosa River. Bishop's hostility to Alabama Power was not even veiled.[131]

In March the governor called a special session of the legislature to deal with several issues, one being utility rate regulation. Throughout February and March 1971, newspapers were filled with stories about companies struggling to make ends meet under inflationary conditions. On March 23 Alabama's Blue Cross–Blue Shield asked permission from the Insurance Commission to raise rates because it had lost $5 million in the previous twelve months. All railroads were requesting a 6 percent freight rate increase in Alabama. As an anti-inflationary move, President Nixon requested that all states suspend the

1931 Davis-Bacon Act, which required contractors on federally funded projects to pay union wages. Governor Wallace refused. On March 31 the governor opened his special session of the legislature with his usual stem-winder speech. Among other things, he asked for tighter control of utility rates and wanted the legislature to force utilities to base their rates on original cost rather than new reproduction cost of their investments.[132]

Hearings began at the Public Service Commission on February 24 on Alabama Power's rate increase request of $19.9 million. They were ongoing while the legislature was meeting in special session considering the governor's anti-utility requests.[133] John Burks, who came to Alabama Power in 1948 and moved to the rate department the next year, recalled these hearings: Joe Farley would testify and "they would ask him the most outlandish questions, and he could come up with the best answer. Farley was calm and collected and took the sting out of Maurice Bishop." Burks did not like to testify, especially when Bishop would ask him questions that should have been asked of Farley, but he understood rates and his testimony was needed to make sure the company's figures were not misrepresented.[134]

As difficult as the times were, Burks recalled that there was close cooperation from the company's people, remembering that as "we all worked together, it helped morale, and the hard times melded us." Hearings and commission meetings meant rides to Montgomery as the sun was rising, breakfasts at Shoney's, and ice cream breaks at Howard Johnson's, where the group always ordered banana splits but the restaurant never had any bananas. One time Elmer Harris, who has a special passion for ice cream, walked in with a whole bunch of bananas. Harris, Walter Johnsey, Jack Minor, Rod Mundy, John Burks, and Bruce Hutchins all ordered banana splits. The waitress, without a smile, looked at the bananas and said, "I suppose this is the bananas."[135] The tension would have been unbearable without the humor and the support of friendships.

Alabama Power accountants and rate experts were critical to the company in these years of rate cases. Johnsey, who had been involved with finances earlier, was made vice president of administration and finance in 1972. Jack Minor, the comptroller, was an important person in this process. He was as much a

Jack Minor

blue-blood Alabama Power child as possible—born in Gorgas and educated in the Alabama Power Company school. Drafted out of Auburn toward the end of World War II, and a graduate of Samford University's accounting program, Minor began employment with the company in 1952. He worked in several district offices, then was transferred to Birmingham and moved rapidly up the ladder to comptroller and vice president. He fought Harllee

Branch when Branch tried to move all the accounting responsibilities to Atlanta under Southern Company. Minor told Branch that he had to testify to the accuracy of Alabama Power's books and that "as comptroller for Alabama Power I can't be responsible for these books if you are going to control it over there." Alvin Vogtle sided with Minor, and accounting stayed in Birmingham under Alabama Power control.[136]

Accountants Jim Elliott, William B. "Bruce" Hutchins III, and Gibson Lanier Jr. were also critically important in these hard years. Jack Minor recruited Jim Elliott from Arthur Andersen in 1964, and he first worked in budgets with Paul Acton. In those days before computers, putting together a budget was done manually, and when the game plan was changed from the top, it meant hours of work to adjust the budget. In 1975 Johnsey pulled Elliott

Jim Elliot

"upstairs" to work with accounting, rates, and the Public Service Commission auditors. Minor recalled that he had never known anyone who was as good with numbers as Elliott was; in fact, he considered Elliott a genius with figures who also had the ability to interpret and explain numbers to other people. Elliott had worked with A. G. Youngsteadt when he was comptroller, and both won the respect of the Public Service Commission staff for their knowledge and integrity. Rolland Casey, a PSC staff member who knew Elliott, called him a "walking encyclopedia of accounts and rates."[137] Whenever a power company executive was testifying, Minor or Elliott would be close by to deliver figures and interpret numbers.[138]

Bruce Hutchins was another second-generation Alabama Power product. His mother worked in the Alabama Power Tuscaloosa office, and his father was an IBEW electrician who worked for contractors doing work for Alabama Power. Growing up working on the family farm convinced Hutchins that he did not want to be a farmer, so he studied hard in school, made good grades, played basketball, and got his first paying job from Alan

Bruce Hutchins

Barton cutting grass in the summers at Alabama Power substations. Hutchins came to Alabama Power in 1966 with his accounting degree, then during the Vietnam War he left for the air force to do quality auditing and accounting. In 1971 Hutchins returned to work with Southern Services and for several years worked with the operating companies on converting to optical scanners. Jack Minor brought him back to Alabama Power in 1972, and Hutchins was immediately thrown into wholesale rate cases before the Federal Power Commission.[139] Gibson Lanier Jr. began working with the

Gibson Lanier Jr.

land department in 1968, left for a two-year tour of duty with the army, and returned to the treasury department where Jack Minor asked him to join the rate case team in 1974. For the next ten years Lanier was closely involved with both wholesale and retail rate cases in Washington, D.C., and Montgomery.[140]

Alabama Attorney General Bill Baxley also announced opposition to Alabama Power's rate increase. In 1971 Baxley appointed the Huntsville law firm of Butler & Potter to represent his office in rate cases. Governor Wallace concurred and approved Ernest Potter's appointment as special assistant attorney general to represent the state.[141] Maurice Bishop still represented the governor. Alabama Power presented economist Dr. John K. Langum of Chicago as an expert witness. Langum was an impressive witness but also quite a character and required a lot of "looking after" and chauffeuring. Langum testified that using fair value instead of original cost over the long haul resulted in lower rates for the consumer. Alabama Power's rate of return on average common equity in 1971 was 11.37 percent. Langum contended that the fair and reasonable rate of return on common equity for Alabama Power should be 14.5 percent.[142]

On April 22, hearings were concluded and the case was submitted to the commission for an order. The people on the commission had changed again. Sibyl Pool had been defeated by Juanita McDaniel, who opposed the increase and presented her own conclusion and finding. Jack Owen and Bull Connor, who was still president, approved an increase.[143] The PSC granted the company a 7.2 percent increase, which would provide $16.9 million in additional revenues effective April 29, 1971. Maurice Bishop, on behalf of Governor Wallace, made a vigorous objection, but the new retail rate schedule went into effect immediately. Fuel and tax adjustment clauses would also increase revenue for the company.[144]

In the 1971 special session of the legislature, Governor Wallace was successful in getting through a property tax classification system supported by the Farm Bureau that required utilities to pay 30 percent of value on their property, while other business and commercial property paid 25 percent and home owners and farm owners paid 15 percent. This system was approved by voters and added to the 1901 state constitution as Amendment 325. Because their businesses were so different, neither Southern Bell nor Alabama Gas owned tracts of real estate. As a result, Alabama Power's total plant investment, which included dams, steam plants, and other property, was many times that of other utilities and thus subject to higher taxes. Some of the land it owned was under the state's lakes. The legislature also addressed utility rate regulation by enacting changes in the procedures in rate cases, giving the Public Service Commission up to six months to suspend a rate filing (instead of sixty days) and eliminating the fair value rate base and substituting "original cost plus new investment proposed to be added in the twelve months following the test period." While Alabama Power Company did not favor the legislation, as Farley noted, it was common in other states and would not significantly damage the company.[145]

Although the fight was brutal in the special session and in the press, these laws were passed on May 11, 1971. Jeff Frederick, historian of the Wallace administrations, wrote that Wallace continued to blame utilities for high rates and criticized them for "unlimited power with the legislature" during the special session. The governor's campaign played well in small towns and rural areas. Wallace claimed that the reason he had such a hard time beating Brewer in 1970 was that the utilities—gas, telephone, and power—raised money to defeat him and elect Brewer.[146]

Joe Farley observed that in the decade of rate cases there "developed a sort of culture of rate hearings." Intervenors were recognized, their agendas known, and they were described as good guys, bad guys, disrupters, self-seekers, and other names. A number of regulars often attended: John Paul Ripp, a Birmingham-Southern College economics professor and self-styled consumer advocate; Robert Crowder, retired businessman who was concerned about strengthening the financial position of Alabama Power; James Brooks of Mobile, who represented large industrial customers; and Stanley Weissman, who represented Legal Services.[147] Buddy Eiland was working out of Alabama Power's Montgomery office during most of these hearings. He remembers power company executives and those who would be testifying setting up shop at the Governor's House Motel, bringing boxes of financial records to use in testimony. They would take over the company's Dexter Avenue office, order food catered from the Elite, Montgomery's favorite eating place, and work through lunch with secretaries finding records and documents and with witnesses and lawyers fine-tuning presentations for the afternoon session. Eiland recalled expert witness Langum saying many times that the only reason he kept coming back to Montgomery was because of the Elite's seafood gumbo. Alabama Power's local office staff, beginning with Vice President Hugh Foreman, was deeply involved in the process and would shuttle people back and forth between the company office and the Public Service Commission.[148]

Hugh Foreman

THE RATE PROCEEDINGS OF 1972

Wallace's vote totals in 1968 had been good enough to place him on the 1972 presidential primary ballots of most states as the candidate of the

American Independent Party, and his followers worked to maintain a party organization in every state. The Alabama governor did surprisingly well in the primaries, then on May 15 as he was campaigning in Laurel, Maryland, he was shot by Arthur Bremer, a man described by a newsman at the rally as being really "weird." George Wallace survived five bullets, but he would never walk again, and for the rest of his life he suffered excruciating pain, which his biographer says could not be soothed by drugs, acupuncture, or "sophisticated neurological surgery."[149] The governor was a very different man after late spring of 1972.

In June 1972 Alabama Power Company filed for its third rate increase in four years, this time for $29.2 million. It was the first time the company had based its testimony on original cost as required in the law passed in 1971. Inflation continued to be a major problem. Large new generating units at Gorgas and Barry went into operation, causing the company to lose income credits available during construction. The company was hit hard by the general accounting principle that mandated interest and capital cost on new construction to be capitalized during construction, which artificially increased the company's income during construction. After the project was completed, the income credit was eliminated and income plummeted. These jolts hit the company hard as new plants came online in 1971, 1972, 1974, 1977, and 1981.[150]

Income performance was critical because Alabama Power was restricted by the company's 1942 mortgage indenture and could not issue first-mortgage bonds unless the before-tax income of the company was twice the annual interest charges on all bonds and securities (2.0). Nor could it issue preferred stock unless the before-tax income was a least one and one-half times the annual interest charges and the dividends on preferred stock together (1.5). To compare, in 1958 the company's coverage on first-mortgage bonds was 5.11 and 2.63 on preferred stock. In 1972 the coverage on first-mortgage bonds had fallen to 2.23 and to 1.61 on preferred stock. The company would fall below these requirements in 1974.

Newspapers, radios, and television stations received invitations from Joe Farley to attend a special press conference on June 14, 1972, at the corporation's general office in Birmingham. Farley was going to discuss the company's request for another retail rate increase and would take questions. At the press conference Farley explained, as he had so often before and would do so for another decade, the effect of inflation on the company's operations. For many years Alabama Power had been able to avoid rate increases by building larger and more efficient generation plants and effecting economies in operations. Farley handed out a table showing the average cost of 750 kilowatts of electricity in fourteen American cities. Alabama Power's cost was lower than all of them, and even with the full $29.2 million rate increase requested, Alabama Power would still have the cheapest electricity.[151]

On July 19, 1972, Joe Farley addressed the members of the Governor's Advisory Committee on Public Utilities to explain why the company needed the 1972 rate increase of $29.2 million, which would raise the average residential bill 5.5 cents a day or $1.65 a month. He explained the nature of a public utility, its responsibility to provide the demands of its customers for electricity, demands that had been doubling each decade, and he detailed the effects of inflation upon the operations of the company. He used the 1970 National Power Survey to anticipate cost increases in the next decade.[152] Some Alabamians, such as John Ebaugh Jr. of Birmingham, realized the importance of a healthy and prosperous electric utility to the future progress of the state. In a letter to the editor of the *Birmingham News*, Ebaugh detailed the taxes paid by Alabama Power and the unreasonable way the company had been treated.[153]

At the Public Service Commission, Bull Connor had promised Jabo Waggoner Sr. that he would not run for reelection in 1972 because of his poor health but would defer to Waggoner to make the race. Connor backed out of this agreement and ran for reelection to the Public Service Commission. He was defeated in the spring primary by Kenneth Hammond. On December 13, 1972, Connor—as a lame duck—Owen, and McDaniel approved a rate increase of $26.6 million for Alabama Power. Maurice Bishop appealed the rate order to the Montgomery circuit court, which at that time was still considering the 1970–71 case. The PSC allowed the increase to go into effect on December 31, 1972.[154] Appeals were filed in Montgomery circuit court by the governor and intervenors to block the increase. The increased rates would mean that the average residential customer would pay about 4.4 cents more per day or $1.32 more a month.[155] Governor Wallace responded to letter writers complaining about their bills with long letters extolling his efforts to prevent rate increases.[156]

Meanwhile in Washington, D.C., the company's November 1971 request for an increase in wholesale rates to municipal and cooperative customers was slowly making its way through the Federal Power Commission's process. The FPC allowed the company to begin collecting (subject to refund) the additional rates on February 2, 1972. In September, Alabama Power appeared before an FPC administrative law judge in a hearing that lasted almost a month. The rate increases were opposed by intervening municipalities and cooperatives, but the FPC administrative judge ruled favorably for Alabama Power. This ruling was affirmed by the Federal Power Commission on December 14, 1973.[157]

Henry Simpson of the law firm of Lange Simpson Robinson & Somerville and Robert E. Steiner III of Montgomery were outside counsels working with Jack Bingham and Rod Mundy on the Alabama Public Service Commission  cases. Mundy also worked with Eason Balch on the Federal Power Commission wholesale case. Mundy was a young man from South Carolina who ended up at Auburn on an NROTC scholarship studying chemical engineering. He did his time in the navy stationed at Key West and was released a few months early to attend law school at the University of South Carolina. His wife Barbara's hometown was Birmingham, so in 1970 he accepted a position with the law firm of Balch, Bingham, Baker, Hawthorne & Williams and was immediately thrown into the rate case before the Federal Power Commission. Years later Eason Balch described Mundy as a brilliant attorney, smart and tough, and a fighter.[158]

Rod Mundy

For some years Alabama Power had planned to develop a steam plant in western Jefferson County. On August 9, 1972, representatives of the Jefferson County Commission, W. Cooper Green and Thomas B. Pinson, joined Eason Balch, Jim Miller Jr., and Joe Farley to visit Governor Wallace while he was at Spain Rehabilitation Center in Birmingham and made the public announcement of plans to construct a coal-fired plant on the Locust Fork of the Warrior River near West Jefferson. The site was some eighteen miles from Birmingham, and the $400 million plant would allow the company to supply the increased demands for electricity that were expected by 1978. The plant would add more than $2.5 million in additional tax revenues to Jefferson County and the state of Alabama. The company had environmental and meteorological studies ongoing at the site, and the plant would be equipped with modern air pollution devices and comply with environmental regulations.[159]

TVA Territory Settled

Alabama Power Company had suffered the loss of its strongest division after the federal government established the Tennessee Valley Authority. Between 1934 and 1941, government-subsidized public power projects in northern Alabama competed with Alabama Power Company, and the territorial jurisdiction was not settled until the passage of the Tennessee Valley Authority Revenue Bond Act of 1959. Herbert Vogel, TVA chairman, recognized the limitations on TVA unless it had the authority to issue bonds. TVA was increasingly wary of appearing before Congress to justify appropriations for any additional generation. Rate payers would pay off TVA bonds. For its part, Congress did not want TVA to have carte blanche to compete with investor-owned utilities and wanted a firm boundary line for TVA territory. The act allowed TVA to issue bonds for additional construction but "fenced in" TVA and restricted its geographical growth. An uneasy truce prevailed between Alabama Power and TVA, its tone usually dependent upon the personalities of TVA directors and the political party of the president.[160] There were times when jurisdictional lines seemed clearly drawn, only to be once more invaded by public power and the subject of controversy. Having as close neighbors the cities of Bessemer and Tarrant City, which were wholesale customers of TVA, and having the TVA transmission line pene-trating south through Alabama Power's territory did not make the situation easier. The World War I interconnection from Gorgas to Muscle Shoals remained, and TVA and Alabama Power currents did flow between the two systems under certain circumstances.

Territorial jurisdiction between TVA and Alabama Power was finally settled with the passage of the Tennessee Valley Authority Revenue Bond Act of 1959.

Communications between Bessemer and Alabama Power improved after Bessemer mayor Jess Lanier called Walter Bouldin during the severe ice storm that hit northern Alabama on the afternoon of March 2, 1960. Miles of fallen power and telephone lines covered the mountains of the northeastern part of the state. The main TVA 110,000-volt transmission line coming from Guntersville Dam to serve Bessemer and Tarrant City was down in so many places on Sand Mountain that it would be impossible to repair quickly. Bessemer was in the dark with no backup, and temperatures were hovering below twenty-eight degrees. Bessemer needed electricity. Mayor Lanier asked Bouldin to please help his freezing citizens. As Dan O'Gara of the Bessemer municipal system noted some years later, "It was cold, and we had a lot of heating load." Despite the fact that Bouldin's own system north of Birmingham was devastated, too, especially at Blountsville and in the mountains around Gadsden and Anniston, Alabama Power had transmission service from the south.

Bouldin stayed on the telephone for hours working with C. T. Hunter, Birmingham Division vice president, and contacting Alabama Power's transmission engineers to determine the quickest and easiest way to tap into Bessemer's distribution system from an Alabama Power transmission line and substation. Brighton was selected and Alabama Power Company bucket trucks and line crews under J. L. Vick were swarming around the area working with crews from Bessemer directed by foreman J. D. Moyes. By midnight, eight hours after Bessemer went dark, they managed to run a 200-foot span of 44-kV line and install the necessary hardware and make connections. Bessemer was hooked to Alabama Power's power. This was, of course, totally illegal, for it was a connection of high voltage to a new customer in spite of no regulatory approval by either the Alabama Public Service Commission in Montgomery or the Federal Power Commission in Washington. Seven thousand Bessemer customers were tied into Alabama Power's transmission lines for five days, and no regulatory agency ever said one word about it.[161]

Problems began, however, when Bessemer started servicing new areas like Greenwood and other promising subdivisions outside the area drawn on old maps defining jurisdiction and began annexing property that was in Alabama Power's territory according to earlier agreements. In March 1966 Walter Bouldin wrote Bessemer mayor Lanier that Bessemer was in violation of Section 15d(a) of the TVA Act of August 6, 1959, which defined its service area.[162] Informal discussions went on for some time, but when they proved unfruitful, Alabama Power sought relief in federal court in November 1969. The issue was congressional intent in the 1959 act. Harold Williams was the attorney directing this case, and he remembered that when the company appealed Judge Seybourn Lynne's first adverse ruling, TVA said "let's talk settlement." After long and intense negotiations, Joe Farley recalled TVA's general manager, James Watson, telling him, "we've got so many problems in this industry, we don't need to argue over a few houses outside of Bessemer. Let's get this settled." An agreement was reached on September 12, 1971, whereby Alabama Power lost some territory but gained access to the TVA Guntersville transmission line, which allowed Alabama Power Company to serve its Blount County customers better. Williams observed that in order to have "peace in the land," Alabama Power agreed to pick up some TVA wholesale industrial customers, a relief to TVA, which would have been forced to invest large sums of money in a higher voltage transmission line without much return.[163] This agreement established the Birmingham "fence" area for TVA.

Before leaving TVA issues, it should be noted that this government power corporation was struggling with the same economic conditions in the 1970s as investor-owned power companies. In 1967, high interest rates, inflation, and high-priced coal forced TVA to raise its wholesale power rates for the first time since 1933. Between 1967 and 1980, rates increased from just over 0.5 cent per kilowatt hour to nearly 3.0 cents in 1980. The increase in TVA rates and a concern over the environment brought strong criticism from Tennessee Valley residents. Power interchange agreements with its former competitors, investor-owned companies such as Alabama Power, were increased, and this interchange reached a total of 2.4 million kilowatts by 1974. TVA, however, did not reduce its construction program to reflect the decreased growth of demand resulting from the energy crisis and the conservation movement as quickly as investor-owned power companies did, and thus TVA overbuilt its nuclear generation capacity and had to stop construction after considerable investment.[164]

MITCHELL DAM AND THE FEDERAL POWER COMMISSION

In 1973 the Fifth Circuit Court of Appeals ruled on a case that had been slowly working its way through the Federal Power Commission's administrative process and the federal courts for years. The case involved Mitchell Dam, and once more Alabama Power took the lead in setting precedent in a case involving a very significant hydro issue. Mitchell was licensed under the 1920 Federal Water Power Act in March 1921, and the dam was completed on August 15, 1923. Mitchell was the first dam to go through the process of relicensing after the original fifty-year license ran out in 1971.[165] One provision

Mitchell Dam was the first company dam to go through the process of relicensing after its fifty-year license expired in 1971. Mitchell was redeveloped in the 1980s. Units 5–7 were added and a new downstream powerhouse replaced the original upstream structure.

of the Federal Water Power Act, Section 10(d), allowed the FPC to determine if there had been surplus or excess earnings from the project based upon the first six years after the initial twenty-year period. The FPC accounting staff began a detailed investigation of the years 1943–49 and in the 1950s determined that indeed there were excess earnings. This finding would have required Alabama Power to establish a reserve fund, which, in essence, would have reduced the price of the dam should the government decide to take it over at the end of the fifty-year lease.[166]

Alabama Power fought the case vigorously and was supported by other utilities with hydro dams who were facing the same ruling by the Federal Power Commission. Alabama Power enlisted the help of the accounting firm Haskins & Sells and its New York partner, nationally known accountant Weldon Powell, who brought Robert Lanka of the San Francisco office into the effort. A critical part of the case involved the meaning of the words "actual, legitimate investment" and exactly what Congress meant when this term was included in the act. Powell testified that accounting practices when the act was passed would not have included a deduction for depreciation and that the accurate interpretation of the applicable Federal Power Commission Regulation 17 dictated such a conclusion. Joe Farley directed the company's legal attack on the FPC's position, aided by testimony from A. G. Youngsteadt, at that time the assistant comptroller of Alabama Power, and the company's outside independent auditor, Arthur Andersen accountant Robert Lyman. Attorney Willard Gatchell, who was a former general counsel for the FPC, was associated with Farley. The presentation of the case was concluded on May 14, 1963.[167]

In October 1963 the opinion of the FPC staff was totally upheld by the administrative law judge Arthur H. Fribourg. Then on September 27, 1968, the Federal Power Commission mostly upheld the administrative law judge. When the FPC undertook to make a new rule applicable to this situation using the term "net investment," the entire electric utility industry banded together to protest. Action on Mitchell Dam was delayed until June 7, 1971, twelve years after the first order. The commission supported the staff position once more. If this opinion had stood, it meant that should the federal government decide to take over a hydro dam from the company that built it, the cost would be relatively small or zero, and the damage to the company, its stockholders, and its customers huge. Alabama Power appealed to the Fifth Circuit Court of Appeals. Jack Bingham and Rod Mundy argued the case. On July 31, 1973, the court upheld the Alabama Power position, with the case turning on early accounting practices. The court ruled that the government would have to pay a reasonable amount to purchase the dam rather than zero if the Federal Power

Commission decided to take over the dam under Section 14 of the Federal Water Power Act.[168]

The Arab Oil Embargo of 1973

As early as 1971 the federal government was discussing the creation of a national energy policy. By the mid-1960s there was realization that the United States was depleting its supply of fossil fuel, causing concern in the growing environmental movement.[169] On March 22, 1973, the first Alabama Energy Advisory Council was called together by the governor to meet in Montgomery to consider the issues as they related to the state of Alabama. Eason Balch represented Alabama Power. John M. Harbert III, Birmingham construction and civic leader, was elected chairman. Harbert announced that the main challenge was to get the people of Alabama to know that the energy crisis was real. Harbert identified other problems as being national and international political considerations, as well as the new environmental demands that placed additional economic burdens on all hydrocarbon production and on the use of oil, gas, and high-sulphur coal.[170] Energy concerns came to a head on October 17, 1973, when the Organization of Petroleum Exporting Countries imposed an oil embargo on the United States. The embargo was initiated by the Arab-dominated cartel because it was unhappy about American support for Israel in the Yom Kippur War. Egypt and Syria attacked the Jewish state on October 6, and the United States backed Israel. Only a small percent of U.S. oil came from the Middle East, but it was enough to upset the markets, and oil prices suddenly shot up. Besides the increase in 1973, oil prices took major price leaps in 1974 and in 1979. Coal prices also rose from $6 a ton in 1972 to more than $35 a ton in 1980. New environmental requirements pushed the cost of electricity up. The drive to conserve energy led President Nixon to announce that for the first time Christmas lights would not be turned on at the White House.

The energy crisis was only one important aspect of these unsettled times, which included an economy that "fretted between recession and inflation," the distraction of the Watergate scandal, the near impeachment of the president, and eventually Nixon's resignation in the summer of 1974. Double-digit inflation adversely impacted the financial activities of every business and especially utility companies that depended so much upon capital. These conditions forced Alabama Power to request another rate increase.[171]

The oil embargo and energy crisis caused a significant change in the company's marketing strategy. Advertising directed customers to save and conserve energy and suggested ways to use electricity wisely. Heat pumps were still pushed as a way to alleviate the uneven load balance caused by air conditioning demand in summer months.[172] Another result of the embargo was to alter the direction of the electric industry. Although Alabama Power used little oil to generate electricity, it was affected by the increase in oil and gasoline prices and the sudden concern for conservation of all energy. Nuclear energy was made even more attractive. The electric industry generally believed that the 50 percent increase per decade in customers' use of electricity in the decades after World War II would continue and that demand would grow unchecked.[173] This growth did not happen in the 1970s because of campaigns to conserve energy, and as the cost of electricity rose, customers began to ration their use, causing the annual growth rates of electrical use in the 1980s to fall to 3 percent.

For the economy, the oil embargo resulted in stagflation—continued inflation with a decline in business activity and increased unemployment. It also triggered a fundamental change in the American economy. The nation's heavy industry such as steel, aluminum, and chemicals operated from worn-out facilities and equipment, and with 18 percent interest it was impossible to raise the capital necessary to modernize. Instead of modernizing plants in the United States, the trend became for investments to be made in industry located overseas.

More Rate Cases: 1974 and 1975

When Joe Farley looked back to the decade of the 1970s, he recalled one fond memory above others: there was no rate case in 1973. That summer he took his wife Sheila and their three children to visit England, Sheila's home.[174] It proved to be the calm between the storms. In order to finance $383.1 million in construction costs for additional generation capacity in 1973, Alabama Power sold $100 million of 8⅞ percent first-mortgage bonds at net interest of 8.92 percent in August and $75 million 8¼ percent first-mortgage bonds and $500,000 shares of $100 par value, 8.16 percent preferred stock in December. As Farley once noted, "It was the best year the company would have for a long time."[175] In fact, the year was so good that on January 2, 1974, the board of directors approved the construction of the long-planned dam on the Tallapoosa River above Wedowee after the Federal Power Commission issued a license in December. Joe Farley announced the dam would require an investment of $49 million. The plant, called the Crooked Creek Dam and later named for Rother L. Harris, was expected to go into service in 1978, but financial difficulties in the next few years after approval slowed construction of the dam and reservoir and delayed the in-service operation of the two generating units with a total capacity of 135,000 kilowatts.[176]

In 1974 George Wallace won the Democratic gubernatorial primary. The state constitution had been changed to allow the governor to serve for two consecutive terms, and Wallace was moving toward the first third-term administration in the state's history. He polled 65 percent of the vote, including 25 percent of the black vote.[177] After the May Democratic primary, on June 14, 1974, the company filed for a $64 million rate increase at the Public Service Commission with the test year ending May 31, 1974. Three days later, on June 17, the company filed a request for a $12.6 million wholesale rate increase with the Federal Power Commission. Inflation, high interest rates, and declining earnings threatened the reliability of service should the company not be able to invest in additional generation. In August, Alabama Power president Farley asked the commission to approve part of the company's request on an emergency basis, noting that this was the first time the company had ever sought an emergency rate increase. Three days of testimony followed in which Farley said that the measure was needed "because our financing is stalled and our services are threatened."[178] The company again presented Dr. John K. Langum, economic consultant and former vice president of the Federal Reserve Bank of Chicago. Langum testified, along with William L. Brownlee, Elmer Harris, John Burks, and Walter Johnsey, who explained the financial condition of the company and justified its needs with figures. Johnsey's testimony was written and included a chart that showed the company's return on common equity had dropped from 13.89 percent in December 1973 to 11.5 percent in June 1974 and was moving downward toward 7.78 percent by May 1975 unless rate relief was granted.[179]

On September 30, 1974, the Public Service Commission approved an emergency increase that would generate about $7.5 million. On January 14, 1975, the Public Service Commission approved a permanent increase of $54.2 million.[180] The commissioners who granted these increases were commission president Kenneth Hammond, Juanita McDaniel, and Jack Owen. A few days later, Owen was replaced by Jim Zeigler, who had defeated Owen in the spring Democratic primary. *Alabama News Magazine* editor Bob Ingram called Zeigler the "miracle worker" for winning and chided Zeigler for promising to deliver reduced rates, a "cruel joke."[181]

During the next twelve months, until December when Hammond was replaced by Chris Whatley, the commission meetings were one of the best shows in the capital city. Zeigler, as Jack Bingham recalls, "was a very assertive political type." He and Hammond verbally battled so much that onlookers wondered which one would throw the first punch. Zeigler and Hammond began vying for control and publicity. Zeigler, who had little technical background, organized grassroots opposition to rate increases, and as Bingham noted, "it was a right uncomfortable atmosphere, having a judge campaigning against you in a case that is supposed to be a quasi-judicial proceeding."[182]

On March 6, 1975, Governor Wallace demanded that utility management reduce rates by curtailing "massive expansion projects which may benefit future customers but which increased cost to present customers," despite the fact numerous Alabama Power people had explained and expert witnesses had testified that current customers did not pay for construction of new generation.[183] Wallace was having some trouble with his legislature, for it had responded to the governor's "doom-and-gloom" speech on the state's economy by voting for a pay raise, the lawmakers' first achievement of the session.[184] Meanwhile, at the Public Service Commission, without discussing it with fellow commissioner McDaniel, Zeigler and Hammond ordered an investigation into Alabama Power Company's rate structure, certificates of convenience and necessity, load projections, and financing methods. The hearings on Alabama Power drew a large noisy, partisan crowd, and the exchanges on the bench between Zeigler and Hammond became hostile, almost "life-threatening at first." People upset with their electrical bills were bused to Montgomery, and numerous Alabama Power employees and their families also came. Some workers representing the International Brotherhood of Electrical Workers joined the group, as well as operating engineers, ironworkers, pipefitters, and building trades unions, arriving with their hard hats on to support Alabama Power. Doug McCrary recalled that Juanita McDaniel was particularly unsettled by the presence of the laborers, and he thought "she was going to panic." The hearing was so crowded and unruly on March 6 that the commission room would not hold everyone, and the hearing was adjourned and moved to the State Highway Department auditorium.[185] David Hinman, who handled security for Alabama Power, was there to escort the company's people and witnesses, and he was very concerned over their safety.[186]

Walter W. Tidwell of Birmingham was one of those customers upset about his electrical bills who planned to be in Montgomery on March 6. He wrote Attorney General Bill Baxley on February 21, sending copies to Governor Wallace, commissioners Zeigler and Hammond, Joe Farley, and U.S. senator Jim Allen, complaining mightily about electricity bills that "have *doubled* in the past sixty days." He hoped "to be with a large group in Montgomery, whose purpose will be to let the Public Service Commission know that we, as consumers, are not at all happy with the electric bills we are being forced to pay. We are not going down there as a radical bunch of people objecting to utility rate increases, as the *Birmingham News* will no doubt report." Tidwell especially objected to "inflated fuel costs."[187] Within a few months, T. Jeff Davis, the governor's assistant, was funneling these letters to Maurice Bishop and asking him to draft Wallace's response. Bishop asked that a file be activated "of all letters, publications or communications that contain any *factual* information" (emphasis Bishop's). This was wise because so much that was being sent to the governor had no basis in fact whatsoever.[188]

The mood at the Public Service Commission meeting on March 6 was one of hostility and tension. During this proceeding a huge, burly man came in and sat beside Rod Mundy and quietly asked him, "Where is Mr. Farley?" Rod did not know if the man was friend or foe, but he pointed out Farley, who was sitting with Jim Miller Jr. The large man moved and sat behind Farley, then leaned over and said to the company president, "I am going to see that nobody gives you any trouble."[189] There were placards and posters, loud comments, and boos or applause from an audience of several hundred.[190] The appearance of hard hats at the commission meeting reminded the commissioners that they were dealing with people's jobs, and Doug McCrary believed "they realized that labor stuck together."[191] The situation might have gotten out of hand except for the quiet and firm presence of Carl L. Evans, who began his career with the Public Service Commission in 1967 as an attorney and examiner and then became an administrative law judge. Judge Evans had a reputation for fairness and integrity and was respected by everyone. He was able to be consistent in balancing government interests and the rights of individuals. In 1978 he became the chief administrative law judge.[192] These rate hearings were his greatest test and surely his success in moderating them had something to do with his promotion.

Carl L. Evans. Courtesy of Carl L. Evans Jr.

Meanwhile, Joe Farley appeared before a special senate committee studying utility regulations chaired by Senator E. C. "Crum" Foshee of Red Level. Farley observed that every other committee he had ever testified before had been "polite and cordial" even if their views were opposite those of the company; however, this committee was hostile and his personal friends in the senate were silent. Foshee announced that "there was a severe mismanagement problem at Alabama Power Company" and they were "going to get to the bottom of it." Farley kept explaining to the committee that the problems the company faced were international in origin, the shortage of available energy and runaway inflation, and could not be solved on a state basis.[193]

One of the things the state senator wanted was a list of Southern Company stockholders. Farley resisted releasing confidential information of 200,000 stockholders but agreed to present a list of the top 50 stockholders on the condition that the list would remain strictly confidential. A few days later, Farley appeared again before the senate committee with the list. Forty-nine on the list were institutions, trust funds, and insurance companies, and the only individual was a respected Alabama war hero. This fishing expedition came up empty, and after the committee adjourned and left the room, Farley found the list on a chair in the hallway. The committee, he noted, "had lost interest, including losing interest in their commitment to keep the list confidential." He picked it up and carried it back to his office.[194]

While the Public Service Commission hearings were going on in early March, the house of representatives joint committee on utility legislation, composed of the house judiciary committee and the ways and means committee, was holding a hearing on utility rates. Farley testified before that committee and explained about runaway inflation and shortages of available energy all over the world. He noted that Alabama Power customers were paying $29.48 for 1,000 kWh, while customers in Los Angeles paid $30.19, San Antonio paid $40.45, Philadelphia paid $49.20, and New York City customers were charged $72.[195] Walter Johnsey also testified, and the company had John Childs, a retired executive of Irving Trust Company in New York, ready to testify, but the questions went on too long. Representative Douglas Johnstone of Mobile did most of the questioning. When the committee adjourned, Childs joined Farley, Johnsey, Jim Miller Jr., and Jack Bingham on a flight to New York where they planned to attend a financing meeting. On the plane Farley and Bingham were saying that they thought things went "reasonably well" in the committee hearing, but Childs confessed he was in a "state of shock" and that "if the financial community in New York had heard the comments and questions from the Alabama legislators, no utility in Alabama would ever be able to sell a security again."[196]

Senator Foshee had sponsored a bill to give the governor the power to "freeze rates," but Governor Wallace said that was the "wrong approach." Instead, Wallace wanted to abolish the automatic fuel adjustment clause and have Alabama Power come back to the Public Service Commission with each increase or decrease in the price of coal, send appeals from the PSC directly to the supreme court, and use original cost less depreciation as a rate base. The governor announced that attorney Maurice Bishop, who, he said, was the most knowledgeable man in Alabama on utility rate making, was preparing the administration's bills.[197]

On March 11, 1975, Governor Wallace called a special session of the legislature to meet on March 17 "to seek relief" from what the governor called "exorbitant rates charged" by major utilities. Because of business before the legislature's regular session, there was a day's delay. When the legislature finally convened in special session on March 18, Wallace addressed it and a statewide television audience and presented eight utility bills drafted by Maurice Bishop. Wallace advocated forcing the company "to curtail, defer or implement other technology with respect to massive expansive projects which may benefit future customers but which increases costs to present customers."[198]

The Wallace bills would redefine the rate base, abolish the automatic fuel or tax rate adjustment, create a new office of the peoples' utility counsel (which the governor would appoint to represent consumers in rate cases), provide for direct appeal of PSC decisions to the Alabama Supreme Court, and change the legal requirements for evidence during an appeal. Other proposed legislation dealt with refunding excessive charges, telephone contracts, and notification of property owners by filing a certificate of convenience and necessity with the PSC before acquiring land for transmission and distribution lines.[199] Farley noted that most of this legislation would be costly to administer, cumbersome to implement, and would reduce the quality of service to the consumer. Despite the nation's economy and the fragile financial markets, Wallace said he was confident the "highly skilled management of our utilities" could surely "find ways and means to provide their services to the people in a manner consistent with their ability to pay for such services."[200] This was the third special session the governor had called since January. Alabama senator Sid McDonald, from northern Alabama, observed that the Wallace administration's utility bills would be about as effective in lowering utility rates as the Wallace administration's bills ten years before were successful in preserving segregation.[201]

Joe Farley responded to Governor Wallace by thanking him for his "temperate approach" to the problems faced by Alabama Power and for recognizing that "there is no magic wand, no instant and simple answers" to fix the problems. While Farley disagreed with Wallace's proposed legislation, he was "pleased the governor referred to the increasing costs faced by utilities and the fact that higher utility rates are a reality not only in our state, but also throughout the United States and much of the world." He expressed concern over any legislation that would drastically increase the cost of electricity to the consumer and suggested careful study of the amendments to the Federal Clean Air Act and the provisions of the surface mining legislation currently before Congress.[202]

Meanwhile, public service commissioner Jim Zeigler announced a plan to lower electrical bills by raising rates for those who used more electricity than 400 kilowatt hours. He proposed a schedule that would shift rate increases to large users of electricity, but industrial customers rallied to oppose it. U.S. Steel Corporation, one of Alabama Power's large industrial customers, said such rates would add $880,000 to the operation of its Fairfield Works.[203] On March 20 the Birmingham Metropolitan Development Board criticized Wallace's eight bills as a "no-growth policy for the state." Central Bank president Harry Brock said that states where politicians had used utilities as a whipping boy "are paying the price of brownouts, curtailment of energy and loss of jobs." Joe Farley responded to the governor's attack with measured words but firmly stated that the governor's utility bills would prevent raising capital necessary for expansion. On the question of fuel cost adjustment, he pointed out that decreases as well as increases would be reflected in consumers' bills. On March 22, 1975, a Birmingham News editorial noted that the governor's own 1971 increase in gross receipts tax on utilities was responsible, too, for raising electrical rates and that the tax should be repealed. The editor wrote that "surely he is as resourceful in finding ways to make up for lost state revenue as he expects the utilities to be in finding ways to operate without seeing rate increases."[204]

By this time, the Public Service Commission members were angry with the governor for intruding onto their turf without any prior communication with them. Commission president Kenneth Hammond called the governor's hand and announced that he was ready to have a "'shootout at the O.K. Corral' over the alleged hypocritical role of Gov. Wallace in utility regulation in Alabama." Hammond said he did not tell the governor how to run the state, and he resented Wallace telling him how to regulate utilities. The Birmingham News quoted Hammond as saying, "I operate a lot like old Al Capone. If you stay out of my business, I'll stay out of yours."[205] Senator Sid McDonald of Arab spoke to the Alabama Forestry Association and said that state government was "anti-business. We're big on attracting business, but small on complementing its viability." McDonald said that the legislature "never did anything to stop full racial equality and they cannot do anything to affect energy costs."[206]

On March 21, 1975, the Birmingham News featured an article on the problems of the nation's electric utilities, which were "the most capital-intensive industry in the entire economy and the nation's largest fuel consumers." Because the rate of growth of electrical use fell to 6 percent in 1974–75, below the historic annual growth of 7 percent, many utilities cancelled or postponed planned construction of new generation facilities. Herman G. Roseman of the National Economic Research Associates predicted "widespread brownouts and blackouts" as results of the industry's struggles.[207]

Meanwhile, in Alabama Wallace's utility bills passed the house by a comfortable margin, "dutifully passed," as Alabama News Magazine noted, "without so much as changing a comma." The senate killed the bills by filibuster. Senators might have enacted some legislation, but the governor had threatened to veto any bill that was not approved exactly as it was written, and there had been no way to compromise.²⁰⁸ Wallace immediately had the bills reintroduced when the regular session reconvened. Alabama Power, its friends, retirees, stockholders, and employees were able to prevent passage of the punitive laws in the legislature during the 1975 session. In the fall, Zeigler called for hearings on abolishing fuel add-on charges. Except for headlines and Zeigler's remarkable quotes, he had no plan to reduce power bills.²⁰⁹

In November 1975 Alabama Power requested a $106.8 million rate increase. Farley explained that the company had been unable to raise funds through sale of long-term securities, so large amounts of money had to be borrowed through short-term loans to cover the costs of construction. There were also restoration costs for damages from Hurricane Eloise, "which churned her way through Alabama" on September 23.²¹⁰ The dynamics of the Public Service Commission changed in December 1975, when Hammond stepped down because he was convicted of soliciting a bribe in a rate case brought by South Central Bell, a conviction the U.S. Supreme Court refused to review.²¹¹

THE BREAK IN BOULDIN DAM

In the early morning hours of February 10, 1975, Tom Sanford, an Alabama Power Company guard, finished his security round at Bouldin Dam, which is below the dam. It was a little after midnight when he sat down in the lobby to read the newspaper. In a few minutes, Sanford noticed water in the drain behind the building and remembers that at the time he thought it was raining. He sensed something was not quite right, and he went to the door and stepped outside. He saw water on the top deck of the plant and water coming through the dam on the eastern side. Immediately, he called the superintendent, Curtis Jones, who was serving as superintendent for both Jordan and Bouldin Dams and was living a short distance away at Jordan Dam.

To save time Sanford went to unlock the gate for Jones, who was arriving with assistant superintendent Jimmy Snow. Snow recalled that Sanford was

Aerial view of the Bouldin breach. The rushing waters opened a gap 400 feet wide in the eastern section of the dam.

eager to get away from the dam. Just as the men arrived, Sanford recalled the water "really broke through the dam with loud noises and electrical pops and flashes." Jones and Snow drove the company car across the western side of the dike, and with the car's headlights they were able to see only that a break had occurred in the earth embankment east of the concrete portion of the dam. They had no idea they were so close to danger, and it was daylight before they knew how badly the dam had blown out.[212] When notified of the trouble, engineers at Jordan Dam immediately opened the floodgates to relieve the water pressure on Bouldin and reduce flooding below the dam. Lake Jordan was lowered twelve feet.[213]

The night the dam broke, engineer Ron Parsons was working out of Montgomery on a power company crew operating on night shifts testing relays in substations. He had just gotten in from Selma and was in bed when his supervisor called and told him something was wrong at Bouldin, that he was unsure what it was, but asked him to go over there immediately. As he drove to Bouldin, Parsons was listening to his car radio and heard a live account from a man standing on the banks of the downstream channel from Bouldin describing all the rushing and rising water pouring through the channel. Parsons knew something bad had happened. He soon learned that the dam had breached and the lake was emptying through a widening gap in the dam that eventually reached some 400 feet.[214]

When Parsons arrived at the dam, water was still rolling over the concrete area where the transformers were. As he looked around, he was amazed to see portions of the dam lodged in the high-voltage transformers on top of steel structures. "When the dam blew," he said, "it sprayed stuff everywhere." Company engineers immediately began an investigation to determine the cause of the failure of the dam. Everyone was grateful there was no loss of life, except for several cows grazing south of the dam. It could have been much worse. In the previous four weeks, there had been some ongoing routine maintenance and repair on unit 1 by Westinghouse engineers. This work required several men to weld in the scroll tubes leading into the water wheel. The men had worked every night for four weeks, but on Sunday morning they decided to take the day off and not report back to the dam until Monday night. If the men had been working on Sunday night and in the tube early Monday morning, Parsons observed, "there was no way they could have gotten out."[215]

Within hours of the dam break, people began to slosh through the muddy lake bed, picking up large fish trapped in pockets of water. As soon as John M. Harbert III heard about the break, he offered his company's heavy earth-moving equipment and manpower to construct a temporary dam across the inlet canal connecting Lake Jordan to Lake Bouldin. Within three days this work had been completed, and Jordan began to fill to its normal level of 252 feet. The Bouldin powerhouse suffered extensive damage, and the generation of 225,000 kilowatts, 4 percent of Alabama Power's generation, ceased.[216] The report from the company's board of inquiry was released on April 29, 1975. Sabotage and earthquake were ruled out as causes, and no evidence was found that the dam failure resulted from any previously identified groundwater seepage conditions nor from any burrowing in the earth dikes by fire ants or rodents. Dispersive clays were also ruled out. The board of inquiry continued to explore "features of design, construction, and operation in the breach area."[217] After the probe showed there had been deficiencies with the compaction of the earthen dam, Alabama Power decided to file suit against the contractor, Blount Corporation, and its subcontractor, Harbert Corporation. John Harbert was not concerned about the money but about the reputation of his company. The Harbert suit presented a conflict of interest because both Harbert and Alabama Power normally used the Balch Bingham firm for their legal representation. Robert McDavid Smith of Lange Simpson handled the Alabama Power case and also its presentations before the Federal Power Commission.[218]

There were two major concerns. Alabama Power was without Bouldin Dam's 225,000-kilowatt generation, and funds were needed to rebuild the dam, both problems devastating considering the company's dire financial condition. Alabama Power believed it was due compensation from the contractor's insurance companies, money that could be used to rebuild the dam, and its position was that its own insurance coverage should compensate the corporation for its loss of the dam.[219] Eventually, Harbert's insurance carriers settled. Bill Reed, who had recently become president of Southern Services and had made a routine visit to Lloyd's of London, worked with Lloyd's to settle the dispute on Alabama Power's policy. Reed and Joe Farley met in New York with a Lloyd's representative who flew over on the Concorde for the day's meeting. A settlement was reached on the company's policy. Enough compensation was received from these lawsuits and from the company policy to cover the estimated cost of rebuilding the dam; however, the cooperative attitude of the Federal Power Commission changed during the fifteen days of trial because of the massive failure of the Teton Dam in Idaho on June 5, 1976. The FPC required Alabama Power to include additional provisions and inspections, and reconstruction of Bouldin Dam eventually cost three times the original estimate.[220]

The Federal Power Commission announced its final decision on the Bouldin breach and closed the case on April 21, 1977. By this time the agency name had changed as part of President Jimmy Carter's emphasis upon energy.

The FPC was now the Federal Energy Regulatory Commission or FERC. The FERC decision noted that the evidence "does not provide a basis for conclusive determination of the precise cause of failure," but it did disclose that "the construction of the earthfill dikes did not comply with the design specifications in one or more critical areas." The report scolded Alabama Power for not inspecting the construction work more closely but said there was no evidence that Alabama Power violated any commission regulation.[221]

New Management Team

In August 1974, Walter Bouldin died. He had retired as chairman of the board on July 31, 1970, and served as an advisory director of the company until his death following an extended illness. He had provided steady and resolute leadership for the company for many years.[222] In May 1975 the Alabama Power board of directors approved recommendations of President Farley for promotions and changes in management structure. These changes were partly

Bill M. Guthrie

necessary because Jim Miller Jr. had assumed the duties of executive vice president of Georgia Power on April 1. Alan R. Barton (transmission and distribution) and Walter Johnsey (administration and finance) were elected executive vice presidents, and Johnsey joined Farley, G. T. Nelson, and Barton as a member of the board of directors; E. Davis Long (employee relations), William O. Whitt (Birmingham Division), and Jesse S. Vogtle (public relations) were elected senior vice presidents and Bill M. Guthrie was elected a vice president. Reporting to Barton would be vice presidents F. L. Clayton Jr. (power supply), Douglas L. McCrary (construction), S. R. Hart Jr. (engineering), C. E. Brackett (fuels), and Elmer B. Harris (operations services). Other members of the vice-presidential team were Sam Booker (marketing), John D. Jones (power delivery), Liston Cook (accounting), and Charles P. Jackson (treasurer).[223]

John D. Jones

Alabama Power began to diversify its professional staff in the late 1960s. One of the first African Americans to be recruited was Robert Holmes, who was born and grew up in Birmingham. In 1969 he secured a summer job in the Alabama Power print shop working with Burney Cannon. Here he made friends, was well respected, and was encouraged to finish school. When Holmes graduated with a drafting and math degree from Alabama A & M University in 1970, he was recruited by Archie Rogers for a perma-

Robert Holmes

nent job with Alabama Power. He went to work on June 15, 1970, in transmission design under the direction of Sam Caldwell, who taught him the ropes and how to lay out transmission lines. Holmes soon rotated to the engineering design department headed by George Leland Howard, who became a mentor to him.

In reminiscing about this time in his life, Holmes observed that Howard began to teach him other things, like reinforced concrete and structural steel design, and encouraged him to return to school for an engineering degree. Holmes entered the UAB program, attending night classes. When he was one course away from graduation, he needed a nuclear physics class that was only taught at four o'clock. Howard told him to take the course and make up the hours. In 1976 Holmes received his engineering degree. Howard not only gave Holmes the support and encouragement he needed to earn his second degree, but he also guided Holmes as he became a professional. Howard once sent Holmes to a meeting in which Holmes recalled being uncomfortable as "the only black face in the whole room," but he forced himself to do the very best job he could. Holmes credits Howard with teaching him "what Alabama Power was all about—family, hard work, taking care of the people you work with." Robert Holmes had a way of gaining people's trust, and he had a reputation for integrity. As he made his way to the eighteenth floor, he passed on to others the contagious devotion to Alabama Power and the mentoring legacy of George Howard.[224]

MARKETING

By 1973 federal and state governments were beginning to be concerned about the long-term adequacy of the nation's energy supplies, and the stage was set for a new marketing policy emphasizing energy conservation. Marketing used statistics generated by the Atlanta billing office to determine residential customers' use of electricity in various parts of the company's service area.[225] The shifting emphasis to conservation was not too difficult for the department because it was well trained and conservation in the use of electricity had been the primary ingredient of the company's marketing efforts. High insulation standards had been stressed. Former home service advisers became residential energy advisers who conducted free energy audits for customers. Commercial and marketing representatives led energy management seminars and assisted in performing energy audits for their clients. The company provided regular energy audits for schools and government office buildings.[226]

In 1974 Nelda Steele became director of home service after Ann Campbell was promoted to director of retirement planning. Steele came to work with the company in 1957 and developed high school and college home economics

Ann Campbell, left, and Nelda Steele, 1971.

programs and home appliance demonstrations for consumers; she also designed lighting and wiring plans for residential customers. She worked with 4-H programs and coordinated training for residential energy advisers and TV energy educational programs.

When Walter S. "Sonny" Seale retired in 1975, James T. Clements and Jerry W. Bell split the responsibilities of a new department, appliance sales and service.[227] The marketing department, with Sam Booker and Walter Baker taking the lead, was responsible for organizing the Inter-University Committee on Energy and Economics. This group met four times a year to discuss the present and future energy requirements of the state of Alabama and provide an opportunity for an interdisciplinary approach to energy solutions and dialogues between business and the faculty at the state's major universities. Alabama Power's Montevallo office, which opened in 1978, was constructed with solar equipment and was monitored by the reorganized marketing department. With rates becoming the focus of such interest by the company and its customers, a separate section on rates and regulatory matters was established in marketing and directed by John Burks. In 1978 the marketing department was renamed the energy services department. Sam Booker explained that Alabama Power was "not abandoning the sale of electricity" but was promoting the conservation of electricity so that customers achieved the "maximum benefit from every kilowatt of energy we sell."[228]

Walter S. "Sonny" Seale, second from right, and James T. Clements, far right, demonstrate new electric ranges to merchandise salesmen, on left, H. J. Mitchell and J. J. Bookout, 1964.

At Mid-decade

The financial crisis that began in 1968 was not over in 1975, but the financial position of the company had somewhat improved. In 1974 coverage on first-mortgage bonds had fallen to 1.66 (with 2.0 required) and on preferred stock had fallen to 1.36 (with 1.5 required). The next year with rate relief, the first-mortgage bond coverage had risen to 2.29 and coverage on preferred stock had risen to 1.57.[229] However, the problems of regulation and rates and balancing return on equity, stockholder share, and acquiring capital were not permanently solved. The rate filings of 1968, 1970, 1972, 1974, and 1975, coupled with attacks by the governor, politicians, and attorneys with vested interests, had resulted in a public relations nightmare for the company.

Pressured by the legal commitment to provide electricity for its service area as customers demanded it and a rising demand for electricity that could be provided only with additional investment in generation financed by more bonds and securities, Alabama Power Company, which had so long prided itself on customer service and reliability, found itself in a catch-22. Other investor-owned electric utilities in other parts of the nation were facing similar problems, and the idea of managing peak demand by cutting off nonessential electrical service so that additional investment in generating capacity would not be necessary was being discussed by these companies, but not at Alabama Power.[230] In Alabama each crisis seemed to roll over into another one, with tensions never ending. Joe Farley in his report to stockholders called 1975 "a year of unprecedented challenge." The company faced not only a rise in the cost of doing business but also the "loss of the generating capacity at Bouldin Dam," the damage from Hurricane Eloise, and reductions in the company's construction program. However, the company had benefited from the January 1975 rate increase and had been able to sell securities for the first time in fifteen months. Hard times were not over and even more severe crises lurked down the road, but the company had inordinate strengths: a people and their leaders who were imbued with integrity, with allegiance to Alabama Power and to each other, and with the conviction that they were on the right and honorable side.

In 1972 Jefferson County commissioners Thomas B. Pinson and W. Cooper Green joined Eason Balch and Jim Miller Jr. (back row left to right) when Governor George Wallace and Joe Farley announced the construction of an Alabama Power steam plant in western Jefferson county.

Alabama Power Company's corporate headquarters
under construction. An atrium connected the new
north tower, completed in 1986, with the south
tower and the original 1925 art deco building.

Chapter Nine

Joseph M. Farley Nuclear Plant at night.

Struggles, Survival, and Prosperity

Corporations, like people, develop through their lives a personality and, indeed, a character that explains much about their actions.

Joseph M. Farley, *Alabama Power Company*, 1988

While Alabama Power Company was fighting to survive the ravages of nationwide inflation and trying to obtain rate relief in the early 1970s, the country was undergoing a leadership crisis. Richard Nixon had been reelected president in 1972, but a bungled burglary at the Watergate headquarters of the Democratic Party and partially erased tapes from the executive office led to an impeachment investigation and President Nixon's resignation in August 1974. Nixon's vice president, Spiro T. Agnew, had resigned earlier after revelations of improprieties while he was governor of Maryland, and Congress had elected twelve-term Republican congressman Gerald Ford vice president.

With Nixon's resignation Ford assumed the presidency and became the only nonelected president in U.S. history. The Ford administration proposed the utility reorganization bill of 1975, which would have reinstated automatic fuel adjustment charges and charges for construction work in progress in states where these had been eliminated. The bill failed to pass, and energy was an important issue in the next presidential campaign.[1]

In 1976, America's bicentennial year, the Democratic governor of Georgia, Jimmy Carter, defeated Ford, which made Carter the first Deep South president elected since 1844. In the campaign, Carter made energy an important issue, and he was critical of Ford's emphasis upon nuclear energy. Carter proposed a national energy conservation plan with a search for new sources of energy, and he made establishing a "long-range energy policy for the nation his top priority."[2] By this time there was "a belated realization that cheap domestic reserves of petroleum and natural gas were depleted," and the increased demand caused prices to rise.[3] In 1977 Carter signed a bill creating the Department of Energy and replacing the Federal Power Commission with the Federal Energy Regulatory Commission (FERC), which had enhanced authority over whole-sale power rates. From congressional debates came the National Energy Act (1978) and the Public Utility Regulatory Policy Act (PURPA) of 1978, which allowed and encouraged independent generators to sell wholesale power. Utilities attacked the law on constitutional grounds and delayed its implementation. Carter had a brief honeymoon with Congress, then the problems of inflation and a failing economy began to overwhelm his presidency.[4] Alvin Vogtle, president of Southern Company, anticipated that 1976 would pull the company from "the worst slide in earning ever experienced by the Southern Company." To prevent such levels as the previous two years, three of its operating companies, including Alabama Power, would be involved in rate hearings

Company executives attended a meeting at the North River Yacht Club in Tuscaloosa in 1976. Many of Alabama Power's future leaders were there.

in 1976.[5] For Alabama Power Company, the period from 1968 to 1975 had been difficult and challenging, but the next seven years would be even worse.

In his letter to stockholders for the company's 1976 *Annual Report*, Joe Farley noted proudly that Alabama Power was "an integral part of free enterprise," which was the basis "of the American system that celebrated its 200th anniversary in 1976." The people of Alabama Power, he wrote, "have worked to develop Alabama for about a third of that time."[6] But the sharp increase in construction costs, the new demands made by the Nuclear Regulatory Commission, and the increased cost of money needed for Farley Nuclear Plant caused Alabama Power to announce on January 22, 1976, that units 1 and 2 of the Alan R. Barton Nuclear Plant near Clanton were being postponed. Alabama Power had originally planned for its second nuclear plant to be located in Dallas County, near Selma, but extensive geological tests indicated the site was not suitable and could not be licensed for a nuclear plant because drilling found hairline fractures in the chalk formations. Technology in 1976 could not date the faults in the chalk, but thirty years later technology was available to date those faults to a million years ago, and a nuclear plant could be licensed on that site.[7] But in 1976 this was not known and a location in Chilton and Elmore Counties was selected instead. Preconstruction costs were $21.6 million, mostly for site preparations, that were completed by 1976 when the company decided to suspend construction. Willard Bowers, who was with the environmental department then, believes that not having the technology to determine the age of those faults in Dallas County chalk was a good thing because if the company had determined they were old faults, then construction would have progressed on the nuclear plant. The necessity of a change in site caused a delay and slowed the process, thus reducing the lost costs that were associated with the cancelled plant.[8]

At the time, Farley thought the delay in building the Barton plant was temporary until the company was stronger financially and could raise the capital needed for the construction of a second nuclear plant; however, there was a great deal of discussion in-house on whether the company should permanently cancel the second nuclear plant. These discussions were long and involved. Rod Mundy remembers one meeting when Walter Johnsey, then an executive vice president, stood up and said, "There is no way in hell we can afford this." On November 18, 1977, the company announced that because of the expense of developing nuclear energy, the Carter administration's hostility to nuclear power, and specifically because of the president's recent speech on energy, the company was suspending indefinitely the Barton project. The growth in demand for electricity in the company's service area, once projected at

8 percent per year, had dropped in 1977 to a projected growth of 6.5 percent, a reduction resulting from energy conservation and the company's load management. The growth in demand would have to be supplied by additional units at the coal-fired steam plant being constructed in western Jefferson County, named for power generation vice president James H. Miller Jr., and by the Farley Nuclear Plant, which was scheduled to go into commercial service in December 1977.[9]

1976 OPENS WITH A NEW RATE CASE

As America's bicentennial year opened, the Alabama Public Service Commission began hearings on Alabama Power's November 1975 rate request. On February 9, Farley presented written testimony to the Public Service Commission reviewing the $106.8 million increase, emphasizing that even with the increase Alabama Power's rates would still be below the rates of many other utilities. Inflation of operating costs was one part of the equation, but the company's growth in demand was clearly "due to an increase in the living standard of our residential customers." Throughout this period Alabama Power regularly sent state editors and news directors copies of the average residential monthly electrical cost surveys conducted by the Jacksonville (Florida) Electric Authority, a municipally owned electric utility. Alabama Power always ranked in the lower half or lower quarter of electric costs of the sixty government-owned and investor-owned utilities included in the survey.[10] Farley noted that these reports were significant in fighting the misconception fostered by politicians and the media in the state that Alabama Power's rates were too high.[11]

In his testimony to the Public Service Commission, Farley explained that if rates could be increased, then the company's senior securities would be more attractive, would cost the company less, and in the long run would permit lower customer rates.[12] Farley gave details of the company's efforts to operate more efficiently to avoid the necessity of rate increases. These efforts included installing more efficient generating units, improving equipment for line crews, and acquiring computers and a new materials management system, which would be operational in mid-1976. Alabama Power had reduced the number of employees even as the number of customers had grown. The company had plans to increase and centralize its salvage operations, selecting and repairing usable items and disposing of obsolete and damaged scrap materials and equipment.[13] After weeks of hearings and testimony, the company waited for the PSC to render a decision.

The General Services Complex (left) in Shelby County, begun in 1973, replaced the North Birmingham shops (below) that were inadequate for Alabama Power's needs.

GENERAL SERVICES COMPLEX

Meanwhile, one of those efficiencies Joe Farley mentioned in his presentation to the Public Service Commission was the new General Services Complex south of Birmingham. For years many of Alabama Power's service operations had been housed in a barnlike structure in North Birmingham; automobiles and trucks were repaired in a facility on Twelfth Street. In the early 1970s Walter Johnsey took Farley over to the North Birmingham shop to show him its deteriorating condition. Johnsey never got him inside the building. When the company president saw the corner of the structure, he said, "Let's get out of here before it falls," and then told his executive vice president to "do something about it." Johnsey hired a consultant to recommend the best location for a new service complex, and in 1972 the company negotiated an option on 318 acres twenty miles south of Birmingham. The main L&N railroad line ran by the Shelby County site, which was near an I-65 exit. The complex, designed by Rust Engineering and built by Harbert Corporation, was started in 1973, and the first buildings were completed in 1974. By 2006 the General Services Complex had 234 acres fenced with security and thirty-six buildings and structures inside.[14]

The General Services Complex proved to be a valuable addition to the company, allowing Alabama Power to work more efficiently and more economically. Building 4 housed the general shops. In 1979 it was under the supervision of John C. Murphy, whose article about the transformer repair and testing programs of Alabama Power was featured in a national magazine. Construction crews were headquartered at the service complex. By concentrating supplies in one warehouse, the amount of money invested in backup transformers, supplies, and other equipment was reduced, inventory management was more efficient, and cost of warehouse space across the state eliminated. The state's interstate highway system and the complex's central location allowed supplies to be transported wherever they were needed in the company's service area, as well as wherever they might be needed by other operating companies of Southern Company. The service complex provided space to rebuild trucks and transformers and conduct salvage operations. There were classrooms, an area for outdoor training for such skills as pole climbing, and laboratories to test water, coal, and rubber gloves.[15] The company was able to complete the construction of the General Services Complex during a period of tight budgets, a remarkable testimony to Johnsey's financial skill and Billy Guthrie's organizational skills.[16]

At the annual meeting of the Alabama Power board of directors in April 1976, few management changes were made. After forty-five years Liston H. Cook retired, along with A. G. Youngsteadt, executive accountant. Jackson W. Minor, comptroller, took on more responsibilities with his election as a vice president. Minor recalled that "when Joe Farley made me vice president of the company, he told me 'I am putting the trust of the company and these accounting records in your hands. We are going to follow the law and follow the rules and regulations of the Federal Power Commission and Alabama Public Service Commission and if anyone pressures you otherwise, you come to me.'"[17]

Elmer B. Harris began as a co-op student in 1958.

Another promotion at this time that proved fortuitous was Elmer B. Harris's elevation to vice president. He was given a new department, corporate finance and planning. Harris, a tall, lanky young man with a quick mind and a talent for winning the confidence of people, would play a key role in solving the financial problems of the company in the next decade. A native of Clanton and the son of a union man, Harris had been encouraged by his cousin R. L. Harris to join Alabama Power co-op program in 1958. After Elmer Harris graduated from Auburn in 1962, he was assigned to the Montgomery office as a junior engineer, where his desk was near that of his friend Nolan Hardin. Harris joined the Alabama Air National Guard, and in 1964 he took leave from the company to learn to fly at Webb Air Force Base in Texas. Flying became an important part of his life. In 1968 the air force invited Harris to the Air Command and Staff College at Maxwell Air Force Base in Montgomery.[18]

One of the favorite stories about Harris, often told in the company and around the state, was about the Sunday afternoon, April 9, 1965, when his Air National Guard RF-84 jet stalled out over central Alabama near Seman in Elmore County. His friend and fellow National Guard pilot, Banks Farris, said that "Elmer ran out of air speed, altitude, and ideas simultaneously." With the ground coming toward him at a rapid speed, Harris hit his ejection button. The plane crashed in a ball of fire; Harris

Banks Farris

was so close to the ground that his parachute swung once and he was on the ground. He landed hard but safe and walked up to a tenant house carrying his parachute and helmet and asked some children, "If you go to the right, do you go to Wetumpka?" No child said a word. After witnessing the crash and the arrival of Harris, the children were terrified. About that time, Nolan Hardin walked up and said, "Hey Elmer, it's funny finding you here." Harris had managed to land on the farm where Hardin had gone blackberry picking with his son Greg. The Alabama Air National Guard commander, General Reid Doster, who was once described as "a burly cigar-chomping six-footer" and who ran his empire with an iron hand, summoned Harris to his office. Doster, not even looking at Harris, bellowed, "Boy, what the hell are you doing busting up my airplane?" For years Harris's explanation was quoted across the power company: "Well, sir, it looked like the right thing to do at the time." After talking to Harris, the general ordered him to go back and fly for another twenty years.[19]

Harris continued his Air National Guard duty and in 1968 returned to Auburn University for a master's degree in electrical engineering, followed by an MBA degree in 1970. He worked in various engineering and operating positions, and then in 1972 Jim Miller sent him to Headland to be district manager. Miller explained that "Elmer was a really bright guy, and I wanted him to learn the business." The time in Headland gave Harris the opportunity to try new ideas and develop his leadership style. He tried his concepts about decentralizing responsibility and found ways for his Alabama Power people to become involved in civic and charity work in the Wiregrass.[20] At Headland, Harris had his first experience with industrial development and his first taste of the economic and political life of a community. A born politician, Harris never met a stranger, and he put his flamboyant personality to work convincing industry to move to Headland. In 1974 Jim Miller brought Harris to the corporate office as his assistant; Harris was later made manager of operations services, which got him into system planning. Walter Johnsey moved Harris over to help him with budgeting and rate cases, responsibilities that Harris managed well. Harris had a brilliant knack for financial matters. He was able to relate to all people and had an uncanny ability to engage people in ways that endeared himself to them. Banks Farris described Harris as a "man of great heart and faith."[21] He would put these strengths and talents to use in the years ahead.

Alabama Power's earnings for calendar 1976 were down 27 percent compared to 1975, but the company was able to sell $50 million in first-mortgage bonds on March 24, 1976. The sale, plus contributions from Southern Company and the sale of preferred stock, funds from industrial revenue bonds, and interim bank loans provided the financing for 1976 construction costs estimated to be $491,139,000 but which came in under budget at $443,951,000.[22] One of the issues that plagued the company, especially in 1977, was the public's lack of understanding about load and capacity. The company had the responsibility to provide the electricity that customers called for whenever they elected to use electricity. In order to service that load demand, Alabama Power had to estimate population and business growth and future requests because it took years to build new generation capacity and put it into service. It is true that the company preferred to err on the side of slightly more electricity rather than slightly less. Customers would be irate, justifiably so, living with brownouts and blackouts, which would also have damaged the system and been costly to repair. Still, people often fell into believing demagogic charges that Alabama Power was overbuilding and using their rates to finance it, which was not true.

Rate Case of 1976—A Zero Order

Throughout the spring of 1976 and into summer, return on common equity for Alabama Power Company continued to fall as the tensions in the corporate office mounted. The Public Service Commission was now under the presidency of Chris Whatley, a former PSC staff member who had worked closely with attorney Maurice Bishop. Governor Wallace had appointed Whatley to Kenneth Hammond's unexpired term after Hammond was indicted and forced to resign from the PSC. The situation for the company was rather grim, and it was shocked by the PSC's response to its rate request. On June 25, 1976, the PSC announced it would not award any of the requested $106.8 million annual retail rate increase filed in November 1975. When Joe Farley first read the order, Banks Farris recalled that Farley never raised his voice or showed any emotion; he just calmly said, "Let's go see Eason and Jack." Joe Farley called the announcement "shocking and dismaying," an action that meant the commission rejected the testimony of its own expert witness. Farley said the "commission's decision ignores the magnitude of the obligation the company has in maintaining service to its customers." A large number of Alabama Power's industrial customers had opposed the rate increase. These customers feared that under the plan they would lose their lower rates, residential customers would not pay their fair share, and the burden on industry would increase because in two prior cases the PSC had changed the percentages between residential, commercial, and industrial customers.[23]

This "zero order" sent Alabama Power's return on common equity down. The next month, Moody's reduced the company's bond rating from A to Baa. Alabama Power appealed to the Montgomery County circuit court, and Judge Frank Embry ordered the commission to give the company an adequate rate increase so it could raise additional capital to fund its future construction program. Despite the Public Service Commission's grant of a $23.3 million increase in August 1976, Standard & Poor's rating of Alabama Power dropped from A- to BBB.[24] The company again appealed to the circuit court, which confirmed the PSC order but did allow the company to put into effect an additional $30.1 million increase that would be subject to refund. The company, knowing this amount was inadequate, appealed both rulings to the Alabama Supreme Court. The high court reversed the circuit court, ordering that only $17 million be subject to refund. With interest, this would be an average of about $7 per customer.[25]

Alabama Power Company kept bankruptcy at bay during these years by negotiating a revolving credit arrangement with a consortium of large banks in New York and Chicago and many local banks, whose loans were a requirement of the larger banks as a condition of credit. Walter Johnsey testified before the Public Service Commission in hearings on the $106.8 million rate increase. He explained that as negotiations on this credit moved forward, "the banks will be looking at what the company is doing to improve its fixed charge coverage ratios and cash flow, as this will be the only way the banks can be assured that the company will have cash to pay off the loan agreement."[26]

On April 30, 1976, Alabama Power filed for a wholesale rate increase with the Federal Power Commission. This increase would affect fifteen municipalities and eleven rural electric distribution cooperatives served by Alabama Power. Senior vice president Jesse S. Vogtle announced that construction to add additional generation had been deferred because the company's inability to sell

Jesse S. Vogtle

senior securities had forced Alabama Power into using short-term bank loans for financing, a loan arrangement good for eighteen months. The interest rates were very high.[27]

THE TERRIBLE YEAR: 1977

In October 1976 Joe Farley explained to customers, once more, that Alabama Power needed additional revenue because of the lag between requesting a rate and putting a new rate into effect and because the company was not able to sell senior securities with its low rate of return on investment. Yet, the company was "locked in," he explained, to certain construction commitments necessary to provide generation to serve its customers. The formal application to the Public Service Commission was made on October 15, 1976, and the increased revenue was expected to be $173.9 million. On an average bill for 800 kilowatt hours, this translated to an increase of $7.71 a month.[28] Letters flooded into the governor's office. Some writers complained that Wallace's attacks on the electrical system would result in brownouts and blackouts and discourage industry from locating in Alabama. Others supported the governor and complained about their high electrical bills.[29]

Montgomery's Garrett Coliseum was the scene of a raucous PSC rate case hearing on January 4, 1977.

For Alabama Power, the financial situation became so critical that the company could not wait for relief until the rate case was decided, so on December 6, 1976, Alabama Power filed for an emergency rate increase to become effective no later than January 6, 1977. The initial hearings generated such hostility and public attention that when they adjourned on December 20 for the Christmas holidays, Public Service Commission secretary Wallace Tidmore issued notice that the next hearing would be on Tuesday, January 4, 1977, and it would be held in the Garrett Coliseum.[30] This huge indoor stadium was the normal place for winter track meets, rodeos, horse, hog, and cattle shows, and even Montgomery high-society Mardi Gras balls. Joe Farley observed it was "almost surreal. You wouldn't think a legal proceeding could go on in front of several thousand people cheering and booing."[31]

The Garrett Coliseum hearing drew people from all over the state, many traveling on buses, who came either to oppose the company or to support it. A stadium atmosphere prevailed, and the crowd was wild and disorderly as if someone were going to be fed to the lions. Some concession stands opened and were selling popcorn. At one time piped-in music played "Bridge Over Troubled Water."[32] Alabama Power's security people were there in force to protect Joe Farley, Alabama Power's management team, and expert witnesses who were prepared to testify for the company. Fifty people spoke for or against Alabama Power's rate request. Stewart B. Clifford, senior vice president of Citibank of New York, explained the financial expectations of Wall Street and said that Alabama Power had lost its A bond rating. Clifford had a sobering effect on the crowd when he testified, Farley remembered, as to "why he, as the lead bank, had decided that we were no longer credit-worthy and they would not lend us any more money." From Farley's point of view, Clifford had a dramatic effect on the commission and the media, "but it was not the place you wanted your banker to have to be to talk. It didn't help the image of the state of Alabama one little bit."[33] Richard R. Hume of Boston's Pru-Lease Corporation, connected with Prudential Insurance Company, confirmed that his company was unwilling to extend credit for vehicles or fuel. Hume and Clifford had probably never before had such an experience.[34]

On the day of the hearing the 1974 and 1975 salaries of Alabama Power officers were published in the *Montgomery Advertiser*. Much was made of the salary increases given to management, but these were small raises, hardly enough to cover the current double-digit inflation.[35] In one editorial following the meeting, the *Montgomery Advertiser* chided Alabama Power for its approach to rate relief, writing that the company had to show customers higher rates provide "a steady orderly growth sufficient to absorb the natural population growth of the state."[36] Of course, this is exactly what Alabama Power had been trying to tell everyone for almost a decade.

The Alabama Public Service Commission announced on January 20, 1977, that it was granting 95 percent of the emergency rates effective that day for industrial and commercial customers and effective March 1 for residential customers, and a storm of protests began. The year 1977 was a controversial year and one of the most stressful years ever for Alabama Power's public relations department.[37] On January 22, Governor George Wallace instructed Maurice Bishop to appeal the rate increase.[38] On April 26 the governor, frustrated by his inability to force his utility legislation through the Alabama Senate, accused Alabama Power of undue influence and manipulation of individual senators. Joe Farley immediately wrote the governor a long letter stating that his charges were "without foundation, and I deny them categorically." The problem was, Farley noted, the unwillingness of many people to understand "that the price of energy must reflect its true cost." Farley observed that if the governor truly believed that Alabama Power should stop building additional generation, then he should "advise the director of the Alabama Development Office and his industrial development staff of your change in position, because it is frankly wrong to encourage economic development and industrial growth if State policy is directed against a continuing availability of electric energy."[39]

The relationship between George Wallace and Joe Farley during these difficult years was an interesting contrast. Personally, their life experiences were worlds apart. Wallace grew up in rural Barbour County, in the small town of Clio. Farley was born in the state's largest city, Birmingham. Wallace, a longtime southern Democrat, was educated at the University of Alabama, while Farley, who had worked for the Republican Party, was a graduate of Princeton and Harvard Universities. While their differences were public, their personal relationship remained cordial on the surface, and Farley occasionally visited with the governor in the capitol. After Walter Bouldin resigned from the Tuskegee board of trustees, Governor Albert Brewer appointed Farley to one of the state's positions on the board. After Farley's term expired in 1972, Wallace, back in the governor's office, went years without making a replacement appointment, leaving Farley on the Tuskegee board. In the 1980s Wallace asked Farley to travel to Korea to represent the governor's office at a luncheon. Whenever Wallace and Farley met, the governor often told Farley there was nothing personal in his opposition to Alabama Power's rate increases. Farley observed that "I had a good personal relationship with the governor, and it was, in his judgment, nothing personal. It was just a matter that [he believed] the public did not want these increases and we would have to find another way. He could not explain how that could be, but, nonetheless, that was the tenor of it."[40]

Alabama Power's financial problems eased somewhat when the Public Service Commission terminated the emergency increase and, on a two to one vote, awarded the company a $91 million rate increase effective April 28, 1977. The revenue Alabama Power needed would have added $2.96 to a normal residential bill. The request, however inadequate for the company, swelled political opposition and criticism, and newspaper articles became vitriolic.[41] Governor Wallace and Lieutenant Governor Jere Beasley vocally opposed the higher rates and had legislation introduced in the senate to allow the governor to reverse any rate increase granted by the Public Service Commission. If the governor's rollback or callback was successful, Farley said it would "leave a cloud over our financial situation and we'd be in worse shape than we were before the emergency rate increase."[42] In a bitter meeting, the senate commerce, transportation, and utilities committee, chaired by Senator Eddie Gilmore, "cut the guts from Wallace's utilities package." The *Montgomery Advertiser* quoted Senator Joe Fine of Russellville, a onetime supporter of the governor, as saying that "George Wallace had made a career out of raising emotional issues and demagoging his way into office. First, he used the race issue, black against white, but [now] that's run out." Gilmore claimed the utilities package was a "political hook," while the governor charged that the "power company's got more control over the Senate than the people themselves."[43] Farley wanted to correct "the streams of misinformation concerning our company and our work in the supplying of electricity to the customers we serve."[44]

On May 6, 1977, Governor Wallace asked the Alabama Supreme Court for an advisory opinion on the constitutionality of the bill pending in the legislature that would allow the governor to "roll back" any increases granted by the Public Service Commission and announced that he already had an order on his desk to roll back rates up to $91 million a year. The *Birmingham Post-Herald* quoted the governor as saying "the people of Alabama are becoming aroused about the way certain members of the senate are doing nothing about the continued escalation of power bills." The governor pointed out that the Alabama House had passed the bills three times.[45] Although Attorney General Bill Baxley argued the roll-back bill was constitutional, the Alabama Supreme Court rendered an advisory opinion that the proposed law was unconstitutional, and the governor called a special session of the legislature to consider utility legislation.[46]

In the governor's opening address to the special session on May 17, 1977, Wallace criticized Alabama Power for, in his words, its "exceeding [sic] extremely high power bills." He gave names and towns of seven Alabama Power customers who complained about their high power bills. A week later, the company released the billings of each of these customers for the past twelve months, listing dates the meter was read, kilowatt hours used, and amount billed. None of the charges made by the governor were substantiated by the records. One Montgomery customer had used five times the kilowatt hours in his highest billing period compared to his lowest bill. In his speech the governor made other charges, and the company explained why these were not accurate.[47] Joe Farley responded with a press release on May 23. He was offended that the Alabama Public Television Network denied "Alabama Power Company a reasonable opportunity to respond to erroneous charges and statements made by

Governor Wallace." Farley also answered these charges in an address to the Birmingham Rotary Club on June 1, and he sent the governor a letter on July 23, 1977.[48]

In the special session of the legislature called to deal with utility bills, all the governor was able to get passed was an act establishing a legislative committee on public utilities that would oversee "a full and complete audit and management study of the Alabama Power Company and Southern Company Services." This committee was to submit its report to the governor, the committee on public utilities, the Public Service Commission, and the legislature. The legislation was approved on June 9, 1977.[49] The governor appointed Alto V. Lee III, a Dothan attorney; state senator Earl Goodwin of Selma; and state superintendent of education Dr. Wayne Teague to this committee. The committee, with the governor's approval, selected the Birmingham office of Price Waterhouse & Company to make the study, and a contract was signed.[50]

In the year in which the Price Waterhouse study was being conducted and before it was released, electrical rates continued to be the focus of debate and hostility, which increased in midsummer 1977 after Alabama Power released its earnings showing the company had "tripled its net income for the first six months of the year" compared to the same period in 1976. Although Joe Farley was quoted in the press release explaining that "we are comparing a fair year with a bad year" and noting that the company's capital expenditures had increased (in 1976 they were $444 million and in 1977 would total about $540 million), criticism was immediate and widespread. The PSC announced it would investigate Alabama Power's profits.[51] The Securities and Exchange Commission required publicly traded companies to publish their earnings quarterly, and the Southern Company, in order to make its bond and stock sales possible on the most favorable terms, needed to portray strong, viable— and of course, profitable—operating companies. Because of the hostile climate, Public Service Commission president Juanita McDaniel, who had voted for the recent rate increase, was given state security protection after two threatening letters and phone calls.[52] The *Alabama Journal*'s opinion was that the officials of Alabama Power Company "were sandbagged from the start" because "the Southern Company, which owns Alabama Power, wants to look good to investors, an audience in a distinct minority among consumers." The newspaper chided the governor for raising the specter of nationalization as a solution to Alabama's electrical prices. The *Journal* drew a parallel to a California city whose venture into minor league baseball had not produced a winning team and suggested the "pitfall in the governor's notion of nationalization" was that, should state government take over electrical production, "he'd get all the demands for better pitching."[53]

SOUTHERN COMPANY PLANE CRASH

On April 28, 1977, the day the Public Service Commission's rate increase went into effect and bills were introduced in the legislature to allow the governor to roll back rate increases, Alabama Power had little time to be concerned with such politicking because later in the evening tragic word reached Birmingham that a Southern Company jet leaving Washington, D.C., and bound for the Magic City had crashed about 8:30 P.M. with no survivors. Clyde A. Lilly Jr., William G. Lalor Jr., and two pilots were aboard.[54] Two other Alabama Power people, human resources vice president Bob Andrews and attorney Bob Collins, were supposed to be on the plane, but they had finished their business in the capital after lunch and decided to take a Delta flight home.[55] Soon after the crash outside Washington, D.C., Joe Farley Jr., who was fourteen, answered the telephone at the Farley home in Birmingham. His parents had flown on a Southern Company plane to Eufaula to attend a retirement dinner for Alabama Power vice president Raymond T. Garlington. The man on the telephone identified himself as with the media and said he knew young Joe's parents were traveling by air and there had been a crash of a Southern Company plane. Then he asked, "Do you know anything about this?" The three Farley children were left for hours worried their parents were dead until their father called from the Birmingham airport as soon as his plane landed from Eufaula and he learned of the Washington, D.C., crash.[56]

Ray Garlington

Lilly and Lalor were popular men and fine engineers who came from General Electric to Southern Services, Inc. (The company name was changed to Southern Company Services, Inc., on April 21, 1976, and a change was recorded in the Alabama secretary of state's office on April 23, 1976.) Lilly, who had served several years as president of Gulf Power, at the time of the crash was president of Southern Services and Lalor was an executive vice president.[57] Under their leadership the service company expanded its role. A nonprofit organization from its inception, the company provided professional, engineering, and technological assistance to the operating companies at cost. It advised on the location and design of plants to assist with geographically spreading generation and helped establish ways to generate as close to the load as possible while maintaining the security of the system. Southern Company Services had always been based in Birmingham, which was a central location for the Southern Company system and where the Southern Electric System Coordination Center was located. Power coordinators in Birmingham monitored and controlled the entire Southern electric system, making certain that the most economical sources of electric power on the system were used at any given moment. This assured the customer the lowest priced electricity possible.[58]

The Atlanta office of Southern Company Services performed financial, accounting, internal auditing, and tax, rate, research, and marketing services. Harllee Branch decided to create a central data control center in Atlanta, and this added to the service company's responsibilities. William B. Reed, who followed Lilly as president of Southern Company Services, gave Lalor credit "for making the data center work." The center had the most advanced computer operation and provided customer billing information for employees working in the four operating companies. In 1979 the data center processed 2.5 million electric bills every month for the four operating companies. Southern Company Services maintained an office in New York as the contact point for financial information. President Bill Reed was a Russellville native and Auburn engineer who also came to Southern Company Services in 1969 from General Electric.[59]

ANOTHER RATE PROCEEDING: THE GOVERNOR'S COMPLAINT CASE

In August 1977, Governor Wallace, Maurice Bishop, and others took Alabama Power's six-months-earnings report and filed a complaint with the Public Service Commission against the company's high rates. The PSC started a fifteen-month investigation while the Price Waterhouse study was also ongoing. The clerk of the Alabama Supreme Court advised Alabama Power counsel Rod Mundy on September 9, 1977, that the court decision on the PSC's 1976 "zero order" case, which would be announced in Montgomery on September 17, would require that substantial refunds be collected under bond. Coincidentally, that day Alabama Power Company was hosting a meeting in New York for financial analysts to discuss the company's plans for a $50 million preferred stock offering. When the telephone rang during lunch, Bruce Hutchins, then manager of financial planning, answered and talked to Rod Mundy, who was reporting the decision. Hutchins informed Farley, who was uncertain whether the company would have enough coverage. The news put Farley in an awkward situation. He sent vice president and treasurer Travis Bowden outside with Hutchins and attorney Mac Beale. Hutchins began making calculations to see if the company could sell the stock. By a slim margin, he determined the company could, and the stock sale was completed within a few days, but with a supplement to its bidding prospectus dated September 6 and approved by the Securities and Exchange Commission.[60]

Mac Beale, whose full name is Walter McFarland Beale Jr., had arrived at the Balch & Bingham law firm in 1970 and began working with corporate financing and the Securities and Exchange Commission. Beale, an Auburn University and Cumberland School of Law graduate, was assigned to work with Jack Bingham on the legal aspects of selling securities and raising capital for the company. His arrival soon after Alabama Power filed its first general rate increase case gave him little time to settle in before the tough times and challenges came for him.[61]

When Alabama Power announced in October 1977 its twelve-month earnings, which had substantially increased over the previous year, there was another immediate attack on the company. Governor Wallace blasted Lieutenant Governor Jere Beasley and the senate leadership for not passing his anti-utility legislation.[62] On December 1, 1977, unit 1 of the Joseph M. Farley Nuclear Plant near Dothan went into commercial operation and produced 395,930,000 kilowatt hours of electricity during the month of December. Nuclear generation was particularly important for consumers and the company for the company's most efficient coal-fired units would have burned 168,000 tons of coal costing $4.3 million to produce the same amount of electricity as

The Joseph M. Farley Nuclear Plant went into service on December 1, 1977.

the Farley plant. A coal strike began December 6, 1977. Alabama Power had large stockpiles of coal, but as the work stoppage continued, the company became more concerned.[63] On January 18, 1978, Alabama Power announced profits had fallen, explaining that under standard accounting procedures and rate-making practice in Alabama, earnings decline immediately after a major plant goes into service because noncash allowances for funds used during construction cease and the depreciation expenses begin. Later in January, Alabama Power sold $100 million first-mortgage bonds at a cost of 9.59 percent interest in order to pay off short-term loans made at a higher interest rate.[64]

As the coal strike continued, Alabama Power urged its customers to conserve energy, and the company used as much hydroelectric generation as practical. Sam Booker and the marketing department began programs encouraging home owners to install more insulation, although always making clear to customers that the company did not sell or install insulation. Alabama Power presented a contingency plan to the PSC should the coal strike continue. The plan would go into effect when the company's coal stockpiles reached certain levels, which would trigger mandatory curtailment of lighting for advertising and displays and calls for customers to voluntarily reduce use of electricity. Other more drastic measures would automatically go into effect when the company's coal reserves fell below other levels. In February the company was able to purchase low-sulfur coal from Australia to replenish the Barry Steam Plant stockpile, but the coal would not arrive in the Port of Mobile for seven weeks. The coal strike ended in late March, and Alabama Power's emergency plans had been effective in keeping electricity flowing to homes and essential services.[65]

Price Waterhouse Report Issued

The long-awaited Price Waterhouse report was completed and presented to the committee on public utilities on April 28, 1978. In explaining the reasons for the study, Price Waterhouse wrote that Alabama Power Company had requested rate increases in 1968, 1971, 1972, 1974, 1975, and 1976 and that the average revenue per kilowatt hour rose from 1.18 cents in 1968 to 3.22 cents in 1977. The price that consumers had to pay for electricity rose 170 percent over ten years.[66] Price Waterhouse investigated seven key functional categories of Alabama Power Company operations: executive management direction, operations planning and control, engineering planning and control, financial planning and control, general administrative activity planning and control, personnel planning and control, and external impact factors.

The Price Waterhouse study was a detailed and thorough document almost one inch thick. Alabama Power cooperated with the Price Waterhouse accountants and management experts, who were working under the direction of Henry McPherson, the partner in charge. Hugh P. Foreman, Alabama Power Company vice president at Montgomery, was given responsibility for serving as liaison with the accounting firm. Foreman made certain that Price Waterhouse's people had all the information, figures, and facts they needed or asked for as they studied the company's operations, management, accounting procedures, financing, and return on investment. The Price Waterhouse study was an extensive assessment of the company, and Alabama Power was pleased to have an outside evaluation. From the company's standpoint, the study and the recommendations were welcome.[67] Adversaries who hoped to use the study to damage the company were disappointed.

In its final report, Price Waterhouse included a number of recommendations for the company. Alabama Power and Southern Company Services, Inc., were given an opportunity to study the recommendations, and the company's response and action on each one was included in the report. The company agreed with or accepted all the recommendations. The report also studied the regulation of the utility by the Public Service Commission and had some recommendations for the PSC. The overall appraisal of Alabama Power was positive, and the report stated that "it is our judgment that the principal factors which have caused rates to increase so rapidly lie beyond the Company's sphere of control." The study noted that:

> Our overall conclusion from the management study is that Alabama Power Company is an effectively managed company, and that Southern Company Services, Inc., effectively manages the principal services it renders to the Company. We found the Company to be organized in a logical manner and staffed with competent and knowledgeable personnel at all levels of management.
>
> The Company's requests for rate increases should continue to be scrutinized carefully, and feasible alternatives should be presented and explored. Opportunities for cost reductions or operational improvements, such as those identified in our recommendations, should be sought out continually and should be exploited fully. Ultimately, however, the Company and the Public Service Commission, as well as the executive, legislative and judicial branches of state government, should be working toward a common goal: pro-

viding the citizens of Alabama with adequate and reliable electric service at the lowest possible rates that will provide the Company with a fair return on its investments devoted to public service.[68]

A few years later, Alabama Power Company invited Price Waterhouse back, at company expense, to review the company's implementation and operation of improvements recommended in the study.

MARKETING BECOMES ENERGY SERVICES

To encourage good energy management, the aggressive five-year program that marketing vice president Sam Booker unveiled in 1976 to educate consumers on the need for conservation, for more insulation, and for proper sizing of heating and cooling units was reaping results by 1978. The program and other company advertisements were in line with recommendations from the Public Service Commission urging that advertising be beneficial to customers. Nonetheless, the PSC's zero order in June 1976 disallowed advertising as an operating expense. This ban caused a storm of protest from newspapers and advertising companies. Alabama Power strongly objected, and the state press association, advertising clubs and councils, and public relations groups filed briefs with the Alabama Supreme Court supporting Alabama Power's filing. To communicate with customers, the company was left with inserts in monthly bills.[69] On April 7, 1978, the supreme court ruled that advertising costs were a reasonable part of operating expenses and that "the function of the Alabama Public Service Commission is that of regulation, and not of management."[70] Alabama Power resumed its advertising program; however, the other part of this court opinion was not favorable. There was still to be no general rate increase and refunds were required from collections under bond between October 12, 1976, and April 28, 1977.[71]

In October 1978, to reflect more accurately its new charge of conservation, public understanding, and customer service, the marketing department became the department of energy services. Sam Booker announced that Alabama Power was "not abandoning the sale of electric energy. We are merely pointing out our responsibility in selling the right kind of load while at the same time promoting conservation. We must," Booker said, "concentrate on achieving the maximum benefit from every kilowatt of energy we sell."[72] Working with Booker were Walter Baker, head of market research and planning, John F. Hollingsworth, manager of marketing services, and W. C. Martin, manager of load research and technical services. Throughout 1978, marketing was challenged by a Public Service Commission mandate to study the costs and possible benefits of four rate concepts: time-of-day pricing, seasonal differentials, interruptible power rates, and load management control. The comprehensive study compiled by Alabama Power became a model for the industry and served as the basis of both the company's and the Public Service Commission's response to compliance procedures required by the Public Utility Regulatory Policy Act (PURPA), which Congress enacted on October 15, 1978.[73]

Alabama Power Company as Extended Family

The trauma of attacks by politicians and newspapers increased the loyalty of Alabama Power Company's extended family, and the hard times had the effect of uniting employees and making them more determined than ever to defend themselves and their company vigorously and to endure, overcome, and succeed. Company people who survived the 1970s shared a special bond. There is an interpretation of history that asserts nations are forged when outside forces cause people to unite to protect their distinctive culture.[74] Companies can be affected the same way. When reminiscing about these difficult times, longtime employees recalled the pain they shared when Joe Farley's wife, Sheila, died in July 1978. During the height of the company's financial crisis, Sheila fell ill with kidney disease, which eventually forced her into a dialysis program and later a kidney transplant. Farley was determined his personal life would not interfere with his leadership of Alabama Power, but the feeling of family shared by his employees meant that they, too, felt the trauma of his ordeal as he looked after his company family as well as Sheila and his three young children.

For a time, Sheila made trips to UAB for dialysis, but when the trips became so time consuming and intrusive to her family's life, arrangements were made for equipment at home and a small room was turned into a dialysis room. The three children, Joe Jr., Tom, and Mary Lynne, helped in ways they could, but their father took the responsibility. The problems faced by the Farley family were increased by the hostile and sometimes threatening telephone

The Farley family, Sheila, Joe, and children Tom, Mary Lynne, and Joe Jr.

calls they received from an anonymous public stirred by political rhetoric. At times guards were stationed in the driveway. Farley refused to have an unlisted telephone number because he considered himself the leader of a public utility and therefore a public servant. He had to be accountable. The children were taught to answer the telephone with courtesy and to take messages. Joe Jr. laughed as he reminisced that at the age of thirteen he could run the customer service office at home.

One incident that Joe Jr. recalled vividly will suffice to show the pressures of Farley's responsibilities during the dark days for his company and the tragic months for his family. It will also illustrate the hostile climate and the intrusive nature of an insensitive public in these years. The dialysis machine had a hand crank so that if the electricity should go off, the person supervising the procedure could quickly begin to pump the large amount of blood in the machine back into the patient. One night during Sheila's dialysis there was a thunderstorm, and the electricity went off in the Farley house. While Tom held the flashlight, his father began frantically turning the hand crank to keep Sheila alive. Soon the telephone rang. A very unhappy man was without his electricity and insisted on talking to Joe Farley. Joe Jr. told him his father could not come to the telephone. The man was not kind, insisting Farley must have electricity in his home and that he was just refusing to talk to him. As the man grew more angry, Joe Jr. blurted out exactly why his father could not speak to him. Needless to say, the man apologized and hung up quickly without giving his name or telephone number.[75]

Unknown to the general public, and two decades before active fathers became national role models, the chief executive officer of one of the state's largest corporations became mother and father to three children. Joe Jr. was fifteen, Tom was twelve, and Mary Lynne was ten. Mary Lynne, recalling these years of her childhood from her perspective as the mother of two young children, appreciated even more "my All-American Dad" and how he kept the family together and thriving. During interviews about the company's history, so many people who were employed by Alabama Power during these years wanted to talk about Sheila's illness in relation to the company that it was evident it had a larger impact on Alabama Power's people than Joe Farley ever realized. Many had special stories to tell. Eason Balch remembered that "Joe never missed a Sunday getting those children to Sunday school." Alan Martin recalled one day: "Mr. Farley was late. I could hear him walking fast down the hall. He stopped in my door to explain, 'Alan, I know I am a little late, but it's my car pool day.'" And when some executives drove shiny sedans, Farley's was a weathered station wagon with one hubcap off.[76]

Although different people in the company remembered the story in slightly different words, a comment Joe Farley made in one corporate meeting must have flown along the office grapevine, for it was never forgotten. During a discussion of ways the company could be saved, someone suggested cutting salaries and letting people go. Farley replied, "We are not in this because our employees have done something wrong. And we are not going to get out of this on their backs. When we do get out of this, and we will, we will need them behind us, and we are going to take care of our employees."[77]

Public Relations and Government Affairs

In July 1978 Alabama Power Company hired Stephen E. Bradley as assistant vice president with responsibility for the company's information program. This move came about after polls showed the company had a poor image in the state and an outside consultant told Alabama Power that it must repair its corporate reputation with the public. Bradley, who was working under executive vice president Jesse S. Vogtle, was born in Birmingham, raised in Florence, and educated in journalism at the University

Stephen E. Bradley

of Alabama.[78] After jobs in California and Texas, he returned home in 1974 to be executive director of the Alabama Press Association. Bradley witnessed the attacks on the company from his position with the press association. He had opposed Wallace's anti-utility legislation, which would have prevented advertising, and the Public Service Commission's ban on advertising as a legitimate business expense, which caused his press membership to lose money. In Bradley's opinion, the company's presence in Montgomery had somewhat declined, and after 1978 it increased.[79] Jesse Vogtle was confident that Bradley had "all the tools we needed to start a public relations program, which we had never had before. All the media knew him and respected him." Joe Farley gives Bradley credit for "insisting that [the media] treat us fairly."[80]

Bradley was a detail person, very aggressive and well suited for leadership at this time. During the fight, Bradley was allied with Vogtle and Clark Richardson, whom Jesse Vogtle had brought in as the manager of state governmental affairs. Richardson was a Eufaula native and a true southern gentleman, very low key, with a smooth style. He was a dynamic individual with a reputation for integrity and was knowledgeable about Montgomery politics. He was also effective.[81] Two other men who were associated with Alabama Power's increased presence in Montgomery were Neal Wade and Bob Geddie. Wade was a Samford University history graduate who was interested in politics, public relations, and lobbying. He worked for Albert Brewer and Sid McDonald and was recruited to Alabama Power by Bradley in 1978.[82] Wade was extremely bright and creative, and Bradley considered him "the perfect person to carry out the nuts and bolts of a public affairs/public relations group." Geddie was considered one of the best governmental relations people in the state. He was extremely smart, had an uncanny insight into people, and was a creative thinker as well as a student of political history. He worked in a smooth, calm manner and was a likable individual. By 1985 Geddie and Joe Fine had combined to form one of the most successful lobbying partnerships in Montgomery.[83]

In 1978 Steve Bradley knew there needed to be one voice for the company, and he decided to place a public relations representative in each division to co-ordinate Alabama Power's messages. The divisional vice presidents were powerful and some viewed Bradley's decision as infringing on their authority, but Farley and Vogtle supported Bradley through these turf wars. Despite everything, Bradley believed "we accomplished a lot, but we would not have succeeded if Farley and Vogtle had not stood behind me." In reorganizing public relations, Bradley was especially concerned over internal communications, because he knew anything published internally would find its way outside the company. Bradley emphasized communications with employees and made certain they understood company positions and that the company knew what employees felt they needed to know.[84] While Southern Company was concerned about this "street fighter," as Bradley described himself, Southern's president Alvin Vogtle, perhaps despite some possible complaints, left Bradley, Farley, and his brother Jesse Vogtle alone.[85]

The next step Bradley took was to deal with newspapers that were printing untrue, incomplete, or biased stories about Alabama Power. "We were," he recalled, "going to call their hand publicly on it." Alabama Power had not been aggressively responsive to the media. Many times reporters failed to ask the company for a comment on a story, and sometimes when the media did contact Alabama Power for information, it took so long to get a response that the story was already written. Bradley hired Chris Conway, a Birmingham-Southern College graduate and well-respected *Birmingham Post-Herald* reporter with an excellent knowledge of state government. Bradley put Conway in the Southern Division where he could be close to capital offices.[86]

Bradley traveled the state to visit newspaper offices and speak directly with editors and reporters. He explained that the company would answer their questions, would not ignore their phone calls, and would tell the good with the bad. He gave out his office and home phone numbers and those of his top staff members and told the media that Alabama Power's representatives would be available seven days a week, twenty-four hours a day. Joe Farley let employees know that all media inquiries would be forwarded to public relations, and a form was designed for quick response to questions. He also told engineers to cooperate with public relations and furnish in a timely way the information requested.[87]

Under the new program, Alabama Power would respond immediately to an inaccurate story with a letter to the editor, a call to the editor, a press conference, or an op-ed piece giving the full and complete information. The Associated Press was also a problem because stories written by its Montgomery staff were often skewed and inaccurate and these stories went statewide. Bradley leased an AP and UPI wire machine for the public relations office and had one person reading every story that came off the machine. The company was thus able to respond to attacks and inaccurate articles immediately, not waiting until the story appeared in print.[88]

In the gubernatorial election of 1978, with Wallace constitutionally barred from running, political pundits decided one of the "three B's" would win—Attorney General Bill Baxley, Lieutenant Governor Jere Beasley, or former governor Albert Brewer. However, a newcomer, given little chance by prognosticators, rode a yellow school bus over the state campaigning for better education for children, led the ticket, and defeated Baxley in the runoff. Forrest James Jr., called Fob, was a former Republican recently turned Democrat for this race and better known as an Auburn football player, state highway

Governor Fob James

engineer, and millionaire entrepreneur. No one knew what kind of governor he would be. During the campaign, James made statements about Alabama Power that disturbed Joe Farley, and since he had known James when the Lee County businessman had been active in state Republican politics, Farley went to Opelika in the summer of 1978 and visited with James to explain the inaccurate statements made against the company and the erroneous perceptions the public had about rate making and Alabama Power's financial difficulties. They had a candid and cordial conversation. Farley hoped that in the James administration the tensions between the governor's office and Alabama Power Company would go away and there could be a serious consideration of the issues.[89]

After the 1979 Alabama legislature authorized corporations to solicit "voluntary contributions to a separate, segregated fund to be utilized for political purposes," the Alabama Power board of directors created a state political action committee to support candidates with positions favorable to the company.[90] Called the Alabama Power Company Employees State Political Action Committee, some 2,000 employees joined to let legislators know how employees viewed proposed legislation. The committee's leadership carefully considers candidates and issues, but by company policy it does not contribute to candidates running for or employed by the Public Service Commission.[91] The federal political action committee predates the state committee and supports candidates for president and the U.S. Congress. By law, the corporation may pay for administrative costs of the political action committees.[92]

The Governor's Complaint Case Decided

Meanwhile, on the national scene, the short recession in 1976 temporarily calmed the nation's inflation, but after President Carter's inauguration in 1977, prices and interest rates increased in a dizzying ascent. When the Organization of Petroleum Exporting Countries (OPEC) nearly doubled prices in 1979, inflation shot above 13 percent. By 1980 the prime interest rate would reach 20 percent.[93] Alabama Power's financial condition continued to decline through 1978. The legislature finally passed some utility laws, but they were ones under which the company could survive, including a law that PSC decisions could be appealed directly to the Alabama Supreme Court, cutting months or years off the old appeal process through the circuit court. The legislature also required utilities to give property owners near a plant site notice of the application for a certificate of convenience and necessity, but transmission lines were excluded. Another act changed the way reasonable value of a public utility's property was determined when used as the rate base. The formula was "original cost thereof less accrued depreciation as of the most recent date available."[94]

In November 1978, constitutional amendment 373 reduced the commercial property ratio from 25 to 20 percent and the Class III assessment from 15 to 10 percent, but kept utilities at 30 percent. That month, the governor's complaint, plodding through fifteen months of hearings, and continuous briefings, all well reported in the newspapers, had become ripe for an order at the Public Service Commission. On November 22, the PSC found that the company's rates were deficient, not excessive as Wallace had alleged, and the company was entitled to an increase. The PSC characterized the proceedings as an emergency rate increase and ordered the company to add a surcharge to its existing rate schedules amounting to 25 percent, which was designed to achieve, prospectively, a 12.27 percent return on common equity. Commissioners McDaniel and Zeigler signed the order; Whatley did not join. Zeigler and Whatley were lame ducks, and it looked as though the PSC would defer any more decisions until after January 1979, when the newly elected commissioners would take their seats and a new governor was inaugurated.[95]

Immediately after the PSC granted the surcharge in November 1978, Governor Wallace and Attorney General Bill Baxley filed complaints in Montgomery circuit court asking for an injunction to suspend the 25 percent rate surcharge. The circuit court issued the injunction on November 28, and Alabama Power appealed to the Alabama Supreme Court. Joe Farley was concerned with the financial crisis looming, especially because units 1 at Plant Farley and at Plant Miller were both going into service. Alabama Power asked the Alabama Supreme Court to allow it to put the rates into effect or into effect under bond. On the same date the filing was made at the supreme court, on December 20, 1978, Alabama Power filed a new rate application at the PSC, this one for a $288.8 million retail rate increase.[96]

On January 4, 1979, the Alabama Supreme Court on a five to four vote denied Alabama Power Company's request to lift the injunction. There was a strong dissent by Justice Hugh A. Maddox because, he stated, the circuit court had no authority to issue an injunction since cases were to come directly to the supreme court.[97] Wallace had only a few weeks remaining in his term, and Baxley was also leaving office. The Birmingham News reported both the governor and attorney general had admitted privately "that the rate increase is needed and inevitable" but both were determined to delay any rate increase until after they left office and the blame could then fall on Governor-elect Fob James.[98] Bill Baxley, in reviewing this time period from the distance of twenty-six years, confessed that although he found very little he would change about his actions and decisions over his political career, his attitude toward Alabama Power Company during this period was one he wished "I could take back."[99]

George Wallace left office and Fob James was inaugurated governor on January 15, 1979. Three days later, on January 18, the Alabama Supreme Court issued a group of orders by eight to one votes refusing to hear Alabama Power's appeal because the "commission did not afford due notice to all interested parties."[100] The court also held that the commission's rate orders were void, then dismissed all appeals. Justice Maddox dissented again. At this stage of its long struggle, Alabama Power was left without any rate relief, earning a record low rate of return, and looking for help from a new PSC in a brand new rate case. Clearly, Alabama Power had to take severe cutback steps immediately.

Before the new year began, Alvin W. Vogtle Jr., president of Southern Company, announced that not one of Southern Company's four operating companies had earned in 1978 what regulatory officials in the four-state area had established as "a reasonable return on our investment."[101] Alabama Power had placed a freeze on officers' salaries, shut down construction sites, and delayed the completion of the second nuclear unit at the Farley plant. The Alabama Power corporate newsletter, *Powergrams*, announced it was reducing the size of the publication, was not using color, had discontinued travel to research stories, and was delivering the newsletter through company mail.[102] On December 29, 1978, Alabama Power announced that it had lost $2.9 million in November, its twelve-month income was down $88 million, and it was beginning a statewide shutdown of construction projects and layoffs of personnel. The company was "facing mounting financial problems because a rate increase had been blocked by a court order since November 28," and it was having to borrow money through short-term bank loans to pay its ad valorem taxes. The company sent checks totaling $21,588,377.50 to sixty-three counties and 243 municipalities. The cash shortage, Joe Farley reported, was "becoming more critical every day." The company would owe $20 million more in the first three months of 1979 to pay municipal license fees to 245 cities or towns.[103] At the end of 1978, Alabama Power's return on common equity was "a disastrous 4.5 percent," and that return was mostly related to noncash accounting items. In order to acquire cash, Alabama Power negotiated the sale of five of its office buildings and leased back the buildings, "an expensive measure, necessitated by its need for cash."[104]

The year 1979 was difficult for Alabama Power Company. Mac Beale recalled that in these hard times Jack Minor, the comptroller, was called the "Administrator of Austerity." Company traveling was curtailed. Memberships in industry organizations and attendance at conferences were things of the past. No one was happy. Minor remembered that at one time the company had "$45 million in unpaid bills. We could not borrow money, could not sell stocks or bonds. We had five big vendors, and any one of them could have put us under." Elmer Harris, vice president for corporate finance and planning, told Minor "to stack all those invoices on that conference table. If anyone demands their money, pull that invoice and pay them. When other invoices come in, pile them on the table, too. Don't pay them until someone demands payment." Many people remembered that large table in Jack Minor's office on the eleventh floor stacked high with bills, all organized in groups by 30, 60, 90, and 120 days due. Minor was aware that some in the law firm were anticipating where the company was headed and were making contingency plans, but Farley and his team did not intend to fail. The word was passed: Alabama Power was not going under. It would remember those vendors who helped it through the hard times and would also remember those vendors who did not. There were some vendors from whom Alabama Power annually had purchased thousands of dollars of supplies, but because of their lack of support during this critical time, the company never did business with them again.[105]

In January 1979, *Birmingham News* reporter Tom Scarritt interviewed Joe Farley and asked him if over the past ten years Alabama Power had been asking for too much in rate increases since the company was still in business and the lights were still on. Farley explained that when "we are hurting for money, the lights don't go off in the next hour. It's difficult for us to bring home to the public that the results of the problems we face are often a year or two or three away." He explained that the company was entitled by law to a reasonable return and faced "a very hostile state government" and that "continued harassment has damaged the company's credit and has increased its cost of capital." This, he explained, had offset the advantage of strong hydroelectric facilities. He warned that all the Alabama hydro sites had either been built upon or were under construction, and that the percentage of generation from less expensive hydro plants would grow smaller as demand forced more production from coal and nuclear facilities. In discussing growth, he noted that most of the increase in electrical usage came from residential customers expanding their usage. Frost-free refrigerators, self-cleaning ovens, color TV, and air conditioning required more electricity.[106] A Montgomery customer agreed with Farley, pointing out that consumers were responsible for their high bills, had control over the power they used, and could reduce their bills by turning off their air conditioners and television sets.[107]

On January 24, 1979, Cumberland School of Law hosted a debate between Alabama Power's Steve Bradley and attorney Maurice Bishop. Bradley began his introductory remarks by giving Bishop a ribbon-wrapped copy of the Price Waterhouse study on Alabama Power. Bishop declined the gift, saying he had a copy. Bradley and Bishop differed on every point, with Bishop hammering the company on its profits, payments to expert witnesses in rate cases, and return on investments. Bradley countered with different statistics and interpretations, noting the 1977–78 Public Service Commission hearings cost the PSC $1.5 million and emphasized that the consequences of delayed decisions stressed the company and hurt the consumer by forcing greater increased rates by 1980.[108]

The membership of the PSC had changed in January 1979, and the new commissioners were faced with the problems left from December 1978, the new rate filing by Alabama Power and the vigorous dissent of Justice Hugh Maddox to the supreme court's refusal to hear the company's appeal. Pete Mathews, a former Clay County legislator, and Jim Folsom Jr., son of Governor "Big Jim" Folsom, had been elected to the commission. Folsom was working in public relations with Reynolds Aluminum in Florence in the fall of 1977 when he decided to run for the PSC, despite being told that politically it was a dead-end street. No one was interested in running because of the current conflict over utility rates and the demagoguery that had dominated the commission for almost a decade. Glenn Browder, a Jacksonville State University political scientist, was an adviser to Folsom's campaign, and Folsom did not run as a demagogue nor did he advocate lowering utility rates. His platform was to have a professional approach with decisions based upon the best advice possible.[109]

Pete Mathews joined Folsom and commission president Juanita McDaniel. Mathews, who had practiced law in his hometown of Ashland before serving twelve years in the legislature, was a venerable politician known for his wit and storytelling. Folsom described as "pure chaos" his first Public Service Commission meeting, which was moved to an auditorium to accommodate the crowd. The hearing was on the company's new rate filing. There were TV cameras and crews from every station in the state and newspaper reporters with pads in hand. The legislature had convened in the capitol, but the media were covering the Public Service Commission hearing. At the end of the first day, Mathews invited Folsom to his office, shut the door, and said, "Jim, we have arrived here at a bad time." Folsom responded, "I think you are right." Folsom recalled that as he listened to testimony and cross-examination and heard reports from the PSC staff it was evident to him that "the company was in dire need of rate relief," but the "question for a young ambitious politician at that time was, how to accomplish that without committing complete political suicide?"[110]

Soon after Governor James took office, he called Joe Farley and invited him to Montgomery to discuss Alabama Power's problems and rate making. Farley took Elmer Harris with him. When the two walked into the governor's office on February 9, 1979, they found the public service commissioners already there. Fob James, in a practical, take-charge manner, had invited everyone and suggested they sit down and solve the problems. The commissioners looked bewildered and more so when the governor's secretary announced that the press was outside and wanted to come in. The governor said no, and shut the door. Farley recalled wondering who was the most uncomfortable—he and Harris or the commissioners—and speculating on just how many Alabama laws were being broken. As Farley observed, "Something good came out of this two-hour meeting. The governor was trying to solve everyone's problems, and he was not trying to bully anybody. The governor thought it was in the state's best interest to have the matter speedily resolved and in the public's interest to have the matter fairly resolved."[111]

The first six months of 1979 were described by Joe Farley as "the most serious financial crisis since the earliest days of [the company's] 74-year history." Alabama Power stopped its generation construction and released over time "about 4,000 construction craft workers, contract personnel, and company employees."[112] John Jones, senior vice president of

PSC administrative law judge Carl Evans, left, Commission president Juanita McDaniel, and commissioner Jim Folsom Jr., 1979.

construction, explained the situation was an unknown for the company because it had never shut down a construction site before and could only estimate what it would cost and what would be the cost of reopening the site.[113] On March 6, 1979, the PSC granted Alabama Power an emergency rate increase of $81.9 million of the $288 million annual retail rate increase request filed on December 20, 1978.[114] On July 19, 1979, PSC commissioners McDaniel, Folsom, and Mathews granted additional relief to the company totaling approximately $208 million annually. Both Alabama Power and intervenors appealed to the supreme court, which allowed a portion of the increase to be collected subject to refund.[115] But the immediate increase helped immensely and allowed some construction work to resume.

Plant Farley

Within a short time, unit 1 of Plant Farley achieved a national reputation for its performance record. The initial fuel loading in July 1977 was credited with being the "most efficient nuclear fuel loading of any large power reactor in the United States." Plant Farley created a record 87.1 percent operational time during its first nine months, while the U.S. average for nuclear plants was 63.9. Plant Farley produced 81.7 percent of its total potential capacity, while the national average for nuclear plants during the first year of operation was only 54.1 percent. The plant was operated by George Hairston, plant manager, Jack Woodard, assistant plant manager, and Dan Poole, operations superintendent. Lee Williams was training supervisor. All of the managers, as well as other plant managers and workers, had an extensive background in nuclear operations and were educated in nuclear technology.[116] The dedication of the nuclear plant to honor Joseph McConnell Farley and his leadership of Alabama Power Company was held on July 10, 1981.[117]

With a background of such excellent performance, Plant Farley and Alabama Power Company were still affected, as was the nation, by an event hundreds of miles away in Pennsylvania. At 4 A.M. on March 28, 1979, a problem with a safety valve occurred at Metropolitan Edison's nuclear plant on Three Mile Island on the Susquehanna River in Pennsylvania. Emergency procedures were initiated, but a series of human and mechanical failures followed, resulting in a partial core meltdown. Two days later a small amount of radioactive gases was released, and the governor of Pennsylvania advised that pregnant women and families with small children should evacuate the area. Fear spread as stories circulated about alleged dangers. Many proved to be inaccurate. At this time, Alabama Power's unit 1 at Plant Farley had operated reliably and safely for seventeen months, and unit 2 was under construction with an anticipated in-service date of late 1980. Immediately after the Three Mile Island accident, Southern Company organized a nuclear safety review task force to investigate the major operational and safety systems of the holding company's nuclear plants. Engineers and consultants from private industry and the academic community were involved. The first report was announced at press conferences in Birmingham and Atlanta on July 23. The task force found that the plants were "designed and operated with large margins of safety," but the task force did make twenty recommendations, all of which had already been implemented before the press conference or were in the process of being implemented.[118]

R. Patrick "Pat" McDonald served on Southern Company's task force. McDonald was vice president of nuclear generation for Alabama Power Company, and in the month following the Three Mile Island accident he answered a number of questions from the Alabama media about the operational and safety features of Plant Farley. McDonald was one of the most talented and experienced engineers in the nuclear field. He had spent twenty-two years in the U.S. Navy, including nineteen years in the nuclear program. He assured Alabamians that Alabama Power's plant had "a different design and different operating parameters and operating instructions" and the likelihood of such an accident at Farley was "very, very remote." Plant Farley was "designed with multiple redundant safety features . . . [and] is extremely safe."[119]

In 1979, while the company's nuclear engineers were dealing with the public relations problems resulting from the Three Mile Island incident, Alabama Power's hydro engineers were struggling to maintain control of the water levels in the company's reservoirs. Heavy winter and spring rains in February and March had saturated the ground, and creeks and rivers were swollen. Alabama Power always followed flood control procedures developed by the U.S. Army Corps of Engineers. The Alabama control and dispatch center had constant current data on river levels and normally was able to anticipate high waters flowing downstream and to drop lake levels by full hydro generation. But it was impossible to accurately predict exact rainfall levels. On Friday, April 13, a torrential downpour began that affected the entire state from northern Alabama to the Gulf Coast. Flood conditions were mitigated by Alabama Power holding as much water as possible behind its dams, but eventually engineers had to open floodgates to protect most of the dams when the reservoirs were full.[120]

A Hurricane Named Frederic

In September 1979 Alabama was keeping a watchful eye on a storm roaring through the Gulf of Mexico toward the Florida Panhandle and Mobile Bay. The storm named Frederic was expected to hit land on the night of September 12, and Alabama Power knew it was a serious and destructive hurricane. Workers in the southeastern part of the state were notified to be ready to go to Mobile. William L. "Bill" McDonough, vice president of the Mobile Division and a Vanderbilt-educated engineer, had everyone check emergency supplies

At the time, Hurricane Frederic's destruction was the worst storm damage ever to a U.S. electric utility.

Robert H. Haubein

Robin Hurst

J. Bruce Jones

William L. McDonough

and had windows boarded where possible. Division manager Robert H. "Bob" Haubein told Robin Hurst that he thought a group should spend the night at the company headquarters to handle media inquiries and answer the telephones. Haubein was a University of Missouri electrical engineer who joined Alabama Power in 1967. He had directed Alabama Power's efforts to help Mississippi Power after Hurricane Camille and was familiar with restoration work. Hurst was an electrical engineer with a degree from the University of South Alabama who grew up in Mobile County. He was hired by Ben W. Hutson, who was the Mobile Division manager in 1971, then had been assigned to Thomasville, Eufaula, and Birmingham and in the fall of 1979 was back in Mobile.[121]

J. Bruce Jones recalled that the decision was made to move employee cars to the Merchants Bank parking deck because the company lot would surely flood. Crews were sent home early in the afternoon and told "to go get some sleep." Frederic was the first test of the new General Services Complex south of Birmingham. Alabama Power already had loaded 60,000 pounds of emergency supplies before the storm arrived. Roy Jones was at the service complex that day, and he recalled "everything that could be cranked, towed, or pushed was loaded and headed south." Georgia Power men and trucks were moving south from Atlanta. Eventually 125 men came from Georgia. Mississippi Power and Gulf Power expected to have their own problems, but Gulf Power and Florida Power were prepared to send help toward Mobile if they were spared. Birmingham immediately sent seven power delivery crews and made plans to dispatch more as soon as any damage in Birmingham, Tuscaloosa, and Montgomery was repaired. Bill McDonough remembered that the Georgia Power crews had done this before and knew how to get maximum publicity. The caravan stopped short of Mobile for the storm to pass, washed their trucks, purchased snacks and supplies, then rolled "into Mobile with flags flying."[122]

The entire state watched reports of the storm's movements on television or listened to the radio, but Alabama Power's people were particularly focused. The hurricane named Frederic blew over Dauphin Island with winds of 145 miles an hour and moved directly through the city of Mobile, its eye crushed by pressure into an ellipse that saved the city from an eastern storm surge that would have brought devastating floods in addition to the catastrophic wind damage.[123] Paula Blevins-Russell worked the phones in the Mobile customer service center until 2 A.M. At the height of the hurricane she took a call from a customer who wanted to know when Alabama Power could get her lights back on. Just as Blevins-Russell was trying to tell her there was a hurricane hitting Mobile, the windows in the customer service center shattered from the storm with a loud crashing sound, startling the customer on the telephone. Somehow, the woman had no idea she was in the middle of a hurricane. John Hart shoved a refrigerator against a window, and the wind blew it over. Haubein recalled that not only did windows blow in, but the building started shaking, and he moved everyone away from the windows into the safest, strongest area of the building, worrying that they all were going to be killed.[124]

The Mobile Division management staff expected the worst, but what they saw at daylight on September 13 was still a shock. Roofs gone. Trees, power poles, and lines down and streets impassable. Devastation was everywhere. Governor Fob James, who had ridden out the storm in a Department of Public Safety command trailer at Spanish Fort, took to the air to inspect the damage at dawn and reported that the destruction was "impossible to believe unless you saw it." Haubein recalled that Governor James bypassed the media and came first to the Alabama Power command center to ask what he could do to help. Division engineers said, "we need a helicopter." He found one for them.[125] Division vice president Bill McDonough and Bob Haubein had 90 percent of their area without electricity, 5,550 transformers destroyed, and 2,700 poles down or snapped. Every transmission line into Mobile was down. Some 290,000 customers, almost one-third of Alabama Power's total system, were without power. McDonough recalls thinking at the time, "I don't believe I'll ever get this back together."[126] Bruce Jones, who was Mobile Division engineering manager then, looked back in 2006 and recalled that restoring the system after Frederic was analogous to going to war: "there was a common enemy and everybody had to pull together."[127] Joe Webb, district manager at Atmore, Bob McCloud, district manager at Theodore, and Bob Martin, divisional operations manager, were significant to the restoration.[128] With the financial condition of the company so weak, bringing in crews from around the nation and outside the Southern Company system would be too costly. That left the responsibility for rebuilding the system to the company's own people. Eventually, Alabama Power had 2,000 men and women in Mobile doing restoration work.[129]

Alabama Power families were as hard hit as everyone else, but as soon as the company's people had their families safe, sometimes with a tarp on the roof, they left downed trees and storm clutter in their own yards, as well as homes without electricity, and went to work getting the power back on for the company's customers. One worker shrugged off such dedication as just "part of the Alabama Power Company tradition." Division heating specialist Gerald "Mike" Strachan, who was told before the storm that division personnel should come in at 6 A.M., awoke to find a huge tree on top of his car. At 5 A.M. he started walking toward the office, some five miles away, the only person on the street. He ended up being driven downtown by a policeman, who stopped him thinking he might be a looter.[130]

The Mobile plan was to restore "priority projects" first–hospitals, radio stations, and water and sewage lift pumps. Downed trees caused the most extensive and severe destruction. The distribution line crews were repairing lines as quickly as they could, but the transmission lines had been destroyed, and no lights could come on until the transmission system was connected. Poor weather continued for another twenty-four hours, so planes could not check transmission lines that ran through swamps. Luckily, Chickasaw and Barry Steam Plants suffered only slight damage. After frustrating hours of trying to restore the power supply, a transmission line near the Tensaw River was found severed. Alabama Power's engineers used creativity to get the main feeder lines back on and to energize the substations. A great deal of improvising and spur-of-the-moment planning was done so power could be restored. Robin Hurst recalled

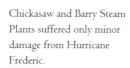

Chickasaw and Barry Steam Plants suffered only minor damage from Hurricane Frederic.

this was the first time the company used automatic line splices, and they worked well, speeding up the repairs.[131]

McDonough had been sent to Mobile in January 1970 to replace R. E. Pride, who had retired. Joe Farley gave McDonough instructions to concentrate on improving Alabama Power's community image in Mobile, where the company's relationship with the newspapers was not always good. The loss of power from Frederic could make things worse. Steve Bradley sent Judy Stone from Birmingham to work with Ed Crosby, who was in charge of public relations for the Mobile Division. Stone and Crosby, McDonough recalled, made the leadership of the Mobile Division respond to the media. After the storm, Griffin Lassiter went to work in Mobile on public relations. To coordinate the storm work, Robin Hurst and Bruce Jones color-coded photo maps of the service area as repair work was completed, and the media could see and report the day-by-day progress. They also came up with the number of customers still without power, and each day the number was lowered. Haubein remembered that the map and the number became important in allowing customers to see how fast the company was working.[132]

Everyone put in twelve to sixteen hours a day for three weeks. At first food was plentiful as folks cleaned out their quickly defrosting freezers and held neighborhood "after-hurricane cookouts" and fed Alabama Power crews working in their areas. The Mobile Division's staff, including Ken Sanders, Barbara Taylor, Suzanne Snypes, and Muriel Boykin, made lunches and cooked at the office, getting breakfast ready at 2:30 A.M. each day, while they also helped keep track of hours and work. Morrison's catered some meals, served unshelled shrimp, and Carlos McKnight recalled watching a Georgia Power lineman, who had obviously never eaten shrimp, trying to eat shells and all. By the end of the first week, however, there was an acute shortage of food in Mobile, and Alabama Power was sending box lunches from Birmingham and Montgomery to its crews. Governor James went on statewide radio and television to ask people to please bring food to National Guard armories and the state would deliver it to Mobile. The outpouring of food donations was amazing.[133]

One set of exhausted Georgia Power crewmen returned to their motel to find it without water or lights, so they got back in their truck, traced the line until they found the trouble, fixed it, and went back to a lighted room. Initially, there was difficulty locating motel rooms for all the crews coming into the area. The city was running out of hotel beds, and Alabama Power did not have enough space to direct the restoration work. The Mobile mayor arranged for the company to use the city auditorium, found 350 army cots, sheets, and towels, and what the crews called "the Empty Arms Hotel" opened for guests.[134]

There was trouble keeping all the trucks filled with fuel. At first utility crews were standing in line waiting for gasoline, ice, and water along with the public. This problem was solved when John Parker, support services manager, acquired a small gasoline tanker truck and went around at night filling up bucket and utility trucks in motel parking lots. Since there were many tree-trimming companies in town, with some working for the telephone company and some for Alabama Power, it was hard to tell which trucks were contracted by the power company, but if it looked like a utility truck, Parker recalled, he put gas in the tank. Georgia Power crews came in with diesel trucks, and diesel fuel was harder to find. Alabama Power personnel put out a call for diesel fuel, and in thirty minutes they had it.[135]

The bridge to Dauphin Island had been destroyed. Almost all of the 44-kV transmission structures to the island were down or heavily damaged and replacing them would take months. N. L. Fields and Bud Robertson from Mobile district operations helped Ronnie Landry, local operations lineman, and local manager John Crist of Bayou La Batre get electricity restored to customers on Dauphin Island. With no transmission line to the island, Alabama Power set up a generation plant on leased land behind a high fence. The small 480-volt system served 300 customers, and as McDonough noted, "Alabama Power was selling electricity to islanders for half what it cost us to generate it." The company leased a house for a mechanic to look after the generator and a local operations lineman to look after the lines on the island. Each one stood a twelve-hour shift, and the two-man crew was swapped every week. Supplies and fuel came by a two-hour ferry ride from Fowl River. Six years later Hurricane Elena hit the island again, but the bridge was not washed away and electricity was quickly restored to the island. After Hurricane Frederic, transmission line engineer Dale Beason designed concrete caissons, which were driven into the floor of the bay; wooden poles were then placed into these caissons to hold the transmission lines. Although some poles were damaged by Hurricane Elena, the company did not lose a single caisson.[136]

While Mobile was the hardest hit by Frederic, the storm also damaged the company's systems in Jasper, Tuscaloosa, and Birmingham. Joe Farley reported that "some 2,100 storm repair workers and support personnel were on the job virtually around the clock." After the first day, experts estimated it would take three months to get the electrical system back up, but "in just twenty-one days of almost superhuman effort, power was restored to nearly every customer."[137] It was, however, months before all the creative and temporary solutions that restored power were reworked into permanent repairs. During the restoration work, Alabama Power's people absolutely took notice of one very obvious thing: the Georgia Power Company trucks that came into Mobile were newer and Georgia Power equipment more modern than Alabama Power's trucks and equipment, the result of a financially strapped Alabama company strangulated by inadequate returns and exhausted from a decade of rate fights.[138]

Alabama Power Company's *Annual Report* for 1979 claimed that Hurricane Frederic's destruction was the worst storm damage ever to a U.S. electric utility.[139] The stories of Hurricane Frederic illustrate the restoration work the company routinely accomplished in ice storms, thunderstorms, and tornadoes—just more severe and more extensive. Hurricane Frederic is also significant because it marked a turning point in the company's history. New and more detailed storm plans were made, and a schedule was created for cutting and trimming trees on a regular basis, something that had been eliminated in the budget crunch. System-wide cooperation was more formalized. The company also realized that it needed service trucks and bucket trucks that could better drive long distances on interstate highways and that had larger fuel tanks. Some of Alabama Power's trucks broke down en route to Mobile.[140]

After more than ten years of being a whipping boy for state politicians, castigated by some media, and criticized by a public swayed by populist rhetoric, Alabama Power received accolades from every quarter for its storm restoration work. Customers applauded the company and sent heartfelt thanks to its people. Not only were the company's employees praised for working heroically to restore electricity to storm-damaged areas, but they were also thanked for working with professionalism and heart. The public appreciated the company's honest communications during the restoration.

From this crisis some people learned that it took "four or five dollars worth of gasoline" and a lot of work to run a generator for less than a day to keep a refrigerator operating. Sam Covert of the Mobile office noted that after Frederic, people had a better understanding that Alabama Power Company was about providing comforts and improving the quality of life. After the storm, Alabama Power's rates seemed more equitable. Governor Fob James, who had once lived in Mobile when he was an engineer for the State Highway Department, publicly praised Alabama Power Company for accomplishing a miracle in rebuilding almost an entire system in twenty-one days. He thanked "the men and women that work for the Alabama Power Company," who, he said, "have probably done the greatest job that's ever been done after any disaster in restoring power."[141] Governor James was a surprise guest at the October employee meeting of the Montgomery district, and he took the opportunity once again to thank the employees for their valiant restoration work. Afterward one Alabama Power Company employee remarked, "It made us feel good, after those long days and nights of hard work, to know that Governor James appreciated what we did."[142]

A New Decade

Alabama Power Company ended the 1970s with one more rate increase filing. On December 28, 1979, the company filed a revised schedule of rates based on the test year ending November 30, 1979. In January 1980 Elmer Harris explained that the rate increase of the previous July was not sufficient to relieve Alabama Power's financial problems. "Until we can get our earnings above minimum requirements, we will have to depend on short-term debt. Not only is this more expensive, but we are limited in the amount we can borrow."[143] These new rates, which would bring revenues of $122.3 million, would help offset national inflation of 12–14 percent, short-term interest rates of 15–20 percent, and the expense of repairing the damage of Hurricane Frederic and restoring service to the state and especially to the Mobile area. Hearings began in March 1980 and were concluded in June. In August the Public Service Commission granted $30.6 million of the request, and Alabama Power appealed to the supreme court because that amount was insufficient by the record.[144]

Jerry Stewart

The political attacks on the company and its financial starvation during the 1970s deeply affected Alabama Power. Jerry L. Stewart, a University of Alabama graduate who started his career with Alabama Power in 1972, was then a young engineer at Barry Steam Plant and later was assigned to the Gaston Steam Plant. Stewart believed the emotional scars left on the company's people were more devastating than the effects of the slowed construction of generation, the deterioration of equipment, and the reduced ability of the company to move forward. "In the old days," Stewart recalled, "no one had credit cards, and you had to write a check at the grocery store. When you did, they asked you where you worked. We all learned to whisper 'Alabama Power Company' so no one else would hear."[145] Roland Cotton, working out of the Southern Division, once had two carts loaded with groceries when the clerk found out he worked for Alabama Power and started berating him. Cotton walked out of the store leaving his unpaid food behind. Jone Davis, whose father "Strut" Burnett joined Alabama Power Company at Gadsden in 1930 and whose husband Rayford began working for the company in Montevallo in the summer of 1955, remembers that in the 1970s when she went to circle club or garden club "all the ladies wanted to talk about was big bad Alabama Power Company." Davis was always proud of the company, and she wanted to do something to help its image. But, she said, "as soon as the media let it go and went on to something else, people forgot."[146]

Alan Martin analyzed the result of those years this way: "The enduring effect was positive. Those who lived through those years were like the World War II generation. We were tougher. Our leadership has been real conservative, but when the company is criticized, we are quick to jump like a tiger to defend it." Robin Hurst explained that in those hard days "we didn't have the luxury of prioritizing things. We just had to put things on the bottom of the stack and service off the top. Customers got mad at us. Today we can take care of our customers' needs."[147]

The 1980s began with a long, hot summer and a high volume of sales. The company's all-time peak (to that time), 7.2 million kilowatts, was reached on July 15, 1980. Rebuilt Bouldin Dam returned to service in late 1980, and Plant Farley's unit 2 was expected to be ready for service in mid-1981. The increased demand coupled with rate increases caused the company's return on equity to rise from less than 6 percent to 11.6 percent by the end of the year, which enabled Alabama Power to sell first-mortgage bonds in June and September 1980 and January 1981. Earnings permitted a preferred stock sale in February 1981, which was Alabama Power Company's seventy-fifth year of serving the state of Alabama.

In 1980 Alan Barton left Alabama Power to become president of Mississippi Power. Two years before, in 1978, Walter Johnsey had retired, causing a realignment of management responsibilities because the same number of executive vice presidents was not maintained. To recognize the importance of Plant Farley, Pat McDonald was named vice president for nuclear generation. Robert E. Huffman was elected vice president for operations services, and J. T. "Jim" Young, who had formerly supervised production, was made vice president of fossil/hydro generation. Price Waterhouse was invited to come back to the company and review and evaluate Alabama Power's progress in addressing the suggestions made in the initial study ordered by the state legislature in 1977. The conclusion was positive, as was the Public Service Commission's mandated audit by Touche Ross & Company of the company's fuel purchases. President Farley expressed his appreciation to the employees of Alabama Power "who have enabled the company successfully to pass through this period of stress and to make so much progress toward recovery."[148]

In the fall 1980 presidential elections, former California governor and conservative Republican Ronald Reagan swept to victory over Jimmy Carter, whose administration had been bedeviled by inflation, the Iran hostage crisis, the soaring price of oil, and his own inability to manage well. The 1980

Republican platform called for deregulation of electricity and gas production. The "Reagan Revolution" was hailed by utilities who had been opposing the National Energy Act of 1978, especially the provision requiring state regulatory agencies to establish standards of efficiency and equity and to promote conservation. The law also required electric utilities to purchase electricity from small independent generating companies, and the general concept was considered revolutionary. Power companies anticipated that Reagan, who had been associated with the industry as the spokesman for General Electric and who went to Washington to dismantle the federal bureaucracy of regulation, would favor the industry he had promoted for so long.[149]

The RICO Case

The last repercussion of the dark days of the 1970s unfolded in May 1980 when U.S. District Judge Frank McFadden began pretrial hearings in Birmingham on a much-publicized trial that Joe Farley once called "a bizarre chapter in the Wallace–Alabama Power story." Media coverage suggested it all began in May 1977 while the governor's special legislative session on utility rates was meeting. Wallace had been increasingly frustrated over his inability to force his utilities legislation through the state senate, and on May 6, 1977, the governor asked the Alabama Supreme Court for an advisory opinion on the constitutionality of his roll-back bill. A few months later, U.S. attorney J. R. Brooks began a white-collar crime unit amid media fanfare.[150] Later testimony and newspaper accounts tied the governor's failed anti-utility legislation directly to the indictment and trial that followed.[151]

A federal grand jury was convened in May 1978 as part of a probe into political corruption.[152] Rumors circulated during the eighteen months it was in session. Dozens of politicians, state legislators, lobbyists, coal operators, and public relations and real estate people were called as witnesses, and names were spread across state newspapers. Wide-ranging charges and issues to be sorted out were eventually made public, including coal contracts (some with Alabama Power), ownership of coal companies, relationships between past and present state legislators and coal companies, real estate purchases, trips to Las Vegas, loans, charges of mail and wire fraud, and a conspiracy in violation of the 1970 Racketeer Influenced and Corrupt Organizations Act (RICO), which had been written to catch the Mafia. Eventually, seven men were charged with violating the racketeering law, including brothers Garry Neil Drummond Sr. and Larry Drummond, state representative Jack Biddle, former state senators Eddie Gilmore and Joe Fine, the secretary of Drummond Company, Clyde

Clifton "Sappo" Black, and Alabama Power's former executive vice president Walter Johnsey, who had already retired. Johnsey passed Maurice Bishop in the lobby of the Frank Nelson Building, and Bishop told him to "go plead guilty." Johnsey just smiled and replied, "The truth shall prevail."[153]

Joe Fine of Russellville had been a member of the state senate's powerful commerce, transportation, and utilities committee, which for five years had refused to vote out Governor Wallace's anti-utility legislation.[154] Eddie Gilmore had chaired the committee. Although Fine had helped Wallace with his 1968 presidential campaign, he broke with Wallace over local issues and the governor's earlier utility legislation, contending that, among other things, Wallace was not concerned with the consumer. The federal government claimed that Fine's investments in the coal industry caused him to oppose Wallace's legislation and that Fine had received inside information on the power company's coal needs.[155]

The case went to trial in May 1980 after the longest jury selection process federal judge Frank McFadden had ever experienced. The seventeen defense attorneys and three federal prosecutors filled all available space in the courtroom that witnessed what *Birmingham Post-Herald* reporter Jim Nesbitt called "complex, colorful, time-consuming" testimony and "high drama."[156] During opening arguments it was evident that prosecutors intended to show that the bribery charges were linked to the bitter legislative fights in 1975 and 1977 "that led to defeats of the Wallace package." Biddle's defense attorney announced in opening arguments that Governor Wallace would testify as a character witness for Biddle, who claimed he had not opposed the governor's legislation. Former lieutenant governor Jere Beasley's name was thrown into the mix, but he denied all allegations. Joe Farley was subpoenaed and questioned by the prosecution. On cross-examination, he testified about the punitive nature of Governor Wallace's utilities package, saying "it would have interfered seriously with our ability to keep the lights on." Farley detailed Johnsey's duties with Alabama Power and said that although Johnsey was responsible for the records of coal purchases, he had nothing to do with the actual transactions, which were handled by the fuel division and a branch of Southern Company.[157] Farley might also have added that Alan Barton, who was responsible for fuel purchases and contracts, would never have allowed Johnsey to have undue influence. Barton later testified that Johnsey "had no impact" on coal service contracts.[158]

One of the government's claims was that prostitutes were provided to legislators, but Judge McFadden ordered one government witness to testify first in closed court without the jury. She was identified by name in the newspapers as a former Birmingham prostitute who was serving time in a New York prison. Among other things, she was supposed to know some of those indicted, but on the stand she failed to identify anyone correctly. Perhaps this was because during recess all the men switched places before she took the stand. Judge McFadden was not satisfied with the relevancy or veracity of what she said and blocked her testimony in open court before the jury. After ten weeks of trial and the conclusion of the government's case, on July 9, 1980, Judge McFadden ruled that the government had failed to make its case of conspiracy and cleared Gilmore, Biddle, Drummond Coal Company, Fine, and Johnsey, then dismissed all charges against the Drummond brothers, Garry Neil and Larry, and Clyde Black. The judge said that any charges left against Fine and Johnsey would have to be tried separately—if at all.[159] All of these small items were later dismissed.

Rate Stabilization and Equalization

In the late 1970s, as the chaos at the Public Service Commission hearings escalated and as Alabama Power was being pushed to the brink of financial disaster, Bruce Hutchins, then general manager of financial planning, and his assistant manager Gibson Lanier began following a decision from the New Mexico Public Service Commission about the same time that Joe Farley heard about the case. All public utility companies in the nation were experiencing identical inflationary conditions, and this particular case involved a New Mexico public utility that was providing electricity and water. On March 7, 1975, the state commission approved a new concept in electric utility rate making for the Public Service Company of New Mexico. The commission would monitor the company's earnings on a quarterly basis and allow it a rate of return on equity between 13.5 percent and 14.5 percent. This was called "rate indexing" or "cost of service indexing," and it meant that when return on investment fell below 13.5 percent, an increase was triggered, but when return went above 14.5 percent, a decrease went into effect. The new idea drew no intervenors and was supported by consumer and environmental groups.[160] Alabama Power was interested in seeing how this new rate method would operate in practice, and Hutchins and Lanier began to debate whether the New Mexico plan would work in Alabama and how it might be adapted to the state. Many hours went into forming models, creating diagrams, and running numbers, but within a climate of so much hostility toward Alabama Power Company, the time was not right to discuss the idea outside the company.[161]

During the Fob James administration, Elmer Harris talked to Farley and requested permission to approach Wallace, believing that while he was out of office would be a good time to develop a relationship with the former governor and explain to him, outside a political context, the financial problems of the company. Everyone believed that Wallace would run for elective office again and would most likely be elected. The former governor thought about running for the U.S. Senate, but instead he joined the faculty of the University of Alabama at Birmingham as director of rehabilitation and lectured occasionally.[162] Billy Joe Camp and other Wallace confidants advised Harris to go see Wallace by himself, to talk about the issues, and to appeal to him on a personal basis. Harris, who was totally unknown to Wallace, recalled visiting the former governor at his office in the old Pizitz building in Birmingham and telling him he knew he would run again and win. In June 1979 Wallace was already talking about another campaign. Harris said, "Alabama Power Company has asked me to be the chief financial officer. I have evaluated the company, and it is a broke company. You and Alabama Power have had a long fight. I have observed it from a distance, and I am here to declare that you are the winner." Harris told the former governor, "Now, I ask you to help me get the company out of the ditch, or I've got to find another job." Wallace looked up from his wheelchair and replied, "Well, son, I'll help you."[163]

Billy Joe Camp. Courtesy of the Alabama Public Service Commission.

Wallace knew that if he ran again it would be his last term, and he probably recognized that he had used utilities for all the political advantages he could. He also probably realized the company actually was in poor financial condition. The most important new development was that now Billy Joe Camp, a man Wallace knew and trusted, was president of the PSC. Camp, a Cullman native and retired army major, had been a member of Wallace's cabinet and a Wallace confidant since 1971. He had worked in Wallace's two presidential campaigns and served as the governor's press secretary and executive secretary. In 1980 Camp had been elected president of the Public Service Commission. On the commission, Camp voted against Alabama Power and never gave the company anything, but he was concerned about the issues. Camp knew Elmer Harris, and one day when Camp was in Birmingham, he called Harris and suggested that they meet. Camp told Harris there had to be a way to regulate utilities based on rate of return. Although Camp recalled not having been aware of the New Mexico experiments with a rate formula, he believed there had to be an arithmetic expression that would work. Harris left the meeting and assigned the challenge to Bruce Hutchins, who Harris knew had a team struggling with the problem of the New Mexico formula. Harris told Hutchins: "Find a way to make this work."[164]

Meanwhile, for months Bruce Hutchins and Gibson Lanier, working from Birmingham, had been writing and running programs on Southern Company's main frame computer in Atlanta. John Burks and Jim Elliott helped with the figures, trying to find the right formula. Hutchins and Lanier could only use the computer at night and on weekends. They suffered frustration after frustration. The main problem was that the mathematical formulas they devised would cause a spiking up and down of rates whenever an adjustment was needed. This was exactly what they wanted to avoid. They had to find a formula that would not jerk rates up and down with a yo-yo effect. If they could not find a formula that would stabilize rates, the concept would not work.[165]

At some point Elmer Harris told Camp about the company's struggle to find the correct formula. The hostile political climate over rates was not good for the state's economic development because new industry needed a stable supply of electricity, nor was the adversarial process securing better service for Alabama Power's customers. Camp recognized that some program of continuous and fair regulation needed to be found, and he knew the contentious attitude that had prevailed for over a decade was damaging to the state as well as to Alabama Power.[166] Finally, Hutchins and Lanier were successful. They wrote a program that worked well in adjusting rates without spiking. They called it Rate Stabilization and Equalization, but it remained to be seen whether this new concept would work when applied to an actual situation.

In 1981, interest rates remained high, costing about 12 to 14 percent on long-term and 15 to 20 percent on short-term loans. Inflation also remained high and eroded the PSC settlements of 1978 and 1979. Under such constantly changing economic conditions, the financial data prepared for a previous twelve-month period were irrelevant and obsolete by the time the PSC considered them. The second unit of Farley Nuclear Plant was expected to go into service in the summer of 1981, which would cause a dive in the company's financial position because of accounting mandates.[167]

To address this crisis, on March 19, 1981, Alabama Power filed a $324.9 million rate request, and the *Montgomery Advertiser* ran a headline ALABAMA POWER ASKS FOR RECORD INCREASE and warned its readers to prepare to pay more for electricity. Attorney General Charles Graddick said he would fight the increase.[168] Hearings began in June. The prospect of dealing with this huge rate increase caused Pete Mathews to resign from the commission. A bachelor, Mathews joked that he had to get off the commission because the only thing pretty girls wanted to talk to him about was their electrical bills.[169] Governor James appointed engineer Lynn Greer, a legislator from northern Alabama, to Mathews's seat on the commission. Camp, as president of the commission, Jim Folsom, and Greer had to deal with this rate request.[170] On October 16, 1981, the Public Service Commission issued another zero order, refusing

Alabama Power Company's requested $324.9 million rate increase. Alabama Power promptly appealed directly to the supreme court to allow collection under bond.[171]

The commission's zero order, Docket No. 18117, is an interesting document because it makes no reference to any testimony or to any facts. The Public Service Commission instead referenced the high inflation and interest rates of the nation's economy and justified the zero order because of high unemployment in the state and because Alabama's poor and those people living on fixed incomes could not pay for electricity and "cannot live humanely without the service." The commission included a strange reference that seemed aimed at the possibility of a statistical formula for rate making. In defending its zero order, the PSC stated that regulation was "largely judgmental. If it were not, some detailed mathematical, scientific formula would have, no doubt, been proposed by now to handle regulation and our offices/positions abolished."[172] Perhaps this zero order was designed for what it actually accomplished the next year: rejection by the Alabama Supreme Court.

On November 20, 1981, the supreme court chided the Public Service Commission for not making specific findings "in a case of this magnitude" and demanded certain documents and findings from the commission by December 11, 1981.[173] On February 12, 1982, the supreme court allowed the company to collect the increased rates under $150 million bond. These funds would increase revenue $75 million. The court in its order pointed out that "neither the legislature, the executive, nor the judiciary can take private property and devote it to public use without just compensation," for the "people in their constitution, both state and federal, prohibit government from taking private property without just compensation." The supreme court was particularly concerned that the effect of Plant Farley's unit 2 on the company's earnings was not justly considered by the PSC. During these hearings, the state supreme court ordered Alabama Power to file its projections of the company's earnings for each of the next twelve months and at the end of each month to give the court an actual accounting of earnings. The projections were remarkably on target, something that impressed the court. But it would be late fall 1982 before the court ruled on the company's appeal of the zero order.[174]

On March 4, 1982, the subject of rate indexing was discussed at the commission as a result of the supreme court order, and the concept was not "laughed at" because of Alabama Power's aggressive efforts in the previous few years to put facts before the people. Advertising and wide use of the Jacksonville Electric Authority's monthly surveys of national utility rates, which consistently showed Alabama Power had some of the lowest rates in the nation, helped—along with the absence of former governor Wallace—to change opinions. The time seemed right to seek a statistical way to regulate rates on a timely basis and not deal with figures a year or two old. Throughout March and April 1982, the PSC discussed the concepts of rate stabilization and equalization and a rate for certified new plants coming online without revenues to offset the cessation of "allowances for funds used during construction." However, after one of the open hearings at the PSC, the representative of the industrial customers did some slanting and startling math and managed to get headlines in a Montgomery newspaper by claiming that Alabama Power would be getting "a billion dollar increase." This caused the commission to back off.[175]

On March 9, 1982, Alabama Power filed for a $453,727,901 rate increase that included the $324.9 million rate increase filed earlier and denied on October 16, 1981, and $129 million in a new filing. This new rate case, Docket No. 18416, was based on data for the twelve-month period ending on December 31, 1981. The next few months were filled with hearings and negotiations between the power company and the PSC, but no consensus was reached. Travis

Travis Bowden

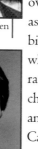

Oscar Walker

Bowden, who was then Alabama Power Company's vice president of finance and treasurer, Oscar Walker, then assistant manager for rates and regulatory matters, and James M. Elliott, the director of corporate financial, accounting, and regulatory services, all testified. Walker had worked closely with John Burks and had taken over his responsibilities. Walker was as knowledgeable on rates as Burks had been and maintained for the company the credibility and respect of regulators. The highlight of the week was when an intervenor presented a Michigan accountant to testify on rate base and operating income. Company attorney Rod Mundy challenged his credentials as a qualified economist or statistician, and the Public Service Commission's administrative law judge, Carl Evans, struck portions of his testimony from the record.[176] Finally, on October 15, 1982, the Public Service Commission issued a second zero order denying any of the Alabama Power rate request on the day before the higher rates would have gone into effect automatically without commission action.

The company appealed the second zero order to the Alabama Supreme Court. While this appeal was in process, on November 5, 1982, the court finally remanded the $324.9 million case (Docket No. 18117) back to the Public Service Commission, ordering it to issue a new order with sufficient rates to allow Alabama Power Company to earn a 15 percent return on its equity. The court ruled that the PSC order was not based upon evidence or fact and was "void of references to record."[177] The court opinion stated that "the 12.43 percent return on equity found by the commission is not supported by the evidence and is confiscatory because the zero order does not allow even this rate of return and because the commission did not consider the effects of the second unit at Farley nuclear plant, we reverse the zero order and remand this cause to the commission." The court ordered the commission on remand to consider the updated evidence submitted by the company and establish "rates which are not confiscatory." The court directed the PSC to accomplish this "in any event no later than December 1, 1982."[178]

By this time, Alabama Power accountants and rate experts were confident their rate stabilization and equalization formula would work and had begun a constructive dialogue with the rate accountants at the Public Service Commission. Everyone realized that some trials and adjustments would have to be made. The big question in everyone's mind was whether the supreme court would approve such a formula system of rate making. Eason Balch quietly began inquiring in Montgomery circles whether the justices might consider it. Billy Joe Camp recalls that attorney Euell Screws, who had sometimes represented the PSC, began asking the same questions to some of the same people. The general response was affirmative.[179] For one thing, the supreme court had other cases to handle and was tired of constant rate cases.

In a series of open hearings the main disagreement was over the percentage range of rate of return for adjustment. Long meetings between the staffs of the PSC and Alabama Power went on into the night while details were hammered out. There were many such details because regulations needed to be adopted for monitoring company operations and for making necessary calculations. Commission staff, representatives of the Alabama attorney general, various intervenors, attorneys, and also media were included. Euell Screws, as special attorney for the PSC and the governor's advisory committee, attended. He was particularly effective. Jack Bingham recalled that "the job got done although some would have predicted the tower of Babel." The *Montgomery Advertiser* reported on November 12 that an increase in rates "was inevitable" after the November 5 supreme court ruling and that the average customer's bills would increase by $4 to $8 a month.[180] Under the terms worked out, the company agreed to a proposal by Camp to devise "an industrial rate discount to attract new and expanding industries into the state." On November 17, 1982, the Alabama Public Service Commission and Alabama Power agreed to the new rate-making concept and a settlement of the 1981 and 1982 rate cases. The Public Service Commission order also included rates for Certified New Plant (CNP), which would allow the company credit for investments in new plants.

The $186 million collected under bond was made permanent, and an additional $120 million annual increase went into effect on December 1.[181]

This new concept, Rate Stabilization and Equalization or RSE, was approved by the Public Service Commission just after George Wallace's unprecedented fourth gubernatorial election. He narrowly defeated Lieutenant Governor George McMillan in the Democratic primary and then handily won over the Republican challenger in the 1982 general election. After a calm period under Governor Fob James, who did not seek re-election, Alabama Power's people wondered what another Wallace administration would mean for their company, which had not fully recovered from its near insolvency in 1978–79. Soon after his inauguration Wallace made two important decisions. He stopped making Alabama Power a political target, and he filled a vacancy on the Alabama Public Service Commission with a person who would assure the regulatory body would have a low political profile and would improve its professional level of regulation and administration.[182]

Jim Sullivan. Courtesy of the Alabama Public Service Commission.

In early January 1983 Wallace called Billy Joe Camp and asked him to give up his Public Service Commission presidency and come to the governor's office to be his press secretary. Camp, who was a loyal friend to Wallace, knew he could not let the governor down, but he was worried about the fragile new rate-making program being worked out at the commission. Camp knew that whoever the governor appointed to fill his unexpired term had to be a professional person who would "not demagogue." Camp and Wallace discussed this appointment and settled on Jim Sullivan, the son of a longtime friend and political supporter, Charles James Sullivan, who was then serving in the governor's cabinet as director of emergency management.[183]

Governor Wallace called the younger Sullivan and told him that Billy Joe Camp was going to be his press secretary and asked if Sullivan would like to fill Camp's unexpired term as president of the Alabama Public Service Commission. Sullivan recalled being "more than surprised" at this "invitation out of the blue" and asked for a few days to think it over. However, the next day Camp called Sullivan and told him things "were popping" and the governor needed an answer that day. Sullivan then remembers inquiring, "By the way, Billy Joe, what is the Public Service Commission and what do they do?" Sullivan immediately called Wallace and asked him, "Governor, if I take this appointment, what do you want me to do?" Sullivan always remembered the brief answer he received: "Be honest and do what you can to help the people of Alabama." Only later, after Sullivan found out that a few previous PSC presidents had been convicted of misconduct, did he fully understand the governor's admonition.[184]

At the time, Jim Sullivan had no idea he was a perfect selection. At six feet, three inches tall, the former Ole Miss wide receiver was impressive and could handle the sometimes unruly meetings. He held an undergraduate degree in business administration from Ole Miss and a master's in banking and finance and a law degree from the University of Alabama. When the governor called, he was, in his words, "running the family furniture store and practicing a little country law." The closest he had ever come to politics was his recent election as chairman of the Andalusia Chamber of Commerce. Besides his education and his political naïveté, Sullivan brought to the Public Service Commission a quiet professionalism, a small-town business view, dignity, rare common sense, an understanding of ethics, and integrity. He also had a sense of humor. He had not been part of the commission when the new rate-indexing idea was approved for a trial operation and thus could not be blamed for it. But he did have the responsibility to watch RSE carefully to make certain that it worked with equity. In one of his first interviews Sullivan said, "I intend to see that we have very reasonable utility rates in an atmosphere of solvency for the utility companies."[185]

The first day Sullivan walked into his new office at the old State Office Building, he found a tall man, a stranger, sitting in the chair before his desk. The man introduced himself as Elmer Harris and said: "I just want to know if you are going to be fair." Surprised, Sullivan responded, "That depends upon what your definition of fair is." Weeks later, after he was somewhat settled in, Sullivan called Harris and invited him to Montgomery to talk. Sullivan and Harris discussed the new rate-making concept.[186] The adoption of RSE changed the political scene in Alabama, took utility rates out of politics, and ushered in an era of financial health for Alabama Power and of stability of rates for the consumer. Under the plan, the electricity section of the Public Service Commission examines Alabama Power Company books and records each month to determine the retail return on common equity (RRCE) to see if it is within the approved range of 13.0 percent to 14.5 percent. The adjustments are limited and relatively small. For instance, the adjustment for April 2002 for 1,000 kilowatt hours was an increase of $1.54. The Public Service Commission's 2002 *Annual Report* noted that this was only "the second base rate adjustment pursuant to Rate RSE in almost ten years."[187]

RSE proved so successful that it was later used by the commission to regulate the Alabama Gas Corporation and in a decade was used by other state regulatory commissions. George Wallace, who had pushed the company to the brink of financial failure, was, through the appointment of Sullivan, responsible for taking rate setting out of politics and putting it on a more businesslike basis.[188] It must be noted that Maurice Bishop, the Birmingham attorney who had been "so obsessed" with opposing Alabama Power and who had been a perennial intervenor in the company's filings before the Public Service Commission, died on July 12, 1982, after a brief illness. It is ironic that in the Sunday edition of the *Birmingham News* that carried Bishop's obituary one of the front-page stories was critical of Alabama Power's long-term coal contracts. Beside the continuation of that story on page two, the *News* printed a long essay of rebuttal and explanation supplied by Alabama Power.[189] Bishop's passing and the enactment of RSE indeed signaled the end of one era and the beginning of another. On September 16, 1983, the Alabama Supreme Court, in a case brought by two of the company's industrial customers, Alabama Metallurgical Corporation and Alabama Textile Manufacturers Association, approved Rate RSE and Rate CNP and approved the Public Service Commission's orders of November 17 and 22, 1982.[190] In 2006, Alabama Power's centennial year, RSE and CNP had operated effectively for twenty-five years.

IBEW Strike of 1982

At midnight on August 30, 1982, 3,900 Alabama Power Company employees who were represented by the International Brotherhood of Electrical Workers walked off their jobs when talks on a two-year contract renewal broke down. The company and the union had been negotiating for weeks, and on August 15 the union rejected the company's first offer. During the ten-day extension, federal mediators were unsuccessful in solving the differences. Rayford Davis, who was vice president of power delivery, believed he caused the strike by insisting that the union agree to use rubber gloves to handle voltages above 4,000 kV instead of using insulated sticks. "We were," Rayford recalled, "behind the times as far as I was concerned. A lot of companies in the country were gloving above 4,000 volts very safely." The *Birmingham News* reported on September 5 that 700 workers had already been trained to use the gloved method.[191] Hours before the strike began, Alabama Power implemented its emergency plan to keep electricity flowing to its customers, and nonunion employees began their emergency assignments. The thirteenth-floor auditorium at the corporate building became the headquarters for the strike emergency operating group. IBEW threw up picket lines at generating plants and district offices. Cots, sheets and towels, and food were stocked in the generating plants as management moved in to keep the plants operating.[192]

On August 31, the 44-kV line serving the construction crews at the dam near Crooked Creek on the Tallapoosa River was sabotaged. A rifle was fired into the Harpersville substation, and rocks were thrown at a train hauling coal to Gorgas Steam Plant.[193] The next day, Wednesday, September 1, a storm disrupted service to 42,000 customers in Birmingham, but power was restored in the morning after thirteen line crews composed of nonunion employees worked through the night.[194] Harold Bowron Jr., a labor relations attorney who was held in high regard by both management and labor, worked seven days a week moving around the state getting injunctions to protect the company's property and the lives of employees and the public.[195] A company proposal was rejected once more on September 8. Meanwhile, general office employees were learning new skills. Ed Orth, manager of corporate planning, was assigned lineman duties in Tuscaloosa; Karen Berquist, stenographer in power generation, was sweeping coal in the lower pulverizer at Plant Gaston; and Gary "Buddy" Parker Jr. was reading meters instead of working in the Birmingham customer service center.

When Alan Martin walked into the Twelfth Street garage, the guys already knew he was "Mr. Farley's assistant." One man asked him, "Can you change a rear axle on a three-quarter-ton truck?" Martin replied, "I've never had any trouble before." Of course, Martin explained twenty-two years later, "I had no trouble because I had never done it." The husband-and-wife team of Donna (supervisor in human resources planning) and Julian Smith (government affairs in Montgomery) rarely saw each other during the strike. She was reading meters in Tuscaloosa, and he was shoveling coal at Gorgas Steam Plant. Ricky Cofer, senior engineer I, Clanton, who had just completed the pole-climbing course at the General Services Complex, was part of Billy Smith's pole-climbing crew. Terri Gast, who was trying to do two jobs at the Tuscaloosa office, hoped "a big storm doesn't come through town."[196] Buddy Eiland's worst nightmare was driving a thirty-foot trailer with poles on it through rush-hour traffic in downtown Montgomery.[197]

IBEW leaders Bill Frederick and Phil Hamilton recalled in 2004 that the 1982 strike was especially hard on families because so many of the union members had spouses who were Alabama Power employees not covered by the union contract. One spouse might be working an emergency job while the other was walking a picket line. The strike was an emotional issue for some. Hamilton added, "Yes, there were divorces over that strike." Frederick recalled that his father-in-law Don Dawson, who began working with Alabama Power in 1958 when Weiss Dam was under construction, was assigned special jobs during the strike and worked irregular hours. They would go fishing together on the Alabama River when Frederick was not walking the picket line. Frederick noted that strikes are always hard on everyone because when the strike is over "both sides have to come back and work together."[198]

Issues in the 1982 strike involved an increase in per diem payments, reading meters in the rain (not in stormy or severe weather), gloving, the discharge of eight employees who participated in an illegal strike in 1981, and overtime guarantees. David Cooper, who began working in the labor relations department in 1977, noted that the gloving issue was most important in 1982 but in 2005 the practice was commonplace. The five-week strike ended on Thursday night, October 14, when IBEW notified the company that the contract had been approved. Meter readers and collectors would be given appropriate rain gear to work during rain, sleet, or snow but would not be expected to work during severe weather conditions. Effective October 12, 1982, wages would increase 7.5 percent, and beginning August 15, 1983, wages would go up 6.5 percent. Benefits were improved, and sick leave accumulation was increased by ten days.[199]

Alabama Power Company Diversifies Its Workforce

In the 1960s and 1970s the law on employment discrimination was still emerging. Southern federal judges were not moving forward swiftly, and George Wallace dominated Alabama politics. Robert Collins, the Balch & Bingham attorney who became the firm's expert on civil rights legislation and employment, recalled that Joe Farley was quite sensitive to these issues and wanted to do what was right, but it was often difficult to determine what the company needed to do, and it was not easy to work out how that could be accomplished.[200] Alabama Power Company always had a diverse workforce but not at management levels or in professional positions. Women, especially in the South, were not encouraged by universities to major in engineering and technical fields, and before the 1970s few females were graduating with these degrees. In 1972 blacks and women accounted for only 1 percent of engineers nationwide. Although traditional black colleges and universities had been turning out engineers for some time, the integration of these professionals into their fields had gone slowly in the South.[201] As for other college majors, Bill McDonough observed that Alabama Power was "an engineer-driven company, and it had trouble recognizing nonengineers and nonlawyers and ways to utilize nontechnical degrees."[202]

The first attention to the company's diversity came from Alabama Power's responsibility to provide electricity to federal installations, military bases, and government operations through contracts with the General Services Administration (GSA). In 1967 the GSA noted that the company "grossed almost $2.5 million" from these contracts. President Lyndon B. Johnson had signed Executive Order 11246 on September 24, 1965, charging the General Services Administration with revising its contracts and adding a provision that companies doing business with the government would not discriminate in employment. GSA had responsibility for oversight, and the Office of Federal Contract Compliance (OFCC) enforced the executive order. GSA's first compliance review of Alabama Power noted that black employees were mostly in unskilled jobs, "almost no black women held white-collar positions," and in a geographical area "where Negroes represent more than 25 percent of the labor force, less than 10 percent of all employees in Alabama Power were Negroes." The GSA noted that the company even maintained segregated facilities. Some suggestions were acted upon, but the GSA reported two years later that the company had initiated little change.[203]

The company's first affirmative action program was developed by Gary D. Grooms, an African American who was recruited by Alabama Power after graduating with a business degree from Miles College in 1972. Grooms supervised and managed the program under vice president E. Davis Long, working closely with attorney Robert Collins and Bob Andrews in personnel. Grooms recalled that the possibility of GSA withhold-

Gary D. Grooms

ing millions of dollars unless the company had a viable affirmative action plan encouraged Alabama Power to develop such a plan. The financial condition of the company could not stand any further erosion of cash flow. Before this time, the industrial relations or personnel department was concerned mostly with benefits and retirement plans, but reacting to its new broader mission of diversification, the department name was changed in 1976 to "human resources." Andrews was elevated to vice president of human resources as the responsibilities of the department grew. The first woman in management in the department, Paula Bryan, was hired in 1979 into the labor relations group. She was an early female graduate in industrial relations at Auburn University, and unbeknown to her, she was employed by Alabama Power under its affirmative action program.[204]

On another track and occurring simultaneously, the Civil Rights Act of 1964 gave individuals the right of redress for discrimination; the federal courts and the Equal Employment Opportunity Commission (EEOC) dealt with these complaints. The first filing against Alabama Power came out of Barry Steam Plant in Mobile, and another complaint on gender was filed by Susan Woods in the accounting department.[205] A charge against the company was also filed by the EEOC on August 14, 1974. This was known as the Telles charge, named for Raymond L. Telles, the El Paso, Texas, native whom President Richard Nixon had appointed chairman of the Equal Employment Opportunity Commission in 1971. Telles signed the complaint charging discrimination by Alabama Power and the International Brotherhood of Electrical Workers. The double complaint by Telles complicated the situation and made it difficult for the company to resolve. One year later, on August 25, 1975, the EEOC rendered a decision that the company "had violated and continued to violate Title VII by discriminating against blacks and women because of their race and/or sex" in hiring, promotion, and pay practices. Federal attorneys searched the company's records and investigated for months. Through the next decade, the responsibilities of the company to its employees increased, and federal laws and regulations applicable to employment expanded.[206]

For years Alabama Power and the EEOC were in a fact-finding mode, and the company's liability for class-action suits kept running. Meanwhile, Alabama Power was recruiting an extraordinary and talented group of African Americans. The company encouraged each one to work on graduate or engineering degrees that would better qualify them for management positions. Many of these young people took leadership roles in the company's diversification effort. Robert Holmes joined transmission design after college graduation in 1970. He received his engineering degree from UAB in 1976. Holmes would be vice president of human resources in 1992. Brenda C. Faush joined the company in 1973 with a position in personnel. She had not completed her college degree but was encouraged by her supervisors to return to school. Taking night courses, she graduated from UAB in 1979 and earned a master's degree from Birmingham-Southern College in 1995. Faush recalled that an informal group that encouraged social events, BAPCOE, Black Alabama Power Company Employees, was an important support group for African-American employees in the 1970s at a time when, in Faush's words, there were "few people who looked like me." Faush became a mentor to many of the young African Americans who came to the company in the next decades. In the mid-1990s Faush was the marketing manager of the Birmingham Division; she retired in 2001 as communications services manager.[207] Bobbie Knight joined Alabama Power in 1978 after graduating from the University of Alabama with a degree in communications. Mary Rollins, one of the few women in a supervisory position then, was Knight's first supervisor in customer service. Knight was soon promoted into management positions and received her law degree in 1985. She was elected vice president of public relations in 2002.[208]

Audrey Vaughan began working in human resources in 1981. Sheila Ash Garrett came to Alabama Power in 1984 and turned her experiences in college recruiting to locating and screening minority engineers for the company, then was promoted to human resources supervisor. In 2006 she was manager of advertising and communications services. Walter Graham, an Alabama A & M business administration graduate, started working for

Left to right, Marsha Johnson, Bobbie Knight, Brenda Faush, Sheila Garrett, and Audrey Vaughan, celebrating Brenda's retirement, 2003.

Alabama Power in 1984 as an equal opportunity specialist with responsibilities for affirmative action and Department of Labor audits.[209] Marsha Johnson began her career with Southern Company in 1986 and came to Alabama Power in 1988. Johnson was in Birmingham for two years, then went to Mobile. After other jobs in the corporate office, she became vice president for the Birmingham Division and in 2005 went to Atlanta to be vice president for diversity and chief diversity officer for Southern Company.[210] Christopher C. Womack was recruited in 1988 by Steve Bradley on the recommendation of Julian Smith to become the company's federal governmental affairs representative. Womack, an African American born in Greenville, Alabama, was a political science graduate of Western Michigan University. He earned a master's degree in public administration at American University while serving as a legislative aide to California congressman Leon E. Panetta.[211]

Donna Smith, a political science major at the University of Alabama, began in corporate training and human resources in 1976. She received her MBA from Samford in 1988, became marketing manager for the Birmingham Division, and later returned to the corporate office to head human resources. In the 1980s one of Paula Bryan's responsibilities in the human resources department was to teach diversity sensitivity classes. Bryan recalled one session when longtime company secretary Richard Bowron was in attendance. After she listed all the things to do and not to do, she thought Bowron captured the essence of her efforts in his comment, "Paula, isn't it all about respecting the equality of all people and having good manners?"[212]

Susan Story

Susan Story was recruited by Alabama Power following her graduation from Auburn in 1981. She was assigned to nuclear generation as a junior engineer and began work January 11, 1982. She was twenty-two years old when the IBEW strike began in 1982 and spent seven weeks at Plant Farley working twelve-hour shifts. In evaluating this experience, Story observed that although it was difficult, it was also interesting and challenging, and she had an opportunity "to really know the plant." Story was the first Birmingham person—Alabama Power or Southern Company Services—to make an A on the Nuclear Regulatory Commission examination, and although she accomplished more than required on any job, she was concerned because she was not getting high evaluations. When she asked why, her immediate supervisor frankly told her he saved those marks for men who had families to support. She never reported this discrimination, but it was eventually noticed by David Varner and George Hairston of nuclear management. They took care of it. From nuclear generation, Story was moved into various management positions in marketing, customer operations, community resources, corporate planning, human resources, and corporate real estate. In April 2003 she was named president and CEO of Gulf Power.[213]

On March 31, 1981, the EEOC filed a second complaint and the company eventually agreed to a consent decree by which Alabama Power would begin a craft and skills testing program. Bob Andrews recalled that Alabama Power engaged Felix Lopez of Long Island who was an expert in competency testing, and he was able to win the confidence of the IBEW leadership. The union and the company were able to develop tests for a broad range of skills. Andrews believed the overall effect of the Telles decree on Alabama Power was positive and the most significant result of Telles was the testing program. Meanwhile, Graham and Grooms spent weeks in Washington with Andrews and attorneys Richard Carrigan and Robert Collins negotiating with the EEOC on remedial relief, back pay, job categories, and what would be adequate company goals on professional, skilled craft, technical, and clerical job categories.[214]

Diversification came to the board of directors of Alabama Power Company in 1984 when Louis J. Willie, executive vice president of the Booker T. Washington Insurance Company, was the first African American appointed to the board. Willie was joined in 1993 by the Reverend John Thomas Porter, whose middle name came from Thomas W. Martin.

By the end of 1988 a number of women were in management positions, including Gail Amburgey, who became the company's first female district manager when she took over the Gardendale district in 1986. Amburgey, who married Alabama Power marketing specialist Royce Willis in 1994, recalled that at the time she believed this was "an incredibly exciting opportunity but also very daunting in that I felt many people were watching and gauging the future opportunities for women based on my performance. It was not only that I was the first female but also one of the first non-operating district managers." Despite the pressure, she found it a rewarding challenge and the people within the community and the company supportive. Cindy Webster, a strategic planning coordinator at corporate headquarters, and Cheryl Thompson, a sales supervisor in Roanoke, were two other women in management positions.

Between 1977, the first full year for which data are available, and 1986, there was a 64 percent increase in the number of women hired, including 8 percent in supervisory positions. Black employment grew 23.5 percent, with the fastest growth in managerial and professional ranks.[215] Looking back, Bob Andrews recalled that the program evolved but not without some struggle within the company. When the civil rights movement touched employment opportunities, Alabama Power first had little interest. Then with affirmative action, the company moved slowly forward in fits and starts and finally became totally committed and dedicated to diversity. Paula Bryan observed that it was a long effort over many years and many people suffered hard knocks and scars from the struggle, but, she said, in the end "what began as a legal battle ended with the realization that a privately held and publicly regulated corporation recognized that it was important for a public service company to reflect the population it served."[216] The federal court approved the settlement in the Telles decree in July 1987.[217] Steve Sprayberry and Curtis Jones, who were in the Southern Division, pointed to the quality people who worked at Alabama Power—people who did the right thing and who constituted one of the strengths of the company—as one reason for the company's success in achieving diversity.[218]

ROTHER L. HARRIS DAM AT CROOKED CREEK

The last hydroelectric dam in Alabama Power's original river development plans was to be on the Tallapoosa River. The dam's location was identified as a potential site in the 1920s, and the company purchased about two-thirds of the land needed for the dam and the reservoir. Decades before the dam was built, Alabama Power designed transmission lines so they would come close to the site, so few new transmission lines were needed when generation started. Beginning in 1967 J. A. Tyson and Clayton Gore directed the drilling of some

The Rother L. Harris Dam, completed in 1983, was the last of fourteen hydroelectric plants built by Alabama Power.

500 core and auger holes to locate the best site for the dam and find possible quarry and borrow pit locations. The company requested a license from the Federal Power Commission to build the dam long planned for Crooked Creek near Wedowee in Randolph County. It was granted in December 1973, and preliminary site construction began in 1974 after the Alabama Public Service Commission issued a certificate of convenience and necessity, but it was two years later when cofferdam construction started. A flood in 1977 washed part of the cofferdam away and construction halted for a time. John D. Jones, vice president of construction, guided the project.[219]

The dam was named the Rother L. Harris Dam for longtime Alabama Power executive Judge Harris. On October 25, 1982, Alabama Power announced that massive steel gates would be lowered to seal off the sluiceway tunnels, openings in the 150-foot high concrete dam. Some 6,000 yards of concrete would be poured in the tunnels. Depending upon rain, it would take one to three months to fill the 11,000-acre reservoir to full pool level. Although the completion date for Harris Dam had been expected in early 1979, poor national economic conditions and the company's financial problems slowed the process and heavy floods in February 1981 delayed work so much that it was not in service until April 1983.[220]

THE MARKETING DEPARTMENT GETS BACK TO BEING MARKETING AGAIN

In 1981 the U.S. Department of Energy mandated that all large utilities provide residential customers who might request it "a prescribed comprehensive home energy audit." Alabama Power trained its home service people, who were comfortable going into people's homes to explain electrical appliances and services, to do the home audits. Over the course of four years, they made 25,115 audits, leaving customers a detailed analysis of recommended improvements covering twenty-three different areas, such as insulation and heating and cooling systems. Through advertising, Alabama Power educated the public about EER, or the energy efficiency rating, which was attached to new appliances. By 1983 economic conditions had changed once more. Although the residential energy advisers continued to make home audits to assist people in conserving energy, the conservation programs had worked so well that Alabama Power had energy to sell, and energy services returned to being the marketing department.

A general marketing meeting was held in Birmingham on January 26–27, 1983, for the first time in five years. Sam Booker, Joe Farley, Elmer Harris, and University of Alabama business professor Dr. Arthur Thompson, who had been a witness in the company's rate cases, discussed the company's position and the opportunities in a new marketing era for Alabama Power.[221] The conference theme was "Back to Marketing: It's the Centsable Thing to Do." Marketing leader and vice president Sam Booker addressed the gathering, saying: "We'll keep selling high-efficiency equipment and full insulation. But in doing this, we must keep foremost in our minds our need for new business and added revenues." Years later, Booker explained that "we were very responsive to the conditions that existed at that time. We responded to the pressures of the times and to the needs of the customers." In 1984 all but four of the residential energy advisers were assigned to marketing. Nelda Steele, who was then home service director, observed that most of the advisers made the transition successfully and enjoyed the new challenge.[222]

Marketing results were soon exceeding quotas in thirteen of seventeen categories. Increased gains in all areas continued in 1984, and the next year Alabama Power developed its first five-year marketing plan, which was part of Southern Company system's sales goal. Walter Baker retired on August 31, 1983, as manager of market research and planning, following a forty-two-year career with Alabama Power that began on January 1, 1941. Other leaders who were involved in marketing in this era were Pete Lester, Edward A. Wilson, William J. Wimberly, Banks Farris, James T. Clements, Charlton McArthur, James P. Scarbrough, Jerry Bell, Virgil Rice, and Terry Waters. Bill McDonough moved from Mobile to become executive vice president with responsibility for marketing. Sam Booker retired in May 1987 after forty years with Alabama Power. For twenty of those years Booker had served as leader of the company's marketing efforts. Alan Martin, who had been an assistant to Joe Farley, succeeded Booker as marketing vice president. By 1988 Alabama Power had surpassed the mark of one million customers and had sold 38.9 billion kilowatt hours of electricity.[223] One of Martin's initiatives was a complete evaluation of the mission of marketing to make it more competitive for the next decade.[224]

In October 1982 Alabama Power announced a new emergency assistance program to help Alabama's low-income families with their energy bills. The program called Project SHARE (Service to Help Alabamians with Relief on Energy) was to be administered through the American Red Cross. Alabama Power made a onetime contribution of $50,000, company employees were given the opportunity to provide funding through payroll deductions, and customers received the opportunity of making a voluntary $1 contribution on their monthly bills. The program went into effect in January 1983. Steve Bradley and Jera Stribling, then consumer affairs coordinator, went to Joe Farley with the initial idea, and Farley supported them, but he was amazed at how many customers supported the program. In the first few months 8 percent of the company's customers participated in the program, providing $170,475 in donations. By 1985, $1.7 million had been contributed to help needy people pay their utility bills. Later other utilities and cooperatives and municipalities began participating in the program.[225]

FEDERAL LEGISLATION ON HYDRO RELICENSING

Alabama Power Company began with hydroelectric generation, and the romance of rivers, dams, and reservoir lakes is significant in its history. The company had always taken a leadership role in hydro-generation issues. Alabama Power's Mitchell Dam was the first large hydroelectric dam licensed under the Federal Power Commission, established by Congress in 1920. After the long hiatus caused by the 1929 depression, World War II, and the dissolution of Commonwealth & Southern, Tom Martin was determined that Alabama Power would convince Congress to repeal certain provisions of the 1945 Rivers and Harbors Act so the company could complete its original plans for the Coosa River. He was also determined to pursue developments on the Warrior River. The company fought the Federal Power Commission's interpretation of the amortization reserve in relicensing older hydroelectric dams, which basically involved the issue of depreciation, and won a favorable ruling on the question.

In the 1970s and 1980s the company's hydroelectric dams were threatened once more, this time on the question of preference in relicensing. In 1980 the Federal Energy Regulatory Commission (FERC, the successor to the Federal Power Commission), with pro–public power Nebraska native Lee White as chairman, gave special preference to public power.[226] This involved the case of the small town of Bountiful, Utah, which challenged the Utah Power and Light Company for ownership of its dam on the Weber River. FERC interpreted the 1920 Federal Power Act's provision of preference for public power in original licensing to hold in relicensing. Challenges to other dams immediately followed, one being from Clark and Cowlitz Counties, which went after Pacific Power and Light's Merwin Dam on the Lewis River in Washington State. Alarms went off across the country in power companies that owned 586 dams worth some $100 billion that were generating electricity under the control of FERC. Private companies, whose customers had paid for these dams through their rates and needed the electric generation from these dams, organized a team through the Edison Electric Institute to gather facts on all the dams in the nation that would be threatened, what they cost, and what the impact would be if FERC's policy stood. Alabama Power's Joe Farley, Howard Allen, CEO of Southern California Edison, and Fred Melke, chairman of Pacific Gas and Electric Company, led the team. [227]

In 1983 FERC, with President Reagan's appointments, overruled its administrative law judge, who used the Bountiful case as precedent in the Merwin Dam case. The commission relicensed the Merwin Dam in Washington State to Pacific Power and reversed the Bountiful rule. The legal situation was cloudy at best. The position of Alabama Power was that the original law did not address the issue of public power having a preference in the relicensing process, and this point was fought in the courts. But obviously some federal legislation was needed to clarify the issue. From 1980 to 1983 Alabama Power was very much involved in the national fight by investor-owned utilities to secure congressional legislation to amend the Federal Power Act of 1920 to protect its hydro investments by securing the right of first refusal for a dam undergoing relicensing.[228]

Julian Smith worked with the Edison Electric Institute hydro-relicensing team in Washington, D.C., in some of the most exciting years of his career with Alabama Power. Smith is a Selma native and a Virginia Military Institute civil engineering graduate with a lifelong passion for politics that began when he was twelve years old and supported C. C. "Jack" Owen for the Public Service Commission. Smith joined Alabama Power in 1974 and was sent to Greene County, then

Julian Smith, left, director of Alabama Power's governmental affairs department, and Donnie Reese, manager of state legislative and agency affairs, at the state capitol, 1986.

Plant Miller, and was later assigned with David Whitt to develop a white paper on the costs of two nuclear plants that the Public Service Commission kept comparing to Alabama Power's Plant Farley—the North Anna Nuclear Plant of Virginia Electric and Power and the Crystal River Nuclear Plant of Florida Power—a study that had far-reaching national influence and effect. When asked, Smith jumped at the opportunity to go to Washington in January 1982.[229]

Julian Smith well remembered that day in February 1983 when "Big Eason" Balch came to Washington to begin the campaign to protect Alabama Power's dams. By this time Eason Jr. was with the law firm, and his father, because his clout was huge, was often called Big Eason to differentiate him from his son. Never was Balch better at his game than in the campaign to protect the billions of dollars in dam investments of the stockholders and customers of private utilities. Tom Bevill advised Balch and Smith to seek out Richard Shelby, who was in the House of Representatives and serving on the energy committee. Smith recalled that Eason and Joe Farley were especially passionate about this bill: when they came to the law firm as young lawyers in the 1950s, one of their first assignments had been to get the Coosa River legislation passed.

The bill was sponsored in the House by Shelby and in the Senate by Wyoming senator Malcolm Wallop. Smith and Steven G. McKinney worked together, and Jesse Vogtle frequently came when he was needed. Joe Farley testified before the House Subcommittee on Energy and Conservation and Power on June 25, 1985. Farley stressed that hydroelectric projects of investor-owned utilities were already serving the public interest. Alabama senators Howell Heflin and Jeremiah Denton supported the bill, but it was Shelby's leadership that steered the bill through compromises and through both houses of Congress. The bill was finally passed on August 16, 1986, and was signed by President Reagan as the Electric Consumers Protection Act of 1986. This law amended the Federal Power Act of 1920 to clarify language and allowed the original owners of a dam first right to the dam on relicensing. There was a provision that should a court rule otherwise, then the investor-owned power companies deserved just compensation for the loss of that asset at current market costs, not depreciated value. As Julian Smith explained, "No one would go after a dam if they couldn't steal it outright."[230]

New Corporate Headquarters

After years of planning, the new Alabama Power corporate headquarters opened in 1986. The eighteen-story tower was connected to the 1958 building

with a dramatic atrium, and the overall plans included a large parking deck. The project began after years of planning when Alabama Power invited six architectural firms to submit preliminary drawings in January 1981. A panel selected Gresham, Smith and Partners of Birmingham and its associated Philadelphia firm of Geddes, Brecher, Qualls, and Cunningham to be architects. Kenneth Penuel of support services was project coordinator. After months of careful geological testing, made necessary by the limestone cavernous stratum that runs beneath the floor of Jones Valley where the city of Birmingham is located, proper caissons were designed. Construction began after competitive bidding, which was won by a joint venture of Doster Construction of Birmingham and Gust Newberg Construction of Chicago, and the parking deck was built by Brasfield & Gorrie of Birmingham. Overall plans called for a complete renovation of the 1958 building and a restoration of the 1925 art deco original building as well as the 1950s annex to that building.[231] These renovations were not completed until several years after the new north tower was finished.

The all-electric complex was designed to be energy efficient and would house all corporate offices in one large facility. Alabama Power Company had facilities scattered in numerous leased spaces from Five Points to Fairfield. The new building would increase efficiency and save money for the company. On March 24, 1983, Billy Joe Camp, press secretary to the governor, represented Wallace at the groundbreaking ceremony. Camp in his remarks noted that

Architects Gresham, Smith and Partners of Birmingham were selected to design the new corporate headquarters. This image shows the construction progress on August 14, 1984.

when he was on the Public Service Commission, he "went through the facts and figures" and determined that the building would "be cost-effective and will benefit the state of Alabama." Camp called the governor, who was in the hospital, and Wallace spoke to the group, noting that 1,000 jobs would be created by the construction of the complex and it would "improve the cost-efficiency of Alabama Power by eliminating leasing expenses, and lowering costs associated with mail delivery, telephone service, and transportation." At the end of his remarks the governor said he hoped this building would be dedicated to the people of Alabama and quipped, "And please, Joe, keep the rates down."[232]

The new parking deck opened on October 1, 1985. In the spring of 1986 the 900,000 square feet of new office space were ready for occupancy. Detailed plans were made for the move and each employee was urged to take time to cull papers, discard what was not needed, send what had to be kept to records retention, and move only the files essential for operation. Senior vice president Ken Allums warned that "we won't have room to maintain files we don't need." Allums had carefully supervised and managed the long planning process for the building, analyzed the space needs, function by function, and anticipated future needs. Ken Penuel was the general office project manager. Moving took place on weekends over several months.[233]

FERC and Washington

Since its incorporation in 1906, Alabama Power Company has had a presence in the nation's capital. Captain William Patrick Lay began lobbying Congress to pass a law allowing the company to build a dam at Lock 12 on the Coosa River. Then in 1912 James Mitchell, J. W. Worthington, and Frank S. Washburn were in Washington trying to get congressional approval for dams at Lock 18 on the Coosa River and at Muscle Shoals on the Tennessee River. During World War I, Tom Martin would ride the afternoon train to Washington, and after the 1950s attorneys and Alabama Power experts would fly out of the Birmingham airport bound for the capital. Years later, they would sometimes fly in a Southern Company plane. Alabama Power was more involved on the federal level than other Southern Company operating companies, working with legislative and regulatory matters, especially because of its large hydro holdings. In the 1960s and 1970s Jack Bingham and Eason Balch worked on cases before the Federal Power Commission, which became the Federal Energy Regulatory Commission; then when Balch later took the lead in the Plant Farley antitrust case and in the lobby efforts for the Electric Consumers Protection Act of 1986, the FERC cases were delegated to Rod

Mundy, whom Balch described as "brilliant and a fighter."[234]

On Mundy's part, he appreciated the confidence Balch had in him to send him to Washington alone, that is, without Washington counsel, to try a case before FERC to raise wholesale rates. Case E8851 lasted, in Mundy's words, "forever" and was finally settled in 1985. Mundy recalled one time in Washington during hearings when he and Jim Elliott were staying at a hotel and preparing for testimony the next day. They had worked late into the night and left papers stacked all over the room. They had hardly gotten to sleep when they awoke to the smell of smoke, fire alarms going off, and an order to evacuate the hotel. Elliott started grabbing his suitcase and clothes, and Mundy said, "To hell with your clothes, grab these papers." They went down the stairs carrying all the briefcases they could.[235] Many of the young people, like Elmer Harris and Bruce Hutchins, who would take leadership responsibility in the next decade, testified in this case. The result of E8851, Mundy recalled, after numerous appeals to the courts and all those years, "was we got over 95 percent of what we asked for."[236]

Balch, Mundy, Steve McKinney, Bob Buettner, who was head of the utility section of the law firm, and a young attorney named Karl Moor, who was following the environmental legislation that became the Clean Air Act and was traveling to the capital every week, decided it would be better to open an office in Washington. The office was eventually established in the 1990s.[237]

Farley Antitrust Case Settled in 1988

One of the longest running legal battles in the history of Alabama Power Company finally came to an end amicably in 1988. Amendments to the 1954 Atomic Energy Act that took effect in 1970 provided that the Justice Department upon complaint must investigate to determine if there were any violations of antitrust laws. The Alabama Electric Cooperative and several municipalities charged that Alabama Power had engaged in conduct that was designed to exclude competition. Eason Balch directed the case, which originated in 1971. Rod Mundy recalled that in these years the case "was all-consuming." The cooperative wanted part ownership of Farley Nuclear Plant. Balch, in reminiscing about the case, said when Joe Farley sent him to Washington to defend Plant Farley, he felt that if he did not win the case he "couldn't come back home." In an April 14, 1971, meeting with Alabama Power, the cooperative demanded the right to purchase an 8–10 percent interest in Plant Farley. Alabama Power was adamant it would sell a percent of unit power capacity but not share ownership of its nuclear plant.[238]

In this case, Joe Farley's testimony covered 600 pages and the entire transcripts and exhibits covered nearly 30,000 pages generated over eighteen years. The case was costly, but Farley considered it absolutely necessary. The Alabama Power president resented the plethora of untrue charges, many of them brazenly wrong, made by the cooperative and the municipal wholesale customers who had intervened against Alabama Power. He was especially disturbed by the Alabama Electric Cooperative's charge that the Coosa rate, a reduction in rates to cooperatives forced on the company by Governor Persons and senators Hill and Sparkman in 1954 as a condition for legislation allowing the upper Coosa to be developed by Alabama Power, "was [an] antitrust misconduct on [Alabama Power's] part."[239]

Joe Farley also was fearful of being forced to work in partnership with a competitor that had hard feelings toward Alabama Power. There were potential management problems, doubly so because a nuclear plant was not a simple operation. Securing financing for a plant with any joint ownership arrangement would be difficult. Alabama Power's position was mostly upheld by the Atomic Safety and Licensing Board, which found a limited problem with the company's conduct; but that, in Farley's words, "had been effectively coerced by a combination of competitors and public officials."[240] The appellate board, however, held that Alabama Electric Cooperative, but not the municipals, was entitled to some small ownership, and in 1981 the Nuclear Regulatory Commission required the sale of approximately 6 percent interest in Plant Farley to the cooperative. Alabama Power appealed the decision through the courts and when the U.S. Supreme Court refused to review the matter in 1983, negotiations began with Alabama Electric Cooperative. At issue was the very high cost involved in purchasing part of Plant Farley, and AEC was unwilling to pay its share of the actual cost of the plant. In May 1988, the long-time co-op manager retired and was replaced by James A. Vann Jr., whom Farley had known for many years. Vann came to see Farley and suggested that nuclear ownership would be difficult for them to accomplish and asked to purchase instead a portion of the new Miller coal-fired plant. In fact, Alabama Power had discussed such a deal in the early stages many years before. In 1988 Alabama Power and Alabama Electric Cooperative agreed to a settlement that gave the co-op an 8.16 percent ownership interest in units 1 and 2 of the James H. Miller Jr. Steam Plant (later called the James H. Miller Jr. Electric Generating Plant when all the steam plants were renamed "generating plants"). Vann and Farley together called on the REA administrator in the Department of Agriculture in Washington to urge the bureaucracy to approve the settlement. The sale was to be finalized between January 1, 1991, and mid-1992.

This arrangement worked well for both Alabama Power and the Alabama Electric Cooperative, and their relationship improved.[241]

ALABAMA RESOURCE CENTER AND INDUSTRIAL DEVELOPMENT

On May 6, 1988, Governor Guy Hunt formally opened the Alabama Resource Center at Meadowbrook Park south of Birmingham. Beginning in 1986 and under the leadership of executive vice president Bill McDonough, Alabama Power began working with two Georgia Tech engineers to design computer programs that would provide information on possible industrial sites in Alabama. The Alabama Power board of directors approved the project in early 1987, hoping to reinvigorate the company's industrial development program and to provide state of the art technology in one place to market Alabama's assets. The engineers warned the company that because of the explosion of new technology, Alabama Power would get only seven years of operation out of the technology before it became obsolete. Although the resource center supported all parts of the state equally, the fact that the resource center was operated by Alabama Power made the co-ops and TVA uncomfortable.

The center was developed as a team effort with the Alabama Development Office, Southern Research Institute, Rust International, and the University of Alabama at Birmingham. The interactive video system provided information on potential sites for industrial parks or plant locations and statistics on a variety of subjects such as transportation, local schools, labor force, water resources,

Developed by Alabama Power, the Alabama Resource Center provided in one location state of the art technology to market all of Alabama's assets.

and demographic profiles of any given area of the state. Local chambers of commerce and community officials kept the data current. Alabama Power built the center and staffed it as a free service to the state. More than 1,400 people toured the facility the first six weeks it was open.[242]

PERSONNEL CHANGES

In 1985 Alabama Power began a process of management restructuring and job recorrelation. Although this process caused some uneasiness, it proved to be valuable for the company. Alan Martin had replaced Sam Booker after he retired in 1987, and in the spring of 1988 there were more retirements. Bill Whitt, who as a child had played on the elevator in the corporate headquarters on Saturdays while his father, the local Alabama Power manager in Haleyville, discussed with Tom Martin how to stop the expansion of TVA north of Haleyville, retired on February 1, 1988. He was replaced by Bill Guthrie, who had grown up in Parrish near Gorgas Steam Plant and came to work with Alabama Power as a co-op student at Auburn University in 1951. Guthrie's responsibility, after eleven years with Southern Company Services, was generation. He came with a philosophy of having more employee involvement, using task forces to solve problems, and expanding performance teams.[243] On March 1, Kenneth Allums retired.

CHALLENGING ISSUES

With talk of deregulation in the electric utility industry, Alabama Power moved in the late 1980s to streamline operations, increase efficiency, and reduce costs. The company committed itself to being, as Bruce Hutchins phrased it in a February 1987 interview, "a low-cost producer." Hutchins warned that a company must not wait to react to changes, such as increased competition and possible deregulation. "You've got to start planning early and be prepared for future changes."[244] Throughout Alabama Power Company and the Southern Company system, the late 1980s was a period of transition. It was a time when there were remarkable advances in the technology of communications and the ease by which everyone could keep in close touch. Personal computers began to appear on every desk. Record swapping and data base sharing increased productivity. Across its system, Southern Company initiated studies, and, as Joe Farley recalled, "a great deal of time and thought went into finding efficiencies and ways to do things less expensively." Farley believed that these initial discussions and studies eventually led to ideas for combining nuclear operations, generation (which Bill Guthrie and Charles McCrary each led for a time), and the functions of human resources that came later.[245]

The Farley Years

During two decades as the president of Alabama Power Company, Joe Farley earned national status as an industry leader. He was widely recognized as one of the nation's most knowledgeable and respected executives in nuclear generation, a leader who could take the most complex issue and write the essence of it on the back of an envelope.[246] Farley was important to the company's sense of historical memory because he bridged the early times with the modern era. Although in 2006 there were many in the law firm who had known and worked with Tom Martin—Jack Bingham, Eason Balch, Harold Williams, Robert Collins, Billy Ward—Joe Farley was the last Alabama Power president to have worked with Martin. Farley was significant, too, because his administration molded the future of the company. Many of the young men, such as Banks Farris, who were assistants to Farley in the 1970s and 1980s rose to executive positions with Alabama Power, the Southern Company, or other operating companies in the system. During one period, in succession, Farley's administrative assistants were Alan Martin, Charles McCrary, and Steve Spencer.

Farley's twenty years were critical years for Alabama Power. He took executive responsibility on the cusp of the Sun Belt population explosion and industrial expansion that increased demands for electricity. He steered the company through years of dangerous political attacks and led with courage. He kept the company from tumbling into financial ruin during times when the nation was in economic crisis with inflation soaring and interest rates in double digits. Farley oversaw the completion of the Coosa, Tallapoosa, and Warrior Rivers development plan and directed the completion of the company's only nuclear plant. He was responsible for building the north tower of the corporate office complex and the General Services Complex. He directed the company through the initial phases of its diversification efforts. On several occasions, Farley led Alabama Power into defensive legal or regulatory positions or lobbying efforts that were supported by the Edison Electric Institute and a consortium of private investment power companies, successes that established precedents invaluable to all power companies. Joe Farley led the company through a decade of financial and rate crises, saw the Public Service Commission adopt a statistical formula for rate regulation, and witnessed the resurrection of the company's reputation in the state and among its customers.

The Water Course
in Clanton is an
Alabama Power
program that teaches
children about the
state's rivers and the
value and uses of
water.

Elmer Harris stressed the traditional Alabama
Power support for education. Here he visits his
grandson Harrison King's class.

Chapter Ten

Ninety-six percent of the over
400,000 Alabama Power customers
who lost power during the blizzard of
1993 had it restored within six days.

CORPORATE CITIZEN

We must never desert those values—respect for fellow employees, ethical conduct, community service, hard work, positive attitudes, providing reliable service, etc.—that have made us successful in the past and that will make us successful in the future.

ELMER HARRIS, *Powergrams*, June 1989

In the mid-1980s, Alabama Power Company was in a better financial position than it had enjoyed in well over a decade. President Joe Farley reported that Alabama's improved economy encouraged the company's growth in residential, commercial, and industrial customers, and profits were up from increased sales and improved operational efficiencies. Alabama Power's return on common equity increased from 14.74 percent in 1984 to 15.41 percent in 1985. In 1987 the rate fell to 13.6 but was up to 14.0 percent in 1988, a great improvement over the return on common equity of 4.5 percent in 1978. The company's bond ratings were raised for the second consecutive year in 1985, and in 1988 Moody's rated the company's first-mortgage bonds A1. In fact the company was doing so well that a rate *decrease* of 2 percent was ordered in July 1985 under Rate Stabilization and Equalization; however, this decrease was offset by a 1.5 increase granted under the Certificated New Plant rate that went into effect with the completion of Mitchell Dam's redevelopment.[1]

As good as things were financially for Alabama Power at mid-decade, all was not well in Atlanta with Southern Company's largest operating company, Georgia Power. In 1974 Georgia Power had survived fiscal problems that put it close to insolvency, but in 1985 the financial situation was grim once more because of large expenditures on the construction of the company's second nuclear plant, which was named for longtime Southern Company president Alvin Vogtle. To strengthen Alabama Power's sister company, Southern Company president Edward L. Addison decided to ask Alabama Power's executive vice president Elmer Harris to go to Georgia Power. Harris had nursed, albeit with a lot of help from many people, the rate stabilization and equalization concept through the political minefields of Alabama politics and the Public Service Commission. Addison hoped Harris could do the same for Georgia Power, which was having difficulty with its rate structure and state regulatory commission. Harris resigned as an officer of Alabama Power on November 30, 1985, and moved to Atlanta where he was elected executive vice president with the chief financial officer of Georgia Power reporting to him. Besides the challenge, there was another attraction for Harris. He had the opportunity to add a second system experience to his résumé and would have the chance to move up the corporate ladder at Georgia Power. Harris immediately went to work on Georgia Power's rate problems and was successful in getting rate relief that solved some of the company's financial difficulties. The next year he was promoted to senior executive vice president.[2] Although Harris was surely a possible candidate for the presidency of Georgia Power, he was not to stay long in Atlanta.

In 1985 Elmer Harris was elected executive vice president of Georgia Power, where he helped develop and strengthen the nuclear and rate programs.

While Elmer Harris was in Georgia, plans that originated several years before in a conversation among senior Southern Company management officials began to materialize. In the early 1980s, at a retreat at Crispen Island near Brunswick, Georgia, Jim Miller Jr., then president of Georgia Power, brought up the idea that perhaps the nuclear plants of Southern Company's operating systems should be consolidated under one management umbrella. Overseeing nuclear plants required, as Joe Farley explained, "a different kind of operating culture" and a special management expertise. Such an arrangement would keep Alabama Power and Georgia Power from having to fund two management structures dealing with the same challenges. Instead, they would have one team to operate all three plants.[3]

There was merit to the idea because Alabama Power had an abundance of nuclear talent and Georgia Power was facing many challenges with the operation of its first nuclear plant, Hatch, near Baxley, Georgia. The first unit of Hatch was placed in service in 1975, and unit 2 began commercial operation in 1979. Plant Vogtle, near Waynesboro, was still under construction. Joe Farley recalled that the group at Crispen Island "concluded that it would be better to wait and let Vogtle get online [before] creating a new entity that would have to go through a transfer from construction to operation."[4] Unit 1 of Plant Vogtle went online in May 1987, and unit 2 was expected to became operational in May 1989.

In 1987 senior executives charged a small group with considering the possibility of creating a functional nuclear subsidiary. The concept was reported favorably. Then a formal task force was organized by Southern Company to study the proposal and make recommendations to the Southern system's board of directors, which was done in 1988. Pat McDonald, who had joined Alabama Power Company in 1974 and had become chief nuclear officer in Alabama, was made an officer of Georgia Power once the project was under way. He divided his time between the two companies. McDonald chaired the team composed of Robert M. "Bob" Gilbert, who studied administrative functions; Louis B. Long, who handled the technical areas; Thomas J. McHenry, who looked at operations; and John O. Meier, who headed task force coordination. The task force presented its report to the Southern Company board of directors. The creation of the new nuclear management company was approved, and its organization was announced on May 18, 1988.[5] The boards of both Alabama Power and Georgia Power then approved the changes.

Before these boards acted, Ed Addison had received a commitment from Joe Farley to head up, eventually, the new nuclear operating company, but the timing had not been finalized. A. W. "Bill" Dahlberg, who moved from the presidency of Southern Company Services to become president of Georgia Power in 1988, recalled that "when we made the decision to form the [Southern Nuclear Operating] Company, we had to make another huge decision at almost the same time. After considering a number of possibilities, we agreed that the absolute best leader for the new organization would be Joe Farley."[6] Ed Addison pointed out that Farley's "seniority and familiarity to the rest of the system" would be beneficial and would help win approval from the boards of Alabama and Georgia Power.[7] Farley took a leadership role as the plans for the nuclear management company developed, and, as he remembered, his selection as the first CEO "evolved from a more or less circumstance of the time." Farley had been associated with the nuclear program longer than any other senior person in Southern Company. Farley himself thought because he had been around for so long and knew many of the people working in nuclear, he might "be able to help overcome the turf problems that someone fifteen years my junior might not be able to do."[8] Along with Farley, it was clear that Pat McDonald, as chief nuclear officer, and George Hairston, his next in line of authority, would move to the new company and bring to it an excellent operating team.

Charles McCrary observed that Farley had been so involved with nuclear and had such national credibility that "he was the one to lead it." Federal regulatory agencies would have to transfer the licenses to the new operating company, and the respect these agencies had for Farley would be invaluable in securing approval.[9] Unfortunately, the process of getting the Securities and Exchange Commission's approval to form the company, which would be followed by the license transfer, was delayed because of objections by Oglethorpe Electric Cooperative, which owned a portion of Plants Hatch and Vogtle. Although the co-op supported the plan for unified management, it had issues with Georgia Power it wanted resolved. The team study recommended Birmingham as the most logical and cost effective location for the nuclear company, near Southern Company Services, which had space available in its offices in Inverness.[10] During organization the operation was called SONOPCO (an acronym Farley did not like) for Southern Nuclear Operating Company, which is what the new company eventually was called. Georgia transferred some of its nuclear people, and Farley had Charles McCrary, who was his assistant at Alabama Power, transferred to SONOPCO to help get the nuclear organization off the drawing boards. McCrary and others, including Farley, were on Southern Company Services' payroll until the nuclear company's formation was finally approved by the SEC in late 1990.

McCrary had a wide range of administrative responsibilities, including finance, human resources, corporate services, information technology, public relations, and procurement. One immediate responsibility was getting the Vogtle and Hatch people and their offices moved from Atlanta, something they were reluctant to do, and having offices redesigned and established with phones, desks, and even trash cans. Although Joe Farley and Pat McDonald were the driving force, McCrary had the responsibility of building an administrative support team. He knew Southern Company's people so well that he was able to select talented individuals for various jobs, such as Robert Bell (human resources), Ed Crosby (public relations), David Cooper (compensation), and Bob Gilbert (comptroller). The pace of the company's organization was slowed so much by regulatory matters that years later McCrary recalled with some humor that after working on the nuclear company project two and a half years, on the very day the company was officially approved by the Securities and Exchange Commission he was transferred to Alabama Power as vice president for external affairs with responsibility for advertising, public relations, governmental affairs, and working with the Public Service Commission.[11]

The decision by Southern Company to cluster the operation of its three nuclear plants into one management company had a precedent in Tom Martin's Southeastern Power & Light's concentration of construction and engineering services in Dixie Construction and its central control and dispatch of the system's power resources. Both these operations saved money for the operating companies and made service more efficient, reliable, and less costly for customers. Southern Company's consolidation of data control and customer billing in the 1950s had been highly successful. The exchange of personnel among Southern's operating companies became more common, and the advances of computers and instant communications, which exploded in the 1990s, made the world a smaller place and Southern's operating companies seem less spread out. The success of Southern Nuclear Operating Company encouraged Southern Company to introduce more systemwide functional organization, such as combining fossil-hydro generation in the late 1990s, a move that would also prepare the operating companies for any deregulation in generation.[12]

On February 24, 1989, Alabama Power Company issued a press release announcing that Joseph M. Farley was named to the new position of executive vice president–nuclear for the Southern Company. He would have responsibility for the Southern Nuclear Operating Company project. Southern Company president Ed Addison noted that Joe Farley "had professional expertise and management skills to ensure that the most exacting standards" were met in the company's nuclear sector, which contained $5.6 billion or 30 percent of Southern Company's assets.[13]

Joe Farley became executive vice president–nuclear for the Southern Company on February 24, 1989.

Joe Farley looked back on his almost twenty-five years at Alabama Power and commented in a *Powergrams* interview that the business was more complex in 1989, that Alabama Power was "no longer a quiet kind of stay-in-the-background business," but it must deal with new challenges, less certainty, and changes in the utilities industry itself. Competition in the industry, independent power suppliers, plus a growth rate that had slowed were other challenges.

Farley thought that "just holding the company together, keeping us function-ing, avoiding running out of cash and just plain ordinary survival" were his biggest challenges over the two decades he led the company. Jack Bingham and Eason Balch analyzed Farley's leadership of the company, commenting that although he had chosen to surround himself with strong people and had the ability to delegate, it was Farley's "quality of knowing not to delegate" that made him so effective. His judgment of when to be "hands on" and his knowledge of the technical, legal, and business aspects were qualities Bingham and Balch believed enabled Farley to give outstanding leadership, not only to Alabama Power but to many charitable and civic organizations in the state.[14]

A New President and CEO

The same press release that explained Farley's move to the new nuclear company announced that Elmer B. Harris would replace Farley as president of Alabama Power Company. For Ed Addison, the time seemed right to make this move for Harris, who succeeded Farley on March 1, 1989.[15] Harris came back to the corporate office with years of familiarity with Alabama Power. He had been gone only four years, so he knew the senior people and middle management knew him. Rod Mundy recalled Harris asking Eason Balch about Alabama Power soon after the announcement that he was returning to Alabama, and Balch told him that "things were going really well right now, he didn't need to do anything."[16] But no one expected that to happen. In his first interview with *Powergrams*, under the headline ELMER HARRIS COMES HOME, Harris stressed that he was "very open and candid" and that he would be out visiting, "talking with employees." In this interview, he gave the first hint of his concept of employee empowerment and his emphasis on customer service, both of which became cornerstones of his leadership. Harris believed in building relationships, and close relationships could not be established by correspondence but by telephone calls and personal visits; therefore, there is little correspondence to track his administration.[17]

Doris Ingram, who came to Alabama Power in 1974 and had been Harris's executive assistant before he left for Georgia in 1985, returned as administra-tive assistant to the president. She knew how Harris wanted things done, and he had confidence in her, telling Ingram that she would have to keep the office functioning without him for at least 50 percent of the time. Harris intended to be out among his Alabama Power employees and the company's customers, listening to people, asking questions, and building relationships with govern-ment officials and community leaders. Harris's first priority was to make courtesy calls on CEOs in Birmingham; then he began to tour the state, meeting business and community leaders. If anyone wished to see him, Harris would say, "call Doris Ingram and get her to set up a meeting."[18]

Banks Farris

One of the first things Harris did after arriving back at Alabama Power was to transfer Banks Farris, his longtime Alabama Power associate and friend, to the corporate office. If Harris was going to be out of the office, he needed strong leadership from his vice presidents. Farris, who at the time was vice president of the Eastern Division, became vice president of human resources on April 10, 1989. Farris was a Kentucky native who came to work at Alabama Power in 1958, the same year as Harris. They first knew each other in the engineering school at Auburn and were pilots together in the Alabama Air National Guard. Farris received his law degree while working in Montgomery, and he became assistant to Joe Farley in 1970. Four years later he became general marketing manager.[19]

Travis J. Bowden

Farris was part of a strong administrative team that kept the company functioning smoothly while Harris was visiting Alabama Power's offices, plants, and industrial customers and state and local governmental officials. The company's executive vice presidents were Travis J. Bowden, who was chief financial officer until February 1, 1994, when he was elected president of Gulf Power; Bill M. Guthrie, who supervised generation; Bill McDonough, who was head of customer service areas until he retired on June 1, 1991; and Pat McDonald, who directed the company's successful nuclear program until he transferred to Southern Nuclear group. Among them, these vice presidents had more than one hundred years of experience at Alabama Power. Farris took a new role on December 3, 1991, when he became senior vice president of customer service and satisfaction, a position that had responsibility for one of Harris's hallmark goals: putting the customer first. Harris recalled that "it was very clear to me, I needed to put Banks Farris, a most experienced person, knowledgeable about district and division operations and customer service, in a key position."[20]

Harris's initial vice-presidential team was composed of Steve Bradley, who resigned in September 1990 (public affairs); Robert A. Buettner (counsel); Rayford Davis, who retired in March 1991, then Robin Hurst (power delivery); John E. Dorsett (generation); R. S. Hardigree (corporate services); R. E. Huffman (operating services); Bruce Hutchins (treasurer); T. H. Jones (fossil generation); Alan Martin (marketing); Charlton B. McArthur (economic development); and Jack Minor (comptroller). Harris's division vice presidents were Homer H. Turner, then Michael D. Garrett (Birmingham); John B. Byars Jr.

(Southeast); Anthony J. Topazi (Western); Jerry J. Thomley (Eastern); Clyde H. Wood (Southern); and J. Bruce Jones (Mobile). These men kept the company running smoothly while Harris was out of the office, and he expected them to get out of the office, too. Harris believed to be successful his team needed to know employees and customers.[21]

When Elmer Harris returned to Alabama Power as president, he set five goals for the company. First, he wanted to make sure that in all matters and decisions the customer was placed first. In his years in district offices and in the field, Harris had witnessed a local engineer trying to do something the customer wanted, especially something that could easily be done, only to be overruled by an engineer at the division or corporate level who would say that it had not been done that way before. In pushing every employee to think of the customer first, Harris encouraged everyone to interact with customers and to thank them for the opportunity to be of service. He recalled that once when he was with a group of employees in a small rural grocery store, he took the opportunity to give an example of what he expected of employees. He paused at the checkout counter to tell the clerk, "I am from Alabama Power Company, and I want to thank you for your business."[22]

Harris's second goal was to decentralize the company. He announced that every employee had the authority to make any decision that was in the best interest of the customer and the company. Harris called this strategy not only empowerment but creating individual initiative and immediate decision making. Over the years, the policies and procedures of the company had been collected and recorded in eight very thick books. Harris was quick "to chuck every one of them." The company wrote a few guidelines, but Harris made sure the first guideline was an exception: "anybody who wants to deviate from any guideline herein has the right to do so." Harris established the criterion for making decisions as "you can make any decision—*any* decision—that's in the

Art Beattie

best interests of the customers of the company and the company. Our number-one objective is that we're in business to have a quality product given to the customers in a pleasing manner."[23] As Art Beattie, who came from accounting and was then corporate secretary, explained it, employees were empowered, but management would hold individuals accountable: "Think outside the box, take more risks, but you will be held accountable." Beattie pointed out that this responsibility made some people nervous.[24]

Third, Harris was committed to maintaining the same rates for the next ten years. The company had gone through two decades of increasing rates, so Harris made it a corporate goal to have the same average revenue per kilowatt hour in 2000 that was in effect in 1990.[25] In order to keep rates as low as possible, he initiated a strict control on all expenses, but it was essential that management and employees bought into this goal, made it their own, and accepted it as a challenge because employees played an important role in reducing expenses. Hiring needed to be held flat. Salary expenses were saved by a gradual decrease in the number of employees through natural attrition and through job changes and retirement. Many of the jobs that were eliminated were supervisory positions.[26] From an employee base of 9,698 in 1989, the number of employees decreased to 6,871 in 2000, but that figure is deceptive because over a thousand Alabama Power employees were formally transferred to Southern Nuclear Operating Company in December 1991; in December 1995 more employees, this time in human resources and information technology, were transferred to Southern Company Services. In August 1997 Alabama Power transferred yet another group of employees to Southern Generation (which will be discussed later), as more functions were centralized.[27]

A fourth point of Harris's new administration was his commitment to holding the return on average common equity to at least 13.5 percent. The return on common equity granted by RSE was actually higher than this, and expert testimony before the Public Service Commission stated that figure was too low, but Harris believed it was wise not to push the rate of return too high.[28] Fifth, Harris wanted the company to increase its civic and charitable activities. Project SHARE, which allowed customers to contribute each month to help the needy with their electrical bills, had been enormously successful, but the donations came from customers. He wanted the company to do more. Alabama Power had always made charitable donations, but Harris had studied and compared corporate giving in Alabama and other southern states, and he determined that Alabama corporations, as a group, were not supporting charitable and civic projects as much as companies in other states. He thought that with the stable economic conditions of the 1990s, Alabama Power should be able to give back more to the people of the state and to local communities. He sought ways to do so. Alabama Power employees had always been involved in civic and charity programs, but Harris encouraged everyone to increase their involvement in the community and work with good projects that interested them. Alabama Power's educational services department, which was created in the late 1980s, increased its outreach efforts. Through the company's Teacher Corps program, Alabama Power employees had been trained to present material in schools, but these programs were downsized and dwindled away as the company found more and different ways to support education and other projects that benefited the people of Alabama.[29]

In 1991 Alabama Power established the Alabama Business and Charitable Trust Fund to help low-income families pay their utility bills. Over time the company donated $35 million to the trust's endowment, and in its first five years 50,000 people were served and 14,000 households received energy assistance. The program gave emergency cooling assistance, help with the "Centsable Energy Use" program, and crisis subsistence. The trust was designed so grants were made to community groups that routinely worked with the poor, such as United Way, the Salvation Army, and the Red Cross. No funds were directly disbursed by the company to individuals. When the trust was established, the name of Alabama Power was not used because Harris wanted and expected other utilities and businesses to contribute to the trust and be part of this charity; however, that did not happen. The Alabama Business and Charitable Trust provided help with the heat wave of 1995, giving 800 box fans in addition to more than 2,500 other fans to social service agencies to give to the needy. The crisis subsistence program of the trust allowed for immediate assistance in an emergency. Project SHARE, started in 1982, continued its highly successful and strongly supported program of assistance.[30]

Empowerment

One example of Harris's new policy of employee empowerment initiative and his emphasis on eliminating policies and procedures, reducing expenses, and saving administrative time was reflected in his concern with travel and expense accounts. He asked Jack Minor to study expense

Empowerment encouraged employees to take ownership of their jobs.

account forms to determine how many hands touched a form before it reached the accounting department. For one month Minor had someone checking forms and counting signatures. He found one form with twelve approval signatures. Harris insisted one signature was enough. Surely, the president reasoned, an employee's immediate supervisor should know if travel was necessary for business purposes, if the travel was actually accomplished, and if the expenses listed were reasonable. Minor observed that with the one-signature method people received their reimbursement more quickly because under the old system the form "might stay on someone's desk three days before it was signed and sent on."[31] Harris was also concerned with other approvals, and he expected everyone to "work on streamlining other type approvals."[32]

Harris always expected the company's employees to do the right thing, but his elimination of policies and procedures created a nightmare for internal auditing and accounting because, as Art Beattie explained, there might be five people doing something five different ways. Harris's management style was to tell people to run the company the right way, "to do your job well, and if you need help, let me know."[33] In his candor Harris could also be tough. After a meeting with employees at Greene County Steam Plant, Harris met an employee who was totally negative about the company and his job. Harris told him, "If I were your boss, with your attitude toward the company and your job, I would fire you, and I hope your boss fires you." This story quickly moved across the company grapevine causing some attitude adjustments.[34] Mobile Division external affairs manager Joe Webb recalled that "Elmer told managers to 'do the right thing,' and he would back us up. He did follow that up with a promise to talk to you if you did something stupid, and if you did something stupid twice, 'you probably would be happier working somewhere else.'"[35] Bruce Jones, who worked in the Mobile Division then, recalled, "Elmer was saying it was OK to be bold, OK to be innovative, but it was not OK to be bold, innovative, and stupid." Curtis Jones observed that "Elmer's empowerment rejuvenated and inspired employees."[36]

The concept of empowerment dominated a well-remembered meeting of district managers who gathered at the Auburn University Hotel and Conference Center June 22–23, 1994. Bill Johnson pointed out that Harris, who had been a district manager at Headland, had placed an emphasis upon district managers when he became president. Banks Farris, Harris's executive vice president, had also once been a district manager, going to Selma in 1965, seven years before Harris went to the Wiregrass district. They both understood that district managers needed more resources and more authority to make decisions. The Southern Company was pushing profits and with its new accounting system, MIRS, it could generate profit and loss statements at the district level. Ben Hutson, longtime division manager at Mobile, thought the origins of the concept of dividing companies into small profit and loss units may have started at General Electric. District managers were encouraged to watch the bottom line. Bruce Jones, at the time Mobile Division vice president, called this idea "overly innovative," but it got the attention of district managers and convinced them their districts could be autonomous organizations and run like an independent business. Customer service satisfaction was also evaluated monthly by district, and managers were able to let their staffs know how closely their districts were living up to profit expectations and customer satisfaction goals and how they compared with other districts in Alabama and other operating companies in the Southern Company system. Jerry W. Johnson, who was then district manager for North Shelby in the Birmingham Division, had regular monthly meetings with his people to go over the figures. Soon district managers believed they should be capable of running their own districts with less supervision from division staff heads and, to some extent, the corporate office. In striving to cut management costs, Johnson and other district managers viewed division staff as an extra layer of management.[37]

Depending upon personalities and issues, down through the years there had been an occasional bit of tension between strong-willed district managers and their division managers, who controlled budgets, and their staffs.[38] As Banks Farris explained, the district was a microcosm of the entire company. In organizational structure, the district reflected the division and the division mirrored the corporate office, and managers at every level who controlled budgets wielded power and influence. Bill Zales, who was then district manager of the Shades Cahaba district in the Birmingham Division, recalled that the district was its own little world with a warehouse, engineers, and marketing. At the Auburn meeting, where all thirty-five district managers were in attendance, there were the usual speeches and pep talks. Then the district managers were divided into five break-out teams and asked to answer several questions, including how costs could be cut and what was the status of empowerment in the company.[39]

Elmer Harris stressed candor, openness, and trust, and that was what he got. Jerry Johnson was selected to present his team's recommendations, which had the consensus of the group. Johnson's team report reflected the concerns and ideas in other reports, but Johnson was remembered for his enthusiastic presentation. Elmer and Banks Farris were more than surprised at what he said and the discussion that followed.[40] The district managers were critical of their division staffs, wanted more resources, wanted authority to handle their own fleets and hire and fire with their own rules, and wanted to control their own budgets. Johnson's report was the first to suggest reducing divisional responsibilities and increasing district authority. In sum, as Bruce Jones recalled, the district managers really got into the swing of empowerment and wanted authority and autonomy. Bill Zales remembered that Harris was sitting next to Farris, and when the reports were given, Farris quietly said to his president, "This empowerment business may be going a little too far, but I think I can fix it." Curtis Jones, thinking back to the Auburn meeting, laughed and said, "When Banks and Elmer got through with that meeting, they decided they didn't need district managers."[41]

For years, the district managers had taken pressure off the division vice presidents. However, when the company began moving them more frequently for promotional opportunities and to broaden their experience within the company, when they did not come up through the ranks and many functions were centralized, district managers did not serve the same purpose they had in earlier years. The customer service representatives (mostly women) who did not move but stayed in the same office became the stable, continuing presence of Alabama Power in the local office, and area managers had responsibility for several offices and assumed key roles in the community.[42] The elimination of a level of management at the division level, which had been suggested at the Auburn meeting, resulted in a level of management being eliminated, but it was the old organization of district managers that was phased out.[43] The demise of the district managers came with a functional reorganization that had managers of engineering, marketing, and accounting instead of geographically based responsibilities. District boundaries were eliminated, districts were combined, and the division acted as one district. Farris noted that this reorganization streamlined the company. One immediate result was a strengthening of division vice presidents, although later reorganizations would weaken their authority. In essence, the streamlining of the company and the functionally based structure that evolved actually concentrated more power at the corporate office.[44]

Probably the most traumatic reorganization was Farris's announcement that the local customer service call centers would be closed and the company would operate with one centralized switchboard connecting to two centers, one in Montgomery and one in Birmingham. All outage calls and customer service calls would come through that switchboard. Two connected centers were designed so that if a severe weather pattern hit the state, one of the centers would not be affected at the same time as the other. In the old days, Charlie Britton recalled, each office had a switch on the telephone, and whoever was on call at night or on a weekend had the office telephone switched to his or her home telephone number. But technology and computers would allow the two central call centers to handle calls more efficiently and certainly more economically. With the new 800-megahertz telephone system, control of transmission lines and substations was later concentrated in Birmingham, and division lines were eliminated. With new technology, using coordinates of addresses and telephone numbers, the company computers could take the information on areas without power and determine what switches, breakers, and transformers they shared. This process allowed crews to go more directly to a problem.[45]

In May 1994, actually before the Auburn meeting, the Eastern Division did some reorganization. W. Ronald "Ronnie" Smith had become division vice president on July 1, 1993. He announced changes were necessary because of the heavy growth on the Highway 280 corridor from Childersburg to Dadeville. The number of districts in the Eastern Division was reduced by one, with Talladega and Pell City becoming part of the Anniston district.[46] In March 1995 the Mobile Division reorganized, doing away with its Metro North and West Mobile districts and organizing its operations, marketing, and customer service responsibilities by function to avoid duplication. That same month, the Birmingham Division announced its reorganization plans, which eliminated a layer of management and organized some responsibilities by function. The Southeast Division announced its reorganization in September 1995 in a plan that eliminated twenty-two positions, including north and south business offices and accounting services, human resources, marketing, and operations departments. All of these reorganization efforts were aimed not only at efficiency but also at reducing the operations and maintenance budget to meet the goal of cost reductions established by the corporate office.[47] In evaluating these reorganizations, executive vice president Banks Farris commented that the division vice presidents and their staffs determined their own reorganizations, and "no two divisions have identical structures" but reflected "their particular customer demographics, division geography and employee talent."[48] Harris observed that the company's "positive progress could not have been accomplished without empowerment, personal initiative, and open discussion and debate," all of which Harris believed "strengthened the company in serving its customers at the lowest price."[49]

Performance Pay Plan

The month before Harris assumed executive responsibility, Alabama Power embarked upon a new salary incentive linked to performance. In late 1987 Southern Company president Ed Addison had asked the operating companies to develop a pay plan that would be tied to corporate strategies and would link individual bonus payments to personal and company performance. After much study, careful thought, and some apprehension on the part of employees, the new plan was implemented at Alabama Power on January 1, 1989. In the beginning, many employees were uneasy over the new idea, despite reassurances that no one's pay would be cut. Although the idea of employee accountability was maintained, the emphasis became measurable outputs and achievement of corporate and individual goals rather than organizational size and budgets. Alabama Power believed that the 1990s would be especially competitive, and the performance pay plan was designed to enable the company to reach "its corporate goal of being the best electric utility." The program was successful, and although it was originally designed for exempt employees, through the 1990s the plan was gradually expanded to include nonexempt employees and also some employees covered by union contracts.[50]

New Ideas

In 1993 changes were made to the company's newsletter, *Powergrams*, which had first been published in 1920. A new design featured a larger size with fewer pages, but the newsletter was produced twice a month. There were fewer personal and professional news items about employees and a reduction in the number of stories, but the editors were committed to continuing the tradition of the newsletter, telling employees they hoped "not only to save significant production money but also to better meet your needs for timely 'news you can use.'"[51]

Elmer Harris encouraged the company to adopt the latest technology. Before he went to Georgia Power in 1985, he sent Doris Ingram, Pat Schauer, and Shirley Thomas to an information technology forum sponsored by the National Secretaries Association, and they came back and reported that the company was behind in office technology. Harris approved a new automated office system, DecMate. Alabama Power also installed a new telephone system with its own switch in the corporate headquarters.[52]

Diversity

In the 1990s Alabama Power faced the challenge of increasing the company's diversity in race and gender. In an audit by the U.S. Labor Department, Harris recalled, the company was "raked over the coals" because there were not enough blacks and females in executive and management positions. To improve diversity at the corporate office, Elmer Harris sent Banks Farris to talk with Robert Holmes, who was then working in the Mobile Division. Farris convinced Holmes to leave his engineering responsibilities and come to the corporate office to be vice president of human resources. In 1995 Holmes was elected vice president of ethics and business practices, and he established a central office where employees could go for advice and guidance on questions of business practices.[53]

Christopher C. Womack, a popular young man who came to the company in 1988, had assumed a leadership role in

Chris Womack

Birmingham's civic activities. In 1993 he was Alabama Power's vice president for public relations. Two years later he was promoted to senior vice president over public relations and corporate services.[54] This was the same year, 1995, that Susan Knight Story became vice president of corporate real estate. Story had been in Atlanta directing community resources for Southern Company Services for three years and then worked in Montgomery briefly on loan to the Business Council of Alabama before coming back to Alabama Power.[55] Brenda C. Faush, who had been with Alabama Power since 1973, became marketing manager for the Birmingham Division in 1994. When she retired in 2001 Faush was communication services manager in public relations. Walter Heglar Jr., who came to work in 1973 with Alabama Power's corporate real estate department after a short career in the U.S. Air Force, was moved from human resources, back to corporate real estate, and then in 1994 to public relations and communications services. Heglar typifies the company's diversity strength at midmanagement positions. An Xavier University graduate, Heglar used his MBA work, law degree, and writing and editing skills to oversee budgets and contracts and to monitor policies and procedures to comply with company and governmental agency regulations.[56]

Cheryl Thompson

Banks Farris encouraged Elmer Harris to send Cheryl Thompson to Mobile as division vice president in January 1998 when Bruce Jones moved to Germany to work with a utility in which Southern Company had acquired an interest. Farris had worked with Thompson when he was vice president of the Eastern Division and was impressed with her people skills and work ethic. Thompson joined Alabama Power in 1972 directly from Auburn University, graduating as a home economist, a professional area where Alabama Power had employed women since the 1920s. Sam Booker gave her responsibilities in sales and marketing. By 1987 Thompson was the sales supervisor in Roanoke, and two years later she moved to Birmingham as sales manager. After a number of different responsibilities and a stint as a regional manager at Georgia Power, In 1998 Thompson became the first woman to serve as an Alabama Power division vice president.[57]

Donna Smith

Donna Smith was the marketing manager in the Birmingham Division in 1989, then became manager of residential marketing. She worked as assistant to Bob Andrews, who was then in Atlanta with Southern Company as vice president of corporate services. Smith moved to Southern Company Generation as human resources director, then in 2002 she moved back to Alabama Power as human resources director. Penny Morris Manuel began her career at Alabama Power in 1982 as a co-op student at UAB and joined the company at Plant Gaston after receiving her degree in materials engineering. She later worked at Plants Gorgas and Miller and in a number of positions—in labor relations, procurement, fuel handling, and others. In 2006 she looked back on her career at Alabama Power from her current position as vice president of Gulf Power Company Generation and recalled that "in 1984 when I transferred to Gorgas Steam Plant as a co-op student, there were only two female engineers in all of Southern Company plants, and they were both at Gorgas. They were Stephanie White and P. J. Hester, who have both retired now."

With the appointment of Jacquelyn S. Shaia as a senior vice president in March 1998, there were three white women and two African-American males serving as officers of Alabama Power Company.[58]

In 2000 two African-American women became officers of the company. Celia H. Shorts was elected assistant secretary in April, and in July Marsha S. Johnson was elected vice president of customer service. Johnson is a bright and witty woman who has great insight and could cut to the chase of problems. She was born and grew up in Jacksonville, Florida, received her degree from Jacksonville University, and completed programs at both Harvard Business School and the Wharton School. She arrived

Marsha S. Johnson

in Atlanta to work with United Way and joined Southern Company in 1986 in management development. In 1988 Johnson became Alabama Power's manager of employee development, then was transferred to Mobile in 1991 as an assistant to division vice president Bruce Jones. She became manager of operations and customer service for the Mobile Division, then moved back to the Birmingham Division as manager of the customer service department. There had been a problem on the question of diversity in customer service because a large number of the employees in this department were women, especially African-American women, but their managers had all been white males.[59] Morale was low, and Johnson, who was never afraid of any challenge, immediately changed attitudes, creating a sunny work atmosphere and leading with a positive attitude and a strong promotion of selling.[60]

Other diversity accomplishments were made across the company. For example, Stephanie White, mother of three and a UAB graduate engineer, became the first female superintendent at an Alabama Power hydro facility when she took over responsibility of Smith Dam in 1994. She had thirteen years of experience with fossil generation working at Barry, Gorgas, and Miller.[61] Paula Martese Marino joined Alabama Power in 1993 with bachelor's and master's degrees in electrical engineering from Auburn University; began work in the south region, Birmingham Division, in power delivery. After responsibilities as senior engineer in power delivery, she was an assistant to Charles McCrary when he was at Southern Company Generation. Marino recalled early in her career when she was a junior engineer in distribution, *Powergrams* wrote a story about her, and Susan Story sent her a note of congratulations and encouragement. This encouragement made an impression on Marino, and "ever since, I have taken every opportunity I have to pass that encouragement and recognition along to others."[62] Debbie Hawkins was a support manager at General Services Complex and later an area manager. Bobbie Knight was an assistant to Chris Womack and Steve Spencer before becoming contracts and compliance manager and then later head of materials services. In the 1990s there were more women working in management positions and there were more opportunities available. Women were even allowed to wear pants. Slacks, once considered unprofessional for women to wear at work, were permitted but only as part of a stylish pantsuit. Denim jeans and sports slacks were not allowed.[63]

Alabama Power has also been a leader in maintaining an all-inclusive workplace by giving people with disabilities opportunities to be contributing employees. Teresa Hendon, who is deaf, was hired in 1983, and Carla Davis, who is blind, joined the company in 1988. Hendon, a staff accounting assistant, processes bank statements and incoming mail. She was recognized with an Alabama Power Presidential Award in 1995 and by the Birmingham Area Governor's Committee on Employment of People with Disabilities in 1999. Davis is a familiar person as she makes her way around the building with remarkable ease. As a communications specialist in the public relations department, Davis's byline appears regularly in *Powergrams* and on *Powerlines*, the newsletter's electronic equivalent. Davis commented that she was grateful for the opportunity to "prove that I can work on an equal footing with people who can see." In 1993 the disability management section was established in human resources to support Alabama Power's efforts in hiring people with disabilities.[64]

ALABAMA POWER FOUNDATION

Alabama Power had always budgeted for charitable contributions and in good years donated about $2 million. Major contributions were made at the general office level, with Richard Bowron as the coordinator, and various amounts were allotted to the divisions for use at their discretion. With return on common equity standing at 14.53 percent because of a stable rate base that allowed long-range planning, Alabama Power was in a position to give back more to the community. The board of directors approved the creation

of a company foundation at its meeting on
October 27, 1989, and the Alabama Power
Foundation was incorporated in Jefferson
County on October 31 with Bill McDonough,
Steve Bradley, A. J. Connor, and Art Beattie
as members of the board of directors.[65] Jera
G. Stribling was executive director of the
nonprofit foundation.

   The money to establish the foundation
came from the stockholders' share of Alabama
Power's profits. Harris insisted that not one cent that went into the foundation
"ever increased any rate for a customer," and the Public Service Commission
regularly reviewed the records to make certain that assertion was correct.[66] The
foundation mission statement was easily written and very simple: "to improve
the lives and circumstances of Alabamians and to strengthen the communities
in which they live." The Alabama Power Foundation would support programs
that helped "raise the standard of living, better the quality of life and enhance
the economic success of the people of Alabama." Besides making grants, the
foundation intended to provide "leadership to expand and improve philanthropy throughout Alabama" and especially to use matching funds to leverage
its own contributions. Harris made certain that office managers and division
vice presidents were given a charitable budget each year with control over how it
might be contributed to support their own communities. In its first three years
the foundation gave 406 Alabama agencies and organizations $6,826,018 and
had become the most important philanthropic arm of Alabama Power.[67] By
April 1992, when the endowment had grown to $55
million, Alabama Power Foundation was the largest
foundation in Alabama.

   One reason for the foundation's rapid growth
was the addition of a payment from the federal government for the company's property at Little River
Canyon in northeast Alabama. Sometime in 1992,
Elmer Harris took a call from Walker County's Tom
Bevill, the dean of Alabama's congressional delegation. At that time Bevill had been in Congress representing the fourth district for twenty-five years. Bevill
told Harris he wanted Alabama Power Company
to give the U.S. government the company's land at
Little River Canyon to create a national park. This

The Alabama
Power Foundation
has supported
many charitable
organizations.
They have
been partners
for Habitat for
Humanity projects
all over the state.

In 1992 Alabama
Power's properties
at Little River
Canyon became
part of a national
preserve.

acreage had been acquired by James Mitchell as part of the electric properties of the Little River Power Company near Blanche once owned by S. Z. Mitchell and Electric Bond & Share.[68] The flume and generation plant had been abandoned for decades, and Alabama Power had no plans to generate electricity there. Harris told Bevill that the company would not totally give the land to the federal government, but he said if the government would pay Alabama Power what the land was worth, the company would put that money in the Alabama Power Foundation and use the interest to fund worthwhile projects in the state.[69]

On October 21, 1992, Congress authorized the establishment of the Little River Canyon National Preserve, which affirmed "the biological, geological, cultural and historical significance of Little River Canyon." Elmer Harris announced that "we are proud to be a partner in making the preserve a reality. We are also pleased that money received from the sale of land for the preserve has been contributed to the Alabama Power Foundation to support educational, charitable and cultural activities throughout Alabama."[70] After much discussion an agreement was reached for the company partially to sell and partially to donate its acreage in DeKalb and Cherokee Counties to the National Park Service. On April 19, 1995, eighty people gathered at an overlook, which had a breathtaking view of the falls and canyon. In a short ceremony Alabama Power transferred the deed for 8,580 acres to the National Park Service. Corporate real estate vice president Susan Story gave credit to Congressman Bevill for supporting the preservation of the canyon. Harris noted that the Little River Canyon was an excellent pump storage site, but Alabama Power recognized it was "too beautiful to cover up. That's why the company formed a partnership to preserve this place."[71] A check for $7,641,750 was deposited with the Alabama Power Foundation.[72]

With a few years of operational experience, in January 1992 the Alabama Power Foundation board began thinking about the foundation's future and establishing goals and strategies that would allow it to have the strongest impact on the state. The board used research from the Alabama Poverty Project to compile data on the poor in Alabama and studied reports on philanthropy in Alabama and the South to determine how the resources of the Alabama Power Foundation could be leveraged to provide the most positive results. One conclusion was that educational improvement was the quickest way for long-term community development. Quality education would stimulate new leadership and provide programs to identify and encourage emerging leadership among the state's youth, and such programs would allow the foundation to partner with other organizations. The foundation announced it would judge programs for their long-range goals, cost effectiveness, and orientation to people, not bricks and mortar, and determined for 1992–93 to allot 40 percent of its donations for educational programs, 40 percent to health and human services, 10 percent to civic and community-based initiatives, and 10 percent to arts and cultural programs.[73]

Grants came only from endowment earnings. In 1993 the foundation awarded $3.2 million to 149 organizations, and almost one-third of those projects were educational programs. In discussing these initiatives, Elmer Harris stressed that while Alabama Power was "proud to assist in efforts to bring about creative solutions for continuing concerns," Alabama's future ultimately depended upon "the willingness of diverse individuals and institutions to join forces. All of us, no matter what our role in life, have a responsibility for helping Alabama grow, for strengthening its communities and for bettering the lives of its citizens."[74]

As the number of grants increased, the foundation stressed the benefits of collaboration and the necessity for accountability so that the foundation's "investments meet our expectations and that they benefit the people of our state."[75] The breadth and the geographical distribution of the projects were extensive. The entire company was involved in the grant process because applications could be turned in at any Alabama Power office or plant. Alabama Power did not add money to the foundation after 1996, and unfortunately the foundation's assets dropped after the stock market decline in 2000.[76]

In 1994 Banks Farris was chairman of the foundation's directors, and Clyde H. Wood was president. On January 1, 1998, Jacquelyn S. Shaia became president and served until December 2000, when she resigned to become president of the Economic Development Partnership of Alabama. She was followed temporarily by Bruce Hutchins and then by Bill Johnson, who began working with the foundation in March 2001 and was elected president on September 11, 2001.[77]

APSO, founded in 1990 by Glenda Harris, emphasized programs in education, child health, and safety.

Alabama Power Service Organization

Alabama Power Company had encouraged its employees to be active in their communities from the early years of the company, but there was no formal program as the new company struggled to survive, grow, and move forward. In 1989, after Elmer and Glenda Harris returned from Atlanta, Glenda was inspired to create a formal organization that could encourage and coordinate the vol-

unteer work of the power company family. She had been part of the Women of Georgia Power, which had evolved from a social organization to a service organization, and she was impressed by its accomplishments. Glenda recognized that an organization composed of both women and men would be stronger, would be an excellent way to involve spouses in company activities, and could accomplish more with help from the corporate office. It took time, however, to get men involved.

The organization she founded, the Alabama Power Service Organization, or APSO, planned to emphasize programs in education, child health, and safety. APSO was formally established as a 501(c)(3) charitable organization on December 28, 1990, with Glenda Harris as president, Dena F. Bowden, vice president, Suzanne W. Snypes, secretary, and Linda E. Jones, treasurer. The board of directors first met on January 7, 1991. An advisory committee was selected and the group spent time planning. At the first formal meeting on March 4, 300 people came to join the organization, and Patsy Topazi was elected as the first president of the newly incorporated Birmingham/Corporate chapter. The organization gradually spread to other divisions, with Topazi organizing an Alabama Power Service Organization in the Western Division in 1992 after her husband Anthony was promoted to vice president in Tuscaloosa. Chapters were established at the Mobile Division, Plant Miller, Plant Gorgas, and Southern Division in 1993; Eastern and Southeast Division chapters were organized in 1994; and the E. C. Gaston chapter was formed in 1998.[78]

The APSO-supported Family Place provides short-term housing for patients or family of patients being treated at Birmingham hospitals.

One early APSO project was The Family Place. At first two apartments, then three furnished apartments were acquired near the UAB medical center and were made available to anyone who needed treatment or to the family of patients in the UAB hospitals, the Veterans Administration Medical Center, or at Children's Hospital. For years the profits from the gift shop in the atrium of corporate headquarters provided support for The Family Place. By word of mouth, the Alabama Power family through local offices and plants around the state spread the word that these apartments could be used by people who needed short-term housing in Birmingham because of health reasons. Karen Garrett, Linda Hurst, and Priscilla Hutchins were actively involved with APSO programs, which were partially supported by grants from the Alabama Power Foundation, though the APSO program was totally separate from the foundation. Within a few years APSO had 3,500 members—Alabama Power employees, their spouses, families, and friends—working statewide to volunteer time and money to such programs as Coats for Kids, Guide Dogs, Reading Is Fundamental, and Habitat for Humanity. APSO also worked with other causes, such as building and placing birdhouses in Alabama state parks.[79]

ENERGIZERS

Tom Martin began inviting retired Alabama Power Company employees to reunions in the 1950s. Although he personally never accepted the idea of retirement, Martin was nostalgic about seeing the "Old Timers," as he called them, and sharing once more the favorite stories of bygone days. Barbecues and reunions continued to be held occasionally in the next decades but became events hosted by divisions as the number of people grew unwieldy. Social functions for retiree groups were co-ordinated by an employee in human resources. In 1987 Joe Farley and Bob Andrews, vice president of human resources, asked retired marketing vice president Sam Booker to study the possibility of creating a more formal organization for the company's retirees. Booker asked his longtime associate, Walter Baker, retired from marketing research, to join him. The support for a retiree organization was enthusiastic, and each division selected two people to join the team as coordinators. Julian Smith of governmental affairs served as liaison from the company. Sixty retirees showed up for the initial meeting on October 15, 1987. Bylaws were adopted in early 1988 and by the end of the year all divisions had retiree chapters.[80]

Energizers, front to rear, Alice Green, Mary Martin, Hugh Bryant, and Claire Mosley, help catalogue the Alabama Power archives collection, 1989.

Retirees were kept informed of the company's progress and activities and briefed on the company's position on political issues. When he became president Elmer Harris suggested that the retiree group follow the Alabama Power Service Organization and incorporate as a 501(c)(3) charitable organization. This was accomplished, and the name Energizers was adopted. When the history of the Old Timers was discussed in 2005, one Energizer commented, "Thank goodness we aren't Old Timers but Energizers!" Jack Minor, retired comptroller, helped with the transition to a tax-exempt organization. By 1996 this move was completed. More Engerizer groups were formed for specific plants and some districts, planning sessions and workshops for leaders were scheduled, and a state retreat was held in 1998.

The Energizers began a travel program, introduced an educational safety program to teach fourth graders about electricity, and wrote and sold cookbooks. The proceeds from the sale of more than 8,000 cookbooks were donated to four charities: American Cancer Society, American Heart Association, Children's Hospital of Alabama, and Camp ASCCA (Alabama's Special Camp for Children and Adults) on Lake Martin. Sarah Relfe was assigned to the Alabama Power Foundation as director of volunteer services. She worked with Energizers and APSO. In 2000 Walter Baker wrote a history of the Energizers, complete with constitution, bylaws, a pledge, and the official song.[81]

Alabama Power and Alabama Education

In the 1990s the need for the state of Alabama to reform its K–12 public education was made evident through a number of revealing statistics, including the fact that the math skills on the 1988 high school exit exam were taught at a fifth-grade, eighth-month level. Businessmen were increasingly concerned about the educational quality of the state's job applicant pool. In a speech at Jefferson State Community College in November 1991, Harris stressed that 25 percent of Alabama students dropped out of school and another 35 percent failed the Alabama Power pre-employment tests. From the remaining 40 percent, Alabama Power hired 250–300 people a year. Harris said that "education, tax reform, and economic development go hand in hand" and if Alabama was going to be able to compete in the international market, public education had to improve.[82]

There were several efforts to improve state education in the 1990s. In October 1993 Harris joined CEOs such as Ted Kennedy of BE&K, John W. Woods of AmSouth, Herbert A. Sklenar of Vulcan Materials, Neale Travis of BellSouth, Bill Smith of Royal Cup Coffee, and Caroline Novak of the Montgomery Museum of Art in organizing A+ to push for reform and funding for public education.[83] As Charles McCrary, senior vice president of external and regulatory relations, explained at that time, "Alabama Power will support a property tax increase to fund the reforms, but only if the tax treats all businesses fairly and equitably." McCrary was referring to the fact that businesses were taxed at 25 percent, but utilities were taxed at 30 percent of the value of their property. He recommended that employees read the material from A+, make up their own minds on the issue of educational reform, and then get involved.[84] On a more personal basis, 700 Alabama Power employees began volunteering their time "putting energy into Alabama schools" as Teacher Corps members during 1994.[85]

Alabama Power was the developer and a sponsor of the Birmingham Early Learning Center, a child-care facility, which was set up as a nonprofit corporation and was built in 1995. On September 24, 2002, the center was named the Elmer and Glenda Harris Early Learning Center. The center provided a state-of-the-art building and a curriculum designed by Auburn University. Students from area colleges and universities interned at the center, which was the first project where a nonprofit corporation was involved with urban revitalization in Birmingham. Numerous businesses also became sponsors of the center and provided some of their employees with the opportunity to send their children to the center.[86]

Finishing Miller

December 1990 marked the end of Alabama Power's continuous construction program that began after World War II. For forty-five years Alabama Power had built additional generation to keep up with the 8 percent average per year increase in demand in its service area. With the demand growth declining to about 2 percent a year, the construction boom ended when the initial start-up of the fourth unit of Plant Miller occurred on December 5, 1990. As *Powergrams* noted, the scaffolds came down with some fanfare. Alabama Power had elected to complete Miller, the largest coal-fired generation plant in the state, and to sell some of its power under contract for several years until the demand increased for electricity in Alabama and the company needed the additional capacity to serve its own customers. Financially, this arrangement was good for Alabama Power's rate payers because the revenue from the sale

The completion of Miller Steam Plant in 1990 marked the end of Alabama Power's forty-five-year generating plant construction program that began after World War II.

helped pay fixed charges and operational expenses. Although Plant Miller's tremendous capacity would supply the increase in demand for some years, the company also began exploring ways to meet peak demands through conservation, to adjust some use to off-hours, and to use solar energy.[87]

Plant Miller was dedicated on October 18, 1991, to James H. Miller Jr., longtime Alabama Power engineer and company officer who retired in 1987 as president of Georgia Power Company. Plant Miller's first unit went into commercial service on October 12, 1978; unit 2 on May 1, 1985; unit 3 on May 1, 1989; and unit 4, the most technologically advanced unit, began commercial operation on March 5, 1991. The construction of Miller took longer than expected to complete because the poor economy and rate inadequacies caused a financial stringency for the company along with reduced level of growth. The plant cost $1.9 billion. At its dedication Miller was producing 660 million watts of electricity, about one-fourth of the company's generation capacity.[88]

Although new construction of additional power plants ceased, at least

The last of nine new combustion turbines at Greene County Steam Plant came online in 1996.

for a while, improvements in generation continued. In June 1994 construction began on the first of nine new combustion turbines at Greene County Steam Plant. Five of these units went into commercial operation in May 1995 and four in 1996. All nine units were designed to provide peaking power and added 720 million watts of power to Alabama Power's capacity. They were completed on time and under budget.[89] To increase efficiency, Alabama Power consolidated seven transmission control centers into one, a change that went into effect in 1995.

Hurricanes and the Blizzard of '93

On September 17, 1989, Hurricane Hugo churned through the Caribbean wreaking havoc on the U.S. Virgin Islands and leaving thousands homeless. The request that came from the Virgin Islands Water and Power Authority for

Alabama Power to send crews to help was unprecedented. The response required the most intense logistical effort with which the company had ever been involved. Transporting mechanized equipment, derricks, and bucket trucks to the islands required a team of people working closely with the U.S. Air Force to load the equipment on C-5A transports at the Birmingham International Airport. The restoration work extended over a month and established Alabama Power Company and Southern Company as a premier service restoration utility.[90]

Alabama Power trucks being loaded on a U.S. Air Force C-5A transport plane in September 1989 to help with power restoration in the Virgin Islands after Hurricane Hugo.

While Alabama Power crews were packing to leave on September 22 to assist the Virgin Islands, Hurricane Hugo, which had crossed the North Atlantic and gained strength, came ashore in South Carolina near midnight on September 21 with sustained winds of 135 miles per hour. Tidal surges reached 19.8 feet above sea level. With some Alabama Power crews already working on St. Croix, on October 1 a contingent of armed and uniformed security forces left Alabama Power to assist South Carolina Electric & Gas with security while another 700 men went to help restore power there and in Gastonia, North Carolina. Some of them stayed three weeks. James Barwick recalled that when the Alabama Power crews arrived in South Carolina, only 2 percent of the power was on, and "when we left for home, 98 percent of the lights were on." Larry Cleveland, who at the time was a lead lineman at Huffman, recalled that none of the crews had any close calls because they worked safely by their own Alabama Power rules.[91]

Three years later, at 5:05 A.M. on August 24, 1992, Hurricane Andrew, an Atlantic category four hurricane, slammed into south Florida near Homestead Air Force Base, killing 15 people and leaving 250,000 people homeless and a devastated electrical system. Alabama Power sent waves of trucks and crews, eventually some 200 employees and 100 vehicles. Wayne Lewis, who was co-director of the Alabama Power storm team with engineer M. Stephen Daniel, kept a diary of his trip to Miami with 22 men and 18 trucks. The Alabama Power crews were headquartered at Florida Power & Light's Princeton Service Center in South Miami and were put to work in Cutler Ridge, one of the most devastated areas. Many of

Alabama Power sent two hundred employees and one hundred vehicles to south Florida to help with restoration after Hurricane Andrew smashed into the state in 1992.

the crews who traveled to south Florida had worked storm damage in Mobile. They understood about the fourteen-hour days, seven days a week. Alabama Power crews set poles, rolled up damaged wire, strung new wire, installed transformers and switches, always trying to accomplish more than the previous day. Florida Power & Light had trouble delivering all the materials they ordered, but Alabama Power's people gave a good account of themselves, working through heat and brief showers and under difficult conditions for three weeks.[92]

Seven months later, on March 12, 1993, a severe late-season winter storm arrived in the Birmingham Division. Hurricane damage can be extensive, but weather following a hurricane usually is not a problem for restoration because the storm moves quickly through an area. A winter blizzard is different because the severe winds may remain and the ice and snow stay on the ground and in the trees for several days. Such conditions make it dangerous to work on poles and driving is sometimes impossible. Called the Blizzard of '93, the winter storm provided a key test for Alabama Power's new home-based customer service program, started the year before by Mike Garrett, who was then vice president of the Birmingham Division. Garrett had discussed the technological feasibility of establishing a home-agent program with David Ellis, manager of technological accounting services. The proposal was for the Birmingham Division to establish some customer service center employees with computers at home. Tina Lewis and Cindy Nix were the first ones in this program, although Mary Story, editor of *Powergrams*, had worked from home after the birth of her second child in late fall of 1987. The home computer program proved very satisfactory, especially after the 1993 winter storm blew through Birmingham with winds of fifty to fifty-eight miles an hour. Snow piled in drifts to seventeen inches, and trees and limbs snapped under the weight of ice and brought down power lines.[93] Lewis and Nix responded to 5,465 customer calls during this winter blizzard called "the storm of the century."

Audra Ezell answered calls at Birmingham Division headquarters for twenty-four hours straight before she was able to get some rest. Suzan Adderholt, supervisor in customer service, had twenty people staying in corporate headquarters. The weather was so severe the cafeteria manager could not get in to prepare meals, so he told Suzan to cook whatever food she could find in the kitchen. When the Western Division crews had their customers' power restored, they moved to Birmingham, set up a staging area at the Hoover Metropolitan Stadium, and assisted the Birmingham Division.

Downed lines, snapped poles, and damaged substations and transformers were not the only challenges faced by Alabama Power in this storm. Fossil plants Gaston, Gorgas, Miller, and Gadsden all had problems caused by ice and snow: frozen conveyor belts and coal crushers, separated ash lines, and wet coal. The crews at Plant Miller struggled, but Joe Hatley, assistant superintendent, recalled that although "Unit 1 got down to about 20 megawatts at one point, . . . we never completely lost a unit." In order to restore power quickly, Alabama Power had 3,200 of its support and field people working with help from outside crews of 2,300 workers. Long-standing reciprocal agreements among utility companies, with costs determined before disaster strikes, allowed companies to assist neighbors without negotiating costs at the time of the crisis. All of these workers had to be fed and housed. Hotel rooms were booked in Birmingham, Tuscaloosa, Anniston, and Gadsden, and caterers responded after arrangements were made by Cindy Bradford and Norma Huguley of conference services.[94]

The cost of restoration after hurricanes and the Blizzard of '93 caused insurance premiums to go so high that Alabama Power found it no longer feasible to carry insurance to cover restoration. For this reason and from experiences with storm damage restoration and to protect customers, the Public Service Commission authorized Alabama Power to establish a natural disaster reserve book entry. By an order dated October 3, 1994, the commission allowed Alabama Power to establish a reserve of up to $32 million to pay for "extraordinary operation and maintenance expense resulting from natural disasters." Judy McLean, longtime director of the advisory division of the PSC, noted that Alabama was one of the first states to allow an accounting reserve for disasters.[95]

The cost of restoration after hurricanes and the Blizzard of '93 was extensive.

The first storm after the reserve was established occurred on August 3, 1995, when Hurricane Erin came ashore on the Florida Panhandle and moved across north Mobile County. Although Erin caused power outages for almost a quarter million Gulf Power customers, only 39,000 Alabama Power customers lost power, and they had electricity restored in forty-eight hours. The previous month, July 1995, high humidity and heat caused Alabama Power customers to set records for the use of electricity over six days, with each day breaking the previous day's record. Temperatures in the high 90s and low 100s set new peak demands, and on July 25 peak demand reached a record 10,010,000 kilowatts.[96]

Before the Gulf Coast had recovered fully from Hurricane Erin, on the night of October 4, 1995, Hurricane Opal came across the Florida Panhandle between Pensacola and Fort Walton. Opal arrived as a category three hurricane with its storm-surge floods bringing the greatest devastation on the coast. Opal weakened just as it hit land, but on its trip north through eastern Alabama and western Georgia to the Tennessee line, it maintained wind strength and cut a swath of destruction. Falling trees brought down power lines, and more than 475,000 Alabama Power customers lost electricity. During major storm restoration, Elmer Harris took an active role in communicating with customers about the extended outages. When Opal crossed the state, Alabama Power's storm reserve of $31 million covered the $23 million restoration cost.[97]

Alabama Power's forests were also victims of the storm. Corporate real estate managed the 134,000 acres of timberland owned by the company and harvested $1 million of timber in 1990. Benny Vinson, land manager, announced after Opal's trip through eastern Alabama that Alabama Power had trees worth $2 million on the ground and that it would take twenty years to replace them. The most severe damage occurred in Tallapoosa, Coosa, Elmore, and Randolph Counties and in Ozark.[98]

ECONOMIC DEVELOPMENT PARTNERSHIP OF ALABAMA

Elmer Harris was committed to Alabama Power's traditional role of recruiting new industry to Alabama. He realized that to be successful, there needed to be a coordinated effort to sell the assets of the state, and Alabama Power could not do the job alone. Harris was instrumental in establishing the Economic Development Partnership of Alabama (EDPA) and getting EDPA privately funded as a nonprofit organization. Many banks, venture capital groups, corporations, and chambers of commerce provided financial support when the organization was established in 1991. Harris recommended Alabama Power's Neal Wade as president, and he was elected.[99]

Wade was a Samford University history graduate who had been involved in political campaigns, advertising, and lobby activities in Montgomery and was recruited to Alabama Power in 1978 by Steve Bradley. Wade became head of the company's public information efforts and served as director of corporate communications. In 1990 Harris asked Wade to work with him to develop his idea for an economic development partnership that would have major corporate players in the state cooperating in funding and working together for economic development for Alabama. The partnership began with an office in Montgomery, but it was moved back to Birmingham in 1996 when it expanded and took over Alabama Power's Alabama Resource Center. Analyzing Wade's leadership from the distance of a decade, Harris believed Wade's key accomplishment was cultivating the image of the organization and building its role in the state. Wade left the partnership in 2000 to work for St. Joe Paper Company in the Florida Panhandle. He returned to Alabama in 2003 to head the Alabama Development Office in Governor Bob Riley's administration and continued to bring the state's economic development entities together in a coordinated effort.[100] The Economic Development Partnership remained a strong force for industrial recruitment.

Ten Islands Historic Park

Tom Martin's interest in state history was a legacy to Alabama Power. One example was the creation of the Ten Islands Historic Park. In 1988 three women from northeast Alabama began researching the area in the Coosa River known as the Ten Islands, just north of H. Neely Henry Dam. Charlotte Hood of Ohatchee and Bette Sue McElroy and Patsy Hanvey of Gadsden detailed the region's rich history and discovered stories that, centuries apart, Hernando de Soto and Andrew Jackson both crossed the Coosa River on the shoals at Ten Islands, which were part of the Creek Path. During the Creek War, General Jackson's men widened the path to a road that ran from Gunter's Landing on the Tennessee River toward Fort Strother, which was constructed in 1813 on the Coosa River. Some of the land at Ten Islands was used as burial grounds for Jackson's men who fell in battle. Hood, McElroy, and Hanvey contacted Alabama Power's Jess Langley. With support from Bill Tharpe, Buddy Eiland, Charlie Brannon, George Williams, and Randy Hardigree, Alabama Power provided a historical marker and agreed to rename what had been called the Neely Henry Park. On May 18, 1993, Alabama Power Company officials, local residents, and county officials met to name the park on the western side of Neely Henry Lake the Ten Islands Historic Park.[101]

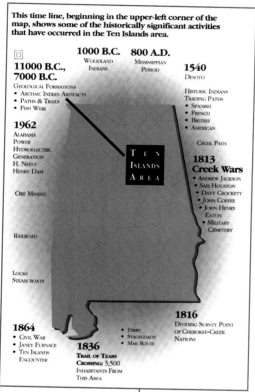

Replica of the historic time line at Ten Islands Historical Park.

Bringing Mercedes-Benz to Alabama

The recruitment of the German automobile manufacturer Mercedes-Benz to Alabama marks a milestone in the state's industrial development and in its economic history. The first inkling Governor Jim Folsom Jr. had about an

Alabama Power worked behind the scenes to help bring the Mercedes-Benz plant to Alabama.

important manufacturing company seeking a new plant site in the United States came from his director of economic development, Billy Joe Camp. From his position as lieutenant governor, Folsom had succeeded Governor Guy Hunt following the latter's April 22, 1993, conviction by a Montgomery jury on a felony charge. Camp was serving in his second year as secretary of state when Elmer Harris suggested to Folsom that Camp might be willing to leave his elected office to work with economic development. Folsom appointed Camp director of the Alabama Development Office (ADO). Earlier in the year, Don Erwin, Alabama Power's senior international development representative, had mailed a letter to ADO and enclosed a news article from the *International Herald Tribune* that he clipped while on a trip to Europe. The article reported that Mercedes-Benz was considering construction of a plant in the United States as part of "its strategy of globalization." The plant would produce "a new all-terrain vehicle."[102] Folsom had been in office only a week or two when, he later recalled, "Camp came over and told me that a major European automobile manufacturer was searching for a U.S. site for a new plant. Everything was very secret, and the code name for the search became 'Rosewood.'" Folsom realized it was going to be a very competitive process and remembered that Camp wanted "my approval to go after the plant and my support and my time to help him." The governor asked Camp if he thought Alabama had a chance to get the plant. Camp said yes, and Folsom told him "to go for it."[103]

Governor Jim Folsom Jr. Courtesy of Alabama Department of Archives and History.

Camp brought Elmer Harris onto the recruitment team. These men understood the importance of the opportunity and what it would mean for Alabama's image to capture a Mercedes-Benz plant. Camp arranged for the governor, Harris, and David Bronner, director of the Alabama retirement programs, to fly with him to Stuttgart, Germany, to meet with the subcommittee of the Mercedes selection team. They managed to do this without any media in

Alabama taking notice. It took a second visit to Germany for the team to work its way up through the committees in order to visit with the search committee and company executives.[104]

Harris recognized the importance of involving the leadership of the state's business community. At the proper time, the Alabama Power president brought in the Economic Development Partnership of Alabama. Neal Wade, then president of EDPA, recalled that prior to Mercedes "we could not get in the door or an appointment with an international company because business leaders viewed Alabama as a backwoods, redneck, football-oriented state." EDPA was providing market research and information on sites to industries seeking Alabama locations but at this time was not doing recruitment.[105] In the few years between 1991 and the Mercedes project in 1993, EDPA had worked with the state on long-range economic development goals and on an ambitious five-year strategic plan to obtain those goals.[106] Alabama Power directors, who represented many of the state's leading bankers and industrialists, were told only enough about the secret negotiations to support Harris and the company's commitment to the project.[107]

Alabama eventually submitted 22 possible locations as part of 150 sites nationwide that Mercedes sent to Fluor Daniel, its site consultant in Greenville, South Carolina. Dr. Hubert Gzik, who was going to build the plant, was on the team that first visited Alabama. By this time, sites in the state had been narrowed down, and there were tours of the proposed site at Vance and the city of Tuscaloosa. Dr. Gzik, as Anthony Topazi, vice president of Alabama Power's Western Division, recalled, was "an engineer's engineer" with a "problem-solving engineer's mind." Gzik and Topazi became good friends, and Gzik came to trust the Alabama team.[108]

Alabama dignitaries met the visitors at the North River Yacht Club, then the Mercedes group flew to Birmingham by helicopter and had lunch at Twin Hills, the Red Mountain home of Peter and Derry Bunting. Don Erwin recalled what he believed was a significant moment in the process of convincing Mercedes to give Alabama a chance. He watched Dr. Gzik on the back terrace of the Bunting home gazing pensively at the Magic City in the valley. There was something about the ambience of his Alabama visit and his feeling he could trust the team that made Gzik convince Andreas Renschler, president of Mercedes and the person in charge of the project, that he should come look at Alabama. Part of the ambience involved the Alabama team locating a Mercedes Gelaendewagen in Birmingham. Known as the G-Wagon and manufactured by Mercedes only in Germany and never sold in the United States, the hosts used the classic vehicle to drive the visitors to the Bunting home and back to the airport. This cross-country vehicle, brought into the United States by a private owner, was one of the thoughtful touches that went into planning the German team's visit to Alabama, creative details that impressed the automobile manufacturers.[109]

When Renschler agreed to visit the state, Camp, Harris, and Topazi flew to Omaha, Nebraska, and brought him to Alabama. Renschler developed a comfortable and confident relationship with the governor and the Alabama group, and Governor Folsom credited Alabama's success in recruiting Mercedes to the close working relationship that he, Harris, and Camp developed.

Anthony Topazi

Anthony Topazi was a key part of the recruitment process and was involved in a dual capacity. As head of the Western Division, he was assigned the responsibility of coordinating all Alabama Power's support activities and personnel relating to recruiting the plant and then negotiating the Alabama Power contract with Mercedes. In 1993 Topazi also happened to be the chairman of the Tuscaloosa County Industrial Development Authority. The IDA, under executive director Dara Longgrear, played an important role because a unique statute in Alabama gave the Tuscaloosa County IDA "greater authority to use state and local funds as incentives for Mercedes than did the State of Alabama."[110]

Topazi recalled that in June, July, and August "the pace was frenetic." The data on the site—infrastructure, educational initiatives, and quality of life as well as a topographical site survey—were due shortly, and David Looney and the power delivery survey crews did in four weeks what normally took five months to accomplish. The Tuscaloosa office provided local arrangements and transportation. Topazi remembered that to capture the plant "Alabama had a lot of obstacles to overcome. But when it was clear that Mercedes-Benz had come in with an open mind—and with the desire to investigate for themselves—we knew we had a chance." During the first site visit, power delivery staff members Darrell Piatt and Dwight Mullis joined Topazi, Larry Ramsey of corporate marketing, and members of the Tuscaloosa County Industrial Development Authority in meetings with the German auto manufacturer's site selection committee.[111]

Mercedes demanded reliable power for its manufacturing process, Topazi recalled, "and we convinced them that we [could] provide that." A number of Tuscaloosa-area industries assured Mercedes people that Alabama Power was "the best electric power situation in the United States." Mercedes estimated that when its assembly line was operational in 1997, the plant would need 18 megawatts. The plant also required the highest quality of power that it could be fed in order to ensure that disturbances in the transmission system would not take its auto-making processes off-line. The Alabama Power Company team, headed by Mullis, designed a loop transmission service that allowed the plant to have electrical service from two substations with either being able to handle the load in case of a service break.

The governor remembered that Renschler was impressed after his first visit to Alabama and pleased with the Tuscaloosa County site. When negotiations became serious the last of August, Mercedes called Alabama and asked Billie Joe Camp and Topazi to come to Stuttgart, Germany. Folsom told Camp not to come back without the plant. Camp and Topazi spent a week in around-the-clock negotiations. David Bronner, Wallace Malone, and many Birmingham and Alabama business and community leaders worked quietly behind the scenes to convince Mercedes to come to the state.[112]

Alabama Power's John Bass (of the material services department) and Larry Sides (of the traffic department) put together a transportation cost study for Mercedes. Dawn Anderson in library services monitored national news reports so the Alabama team would know exactly what was happening in other areas bidding for the plant. The Tuscaloosa Industrial Development Authority optioned the land for Mercedes, and Alabama Power's corporate real estate department under Milton Jerrell "Jerry" Johnson, working days, nights, and weekends and using every right-of-way agent in the company, managed to option thirty-two parcels in two weeks. The last piece was optioned ten minutes before the deadline to turn the paperwork over to Mercedes. Elmer Harris was proud that Alabama was the only state that met every deadline established by Mercedes, an accomplishment that also impressed the German leaders.[113] Mercedes wanted to negotiate with one attorney, and James F. Hughey Jr. of Balch & Bingham was appointed a special attorney general to represent Alabama's interests. He spent time with the Mercedes lawyer going over the details. Hughey recalled that Elmer Harris was always nearby monitoring these meetings but was never in the meetings.[114]

When Mercedes had narrowed the field to three states—South Carolina, North Carolina, and Alabama—Folsom recalled that most Alabama news media had already counted Alabama out. During the Southern Governors' Conference in Virginia, Folsom was told within earshot of the governors of North and South Carolina that he had an emergency call from Germany. Folsom found Renschler on the telephone, and he revealed to Folsom that the plant would be located in Alabama but warned the governor not to tell anyone. Jubilant on the inside, Folsom put on a sad face as he returned to the group. When the Tennessee governor queried him, Folsom shrugged his shoulders and mumbled something about an update from his economic recruiter.[115] The day Folsom returned to Alabama, national networks reported that Mercedes was going to North Carolina, and, the governor remembered, later that week the Alabama Public Television news program "For the Record" featured state editors expressing pride that Alabama had at least made the top three. The two weeks before Mercedes made the public announcement seemed to Folsom an eternity. The governor credited Alabama Power with doing everything the state asked it to do in the recruitment process, even, after the announcement was made, helping to fulfill Renschler's request to place a huge Mercedes encircled star over Legion Field before the Alabama-Tennessee football game.[116]

When it was all over, Topazi praised his division people for coordinating aircraft, buses, and signs and for installing telecommunications for the final press conference. The Western Division cleaned up roadways, trimmed trees, and "dressed up the city in what was," said Topazi, "a team effort. You can't single out any particular person. But I do feel Alabama Power helped provide the glue to hold the effort together." Topazi observed that "Elmer Harris provided leadership all along the way. I think his insistence that we all take active roles in our communities is one reason that Alabama can be effective in efforts like this. We've built solid relationships with government, business and education leaders." Topazi pointed out that the resources of Alabama Power "helped the state and county respond with facts about Alabama."[117]

Dr. Dieter Zetsche of the board of management for Mercedes-Benz said that "if anybody still asks why we chose Tuscaloosa, my answer will be short and simple—have you ever heard of the State of Surprises?" Helmut Werner, president and CEO of Mercedes-Benz, noted that while the incentive package the state of Alabama offered was important to his company, "it wasn't the deciding point. In Alabama, we found an open-minded atmosphere, entrepreneurial spirit and very little bureaucracy."[118] Alabama Power's governmental affairs leaders supported the incentive package through the legislature. Public relations worked behind the scenes to make certain that citizens understood the importance of this $300 million plant to the state of Alabama, while downplaying any role played by Alabama Power.[119]

On May 4, 1994, Governor Jim Folsom Jr., state officials, several Alabama Power Company people, and the Mercedes leaders gathered at the 966-acre site in Vance for the groundbreaking ceremony. The governor stressed the new jobs being created and the importance of positioning Alabama to recruit other international companies; Elmer Harris emphasized that Mercedes would be a "good customer for Alabama Power," requiring 18 megawatts of power initially and more later; and Dr. Dieter Zetsche said that as he had watched relationships develop he was "more sure than ever that Mercedes-Benz made the right decision to come to Tuscaloosa."[120]

Safety Is Always First at Alabama Power

In February 1994, workers at Lay Dam celebrated fifty years without a lost-time accident. Part of Lay Dam's history included one of the most tragic accidents in Alabama Power's past. Fifty years before, on Valentine's Day in 1944, three employees were killed and one was fatally injured when Lay Dam's No. 4 generator spun out of control. Danny Tignor, group supervisor at Lay in 1994, observed that "there are so many days for an accident to occur during fifty years.

View of the 1944 Lay Dam unit 4 generator that failed and killed three men and fatally injured another. In the fifty years between the 1944 tragedy and 1994 there were no lost-time accidents at the dam.

I'd have to say that it's pretty rare for any generating plant to go that long." Lay Dam's employees were part of the same safety programs that were in place at other Alabama Power plants, but Tignor speculated that because of the 1944 accident each generation of workers at Lay made a special effort to stress the importance of safety. As the record rolled on through the decades, employees worked more carefully so they would not be the one to break the long-standing safety record.[121]

Hydro Issues

In 1993 Yates and Thurlow Dams came up for relicensing. Work on the renewal application began in 1988 and included what Barry Lovett, then power generation engineer, called an aggressive proposal to increase the minimum water release from Thurlow from 70 cubic feet per second (cfs) to 1,200 cfs. This would provide a more constant water flow and improve fish habitat and recreational opportunities downstream. The company worked closely with state and federal environmental and wildlife agencies to implement the plan long before the final relicense request was presented to Federal Energy Regulatory Commission, which granted forty-year operating licenses to Alabama Power for both dams on February 3, 1994. The relicense included an upgrade to increase the generating power to a total of 38 megawatts. This relicense process went so smoothly that the FERC staff called the Alabama Power relicense application and process a model for other utilities.[122]

The summer of 2000 brought another challenge for Alabama Power's hydro facilities. Alabama suffered a severe drought, which the National Weather Service reported actually began two years earlier. Water levels in Alabama rivers were reduced and hydro generation was affected. The hydro team used all the water they could to generate electricity, but they had to make certain there was adequate water for industrial use, aquatic environments, and navigation and that water supply and water quality were maintained.[123] Alabama Power was using computers to analyze data on plant discharges, water elevations in the reservoirs, rain gauges, and stream gauges and hourly meteorological and hydrological information from the National Weather Service to manage its hydro generation and water levels in order to make maximum use of its hydro generation.[124]

ENVIRONMENTAL ISSUES OF THE 1990S

As the decade of the 1990s opened, Alabama Power was supporting research on solar energy, sulfur dioxide, fly ash, acid rain, nitrogen oxides, and the effects of acid rain on lakes and trees. In 1990 Alabama Power was meeting or doing better than required on all standards for clean air that were then mandated. To make certain the public understood the company's positions and activities, it began a well-coordinated environmental program in the 1990s that included Alabama Power employees volunteering in the Teacher Corps program to promote reading and to teach about the environment and safety rules. The program also included environmental kits and animal puppets. To encourage roadside cleanups, the company provided garbage bags, with Alabama Power Company/Keep America Beautiful printed in large letters on the side. Many of these plastic sacks were distributed in northern Alabama and so many were being used by volunteers cleaning up trash along roadways that TVA supporters noted the community support. The company established The Water Course in Clanton, where students could participate in interactive programs to learn about Alabama waterways and how to protect this natural resource. Alabama Power began participating in Earth Day, expanded its Christmas tree recycling program, and planted six million trees in Alabama.

The company's first proactive environmental publication came from its involvement with Earth Day in 1990. The ten-page booklet traced the history of the company and its commitment to environmental issues, while touting the advantages the state had from its large coal reserves and abundant rivers and expressing the company's apprehension about pending congressional legislation that would add costs to electrical users. In 1993 the company began a reintroduction program with ten baby peregrine falcons raised in a hacking box on the roof of the power company building. People dressed in bird outfits fed the falcons so they could more easily be reintroduced into the wild. Although there have been numerous sightings, in 2006 no one had been able to read a leg tag to verify that the falcons stayed in this area. Alabama Power supported the Forever Wild legislation that called for the purchase of valuable wildlands and placing the lands in trust. The constitutional amendment that established Forever Wild passed with 80 percent of Alabama voters approving.[125] In 1993 Elmer Harris joined and later became a trustee of the Nature Conservancy of Alabama.

Clean air and clean water were the two dominant issues of federal environmental concern in the 1990s. Water was important to the company's operation because it was used for cooling in coal-fired and nuclear plants and to produce electricity in hydro plants. Alabama Power had always supported programs of pollution prevention and used weirs, deflector plate turbine aeration systems, and, at Logan Martin Dam, the Speece Cone to increase the dissolved oxygen in its hydro plant discharges. The company increased testing of water quality in its reservoirs and rivers and improved the quality of its technology. It created a three-acre, specially designed wetlands area at Plant Gorgas to research its effect on cleaning water runoff from the coal pile.[126]

But it was clean air legislation that gave the company the most concern. After 1977 there was increased interest in acid rain and a concerted effort in Congress to strengthen the Clean Air Act of 1970. The Southern Company electric systems lobbied for changes that would be based upon sound science, regulations that realistically could be implemented and were not too costly for consumers of electricity.[127] In August 1990 Ed Addison, president of Southern Company, circulated the company's 1991 strategic plan that included an environmental commitment that the company would "meet or surpass all environmental laws and regulations" and that its business would be conducted "to enhance the quality of the environment."[128]

In 1990 amendments to the Clean Air Act finally passed Congress and were signed into law, a law that has been described as "the most comprehensive, complicated, and far-reaching environmental statute ever enacted."[129] The amendments were so broad that the Environmental Protection Agency had to write extensive regulations and interpretations. These regulations addressed the emissions of fine particles, sulfur dioxide, nitrogen oxides (by-products

Alabama Power has an ongoing program to evaluate different sources of renewable engergy, including switchgrass and other biomass. Of primary concern is that there be environmental benefits and the cost is commensurate with that benefit.

of fossil-fuel combustion and other chemical processes), ozone, carbon monoxide, and lead. The amendments established Title IV of the Clean Air Act that required significant reductions of sulfur dioxide and nitrogen oxide and established the use of allowances.

The Title IV amendments were implemented in phases. Southern Company's initial compliance strategy for Phase I was to switch to low-sulfur coal to reduce the emission of sulfur dioxide, to begin plant upgrades, and to purchase annual emission allowances under EPA regulations. These actions would give the company time to see how the EPA regulations would be applied and what the courts would rule before spending millions (eventually billions) of dollars on technology that in the end might not be required or would not work. Southern Company initiated its environmental strategic plan in 1992 with the goal of becoming an electric utility industry leader in environmental stewardship.[130] In January 1992 Elmer Harris issued corporate policy statements that defined the company's commitment to compliance with laws and regulations.[131]

On September 16, 1992, Harris released an Alabama Power Corporate Policy Statement on Environmental Policy. It detailed the company's commitment to "meet or surpass all environmental laws, regulations, and permit requirements and verify this commitment through environmental auditing," while seeking "to ensure that environmental laws, regulations, and permit requirements are based on sound science and cost-effective technology."[132] By 1995 Alabama Power had spent $25 million for control equipment to comply with nitrogen oxide emission limits. Phase II compliance involved further reduction of emissions beginning in 2000 with expenditures totaling $63 million by that year.[133]

Meanwhile, Alabama Power had built electrostatic precipitators, which were able to clean the exhaust gases of fossil-fuel plants by removing more than 99 percent of the fly ash particulates, and was working to improve the ground-level ozone conditions in the Birmingham area.[134] While Title IV implementation was ongoing, renewed interest in the ozone standard focused on Alabama Power's coal-fired power plants when studies conducted during 1998 called for nitrogen oxide emission reductions beyond those required to comply with the acid rain provisions of Title IV. Additional construction to comply with the one-hour ozone nonattainment standards for the Birmingham area were to be implemented by May 2003 with an estimated cost of about $230 million.[135]

By 2000 Alabama Power announced that it had eliminated 30 percent of its per-megawatt-hour emission of nitrogen oxides by using cleaner fuels and by installing low-nitrogen oxide burners on eleven of its generating units. Sulfur dioxide emissions had been reduced 28 percent per megawatt hour. Alabama Power had also added natural gas to its fuel mix, thus reducing carbon dioxide emissions.[136] The company set a goal for its employees to be committed to the company's environmental plans. Much effort went into writing and printing brochures and updates on the company's environmental programs. In the 1993 Vision Progress Survey, 86 percent of the company's people showed they understood these programs by their answers to questions about the company's environmental programs.[137] Alabama Power continued to recognize the importance of employee support for environmental issues in the community and encouraged involvement.

Politics and TVA

In the 1990s Alabama Power took an active role in working with state officials. Elmer Harris, always careful not to become identified with any political party or candidate, was supportive of whoever was elected to office, especially the governor. In the 1994 gubernatorial elections, Fob James ran as a Republican and defeated incumbent Democratic governor Jim Folsom Jr. by a slender margin. Harris, who had worked closely with Folsom on the Mercedes recruitment and had also worked with James in his first administration, anticipated a probusiness administration in Montgomery.[138] Alabama Power did publicly support certain issues in these years, favoring, for instance, both tax and educational reform.

In Washington, lobbying activities in the 1990s were directed by Julian Smith and Phillip Wiedmeyer. Some assistance came from Karl Moor and Gordon G. Martin, who were with a Washington law firm. The group was particularly focused on trying to get two outdated acts—the Public Utility

Holding Company Act (PUHCA) and the Public Utility Regulatory Policies Act (PURPA)—repealed because a nationwide restructuring of the electricity industry threatened to pit Alabama Power and other investor-owned utilities against generators of power not regulated under these acts. Alabama Power especially was opposed to the heavier taxes assessed against public utilities compared to the taxes independent generators were required to pay. The different tax structure for nonutility generators would create an unfair advantage for those suppliers in a competitive market and the dual regulations caused higher costs for customers.[139]

The Washington, D.C., office also kept close tabs on the Tennessee Valley Authority. One of the challenges Alabama Power faced in 1995 was an aggressive attempt by TVA to expand and compete with private power producers. Chris Womack, vice president of public relations, represented Alabama Power and took a leadership role in opposing this move. Womack responded firmly to TVA director Craven Crowell, who had announced that TVA wanted congressional approval to compete with Alabama Power. TVA began paying for television advertisements in the Birmingham area and sending marketing representatives into Alabama Power's territory to conduct free energy audits. Womack noted that TVA had "enjoyed an unnatural and artificial competitive advantage since it was set up by President Franklin Roosevelt sixty-two years ago," concluding that "if the 'fence' that keeps TVA from competing outside its service territory comes down, the agency's current advantages must be eliminated." Womack pointed out that the agency paid no federal income taxes, and the amount it paid in lieu of state and local taxes was much lower than the taxes paid by Alabama Power. In 1993 Alabama Power paid 13.9 cents of every dollar it earned in taxes while TVA paid 5 cents based upon wholesale prices. TVA also borrowed money at a much lower rate than private companies could obtain in the marketplace. Womack noted that in 1995 Alabama Power was charging 3.72 cents a kilowatt hour while TVA's charge was 4.19 cents.[140]

The operating companies of Southern Company discovered that TVA was selling to a power marketing affiliate of a Kentucky utility. On January 12, 1996, Alabama Power, Georgia Power, and Mississippi Power filed suit against the Tennessee Valley Authority for violating the congressional mandate that TVA be confined to selling power in the area it served in 1957.[141] On August 28, federal judge Robert Propst ruled that TVA was in violation of selling power outside the 1957 "fence" and in a fifty-page memorandum opinion wrote that TVA's argument that is was not "selling" power but was "exchanging power" was a "stretch of realism."[142] The case was settled out of court to Alabama Power's satisfaction. In February 1997 Karl Moor organized TVA

Watch, a group coordinated by Gordon Martin with David Ratcliffe as its first head. TVA Watch was to make certain that TVA did not attempt to market its federally subsidized power outside its boundaries. Martin explained at the time that "if TVA is allowed to enter into a competitive market without significant reform, it could have a dramatic effect on our company."[143]

ECONOMIC DEVELOPMENT

Throughout the 1990s Elmer Harris pushed his economic development team to recruit international industry. Although some questioned the generous incentive package the state offered Mercedes, it proved to be the beginning of a significant automobile manufacturing component in the state's economy. With the support of the Eastern Division office, Honda was recruited to Lincoln, Alabama, in 1999. The manufacturing investments in the automotive industry helped replace the jobs and power loads being lost in the textile industry. Harris made a number of international visits to sell Alabama to companies considering locating a plant in the United States. In an economic conference called by President-elect Bill Clinton in Little Rock in December 1992, Harris stressed to the gathering the strength of private enterprise and how partnerships between government and business could be successful.[144]

Charlton B. McArthur, vice president of economic development, retired and was replaced by Phillip R. Wiedmeyer, who headed up industrial recruitment in 1994 and 1995. C. Stephen Fant took over in 1996 and held those responsibilities until May 2001. With the success of the Mercedes-Benz recruitment still fresh, in 1994 Alabama Power helped convince Packard Electric, a General Motors subsidiary, to come to Gadsden. In analyzing the success of the recruitment of this 1,200-worker plant, Jim Wible, senior economic development

The Honda plant in Lincoln is the second largest automobile plant to locate in Alabama.

representative, pointed to the cooperation with the Alabama Development Office and the use of company planes and helicopters to transport the Packard team to Alabama and tour it around the state.[145] Alabama Power also worked with the Birmingham Metropolitan Development Board in the fall of 1998 through the spring of 1999 to recruit Honda to Lincoln.

Federal Energy Policy Act and Deregulation

In the early 1990s Alabama Power identified several areas of concern for the company. One was the push for deregulation of the electrical industry. Since the early 1980s, the climate favored less governmental regulation, which was manifested in various industries from airlines to telecommunications with mixed results. Regulated utilities were required by statute to build electric generating plants to serve all customers in its territory. In many parts of the country (notably California and the Northeast), state regulatory commissions required utilities to build or purchase inefficient and costly generation facilities (such as solar or wind) to meet environmental or social objectives. Utilities that had constructed expensive nuclear plants or were forced to buy from so-called PURPA machines at inflated prices did so with the implied promise that they would be able to recover these inflated costs in retail rates. PURPA, the Public Utility Regulatory Policies Act, included "must buy" provisions for cogeneration and small power production facilities if certain conditions were met.

As a result of these forced federal initiatives, regulated utilities were understandably concerned about the new law that would allow customers, for which these huge investments were made, to now buy power from a nonregulated independent power producer, thus leaving these expensive generation facilities stranded and uncompetitive.

Stranded costs, as they were called, were a national issue. Alabama Power believed it only fair that it should be reimbursed for these costs, but it was less concerned about the problem than most utilities because its regulators—the Alabama Public Service Commission—had not required the company to make inefficient and costly investments in noncompetitive generation. Furthermore, Plant Farley, the company's only nuclear plant, although expensive, was operating well and proving to be quite competitive. Alabama Power was never concerned about competing on a level playing field, but it was anxious about marketplace competition when it remained so heavily regulated on the federal and state levels, while new independent power producers would not be regulated. The company was not threatened by transmitting power because voluntary wheeling of electricity across transmission lines occurred on the Southern Company system every day.[146]

Just before the presidential election of 1992, on October 24, Congress passed the long–debated National Energy Policy Act, which allowed competition with regulated investor-owned utilities. The complicated law encouraged conservation of energy and made it easier and less costly for new and independent investments in generation to have access to established transmission lines, thus making it easier for new generation companies to compete and reach customers of the older utilities. This competition in generation made no allowance for compensation to the utilities for stranded costs. Across the nation, these stranded costs were estimated to be in the billions of dollars, costs that could be legitimately passed on to rate payers in the form of higher power bills. It was a huge issue nationally, as utilities tried to specify how these costs would be covered.[147]

As 1995 opened, Elmer Harris was approaching his sixth year as chief executive officer. When asked if there would be layoffs in 1995, he replied that was not on his mind because he thought the company could achieve its goals of becoming more efficient and productive by attrition. Since 1989 the number of employees had been reduced from about 9,698 to 7,261 through early retirements, natural attrition, and the transfer of people on Alabama Power's payroll to other subsidiaries of Southern Company; Harris thought this pattern would continue. Alabama Power was one of the lowest priced utilities in the nation and had managed since 1985 to keep prices stable while the consumer price index increased 40 percent. Harris saw the biggest challenge for Alabama Power to be increased competition from deregulation, which would necessitate decreasing prices. Harris stressed that operations and maintenance budgets would be slashed again, and he expected that by 1999 capital expenses would be cut $100 million.[148]

As the national debate over deregulation and stranded costs continued, Harris decided that Alabama needed a state law to protect the company and its customers. He began efforts to prevent an independent power producer from "cherry-picking" large industrial customers, which would result in increasing the cost of electricity to the remaining residential customers. Donnie Reese, who was on Alabama Power's team working for the legislation, recalled that most of the municipal systems, the Alabama Electric Cooperative, the Alabama Rural Electric Association, and TVA all joined Alabama Power in support of such protection. Reese, who began his career with Alabama Power in 1969 as a junior sales representative in Phenix City and moved to the Wiregrass area in 1975, began lobbying for support for Alabama Power in 1985.[149]

Governor Fob James and Elmer Harris discussing issues affecting the state of Alabama.

In the spring of 1996, when Alabama Power pushed for legislation to protect its customers and its investments, Reese was deeply involved. A bill was introduced that provided a review process through which the stranded costs of a utility were determined when a customer left one system for another supplier. The debates were heated and contentious, and the Business Council of Alabama split over the bill. During the legislative process, on April 24, the Federal Energy Regulatory Commission issued a ruling that electric utilities must open their transmission lines to wholesale competitors. Harris recalls that the stranded costs bill passed the Alabama legislature without a single negative vote. On May 6, 1996, Governor Fob James signed the Alabama Electric Consumers Act, which would have the Public Service Commission and the circuit courts review contracts to see if they were in the public's best interest.[150]

With its nuclear plants being successfully operated under Southern Nuclear Operating Company and in anticipation of deregulation, in 1993 Southern Company organized its fossil and hydro generation into one group. Bill Guthrie, who had been in charge of Alabama Power's generation since January 1, 1988, was Southern's choice to head up generation. He worked with this matrix organization for five years and made giant strides toward making the generation plants more efficient. At the end of his tenure, Southern Company's generation cost was one of the lowest in the nation. As Guthrie approached retirement, Charles D. McCrary was selected to replace him on March 3, 1998, as executive vice president of Southern Company's Fossil/Hydro Group. McCrary changed the name to Southern Company Generation, which better explained the organization's responsibilities and helped with the group's image. In the generation organization, McCrary faced employee morale problems borne of uncertainty about their own and their plants' futures because of what was happening nationwide in the industry, and he also faced a wild rumor mill churning out speculation about what Southern Company intended to do with its generation facilities. The popular notion among gurus at the time was that utilities needed to divest their investments in generation plants. Some preached that real profits came from trading, not from generation. California had not yet suffered its long summer of rolling blackouts and skyrocketing electricity prices in 2000, and Enron had not yet imploded.[151]

McCrary visited his plants and talked and gathered his troops for a strategy meeting on September 14, 1998. He said he knew they were tired, and the plants were tired. They had gone through a brutally hot summer with exceptionally high demand, and they had kept the equipment operating efficiently. McCrary told his people he was not going to announce any restructuring, but change was coming. He was not certain what it might be. McCrary challenged his people to change the culture of generation, to adopt a best-practices culture, because with competition, they would have to improve even more. He said, "When I look and see you walking around, you've got your heads hanging down, and there is no joy in your life, no joy in your work." McCrary told them they were the best generation people in America: "If you are not the best, become the best. If you are the best, act like it. I want to see you swagger."[152]

The movement for competition that McCrary was preparing generation to win kept moving forward in 1999. The rationale for competition was that free markets always lowered costs, but that was not exactly what the results were in the few states that moved to deregulation, most encouraged by heavy lobbying by trading companies like Enron. As the Alabama Public Service Commission watched the national deregulation trend move onward, it was keenly aware that with Alabama having some of the lowest power rates in the nation, the talk of equalizing rates across the country translated into Alabama's electricity rates going up. Nationally, deregulation produced mixed results, but generally the cost of electricity rose. The widely publicized events in California in 2000 had a chilling effect upon the push for deregulation. In a complex set of circumstances, too involved to retell here, deregulation of California's energy market, coupled with a shortage of electricity in the hot summer of 2000, sent electrical prices sky-high, resulting in rolling blackouts and brownouts and ultimately placing some $20 billion to $28 billion of stranded costs on the bills of California rate payers. On the heels of that California summer came the Enron collapse, which gave more credence to charges that the nation's largest electrical trading company made enormous profits by manipulating the price of electricity in California that summer. The debacle sent shock waves through the industry and brought the impetus for deregulation almost to a halt.[153]

In January 2001 Southern Company announced the formation of a new subsidiary, Southern Power Company, which would own, manage, and finance future competitive wholesale generating assets in the Southeast. The fundamental purpose of Southern Power was to grow Southern Company's longer-term market-based energy business through multiyear negotiated contracts predicted on these new generating assets. McCrary, who was responsible for setting up Southern Power in addition to the Southern Company Generation organization, served as Southern Power's first president and CEO. In meeting these challenges, McCrary had to focus on business results in terms of both increased efficiency as well as financial performance. In the process, he acquired valuable knowledge and experience that would serve him well in the future.[154]

Technology

The 1990s witnessed an explosion of computer technology and innovations. Alabama Power supported research in geothermal heat pump technology and trained technicians at its center at Mitchell Dam.[155] The advent of new technology encouraged Alabama Power to consolidate seven transmission control centers into one at the Alabama Control and Dispatch Center at the corporate headquarters. When Banks Farris announced the consolidation, he said that the change would allow the company to meet the challenges of the future by ensuring that decisions are made quickly by the appropriate individuals. A new energy management system and an 800-megahertz communication system provided operational efficiencies. New technology allowed Alabama

Heat pump center at Mitchell Dam trains technicians in heat pump technology.

Power to determine from a remote location the amount of electricity a customer used, and in 1995 the company froze the hiring of new meter readers and began a skills training program for meter readers so they could take jobs in other areas of the company.

Alabama Power adapted the latest technology in transmission and distribution systems so that substations and distribution lines could be automated and power restored if lines were not down. In 1991 a team headed by Larry Clark, principal engineer, and Homer Cotton, real time systems manager, developed an ambitious plan to extend automation on the transmission and distribution system through deployment of supervisory control and data acquisition (SCADA). SCADA radios were used to control substation breakers and automated line devices were placed on the poles to tell which lines were out. Armed with a sound technical plan and management support, it is one of the premier automation efforts in the country, and it positions the company to move forward in its plans to take automation technology to new levels in the twenty-first century.[156]

Distributed resources, also known as distributed generation, are customer-owned sources of electric power that can provide emergency or backup power. Alabama Power first negotiated an agreement with an industrial customer, purchasing excess electricity from its plant about 1985, and about 1992 began utilizing customer-owned standby generation to reduce electric system peak demands. By 2005 the company was purchasing excess power from seventy-six customers, and this distributed generation provided up to 84 megawatts of capacity to the system during peak times and under contingency conditions. Use of this capacity improves reliability and allows the company to defer construction of a plant to provide peaking capacity.[157]

The company was rapidly developing technology systems for everything it did. In January 1998 the Birmingham Division installed computers in the trucks of nine local operations linemen. Work orders were assigned automatically through the Automated Resource Management System that combined laptops, software, and a 900-megahertz data radio frequency.[158]

The Harris Years

The computer-related catastrophes predicted for January 1, 2000, did not materialize, and the new year rolled in with celebrations and no glitch in electrical supply and no crises, perhaps because of the effort that went into making certain automated systems and controls would work well when the new year arrived. Alabama Power's net income for 2000 was $420 million, an increase of $20 million over 1999. A long hot summer in 2000 increased sales by 4.7 billion kilowatt hours, and despite an extensive drought, Alabama Power's electric service was 99.95 percent available, which exceeded the company's previous reliability record. The company's use of a diverse fuel mix for generation—hydro, coal, oil, natural gas, and nuclear—allowed the company flexibility, which enabled it to somewhat mitigate increasing fuel costs. Cogeneration agreements and contracts where power could be interrupted during peak periods reduced the demand on the system. A strong economic climate in Alabama also caused sales of electricity to increase in 2000. The company's average rate of return on common equity was at 13.58 percent, down slightly from 1999's return of 13.85 and 1998's return of 13.63. The decrease was due to an increase in expenses.[159]

By stressing efficiency and by cutting operation and maintenance budgets and implementing new technologies, the company was able to function and move forward with only minor rate increases. The lean budgets had, however, affected routine upkeep on plants and lines as nonessential repairs were placed on hold. The company's employees were more diverse at the end of the twentieth century than they had been ten years before. By gender Alabama Power's employees were 76 percent male and 24 percent female. The workforce of 6,792 employees was 80 percent white, 19 percent black, and 1 percent Asian, Hispanic, or American Indian. Alabama Power employees owned 17.9 million shares of Southern Company stock in savings and stock ownership plans. Twenty-two percent of the company's employees worked in plants and dams, while 19 percent worked in the corporate headquarters. Other employees were scattered across the company and the divisions.[160]

Elmer Harris often said that "ten years is enough" to be a chief executive officer and shoulder the responsibilities of leadership for Alabama Power. By 2001 he had served twelve years.[161] To many of the state's people, Elmer Harris had become synonymous with Alabama Power, and to the power company's family he was simply Elmer. John Young, who had worked with Harris from his position at Southern Generation in the 1990s and who in 2005 was the chief financial officer of Exelon Corporation in Chicago, observed that one of Harris's finest attributes was "to allow and encourage unknown talent to be successful."[162] Joe Farley pointed to Elmer's "bright mind and keen understanding of utility rate making and his understanding of the realities of the rate-making process" as valuable talents that "enabled Elmer to have been the key figure in achieving a far better approach in Alabama." Allen Franklin, who was chief executive officer of Georgia Power (1994–99) and president and chief operating officer of Southern Company from 1999 to 2001, when he was made chairman and CEO, noted that "when you look back on the last thirty years, one of the most important things for Southern Company was getting Plants Farley and Vogtle in the rate base. Elmer deserves a good deal of credit for both."[163]

Harris's insistence on putting the customer first and making Alabama Power respond quickly to customers' needs changed the way employees served customers. His twelve years of leadership saw Alabama Power's image improve and the company's presence in the state solidified. Harris knew that the marketplace was growing more competitive every day, and he had positioned the company to compete, making it lean and efficient. In analyzing why Elmer Harris had been successful in his leadership of Alabama Power Company, his friend Walter Johnsey observed that "Elmer has a unique persistence. He never recognizes rejection."[164] This was a characteristic Harris shared with Thomas W. Martin, who never accepted no for an answer when he wanted a yes. Harris's decentralization of decision making transformed the way the company operated. Bill Johnson, who was once Harris's assistant, pointed to the changes Harris made, comparing the way the company did business in 1990 with the way the company operated in 2005. Johnson also appreciated how far the company had come from those days of being "unjustly beaten up" and the "wonderful things accomplished through the Alabama Power Foundation."[165]

On October 26, 2001, the board of directors of Alabama Power Company adopted a resolution commending Elmer Harris's forty-four years of service to the company and detailing his leadership, which ended on January 11, 2002. Four days later his friends and colleagues gathered to send Harris and his wife Glenda into retirement with a gala dinner celebration that included the announcement by Southern Company CEO Franklin that the Southern Power Company's combined-cycle facility in Autaugaville was being named Plant Harris to recognize Elmer Harris's leadership of Alabama Power.

Renew Our Rivers, started by Alabama Power employee Gene Phifer in 1999 on the Coosa River, is the Southeast's largest organized river-system cleanup. Tom Cooper of Alabama Power and other community volunteers collect trash.

target
ZERO
Every day, every job, safely.

MADELYN COUCH COUNTS ON
HER DADDY.

WHETHER IT'S BAITING A FISH
HOOK OR HELPING WITH
HOMEWORK, 7-YEAR-OLD
MADELYN COUNTS ON HER
DADDY, DEMOPOLIS LOCAL
OPERATION LINEMAN JEFF
COUCH. SHE COUNTS ON HIM
EVERY DAY, JUST LIKE ALABAMA
POWER DOES TO HELP KEEP THE
LIGHTS ON FOR OUR CUSTOMERS.
AND, MORE IMPORTANTLY,
MADELYN AND ALL OF US AT
ALABAMA POWER COUNT ON
HER DADDY TO ENSURE THAT
SAFETY IS THE NO. 1 PRIORITY IN
DOING HIS JOB.

TARGET ZERO. EVERY DAY.
EVERY JOB. SAFELY.
WE'RE COUNTING ON YOU!

ALABAMA
POWER
A SOUTHERN COMPANY

Target Zero was introduced at Alabama Power in 2004. It establishes the mindset that no accident is acceptable.

At the March 2006 Business Forum, on behalf of the company, Charles McCrary accepted from Anthony Topazi, president of Mississippi Power, a poster signed by hundreds of Mississippi Power employees thanking Alabama Power for its help in restoration after Hurricane Katrina.

Chapter Eleven

Alabama Power has developed techniques for
storm restoration, and its crews have achieved
national recognition for their ability to restore
service quickly using the highest safety standards.

INTO THE TWENTY-FIRST CENTURY

*In 2005, we cannot afford—literally or figuratively—to live in a vacuum.
We cannot afford to focus solely on ourselves, because we are increasingly
impacted by national and global issues and events.*

CHARLES D. MCCRARY,

ALABAMA POWER COMPANY BUSINESS FORUM, MOBILE, 2005

At a special meeting of the Alabama Power Company board of directors
on April 26, 2001, Charles D. McCrary was elected president and chief operating officer of the company in a move that caught few people by surprise.[1]
Astute observers of Alabama Power and Southern Company's top management
realized it was coming and was only a matter of time, especially after H. Allen
Franklin became president of Southern Company in June 1999.[2] He had been
a mentor to McCrary and had watched him handle several challenging responsibilities with remarkable success. Elmer Harris, who agreed with Franklin that
McCrary should be his successor, made the public announcement and said he

would stay on as chief executive officer and chairman of the board during a transition period.[3]

Previously, the administrative authority at Alabama Power went to the new president and the retiring executive took the position of chairman of the board. The title of CEO had only occasionally been used by Joe Farley, because it was clear in the bylaws that the president was the chief executive officer. The title was used at Georgia Power and Gulf Power at least by 1987. Farley recalled signing some documents, especially from the Securities and Exchange Commission, as CEO when that was required. The title CEO had been given to Elmer Harris in March 1989 in addition to his title of president. In October 1949, when James M. Barry became president, Tom Martin maintained his control of the company from his new position as chairman of the board, and he did so for fourteen years. When Walter Bouldin stepped down in 1969, he moved into the position of CEO and chairman of the board for a one-year transition period. When Farley was elected president and CEO, Bouldin, who stayed as chairman of the board for another few months, told him, "I'll be down the hall if you need me."[4] Farley recalled that the position of chairman was favored at that time by Southern Company to facilitate the transition of responsibility, and company bylaws were amended to provide for or remove the titles and positions and facilitate retirement.[5] In 1989, since Farley was moving directly to Southern Nuclear Operating Company, he did not remain at Alabama Power.

In 2001 Elmer Harris retained executive authority until McCrary was elected CEO at the board's quarterly meeting on October 25, 2001. In making this announcement, Harris told the *Birmingham News* that "our industry, our state and our nation are facing a time of great challenge and uncertainty. It is a time that requires great leadership and strong leaders. Charles McCrary offers both."[6] Harris retired on January 11, 2002. The title CEO was required under certain provisions of the Sarbanes-Oxley Act of 2002, which has been described as the most significant change to U.S. securities laws since the New Deal. The new law places certain responsibilities on the chief executive officer of a company, and one early challenge McCrary faced was making certain Alabama Power was in compliance with the new law.

Charles McCrary had been on a fast track for executive leadership since the mid-1980s. He grew up in the company and understood the power business. His mechanical engineering and law degrees provided a broad educational base, and, as Allen Franklin recognized, McCrary was a leader who was extremely serious about his work and his principles, "a bright guy who worked hard, who had no political motivations, and had the ability to tell people what the facts were and not upset people." Franklin observed that McCrary was also a "fun-loving guy" who got along well with people, instilled confidence, and had the ability to lead. Joe Farley recalled that when McCrary was his assistant and later when he went to Southern Nuclear Operating Company with him, McCrary succeeded at the jobs assigned to him and stayed focused on the challenges at hand.[7]

McCrary's first job out of Auburn University was with the engineering department of Southern Services in 1973. A short time later, his father moved from Alabama Power to Southern Services to direct the department where Charles was working. Both admit this was not fun for either one of them. Charles started calling his father

Charles D. McCrary

"Douglas" because, as he explained, "I could not call him 'Daddy' in a meeting," and Doug remembered that he "never gave Charles a break, and I understand why he wanted to get out of there."[8] Despite the tensions, a longtime father-son closeness based upon common interests, especially all things mechanical and most especially old jukeboxes, survived and deepened. It was Charles's well-known love for repairing mechanical things that caused Bill Frederick, business manager of IBEW, to comment that the union believed Charles could relate more to them because he worked with his hands.[9]

In 1982 Allen Franklin was a senior vice president at Alabama Power, which was struggling with a critical environmental survey, and Franklin offered the younger McCrary a job heading up the company's environmental compliance department.[10] If McCrary realized what kind of quicksand he was stepping into, he never shared it at the time. As a young man, he was directing older, senior management personnel to do things a new way, and he was responsible for making certain they did it that way. In the generation plants the common attitude was that environmental staff came by occasionally and told them what to do. Senior generation leaders tended to side with their own people. Given an unpopular role, McCrary had to figure out how to maintain sufficient personal popularity to win the generation workers and their leadership over to new ways of meeting new challenges. He put a permanent environmental compliance team in every Alabama Power generation plant. Through hard work and determined effort, he and his staff were able to develop a dedicated environmental program.[11]

After serving as Joe Farley's assistant and as vice president of Southern Company Services with the Southern Nuclear Operating project, McCrary came back to Alabama Power in 1991 as vice president of external affairs, becoming executive vice president three years later. In this position, he was responsible for public relations, governmental affairs, and the company's relationship with the Public Service Commission, where he worked closely with the staff, commission president Jim Sullivan, and commissioners Charles B. Martin and Jan Cook. Martin served from November 1986 to November 1998 and took a leadership role on the commission. Cook, a native of Dozier in Crenshaw County, joined the commission in 1990 from the state auditor's position. She had a special concern for Alabama agriculture and wanted to make certain commercial farmers could compete in a global market. She once encouraged Alabama Power to establish a special rate for poultry and catfish farmers.[12]

In Montgomery McCrary developed a reputation for being a straight shooter and someone who could be trusted. As vice president for external affairs he testified in 1992 before a congressional subcommittee considering the creation of the Little River Canyon National Preserve, in part reiterating the company's commitment to the environment, saying that Alabama Power had "to demonstrate our commitment every day through our deeds."[13] In his leadership of the company's external programs, McCrary insisted on extensive educational programs so Alabama Power's people understood what the applicable environmental laws were. He once said he was "more concerned about accidental violations—taking actions without knowing what the governing statute is."[14]

McCrary moved to Southern Company Generation in 1998, where he directed the formation of Southern Power Company to handle Southern Company's wholesale unregulated electricity sales and honed his skills while bringing that company together.[15] John Young, who worked closely with McCrary as executive vice president of Southern Generation, noted that at the time the conventional wisdom was to sell generation assets, but "Charles had the patience to study the issue, to encourage diversity of thought, to withhold judgment until he had all the facts, and to come up with the right decision. It was not an easy place for him to be, for the hierarchy was heading off in the opposite direction. It was easier to go along to get along, but Charles held his ground, encouraged good debate, and made financially sound decisions." Young believed that Charles's actions were a leadership skill as much as anything.[16]

C. Alan Martin

In his first press release as president of Alabama Power, McCrary tapped into history by thanking "all my fellow employees of Alabama Power for their support and encouragement," a phrase used almost continuously since the days of Thomas W. Martin. McCrary made three staff assignments. He moved C. Alan Martin into the executive vice president's position, vacant since Mike Garrett's election as president and CEO of Mississippi Power. Alan Martin was widely respected in the company and had taken over the responsibilities of Banks Farris when he retired. Martin had broad experiences in senior leadership, once serving as vice president of the Birmingham Division, and had returned to Alabama Power in 2000 after five years with Southern Company in Atlanta. Martin took over customer and corporate services and began to focus on Alabama Power regaining the number-one position in customer satisfaction, which it had lost in the previous few years. Because of the anticipation of competition, price and budget cuts had reduced the ability of the company to answer customer requests as quickly as before. Martin would focus on emphasizing local offices and community involvement, the Target Zero safety program he had initiated, and encouraging the corporate real estate department to utilize its land assets to produce net income.[17]

McCrary announced that Steve Spencer, who had worked with external affairs at Southern Nuclear Operating Company and was then senior vice president for external affairs, would replace Alan Martin as executive vice president, external affairs. Spencer had returned to Alabama Power after several years in Atlanta, where he was Southern Company chairman Bill Dahlberg's assistant and later was senior vice president for external affairs at Southern Company. Spencer was now responsible for Alabama Power's

Steve Spencer

economic development, state and federal government relations, community relations, environmental affairs, public relations, and advertising. Spencer was another second-generation Alabama Power employee; his father was a district manager in Birmingham for almost twenty years before his death in 1981, when he was serving as manager of the Huffman district. Spencer was an Auburn psychology major who joined Alabama Power's real estate department in 1978. He used his easygoing personality and people skills in human resources and employee relations and then moved into external affairs. McCrary valued his astute political mind and his ability to see and balance all the issues; he called Spencer "a great ambassador for this company."[18]

Robert Holmes, who had been part of the management team since his move from Plant Barry in 1992, was elected senior vice president of ethics and business practices. McCrary complimented Holmes on his community leadership and gave him the additional responsibility of serving as chairman of the Alabama Power Foundation.[19]

McCrary tapped John O. Hudson III, who had been hired by Chris Womack in 1996 and was then working in external affairs under Alan Martin, as his first assistant to the president. Hudson, the son of educators, grew up in Birmingham and was a political science graduate of Alabama A & M University. A gifted writer, Hudson worked on the staffs of the *Huntsville*

News, Huntsville Times, and the Birmingham News before joining Alabama Power. He later earned a law degree from Miles College and did postgraduate work at the Wharton School of Business at the University of Pennsylvania. Hudson first worked with McCrary when he handled communications for Southern Company Generation. McCrary recognized untapped potential and wanted to give Hudson opportunities to broaden his experiences.[20] After three years, Hudson became area manager for the Birmingham Division, and Elaine Kwarcinski moved from transmission and customer service to become assistant to the president. McCrary knew Kwarcinski was a talented and hard-working engineer, and he again used the assistant to the president position to develop leadership potential. Kwarcinski is a Birmingham native who had co-oped with Alabama Power while she earned her electrical engineering degree at UAB. A well-organized and detail-oriented person, Kwarcinski had experience in substations and generation planning and development before becoming the first woman to be named assistant to the president.[21]

In the weeks after assuming the presidency of Alabama Power, McCrary began traveling to the offices and plants, meeting the 6,700 company employees. One of the themes that emerged from those discussions was that Alabama Power needed to rediscover its sense of employee community. Employees needed to continue the company tradition of "not only being a highly efficient team, but also a family" and to have more fun together. In the months ahead, McCrary would find ways to address these ideas.[22] On one trip to Mobile in May, Birmingham News staff writer Ted Pratt tagged along to record what McCrary described as "like being on a campaign trail, except at the end, I don't ask them for their vote." On that trip, he was able to visit with employees at four offices and substations, meet with two mayors, and see a new Alabama Power board member. He talked about safety, working hard but enjoying your work, having fun in life, smiling.[23] McCrary also visited with the media around the state. The Birmingham Business Journal found the new Alabama Power president "remarkably candid and open, displaying a vibrant sense of humor."[24]

Circumstances over which McCrary had no control affected Alabama Power in the six months after he became president. The weather, for one thing. The summer of 2001 was mild, less air conditioning was needed, and Alabama Power lost $29 million in revenue compared to the previous year. In August financial results were falling so far short of goals that McCrary asked for immediate reduction in costs.[25] The power deregulation debacle had hit California the summer before, leaving, as McCrary noted in January 2002, the energy future "more murky than clear" and many questions about what the government's policy might be.[26] In September 2001 Enron imploded from its own failures and that same month terrorists flew two airplanes into the World Trade Center and one into the Pentagon.

Just after noon on September 11, 2001, McCrary sent an e-mail to his fellow employees asking for their prayers for those who were suffering, thanking them for their dedication and for staying focused on their jobs, and assuring them that the company had immediately taken appropriate precautionary measures and heightened security at all of Alabama Power's offices and plants.[27] Because of the drop in revenue and the uncertainties, McCrary again asked employees to find cost savings, cut back on travel and entertainment, and reduce advertising budgets. He cancelled outside consultant contracts and all Christmas parties, which he confessed earned him some grief and the nicknames "Scrooge" and "Grinch." But he defended the belt-tightening to help the company cope with added expenses such as the increased security that was necessary after the terrorist attacks.[28]

The events of 9/11 brought shock and disbelief to Alabama Power as they did to the entire country and all Americans. McCrary immediately requested a study of Alabama Power's security and asked for recommendations to tighten it. Alabama Power had not even had a security department before the 1966 strike but had employed off-duty law enforcement officers for specific tasks when needed. Although contract security was less expensive, the company wanted security officers who were identified with the company and who felt a sense of ownership toward it. After the 1966 strike, a small security department was created under David Hinman, and later much of the security detail was concentrated at Plant Farley.[29]

In September 2001 Randy Mayfield was in charge of security. He began working at Alabama Power in 1981 and had come to the corporate office from nuclear security in March 2001 as security manager. Lyle Mitchell, who was attending a session of a leadership program in Shelby County on the morning of September 11, 2001, rushed back to corporate headquarters to attend a hastily called management team meeting to discuss what needed to be done. Mitchell had joined Alabama Power in January 1981 as a general investigator after years working in law enforcement. A Haleyville native, Mitchell was working with both security and governmental affairs. After 9/11, immediate steps were taken to protect the company's infrastructures, and the number of people working in the company's security department almost doubled within a few months. Mayfield and Mitchell were on the Southern Company team that helped write the Edison Electric Institute and North American Electric Reliability Council's security guidelines, which were also adopted by Alabama Power. All employees were required to wear photo identification badges.

Mayfield recalled that McCrary was "a first-name CEO, and he wanted the first name printed on the badge much larger so he could read it."[30]

Economic and Community Development

McCrary knew that one of the challenges the company faced was rebuilding its legendary economic development department. Following the successful recruitment of the Mercedes plant, an expansion of the Economic Development Partnership of Alabama, and a higher profile for the Alabama Development Office, Alabama Power's industrial development department was weakened by the loss of key people. Some recruiters opted for the career transition plan instituted by Alabama Power Company as a cost-cutting program, giving employees the opportunity for early retirement. Also, Alabama Power management included the resources of the economic development department in its cost reductions, cutting back on international recruitment. During the last years of Elmer Harris's presidency, an increased emphasis was placed and more dollars invested in EDPA. There was the thought that a strong EDPA, working with ADO, meant there would be less need for Alabama Power's industrial recruitment activity. The career transition plan resulted in some of Alabama Power's staff transferring to EDPA, and others left or retired.[31]

Steve Fant was one of those economic recruiters who began planning for early retirement months before he left on April 30, 2001. In looking back on his years in selling the state of Alabama as a good place to build a new plant, he pointed to the number-one problem the recruitment team faced: the negative perception of the state of Alabama, especially in Europe. "We knew," he said, "that if we ever got those people to visit Alabama, we could change their perceptions." Fant explained that with Alabama Power serving two-thirds of the state, the company preferred new industry to locate in its service territory, but if for whatever reason a company was interested in an area served by TVA or a co-op, Alabama Power remained part of the team selling Alabama.[32]

In analyzing the challenges he faced leading Alabama Power, McCrary saw economic recruitment as significant and was determined that Alabama Power would not abandon its own economic development mission, which had played such a key role in the company's history. Helping to develop Alabama had been a theme in Alabama Power's story since James Mitchell acquired the company in 1912. Looking at the bottom line, McCrary wanted increased industrial, commercial, and residential loads for his company. Economic development directly affected Alabama Power's growth and income, and he was unwilling to place direction and responsibility for this in other hands. Personally, McCrary had a deep southern sense of place and commitment to his state and he realized that new industries created wealth. He was steadfast in wanting more jobs and better lives for Alabamians, which would also translate into a larger commercial and residential load for Alabama Power. He once said, "the only way to build a better, stronger Alabama Power Company is to first build a better, stronger Alabama."[33] McCrary appreciated that economic development was a team effort and that the governor was the number-one recruiter. The key to his company's growth and profits was economic development, and he knew he needed a new plan.[34]

McCrary and Spencer placed the responsibility for rebuilding economic development on the shoulders of Christopher T. Bell, who was elected vice president of economic development on May 1, 2001. Chris Bell, a Birmingham native, had joined Alabama Power in 1984 as a junior engineer at Plant Miller. He worked as manager of corporate planning and added a University of Alabama at Birmingham MBA to his Auburn civil engineering degree. Bell gained experience in public relations and external affairs. He was McCrary's assistant in 1997, then transferred to business development in Southern Company's energy marketing group. Soon after Bell accepted McCrary's and Spencer's challenge and moved to economic development, he attended a working lunch with them. The three plotted a new future for economic development expressed in this charge to Bell: regroup and return to dominance.[35]

Chris Bell

From this meeting came a brief 2002–07 five-year strategic plan designed to guide the rebuilding of economic development beginning with present strengths—such as credible, competent, and talented resources, a proven track record, strong network, and competent professionals across the service territory. If these assets were well used, they could overcome current weaknesses of staff size and diversity, a lack of presence in international recruiting, and a failure to link community development, among others. Through specific programs, the economic development team planned to regroup and return to dominance within five years.[36] One of the important first steps was to form a closer partnership with the company's community development staff because communities had to prepare for economic development and prosperity before the recruitment process went forward. Alabama Power recognized that it needed to help communities build the infrastructure and to develop their assets before moving to attract new business and industry.[37]

The focus of the company's 2002 business forum, where some 600 Alabama Power leaders came together to discuss the company's past year and its future direction, was RESULTS COUNT. McCrary challenged Alabama Power's people to do what they did best: "run the best electric company in America." He explained that only by measuring "our results can we make sure we're moving forward and taking care of all our stakeholders. Making a profit is the first measure of how we're doing as a company. If we don't make money, if we don't have earnings, we won't be here. So we must have financial results." He was fully aware that "this company has led the industry in empowering employees, now we must lead in accountability." McCrary emphasized that Alabama Power would not "round any corners" and would "continue to achieve its goals by acting legally, ethically, morally, and honestly. There is no other option. This is the first test we must apply to every action." Steve Spencer stressed that economic development was important and that the entire company needed to become involved to achieve results. He challenged the customer service managers to use their relationships and community involvement to focus on the company's economic development initiatives as well. Alan Martin stressed the same message to customer service and sales representatives.[38]

A few weeks after the business forum, Spencer announced that since "an essential part of our economic development process is ensuring our communities are prepared for economic growth," the community development group, which was then in corporate relations, would be transferred to economic development and the name changed to economic and community development.[39] The next month, Chris Bell gave a presentation to the Alabama Power board of directors and updated twenty-seven announced projects in which Alabama Power had played a significant role in the recruitment process. These projects represented a $550 million investment, brought almost 5,000 jobs to the state, and provided an additional annual load of 80–90 megawatts.[40] In early December 2002, two forums were held to explore economic and community development strategies and to make the leadership in divisions and business offices accept ownership in developing the company's service territory and growing earnings through economic and community development. These forums clarified roles and set expectations.[41]

Charles McCrary was serious about selling electricity, but above that he wanted to make certain the company made a profit on what it sold. As generation vice president Jerry Stewart noted, "Charles focuses on the bottom line. He wants to sell electricity, but he wants to make money." McCrary's experiences in operating Southern Generation had focused his attention on profit. McCrary's leadership style is all about results and measuring those results. As Stewart observed, at the end of the day, McCrary wants to know who is responsible.[42] McCrary carries calling cards with the motto: NO RESULTS PLUS EXCUSES DOES NOT EQUAL RESULTS.

Honda, which built a plant in Lincoln, was the second automobile company recruited to Alabama; Hyundai's plant south of Montgomery was the third. In 2003 McCrary asked the economic development staff to find a way to quantify the effect Hyundai's arrival in the state had on Alabama Power. What would be the effect of

Hyundai, with a plant located south of Montgomery, was the third automobile manufacturer recruited to Alabama.

Hyundai suppliers on Alabama Power's load? Tentative estimates were that by 2009, Hyundai suppliers would be generating about $5 million a year in additional revenue for Alabama Power.[43] This would include the $22 million manufacturing plant located in Enterprise by HS R&A, a Korean supplier for Hyundai rubber parts.[44] The impact of the automotive industries on Alabama Power and on the state was updated in 2004 but was still not firm because of uncertainties over the extent of expansions announced by both Mercedes and Honda; regardless, the revenue from these industries had increased Alabama Power's profits.[45]

Despite the revenue increases these automotive projects represented for the power company, they were only 30 percent of the active economic and community development projects of the department, which by 2006 had five recruiters and four community development representatives. Bob Howard guided the Alabama Communities of Excellence program, Cecil Medders was a leading resource on the recruitment of agribusinesses, Roger Wehner recruited internationally, and Ted Levi was a significant leader in many economic development projects. Steve Spencer, who chaired the Metropolitan Development Board of Birmingham in 2003 and 2004, led the most successful capital campaign in the board's history, raising $13 million. This support strengthened the board's ability to recruit projects to its seven-county region. Alabama Power's economic development department works closely with the Economic Development Partnership of Alabama and the state agency, Alabama Development Office, and with communities to reach viable prospects. The estimated new load generated in 2005 due to economic development was 155 megawatts of power that resulted in almost $36 million in new revenue for Alabama Power.[46]

Environmental Programs

To underscore Alabama Power's dedication to environmental programs, Charles McCrary, for the first time in the company's history, named a vice president to lead Alabama Power's environmental affairs, elevating Willard Bowers to this new position. McCrary stressed accountability in environmental issues, and under his leadership Alabama Power began working closely with a number of environmental groups, including The Nature Conservancy of Alabama, the Alabama Wildlife Federation, Legacy Partners in Environmental Education, and Keep Alabama Beautiful. McCrary appreciated the opportunity to discuss issues and exchange ideas with these organizations.[47]

Environmental issues provided some of the important and difficult challenges Alabama Power faced as it moved into its second century. The company was always in compliance with the Environmental Protection Agency and the Alabama Department of Environmental Management's (ADEM) air quality and emissions regulations, but in the early years of the twenty-first century, this became an even more expensive problem to solve and a contentious public relations issue that required educating the public and the company's customers and employees. As Bowers explained, public understanding was especially necessary because environmental groups such as the Southern Alliance for Clean Energy and the U.S. Public Interest Research Group released information that was not balanced, sometimes inaccurate, or did not give the company credit for its success in reducing air pollutants. Alabama Power's customers supported a strong environmental program and were willing to pay something for these efforts, but they also wanted to keep their bills low.[48]

The company moved cautiously, uneasy over spending billions of dollars before it was certain what the final rules and requirements of the federal Environmental Protection Agency and ADEM might be. McCrary was aggressive in his environmental stewardship, and Alabama Power worked closely with the Public Service Commission to ensure environmental issues were addressed at the least cost to consumers. The company wanted upgrades implemented before deadlines. In the fall of 2004 the PSC agreed to establish an environmental clause that would serve as a way to cover costs of environmental technology, allow Alabama Power to move forward in installing equipment to reach federally mandated standards, and minimize the impact on the rate payer.

While Alabama Power was committed to following the laws and regulations of government and regulatory agencies and to working diligently with responsible environmental groups, the problems were huge, solving them expensive, and satisfying everyone impossible. Environmental science was steadily evolving, and Alabama Power needed time to study data used as the basis of decisions by the EPA. The company recognized it had a responsibility to its customers and stockholders to invest only in proven technology that provided the best results within costs that were manageable. On the other hand, in environmental politics there was more involved than just clean air and water. There was the fact that Alabama plants burned coal, local Alabama coal along with western low-sulfur coal, and for years coal had been less costly than natural gas or oil. Eastern states used cleaner burning natural gas, a more expensive fuel that resulted in more costly electricity. They also had access to Canadian hydro. Simply put, many believed there was a component of Rust Belt vs. Sun Belt politics in the environmental equation.[49]

Improving the air quality in Birmingham was especially important to Alabama Power. When author Carl Carmer visited the city in the 1930s, he called it "the valley of the furnaces . . . an inferno."[50] By the 1990s much of the steel and heavy industry of the city had vanished, and the tall stacks, if they remained standing, no longer billowed black smoke. With no widespread public transit system, vehicle emissions were high, and, according to the Environmental Protection Agency, diesel engines were the main cause of hazardous air pollutants.[51] The area's hills and mountains trapped the smog. The city had difficulty attaining federal air pollution standards, and this failure handicapped the economic development of the immediate area.[52] Between 1996 and 2004 Alabama Power had reduced seasonal nitrogen oxide emissions by half and annual sulfur dioxide by 22 percent.[53] Three of Alabama Power's generation plants—Gorgas, Miller, and Gaston—are miles from the city but are in the metropolitan area and were the first plants the company scheduled for selective catalytic reduction (SCR) technology. This expensive equipment washed pollution from the air before it left the stacks and reduced nitrogen oxide emissions by 80 to 90 percent.[54]

A $60 million SCR system at Gorgas was unveiled with ceremony on June 17, 2002. McCrary noted that "By the time we complete our expenditures, we will have almost as much invested in environmental control equipment as we do in the plants themselves." He pointed out that "from now until 2010, we expect to spend $1.5 billion on environmental upgrades to meet future air standards."[55] The next year, on May 17, 2003, a fourteen-story $170 million selective catalytic reduction facility at Plant Miller on units 3 and 4 was unveiled by the company. In 2005 SCRs were completed and put into service on Miller units 1 and 2. As a result of

Charles McCrary unveils the $60 million SCR system at Gorgas, now called Gorgas Electric Generating Plant, on June 17, 2002.

these improvements and the required use of lower-emission gasoline by auto-mobiles, the Birmingham area achieved compliance with the ozone standard in 2005.[56]

More than $800 million in pollution controls will be in place at Plant Barry by 2010.

The Environmental Protection Agency's 2003 Particle Pollution Report noted the nation's success in reducing sulfur dioxide emissions, which dropped 33 percent between 1990 and 2003. By 2005 Alabama Power had reduced its emission rates of nitrogen oxide, a component of ground-level ozone, by 57 percent and had reduced its emission rates of sulfur dioxide, a contributor to acid rain and fine particle pollution, by 48 percent. This reduction occurred

while the company's fossil generation increased 63 percent.[57] In March 2005 Alabama Power announced the next phase of its clean-air initiative, additional selective catalytic reduction technology and the addition of scrubbers to further reduce emission of nitrogen oxide, sulfur dioxide, and mercury. By 2005 the scope of controls had increased, and the company planned to spend over $2 billion on environmental technology by 2010. Scrubbers would be in operation at Gorgas in 2008. New technology costing $800 million was planned for Plant Barry

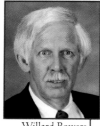

Willard Bowers

in Mobile and would be in operation in 2010, and new technology was scheduled for Plant Gaston in Shelby County in 2006. Willard Bowers, responding to criticism of the company on its environmental policies, wrote the *Anniston Star* that the bottom line was that "as a good corporate citizen, we take responsibility to reduce emissions seriously, and our accomplishments are making a difference. Meanwhile, we must balance these costs with our responsibility to provide reliable and affordable electricity."[58]

In 2005 a suit filed six years earlier by the Environmental Protection Agency against Alabama Power and a number of other generating companies, including TVA, moved toward conclusion. The dispute was over regulations and interpretations of the meaning of the New Source Review provisions of the Clean Air Act. In the spring of 2001, Alabama Power's case was stayed while the TVA case was being appealed. The TVA case was decided in TVA's favor, and in June 2004 the Alabama Power case moved forward. In 2005 the federal court in Birmingham agreed with Alabama Power's position on the legal issues regarding Plants Barry, Gaston, Gorgas, and Greene County, leaving the Miller issues to be resolved. U.S. District Judge Virginia Hopkins ordered EPA and Alabama Power to mediation.[59] On April 24, 2006, the federal government and Alabama Power filed a consent decree with the court. The consent decree settled the remaining issues involving Plant Miller with a $100,000 payment and a donation of emissions allowances. Alabama Power also agreed to meet certain deadlines and emissions targets in installing environmental technology on Plant Miller units 3 and 4, an agreement that was in line with the company's overall environmental plans. On August 14, 2006 Judge Hopkins resolved all remaining claims in favor of the company.[60]

One of Alabama Power's most popular and successful environmental efforts started when Plant Gadsden's compliance team leader Gene Phifer became disgusted with the debris he discovered around the plant's discharge units on Neely Henry Lake. What started as a one-man Coosa River clean-up effort in 1999 attracted volunteers from across the company and from various communities and organizations and spread from "Renew the Coosa" to the state's other rivers as "Renew Our Rivers." In Etowah County, the Keep Etowah Beautiful Committee founded by Alabama Power's Tom McKenzie and Peter Greggerson supported the project. In 2002 the program drew 1,700 volunteers who donated 15,000 hours to removing 142 tons of trash from the Coosa River.[61] That year the program received Keep America Beautiful's National Litter Prevention Award in the business/professional organization category. In 2003 the Renew Our Rivers program received the Alabama Wildlife Federation's Water Conservationist of the Year Award. Gene Phifer was recognized with Keep America Beautiful's 2004 Volunteer Leadership Award.[62]

Another environmental project was initiated at Plant Gadsden. This project involved the use of renewable energy. Gadsden began experiments with mixing switchgrass and coal in a 70-megawatt unit. Initial results proved the switchgrass did reduce emissions of carbon dioxide, sulfur dioxide, and mercury, and research continues on the effects and economy of using switchgrass, a renewable energy source, as a fuel.[63] In 2003 Alabama Power offered its customers the option of purchasing blocks of renewable energy each month. A 100-watt block of energy cost an extra $6 a month, which was the cost difference between regular and renewable generation.[64]

The environmental issues that Alabama Power faced at the beginning of 2006 continued to be driven by air quality. While tremendous strides had been made to reduce emissions of nitrogen oxide and sulfur dioxide, new challenges in the form of mercury and global climate change were moving to the fore-front. Other issues involving water and lake levels were gaining importance and placing new pressures on the company as it began its centennial year. Alabama Power, with its twelve hydroelectric impoundments, controls more water than anyone else in the state. As demand for water grows, these reservoirs may be eyed to satisfy those needs. In addition, the recreational use of Alabama Power's lakes increases each year and pressures mount for higher lake levels. As 2006 opened, once again water was emerging as one of the most critical challenges for Alabama Power, a challenge that started in 1958 when John Farley asked what limnology meant.[65]

Operation Enduring Family

Operation Enduring Family recognizes employees called to military service and provides support to their families.

After 9/11 when the United States called members of the Alabama National Guard to active duty as part of the inva-sions of Afghanistan and Iraq, Alabama Power was committed to helping employ-ees' families. Operation Enduring Family was a plan to recognize employees who were called to military service and to provide support to their families during their service. Periodically, the plan was revised, but it involved a continuation of benefits the company normally pro-vided and a person assigned to maintain contact with the family to see what type of support might be needed. The plan also established protocols so the company could react quickly and effectively in any contingency. Key contacts worked with human resources representatives and a weekly update was pro-vided to Charles McCrary. McCrary maintained contact with families and with company employees on active duty.[66]

The stress of the times caused Alabama Power's management council to sponsor old-fashioned family picnics for the company's people. On September 21, 2002, Alabama Power held its first Family Counts Day. The General Services Complex hosted 3,300 adults and children representing all divisions. Hot dogs, hamburgers, and barbecued pork were consumed along with forty gallons of baked beans, thirty gallons of slaw, 5,000 soft drinks, and 2,700 snow cones. With the good food there were games and contests. A second Family Counts Day was held at Barry Steam Plant on April 12, 2003. The menu featured fish and shrimp instead of barbecued pork.[67] The 2006 Family Counts Day was held at Neely Henry Dam.

"You Can Count on Alabama Power, Even in Virginia"

In September 2003 a category three hurricane named Isabel swept ashore on the southeastern Atlantic coast, leaving devastation in North Carolina and Virginia and 3.3 million people without electricity, most of them in Virginia. Alabama Power sent nearly 300 of its most experienced storm restoration people to help get the lights back on for customers of Virginia's Dominion Power, which reimbursed Alabama Power for this service. Alabama crews were assigned to an area of downed trees and rear-lot service in heavily wooded terrain that forced them to work without the power equipment they usually used. Charlie Harrison was foreman from Mobile's Eight Mile Crew headquarters, and the group included Lew Sumerlin, Ricky Riego, James Tate, and Terence Logan. Eufaula's Chuck Robertson, Phil Shelley, and Jeff Bonner were in Virginia two weeks. Kim Miller, an engineer with the Mobile Division, Tim Glover of Headland, and Andy Short of Auburn were part of the group. Hundreds of calls, e-mails, and letters of appreciation (many coming from schoolchildren) were sent by grateful people, thanking Alabama Power crews for getting their lights on after a week to ten days without power. In a resolution commending Alabama Power for its work, the Public Service Commission quoted Charles McCrary: "You can count on Alabama Power, even in Virginia."[68]

Ivan, Dennis, and Katrina—Unwelcome Visitors

For days in September 2004, the Alabama Power Storm Center had been tracking a large hurricane named Ivan as it swirled through the Gulf of Mexico. Storm plans were readied should the hurricane come into Alabama Power's territory. In the early hours of September 16, Hurricane Ivan came ashore near Gulf Shores, Alabama. The category three storm then moved north into Alabama Power's service area. Its heavy rains and winds left a trail of destruction, setting a record for the highest number of collective storm outages in Southern Company history.

In 2004 Hurricane Ivan set the record for the highest number of collective storm outages in Southern Company history.

Damages were incurred in four of Southern's five operating companies, leaving 1.2 million Southern customers without power, 825,701 of them Alabama Power customers.[69] Previous to Ivan, the record outage for Alabama Power had been 475,889 customers without electricity in October 1995 after Hurricane Opal. Mike Neighbors, crew methods and training manager assigned to lead the restoration effort at Atmore, looked over his area after Ivan struck and called Robin Hurst, senior vice president for power delivery, and told him, "We can't fix this. It's too much." Hurst observed that in restoration work "you can't get lost in the hugeness of the destruction."[70]

Before the storm hit land, Alabama Power had activated the company's extensive and detailed storm damage plan. In the aftermath of this hurricane, dubbed "Ivan the Terrible," Alabama Power gathered one of the largest restoration teams in Southern Company history. Crews came from twenty-six states to help Alabama Power because the other Southern Company operating subsidiaries had their own problems to handle immediately following the storm's impact. Vicki Grimsley, administrative assistant to Charles McCrary, observed that "this company is always in its finest hour when it goes into storm restoration."[71] Ivan struck on a Thursday. Alabama Power customers were urged to call the company from their home telephones if possible to report their power off. Using the telephone numbers, the computer system instantly plotted outages while SCADA (supervisory control and data acquisition) information told transmission and distribution engineers where circuits were out. Customer service centers handled over 900,000 calls in the days after Hurricane Ivan's destruction. Meanwhile, engineers in trucks were spot-checking distribution damage from the ground, and transmission lines were surveyed in helicopters or small planes to locate any problems. Luckily, Ivan did no great damage to transmission lines and towers. Final restoration plans were made when damage assessments were completed.

On Saturday morning, McCrary called a meeting of his management and communications teams. He and Robin Hurst had gone over the company's storm plan, and they understood the destruction. Carrie Kurlander, director of corporate communications, recalled that McCrary did something that had never been done before. "He told us we were going to set goals and set expectations. We were going to give customers hope." McCrary then addressed an unusual Saturday press conference and announced that in eight days Alabama Power would have 99 percent of its electricity back on. He said, "Ladies and gentlemen, the light is in sight," which the Birmingham News adopted for its Sunday morning headline: THE LIGHT IS IN SIGHT.[72] Kurlander and Bobbie Knight, vice president for public relations, initiated a new effort for Alabama Power by deploying journalists with the crews so they could cover the restoration efforts firsthand. This embedded journalist approach proved helpful to the company in making customers aware of progress and in communicating its efforts to the public.

McCrary's challenge to Alabama Power's engineers and crews to get the lights on in eight days came after he reminded his teams to work safely and never to place themselves in danger as they began restoration work. Employees knew the responsibilities they had, the equipment they needed, and where to go. The atrium of corporate headquarters, usually busy with people, suddenly fell silent as men and women assumed their storm team assignments. They walked toward the parking deck or cafeteria, not dressed in coats and ties, high heels and silk blouses, but wearing jeans and boots and carrying hard hats. Some pulled suitcases and had laptop computers slung over their shoulders. They were going to coordinate and support the restoration work or to the staging areas set up in the hardest hit areas throughout the state.

Alabama Power is a member of the regional Southeastern Electric Exchange, an organization of investor-owned utilities that have reciprocal agreements in which members provide assistance in personnel and equipment to aid participating companies in storm restoration. The requesting company pays at actual cost for the crews. Donald Boyd, Alabama Power's director of emergency operating procedures in the storm center, noted that since there was a previous agreement on terms and conditions, "no paperwork is exchanged at the time of the request."[73] Those people responsible for contacting outside help coordinated what the company needed in terms of numbers, crews, and types of skills and equipment. Storms generally strike Mobile first, and Alabama Power is able to make decisions, ask for help, and have assistance moving toward Alabama before the hurricane arrives.

Robin Hurst, who has directed more storm restorations than he cares to remember, believes that doing restoration work "is the best time in the world because there is no bureaucracy, no paperwork. We're just building and fixing things. The best time is at the end of the day, and the lights come on. The worst time is when you close a switch, and the lights don't come on. Many times our people will just stay and work into the night until they can find the trouble and get those lights on before they quit." During the restoration everyone had a job. Climbing poles and operating bucket trucks required a special skill set, but dealing with the logistics of feeding and housing several thousand contract employees was another. These contract crews were strangers in the area and needed maps and special directions. They were given manuals that explained how the Alabama Power system was engineered and specific assignments to repair destruction on the system. These assignments were carefully coordinated so the maximum number of customers would have power restored in the shortest time. Alabama Power provided fuel for their trucks, a good breakfast, water and high-calorie snacks, lunches delivered to them in the field, a hot nutritious supper, and a place to sleep. In Birmingham the mostly vacant Eastwood Mall was one staging area for Ivan crews; the Hoover Metropolitan Stadium was another. Tables and chairs were set up, electrical wiring was run for computers, refrigerators, and hot boxes, and meals were ordered from caterers. Hundreds of rooms were reserved at local motels, keys collected, and registration tables set up for crews to pick up room keys and time schedules. Buses were chartered to carry crews after supper from the staging area to the motels and then to pick them up at 5:00 A.M. to have breakfast at 5:30 so they were rolling by 6:00. Bucket trucks and utility vehicles were left in the parking lot overnight where mechanics checked tires and oil, filled fuel tanks, and resupplied the trucks with materials needed for the next day's assigned tasks. This pattern was repeated in Mobile and other areas where extensive damage occurred across Alabama Power's service territory. Joe Farley recalled that the storm damage in his neighborhood was repaired by crews from Pennsylvania Power & Light.

As successful as the Hurricane Ivan restoration was, the power company family will always remember it sadly because of the tragic death of Bobby Jay Turnbloom, who was in the bucket of a utility truck when the boom failed while he was working near Lay Lake. Turnbloom's father, Bobby Ray, had recently retired after thirty-six years working at the Gaston Steam Plant. Bobby Jay's twin brother, Barry Ray, also worked for Alabama Power, and that day he was restoring power in Mountain Brook, while his parents were at home without electricity. Alabama Power president Charles McCrary announced the sad news of Bobby Turnbloom's death to the company. For such a large company, the close family feeling is never stronger than in times of trouble. In his message, McCrary included a reminder to work safely for "nothing, absolutely nothing, is more important to me than sending you safely home to your families."[74]

On July 11, 2005, Hurricane Dennis, another category three storm, made landfall between the Navarre and Pensacola beaches, moved straight north, crossing the Florida Panhandle and moving into Alabama Power territory. The storm weakened over land, but its winds and the tornadoes it spawned knocked out power for 241,000 Alabama Power customers. The critique of the company's storm response to Hurricane Dennis was barely completed when seven weeks later Katrina arrived, just over a year after Hurricane Ivan devastated the company's system. Beginning as a small category one storm in the South Atlantic Ocean, it attracted only passing public interest, but the

Alabama Power Storm Center was carefully monitoring the swirling circle as it moved north and west.

The hurricane touched Cuba and blew through Miami-Dade County on August 25, 2005. Torrential rain and high winds left one million people in southern Florida without electricity. As extra crews from southeastern and midwestern utilities rushed toward Miami to restore power, Hurricane Katrina left the Florida peninsula and whirled slowly northwest into the Gulf of Mexico. The storm gained strength to a category three storm, headed straight toward New Orleans, and a mandatory evacuation of the city was ordered. It seemed the storm would only brush Mobile Bay and Alabama's Gulf Coast, yet in case the storm path changed, Alabama Power was in constant contact with the Alabama Emergency Management Agency's communication center near Clanton. The year before, when Hurricane Ivan was threatening the Alabama shore, Governor Bob Riley requested that Alabama Power have a representative with him in the EMA center, which is called "the bunker." Keith Karst from the Southern Division was designated the liaison between the power company and the governor's office. Alabama Power learned from Hurricane Frederic (when 239,400 outages were restored in twenty-one days) to delay crew arrivals until arrangements were made for housing, food and fuel and applied this lesson in the restoration work after Hurricane Ivan (when power to more than 825,000 customers was restored in less than nine days).

Keith Karst from the Southern Division, far right, was selected as Alabama Power's spokesman to be with Governor Bob Riley, second from right, in the EMA center, the "bunker," when Hurricane Ivan came ashore.

Just before landfall on August 29, Hurricane Katrina turned slightly to the east, away from New Orleans, and slammed into the Mississippi coast. Biloxi and Gulfport were damaged more extensively than during the area's benchmark of hurricane destruction, Camille, which leveled the same area in August 1969. The Mississippi Power Company system was destroyed, along with many homes of its employees and residential customers. Mobile, on the eastern side of the storm, received high wind and rain and heavy flooding. Alabama Power's Mobile Division headquarters on St. Joseph Street was flooded, with water up to customer service manager Eric Patterson's neck. The *Mobile Register* reported that "the last people to leave the building did so in a boat."[75] Alabama Power's underground electrical system for downtown Mobile was flooded for the first time ever, and streets went dark. The beachfront home of Bayou La Batre office manager Bud Robertson simply vanished. Only the pilings that had supported the house remained.[76]

As Katrina swirled north through Mississippi, it curled eastward again, blowing through Alabama Power's Western and Birmingham Divisions, leaving 636,891 Alabama Power customers from Bayou La Batre north to Birmingham without power. Although this was almost 190,000 fewer outages than Hurricane Ivan's total outages the year before, Katrina caused more severe damage to the company's system because hurricane winds were recorded farther inland than usual. Transmission lines and towers were destroyed and the storm covered a wider area, making restoration more difficult and more expensive.[77] Danny Glover, who was working in the Western Division, noted that Katrina was "the worst storm ever recorded" for the Western Division and Tuscaloosa area.[78] Both Mississippi Power and Gulf Power had their own troubles and could not help, and most of the personnel from other utility companies that might come were already working in southern Florida to restore power there.

As damage assessment began, Charles McCrary placed the company and all its resources in the hands of power delivery senior vice president Robin Hurst, who directed the restoration. Hurst told Rebecca Smith of the *Wall Street Journal* that "It's nothing to put up poles and wire. We're good at that. The hard part is housing and feeding 3,000 people where there's none of the infrastructure left to support them."[79] Alabama Power learned from Ivan that it needed to provide more logistical support in storm restoration. Power delivery

Robert M. "Bob" Waters

services manager Robert M. "Bob" Waters explained that when Katrina hit, the decision was made to delay the arrival of crews to allow Alabama Power time to prepare for them. He also noted that in this restoration, "GIS [geographic information systems] mapping was utilized to assist in the restoration effort more effectively than ever before, and media relations painted a realistic picture of the magnitude of the storm as it struck the coast and moved inland."[80]

Waters noted that "we used satellite communications at some staging areas, making communications more efficient." The support teams set up thousands of cots and air mattresses in Mobile at the civic center and fairgrounds and ordered thousands of meals from caterers across the area. Many of Alabama Power's Mobile employees suffered severe damage to their own homes, and while they were working to get power back on for their customers, other Alabama Power staff were helping their families. Across the Southern system checks were being collected for the Southern Company's Employees Helping Employees fund.

Despite its own problems, Alabama Power managed to answer every call for help from its former vice president and friend, Mississippi Power president Anthony Topazi, including releasing its helicopter to Mississippi Power.

When service in Alabama was restored to every structure that could receive power, Alabama Power sent crews to Mississippi where the work was far more difficult, and there was no infrastructure to accommodate either the relief workers or utility crews pouring into the region to help. Topazi, who had spent so many years with Alabama Power, told his people in the Hattiesburg area to just hang on. Topazi explained that this small rural area was concerned about taking care of the large number of people Alabama Power was sending, and he assured them that Alabama Power would come well prepared and not to worry about managing this group.[81] The first day in the Hattiesburg area Alabama Power set 109 poles and put up enough wire to build a twenty-mile line. At the end of four days they had set "some 300 poles and put up over 2,000 spans of wire." Communication was a problem. With cell towers on the ground, as Robin Hurst explained to *Wall Street Journal* reporter Smith, SouthernLINC, Southern Company's cellular service, was "the only radio and phone working on the Gulf Coast."[82]

Scott Bishop, line crew foreman from the General Services Complex, was one who went to Mississippi. Bishop is a second-generation Alabama Power employee. His father Stanley "Dude" Bishop Jr., who "elected to take early retirement after forty-two years," had been hit in the head in the 1950s and, Scott recalled, that accident was one reason the company began to require all employees to wear hard hats. After Hurricane Katrina, the younger Bishop and his crews worked five days in the Birmingham area, around Pelham and Patton Chapel, then packed and left Sunday, September 4, for Mississippi. They were housed in barracks at Camp Shelby, an army training facility with a history dating to World War I and located twelve miles south of Hattiesburg. Bishop's crews were assigned to restore power in Poplarville, Mississippi, a small town of less than 3,000 people about forty miles north of the Gulf of Mexico. Bishop, a veteran of Alabama Power's roving crew and storm restoration team, was surprised to find such extensive destruction so far inland.

The Alabama Power crews started their day at 5:30 A.M. with breakfast in Hattiesburg, followed by a bus ride to their trucks, which had been refueled and resupplied during the night. Lunch and snacks were delivered to them where they were working until dark, and dinner was back in Hattiesburg. The heat and high humidity made work more difficult. Bishop and his men were repairing lines on Poplarville's Ida Avenue when a man told him the governor of Mississippi was coming and wished to talk to his crew. The motorcade that rounded the corner included the press, Secret Servicemen, the governor of Mississippi and his wife, and President and Mrs. George W. Bush. The Alabama Power crews came down from poles and buckets and were intro-

President George W. Bush visits with an Alabama Power crew in Poplarville, Mississippi, during the Hurricane Katrina restoration. Courtesy of George Clark, Hattiesburg American.

duced to the president of the United States. President Bush signed autographs, posed for photographs, and asked questions about the restoration. Residents came from their houses with cameras. When one Ida Avenue home owner thanked the president for getting their lights back on, Bishop remembers President Bush responding that he was not responsible for getting their lights on, the Alabama Power crews were.[83]

Marshall Ramsey, the political cartoonist for the Jackson, Mississippi, *Clarion-Ledger*, recalled that more than a week after the storm came through his power was still out, "and our spirits were crushed. Then the lights came on. And hope soon followed." Ramsey recalled Associated Press photographer Joe Rosenthal's iconic image of U.S. servicemen raising the American flag on Iwo Jima during World War II, and on September 6 he drew a parallel heroic moment for those in the hurricane zone. The cartoon showed a line crew raising a power pole amid the destruction of the storm. The drawing was reprinted, copied, made into posters, and tacked on the walls of line crew headquarters across the gulf coastal region and beyond.[84]

The state of Alabama was lucky once more when, less than four weeks after Katrina hit Mississippi and Louisiana, another category four hurricane, this one named Rita, moved west through the Gulf of Mexico, missed Alabama, and crashed into the coast at the Texas-Louisiana state line. Galveston's seawall protected the city, but major flooding occurred there and in Houston, and unfortunately water overtopped the newly repaired New Orleans levees and that city's low-lying areas were flooded once more. More than one million people were without electricity in Texas and Louisiana, and national news media predicted it would be over a month before all repairs could be made. Two days before the storm hit land, Scott Bishop and his Alabama Power roving crew were busy packing their trucks again. They would have forty-eight hours to rest, then they would leave for Texas to help with restoration as soon as the storm named Rita passed.[85]

TECHNOLOGY

Alabama Power, always on the cutting edge of new ideas, continued to adopt the latest technology that would benefit its customers. After years of testing and trial use of automated meter reading for industrial customers, in

2005 residential use of automated meter reading took another step forward. Reggie Murchison, metering services manager, reported that the company had reached a major milestone in technology and was able to read a customer's meter through automation and communicate the information to the customer service system, which would process a bill for the customer. This technology required a special automated meter, and 50,000 were in place in the Birmingham Division by the end of 2005.[86]

State of the art equipment in generation was also a priority. Technology expert Ron Campbell noted that whenever "a new design of power plant equipment became available that would improve the operating efficiency of a plant, those designs would be incorporated into the next generation of plants." Campbell pointed to the technology called supercritical, which was installed at Plant Barry in the 1970s and improved the plant's production by 10 to 15 percent, and to the new technology implemented at the turn of the twenty-first century called the combined cycle plant, which improved efficiency of gas-fired generation in 2005 by another 20 to 30 percent.[87]

Transmission and distribution are two of the most technologically advanced areas in the company. The Southern Transmission Operations & Maintenance Program, called STOMP, was originally designed at Alabama Power in 1993, Randy Plyler explained, "as an inventory of substation equipment, a tool to schedule maintenance activities, and a cradle-to-grave history of maintenance completed on the equipment." But after the concept was proven, it became obvious that transmission lines needed the same kind of tool and that Southern's other operating companies could benefit from the program. Since 1995 it has been used across Southern Company. Another technological breakthrough was the drawing image database (DID), a system that allows employees to view and plot all Alabama Power transmission drawings online, an advantage Plyler explained would allow design projects to be electronically transmitted. Although the initial product was commercially available, Alabama Power's in-house experts wrote a special program in 1999 that allowed documents to be printed, sorted, collated, and delivered to field forces.[88]

Power delivery uses the transmission estimating and management system, called TEAMS, which was originally written by Southern Company for Georgia Power. In 1997 Alabama Power modified TEAMS to fill its need to estimate the cost of substation and transmission line projects. The program works with supply chain programs and, as Plyler stated, "allows users to order material and track those orders." After a successful pilot program in 1991, distribution substation automation began across the Alabama Power system. By September 2005, 585 distribution substations were automated. The project will be completed in 2007.[89] Richard H. "Rick" Greene has developed a computer program that consolidates information across the company into one "dashboard" that can be viewed on a computer. Called Gabrielle, the system has evolved, as Greene explained, "from a combination data warehouse, decision support system, web portal, to an 'Enterprise Information Portal.'. . . The system integrates customer and asset data with large amounts of complex, real-time, power grid data. To our knowledge, this concept is unique to the industry."[90]

The work of transmission control centers is crucial to the successful operation of any electric system. The company's Alabama Control Center monitors and controls the flow of power, making certain power is balanced and adequate throughout the state. Ron Parsons, who in 2006 was the manager of transmission interconnections and operations, explained that the transmission control center "must have the ability to document the current status of every operable device that is a part of the transmission system in order to maintain the safe and reliable operation of that system through time." This operation is typically done by using map boards on the walls of the center, but these are difficult and time consuming to update and maintain. Parsons noted that in 1996, when several regional transmission control centers were folded into the central control center, Alabama Power "developed an electronic map board that could be easily operated and maintained on standard computer workstations in the consoles of the control center." Almost ten years later, Parsons said, Alabama Power was "not aware of anyone else in the industry having developed this same capability." In 2005 other operating companies within the Southern Company were beginning to implement the technology in their transmission control centers, and within Alabama Power the "distribution function has modified the Transmap application for its use in all our Distribution Control Centers."[91]

Transmission and distribution also uses geographic information systems (GIS). Although the technology appeared in the 1980s, it was not until 2000 that advances made it feasible for a large utility to support this technology in asset, outage, and work management. The use of outage management systems has evolved over the past twenty years and has resulted in reducing customer outage durations and costs associated with outage restoration and in helping Alabama Power become one of the nation's leading companies in the area of customer satisfaction. In 2006 Bill Mintz and Clyde Herring were developing the concept of a third-generation outage management system. The utilization of wireless automated resource management systems to assign service and meter type orders to service technicians across the state effectively manages the workload and reduces the cost of providing service to customers.

The technology program was strengthened by the engineers-in-training program started by Robin Hurst. In 1993 Hurst asked Bob Waters to recruit top engineering graduates with academic and leadership skills. Concerned about impending retirements of key operating and engineering personnel, Waters's organization designed and initiated a program that provided classroom and hands-on training to give young people the skills necessary to provide leadership of Alabama Power into the twenty-first century. The program is constantly updated. By 2005 Alabama Power had a talented pool of 123 engineering graduates of this program who were holding key positions of responsibility not only at Alabama Power but across the Southern Company system.[92]

As the twenty-first century opened, experiments with technology were evident across the company. Laptop computers in trucks allowed crews to receive assignments immediately and proceed to a trouble spot. Julia Segars, who joined information technology in 2001, noted that "we have gone from operating in total silos with hard copy distribution by mail to technology systems for everything we do." Segars added that "technology has allowed us to communicate more freely across departments, across subsidiaries, and has given us immediate access to the information and data we need to do our jobs better." Segars noted that "e-mail has changed the workforce."[93]

EDUCATIONAL AND VOLUNTEER SERVICES AND THE ALABAMA POWER FOUNDATION

In 2004 Alabama Power consolidated programs to support stronger community involvement by putting all the volunteer work—the Alabama Power Service Organization and Energizers—under one department headed by Carla Roberson, who had been working with the Alabama Power Foundation and with the company's education programs for some years. Under the leadership of executive vice president Steve Spencer, Roberson was the lead person working with the Alabama Department of Education to produce the well-received *Patriots & Pioneers: The Tuskegee Airmen*. This fifty-six-minute documentary was developed by Alabama Power after Charles McCrary was presented with the idea by

Former president George H. W. Bush, second from left, and Charles McCrary, far right, pose with Tuskegee Airmen, from left, Roscoe C. Brown, Hubert Carter, and Percy Sutton, at the premiere of the documentary *Patriots & Pioneers: The Tuskegee Airmen*.

local producer Giles Perkins. McCrary saw the value in preserving and highlighting the experiences of these pioneer African-American airmen, who were trained in Alabama, their contributions toward winning World War II, and the role they played in breaking down racial barriers at home. Roberson directed the development of teaching materials with lesson plans, primary sources, and learning activities, which had flexibility for different grade levels. These plans were distributed to every school system in Alabama and are being taught every year in grades four, six, seven, and eleven.[94]

The documentary was premiered at the Alabama Theatre with former president George H. W. Bush making a few introductory remarks. To recognize the importance of this project, the Tuskegee Airmen Foundation bestowed on Charles McCrary the Distinguished Service Award at the Tuskegee Airmen's annual convention on August 4, 2004, in Omaha, Nebraska. McCrary's acceptance remarks centered on the need to share the heritage and the story of these brave men, to tell the "story the younger generation needs to hear and older generations must never forget."[95]

Roberson saw that her challenge was to focus strategically on the volunteer efforts of the company and its retirees, to support the volunteers with staff, and to evaluate the programs to see what the results were. Roberson noted that this approach fit with McCrary's results-oriented philosophy. He wanted to know which programs were improving the quality of life in communities and which ones were more successful in building relationships between the company and the community. One successful program began when the Birmingham chapter of APSO organized an annual cleanup of Five Mile Creek, which fit in well with the company's focus on environmental stewardship. The company continues to be interested in supporting education, especially literacy and environmental programs, and providing projects for local schools.[96]

Meanwhile, Bill Johnson, who was elected president of the Alabama Power Foundation on September 11, 2001, had to deal with the repercussions of the stock market fall after 9/11.

The attack on the World Trade Center forced the foundation to reduce its level of funding. Some programs on multiyear commitments had run their course, and the foundation had more flexibility at this crucial time. By 2005, with good management and a careful allocation of earnings, the foundation's assets had recouped; however, by 2006 the endowment had yet to recover to its highest value. When asked to evaluate the foundation, Johnson commented that "we have been able to do some wonderful things through the foundation, contributing by the end of 2006 well over $90 million to projects all over Alabama. While we will never get the credit for all we have done, we have certainly lived up to our mission of improving the lives of Alabamians and the communities where they live."[97]

MARKETING

Marketing is particularly susceptible to the effects of current events, and the terrorist attacks on September 11, 2001, coupled with a general economic recession, sent charts of revenue, megawatt hour sales, and retail energy sales into a steep decline. But recovery was evident during 2002.[98] In 2001 Alabama Power's retail market-

Mike Scott

ing strategy, built upon a decade of customer-oriented philosophy, was to empha- size customer satisfaction, motivate every employee to identify the customers' needs, and find innovative, effective, and profitable ways to meet those needs. This strategy had served the company well and had resulted in electric technolo- gies from 2000–2005 capturing over 60 percent of the home heating market and winning customer choice opportunities. Mike Scott, senior vice president for customer service and marketing, believed Alabama Power's strength in marketing came from its emphasis upon building relationships with customers and from its willingness to individualize service and rates for all customers, especially large industrial and commercial customers. Scott says it is important to involve every employee in the company's customer service and sales strategy.[99]

For the future, Scott saw even more reliance on market research and infor- mation. Alabama Power must explore new ways of doing things the customer wants. Scott observed that Charles McCrary is "very analytical and that market- ing strategy is very analytical." Scott noted that "McCrary has made two things clear. Any new business has to be, first, a good deal for our customer and then, second, a good deal for our company. He doesn't just want us promoting any new business that will increase our top line number of total sales. He wants busi- ness that is good for our customers, so we can keep the business over time. And he wants business that has a good margin for our company so we increase our bottom line." Scott notes the challenge of a changing market. The textile indus- try has declined—and in some towns vanished—and the automotive industry has arrived. Alabama Power must be efficient enough to keep its prices competi- tive without decreasing its ability to provide the customer with service and reli- ability at a cost that will allow industries to compete in a global market.[100]

In 2005, compared to sixteen peer utilities, Alabama Power placed in the top spot for the second consecutive year in Southern Company's customer value benchmark survey. The rank has consistently improved: sixth in 2001, third in 2002, second in 2003, and first in 2004 and 2005. Larry Crocker, customer satisfaction and value manager, and Myrna Pittman, customer services vice president, gave credit to all employees responding to customers' needs. Pittman noted "that the bar has been set at a higher level now" and maintaining the number one rank would continue to be a company goal.[101]

The Divisions

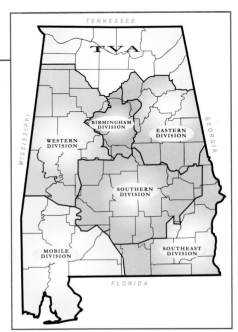

The six divisions of Alabama Power Company.

In 1919 Alabama Power was serving forty-one communities in twenty-seven counties when management decided the company could be strengthened if more local authority was placed in various regions of the state. Directing a large company that operated in a widely scattered area during a time period when train rides and tele-grams were the quickest way to commu-nicate presented challenges. The Alabama Power general manager reported in 1919 that "after carefully trying out various suggestions, it was decided to establish four divisions." George H. Middlemiss supervised these changes. James M. Barry was sent to the Eastern Division, head-quartered in Anniston. Lonnie P. Sweatt Jr. became manager of the Western Division, with headquarters in Birmingham and serving towns from Jasper to Tuscaloosa and including Bessemer and portions of the Birmingham district not served by Birmingham Electric. The Northern Division, with offices in Huntsville, was headed by Wells M. Stanley. Because of expansion in the south, E. C. Wilson was sent to head the Southern Division serving the towns of Selma and Marion. Montgomery was not yet part of the system.[102]

James M. Barry

Lonnie P. Sweatt Jr.

The heads of the divisions were first called managers, then the position was elevated to a vice-presidential rank and division heads were made officers of the company. A second person was designated as division manager. The divisional vice presidency was a powerful and distinguished position with the authority to make decisions within wide latitudes. Division vice presidents controlled the hiring, advertising, repairs, and the operations of

Alabama Power Company within their divisions. These men, and they were all men until Cheryl Thompson went to Mobile as vice president in 1998, were the company's representation in their geographical areas and served important public relations functions as well as being responsible for making certain the lights stayed on in their divisions.

The autonomy of the division vice president gradually decreased as changes in transportation and communication made it easier for the corporate office to influence activities in distant areas and as financial stringency and cuts in operation and maintenance budgets encouraged reductions of personnel. Organization along functional lines, which had certain people in the divisions reporting to senior or executive vice presidents at the corporate level as well as to their division vice presidents, began to erode the division vice president's authority, but the power that remained was still impressive. A precedent began in the 1970s when Steve Bradley initiated public relations efforts that were coordinated from the corporate office across the company. The district offices, which had been a level of management for decades, began to disappear in the mid-1990s, and some local offices were closed or combined with other offices.

EASTERN DIVISION

The Eastern Division, which touches the Georgia line, encompasses the end of the Appalachian Mountains and the Piedmont sections of the state, including Mount Cheaha. The Eastern Division has a special place in the story of electricity in Alabama because the first practical use of electricity in the state occurred at the Woodstock Iron Company in Anniston in April 1882. Alabama Power founder William Patrick Lay constructed a generating plant in Gadsden in 1887, and in 1902 he rebuilt a dam on Bill Wills Creek near Attalla. He sold both several years before he founded the Alabama Power Company in Gadsden in 1906. When James Mitchell purchased the Alabama Power Development Company from S. Z. Mitchell and Electric Bond & Share on July 22, 1912, he acquired a company that was generating electricity from a dam at Jackson Shoals on Choccolocco Creek in eastern Alabama and transmitting and distributing it around Anniston, Gadsden, and Talladega. James Mitchell's purchase from EBASCO also included small companies in Anniston,

The electriciy generated at Jackson Shoals in 1912 was sold by James Mitchell through Alabama Traction. Gadsden Steam Plant, completed in 1913, generated the first electricity sold by Alabama Power Company.

Decatur, and Huntsville and the Etowah Light and Power Company.[103]

The city of Anniston, site of division headquarters, was founded toward the end of Reconstruction as a model city of the New South with an economy based upon iron furnaces, cotton mills, and manufacturing. It was the commercial center for farmers in the surrounding counties. As the years passed, other towns in the area developed important industrial loads—Gadsden (rubber, iron, and steel), Sylacauga (textile mills), Alexander City (textile mills), Childersburg (paper mills), and Talladega (textile mills). The war industries that were constructed during World War II, and later converted to peacetime use, were an important part of the division's load. Fort McClellan, a major army base dating from 1917, and the Anniston Army Depot, which was authorized in 1940, gave the division a military presence.[104] The Gadsden Steam Plant played an important role in Alabama Power's history, and the division was influenced by the Coosa and Tallapoosa Rivers flowing through its area and by the company's dams on these rivers.

Eastern Division vice presidents Homer Turner and W. Donald Bolton were powerful influences in the development of the Eastern Division's culture. Bolton offered that the booming areas of the division in 1983 were around Oneonta, where people from Birmingham were moving to larger tracts of land, and in the Pell City region near Logan Martin Lake and in the area around Lake Martin. Within a short time, he expected a building boom in Randolph County near Harris Lake.[105] The Eastern Division always had strong leadership, and many future company executives, like Banks Farris, came through the division. Farris became division vice president in 1985 and pushed teamwork and innovative changes aimed at recognizing and rewarding employees who did their jobs well. Farris inaugurated family events and a week when employees were thanked for "the blood, the sweat, and the tears that go into keeping the lights burning." Farris left his imprint on the division, encouraging employees to work together, to feel their job was important, to think in innovative terms, and to make a difference.[106]

When asked what was unique about the Eastern Division, retired Gadsden district manager Tom McKenzie said it was ice. During almost twenty years in Mobile, McKenzie had dealt with hurricanes but had not encountered anything like the ice storms on Chandler Mountain. He also observed that it was a lot easier to sink a pole in the sandy soil around Mobile than in the rock he found so prevalent in northeast Alabama. Ken Deal, area manager, pointed to the industrial base of the region as the main force in shaping the customer base of the Eastern Division and making it unique. Bill Morrow noted the presence in the division's area of strong municipal systems—Sylacauga, Alexander

City, Piedmont, and LaFayette—which were wholesale customers of Alabama Power. Sophia Christian, who was in customer service, recalled stories of a Mr. Snow, who called every month to ask Alabama Power to extend its service to him. He got his electricity from a co-op, and he wanted to be served by Alabama Power. Everyone at the division office knew about Snow; many had talked to him, and he became a legend in the Eastern Division. Finally, a way was found to serve the man's residence, and Walter Bouldin himself approved running a line to the man's house. Pat Martin, senior clerk, noted that following storm restoration, when Alabama Power had its customers' electricity restored so much sooner than municipals or co-ops, there were always more petitions for Alabama Power service.[107]

Clay County's contribution to Alabama Power was noted by Ron Dewberry. The business office manager said he felt certain Alabama Power had more Clay County employees than from any other county if you compared company employment as a percent of total county population. Chilton County, which is in the Southern Division, was another place where large numbers of residents sought employment with Alabama Power. The company offered greater opportunities than most could find close to home. In looking at the contributions of Alabama Power toward quality of life issues in the state, marketing specialist Doug King put heat pumps in rural homes at the top of the list. King compared rural life before central heating and cooling by heat pumps and credited the heat pump with making it more comfortable to live on farms and isolated wooded land.

Barbara Curry, who came to work in the Eastern Division in 1969 fresh from Jacksonville State University, was the first African-American home service specialist in the division and the second one in the company. Susan Nelson, who was hired in Tuscaloosa in 1968, was the first. Curry remembers her most gratifying experience as getting to work on Sand Mountain. For generations in Alabama, stories were told that blacks were not welcome on Sand Mountain. Curry recalled that in her first days on the job, she was as frightened of these white farm families as they were of her. But by the end of summer, Curry had made friends all across the mountain and was invited to have lunch here and tea there. As she headed for home at the end of the day, her little Dodge Charger was loaded with hospitality gifts of garden fresh vegetables and once a live chicken in her trunk.[108]

Barbara Curry, the first African-American home service specialist in the Eastern Division, with home service specialist Judy Baker.

By the beginning years of the twenty-first century, the composition of the industrial load in the Eastern Division had changed. Tire and rubber continued to be significant but were struggling, while iron and steel were either closed down or struggling, too. Textiles had moved offshore. The Honda plant at Lincoln and the automotive parts and manufacturing plants it spawned were growing. In June 2005 Kronospan, an Austrian company that is the world's largest wood-based flooring and paneling producer, announced it would invest $500 million in Oxford, a victory for Calhoun County and eastern Alabama. This was Kronospan's first American location, and when the plant was in operation, it anticipated employing 700 people and requiring 18 megawatts of electricity.[109] Wood products manufacturing would replace some of the lost steel and textile loads.

Although on several occasions Alabama Power worked with local people to keep Fort McClellan from being deactivated, the government closed the fort in 1999. The property was turned over to the city of Anniston to be operated by the Joint Powers Authority. Alabama Power, which always furnished the electricity for the fort, purchased the distribution system on the base. The electrical load was much smaller in 2005, but with strong support from the Eastern Division, the 21,000 acres of the former military base were being redeveloped with a variety of new tenants, including businesses and private homes, the Center for Domestic Preparedness, and in September 2005, evacuees from Hurricane Katrina. The Anniston Army Depot remained strong into the new century as the primary site for repairing all tracked army vehicles (except for the Bradley) and was the area's largest employer.[110]

In 2005 the division vice president was W. Ronald "Ronnie" Smith, who had been a division vice president longer than any company vice president serving that year. Smith was a manager at Anniston for a number of years and had strong community connections before becoming vice president in 1993. Smith believes that the strong commitment to community service is a hallmark of the division, pointing out that the Renew Our Rivers environmental program began in Gadsden and that the division has always supported Camp ASCCA (Alabama's Special Camp for Children and Adults), which opened on Lake Martin in 1976 and became the world's largest camp for the disabled. Jerry Thomley, who was Eastern Division vice president 1989-93, was deeply involved in Camp ASCCA and left a legacy of community involvement for the division.

W. Ronald "Ronnie" Smith

Smith was one of the first in the company to foresee the changing industrial loads in eastern Alabama. During the mid-1990s Smith told Elmer Harris and Banks Farris "that east Alabama was an economic time bomb. We faced the closure of Fort McClellan, the decline of the textile industry, the shutdown of Gulf States Steel, and difficulties facing the paper and pulp industry." Smith knew this would "directly or indirectly have a negative impact on employment, the economy, and ultimately Alabama Power." Smith recognized that the employees of the Eastern Division "were strategically positioned in community economic development leadership roles, allowing them to positively affect the redevelopment of the region."[111]

This Alabama Power group was instrumental in recruiting the Honda plant to Lincoln, during the period between September 1998 and May 1999. Partnering with the Birmingham Metropolitan Development Board, which served seven counties in 2005 (Jefferson, Shelby, St. Clair, Walker, Chilton, Blount, and Bibb), Ronnie Smith assisted in the recruitment from his position in the Eastern Division. Since the fall of '98 was an election year, the recruitment team decided not to let this project become involved in politics and deferred any gubernatorial participation until after the election. The project later landed in Governor Don Siegelman's lap.[112]

In the twelve-month period ending June 2005, the Eastern Division ranked third among the Alabama Power divisions in number of customers, 223,148, with annual sales of 7.3 billion kilowatt hours producing annual revenues of $451.7 million. The division employed 507 people, but that figure did not include staff at the Gadsden Steam Plant or the hydroelectric dams in its area. In 2005 Ronnie Smith recognized the division had gone through some hard years of change and adjustment, but he believed it had recovered and was entering a new phase of development. In June 2006 Smith retired, and Julia H. Segars, who was vice president and chief information officer, moved from directing the information technology area of the company to become vice president of the Eastern Division.[113] Segars had broad experience in corporate communications, operations, and human resources and served as assistant to Anthony Topazi when he was vice president of the Birmingham Division. She also had worked with leadership development and was honored to follow Mobile Division's Cheryl Thompson into divisional leadership.

Julia H. Segars

Segars knew she had "big shoes to fill" in the Eastern Division. She saw Ronnie Smith's leadership as a compass, and she looked forward "to meeting and learning from all the employees in the division who do such good work."[114]

NORTHERN DIVISION

Alabama Power's old Northern Division, which was abolished after TVA took over power generation in the Tennessee Valley, grew from the small power companies James Mitchell began acquiring in northern Alabama for his holding company, Alabama Traction, Light & Power. Companies in Decatur and Huntsville and the Little River Power Company, which owned undeveloped dam sites on the Little River, were part of Mitchell's purchase from S. Z. Mitchell and EBASCO in 1912. The companies were folded into Alabama Power in 1913. Those companies had some generation and short transmission and city distribution lines and with the Jackson Shoals dam produced the first electricity that Mitchell had to sell. When the power from Gadsden Steam Plant, and eventually the power from the Lock 12 (Lay) Dam and Western Reserve Steam Plant at Gorgas, reached northern Alabama through Anniston and Gadsden before World War I, these towns had central station power for the first time.

Alabama Power constructed its first rural line in Madison County in 1920, and some of Alabama Power's early leadership joined the corporate office from the old Northern Division. Men like Wells Stanley, who began his work as a meter reader with the Huntsville Railway Light & Power Company, came to Alabama Power, worked to integrate Gulf Power into Southeastern Power & Light, and became a vice president of Alabama Power. The Northern Division became the foundation of cooperative and municipal systems receiving power from TVA.

Workers reeling in wires during the dismantling of the Northern Division distribution system, 1940.

In 2005 Roy Lamon, who came to Alabama Power in 1950 and retired as human resources manager of the Western Division, wanted to make certain that in any discussion of the company's divisions, the old Northern Division was not forgotten. He recalls when he was a young man J. O. Henkel, who was in human resources, vividly told him about the early days of the company and the Northern Division's progress in bringing electricity to the Tennessee Valley. Henkel told him what a "blow it was to have it taken in such a manner," and it left Lamon and others "knowing that a great wrong had been committed." It was, Lamon believes, "without a doubt one of the nation's greatest wrongs against a free enterprise system."[115]

SOUTHERN DIVISION

The Southern Division, with headquarters in Montgomery, stretches across the south-central part of the state from Selma to Auburn and Clanton to Greenville. In 1982 Southern Division vice president Hubert Park Foreman noted that his division was unique because the first office for Alabama Power's holding company, Alabama Traction, was located in Montgomery. James Mitchell and Tom Martin began their association in the capital city in November 1911. In the fall of 1912 the corporate office was moved to Birmingham, and in 1919 Alabama Power organized the Southern Division with headquarters in Selma. Alabama Power came back to Montgomery in 1923 when it acquired the franchise to provide electricity to the city. James M. Barry, who was the first head of the Eastern Division, was sent to Montgomery to supervise the transfer of two financially strapped electric companies to Alabama Power and also to direct the company's construction of distribution lines and upgrades of substations.[116]

Foreman, leader of the Southern Division for many years, put his own stamp upon the division's culture. He observed that "because we are located in the capital city, we maintain a working and personal relationship with state officials and important agencies, such as the Public Service Commission." He noted that the Southern Division people "see these officials socially as well as during business hours," and he believed that these responsibilities of the division differed from those of other divisions throughout the company. Lucy Wallace, who retired from the company in 1990 with more than thirty-seven years of service, noted that the Southern Division employees "knew when we saw Clarence Wilbon, Mr. Martin's chauffeur and special messenger, that Mr. Martin was in the building or close by."[117]

But there were other reasons why Montgomery and the Southern Division were important in the life of Alabama Power beyond corporate executives using the divisional office as headquarters when visiting the capital. Dot Scott, who started working for Alabama Power in the Western Division, pointed out that another effect on the division was being one block from the Alabama Public Service Commission, which meant any customer dissatisfaction, no matter how minor, might result in a complaint being filed with the PSC. Elaine Lassiter, who served in the Southern Division for thirty-eight years, noted that for most of those years the office of the *Montgomery Advertiser* was located directly behind the Alabama Power Company headquarters, and "they watched us like a hawk."[118]

Besides the importance of being in the capital city, in 2006 the Southern Division had a strong educational and agricultural presence. It serves Auburn University, Auburn University Montgomery, Alabama State University, and Troy University Montgomery. The fertile and flat lands in the area have long been home to large cotton-growing operations and the rolling hills north of the Alabama River are home to extensive peach orchards. Commercial traffic on the river was more important to the city in the nineteenth century, but forest products and pulp continue to be shipped downriver. A number of the state's significant historical places—such as the 1820 capital site at Cahawba, the industrial complex founded by Daniel Pratt in the antebellum period, and important sites of the modern civil rights movement—are located there. Montgomery also has a strong military influence because of the location of Maxwell and Gunter air force bases. Maxwell, originally a cotton field northwest of the city, was first converted to an airfield in 1910 when Wilbur and Orville Wright opened a flying school there. In 2005 the Maxwell–Gunter load was 30 megawatts, which placed the bases among the top five customers of the Southern Division.[119]

In a discussion of the influences on the division, retiree Curtis Jones thought that because top corporate executives spent so much time in the Southern Division while they were working with state government or the PSC they had a familiarity with the personnel in the Southern Division office. Gordon Martin pointed out that the dams on the lower Coosa and Tallapoosa were in the district and that many of the capital city residents had cottages on those lakes and Lake Martin (which is partly in the Southern Division and partly in the Eastern Division) so "lake levels and lake activities were important to Southern Division customers." In the final analysis, Steve Sprayberry, who was serving his thirty-ninth year with the company in 2005, believed that Alabama Power Company was successful because of the quality of its people, and the Southern Division always had good people. He thought that the company's organizational structure did not matter because good people adapted to whatever business structure they were given and sometimes, he said, succeeded in spite of the organization.

Charlie Britton agreed but noted that the division did not always have the smoothest manager-union relationship in the company. In the last few occasions when the IBEW contract came up for approval, the brotherhood members from the Southern Division and Greene County Steam Plant voted it down the first time. Jones added that it was "the grassroots of the entire company that gave it strength." Alabama Power's employees lived all over the state and were active in their communities, and he thought the people of the state backed Alabama Power Company because of its employees.[120]

Gordon Martin, who became Southern Division vice president in 2001, received his law degree from the University of Alabama, worked for U.S. senator Howell Heflin in Washington, and later was a legislative lawyer for Hogan & Hartson, the largest law firm in the nation's capital. While at the firm, Martin worked with Alabama Power lobbyist Phillip R. Wiedmeyer. Later, Martin was manager of external affairs at Southern Company Generation.[121] Martin pointed out that as Alabama Power moved toward its cen-

Gordon Martin

tennial year, the Southern Division's largest customer was GE Plastics, which started in 1989 and "makes high-quality plastics used in everything from water jugs to CDs, automobile bumpers to football helmets." Other large customers were Simcala and the Hyundai automotive plant in Montgomery. Hyundai, Martin added, invested more than $1.1 billion in its plant, which employs more than 2,500. Alabama Power helped to recruit many of Hyundai's forty-plus suppliers in the state, which represent an additional investment of more than $700 million and jobs for 6,000 Alabamians.

In 2005 the Southern Division's 216,918 customers ranked it fourth in number of customers by division. Its revenues of almost $546 million, kilowatt hours sold of 9 billion, and its kilowatt hours of industrial load at 3.6 billion placed it third behind Birmingham and Mobile. A sense of pride in the division is evident among its employees and recent retirees. But those who came aboard decades ago and have long been retired can be nostalgic in their recollections of the old days, a time when they believed there were more employees and more time to train new people, when everyone shared the midnight calls about power being out, when folks began as meter readers and moved on to be vice presidents, when, they thought, more people came up through the ranks.[122]

The Southern Division has a feeling of being an extended family, unusual in today's corporate world, Gordon Martin noted. He points out that "we still get birth and death announcements, and have breakfast with our local retirees every quarter."[123] Perhaps the Southern Division's feeling of extended family is more a company trait and shared by all the divisions, but longtime Southern Division employees believe it is significant to the division's sense of identity. Martin summed up this feeling when he observed that "I once saw an ad for an expensive watch which said something to the effect that 'You never really own one, you just hold it for the next generation.' That's the way I think most employees feel about Alabama Power. We are the beneficiaries of those who came before us, and we want to be good stewards of the company for our customers, our communities, our retirees, and our successors."[124]

Western Division

The Western Division was created in November 1923 after Alabama Power acquired the electric, gas, and street railway systems in Tuscaloosa, and for many years the division operations were based in Birmingham and included areas of the Birmingham district not served by Birmingham Electric Company. Then in February 1953, after Alabama Power acquired BECO, the Birmingham area was removed from the Western Division and the office was moved to Tuscaloosa. Roy Lamon remembered Henry Maulshagen as the first vice president of the Western Division after it located in Tuscaloosa. He also recalled that forty-six families were transferred from Birmingham, and it was very difficult to find suitable housing in the area for all these families. The division office was situated above the Tuscaloosa district office until 1966 when it moved to a new building at the corner of Paul Bryant Drive and Queen City Avenue, where the division was located in 2006.[125]

At the beginning of the twenty-first century, the Western Division extended from Hamilton and Haleyville to the north, Centreville on the east, Demopolis and Linden to the south, and west to Reform on the Mississippi state line. A. Clayton Rogers Jr., who became vice president of the Western Division in

A. Clayton Rogers Jr.

1968, noted in 1982 that his division was important because the connecting link between TVA and the Mississippi state line ran through the Western Division. Rogers also observed that the Western Division served all the rural territory between the towns it served and had "more lines, more poles, and more miles of lines to maintain than any other division in the company."[126] The Western Division was also in the middle of weather patterns coming from the south and west and was part of "Tornado Alley," where tornadoes that originate in western Mississippi begin their pass through the state.[127]

The Western Division was influenced by the Black Warrior River running through it, with ports and barge traffic to the Gulf and sites for industrial plants that needed water for production. Paper mills and wood product companies were attracted to the area. The Tenn-Tom Waterway, which opened in 1985 and connected the Tombigbee River north of Demopolis through northern Mississippi to the Tennessee River, has not affected western Alabama with as much river traffic and support investments as was predicted, but it is still important. The University of Alabama has a strong influence on the division, as do other area educational institutions such as Stillman College, Shelton State College, Bevill State College, and the University of West Alabama. These schools provide educational opportunities for the division's children and supply a solid well-trained and educated pool of applicants for jobs. The University of Alabama also offers opportunities for Western Division employees to pursue advanced degrees. With Tuscaloosa only an hour's drive from corporate headquarters, many officers visit the division office frequently, and there is strong corporate interest in the division.[128]

J. G. Brazil and Elaine Acker, both retired longtime Western Division employees, believed the influence of Clayton Rogers, vice president 1968–86, was significant in developing the culture of the division. Rogers came to the general office as a rural service engineer working under E. C. Easter in 1941. After his service in World War II he returned to the company in the Southern Division where he credited Hugh Foreman, B. B. Marsh, and Joe Hickson for teaching him the business of Alabama Power. Rogers was remembered as a kind man who created a warm and inclusive atmosphere at the Western Division, a "strong camaraderie between management and the employees that extended into the relationship with the communities." Brenda Randall believed this bond was "the glue that held it together and crossed boundaries of covered/non-covered/supervisory" personnel.[129]

Tuscaloosa district manager J. W. Cruse was remembered by Mildred Hutchins, retired executive secretary, as being known as "Mr. Tuscaloosa" for his community activities. Division vice president Robert Haubein initiated the "West Best" theme, emphasizing productivity and economic growth, Brenda Randall recalled. She also remembered him as being very involved with the University of Alabama and thus making the division ready for vice president Anthony Topazi to rally the division to recruit the Mercedes plant. Topazi was, as Michael R. Burroughs, safety specialist in the Western Division, noted, "the right man in the right place at the right time." Bobby Jack Kerley, then division manager of operations and in 2006 a vice president, also played a key role in the Mercedes recruitment and in the design of the electrical system serving Mercedes.[130]

The Western Division was always active in industrial recruitment. For years Gulf States Paper, B. F. Goodrich, Phifer Wire Products, and Hunt Refining were some of the industries supplying industrial load and employment in the area. While some employees such as Bill Faurot pointed to gaining the Demopolis district from the Southern Division and Gulf States Paper closing its Tuscaloosa plant and opening a new plant in Demopolis as turning points in the Western Division's story, all agreed that the location of the Mercedes-Benz plant at Vance was the most important development in the division's recent history.

Roy Lamon offered another area in which the Western Division excelled—the affirmative action program. When it was developed, implemented, and became a company priority in the early 1970s, Lamon noted that "the Western Division immediately began to meet all the requirements in employment and advancement of females and minorities." In fact, the division became so accomplished at developing new employees, many of the divisions's talented people ended up at the corporate office.[131]

Terry Waters

When Anthony Topazi left the Western Division for the Birmingham Division in 1995, Terry H. Waters, who was the division manager in Birmingham, took Topazi's place as Western Division vice president. Waters, an electrical engineering graduate of the University of Tennessee, joined Alabama Power in 1972 as a junior engineer. Waters was an assistant to Rayford Davis when Davis was vice president of power delivery. Waters recalled Davis as "tough, old school, who taught us to be disciplined and to watch out for the company's money and spend it wisely." Waters developed a keen business sense, the ability to inspire his fellow employees, and a broad understanding of the company's challenges in providing services, promoting budget restraints, and moving forward with environmental upgrades. Waters became active in promoting Tuscaloosa and western Alabama, industrial development, and community services, especially the United Way.[132]

In 2005 the Western Division served 213,985 customers and sold 8 billion kilowatt hours of electricity, which produced $485 million in revenues. Sales of 3.3 billion kilowatt hours of industrial loads ranked the division fourth in the company. In reminiscing about his years in the division, E. T. "Foots" Mathews recalled falling from a pole and hurting his back but the company keeping him on and transferring him into the service department. He said, "I loved my job. I really worked at it. In my life, the Lord was first, my wife second, and Alabama Power Company third." Mildred Hutchins remarked, "If anyone loves the Alabama Power Company more than I, I would like to meet them."[133]

Mobile Division

Electricity came to Mobile in 1884, and after years of various companies competing and then consolidating, a subsidiary of Alabama Power, Gulf Electric, acquired the assets of the Mobile Electric Company in 1925. Two years later, Gulf Electric was merged with Alabama Power, and the Mobile Division was organized with T. K. Jackson, who had been head of Mobile Electric, as the manager. In 1950 Frank S. Keeler, who went to work for the

Mobile Electric Company in 1920 and was vice president of the Mobile Division from 1948 to 1960, wrote a history of power supply to the city and its industries. Keeler detailed the boiler explosion at 8:25 P.M., February 22, 1919, at the Mobile Electric Company's powerhouse on Royal and St. Louis Streets. Fire broke out at 1:20 in the morning and the building and the machinery were completely destroyed. The *Mobile Register* reported that one man was killed and ten were injured. It took ninety-six hours to restore electricity to Mobile.[134]

A boiler explosion and fire at Mobile's Royal Street station on February 22, 1919, destroyed the building and equipment.

Because of the distance from the corporate office to Mobile and the difficulty in communicating, the Mobile Division, as longtime Alabama Power employee Chuck Hrabe phrased it, "continued to operate as a local utility." His wife Mary Jo, also a retiree from Alabama Power, added that because of the division's isolation from the corporate office, employees accepted the challenge of being responsible for solving problems.[135] Eight decades after Mobile became part of Alabama Power, the division was still teasingly called, both within the company and in the division's area, "Mobile Power & Light Company."[136]

During the early years of Alabama Power's presence in Mobile, T. K. Jackson was the divisional leader, directing the reconstructed powerhouse on St. Louis and Royal Streets. In 1927 Alabama Power completed a new transmission line connecting Mobile with Jordan Dam. With great ceremony Mayor Harry Hartwell pushed a button and, as the *Mobile Register* described it, "hydro electric current from the Coosa River flowed into the metal veins of Mobile's electric system."[137] After serving the company for thirteen years as division manager, A. D. Quackenbush became division vice president in 1941 on the eve of World War II. The next year, 1942, the demand for electricity in Mobile, compared with 1940, increased 48 percent. To support new war industries, the steam plant at Chickasaw was expanded.[138] After the war Barry Steam Plant was constructed to provide most of Mobile's power, and the Chickasaw plant was phased out.

The Mobile Division is unique, affected by the geography of its location on the bay at the mouth of the state's major river systems. The saltwater breezes are hard on equipment, and the swampy land and waters of the Mobile Delta make repairs difficult, especially on transmission lines that cross the rivers. The land is low, the water table high, and the soil is mud or sand, making setting poles, said assistant manager of distribution Bill Patterson in 1982, "sometimes like trying to dig a hole in a bowl of oatmeal."[139] The northern Gulf Coast is often the destination of tropical storms and hurricanes, and the Mobile Division has perfected storm restoration techniques that have been adopted and adapted by other divisions. The numerous creeks and rivers that flow into the bay and the swamps infested with snakes and alligators make setting transmission towers and distribution poles a challenge. The division's territory is clustered around the state's oldest city and stretches north to Thomasville and Monroeville and south to Dauphin Island and the Gulf fishing villages of Coden and Bayou La Batre. Mobile, on the western side of the bay, is on low land prone to flooding, often a problem for access to transmission lines the company owns and the reason the transmission group has several boats.

The coastal location fosters maritime industries. Shipbuilding, chemical and paper industries, the nearby state docks, and until it closed, Brookley Air Force Base have given the division Alabama Power's largest industrial load. By 2006 the economy of the region was more diversified. Bernie Fogarty, head of public relations for the Mobile Division in 2006, reported that natural gas production, medical research stimulated by the state's second medical school that was located in Mobile at the University of South Alabama, aerospace projects, steel making, and a cruise line that makes Mobile a home port helped diversify the region's economy and increased the division's industrial load. In 2005 the industrial load ranked first in the company with almost 7 billion kilowatt hours and included the company's largest customer, Olin. The Mobile Division had the company's second largest number of customers (226,930) and ranked second in total revenue (almost $700 million) in 2005.[140]

The unique culture of the area has also affected the division. The largest city in the state until the rise of Birmingham in the late nineteenth century, Mobile is a cosmopolitan three-hundred-year-old city proud of its French, Spanish, and British heritage and its standing as the state's first commercial center with a typical port's view of the world. Yet its social culture is conservative, influenced by "old Mobilians" with roots that go back generations. There is a decided Catholic influence, and its city politics has a unique flavor. Sam Covert, Mobile Division area manager, commented that Mobile is so different from the rest of the state that it has been described as being "three hours south of Alabama." Bruce Jones, who was vice president of the division from 1989 to 1997, observed that the division was viewed by some in the company as having unconventional leadership, but the division was usually positioned on the cutting edge of changes in the industry and involved with pioneering innovations. He suggested the division was a bit inbred, which was exacerbated by employees being less likely to relocate to other divisions. Bill McDonough, another former Mobile Division vice president, believed the Mobile Division was "the most interesting and enjoyable place to work in the whole company." In 1982 *Powergrams* reported that Alabama Power's human resources department was "singing a new version of an old song, 'How ya' gonna get 'em outa Mobile after they've seen the bay?'" Yet many of Alabama Power's corporate leaders came out of Mobile or passed through the Mobile Division.[141]

Beyond Mobile, there are other towns in the Mobile Division that also have a unique heritage: Butler, in an isolated part of the state in Choctaw County; three Clarke County towns—Jackson, Grove Hill, and Thomasville; Baldwin County's Bay Minette; and Atmore, Flomaton, and Brewton. Monroeville produced one of the division's most enduring characters, John H. Finklea, whose memories go back to the early days of Alabama Power when the company made and sold ice as well as electricity in Monroeville. He would entertain for hours with stories about Alabama Power, its people, its substations, and its lines. One of Finklea's favorite stories is about the time he froze a dozen red roses in a block of ice, then chipped out a hole for the punch bowl at a women's club meeting, endearing Alabama Power to the real power brokers in the community.[142]

One example of Mobile's uniqueness is that it has the distinction of having the first female division vice president, Cheryl Thompson, who took over the division in January 1998. One of the first things Thompson did was to join the chamber of commerce's economic development committee, and in 2003 she chaired the Mobile Area Chamber of Commerce. Later she was in charge of the chamber's Partners for Growth, 2004–2008, a plan to promote retention and expansion of business, recruit new businesses, and support improved infrastructure in the area.[143]

Cheryl Thompson

Many leaders have influenced the character of the Mobile Division but perhaps none more than Ben W. Hutson, who came to the company on June 1, 1935, with an Auburn electrical engineering degree. Hutson was at Brookley Field during most of the war years, returned to Alabama Power as a division engineer in Mobile, and was division manager at Mobile from 1967 to 1981. A rapid talking and enthusiastic engineer, Hutson believes he is responsible for the stories that Alabama Power engineers from corporate headquarters could not go into the Mobile Division without letting the division manager or vice president know their intentions. The old Courtaulds Fibers plant had delicate rayon manufacturing operations that could not stand any interruption in service, and Hutson did not want anyone coming in without

Ben W. Hutson

his being aware of what changes or repairs they intended to make, especially with any interruption of power.[144] Hutson stressed safety and developed a strong safety program in Mobile. Because working conditions were complicated by the low swampy areas around the rivers, the Mobile Division has always stressed safety. The division was nationally recognized by the Edison Electric Institute when it achieved four million work hours without a lost-time accident. The division actually worked 4,000,024 hours without a lost-time accident between July 17, 1989, and September 29, 1992.[145]

In the fall of 2005 the Mobile Division was recovering from its third hurricane and one tropical storm that had arrived over a short eleven-month period, each one inflicting devastation upon the electrical system of the division. Vice president Thompson explained that only by teamwork, commitment, and professionalism could the division employees have restored power in three days to 48 percent of the customers who lost power during Hurricane Katrina, and in nine days they had 99 percent of the division's customers with their lights back on.[146]

Southeast Division

The Southeast Division began after the Gulf Electric Company merged with Alabama Power Company on November 10, 1927, and in January 1928 the properties were divided between the Mobile and Southeast Divisions. Southeast Division headquarters was established in the quaint Chattahoochee River town of Eufaula, founded in 1823 on the site of a Creek Indian village that gave the town its name. A commercial center and river port for the cotton and later peanut farmers of the surrounding area, Eufaula was a wealthy community noted for its nineteenth-century architectural gems and for having five of its Barbour County native sons elected governor of Alabama, more than any other county. Members of its legislative delegation were always powers to be reckoned with. In fact, in the 1980s when Alabama Power's boundary committee was meeting and rumors began circulating that the division might be abolished, Barbour County legislator and speaker of the Alabama House of Representatives James S. "Jimmy" Clark, whose clout was huge, merely whispered that would not be a good idea. Charles McCrary, who served on that committee, commented that Joe Farley would never have divided the Southeast Division and abandoned its headquarters in Eufaula, but the story persisted.[147] Alabama Power Company's Southeast Division headquarters had contributed payrolls, taxes, and talented hard-working leaders to the community. Clark was aware that by Alabama Power policy, supplies, automobiles, building materials, and other items were to be purchased locally when possible, and for over half a century this policy had contributed to Eufaula and Barbour County's economic prosperity.[148]

The first cotton mill arrived in Eufaula in 1888, and others followed; after 1927 many of them were recruited by Alabama Power. Eufaula historian Robert H. Flewellen noted that the Glorie Knitting Mills came to Eufaula in the late 1920s because of a new bridge over the Chattahoochee River and because Alabama Power had completed a transmission line to Eufaula from Union Springs that would provide more electric power for the city.[149] In 1948 the Cowikee Mills owned by the Comer family was Barbour County's largest employer. The construction of the Walter F. George Lock and Dam between 1959 and 1963 and the creation of Lake Eufaula increased commercial activity in the division and promoted recreational boating and bass fishing with a national following.[150]

The Southeast Division stretches across the Wiregrass to the Florida line and north to Russell County. Fort Rucker was activated in 1942; the U.S. Army base between Enterprise and Ozark became a significant load. In 1983 Fort Rucker was the largest Alabama Power customer in Ozark. In 2005 the Southeast Division was the smallest division in the company by number of customers, 105,162; revenue generated, $215 million; industrial load, 1.4 billion kilowatt hours; and by total kilowatt hours sold, 3.4 billion kilowatt hours (for twelve months ending June 30, 2005). The areas largest city is Dothan, which has a municipal system and is a member of the Alabama Municipal Electric Authority, a wholesale customer of Alabama Power. The most significant economic factor in the area is Alabama Power's Farley Nuclear Plant, a large employer that provides abundant inexpensive power and helped fuel growth in in the Houston County area in the last decades of the twentieth century.[151]

The rest of the Southeast Division area is composed of small towns and rural communities. Alabama Power retiree John R. Mills, who over the course of his career with Alabama Power worked in four divisions and in corporate headquarters, believed rural Wiregrass residents recognized that Alabama Power was one of the best things that ever happened to their towns because power company people lived and worked there and were actively involved in improving their communities and selling southeastern Alabama to industry. John Grimes, retired division transmission line engineer, pointed out that the rural nature of the Southeast Division was one of its strengths because Alabama Power's employees not only worked together but also raised their children together.[152] Longtime Southern Division manager William C. "Bill" Long considered the division "as a training ground—a place where outstanding young people are trained and promoted into the mainstream of Alabama Power operations."[153] Margaret Slade from accounting added that "at one time every division accounting manager in the company had worked in Eufaula."[154]

Sales and marketing were a traditional strength of the Southeast Division. Fred Cherry was called "Mr. Heat Pump" because of the large volume of his heat pump sales. Cherry knew every builder in the division's area, and if any one of them needed some guy wires or poles changed, he managed to get it done. Bobby Lockwood became a legendary district manager, serving Eufaula after he arrived in 1965. He called everyone "Captain," knew everybody, including being personal friends with George and Lurleen Wallace, and was a great raconteur. George Simpkins recalled that Lockwood quietly helped the poor of the community pay their power bills in hard times.[155]

Mike Saxon

Vice presidents Charles T. Hunter (1941–52), Marvin Wade (1952–54), Murray Greer (1954–66), Ray Garlington (1966–77), and John Byars (1977–93) were leaders who served the division for decades and influenced the culture of the division. Mike Saxon, who became vice president of the Southeast Division in 2003 (following Roy Crow and Bobby Kerley), anticipated a new flourish of industrial growth in the region, especially "as the automotive industry continues to grow in southeast Alabama." He expected the strong military presence to continue with significant growth at Fort Rucker.[156]

Birmingham Division

The Birmingham Division, located in the state's largest metropolitan area where roughly one-third of the population of Alabama resides, is the youngest division in Alabama Power's organizational structure. In 2005 it had the most customers (407,757), generated the most revenue ($947 million), and sold the most kilowatt hours (almost 15 billion kilowatt hours) but came in second to Mobile in industrial sales. After Alabama Power acquired the Birmingham Electric Company in 1952, BECO became the nucleus for the division with former BECO president Charles S. Thorn elected a vice president of Alabama Power, Birmingham Division, and Charles T. Hunter, who had been division vice president of the Southeast Division at Eufaula, being assigned to the Birmingham Division as a vice president in a transitional move.[157]

One hallmark of the Birmingham Division was stable leadership. In the thirty-nine years between 1952 and 1991, only three men were division vice presidents—Hunter, Bill Whitt, and Homer Turner, who served the division the longest, sixteen years. Since 1991, vice presidents of the Birmingham Division have not stayed longer than four and a half years as the position has become a proving ground for executive leadership. Birmingham vice president

Mike Garrett within a few years after he left the division (and after a stay as executive vice president of Alabama Power) became president of Mississippi Power and then was elected president of Georgia Power. Anthony Topazi was elected president of Mississippi Power after serving as vice president of the Birmingham Division, then moving to Southern Company Generation. Jim Miller III was vice president of the Birmingham Division before leaving to join Southern Power as corporate counsel. Alan Martin left the division to become executive vice president of Alabama Power, and Marsha Johnson moved from vice president of the Birmingham Division to a vice presidency at the Southern Company.

The Birmingham Division was noteworthy, too, because with Marsha Johnson it had the first African-American woman as a vice president and with her replacement, Gerald Johnson, the first African-American man to lead a division. A North Carolina native with degrees in accounting and economics and a career as a wide receiver for the Dallas Cowboys, Johnson came to Alabama Power in 2001 after twenty years with Georgia Power and extensive experience in customer operations, nuclear, governmental regulatory affairs, finance, and accounting.[158] He followed custom in playing an active role in the civic life of the Birmingham area.

Gerald Johnson

The Birmingham Division was so close to corporate headquarters that it was often overshadowed by the officers of the company, and residents of the area did not always differentiate between division and corporate leadership. Bruce Jones observed that it was always hard to be head of the Birmingham Division because that vice president "had so much help." Problems within the division were recognized sooner by top management, and the division's leadership successes and failures were more visible. On the other hand, having many of the corporate departments, such as the storm center, public relations, and the Alabama Power Foundation, in the division has been an advantage.[159]

In 2005 there were four members of the Alabama Power board of directors living in the division. Many of the state's most important CEOs called Birmingham home, and if their power went off, they were more likely to call friends or neighbors in the corporate office, perhaps not even being aware of the difference between the two. Many of these CEOs lived in heavily wooded areas where rear-lot service is required. The large trees come down in high winds, and their lights go out more frequently; yet the company maintains its orderly process for restoration. Making repairs of broken poles and heavy transformers in such conditions is an extremely difficult and lengthy process.[160]

The Birmingham Division consists of Jefferson and Shelby Counties. Shelby is the fastest growing county in the state. One of the company's two customer call centers is located in the division. Gerald Johnson pointed out that other Southern Company subsidiaries, such as Southern Company Services, Southern Generation, Southern Nuclear, and SouthernLINC are in the division and some coordination is needed in managing external activities and maximizing support for the community, such as in United Way drives. Many of the main company computer systems for each subsidiary are also located within the Birmingham Division.[161]

The industrial load of the company was once centered in the Birmingham mineral district, but after World War II the move away from heavy industry, iron, and steel to service jobs allowed Mobile to assume the number-one industrial load rank. The growth of the University of Alabama at Birmingham and its medical center and other hospitals in the area helped change the city's economy. The Birmingham Division is unique because when Alabama Power acquired BECO, it also assumed responsibility for providing steam service to the downtown area and to the University of Alabama's medical center hospitals. Low-pressure steam was sold downtown beginning in 1904.

Homer Turner

Homer Turner recalled that his greatest challenge as Birmingham Division vice president was to live within his budget and at the same time give the customer quality service. He was lucky to have talented people in managerial positions to help him: James Roland Ivy and Anthony Topazi were two of many. The leadership of the Birmingham Division worked hard to maintain good relationships and stay involved in the community and were active in the chamber of commerce, United Way, and civic clubs and special educational and charity drives.[162]

Bruce Jones observed that to organize sales and other jobs in divisions by function and place them under some central responsibility does not diminish the authority of the division vice presidents. As a practical matter, it gives the vice president more time to do those things that are vital for vice presidents to be involved in—work with the local industrial development boards and push for economic development. Building credibility in the communities and creating a foundation of trust, community development, and common goals cannot be accomplished across Alabama from the corporate office in Birmingham.[163]

INTO THE FUTURE

The six divisions of the company remain the touchstone for Alabama Power's relationship with its customers and the people of the state and the key to implementing company policies, accomplishing corporate goals, and keeping Alabama Power's customer service ranking at number one. The local, district, and division personnel are on the front line of winning and maintaining the confidence and hearts of customers on a daily basis. They are the face of Alabama Power, just as everyone is who drives a truck with an Alabama Power logo, who restores service after a storm, who keeps generation going, or who sells or works behind the scenes in human resources, risk management, appliance sales, public relations, or performs any of the hundreds of tasks necessary for Alabama Power to provide electricity for its customers. While technological advances have made the company more efficient, the personal touch delivered with integrity is still the key to Alabama Power's success.

Charles McCrary was deeply troubled by the national business scandals that surfaced in the summer of 2001 only months after he became president of Alabama Power. He was concerned over the failure of leadership and the absence of integrity at large American global corporations that came crashing down with devastating results for employees, investors, and the economy. These events caused him to emphasize models of behavior that for years had simply been taken for granted at Alabama Power. In an interview in 2003 McCrary said that "nothing is financially right if it's morally wrong. You have to start by running your business with honesty, integrity and by telling the truth. Once you do that, you can then start focusing on results."[164] The 2003 and 2004 business forums stressed ethical conduct and performance while celebrating the good financial results from those years.[165]

From 2002 to 2005 the average return on common equity exceeded the target of 13.5 percent. A hot summer in 2002 boosted income. The company's 2004 net income of $481 million was an $8 million increase from 2003. The target for the peak season equivalent forced outrage rate (EFOR) in 2004, which is an indicator of plant availability and efficient generation, was 2.8 percent or less, and the actual EFOR rate was 1.86 percent.[166] The unusually hot September in 2005 helped increase revenues for that year but also placed stress on generation plants, which still managed to produce a yearly 2.88 percent EFOR and a peak season rate of 4.48 percent, a testament to the dedicated work of all plant employees. At the 2006 business forum Jerry Stewart, executive vice president of generation, noted that since 1990 the company had reduced nitrogen oxides and sulfur dioxide emissions by 50 percent while increasing generation 60 percent. Despite these demands on the system, Stewart noted that the Target Zero safety campaign had resulted in Plants Gadsden, Gaston, Gorgas, and Washington County CoGen having zero recordable accidents, and the total number of lost-time accidents for generation in 2005 was one. Plant Gorgas had worked over one million hours safely from April 14, 2004, to January 2, 2006. Alan Martin stressed safety values, announced that ninety-seven of the company's high-risk work groups had worked injury-free in 2005, that the recordable incidence rate for the company was 1.54, which was the best rate in the company's history in safety performance, but noted that "even with our best, there is still work to do." He touted the new Target Zero slogan BELIEVE IT! EXPECT IT! LIVE IT![167]

In order to achieve corporate income goals in 2005 and 2006, McCrary expected his people to keep a tight rein on operation and maintenance budgets, which would allow Alabama Power to maintain its electricity costs at least 15 percent below the national average while keeping its promises to its stakeholders. Although the price of Alabama Power's electricity runs closer to 20 percent below the national average, the company prefers to advertise the more conservative figure of "at least" 15 percent. Challenges to maintain this pricing will be most demanding in environmental and fuel cost areas where the company has little control.

Looking to the future, one of the themes McCrary stressed in his leadership of the Birmingham Regional Chamber of Commerce in 2002 was promoting just that—companies, people, and organizations working together to solve regional problems. McCrary believed there was strength in numbers and unity, saying "we cannot survive without supporting each other." He advocated the chamber's involvement in the Growth Alliance, which was a partnership of eighty governments in the region and businesses, especially those that employed large numbers of people.[168] Writing in an op-ed piece in the Birmingham News, McCrary explained the private nature of the Growth Alliance and the exciting possibilities for the region around Birmingham if governments and private corporations worked together.[169] Whether turf wars and political differences in the Birmingham and Hoover metropolitan area can be overcome by a common vision for the future remains to be seen.

One of the best examples of McCrary's dedication to working with many groups and his ability to bring people together drawing on their common interests rather than their real or perceived differences is in the areas of community and economic development and industry recruitment. Under the direct leadership of Steve Spencer, Chris Bell, and Mike Saxon, Alabama Power began cosponsoring with the Alabama Electric Cooperative a series of economic development summits. The evolution of a cooperative spirit was remarkable considering the histories of Alabama Power and the AEC and was a testament to the leadership of both organizations, which recognized that a healthy Alabama economy benefited everyone and that competition should come after prospects were sold on Alabama as a place for the location of their new industries.

The initial contact was made while McCrary was head of Southern Generation and after frank negotiations and trust building occurred during talks on the AEC purchase of a block of coal-fired wholesale power from Southern Company. This was the first long-term contract between Alabama Power and Alabama Electric Cooperative. Communication and cooperation in mutually beneficial programming began. The successful economic seminars in southeast Alabama were replicated in southwest Alabama in 2006. The Alabama Communities of Excellence program and Impact Alabama are two other initiatives that Alabama Power was cosponsoring along with AEC. The North Alabama Industrial Development Association, in the heart of TVA land, is another cosponsor of Impact Alabama under executive director Tate Godfrey. Alabama Power has joined TVA in programs that market the state of Alabama, and McCrary chairs the board of the Economic Development Partnership of Alabama. Gary Smith, CEO of AEC, and Glenn McCullough Jr., from May 2004 until May 2005 when he left the chairmanship of TVA, were both serving on the EDPA board with McCrary.

Customer service remains at the top of Alabama Power's concerns as it begins its second century. Surveys to gauge customer opinions on a variety of specific issues continued, and Alan Martin announced at the beginning of 2006 that, for the second year in a row, the company ranked number one in customer service. Martin, Mike Scott, Gerald Johnson, and Myrna Pittman credited this success to everyone in the company, especially customer service representatives. Alabama Power has a special relationship with its longtime public affairs consultant, John Ashford, CEO of the Hawthorn Group, a friendship that goes beyond the professional

The 2006 meeting of the Alabama Rural Electric Association of Cooperatives (AREA) featured a panel discussion with, top left to right, Charles McCrary, CEO of Alabama Power; Tom Kilgore, CEO of TVA; Dudley Reynolds, CEO of Alabama Gas Corporation; Gary Smith, CEO of Alabama Electric Cooperative; and, bottom from left, Gary Harrison, general manager of Dixie Cooperative, and Fred Braswell, CEO of AREA.

connection with the founder of the Washington, D.C., public relations firm. Ashford knows the company and its people well, and he observed that "better than any corporate executive—and I've worked with a lot of his Fortune 100 counterparts—Charles McCrary understands the external as well as the internal dynamics of running a corporation that is a public franchise, dependent on the goodwill of the public." Ashford went on to explain that Alabama Power invests "more and smarter" than any other U.S. company in "listening to their customers, polling them, talking with them, hearing their concerns, answering their questions, working with them, helping them." The company's constant measuring of customer satisfaction and taking corrective actions when problems are discovered is the reason why, in Ashford's opinion, "Alabama Power under McCrary has achieved the highest customer satisfaction rating of any electric utility in America. And it's also why a majority of their customers rate Alabama Power as the best corporation in Alabama."[170]

Only time will tell what the repeal of the Public Utility Holding Company Act of 1935 will mean for the future of Alabama Power and all investor-owned power producers and their customers. On August 8, 2005, the president signed the Energy Policy Act of 2005, which repealed PUHCA beginning February 8, 2006, and increased the power of the Federal Energy Regulatory Commission. Holding companies were freed of the "integration" requirement of PUHCA and could now own operating companies that were not interconnected. The Public Utility Holding Company Act was costly to customers and shareholders and was not compatible with the new world of competition in power generation.

As Alabama Power looks to the future, economic and community development remains an important part of the company's plans. Chris Bell and Bob Howard's programs of preparing communities for economic development will be critical to economic success for the state in the twenty-first century. Cooperative programs with universities and local organizations will leverage efforts to replace some of the thousands of jobs lost in Alabama between 1996 and 2006. McCrary has taken a special interest in the Alabama Black Belt, a region of some eleven counties where the quality of life ranks near the bottom nationally in many indicators. Some of these counties are not in Alabama Power's retail service territory, but McCrary understands that improving the quality of life in these areas is critical to the state's overall prosperity. His solution is not just to throw money at problems but to change the way things are done so that these communities are self-reliant and realize their potential for long-term change.[171] In a major address to the Birmingham Kiwanis Club on March 14, 2006, McCrary challenged the business and political communities of the city and county to put aside turf conflicts and cooperate to prevent the state's largest metropolitan area from falling behind other Alabama and southern cities where economic indicators were up and creative programs booming. His speech was given wide publicity and became the topic of conversations. In an editorial two days later, the *Birmingham News* urged the city's leaders to heed McCrary's warning that Birmingham and Jefferson County's longtime state leadership was in jeopardy.[172]

While focusing on his business and his state, Charles McCrary is also keeping a wary eye on today's global economy where China's competition and India's outsourcing are challenges. The opportunities for manufacturing and industrial recruitment will be more limited in the future. Partnerships with universities and research institutions will become even more significant. Chris Bell has suggested that an increase in "wealth-creating, knowledge-based jobs will require the development of non-manufacturing product development and recruiting strategies" and a significant attention to "education and alignment issues to ensure Alabama's children can compete intellectually in the new economy."[173] Since the recruitment of Mercedes, the state has been attractive to the automotive industry and its suppliers, which in the early years of the twenty-first century brought 11,000 jobs to Alabama. The state has also been attractive to biotech and biomedical companies, especially around Huntsville and the University of Alabama at Birmingham.[174]

Charles McCrary is described as a caring and fair person who leads the company with justice and integrity. When asked a question, he is deliberative and not afraid of silence while he weighs his thoughts and formulates his answer. He is very good at listening. He wants facts to back opinion and research to support action. His wife Phyllis describes him as calm, sincere, and steadfast. In an age with so many environmental problems, he is well versed and experienced in the issues and the technology, dedicated to solutions within the range of possibilities of his corporate resources. Willard Bowers credits McCrary with changing the culture of the company on environmental issues so that everyone is committed.[175] McCrary has literally spent his life with Alabama Power, growing up in an Alabama Power family and spending his entire career with the company or its related service, nuclear, or generation companies. This background has given him a special appreciation for the traditions and history of Alabama Power Company and a willingness to shoulder the responsibility of leading the company into its second century, and he has assembled a strong team to lead with him.

Crews used Garrett Colliseum in
Montgomery as a staging area during
Hurricane Dennis in 2005. Courtesy
of Barry Chrietzberg.

Chapter Twelve

Family Counts Day, April 1, 2006,
at H. Neely Henry Dam.

ONE HUNDRED YEARS:
HELPING TO DEVELOP ALABAMA

*The Alabama Power Company believes that it has been of service to the
public and that it can be of still greater service in the future.*

JAMES MITCHELL, 1918

When electricity began to surge through Alabama Power's transmission
lines from the Coosa River dam in 1914, only then did the state of Alabama
begin its transition to modern times, for there can be no modernization without
an affordable and reliable supply of electric power. Industries in the twentieth
century required electricity, and the initial river development plans of James
Mitchell and the early leaders of Alabama Power Company were designed to
provide inexpensive hydropower backed by coal-fired steam generation, first
at Gadsden and later at Gorgas, to give Alabama all the electricity the state
needed to push forward with its industrial revolution.

From the beginning, Alabama Power had a policy of encouraging new industries to locate in Alabama because it needed to sell electricity. As early as 1913, months before Coosa River hydropower was available, Alabama Power's organizational chart showed a new industries as well as a new business department. In the decades that followed, the growth of the state of Alabama and Alabama Power Company were inextricably entwined. President William H. Taft's 1912 veto of a bill to allow the company to construct a dam at the Lock 18 site on the Coosa River above Wetumpka delayed the development of additional dams on the company's sites on the state's rivers. Only after the Federal Water Power Act passed in 1920 would these dams be constructed. Wars in the Balkans and a general European war caused financial hardships for the company, initially dependent upon English capital. At least once during this early period, Alabama Power was technically insolvent and for many years was financially strained. World War I stimulated American industry, and in 1917 the steam plant at Gorgas added critical capacity for the state's industries as German U-boat attacks on merchant shipping pushed the United States to enter the war. The federal government's insistence upon controlling the company's site on the Tennessee River at Muscle Shoals in order to build a dam to produce atmospheric nitrates for explosives resulted in James Mitchell's decision to donate the land, plans for the dam, and the company's river bottom and water flow studies. Following the armistice in 1918, a long and heated political controversy began over the future of the dam then still under construction at the Shoals.

James Mitchell's untimely death in 1920 might have been disastrous for the young company carrying such heavy debt and would have been a serious setback for the state of Alabama had not a bright young attorney, Thomas W. Martin, stepped into the leadership role and kept Alabama Power moving forward. Economic development and the expansion of central station power in the state would have been delayed. Surely investment capital for power development eventually would have come to Alabama, but how long might it have taken? The next decade, the Roaring Twenties, tested Tom Martin's mettle. There were great accomplishments for the company as well as bitter political attacks and heartbreaking setbacks. Under the Federal Water Power Act of 1920, Alabama Power built Mitchell, Jordan, Martin, Yates, and Thurlow Dams. The recruitment of new industry was accelerated to use the hydro-electricity being generated and an interstate connection was completed with Georgia utility companies so power could be exchanged all the way to the Carolinas. During the 1920s the commercial market exploded with new electrical inventions for the home and farm and demand for electricity increased. Martin's goal of the ownership of Alabama Power being vested in the citizens of the state of Alabama, his emphasis upon stock sales, and his commitment to keeping the price of that stock affordable encouraged many employees, workers, and the state's middle class to begin buying small amounts of stock on a regular basis for investment and for their retirement years.

The Muscle Shoals controversy raged for most of the 1920s, and Martin formed an American holding company to quiet opposition in the state of Alabama to Alabama Traction's Canadian incorporation and its English capital. His loss of control of that new holding company, Southeastern Power & Light, and its acquisition by a J. P. Morgan–backed holding company, Commonwealth & Southern, occurred on the eve of the nation's Great Depression. Franklin D. Roosevelt's election in 1932 brought the New Deal. Roosevelt's solution for the Muscle Shoals and the problem of dispersing government power produced at Wilson Dam was to create the Tennessee Valley Authority, a government corporation that took over Alabama Power's second Tennessee River dam site, built Wheeler Dam on that site, and initiated competition that eventually led to the loss of the company's Northern Division, one of the company's strongest and most profitable divisions. Tax-exempt and federally subsidized municipal and rural electric cooperatives, which were supplied by federally supported electricity, threatened the company's ability to compete. The beginning of war in Europe in 1939 and the Japanese attack on Pearl Harbor in 1941 shifted the nation's focus to war production that depended upon electricity. Defense and war spending brought a billion-dollar economic development program to Alabama, in part because the state had an abundant supply of electricity.

When the war was over in 1945, Alabama Power took a leadership role in recruiting private industries to take up the infrastructure abandoned by war industries in Alabama. Tom Martin's major challenge after the war was to make certain that when the Public Utility Holding Company Act of 1935 was applied to Commonwealth & Southern, Alabama Power's holding company would be a southern company not dominated by northern utility leaders or served by a northern service company. Martin met this challenge when the Southern Company began operating in 1949 and during the following few years as the company's board of directors became dominated by southern voices.

In the postwar economic boom of the 1950s, demand for electricity in Alabama soared. Alabama Power was able to convince Congress to remove its reservation of the upper Coosa River for federal power projects and possible TVA expansion. Alabama Power was able to complete its original river development plans by building Weiss, Logan Martin, Neely Henry, and Bouldin Dams on the Coosa. The company redeveloped Lay Dam, increasing the height of the dam by fourteen feet and installing new turbines, and completed

Harris Dam on the Tallapoosa. Alabama Power also constructed Smith Dam and generation plants at the U.S. Army Corps of Engineers' Bankhead and Holt Locks and Dams on the Black Warrior River. Steam plants—Barry (in Mobile), Miller (in northwest Jefferson County), Greene County, and Gaston (near Childersburg)—were constructed, and the company's first nuclear plant, Farley, was built on the Chattahoochee River near Dothan. In 1968 inflation and the national economic climate forced Alabama Power to request its first-ever general rate increase. The next fourteen years were dominated by hostile political attacks on the company and one financial crisis after another. The dire situation was solved by the Alabama Supreme Court's intervention and subsequent approval of a formula to take rate making out of politics. Alabama Power was then free to concentrate on being the most efficient and consumer-minded utility in the state and making certain its rates stayed where they had been throughout the company's history: among the lowest rates in the country.

In the one hundred years since Captain William Patrick Lay incorporated Alabama Power in Gadsden on December 4, 1906, the company has made significant contributions to the state of Alabama. In addition to its years of promoting economic development, Alabama Power pushed beyond the urban areas and brought electricity to small towns and rural regions. The company financed research on how farms could use electricity to become more profitable and each year built as many rural lines as possible without endangering its financial solvency. Alabama Power pioneered the development of technological equipment and ways of designing transmission lines and transformers that made it less expensive to serve these isolated areas. Electricity improved the quality of life in rural parts of the state by bringing lights, electric irons, refrigerators, water heaters, and motors that pumped well water into homes for indoor plumbing. Electricity soon became not just a luxury but a necessity. On NBC's *Today Show*, October 10, 2005, Zainab Salbi, a native of Iraq who founded Women for Women International, was discussing her work in war-torn areas of Iraq. She said that "people need water and they need electricity." It is striking that she coupled electricity with life's first necessity, water, which illustrates the modern world's dependence upon electricity as a sustainer of life, not just an enhancement of the quality of life. And so it was in Alabama.

Over its long history Alabama Power Company provided employment for the state's people. These good jobs were located all across the state and, after the coming of TVA, in the southern two-thirds of the state. For thousands of men and women, especially people living in Alabama's rural areas, getting a job with the power company was an opportunity to leave the farm and provide a good living for the family. Once a family member secured a job with Alabama

Power and proved to be a dependable and capable worker, other relatives followed. The family of Leitha Shaw McKenzie is only one example. In the early 1950s her picture appeared in *Powergrams* with the caption that she had five sons and two stepsons working for Alabama Power, two at Gorgas Mine, three at Gorgas Steam Plant, one at Yates Dam, and one with the construction force at Montgomery. In the company's centennial year, one grandson, Theron David Shaw, was retired from Smith Dam and one great-grandson, Billy Eugene Jent, was working at Miller, by then called the Miller Electric Generating Plant. These extended families and generations of families working for Alabama Power meant that the culture of the company, its expectations of a good work ethic and strong integrity, were passed to a new generation not just in the plant, line crew, or office, but at home, too.

"Going with the power company," as it was phrased, meant not just a good job but a chance for advancement. Biographies of company vice presidents and leaders in the 1920s and 1930s list beginnings as meter readers and surveyors. In the first half of the twentieth century, Alabama Power provided engineering graduates of the Alabama Polytechnic Institute at Auburn and the University of Alabama opportunities to be employed in the state, and later, after other schools organized engineering programs, employment opportunities for graduates of these schools, as well as college graduates with other majors and degrees. The company's early home services department offered women with college degrees professional employment. Through the decades, thousands of young men and women stayed home in Alabama and used their talents to move the state forward because there were professional and well-paying jobs available at Alabama Power. The company nurtured leaders without really having a leadership program and used mentors to tutor young and new employees long before that approach was fashionable. Training courses and professional development opportunities produced competent employees. Many of the state's economic, civic, and political leaders in the early twenty-first century speak fondly of beginning their working careers at Alabama Power.

Alabama Power encouraged its employees to contribute their talents and leadership abilities in activities that would make their communities stronger and a better place to live. Early Alabama Power leaders realized they were building a company with a new vision, serving the public in a new way. They wanted to inspire Alabama Power's employees to become leaders in their communities and to participate in the civic life of their towns. This tradition of service has continued. The company supported the economy of small towns by purchasing supplies locally, by working with youth organizations and local charities, and by providing leadership for civic clubs and later industrial development boards to attract new industries to the town. If in the course of community life something unusual or challenging came up, it was common for the first response to be "Let's bring in the local Alabama Power people to help us figure out how this task can be accomplished." By the end of 2006, through the Alabama Power Foundation the company had contributed $90 million to programs of nonprofit groups to improve the quality of life for the citizens of the state.

Over its history Alabama Power attracted good people, many of them young and just entering the workforce, and many of them stayed throughout their working careers. Length of service to the company produced a deep sense of loyalty, and pride was always strong among employees who considered themselves part of an extended family. Alabama Power's newsletter, *Powergrams*, was created in 1920 to communicate with employees and to bring the company and its people closer together. A study of the contents over eighty-six years illustrates how the birth, death, wedding, retirement, and promotion announcements were significant in creating a closeness in the workforce at a time when telephone calls were expensive or service nonexistent and travel was difficult. News of people at local, divisional, and corporate offices and at dams or plants brought familiarity with names, and photographs put faces to the names.

One of the constant themes of Alabama Power's history is the company's ability to stay on the cutting edge of emerging technology. The Thurlow Backwater Suppressor was used on many dams around the world; the company created one of the first hydraulic laboratories in the nation; the designs of rural line equipment were adapted across the United States; the first radio station in Alabama went on the air with equipment designed and built by Alabama Power engineers. In the 1940s the company pioneered research in coal gasification, and inventions and research are ongoing and include programs such as the Power Systems Development Facility in Shelby County, where the goal is to help power plants generate the same amount of electricity while burning a third less coal. Alabama Power ranks near the top of all utilities for investment in equipment, research, and technology to improve the environment. From automated meter reading to advanced generation technology, from innovative software that monitors and controls the flow of power to computers that operate switches remotely, from computer grids that tell engineers exactly where there are interruptions of service to experiments with switchgrass as a renewable source of energy that helps coal burn cleaner, Alabama Power has always been a leader in power technology.

The emphasis upon safe work practices is another theme of the company's history. From the first safety meetings to the 2006 TARGET ZERO: BELIEVE IT! EXPECT IT! LIVE IT! mind-set, the company has stressed safety, supported meetings where safety methods were explained and emphasized, published articles in *Powergrams*, and sent representatives to the earliest national safety conventions. Alabama Power always had women and blacks in its employment, but as the nation's culture modernized and the state's educational institutions filled the work pool with women and African Americans with engineering and professional degrees, the company's middle and upper management became more diverse. Thumbing through *Powergrams*, the sociological changes are evident. For one thing, men stopped wearing hats, and women left hats and white gloves at home. In the latter part of the twentieth century, men sometimes did not wear coats and ties and women began wearing dress pants to the office. Not unlike other large corporations of the twenty-first century, Alabama Power has become a first-name company where even the president is called by his first name.

The motto of the state of Alabama is WE DARE DEFEND OUR RIGHTS. The words also encapsulate a theme in Alabama Power Company's history. From the 1914 mosquito lawsuits over the first Coosa River reservoir to threats from federally subsidized power, from what the company believed were unfair rulings by government regulatory agencies to erroneous charges made by rabble-rousing politicians, Alabama Power has always taken appropriate action to protect the interest of its customers and the public's short-term and long-term interests, even when the customers themselves were not paying attention or disagreed with the company's approach.

In a draft of a speech about his company, Tom Martin once used a quotation from early twentieth-century writer Fletcher Bascomb Dresslar that "the artists of the world do not find inspiration in a tree which has grown without struggle, whose branches are straight and even, and whose trunk reveals no scars." To Martin, the struggles of Alabama Power made for a richer history: in his *Story of Electricity in Alabama*, Martin ended with the observation that "there has scarcely been a year in [the company's] history when it has not been visited by some disaster." Lightning, tornadoes, and ice storms, he pointed out, caused difficulties for the company. More than fifty years later, Hurricanes Ivan, Dennis, and Katrina came calling, creating far more than just difficulties. In its history Alabama Power has been impacted by forces of nature and actions of government over which it had no control. But the company's vision, its leadership, its technological innovation, and its culture, which above all else values the people and customers of Alabama Power, allowed it to meet and overcome those challenges. Adversity has only made the company stronger, and despite all, Alabama Power Company has survived, prospered, and served the people of its state with an unwavering commitment that draws strength from its past as the company moves into its second century.

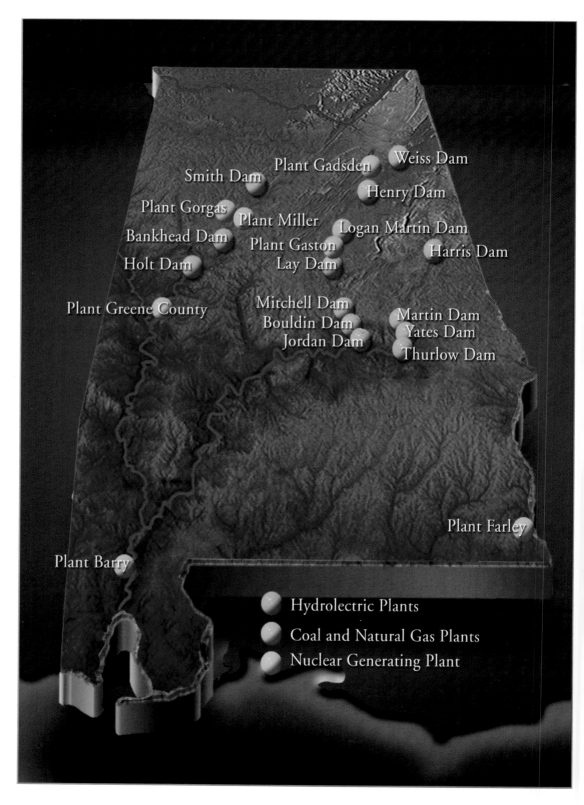

Smith Dam

Plant Gadsden

Weiss Dam

Henry Dam

Plant Gorgas

Plant Miller

Logan Martin Dam

Bankhead Dam

Plant Gaston

Harris Dam

Holt Dam

Lay Dam

Plant Greene County

Mitchell Dam

Bouldin Dam

Martin Dam

Jordan Dam

Yates Dam

Thurlow Dam

Plant Farley

Plant Barry

○ Hydrolectric Plants

○ Coal and Natural Gas Plants

○ Nuclear Generating Plant

Alabama Power Company Generation Plants

Alabama Power owns or operates eighty-two electric generating units with total nameplate capacity of nearly 13 million kilowatts. These generating units are located at twenty-four facilities.

In 2006 Alabama Power generated 68.2 percent of its electricity using coal-fired units, 18.5 percent using nuclear units, 7.3 percent using gas-fired units, and 6 percent using hydroelectric units.

Coal and Natural Gas Plants

James M. Barry Electric Generating Plant
Location—along the Mobile River in Bucks
Construction started: August 1951
In-service date: February 12, 1954
Total nameplate generating capacity—2,657,200 kW
Generating units—7
Type of fuel—coal and natural gas

Gadsden Electric Generating Plant
Location—along the Coosa River in Gadsden
Construction started: 1912
In-service date: 1913
Total nameplate generating capacity—120,000 kW
Generating units—2
Type of fuel—coal, oil and natural gas

Ernest C. Gaston Electric Generating Plant
Location—along the Coosa River in Wilsonville
Construction started: July, 1957
In-service date: May 1, 1960
Total nameplate generating capacity—1,880,000 kW
Generating units—6
Type of fuel—coal and oil

William Crawford Gorgas Electric Generating Plant
Location—along the Black Warrior River near Parrish
Construction started: 1916
In-service date: 1917
Total nameplate generating capacity—1,290,000 kW
Generating units—5
Type of fuel—coal

Greene County Electric Generating Plant
Location—along the Black Warrior River near Demopolis
Construction started: February 1963
In-service date: June 11, 1965
Total nameplate generating capacity—1,220,000 kW
Generating units—11
Type of fuel—coal, oil and natural gas

James H. Miller Jr. Electric Generating Plant
Location—along the Black Warrior River near West Jefferson
Construction started: September 1974
In-service date: October 12, 1978
Total nameplate generating capacity—2,640,000 kW
Generating units—4
Type of fuel—coal

Nuclear Generating Plants

Joseph M. Farley Nuclear Electric Generating Plant
Location—along the Chattahoochee River east of Dothan
Construction started: August, 1972
In-service date: December 1, 1977
Total nameplate generating capacity—1,720,000 kW
Generating units—2
Type of fuel—nuclear

Hydrolectric Plants
Coosa River

Walter Bouldin Hydroelectric Generating Plant
Named for Walter Bouldin
Location—on the Coosa River near Wetumpka
Construction started: August 20, 1963
In-service date: July 27, 1967
Total nameplate generating capacity—225,000 kW
Generating units—3
Elevation above sea level—252 feet
Reservoir area when full– 6,800 acres

Jordan Hydroelectric Generating Plant
Named for Elmira Sophia Jordan
Location—on the Coosa River near Wetumpka
Construction started: June 15, 1926
In-service date: December 31, 1928
Total nameplate generating capacity—100,000 kW
Generating units—4
Elevation above sea level—252 feet
Reservoir area when full—6,800 acres

Lay Hydroelectric Generating Plant
Named for William Patrick Lay
Location—on the Coosa River near Clanton
Construction started: original—1910; redeveloped—August 31, 1964.
In-service date: original—1914; redeveloped—February 24, 1967.
Total nameplate generating capacity—177,000 kW
Generating units—6
Elevation above sea level—396 feet
Reservoir area when full—12,000 acres

Logan Martin Hydroelectric Generating Plant
Named for William Logan Martin
Location—on the Coosa River near Vincent
Construction started: July 18, 1960
In-service date— August 10, 1964
Total nameplate generating capacity—128,250 kW
Generating units—3
Elevation above sea level—465 feet
Reservoir area when full—15,263 acres

Mitchell Hydroelectric Generating Plant
Named for James Mitchell
Location—on the Coosa River near Verbena
Construction started: July 1, 1921
In-service date: August 15,1923; redeveloped—April 1, 1985
Total nameplate generating capacity—170,000 kW
Generating units—4
Elevation above sea level—312 feet
Reservoir area when full—5,850 acres

Neely Henry Hydroelectric Generating Plant
Named for H. Neely Henry
Location—on the Coosa River near Ohatchee
Construction started: August 1, 1962
In-service date: June 2, 1966
Total nameplate generating capacity—72,900 kW
Generating units—3
Elevation above sea level—508 feet
Reservoir area when full—11,200 acres

Weiss Hydroelectric Generating Plant
Named for Fernand C. Weiss
Location—on the Coosa River near Leesburg
Construction started: July 31, 1958
In-service date: June 5, 1961
Total nameplate generating capacity—87,750 kW
Generating units—3
Elevation above sea level—564 feet
Reservoir area when full—30,200 acres

Tallapoosa River

R. L. Harris Hydroelectric Generating Plant
Named for Rother L. Harris

Location—on the Tallapoosa River near Lineville
Construction started: November 1, 1974
In-service date: April 20, 1983
Total nameplate generating capacity—135,000 kW
Generating units—2
Elevation above sea level—793 feet
Reservoir area when full—10,600 acres

Martin Hydroelectric Generating Plant

Named for Thomas W. Martin
Location—on the Tallapoosa River near Dadeville
Construction started: July 24, 1923
In-service date: December 31, 1926
Total nameplate generating capacity—154,200 kW
Generating units—4
Elevation above sea level—490 feet
Reservoir area when full—40,000 acres

Thurlow Hydroelectric Generating Plant

Named for Oscar G. Thurlow
Location—on the Tallapoosa River at Tallassee
Construction started: April 5, 1928
In-service date: December 31, 1930
Total nameplate generating capacity—85,000 kW
Generating units—3
Elevation above sea level—287.50 feet
Reservoir area when full—574 acres

Yates Hydroelectric Generating Plant

Named for Eugene A. Yates
Location—on the Tallapoosa River near Tallassee
Construction started: January 18, 1927
In-service date: July 1, 1928
Total nameplate generating capacity—58,000 kW
Generating units—2
Elevation above sea level—344 feet
Reservoir area when full—2,000 acres

Warrior River

Bankhead Lock and Hydroelectric Generating Plant

Named for Senator John Hollis Bankhead
Location—on the Black Warrior River near
 Northport
Construction started: February 13, 1961
In-service date: July 12, 1963
Total nameplate generating capacity—52,400 kW
Generating units—1

Elevation above sea level—255 feet
Reservoir area when full—9,200 acres

Holt Lock and Hydroelectric Generating Plant

Location—on the Black Warrior River near
 Northport
Construction started: April 27, 1966
In-service date: August 15, 1968
Total nameplate generating capacity—40,000 kW
Generating units—1
Elevation above sea level—187 feet
Reservoir area when full—3,200 acres

Smith Hydroelectric Generating Plant

Named for L. M. Smith
Location—on the Sipsey fork of the Black Warrior
 River near Jasper
Construction started: November 25, 1957
In-service date: September 5, 1961
Total nameplate generating capacity—157,500 kW
Generating units—2
Elevation above sea level—510 feet
Reservoir area when full—21,200 acres

ADDITIONAL GENERATING FACILITIES

Theodore Cogen Facility

Location—in Mobile County
Total nameplate generating capacity—273,870 kW
Generating units—1
Type of fuel—natural gas

Washington County Cogen Facility

Location— near McIntosh in Washington County,
 north of Mobile
Total nameplate generating capacity—122,579 kW
Generating units—1
Type of fuel—natural gas

GE Plastics Cogen Facility

Location—at the GE Plastics plant in Burkville,
 west of Montgomery
Total nameplate generating capacity—105,100 kW
Generating units—1
Type of fuel— natural gas

Symbols of recognition

Over the years, Alabama Power has used a variety of symbols to identify the company. These symbols have changed but one factor remains the same. The trademarks and logos show the company's continuing efforts to promote the economic growth of the state.

1913–1920s

Early 1920s

Mid-1920s–early 1950s

1954–early 1960s

1960s–1973

1973–1977

1977–1996

1996–present

Appendix B

ALABAMA POWER COMPANY BOARDS OF DIRECTORS

Name	Date Elected	Date of Termination	
W. P. Lay	12/04/1906	05/07/1912	Resigned
	08/05/1913	09/01/1915	Resigned
Earl Lay	12/04/1906	05/07/1912	Resigned
O. R. Hood	12/04/1906	05/07/1912	Resigned
James Mitchell	05/07/1912	07/22/1920	Died
Thomas W. Martin	05/07/1912	12/08/1964	Died
Frederick S. Ruth	05/07/1912	09/07/1912	Resigned
	10/04/1913	02/15/1915	Resigned
W. W. Freeman	09/07/1912	10/04/1913	Resigned
Lawrence Macfarlane	08/05/1913	10/04/1913	Resigned
	02/16/1920	11/14/1921	Resigned
	02/20/1922	12/29/1932	Resigned
J. W. Worthington	08/05/1913	12/01/1915	Resigned
Frank S. Washburn	08/05/1913	03/10/1916	Resigned
Frederick Darlington	08/20/1913	02/23/1914	Resigned
E. Mackay Edgar	02/23/1914	03/05/1915	Resigned
H. S. Swan	02/15/1915	05/01/1920	Resigned
	02/21/1921	02/19/1923	
	05/30/1923	08/18/1923	Resigned
Gerhard M. Dahl	09/01/1917	08/18/1923	Resigned
	02/18/1924	09/09/1935	Resigned
George E. Chaflin	09/01/1917	04/18/1919	Died
W. H. Hassinger	09/01/1917	03/28/1935	Died
W. J. Henderson	09/01/1917	06/11/1930	Resigned
W. H. Weatherly	07/05/1918	03/17/1947	Died
R. A. Mitchell	08/26/1918	01/10/1937	Died

Name	Date Elected	Date of Termination	
C. E. Groesbeck	06/02/1919	08/18/1923	Resigned
	02/18/1924	12/29/1932	Resigned
W. N. Walmsley	10/15/1919	12/30/1924	Resigned
S. Z. Mitchell	02/16/1920	12/29/1932	Resigned
Richard M. Hobbie	02/16/1920	03/01/1920	Resigned
	05/27/1920	12/24/1940	Died
Walter M. Hood	02/16/1920	02/18/1924	Resigned
Frank M. Moody (Sr.)	05/27/1920	09/20/1940	Resigned
E. C. Melvin	08/18/1923	04/18/1949	Resigned
D. P. Bestor Jr.	10/19/1923	03/21/1933	Resigned
R. I. Ingalls	09/09/1924	04/21/1941	Resigned
O. G. Thurlow	05/28/1925	04/21/1930	Resigned
W. E. Mitchell	05/28/1925	11/06/1930	Resigned
Theo K. Jackson	04/19/1926	09/24/1945	Died
J. E. Z. Riley	11/10/1927	10/16/1935	Died
L. H. Sessions	11/10/1927	04/18/1932	Resigned
R. D. Thomas	11/10/1927	01/06/1951	Died
B. C. Cobb	09/12/1929	12/29/1932	Resigned
Oscar Wells	02/27/1930	04/18/1938	Resigned
	04/15/1940	04/18/1949	Resigned
P. W. Turner	04/21/1930	04/15/1940	Resigned
F. P. Cummings	04/21/1930	11/12/1931	Resigned
Wendell L. Willkie	12/29/1932	02/13/1936	Resigned
Crawford T. Johnson	02/09/1933	02/13/1936	Resigned
Thomas Bragg	04/15/1935	10/30/1943	Died
W. M. Stanley	04/15/1935	04/18/1949	Resigned
Justin R. Whiting	02/13/1936	11/07/1938	Resigned
Algernon Blair	04/19/1937	04/17/1950	Resigned
David R. Dunlap	04/19/1937	04/19/1943	Resigned
C. A. Bingham	04/18/1938	04/15/1940	Resigned
Carl James	11/18/1938	11/16/1951	Resigned
Al C. Garber	04/21/1941	02/18/1946	Died

Name	Date Elected	Date of Termination	
B. Lonnie Noojin	11/15/1946	09/07/1950	Died
E. A. Yates	02/19/1923	04/21/1930	Resigned
	11/12/1931	10/05/1957	Died
J. M. Barry	11/06/1930	04/15/1963	Retired
Crawford T. Johnson Jr.	04/18/1938	04/18/1969	Retired
E. W. Robinson	04/15/1940	12/17/1954	Resigned
Gordon D. Palmer	02/21/1941	04/16/1956	Resigned
Joseph Linyer Bedsole	12/18/1942	04/15/1963	Retired
Wm. Howard Smith	11/19/1943	04/15/1963	Retired
John C. Webb Jr.	12/19/1945	04/22/1977	Retired
Ervin Jackson	04/15/1946	05/19/1974	Retired
Walker Reynolds	04/21/1947	04/15/1963	Retired
W. C. Bowman	04/18/1949	04/15/1963	Retired
J. Finley McRae	04/18/1949	04/21/1967	Retired
John C. Persons	04/18/1949	04/15/1963	Retired
Alfred M. Shook III	04/18/1949	10/25/1955	Resigned
Lewis M. Smith	04/18/1949	03/04/1958	Died
Wm. Logan Martin	11/16/1951	02/25/1959	Died
Earl M. McGowin	02/15/1952	05/19/1972	Retired
William J. Rushton	05/26/1952	09/18/1970	Resigned
Walter Bouldin	12/17/1954	09/18/1970	Resigned
H. Neely Henry	12/17/1954	12/01/1968	Resigned
Everett Lay	12/17/1954	04/19/1956	Retired
L. Y. Dean III	04/16/1956	04/22/1977	Retired
Frank M. Moody	04/16/1956	04/25/1986	Retired
D. H. Morris III	04/16/1956	04/23/1982	Retired
Fernand C. Weiss	04/16/1956	05/28/1959	Died
Harllee Branch Jr.	10/18/1957	10/29/1969	Resigned
Edwin I. Hatch	08/01/1958	05/16/1962	Resigned
E. C. Easter	04/03/1958	04/20/1964	Retired
W. Cooper Green	10/16/1959	04/01/1965	Resigned

Name	Date Elected	Date of Termination	
Alvin W. Vogtle	04/20/1959	12/27/1960	Resigned
	05/31/1962	11/19/1965	Resigned
	1968	11/01/1983	Resigned
T. Massey Bedsole	04/15/1963	04/22/1988	Retired
John A. Hand	04/15/1963	05/19/1972	Retired
Marshall K. Hunter	04/15/1963	05/19/1972	Retired
Walter Kennedy	04/15/1963	04/18/1969	Retired
Howard Murfee	04/15/1963	04/22/1983	Retired
Joseph M. Farley	04/19/1965	03/01/1989	Resigned
Rother L. Harris	04/19/1965	12/01/1968	Resigned
James C. Inzer	04/19/1965	04/23/1993	Retired
E. R. Coulbourn	11/19/1965	06/01/1967	Retired
E. Ward Faulk	04/21/1967	04/19/1974	Retired
George B. Campbell	05/19/1967	06/20/1969	Retired
Alan R. Barton	12/01/1968	06/01/1980	Resigned
James H. Miller Jr.	12/01/1968	03/31/1975	Resigned
Crawford T. Johnson III	04/18/1969	04/28/1995	Retired
Frank A. Plummer	04/18/1969	04/22/1983	Retired
G. Thornton Nelson	06/20/1969	04/22/1983	Retired
S. Eason Balch	09/18/1970	04/27/1990	Retired
William J. Rushton III	09/18/1970	04/23/1999	Retired
John W. Woods	04/20/1973	04/25/1997	Resigned
Philip C. Jackson Jr.	04/19/1974	07/18/1975	Resigned
Ernest F. Ladd Jr.	04/19/1974	04/23/1982	Retired
Emil Hess	10/17/1975	04/20/1986	Retired
Walter Johnsey	05/16/1975	04/20/1979	Resigned
Fred Morgan Clark	04/22/1977	04/27/1990	Retired
John C. Webb IV	04/22/1977		Active
Jesse S. Vogtle	05/18/1979	12/16/1988	Resigned
William O. Whitt	05/18/1979	02/01/1985	Resigned
Elmer B. Harris	09/18/1980	11/30/1985	Resigned
	03/01/1989	01/11/2002	Resigned

Name	Date Elected	Date of Termination	
Robert H. Radcliff Jr.	07/23/1982	04/22/1988	Retired
Whit Armstrong	09/24/1982		Active
James H. Sanford	08/01/1983		Active
Edward L. Addison	11/01/1983	04/22/1994	Resigned
Louis J. Willie	03/23/1984	04/22/1994	Retired
William L. McDonough	12/20/1985	02/22/1991	Resigned
Gerald H. Powell	02/28/1986	04/25/1997	Retired
Winton M. Blount III	03/28/1986	04/23/1993	Resigned
Dr. Joab L. Thomas	04/25/1986	09/23/1990	Resigned
Travis J. Bowden	02/01/1988	02/01/1994	Resigned
Carl E. Jones Jr.	04/22/1988	04/28/2006	Resigned
Dr. John W. Rouse	04/22/1988	04/24/1998	Resigned
Bill M. Guthrie	12/16/1988	06/01/1998	Resigned
Wallace D. Malone Jr.	06/22/1990	04/28/2006	Resigned
Dr. Philip E. Austin	01/25/1991	10/25/1996	Resigned
Robert D. Powers	01/24/1992		Active
Margaret A. Carpenter	02/26/1993	04/26/1996	Retired
Dr. William V. Muse	02/26/1993	04/26/2002	Resigned
Peter V. Gregerson Sr.	10/22/1993	04/23/1999	Retired
Dr. John T. Porter	10/22/1993	04/27/2001	Retired
A. W. Dahlberg	04/22/1994	10/22/1999	Resigned
Patricia M. King	07/25/1997		Active
James K. Lowder	07/25/1997		Active
C. Dowd Ritter	07/25/1997		Active
Andreas Renschler	01/23/1998	04/25/2003	Resigned
David J. Cooper Sr.	04/24/1998		Active
Dr. Thomas C. Meredith	10/23/1998	04/26/2002	Resigned
H. Allen Franklin	10/22/1999	07/01/2004	Resigned
R. Kent Henslee	10/22/1999	04/28/2006	Retired
Mayer Mitchell	10/22/1999	04/25/2003	Retired
James W. Wright	07/28/2000		Active

Name	Date Elected	Date of Termination	
Charles D. McCrary	04/26/2001		Active
Dr. Malcolm Portera	02/24/2003		Active
Dr. William F. Walker	02/24/2003	04/23/2004	Resigned
John D. Johns	01/23/2004		Active
David M. Ratcliffe	07/23/2004		Active

Downstream view of upper Tallassee
Hydro Plant, May 1, 1924.

Cities and Towns Served by Alabama Power Company and Date of Service

Communities and the dates (through 1941) when they were first served by Alabama Power Company

*Northern Division communities now part of TVA

1912
Attalla
Anniston
Blue Mountain
Hobson City
Oxford
Huntsville*
Austinville*
Decatur*
Talladega

1915
Eden
Pell City
Leeds
Lincoln
Ragland
Blocton
West Blocton
Hartselle*

1916
Sherman Heights
Gurley*
Jacksonville
Ashland
Lineville

1917
Wilton
Camp Hill
Montevallo

Jasper
Marion

1918
Roanoke

1919
Dora

1920
Madison*
Bellvue Highlands
Oakman
Gadsden
Clanton
Selma
Lily Flag*

1921
Notasulga

1922
Fairview*
Scenic Heights
Marion Junction
Parrish
Normal*

1923
Delraida
Shades Mountain
Warrior

Childersburg
Waverly
Holton Heights
Chase*
Alberta City
Bryce Hospital
Kaulton
Northport
Tuscaloosa
University
Brent
Centreville
Dadeville
Albertville*
Union Springs
Wetumpka
Prattville
Russellville*
Boaz
Montgomery
Oakwood*

1924
Nauvoo
Gardendale
Morris
Trafford
Kimberly
New Merkle
Fulton Springs
Guin
Upper Lewisburg

East Brookwood
Huffman
Oak Grove
East Jefferson County
Hueytown
Winfield
Edgewood Lake
Calera
Greenville
Helena
Five Points
White Plains

1925
Pelham
Eclectic
Fort Deposit
Chapman
Courtland*
Georgiana
Leighton*
Town Creek*
East Parrish
Coaldale
Boston
Eldridge
West Bessemer Highlands
Bankston
Berry
Cherokee*
Creeltown

Apex
Cottage Hill
East Mulga
McDonalds Chap.
Minor High
Pleasant Grove
Smith Hill
Pinson
Ashford
Carrville
Gantts Quarry
Center Point
East Florence*
Florence*
Sheffield*
Tuscumbia*
Demopolis
Knoxwood
Fayette
Faunsdale
Uniontown
Crichton
Plateau
Pritchard
Spring Hill
Magazine
Whistler
Mobile
Abbeville
Enterprise
Eufaula
Midland City
Newville
Thorsby
Deatsville
Elmore
Speigner
Asbury
Letohatchie
Mount Meigs
Boiling
Burlington

1926
Belle Mina*
Mooresville*
Jemison
Rock Springs
Flomaton

Weaver
Columbiana
New Brocton
Moulton*
Doleville
Falkville*
Altoona
Midway
Springville
Wadley
Linden
Trussville
Crestline Heights
Walker's Chapel
Coalburg
Ketona
Glencoe
Part of Homewood
Crumley's Chapel
Sandusky
Wylam Heights
Sherman Heights
Vernon
East Valley
Industrial City
Curtiston
Minnieville
Cardiff
Blossburg
Brookside
Adamsville
Pinckey City
Dolomite
Graysville
Little Italy
North Bessemer
    Highlands
Shortleaf
Chalkville
Heflin
Oneonta
Wedowee
Goodwater
York
Haleyville
Cuba
Sulligent
Livingston
Townley

Thomasville
Columbia
Atmore
Slocumb
Pinckard
Ozark
Munford
Norman Bridge
Choccolocco
DeArmanville
Iron City
Gallion
Coopers
Marbury
Mountain Creek
Verbena
Remlap
Village Springs
Calhoun
Mobile Junction
Alton
Weeden*

1927
Concord
Brookwood
Powderly Com.
Roberta
Brilliant
North Johns
Kansas
Monte Sano*
Mountain Brook Estates
Seloca
Waddell
Webb
Ashville
Alabaster
Bear Creek
Hackleburg
Hamilton
Phil Campbell
Thomaston
Hurtsboro
Clayton
Louisville
Geneva
Carbon Hill
Holt

Carrollton
Gordo
Reform
Aliceville
Florala
Jackson
Eutaw
Bay Minette
Odenville
Mount Andrew
Hornsbytown
Cropwell
Spruce Pine
Barton*
Stroud
Newala
Isbell*

1928
Rainbow Drive
Quintown
Old Jonesboro
Sumiton
Nolanville
Virginia
Flint*
Hodges
Vina
Akron
Boligee
Epes
Moundville
Grove Hill
Arab
Rogersville*
New Hope*
Vincent
McKenzie
Rock Mills
Dwight Village
Kennedy
Millport
Brewton
East Brewton
Buffalo
Stones Tank
Patton Church
Millbrook
Robbins Cross Roads

West Sayre
Grants Mill
Greenwood
Morgan
Mount Olive
Gary Springs
Clay
Hope Hull
Easonville
High Point
Owen's Cross Roads*
Moody's Cross Roads
Whites Chapel
Alexandria
Harpersville
Ohatchie
New Market*
Eastaboga
Webster
Woodstock
Green Pond
Branchville
Dogwood
Bell Factory*
Mitylene
Wheeler*
Molton Heights*
Elgin*
Greenbrier*
Center Star*
Killen*
Canoe
Perdido
Shores Acres
Navco
Burnwell
Wyatt
Pleasant Hill
Atwood
Farley*
Paint Rock*

1929
Hayneville
Rockford
Cordova
Newton
Red Bay
Center*

Collinsville*
Crossville
Fort Payne*
Greensboro
Newbern
Valley Head*
Hanceville*
Steppeville*
Monroeville
Beatrice
Grand Bay
Bridgeport*
Hollywood*
Scottsboro*
Stevenson*
Gordon
Goodyear
Blountsville
Cleveland
Maplesville
Double Springs
Plantersville
Malvern
Beavertown
Burnsville
Woodville*
Pollard
Walnut Grove
Anderson*
Eva*
Lexington*
Tanner*
Capshaw*
Fairview*
Grimes
Trinity*
Elkmont*
Kellyton
Brownsboro*
Maysville*
Ryland*
Glen Allen
Pansy
East Irondale
Whitney
Lowndesboro
Saint Clair
Abanda
Floyd

Liberty City
Horton
Hazel Green*
Meridianville*
Highland Home
Lapine
Palos
Ramer
Sellers
Corner School
Jappa
Douglas
Hissop
Mount Caramel
Stanton
Dawson
Geraldine*
Kilpatrick*
Lebanon*
Leesburg*
Mentone*
Porterville*
Skirum*
Good Springs
Garden City*
Peterman
Tunnel Springs
Uriah

1930
Sayreton
Bellwood
Coffee Springs
Cedar Bluff*
Lisman
Butler
Gilbertown
Toxey
Part of Mulga
Kushla
Auburn
Headland
Lockhart
Phenix City
Sycamore
Citronelle
Coden
Bayou La Batre
Pine Hill

Fackler*
Larkinsville*
Mount Carmel*
Hillsboro*
Ardmore*
Wilsonville
Autaugaville
Shelby
Gaylesville*
Comer
Loachapoka
McCullough
Goodway
Hatcheechubee
Whatley
Dixon's Mill
Chancellor
Cowarts
Robinsonville
Huxford
Seale
Peterson
America Junction
Coosada
Blount Springs
Cragford
Snead
Clarence
Armstrong
Fort Davis
Snowdoun
Bangor
Delchamps
Irvington
Rolston
Saint Elmo
Theodore
Sunny South
Calvert
Mount Vernon
Brickyard

1931
Republic
Gorgas
Axis
Creola
Satsuma
Semmes

Coker
Billingsley

1932
Gainesville
Grady

1933
Siluria

1934
Cranford's Chapel
Hokes Bluff
Woodland-Lamar

1935
Cottonwood
Palmerdale
Orrville
Almont
Daviston
Jasper Homesteads
Cottondale
Manchester
Pittsview
Jeff*
Monrovia*
Fayetteville
Talladega Springs
Hazen
Baileyton*
Holly Pond*
Oxmoor
Harrisburg
Alberta
Catherine
Gastonburg
Martin's Station
Prairie
Safford
Princeton*
Trenton*

1936
Gardendale
Greenwood
Chickasaw
Smith's Lake
Covin

Sweetwater
White City*
Dayton
Oak Grove West
    Jefferson
Havana
Standing Rock
Saint Clair Springs
Reeltown
Martling
Vinemont*
Smith's Station
Wellington
Wallsboro
Riverside
Harvest*
Kinsey
Lynn
Saraland
Union Grove
Chavies*
Fyffe*
Rainsville*
Section*
Belk
Edwardsville
Fruithurst
Bleeker
Milltown
Dutton*
Calcis
Salem
Sterrett
Jackson's Gap
Inverness
Perote
Steele
Hayden
Heneger*
Pisgah*
Sylvania*
Wilmer
Tenbroeck*
Wattsville
Painter
Collins Chapel
Mexia
Perdue Hill
Duke

Argo
Taylor
Tumbleton
Arkadelphia*
Bankhead
Brooksville
Oak Grove (Talladega)
Detroit
Nixon's Chapel
Old Spring Hill
Summit
Ethelsville
Cold Springs*
Center Hill*
Beulah
Marvyn
Society Hill
Keener
Stewart
Arlington
Lamison
Grant*
Browntown*
Millerville
Mineral Springs
Chigger Hill*
Alpine
Flattop
Muscadine
Claiborne
Danville

1937
Palmerdale
Cahaba Village
Bay View
Castleberry
Cedar Cove
Coaling
Chelsea
Four Mile
Lawley
Randolph
Buhl
Elrod
Shortersville
Adamsburg*
Good Hope
Forney*

Nanafalia
Pike Road
Hodgesville
Madrid
Friendship
Rock Run*
Spring Garden*
Garland
Maylene
Coppinsville
Pickensville
Black
Brierfield
Colbran*
Eoline
Round Mountain*
Equality
Seman
Sipsey
Lawrenceville
Ranbourne
Graham
Cook's Springs
Keystone
Geiger
Panola
Delta
Moore's Brook
Tait's Gap
Weogufka
Bradford
White Plains
Pleasant Hill
Eunola

1938
Clinton
Cusseta
Emile
Falliston
Jefferson Park
Maxine
Pea Ridge
Sumpterville
Thornton
Wick
Wicksburg

1939	Mississippi Town	Chandler Mountain	1941
Adjer	Newsite	Cochrane	Nashua Mill Village
Agricola	Suttle (Felix)	Cypress	Abernant
Booker Heights	Sand Ridge	Dawes	Clough
Duncanville		Dancy	Howard
Erin	**1940**	Delmar	Kellerman
Fadette	Martintown	Echola Community	Key Camp
Hackneyville	Sloss Village	Summerfield	Searles
Hopewell	Bibby	Tanner Williams	
Hamburg	Buttson		
Hollins	Chunchula		

Taken from Electric Rate History of Alabama Power Company, exhibits 104 and 105. Found in List of Exhibits, APC Corporate Archives, 3.1.1.19.12.

Coffer dam at Lock 12, 1912.

Gadsden outdoor substation
transformers, August 4, 1912.

Appendix D

Division Managers/ Division Vice Presidents

Eastern Division Managers/ Vice Presidents

The Alabama Traction, Light & Power Company purchased the Anniston Electric & Gas Company in 1912 which was merged into the Alabama Power Company in 1915. The first four managers administered the Anniston area only.

A. L. Kenyon	1915–1916
L. W. Jackson	1916–1918
D. M. Dunn	1918
J. M. Barry	1918–1920

In 1920 the Division Manager position was created.
Division Managers

J. M. Barry	1920–1921
L. P. Sweatt, Jr.	1921–1923
O. K. Seyforth	1923–1941

In 1941 the Division Vice President position was created.
Division Vice Presidents

O. K. Seyforth	1941–1959
D. R. Allen	1959–1966
Floyd Otto Miller	1966–1972
Homer H. Turner, Jr.	1972–1975
W. D. Bolton	1975–1985
Banks H. Farris	1985–1989
Jerry J. Thomley	1989–1993
W. Ronald Smith	1993–2006
Julia H. Segars	2006– present

Northern Division Managers/Vice Presidents

W. M. Stanley	1920–1925
C. B. McManus	1925–1927
J. O. Henkel	1927–1941

In 1941 the last of Alabama Power's Northern Division properties were taken over by Tennessee Valley Authority.

Southern Division Managers/ Vice Presidents

Division Managers

E. C. Wilson	1920 –1923
J. M. Barry	March 1923–November 1923
L. P. Sweatt, Jr.	1923–1925
A. S. Coleman	1925–1936

Division Vice Presidents

A. S. Coleman	1936–1957
B. B. March	1957–1965
Hugh P. Foreman	1965–1982
Clyde Wood	1982–1995
Andy Dearman	1995–1997
Bill Cooper	1997–2001
Gordon G. Martin	2001–present

Western Division Managers/ Vice Presidents

When divisions were established and Division Manager position was created in 1920, the Western Division office was located in Birmingham. These first five managers actually had offices in Birmingham:

L. P. Sweatt Jr	1920–1921
O. K. Seyforth	1921–1923
C. B. McManus	1923–1925
R. W. Williamson	1925–1928
Henry Maulshagen	1928–1941

In 1941 the Division Vice President position was created

Henry Maulshagen	1941–1952

In 1952 the Western Division office was moved to Tuscaloosa.

Henry Maulshagen	1952–1954
W. M. Wade	1954–1967
Leon B. Murray	1967–1968
A. Clayton Rogers	1968–1984
Robert H. Haubein	1984–1990
Michael D. Garrett	1990–1991
Anthony J. Topazi	1991–1995
Terry H. Waters	1995–present

Mobile Division Managers/ Vice Presidents

Mobile Electric was founded in 1906. Gulf Electric Company purchased Mobile Electric in 1925 and merged with Alabama Power Company on January 1, 1928.

Division Managers

A. Sidney Quackenbush	1928–1941
Frank S. Keeler	1941–1949
Earl A. Benson	1949–1960
R. E. Pride	1960–1967
Ben W. Hutson	1967–1981
Robert H. Haubein	1981–1983
J. Bruce Jones	1983–1989
Henry Holt	1989–1993
(No Division Manager during this period)	1993–1995
William B. Johnson	1995–1999
Robert W. Holley	1999–present

Vice Presidents

A. Sidney Quackenbush	1941–1948
Frank S. Keeler	1948–1960
Earl A. Benson	1960–1967
R. E. Pride	1967–1970
William L. McDonough	1970–1985
John Richardson	1985–1989
J. Bruce Jones	1989–1998
Cheryl G. Thompson	1998–present

Southeast Division Managers/Vice Presidents

Gulf Electric merged with Alabama Power Company in 1928. At that time, Gulf Electric Company provided service to the south Alabama area. Upon the merger, the south Alabama area was divided into two divisions—Mobile and Southeast.

Division Managers

A. L. Couch	1928–1929
C. T. Hunter	1929–1941

In 1941 the Division Vice President position was created.

Division Vice Presidents

C. T. Hunter	1941–1952
Marvin Wade	1952–1954
Murray Greer	1954–1966
Ray Garlington	1966–1977
John Byars	1977–1993
Roy Crow	1993–2001
Bobby Kerley	2001–2003
Mike Saxon	2003–Present

Birmingham Division Managers/Vice Presidents

C. S. Thorn*	1952–1954
C. T. Hunter	1952–1965
Bill Whitt	1965–1975
Homer Turner	1975–1991
Michael D. Garrett	1991–1993
C. Alan Martin	1993–1995
Anthony Topazi	1995–1999
Jim Miller III	1999–2001

(Jim Miller was reassigned from the External Affairs organization as Senior Vice President and retained this title during his tenure in Birmingham Division.)

Marsha Johnson	2001–2005
Gerald Johnson	2005–present

*President of Birmingham Electric Company became Vice President of Birmingham Division in 1952, when BECO merged with Alabama Power Company. C. T. Hunter served also as Vice President and reported to C. S. Thorn 1952–1954.

SEATED
(Left to Right.)
W. H. Hassinger   S. Z. Mitchell
Frank M. Moody   W. H. Weatherly
E. C. Melvin   R. A. Mitchell
Richard M. Hobbie
STANDING
E. A. Yates   W. J. Henderson
Thomas W. Martin

Alabama Power Company Board of Directors at Lock 12 Dam, August 18, 1923.

Placing the No. 2 rotor and shaft at
Martin Dam, July 20, 1926.

A Note on Sources

Corporate records and the collections housed in the Alabama Power Company Corporate Archives provided the primary source materials for this centennial history of Alabama Power Company. Unless otherwise stated in the endnotes, all manuscripts, speeches, reports, correspondence, company publications, and materials cited in the notes may be found in the corporate archives. Company archivist Bill Tharpe is the custodian of these records and was an important part of my process of researching and writing this history. The corporate archives includes government documents, company pamphlets and printed materials, scrapbooks, some newspaper clippings, annual reports, magazines, regulatory documents, testimony, and depositions. There are reports and various filings before the Securities and Exchange Commission, the Alabama Public Service Commission, and the Federal Power Commission and its successor, the Federal Energy Regulatory Commission. Most of the correspondence dates from the period before 1924. The records of the Birmingham Electric Company are also housed in the Alabama Power Company Corporate Archives. The photographic collections are especially rich and extensive but are concentrated in the period before 1940; most of the photographs and negatives for the 1980s and 1990s have been lost. Unless otherwise noted all photographs came from the corporate archives.

The company's archives has a complete set of *Powergrams* beginning with the first issue in 1920. When *Powergrams* is cited, the documentation is inconsistent because the form and style of the magazine changed frequently over the years from once a month, to twice a month, sometimes with a day and sometimes with only a month noted. The quality of *Powergrams* as a historical record declines over the decades as the length of the journal decreases and the number of articles and the subjects covered are reduced for cost reasons or by changing editorial philosophies. Although after the late 1980s detailed historical information is reduced in *Powergrams* (compared to earlier years), the company magazine and the Alabama Power Company *Annual Report* remain the most valuable company records because of their continuity and length of publication. When there was a discrepancy in figures or dates, I elected to use the facts as stated in the *Annual Report*.

Many versions of numerous histories of the company are also in the collection, nearly all of them in typescript. Some of these histories foreshadowed Thomas W. Martin's 1952 history, *The Story of Electricity in Alabama*, and others were written for federal regulatory agencies, for hearings, or for court cases. None has endnotes or documentation and all tend to give generally the same information. Some of these typed manuscripts have Tom Martin's notes in pencil between the lines and in the margins. Most all of these histories were written before 1952.

In fact, the corporate archival holdings are generally thin after 1950. Exceptions are a box of materials about Hurricane Frederic, a series of interviews on tape, audio and video, and four volumes of Joe Farley's testimony before the Nuclear Regulatory Commission that include copies of documents. Jim Clements has spent almost two decades creating biographical files on Alabama Power employees by clipping news, notices, and photographs that appeared in *Powergrams*. These biographical files were invaluable in determining dates and career paths for the company's people.

Most of the corporate archival material is stored in file folders in boxes by accession numbers, and when there is a number, it will be found, usually in brackets, in the endnotes. Materials are sometimes filed by subject matter, such as "Martin Dam," "Dedication Programs," or "Ten Islands Park." Duplicate materials are often located in several different files. Thomas W. Martin had many of his speeches printed, and these pamphlets are filed together, although they may also be found in other files. Some recently acquired materials have not yet been accessioned. The archives also has a collection of books. Most books are duplicates of those found in the library of research services, old books discarded from the library, or books donated to the archives by retired employees. The archives has an extensive collection of plans, drawings, maps, and surveys.

Corporate Archives also has a large collection of oral histories. Some interviews were sponsored by Southern Company, others by Alabama Power, and some have been videotaped. A few interviews are also transcribed. Samuel R. Heys did interviews with a number of Alabama Power leaders for a history of Southern Company and had transcripts made from the video; these are in the archives. Although I listened to most of the tapes, if there was a transcription, I used that because of the pressure of time. There are many cassettes of old tape recordings of interviews that were valuable for information on certain subjects. In the late 1980s and early 1990s, Chris Conway conducted a number of interviews, and he made a typed transcript of most of them and generously lent them to me. These were especially valuable because several men he interviewed were no longer living when I started this project in January 2003. Conway has generously agreed to donate his files to the archives. On other interviews cited, I conducted the interview unless otherwise noted. My interviews were documented by handwritten or typed notes. Some interviews were an hour to two-hour formal interviews, and others were telephone interviews or conversations about specific points or follow-up questions. Interviews at division offices were group interviews, which proved to be significant and useful. The short timetable for the completion of the manuscript precluded taped and transcribed interviews.

Alabama Power Company has a huge volume of records stored in a documents storage facility and others deposited with a professional storage company. It would take two or three lifetimes to read all this material. Most of these records are personnel, financial, and tax records, but press releases were helpful in tracking the company's issues. There were a number of purges of records in the company's history. When the two new buildings were constructed, the south tower in the 1950s and the north tower in the 1980s, materials were discarded as departments moved into new offices and space was tight. In the mid-1980s, the *Records Management Quarterly*, a respected national professional journal, published many articles, including an explanation of the Paperwork Reduction Act of 1980 and a discussion of records retention programs in relation to subpoena of records. In the 1980s attorneys began to advise clients not to save records; thus, across the United States, archival holdings for these years are slim, as they are at Alabama Power. At the beginning of 1994, Alabama Power made a New Year's resolution to rid office files, desks, and storage areas of as much unnecessary paper as possible, especially records that had no regulatory or operational purpose or value. In this housecleaning operation, called Pound for Pound, fifty-three tons of paper were hauled away. The company agreed to donate a pound of food for every pound of paper thrown away and in March gave $20,000 to the Birmingham Food Bank. Bob Buettner called it a "great weight-reduction program." Karen Smith, supervisor of office services, recommended that documents not needed for the Federal Energy Regulatory Commission or the Alabama Public Service Commission be destroyed because "it doesn't make good business sense to keep them around" (*Powergrams*, May 2, 1994, 2).

Despite these records purges, many valuable documents that tell the story of Alabama Power remain in the files of various departments. The location of the records I used are so noted. The public records collection, published government documents, regulatory records, relicensing files, court decisions, PSC and FERC testimony, and rate case materials in the Balch & Bingham files were very helpful for the latter years. The Public Service Commission records at the Alabama Department of Archives and History are not complete. A number of people, especially Jack Minor, Elmer Harris, Steve Bradley, Chris Conway, Charles McCrary, Jim Sullivan, Douglas McCrary, and Joe Farley, let me use materials from their personal files and memorabilia. Gibson Lanier has the most complete files of PSC decisions and court rulings, and I was able to find there originals or copies of court documents that the Alabama Supreme Court clerk could not locate in the court's files.

The library that Tom Martin started is now part of research services and this collection of books was valuable. The staff was able to find books I needed on interlibrary loan or purchased out-of-print volumes from the Internet for my use. Staff members searched various indexes to which I had no access and found many items I surely would have missed. For published works and articles and for newspapers and magazines on microfilm, I also used the libraries of the University of Alabama, Auburn University, Samford University, and the University of Alabama at Birmingham, as well as the Birmingham Public Library. Samford University recognized my fourteen years on the faculty there and graciously ordered newspapers on microfilm for me, allowed me to use its Internet computer indexes, microfilm readers, books, and manuscript collections. Samford University Special Collections has a number of Alabama newspapers on microfilm and a small collection of materials on Alabama Power; it also contains the papers of William H. Brantley Jr. Dr. Ralph Draughon's collection of Thomas W. Martin materials in the Auburn University Draughon Library was helpful, as were other books and manuscripts in the library's Alabama Collection and its computer and Internet indexes. Auburn's bound volumes of *Manufacturers Record* were easier to read than the microfilm versions that I read at the Birmingham Public Library.

The Birmingham Public Library's books, and especially the materials in the Tutwiler Collection of Southern History, were valuable. The indexes, census records, newspapers on microfilm, government documents, clipping collections, and the manuscript collections in the library's Department of Archives and Manuscripts were important, especially the Worthington family papers. The University of Alabama's Gorgas Library has a complete set of government documents, as well as extensive secondary sources, and the Hoole Special Collections Library houses the Lister Hill Papers, the Agee Collection, and other documents, microfilm, and papers. The Alabama Department of Archives and History is the depository of governors' papers, state government documents and records, newspapers, and manuscripts. The Thomas W. Martin Library at Southern Research Institute has valuable holdings of Martin materials, although these books, papers, photographs, and scrapbooks have not had the care of an archivist and have not been accessioned. Other books came from my personal library, some of them out-of-print copies I purchased from Internet book dealers. This is the first research project for which I used the

Internet, and I have been amazed at what I have been able to find, including Alabama Power Company's news releases beginning in January 1995.

The Lilly Library of Indiana University, Bloomington, holds the Wendell Willkie Papers. Unfortunately, all of Willkie's papers from the Commonwealth & Southern period of his life, although once listed as part of the Willkie estate, vanished some years ago from the filing cabinets before they were transferred to Indiana. The papers of Henry Evans Howell Jr. are found in the library of Old Dominion University. The Benson Ford Research Center in the Henry Ford Museum at Greenfield Village houses the correspondence of Henry Ford, which includes the letters exchanged between his general secretary E. G. Liebold and John W. Worthington.

Initially, I considered traveling to New York to search the materials in the Franklin D. Roosevelt Presidential Library at Hyde Park and several collections in the Library of Congress and the National Archives in Washington, D.C. As I read through the enormous amount of materials housed in the Alabama Power Company Corporate Archives and in the state of Alabama and balanced the richness of these resources against the time and my estimate of the value of research trips to New York and Washington, D.C., I elected not to spend time in these archival institutions. Information that might be found in these places I leave to others who I hope will delve deeper into some topics to which I've given only scant attention.

Bill Tharpe, who selected the photographs, would like to thank the Selma-Dallas County Library and Becky Nichols; the Department of Archives and History and Debbie Pendleton, Cynthia Luckie, Ken Tilley, Bob Bradley, and Bob Cason; the University of South Alabama Archives and Dr. Michael Thomason and Carol Ellis; the Department of Archives and Manuscripts of the Birmingham Public Library and Jim Baggett; the Special Collections Department of Samford University's Davis Library and Elizabeth Wells; Alabama Power Company's Research Services and Sherie Mattox, Arnita Hines, and Dawn Anderson; and Alabama Power Company's Corporate Communications and Marvin Gilmore, Bill Snow, Phil Free, Clyde Adams, and Tim Towns; W. S. Hoole Special Collections Library, University of Alabama Libraries and Clark Center; Museum of Fine Arts, Boston and Jennifer Riley; Ayer Company Publisher, and Paula Howland; Associated Press, New York, and John O'Sullivan; Special Collections and Archives, Auburn University Libraries, and Dwayne Cox and John Varner; Coosa-Alabama River Improvement Association, Inc., and Jerry Sailors; Russell Record, and Thomas Byron Saunders, Sr.; Henry Stern, Opelika; Chuck Hrabe, Mobile; Mrs. John Porter, Birmingham; and TVA and Todd Winkler.

Transmission line construction on
the Mobile-Flomaton line, 1926.

"Developed for the Service of Alabama"

Preface

1. C. Vann Woodward, *Origins of the New South, 1877–1913*, vol. 9 in *A History of the South*, ed. Wendell Holmes Stephenson and E. Merton Coulter, 11 vols. (Baton Rouge: Louisiana State University Press, 1951).

2. George Brown Tindall, *The Emergence of the New South, 1913–1945*, vol. 10 in Stephenson and Coulter, *History of the South*, 71–74.

3. William Warren Rogers, Robert David Ward, Leah Rawls Atkins, and Wayne Flynt, *Alabama: The History of a Deep South State* (Tuscaloosa: University of Alabama Press, 1994), and Wayne Flynt, *Alabama in the Twentieth Century* (Tuscaloosa: University of Alabama Press, 2004), 166, 153.

4. D. Clayton Brown, review of *Electrifying the Piedmont Carolinas: The Duke Power Company, 1904–1997*, in *Journal of Southern History* 69 (February 2003): 216. Professor Brown has written a book on the Rural Electrification Administration and *Pacesetter: The Southwestern Power Administration: 50 Years of Service* (Washington, D.C.: Army Corps of Engineers, 1987).

5. Robert J. Norrell to Richard Bowron and Angela J. Wier, Alabama Power Company, November 10, 1987. Portions of this letter were also quoted in *Powergrams*, August 1991, 17.

6. *Birmingham Post-Herald*, June 29, 2005.

7. *Washington Post*, November 19, 2003.

8. *Birmingham News*, December 13, 2003.

9. Interview with Rod Mundy, June 1, 2005; interview with Banks Farris, September 12, 2005.

10. Thomas W. Martin, *The Story of Electricity in Alabama Since the Turn of the Century, 1900–1952* (Birmingham: Birmingham Publishing Co., 1952), vi. All citations from *The Story of Electricity in Alabama* are from the first edition unless noted otherwise. The second edition (1953) has some added material and a slight difference in page numbers.

Chapter One

1. James Thomas Flexner, *George Washington and the New Nation, 1783–1793* (Boston: Little, Brown & Co.), 308; Robert Irving Warshow, *Alexander Hamilton: First American Business Man* (New York: Garden City Publishing Co., 1931), 138; Ron Chernow, *Alexander Hamilton* (New York: Penguin Press, 2004), 374–78.

2. Rogers et al., *Alabama: History of a Deep South State*, 8, 20, 38; Leah Rawls Atkins, "Introduction: Made in Alabama, 1819–1930," in *Made in Alabama: A State Legacy*, ed. E. Bryding Adams (Birmingham: Birmingham Museum of Art, 1995), 13–15.

3. Harvey H. Jackson III, *Rivers of History: Life on the Coosa, Tallapoosa, Cahaba, and Alabama* (Tuscaloosa: University of Alabama Press, 1995), 1–6.

4. James Graham to Thomas Ruffin, November 9, 1817, in *The Papers of Thomas Ruffin*, 4 vols., ed. J. D. deRoulhac Hamilton (Raleigh: North Carolina Historical Commission, 1918), 1:198.

5. Harper Lee, *To Kill a Mockingbird* (New York: J. B. Lippincott, 1960), 9.

6. George R. Leighton, *Five Cities: The Story of Their Youth and Old Age* (New York: Harper & Brothers, 1939), 105–06. Leighton was writing about the rise of Birmingham and its need for outside capital. In his background on the state of Alabama prior to the city's birth, Leighton discusses Alabama's need for northern capital to be invested in the state, writing that the first northern capital, $2 million of Boston money, came in by way of Mobile in 1795.

7. Quoted by Clarke Stallworth, "JSU prof exorcises lore of demons and politics," *Birmingham Post-Herald*, April 4, 2003.

8. Lance E. Davis, "Capital Immobilities and Finance Capitalism: A Study of Economic Evolution in the United States, 1820–1890," *Explorations in Economic History*, 2d series, 1 (Fall 1963): 88–105.

9. An old but still the best treatment of the early period is Thomas Perkins Abernethy, *The Formative Period in Alabama, 1815–1828* (University: University of Alabama Press, 1965). J. Mills Thornton III emphasizes the political aspects in his award-winning book, *Politics and Power in a Slave Society: Alabama, 1800–1860* (Baton Rouge: Louisiana State University Press, 1978). While he does not treat Alabama specifically, Gavin Wright's *The Political Economy of the Cotton South: Households, Markets, and Wealth in the Nineteenth Century* (New York: W. W. Norton, 1978) explains the cotton culture in Alabama.

10. Weymouth T. Jordan, "A Southern Manufacturer 100 Years Ago," *Progressive Farmer* (March 1954): 94b.

11. Curtis J. Evans, *The Conquest of Labor: Daniel Pratt and Southern Industrialization* (Baton Rouge: Louisiana State University Press, 2001), 17–21; Thomas W. Martin, *Economics of Power in Alabama* (Newcomen Address, 1939), 12–13.

12. David Wilhelm, *A History of the Cotton Textile Industry of Alabama, 1809 to 1950* (Montgomery: n.p., 1950), 11.

13. There are numerous discussions of demagogues in early Alabama and their practice of pitting the common man against wealth and an aristocracy. See Wayne Flynt, *Poor but Proud: Alabama's Poor Whites* (Tuscaloosa: University of Alabama Press, 1989), 6–10; Leah Rawls Atkins, "Southern Congressmen and the Homestead Bill" (Ph.D. diss., Auburn University, 1974), 86–120; and Thornton, *Politics and Power*, 105, 107–15. William H. Brantley in his *Banking in Alabama, 1816–1860*, 2 vols. (Birmingham: Birmingham Printing Co.,1961) discusses how banks were targets of disdain in early Alabama. See 1:46–50. Larry Schweikart, *Banking in the American South from the Age of Jackson to Reconstruction* (Baton Rouge: Louisiana State University Press, 1987), discusses the opposition to banks and corporations as a "battle against privilege," 18.

14. Harvey H. Jackson III, *Inside Alabama: A Personal History of My State* (Tuscaloosa: University of Alabama Press, 2004), 72.

15. Thornton, *Politics and Power*, 101, 105–06.

16. Flynt, *Poor but Proud*, 6.

17. Emma Lila Fundaburk, "Business Corporations in Alabama in the Nineteenth Century" (Ph.D. diss., Ohio State University, 1963), 227–28.

18. *Montgomery Advertiser*, February 14, 1855.

19. Ethel Armes, *The Story of Coal and Iron in Alabama* (1910; reprint, Birmingham: Book-keepers Press, 1972), 15, 48–51.

20. U.S. Department of Commerce, *Historical Statistics of the United States, Colonial Times to 1970*, 2 parts (Washington, D.C.: 1975), part 2:899. The cotton exports of 1880 were 1,822,000 pounds, compared to the 1860 cotton exports of 1,768,000 pounds.

21. Raymond Nixon, *Henry W. Grady* (New York: Russell & Russell, 1969), 317.

22. Thomas Pearsall, *Report of Thomas Pearsall, Commissioner to Survey the Coosa River* (Montgomery: J. G. Stokes & Co., 1870), 5, 11, 13.

23. Marlene Hunt Rikard, "An Experiment in Welfare Capitalism: The Health Care Services of the Tennessee Coal, Iron and Railroad Company" (Ph.D. diss., University of Alabama, 1983), 29–33, and W. David Lewis, *Sloss Furnaces and the Rise of the Birmingham District* (Tuscaloosa: University of Alabama Press, 1994), 217–18. The classical account of industrial development and politics in the post–civil war era in the South is C. Vann Woodward's *Origins of the New South, 1877–1913*, vol. 9 in *A History of the South*; however, the development of southern electrical power was so insignificant in 1913 that he ignores it.

24. Fundaburk, "Business Corporations in Alabama in the Nineteenth Century," 494–97.

25. *Manufacturers Record*, February 22, 1912, 11.

26. Donald B. Dodd and Wynelle S. Dodd, *Historical Statistics of the South, 1790–1970* (Tuscaloosa: University of Alabama Press, 1973), 4–5.

27. Alice Galenson, *The Migration of the Cotton Textile Industry from New England to the South: 1880–1930* (New York: Garland Publishing, 1985), 2; Patrick J. Hearden, *Independence and Empire: The New South's Cotton Mill Campaign, 1865–1901* (DeKalb: Northern Illinois University Press, 1982), 42; and Mary J. Oates, *The Role of the Cotton Textile Industry in the Economic Development of the American Southeast, 1900–1940* (New York: Arno Press, 1975), 8–9.

28. Woodward, *Origins of the New South*, 132–33.

29. *Manufacturers Record*, February 22, 1912, 74.

30. William Warren Rogers, *The One-Gallused Rebellion: Agrarianism in Alabama, 1865–1896* (Baton Rouge: Louisiana State University Press, 1970), deals with the period leading up to the constitutional convention. Samuel L. Webb's *Two-Party Politics in the One-Party South: Alabama's Hill Country, 1874–1920* (Tuscaloosa: University of Alabama Press, 1997) presents evidence of continued Republican Party strength in north Alabama after Reconstruction. The constitutional history of Alabama is best covered in Malcolm C. McMillan, *Constitutional Development in Alabama, 1798–1901: A Study in Politics, the Negro, and Sectionalism* (1955; reprint, Spartanburg, S.C.: Reprint Co., 1978). A more general and modern treatment of the Constitution of 1901 is found in essays edited by Bailey Thomson, *A Century of Controversy: Constitutional Reform in Alabama* (Tuscaloosa: University of Alabama Press, 2002), and the specific fraudulent nature of the ratification election is treated in the essay of Harvey H. Jackson III, "White Supremacy Triumphant: Democracy Undone," 30–31.

31. Dodd and Dodd, *Historical Statistics*, 4–5; Flynt, *Alabama in the Twentieth Century*, 3–5.

32. *Fortune*, March 1952, 93, clipping [1.1.2.20.16]. The writer describes Martin as "a cricket-bright little man of seventy" who "combines a scholarly interest in history with a passionate advocacy of science."

33. Matthew Josephson, *Edison: A Biography* (1959; reprint, New York: John Wiley & Sons, 1992), 105.

34. The best study of the social ramifications of electricity is David E. Nye, *Electrifying America: Social Meanings of a New Technology* (Cambridge: Massachusetts Institute of Technology Press, 2001).

35. Francis Jehl, *Menlo Park Reminiscences*, 2 vols. (Dearborn, Mich.: Edison Institute, 1938), 2:780–85.

36. Josephson, *Edison*, 251–65.

37. Gene Tollefson, *BPA and the Struggle for Power at Cost* (Portland, Ore.: Bonneville Power Administration, 1987), viii.

38. Martin, *Electricity in Alabama*, 11. Grace Hooten Gates, *The Model City of the New South: Anniston, Alabama, 1872–1900* (Tuscaloosa: University of Alabama Press, 1978), 41–42.

39. Josephson, *Edison*, 265.

40. H. M. Caldwell, *History of the Elyton Land Company and Birmingham, Alabama* (1892; reprint, Birmingham: Southern University Press, 1972), 21. The Thomson Houston Electric Company was founded by Elihu Thomson and Edwin Houston and was later one of three companies combined into the General Electric Company. It is incorrectly spelled "Thompson" in some publications (including Martin's *Electricity in Alabama*) and was originally called Thomson & Houston Electric Company. See Charles J. Fitti, "Elihu Thomson," in American Philosophical Society Library Bulletin, new series, vol. 1, no. 1, 2001.

41. *Montgomery Advertiser*, November 3, 1885; *Selma Times Journal*, August 4, 1886.

42. Thomas W. Martin, *The Lightning Route: A Milestone in the March of Progress, 1886–1936* (Birmingham: Alabama Power Co., 1936), 3–6; Mary Ann Neeley, "'The Lightning Route': The Development of the Electric Streetcar and Its Effect on Montgomery, 1885–1900," *Alabama Review* 40 (October 1987): 243–58; Martin, *Electricity in Alabama*, 13–14.

43. *Electrical World*, August 14, 1886, 75–76; March 12, 1887, 133; April 30, 1887, 201–02, full pages in Scrapbook No. 2, Thomas W. Martin Library, Southern Research Institute (hereafter SRI); Martin, *Lightning Route*, 4.

44. Alvin W. Hudson and Harold Cox, *Street Railways of Birmingham* (privately printed, 1976), 34–35. The horse was killed but only because the capital city design did not include an adequate current return system. Neeley writes that Governor Thomas Seay's horse was electrocuted on July 25, 1887, when a wire on Court Street fell. Neeley, "Lightning Route,'" 251.

45. Martin, *Electricity in Alabama*, 13–17.

Chapter Two

1. Mitchell's father, William Mandon Alexander Mitchell, was a medical doctor. His first wife was Julia Shackleford, and he married his second wife, Elmira Sophia Jordan on July 9, 1849. Edna Beasley McGalliard, *Marriage Records of Coosa County, Alabama, 1834–1865* (Weogufka, 1972), 89; Coosa County Records, vol. 1, Cemeteries (Coosa County Historical Society), 112.

2. U.S. Agricultural Census, Tallapoosa County, 1850, 1860.

3. Sidney Alexander Mitchell, *S. Z. Mitchell and the Electrical Industry* (New York: Farrar, Straus & Cudahy, 1960), 4–30, 40–41. Mitchell was named for Confederate generals Felix Kirk Zolli-

coffer and Albert Sidney Johnson. Although Mitchell's biography does not name the Union troops, Rousseau's raid was the only one that came near the Jordan farm and passed through Dadeville. U.S. Census, 1850, Tallapoosa County, 35; U.S. Census, 1860, Tallapoosa County, 99–100. Dr. Mitchell is not listed in any index of Confederate soldiers.

4. Elmira Sophia Jordan Mitchell died October 3, 1865, and is buried in the Jordan private cemetery near Kellyton. *Coosa County Records*, vol. 1, Cemeteries, 112. The 1985 biographical essay in the Alabama Business Hall of Fame program noted that Dr. Mitchell moved to Pensacola, but at some point he returned to Dadeville. His will dated May 3, 1873, requested that he be "buried on the west side of my wife Julian [sometimes spelled Julia] Schackleford at the public graveyard at Dadeville." Tallapoosa County Records, Will Index, Will Book No. 2, 82–85.

5. Mitchell, S. Z. *Mitchell*, 8–10.

6. "Remarks of Sidney Z. Mitchell," Jordan Dam Dedication, November 21, 1927, 21 [1.1.2.20.4].

7. Sidney and Reuben's grandmother died in 1888 and left the farm to Reuben. After his retirement, Sidney purchased most of the land from his brother, added several thousand acres, and constructed a hunting lodge he named Ann Jordan Farm for their grandmother. In 2006 the hunting preserve was called Five Star Plantation.

8. *Heritage of Coosa County, Alabama* (Clanton: Heritage Publishing Co.,1999), 69–70; Mitchell, S. Z. *Mitchell*, 4–19, 40–42.

9. Tollefson, *BPA and the Struggle for Power at Cost*, 14.

10. Mitchell, S. Z. *Mitchell*, 61–66; Curtis E. Calder, "S.Z": *Sidney Z. Mitchell (1862–1944), Electrical Pioneer* (New York: Newcomen Society in North America, 1950), 9–11; Tollefson, *BPA and the Struggle for Power at Cost*, 61.

11. "Sidney Zollicoffer Mitchell, Colossus of Kilowatts," *Business Week*, June 1930, 22–23.

12. Thomas W. Martin, Black Zip Notebook, December 17, 1963, Martin Library, SRI.

13. "Col. Reuben Alexander Mitchell," in Marie Bankhead Owen, *The Story of Alabama: A History of the State*, 5 vols. (New York: Lewis Historical Publishing Co., 1949), 5:1380–81; Nelson P. Hoff, ed., *Alabama Blue Book and Social Register* (Birmingham: Blue Book Publishing Co., 1929), 145; Thomas Martin, talk on the "Opening of Reuben Alexander Mitchell School in Gadsden," February 4, 1949; resolution on the death of Colonel Reuben Alexander Mitchell by the board of directors of Alabama Power Company, April 30, 1937.

14. B. C. Forbes, "Mitchell, the Man Who Saves Millions for Investors," *Forbes*, June 15, 1925, 315–18, 354–69.

15. "Sidney Zollicoffer Mitchell," *Business Week*, June 1930, 22–23.

16. On old maps and in correspondence and newspaper accounts Cherokee Bluffs always appears plural. Modern maps sometimes use the singular, bluff, but this is not correct.

17. Clinton Jackson Coley, *Recollections* (privately printed, 1989), 24; telephone interview with C. J. Coley Jr., February 5, 2003.

18. Martin, *Electricity in Alabama*, 25; Leah Rawls Atkins, "Empowering Alabama: The James Mitchell Story," *Alabama Heritage* (Summer 2006): 8–16.

19. Mitchell Family Genealogy and Records, courtesy of Ivan Stancioff (grandson of James Mitchell); W. E. Mitchell, *James Mitchell: An Industrial Pioneer*, printed speech on the presentation of a portrait of James Mitchell, April 22, 1930, 2, writes that his family came to the United States when his brother was a year old. In 1912 W. E. Mitchell, called Will, joined Alabama Power Company. In

1930 when he gave this talk, he was vice president and general manager of Georgia Power Company. Martin in *Electricity in Alabama* (page 25) writes that the Mitchell family moved to Massachusetts in 1881, but this is not correct. An Alabama Power Company board resolution on August 5, 1920, says James Mitchell arrived in the United States when he "was about three years old." *Powergrams*, September 1920, 3. In his autobiography, published in the September 1920 *Powergrams*, James Mitchell does not mention his family's move from Canada. The 1880 United States Census for Massachusetts lists Charles C. Mitchell and wife Mary living in Milton with six children. James was fourteen years old, born in Canada. His sister Annie was eleven, born in Massachusetts. The Mitchell family was living in the United States by 1868 [FHLF1 254547, NA, T9-0547, p. 168B].

20. W. E. Mitchell, *James Mitchell*, 2–3.

21. James Mitchell, "Autobiography," *Powergrams*, September 1920, 2; Martin, *Electricity in Alabama*, 25–28.

22. W. E. Mitchell, *James Mitchell*, 4–5.

23. Carolyn Marion Mitchell Stancioff, "James Mitchell: Biographical Essay," n.d., Mitchell-Stancioff Family Papers, copy courtesy of Ivan Stancioff. James Mitchell first married the daughter of the Swiss consul in Rio de Janeiro, Ozelah Brelaz, ca. 1895. They had three children, a son, Charles Malcolm Mitchell (born 1897), and two daughters who died of diphtheria in 1901. After a divorce, Mitchell married Carolyn Marie Stevenson Cook, and they had one daughter, Carolyn Marion Mitchell, born in São Paulo on August 7, 1903. Marion spent most of her time in London with her mother but did visit Alabama once in 1920. She married Ivan D. Stancioff, son of a Bulgarian diplomat stationed in London, on February 17, 1925. They had seven children. For the story of this extraordinary family, see Ivan D. Stancioff, *Diplomat and Gardener: Memoirs* (Sofia, Bulgaria: Petrikov, 1998).

24. Mitchell's daughter Marion writes that at this time, late 1906, her father became interested in possibilities in the southern states; however, Mitchell himself gives 1911 as the beginning of his interest. Stancioff, "Mitchell: Biographical Essay"; "History and Development of Alabama Power Company and Its Property," 16, files of J. M. Barry, no author, ca. 1948 [2.1.1.56.20]. Gilmore G. Cooke, "Electrical Engineering Connections," IEE *Transactions on Industry Applications* 31 (May–June 1995): 444, writes that Mitchell left Brazil in 1907.

25. Stancioff, "Mitchell: Biographical Essay"; James Mitchell (Imperial Hotel, Tokyo) to Sperling & Company, November 5, 1909, in James Mitchell Personal Papers, Alabama Power Company Corporate Archives.

26. Stancioff, "Mitchell: Biographical Essay," 1.

27. James Mitchell to Mons. R. Orner, February 21, 1911, and James Mitchell to J. Beaver-White, July 10, 1911, James Mitchell Personal Papers.

28. Depositions in *Horne v. Schuler*, March 3, 1914, Martin Library, SRI. Mitchell was living on Caesar's Camp Road in Wimbledon in July 1911 just before he returned to the United States. See correspondence and papers in James Mitchell Personal Papers.

29. George Westinghouse, "Electricity in the Development of the South," an address before the Southern Commercial Congress, Atlanta, Georgia, March 1911, *Electric Journal*, April 1911, reprinted by Alabama Power Company, November 15, 1951 [1.1.2.20.21]. Two Westinghouse associates, Paul T. Brady and Frederick Darlington, would work closely with Mitchell in the following years. Darlington was Mitchell's personal consulting engineer who developed the first rates for Alabama Power Company. He served as vice president of the company in 1913. Martin, *Electricity in Alabama*, 2d ed., 171.

30. "Charles Hinckley Baker," in *Who's Who in America*, vol. 6, 1910–1911 (Chicago: A. N. Marquis, 1910), 76. See Depositions in *Horne v. Schuler*, March 3, 1914, Martin Library, SRI, and Charles H. Baker to Mrs. James Mitchell, July 26, 1920, copy of letter courtesy of Peter Stancioff. Mitchell's daughter Marion writes that "by 1909 he [James Mitchell] was confident of establishing a large scale electric power development in Alabama," but this date seems too early according to Mitchell's own deposition in the Horne case, which involved a dispute between stockholders of companies purchased by Mitchell. See also Stancioff, "Mitchell: Biographical Essay," 2, and "History and Development of Alabama Power Company and Its Property," 6–7; Mitchell, "Autobiography," 2–3; and James F. Crist, *They Electrified the South* (privately printed, 1981), 11–12.

31. See two letters from Paul T. Brady, Westinghouse Electric Manufacturing Company, to W. P. Lay, Gadsden, October 14, 1909, January 20, 1910 [2.1.1.56.17], and "History and Development of Alabama Power Company and Its Property," 15 [2.1.1.56.20]. One manuscript history of the company (with no author identified) tells that Henry Horne of Macon, Georgia, and Captain James R. Hall of Dadeville interested Paul T. Brady, and Brady told Mitchell [2.1.1.56.17]. Mitchell's deposition in the *Horne v. Schuler* case seems to be his version. Deposition in Martin Library, SRI. An outline history of the company, typed with handwritten notes by Tom Martin, says that "Horne put WPL [Lay] in touch with Brady. Paul T. Brady got JM [Mitchell] over here. Brady put JM on to Coosa." This is an interesting document that records that Gabriel R. Solomon, who was associated with the Henry Horne group, gave Mitchell a Coosa River report in 1911 [3.1.1.19.2].

32. *Powergrams*, August 1924, 4–5, and Mary Lee Carter and Elizabeth Wright Strother, "The Mother of Cherokee Bluffs: Nora E. Miller," paper presented at the program, "The Land and the Lake: Tallapoosa County and Lake Martin," at Children's Harbor, October 14, 1990, 1, 8–9.

33. An Act to Incorporate the Cherokee Development and Manufacturing Company, No. 91, H 466, approved December 8, 1900, copy in section number 10 [1.1.2.79.6].

34. Martin, *Electricity in Alabama*, 16, 19–20.

35. Ibid., 19–21.

36. *Manufacturers Record*, September 14, 1916, 59; Martin, *Electricity in Alabama*, 20; *Commercial Fertilizer* 25 (November 1922): 24; obituary, Frank S. Washburn in the *Vanderbilt Alumnus* 8, no. 1 (October 1922): 23. See also Mary S. Miller's work on Worthington and Muscle Shoals, Miller file.

37. Williams Haynes, *Chemical Pioneers: The Founders of the American Chemical Industry* (1939; reprint, Freeport, N.Y.: Books for Libraries Press, 1970), 244–45; Frank S. Washburn, in the *Vanderbilt Alumnus* 3, no. 4 (February 1918): 102.

38. On December 7, 1908, Frank S. Washburn presented a paper to the Southern Commercial Conference that was published as "The Power Resources of the South," *American Political Science Review* 35 (January 1910): 81–98.

39. Adrian George Daniel, *Formative Period of TVA: The Muscle Shoals Project, 1783–1916* (New York: Carlton Press, 1973), 137–38; Tollefson, *BPA and the Struggle for Power at Cost*, 44. Snoqualmie Falls was organized in 1898 by Charles Hinckley Baker with his father's financial support. When his father, William T. Baker of Chicago, died in 1903, the estate's lawyers did not recognize the son's partnership. See Biographical Note, University of Washington Libraries, Charles H. Baker Photographic Collection No. 649. See Charles H. Baker, *Life and Character of William Taylor Baker* (New York: Premier Press, 1908).

40. Adrian George Daniel, "J. W. Worthington, Promoter of Muscle Shoals Power," *Alabama Review* 12 (July 1959): 200.

41. Charles Hinckley Baker is listed as "H. C. Baker"; Washburn, who was president of Alabama Power Company in 1913, is mentioned a few times by name, and Worthington, who served as vice president during the same time period, is only listed as a member of the board of directors. See Martin, *Electricity in Alabama*, 19, 29, 32, 33, 95, 98, 162.

42. One of the questions Tom Martin asked Mitchell's daughter when she came to unveil her father's plaque in the Industry Room of the Alabama Department of Archives and History in Montgomery was what caused her father to come to Alabama. She confessed she did not know. Remarks of Mrs. Marion Mitchell Stancioff, daughter of James Mitchell, Alabama Department of Archives and History (hereafter ADAH), September 14, 1962. Program in the files of the ADAH.

43. *Powergrams*, September 1920, 14.

44. "Remarks of Massey Wilson," program, Butler County High School, July 6, 1945, 17, William S. Hoole Special Collections Library, University of Alabama (hereafter Hoole Library, UA). By mergers and acquisitions Wilson built the St. Louis company into a giant in its field. The company suffered during the 1929 depression, and he poured his own fortune into the company to safeguard the investments of policyholders. In 1937 Wilson retired to Oak Hill in Wilcox County to live with his wife's family. Wilson was Tom Martin's guest at special events and speaking engagements around the state, and Eason Balch and Joe Farley recalled that at "Mr. Martin's suggestion" they often sent abstracts to Wilson to write title opinions on. Wilson died in 1966. See also *Wilcox County Heritage Book* (Clanton: Heritage Publishing Consultants, 2002), 315; Massey Wilson to Charles H. Baker, March 2, 1910 [4.1.1.7.2]. Interview with Eason Balch, April 10, 2003, and interview with Joe Farley, May 30, 2003.

45. The Thomas W. Martin Library at SRI holds letters that William Logan wrote to his parents from Cumberland and a notebook, "Martin-Harris Family," which traces the family back to Halifax County, Virginia.

46. Webb, *Two-Party Politics*, 61.

47. W. Jerry Gist, *The Story of Scottsboro, Alabama* (Nashville: Rich Printing, 1968), 82, 134; William M. Murray Jr., *Thomas W. Martin: A Biography* (Birmingham: Southern Research Institute, 1978), 5–8.

48. There were six children in the Martin family, four girls and the two boys.

49. Crist, *They Electrified the South*, 17–18.

50. Dr. J. M. Starke, "Remarks," Martin Dam Dedication, October 16, 1936, 33, Martin Dam file.

51. *Huntsville Herald*, May 10, 16, 1902; clipping, "Gubernatorial Boom Started for Martin," special to the *Banner*, May 6, 1902, Thomas W. Martin Scrapbook, n.d. (begins in 1891), Martin Library, SRI.

52. Murray, *Martin*, 8–11, 19–23; Louis M. Finlay Jr., "The Wilson Family," *Clarke County Historical Quarterly* 23 (Summer 1998): 18–21; Thomas McAdory Owen, *History of Alabama and Dictionary of Alabama Biography*, 4 vols. (1921; reprint, Spartanburg, S.C.: Reprint Co., 1978), 4:1171, 1786. Owen gives a different death date for Martin Sr.

53. *Alabama Official and Statistical Register*, 1907, 16, 34, 79.

54. Martin, *Electricity in Alabama*, 21; Murray, *Martin*, 26; *Code of*

Alabama, 1907, 2:467–70; sect. 3627–37; 1477–69; 6148–50.

55. Code of Alabama, 1907, 2:467–70; sect. 3627–37; 1477–79; sect. 6148–50; General Laws and Joint Resolutions of the Legislature of Alabama, 1907, 520. The bill that allowed a tax exemption to water-power development (H 1129) was a companion bill to one that gave a ten-year tax exemption for the manufacture of calcium cyanamide (H 1130). An amendment was added that the tax exemption applied only to new hydro developments. Journal of the Alabama House of Representatives, 1907, 2:2702, 2865, 2886, 3676, 3714. Both bills became law.

56. Murray, Martin, 24–27.

57. See the Scrapbook on Logan Martin Sr.'s death, especially the front page of the Montgomery Advertiser, March 6, 1907. The newspaper noted that Governor Comer had lost his right-hand man. Martin Library, SRI.

58. Martin gives the month in notes he wrote on an outline of a proposed history of the company [3.1.1.19.2] and in Electricity in Alabama, 28.

59. Private and Confidential Memorandum to the Directors of the Alabama Traction, Light & Power Company, Ltd., n.d. but ca. 1914 [2.1.1.26.6].

60. B. C. Forbes, America's Fifty Foremost Business Leaders (New York: B. C. Forbes & Sons Publishing Co., 1948), 313.

61. Martin, Electricity in Alabama, 19; Murray, Martin, 31–32.

62. Martin, Electricity in Alabama, 22–23; John R. Hornady, Soldiers of Progress and Industry (New York: Dodd, Mead & Co., 1930), 63.

63. Marvin B. Small, "Steamboats on the Coosa," Alabama Review 4 (July 1951): 193.

64. "Founder Alabama Power Company Former Cross Plains Lad," reprinted from the Piedmont Journal in Powergrams, September 1939, 19–20. Lay was obviously remembering the July 11, 1870, death of William Luke, whom Lay called only "the Yankee school teacher." See Gene L. Howard, Death at Cross Plains: An Alabama Reconstruction Tragedy (Tuscaloosa: University of Alabama Press, 1984).

65. William Patrick Lay to C. A. Kittredge (manager, Alabama Power Company, Gadsden), March 27, 1939. In this letter, Lay gives Kittredge "a short historical sketch of the little water power plant I developed on Big Will's Creek in 1902 and 1903." The financial and technological success of Big Will's Creek that actually followed Lay's sale of the property encouraged Lay to push for congressional approval and private funding for a dam at the Lock 12 site on the Coosa River, but the Alabama Power Company was incorporated in Gadsden in 1906. See file, William Patrick Lay.

66. Martha Lou Riddle, ed., Who Turned on the Lights in Attalla? (Bloomington, Ind.: AuthorHouse, 2004), 45–46, 106; Hugh Reynolds, The Coosa River Valley from De Soto to Hydroelectric Power (Cynthiana, Ky.: Hobson Book Press, 1944), 241.

67. "Navigation Charts of Tombigbee, Warrior and Black Warrior Canalized System," U.S. Corps of Engineers, Mobile, 1941; Leah Rawls Atkins, The Warrior and the Tombigbee: Rivers Flowing through History (pamphlet, Warrior-Tombigbee Waterway Association, Mobile, 2000), 11.

68. William Patrick Lay, The Great Coosa–Alabama River and Valley in Georgia and Alabama: Memorial and Statements of Facts Presented to the Board of Engineers for Rivers and Harbors, October 26, 1911 (Gadsden: 1911), 1–5.

69. Alabama Power Company, Articles of Incorporation (Birmingham: Roberts & Son, 1908) in 1.1.1.79.1.

70. Hornady, Soldiers of Progress, 211. Dams and locks on the Tom-

bigbee-Black Warrior River system are numbered by the Corps of Engineers beginning with Lock 1 in Jackson to Lock 17 below Birmingport. The Corps of Engineers numbers on the Coosa lock and dam sites use a reverse order with the numbers decreasing as the river flows south so that Lock 12 is above Lock 18.

71. Ibid., 39. When the South Fork Dam failed it dumped twenty million tons of water down the Conemaugh Valley toward Johnstown, a steel company town of 30,000, where 2,200 people were killed. See David G. McCullough, The Johnstown Flood (New York: Simon & Schuster, 1968).

72. Hornady, Soldiers of Progress, 57–61; Owen, Story of Alabama, 1:318.

73. Edmund Morris's biography probably best captures Roosevelt's spirit. Edmund Morris, Theodore Rex (New York: Random House, 2001).

74. Judson King, The Conservation Fight: From Theodore Roosevelt to the Tennessee Valley Authority (Washington, D.C.: Public Affairs Press, 1959), 12–13. King participated in the movement as an associate of Gifford Pinchot and George Norris. He was an avid partisan of conservation and was opposed to corporations and private, investor-owned power companies.

75. See the long letter from James Mitchell to J. W. Worthington, May 15, 1916, in Martin Library, SRI.

76. Thomas W. Martin to Frank S. Washburn, November 28, 1911 [1.1.1.4.1].

77. Annual Report, Alabama Traction, Light & Power, 1913, Auditors' Certificate, 5. By March a full board was named in advertisements for bond sales in London. Members of the board of directors were Mitchell, Congressman Martin Littleton of Long Island, John F. Wallace, president of Westinghouse Church Kerr Company, James R. Morse, president of American Trading Company, solicitor Lawrence Macfarlane of Montreal, W. D. Ross of the Metropolitan Bank, Toronto, Frank S. Washburn, president of American Cyanamid Company, J. W. Worthington, president of Sheffield National Bank, and John Beaver White, director, J. G. White and Company, Ltd. See photostatic copy of advertisement [2.1.1.56.20]. There is a typographical error on J. W. Worthington's initials. He is listed as "J. S. Worthington, president of the Sheffield National Bank." J. W. was president of this bank. See also Poor's Manual of Public Utilities, 1913, 1497–98. Poor's states that Alabama Traction "owns or controls the entire stock and bonds of the Alabama Interstate Power Co., and its subsidiary companies, Birmingham, Montgomery and Gulf Power Co. (Originally the Cherokee Development and Mfg. Co.), and the Muscles [sic] Shoals Hydro-Electric Power Company."

78. At the Alabama Power Company board of directors meeting on March 1, 1915, the board authorized payments to James Mitchell of $35,000 for expenses from October 1911 to February 28, 1915. Corporate Minutes, Alabama Power Company, March 1, 1915, 198. Minutes are in the office of the corporate secretary.

79. See various copies of telegrams in the leather-bound book for 1912–13 [1.1.1.4.3]; Murray, Martin, 32.

80. "James Mitchell, Director and Consulting Engineer, to the Company [Sperling & Co.], 10th January, 1912," printed [1.1.1.43.5]; for the typed draft see 2.1.1.26.6.

81. Private Cable, Wm. P. Bonbright & Co., N.Y., to London office, January 29, 1912 (copy) [3.1.1.17.9].

82. Fortune, March 1952, 93.

83. Private Cable, Wm. P. Bonbright & Co., N.Y., to London office, January 29, 1912 (copy); E. Mackay Edgar, Sperling & Co., Basildon House, London, to James Mitchell, January 29, 1912 (copy);

letter, E. Mackey Edgar, Sperling & Co., to James Mitchell, March 27, 1916, in correspondence of Thomas W. Martin [3.1.1.17.9]. The only reference to this event in histories of the company may be found in 2.1.1.56.20, page 67, where the unknown writer notes that on Mitchell's first trip to England "while negotiating with bankers the plans which later matured in the organization of the holding company," certain other people notified him of their interest in the Alabama waterpower sites. "This was a remarkable telegram to be sent." E. Mackay Edgar frequently visited the United States. A few months after these telegrams were sent, he was at Huntington Bay, Long Island, in 1912 to race his speedboat, *Maple Leaf IV*.

84. *Montgomery Advertiser*, January 23, 1912.

85. Algernon S. Norton to Charles H. Baker, December 22, 1911 [1.1.2.26.1]. Charles H. Baker, New York, to Tyson, Wilson & Martin, January 2, 1912; Frank S. Washburn to Tyson, Wilson & Martin, January 9, 1912; telegram, Paul T. Brady to Tyson, Wilson & Martin, January 25, 1912; Charles H. Baker to Thomas W. Martin, February 6, 1912; telegram, Fulton Pace, Dadeville, to Charles H. Baker, New York, February 6, 1912 [4.1.1.7.2]. In his February 6 letter to Tom Martin, Baker wrote that he had told Pace not to use Russell's name in a telegram, so in the telegrams Benjamin Russell is called Julius Caesar, Baker is Hamlin, and Montgomery is Babylon. Using codes, especially for names, was not unusual in that time for business and legal matters being sent in the open through Western Union. Sometimes elaborate codes were established; for instance, when James Mitchell sent W. W. Freeman to Mexico to deal with the Mexican Northern dam problems, all Freeman's telegrams to New York were sent in code. See telegrams and code list in 3.1.1.41.9.

86. Martin, *Electricity in Alabama*, 37.

87. Thomas W. Martin to Charles H. Baker, January 25, 1912 [4.1.1.7.2].

88. In explaining these legal proceedings twenty-seven years after they happened, Martin testified that "We had, I think, 12 or 15 different phases of litigation in various courts which proceeded with a good deal of feeling throughout the period of December of 1911, and January 1912." Testimony of Mr. Thomas W. Martin before Federal Power Commission, Re: Actual Legitimate Original Cost of Mitchell, Martin, and Jordan Dams, Washington, D.C., December 11, 1939, 1265–75 [3.1.1.11.31].

89. Benjamin Russell to Alabama Power Company, letter published in *Powergrams*, September 1920, 12. For more on the Russell view of the New York negotiations with Alabama Interstate Power see Virginia Henderson Dillon, *Fiftieth Anniversary of Russell Manufacturing Company* (Alexander City, 1952).

90. Testimony of Thomas W. Martin before Federal Power Commission, 1265 [3.1.1.11.31]. Thomas D. Russell, *Russell of Alabama* (New York: Newcomen Society of North America, 1960), 15.

91. Thomas W. Martin to Frank S. Washburn, January 11, 1912 [1.1.1.4.1]; Charles H. Baker to Frank S. Washburn, January 13, 1912. Baker writes that he "wired Tyson, Wilson, & Martin to file the Alabama Interstate Power Co. condemnation at once" but to set the hearing in April or later so that the award of damages would be postponed as long as possible to give the company time to have funds flowing into its account so it could move ahead [3.1.1.44.24].

92. Owen, *History of Alabama and Dictionary of Alabama Biography*, 4:1478, 1635.

93. *Report of Cases Argued and Determined in the Supreme Court of Alabama, 1913–1914*, 186, 622–59; Murray, *Martin*, 35–36; Martin, *Electricity in Alabama*, 38–39.

94. After the Cherokee Dam was completed, the Mount Vernon–Woodberry Mills "discarded the old water wheels, more picturesque than efficient, and installed electric drives throughout the plants." Virginia Noble Golden, *A History of Tallassee for Tallasseeans* (Tallassee: Tallassee Mills, 1949), 66.

95. James Mitchell, deposition in *Horne v. Schuler*, March 3, 1914, Martin Library, SRI.

96. Murray, *Martin*, 32–33.

97. *Manufacturers Record*, January 11, 1912, 55; January 25, 1912, 65; February 11, 1912, 53. See also Minutes, Special Meeting of Alabama Interstate Power Company, April 12, 1912, and Charles H. Baker to Frank S. Washburn, April 12, 1912, and other correspondence, affidavits, and papers [3.1.1.41.8]. Following this transaction illustrates that Mitchell was working through Lawrence Macfarlane in Montreal, who was also president of Southern States Securities Company, another Mitchell-Macfarlane company, which was handling the Alabama Interstate Power Company, Muscle Shoals Hydro-Electric Power Company, and Birmingham, Montgomery and Gulf Power Company stock and securities transfers from the Nashville Savings Bank & Trust Company to Alabama Traction.

98. Corporate Minutes of Alabama Power Company, 2:2.

99. *Manufacturers Record*, April 11, 1912, 49, 51. Washburn spelled his company name Cynamid. The preferred spelling for the chemical is cyanamide, but in the early twentieth century it was usually spelled cyanamid.

100. Telegrams, James Mitchell to Lawrence Macfarlane, Quebec Bank, Montreal, April 26, 1912, and James Mitchell to W. D. Ross, Metropolitan Bank, Toronto, April 27, 1912, bound correspondence, 2–3 [1.1.1.4.3].

101. Telegram, F. S. Ruth to James Mitchell, New York City, April 30, 1912, bound correspondence, 6 [1.1.1.4.3].

102. Tom Martin wrote in *Electricity in Alabama* that the Lay companies were "taken over on May 1, 1912," and in "a brief ceremony in my law office in Montgomery, Captain Lay said to James Mitchell: 'I now commit to you the good name and destiny of Alabama Power Company. May it be developed for the service of Alabama'" (page 31). There is no question that a transfer of ownership was made on May 1, and Lay probably said something like Martin remembered and perhaps at some time he said it to Mitchell, but on May 1, 1912, Mitchell was at the Ritz-Carlton Hotel in New York City; bound correspondence [1.1.1.4.3]. Martin probably wrote the press release over Mitchell's name.

103. Martin, *Electricity in Alabama*, 31.

104. Remarks of Thomas W. Martin in program, "Unveiling the Plaques of William P. Lay, James Mitchell, Thomas W. Martin," September 14, 1962, ADAH.

105. Cablegram, James Mitchell, Montgomery, to Canadian Bank of Commerce, Toronto, May 7, 1912, and James Mitchell to R. C. Brown, Mexican Light and Power Company, Toronto, May 8, 1912, 11–12, bound correspondence [1.1.1.4.3].

106. James Mitchell to Frank S. Washburn, April 27, 1912 [3.1.1.39.37].

107. John Benson's owners were probably James Benson and his son Enoch, who were living at Kowaliga in 1860 with nineteen slaves. Tallapoosa County, U.S. Population Census, 1860, U.S. Slave Census, 1860. See also Michael Sznajderman and Leah Rawls Atkins, "William Benson and the Kowaliga School," *Alabama Heritage* (Spring 2005): 22–29.

108. *Montgomery Advertiser*, March 29, 1914, special section on

progress, 52–53. Richard Bailey, *They Too Call Alabama Home: African American Profiles, 1800–1999* (Montgomery: Pyramid Publishing, 1999), 37–38. Although many of the Kowaliga graduates went on to Talladega College or Tuskegee Institute, Benson's main goal was to help the community become prosperous through agriculture and industry. Benson was supported by northern philanthropists, and at one time Booker T. Washington served on the Kowaliga board. By the time James Mitchell visited the Bensons, Washington had resigned in a disagreement with Benson over funding. The planted fields in the valley of Kowaliga Creek were flooded by the Cherokee Dam, but the school buildings were not. The fields were approximately in the lake area east of the Kowaliga bridge.

109. *Powergrams*, September 1942, 16. In the early correspondence and records in the company files there is no reference to the Bensons' race, surprising for the times, but perhaps an illustration of the influence of Mitchell's sixteen years in the multicultural society of Brazil.

110. James Mitchell to Frank S. Washburn, April 27, 1912 [3.1.1.39.37].

111. Murray, *Martin*, 37.

112. Crist, *They Electrified the South*, 105–06.

113. *Powergrams*, February 1923, 3.

114. "Alabama Power Dedicates Yates Dam," *Alabama Purchaser*, July 1947 [2.1.1.56.19].

115. Cherokee Bluffs Reports, 1906; K. F. Cooper to Charles Baker, August 14, 1907 [3.1.1.41.23], and Alabama Power Company, Tallapoosa River, 1939 [1.1.2.79.6]; Robert A. Russell, "Gold Mining in Alabama Before 1860," *Alabama Review* 10 (January 1957): 5–14. A number of old gold mines were flooded by the lake, two that were on property of the B. E. Kidd family. The Blue Hill mine, owned by the Phillips family of Dadeville, and several other mines were not flooded.

116. James Mitchell to Frank Washburn, April 27, 1912 [1.1.1.4.3]; Eugene A. Yates to James Mitchell, May 31, 1912 [3.1.1.41.8].

117. Eugene A. Yates to James Mitchell, May 31, 1912 [3.1.1.41.8]. Captain W. P. Lay paid Colonel Hugh L. Cooper to design a dam for Lock 12 in 1908. There are dam plans in the corporate archives for Lock 12 that are dated July 29, 1912, and designated as drawn by EBASCO engineers (D-2824, T-C-2437, superseded by D-2908). Yates had to begin with Lay's drawings because time was so critical. Cooper's report on the Coosa site is dated November 24, 1908. See "History and Development of Alabama Power Company and Its Property," 12 [2.1.1.56.20].

118. W. E. Mitchell, *James Mitchell*, 1–2; *Powergrams*, August 1920, 3.

119. Martin, *Electricity in Alabama*, 33.

120. Various telegrams in Mitchell, bound correspondence [1.1.1.4.3], and W. W. Freeman to James Mitchell, July 2, 1912 [3.1.1.39.2].

121. Heys interview with Jack Bingham, March 25, 1999, 1.

122. Thomas W. Martin to Frank W. Lull, November 12, 1913; Frank W. Lull to Thomas W. Martin, November 19, 1913 [3.1.1.37.3].

123. James Mitchell to Frank S. Washburn, June 6, 1912 [3.1.1.39.37].

124. The Alabama Power Development Company had been incorporated in Talladega County, March 29, 1907, by J. H. Hanson, J. K. Dixon, and Reuben Mitchell. The purchase agreement was signed on July 22, 1912, to Alabama Traction, and James Mitchell and Alabama Traction took over these properties on July 28, 1912.

Alabama Power Development Company was folded into Alabama Power Company, July 28, 1913. (The agreement was signed June 18, 1913, and ratified by the stockholders on July 28, 1913.) The steam plant began operation on August 1, 1913, and was in service by September; see D/C 704-455, Corporate Files, Office of the Secretary of State, Alabama; "History and Development of Alabama Power Company and Its Property," 26–27 [2.1.1.56.20]; *Annual Report*, Alabama Traction, Light & Power Company, 1913, 1–5; Martin, *Electricity in Alabama*, 31, 35–36. The power from the Jackson Shoals dam represented the first electricity that James Mitchell and Alabama Traction had to sell. Since the Alabama Power Development Company was not merged into Alabama Power Company until the next year, July 28, 1913, Martin in *Electricity in Alabama* gives the first power sold by Alabama Power to come from Jackson Shoals and the Gadsden Steam Plant on July 28, 1913, although Alabama Traction had been selling power from Jackson Shoals for almost a year. Net earnings for Alabama Power's first year of operations in 1913 were $26,268. Martin *Electricity in Alabama*, 40.

125. *Manufacturers Record*, January 18, 1912, 64.

126. W. E. Mitchell, *James Mitchell*, 7.

127. *Wall Street Journal*, September 26, 1912.

128. *Manufacturers Record*, September 10, 1912, 53.

129. Martin, *Electricity in Alabama*, 31–32; Alabama Traction, Light & Power Company, Ltd., Auditors' Certificate, April 30, 1914 [1.1.2.111.1].

130. Martin, *Electricity in Alabama*, 40.

131. F. T. Tone, works manager for the Carborundum Company, Niagara Falls, New York, to Frank S. Washburn, August 3, 1912, and Washburn to Tone, August 8, 1912 [3.1.1.39.37].

132. *Congressional Record*, 62d Cong., 2d sess., Senate, August 24, 1912, 11797. Taft, in an opinion he later told Senator John Bankhead Sr. was actually written by his "Bull Moose" secretary of war Henry L. Stimson, vetoed the bill. The "fatal defect" was not providing some compensation to the federal government that could be assigned to the cost of navigation improvements. See also King, *Conservation Fight*, 26, who gives an incorrect date for the veto. At this time it was evident that Taft as the Republican nominee would be facing a three-way race with former president Theodore Roosevelt running on the Progressive/Bull Moose Party ticket and Woodrow Wilson on the Democratic ticket. Alabama was a strong Democratic state, and Taft would not be alienating many voters in Alabama.

133. W. P. G. Harding to Oscar W. Underwood, July 29, 1912; Robert Jemison to Oscar W. Underwood, July 29, 1912, in Oscar W. Underwood Papers, ADAH.

134. *Congressional Record*, 62th Cong., 2d sess., Senate, August 24, 1912, 11796. O. R. Hood to Thomas W. Martin, May 4, 1912 [3.1.1.17.7]. James Mitchell to J. W. Worthington, May 15, 1916, in Martin Library, SRI. Mitchell wrote Worthington in 1916 about several matters and commented that the company's first lobby effort "was successful before Congress, but President Taft defeated our perfectly just and legitimate pretensions by vetoing the act of Congress for purely political reasons." On August 29, 1912, Mitchell told the *Manufacturers Record* (page 1) that Taft's veto would not interfere with the dam the company had under construction at Lock 12.

135. *Montgomery Advertiser*, August 8, 17, 23, 24, 1912.

136. *Birmingham Age-Herald*, August 25, 1912; Evans C. Johnson, *Oscar W. Underwood: A Political Biography* (Baton Rouge: Louisiana State University Press, 1980), 115–16.

137. Montgomery Advertiser, August 27, 1912.

138. Martin, Electricity in Alabama, 32.

139. Haynes, Chemical Pioneers, 250–52. Haynes seems to have confused the vetoes of President Theodore Roosevelt and President W. H. Taft; Stephen H. Cutcliffe, "Frank Sherman Washburn," in American National Biography Online.

140. Haynes, Chemical Pioneers, 250–52; Cutcliffe, "Washburn"; "American Cyanamid Company," International Directory of Company Histories, 68 vols. (Chicago: St. James Press, 1988), 1:300; David E. Newton, Chemical Elements (Detroit: U-X-L, 1999), 387–88, 495; Frank S. Washburn, "The Relation of Water Power to Crop Production," Manufacturers Record, September 14, 1916, 61; W. L. Faith, Donald B. Keyes, and Roland L. Clark, Industrial Chemicals (New York: John Wiley & Sons, 1950), 78–79; William Haynes, ed., American Chemical Industry: The Chemical Companies, vol. 4 (New York: D. Van Nostrand Co., 1949), 21–22. Mitchell may have known Washburn before he visited Alabama in 1911, because Sperling invested money (at some point in time) in the Ontario plant of American Cyanamid, but there are no references to Mitchell knowing Washburn before January 1912 in depositions or company records left by Mitchell. James Mitchell never mentioned Washburn as a reason for his decision to visit Alabama in 1911. In 1916, Mitchell reported that he was then heavily invested in American Cyanamid. Manufacturers Record, August 29, 1912, 1, and James Mitchell to J. W. Worthington, May 15, 1916, Martin Library, SRI.

141. Birmingham Age-Herald, February 26, 1914. James Mitchell announced cooperation between American Cyanamid Company and Alabama Power to locate the plant that was intended to be built near Montgomery on the Coosa River to Muscle Shoals before President Taft's 1912 veto ended these plans. The new plant was expected to make Muscle Shoals the "largest electro-chemical manufacturing center of the world." The Huntsville Mercury Banner, February 25, 1914, announced that "Sperling was ready to spend $30 million" on the Tennessee River [4.1.2.27.11]; Martin, Electricity in Alabama, 32.

142. James Mitchell to J. W. Worthington, May 15, 1916, Martin Library, SRI.

143. James Mitchell noted that the dam would produce 12,500 kilowatts, that transmission lines were under construction, and that the company was backed "by some of the strongest financial concerns in England, its bonds marketed through Sperling & Company by Parr's Bank, Ltd." Manufacturers Record, August 15, 1912, 55.

144. Harvey H. Jackson III, Putting "Loafing Streams" to Work: The Building of Lay, Mitchell, Martin, and Jordan Dams, 1910–1929 (Tuscaloosa: University of Alabama Press, 1997). Manufacturers Record, August 15, 1912. Readers are referred to Jackson's book for detailed accounts of the construction of these dams.

145. For details of this construction see Jackson, "Loafing Streams," 14–36, and Harvey H. Jackson III, "Taming the Coosa," Alabama Heritage (Fall 1995): 26–33.

146. See various letters in file 1.1.1.85.8, especially R. A. Mitchell to Thomas W. Martin, January 16, 1914, and Eugene A. Yates to Thomas W. Martin, February 23, 1914.

147. Jackson, "Loafing Streams," 16–30.

148. Ibid., 31–36.

149. Powergrams, December 1920, 1; April 1922, 6; May 1922, 3; July 1922, 15; August 1922, 3.

150. Flynt, Alabama in the Twentieth Century, 129–32.

151. Martin, Electricity in Alabama, 89.

152. W. W. Freeman to J. W. Worthington, Hotel Raleigh, Washington, D.C., August 16, 1912, bound correspondence [1.1.1.4.3]. The first office of Alabama Interstate Power Company was at 1116 Bell Building, but much of the legal and secretarial work was carried on at Tom Martin's law office in the First National Bank Building in Montgomery. The company rented several rooms in Birmingham in the fall of 1912, but the main office was No. 932 Brown-Marx Building, which was located in the center of business activity in the city in 1913. See 1.1.2.067.15, pages 67–69.

153. Birmingham Ledger, August 23, October 1, 1913; Birmingham News, November 22, 1913. The Birmingham Age-Herald covered the opening of Lock 17 on May 11 and 13, 1915, noting that 20,000 people gathered to celebrate the completion of the Warrior-Tombigbee navigational improvements.

154. Manufacturers Record, October 31, 1912, 48.

155. Ibid., December 5, 1912, 87.

156. Wall Street Journal, January 17, 1913. Sperling & Company was also heavily invested in American Cities Company, a utilities investment and holding company in which Mitchell personally held a large interest. Wall Street Journal, February 20, 1913.

157. Birmingham Age-Herald, January 5, 1913; Birmingham News, January 1, 1913; "Report of Work in Progress," Alabama Traction, Light & Power Co., Ltd., February 1913 [1.1.2.62.2]; Birmingham Age-Herald, December 30, 1913 [4.1.2.27.11].

158. Montgomery Advertiser, September 5, 1913.

159. James Mitchell to Carolyn Mitchell, December 4, 1914, Mitchell Personal Papers.

160. James Mitchell to W. W. Freeman, June 6, 1913 [3.1.1.41.9].

161. Wall Street Journal, August 5, 1913.

162. W. W. Freeman to James Mitchell, June 10, 11, 16, 1913 [3.1.1.41.9]. In this extensive correspondence there is always the mention of cablegrams (but no copies of any cablegrams), so the essence of the discussions was being exchanged immediately. One thing surprising from this exchange is how rapidly letters crossed the ocean and were delivered to London or New York offices.

163. Frank S. Washburn, Memo to the File, January 15, 1914; Memorandum of Agreement between Theodore Swann and Frank S. Washburn, President, Alabama Power Company, February 9, 1914 [3.1.1.41.4]. Edward Griffith and Carolyn Green Satterfield, The Triumphs and Troubles of Theodore Swann (Montgomery: Black Belt Press, 1999), 30–31; and Theodore Swann's weekly reports to Washburn listing his contacts for the week [3.1.1.41.3]. Walter Baker, Milestones in Marketing (Birmingham: Alabama Power Co., 1989), 2.

164. Frank S. Washburn to Editor of the Birmingham Age-Herald, January 6, 1914 [1.1.1.4.1].

165. Frank S. Washburn to Alabama Power Company Board of Directors, October 13, 1913 [2.1.1.56.2].

166. James Mitchell to Frank S. Washburn, November 13, 1913 [3.1.1.39.37]; letter, W. J. Henderson to Editor, Powergrams, September 1920, 10; Frank S. Washburn to Thomas W. Martin, February 9, 1914 [3.1.1.17.7].

167. Birmingham Age-Herald, December 30, 1913; Birmingham News, January 2, 1914 [4.1.2.27.11].

168. Thomas W. Martin to Secretary of War, February 11, 1914 [1.1.1.4.25]. The law required the dam to be completed by March 4, 1914. Martin, Electricity in Alabama, 39. The company's first Annual

Report, covering 1913 and issued at the shareholders meeting on July 28, 1914, stated that electricity was being generated and distributed over 160 miles of 110-volt transmission lines through three substations to 116 miles of circuit operating at 22,000 volts. This electricity was coming from Gadsden Steam Plant and from the hydro unit at Jackson Shoals. *Annual Report*, Alabama Power Company, 1913, 2. By the next year, all the Lock 12 units were generating through 60 miles of 44,000-volt distribution lines as the connection to the 110,000-volt transmission line was under way. The company's largest industrial customers were not connected until late in 1914 when the operation of the Gadsden Steam Plant was discontinued except for reserve capacity. *Annual Report*, Alabama Power Company, 1914, 1–3.

169. *First Annual Report*, Alabama Traction, Light & Power Company, Ltd. [1.1.2.111.1].

170. Murray, *Martin*, 41.

171. Black Zip Notebook, December 17, 1963, chapter 7: 2, Martin Library, SRI. These notebooks are most interesting and illustrate the heavy editing that Martin gave the manuscript of his biography before he died. In one place the galley reads that Thomas Martin "was an old man now," and Martin marked through it to make it read "was still a young man now." In another place when he is called Thomas, he marked through his first name and changed it to "Martin." See chapter 11, 2. Joe Farley recalls that he never heard anyone call him Tom to his face other than his brother Logan and his sister Susie Milner.

172. Black Zip Notebook, January 9, 1961, chapter 8, 7, Martin Library, SRI. The Alabama Traction bond indenture stipulated a rule by majority of those present "and voting," and Martin was never clear about whether Weathers overlooked the "and voting" clause.

173. *Wall Street Journal*, July 30, 1924.

174. Jackson, "Loafing Streams"; Dr. W. H. Sanders, Dr. J. T. Hunter, Dr. C. J. S. Peterson, Dr. C. K. Maxwell, and Dr. Julius Jones to Thomas W. Martin, October 29, 1914 [1.1.1.85.4].

175. E. A. Yates, "Clearing Lock 12 Reservoir," January 26, 1913, and Thomas W. Martin to Dr. W. H. Sanders (state health officer), March 8, 1913 [3.1.1.41.18]; J. A. Le Prince, *A Study of Impounded Waters on the Coosa River in Shelby, Chilton, Talladega, and Coosa Counties*, U.S. *Public Health Service* (Montgomery: Brown Printing, n.d., but late 1914). See copy in 1.1.2.85.5.

176. Oscar G. Thurlow to Dr. Henry Rose Carter, February 17, 1915, Philip S. Hench Walter Reed Yellow Fever Collection, University of Virginia.

177. Gorgas testimony, excerpts [1.1.2.65.1]; Robert L. Hughes, comp., *The Great Destroyer* (n.p., n.d.), includes the testimony of General Gorgas in the Hand trial. Copy courtesy of Joe Farley. Murray, *Martin*, 42–43; Jackson, "Loafing Streams," 50–53.

178. Heys interview with Jack Bingham, March 25, 1999, 5.

179. Judge John McElderry Chilton was born in Tuskegee and practiced law in Opelika with William J. Samford, who died in office in 1901 after one year of a gubernatorial term. Chilton was appointed judge of the third circuit in 1882, then retired and in 1889 moved to Montgomery and established a law firm with Samuel Rice and Thomas G. Jones, who was certainly no populist. Chilton died December 29, 1915, before the final decision of the U.S. Supreme Court was rendered in January 1916.

180. James Mitchell to Thomas W. Martin, December 9, 1913; Thomas W. Martin to James Mitchell, February 3, 1914; James Mitchell to Thomas W. Martin, February 9, 10, 1914 [2.1.1.42.8].

181. Brief, *Alabama Interstate Power Company v. Tallassee Falls Manufacturing Company, Mount Vernon–Woodberry Duck Company, et al.*,

Alabama Supreme Court Library, 1–2.

182. The Orange Judd *Southern Farming*, January 4, 1913 [1.1.2.74.6].

183. James Mitchell to Thomas W. Martin, April 21, 1914 [2.1.1.42.8]; Murray, *Martin*, 46–47.

184. Brief, *Alabama Interstate Power Company v. Tallassee Falls Manufacturing Company, Mount Vernon–Woodberry Duck Company, et al.*, Alabama Supreme Court Library, 1–3.

185. Jackson, "Loafing Streams," 58.

186. James Mitchell, *Memorandum Relating to Water Power Developments of Alabama Power Company*, May 4, 1914 [1.1.2.15.10].

187. Martin, *Electricity in Alabama*, 39.

188. *Birmingham Age-Herald*, August 30, 1913; *Birmingham Ledger*, August 29, October 4, 1913; *Birmingham News*, October 4, 1913.

189. As one would expect, this new policy was not well received by the press. *Birmingham Age-Herald*, September 5, 1913.

190. See reports and lists in 3.1.3.37.58.

191. See Executive Bulletin, Alabama Power Company, October 15, 1913 [1.1.2.26.6]. This also includes the company's first organizational chart.

192. For Theodore Swann's reports see 3.1.1.41.3, and for Washburn's letters to Mitchell (beginning August 30, 1913) see 3.1.1.39.16.

193. Executive Department Bulletin, Policies and Procedures, September 20, 1913 [3.1.1.37.54]; Notebooks on Orderly Interruptions to Service [3.1.1.37.53].

194. Executive Bulletin, September 20, 1913 [3.1.1.37.54], and Frank S. Washburn to Executives in Various Departments of the Alabama Power Company, October 20, 1913 [3.1.2.37.58]. Washburn's instructions got longer and more detailed as the months passed.

195. United Gas & Electric Corp., board of directors flyer, May 31, 1914 [3.1.1.41.31].

196. Alice Worthington Fisk to Hill Ferguson, June 19, 1953, Hill Ferguson Collection, Archives, Birmingham Public Library (hereafter BPL). This recollection may be questioned because I found no other reference to any European trip by Worthington. There are times in his career when nitrates seem to be only a way for Worthington to obtain his goal of opening the Tennessee River to navigation and hydroelectric production. See also Mary S. Miller, "Proposal for a Book: Muscle Shoals," 4–6, copy of this paper in the Alabama Power Company Corporate Archives. Miller's work centers on Worthington, Muscle Shoals, Frank Washburn, and the chemical industry's interest in the Shoals. Although many books have been published on Muscle Shoals, none has appeared from Miller's point of view. Although she covers the Shoals in much greater detail and from a different perspective than I do, and we sometimes disagree on interpretations, her work will add to our understanding of the subject and will be a valuable source when it appears. See also Daniel, "Worthington," 196–98. Adrian George Daniel's essay on Worthington is the best published piece on the former Alabama Power vice president; however, Daniel, a University of North Alabama history professor in the 1960s, is incorrect in some details and did not use Alabama Power materials.

197. Claude Williford to J. W. Worthington, November 6, 1918 [3.1.1.39.37]; Alice Worthington Fisk to Hill Ferguson, June 19, 1953, Hill Ferguson Collection, Archives, BPL.

198. James Mitchell to Frank S. Washburn, November 18, December 12, 1913 [3.1.1.39.37].

199. Daniel, "Worthington," 207.

200. Olis Woody to Tom Worthington, April 7, 1942, Worthington Family Papers, Archives, BPL. Woody was J. W. Worthington's secretary in the last years of Worthington's life.

201. Thomas W. Martin to Frank S. Washburn, September 1, 9, 1914 [1.1.1.4.1].

202. Thomas W. Martin to Frank S. Washburn, April 21, 1915; J. W. Worthington to Frank S. Washburn, June 7, 1914 [1.1.1.4.1].

203. The closest that Martin came to recognizing Washburn's contributions to the early years of the Alabama Power Company came in testimony given in 1939 when he said that the Alabama Power Company progressed "under very fine leadership of Frank S. Washburn." Testimony of Thomas W. Martin before Federal Power Commission, 1276 [3.1.1.11.31].

Chapter Three

1. Donald Davidson, *The Tennessee,* vol. 1, *The Old River, Frontier to Secession* (New York: Rinehart & Co., 1946), 281.

2. The U.S. Board of Geographic Names selected "muscle" as the official spelling in 1892. Virginia O. Foscue, *Place Names in Alabama* (Tuscaloosa: University of Alabama Press, 1989), 99.

3. "John Donaldson's Journal," in Tennessee Historical Commission, *Three Pioneer Tennessee Documents* (Nashville: Tennessee Historical Commission, 1964), 6–7.

4. Adrian George Daniel, "Navigational Development of Muscle Shoals," *Alabama Review* 14 (October 1961): 253–55.

5. Daniel, *Formative Period,* 32–33, 91–99; Cinda Kay McMurtrey, "Opening the Tennessee River in Alabama: The Problem of the Muscle Shoals, 1818–1933" (master's thesis, Samford University, 1983), 1–10, 14–16.

6. Lewis, *Sloss Furnaces,* 238–39.

7. Adrian George Daniel, "The Formative Period of Muscle Shoals Power, 1896–1916" (master's thesis, University of Alabama, 1959), 11.

8. Adrian George Daniel, "The Origins of Muscle Shoals Power, 1896–1906," *Alabama Review* 15 (October 1962): 253–54.

9. *Florence Times,* November 15, 1901.

10. Daniel, "Formative Period," 12–18. President Roosevelt vetoed the bill because he believed that private industry developing hydroelectricity should help pay for navigational improvements incurred by the federal government. See *Messages and Papers of the Presidents, 1789–1905,* 10 vols. (1907), 10:595–96.

11. Daniel, *Formative Period,* 120–21.

12. King, *Conservation Fight,* 6–7.

13. *Florence Times,* October 19, 1906.

14. Muscle Shoals Hydro-Electric Power Co., "Articles of Incorporation and Certification of Incorporation," October 10, 1906 [3.1.1.41.36].

15. Daniel, "Formative Period," 29–30; *Manufacturers Record,* December 20, 1906, 573.

16. *Florence Times,* November 14, 16, December 7, 1906.

17. Johnson, *Underwood,* 447.

18. "Water Power Development," *Florence Times,* September 12,

1912. In the secondary sources, there is no mention that the $55 million came through James Mitchell from English sources and almost none cite Martin's *Electricity in Alabama.* Judson King says that Alabama Traction, Light & Power Co., Ltd., was a "Canadian concern heavily financed from London," but he writes that "the British connection was kept secret." Alabama newspapers of the period readily made the source of the money well known in the state, and articles in regional and national publications did also. See *Birmingham Age-Herald,* September 19, 1913 [3.1.2.37.57] and *Anniston Evening Star,* February 25, 1914 [3.1.2.37.58]. King made much of the evils of "interlocking directorates" of the Alabama companies, something that had no sinister motive as King implies but was the natural business result of Mitchell's mergers and acquisitions. King, *Conservation Fight,* 36.

19. Charles H. Baker to Thomas W. Martin, February 9, 1912 [4.1.1.7.2]; Charles H. Baker to Frank S. Washburn, January 13, 1912 [3.1.1.39.37].

20. Alabama Interstate Power Co. to E. A. Yates, December 6, 1912 [3.1.1.41.36]. The partial list of reports that James Mitchell had available to him may be found in "History and Development of Alabama Power Company and Its Property" [2.1.1.56.20].

21. James R. Hall to Frank S. Washburn, February 21, 1914 [3.1.1.64.17].

22. *Birmingham Age-Herald,* January 26, 1914 [3.1.2.37.58].

23. *Montgomery Advertiser,* April 27, 1916 [1.1.2.74.24].

24. Ibid., March 18, 1914; Marie Owen, *Story of Alabama,* 5:1255; Harold Williams, comp., "Some Background Material Concerning the History of Balch & Bingham, 1922–1999," 5.

25. Margaret Pace Farmer, "Governor Charles Henderson," *Alabama Review* 9 (October 1956): 244–47; *Montgomery Advertiser* for January–March 1914.

26. Press release from James Mitchell, February 25, 1914 [3.1.1.29.9]. Although the preferred modern spelling is cyanamide, Washburn's company name took the common spelling used in the United States at that time.

27. *Birmingham Age-Herald,* February 26, 1914; *Birmingham News,* February 26, 1914.

28. *Anniston Evening Star and Daily Hot Blast,* February 25, 1914; *Birmingham Age-Herald,* February 26, 1914 [3.1.2.37.58].

29. *Montgomery Advertiser,* March 19, 1914. O'Neal did not mention, and he may not have known, that the law had been drafted by Massey Wilson and Tom Martin with the Cherokee Bluffs group in mind. Later political charges were made that the law was written especially for Alabama Power Company, chartered in 1906.

30. Ibid., April 26, 1914.

31. Thomas W. Martin to Frank S. Washburn, September 17, 1915 [1.1.1.4.1]. J. C. McMichael was the man in charge.

32. *Montgomery Advertiser,* March 23, 24, 25, 1914.

33. Frank P. Glass to Oscar W. Underwood, January 14, 1915; J. W. Worthington to Frank P. Glass, January 16, 1915, Underwood Papers, ADAH; Johnson, *Underwood,* 344–45.

34. Steve Suitts in his biography of Hugo Black details the Martin family's ties to former governor Comer and Attorney General Logan Martin's fight against Governor Henderson over the cleanup of illegal whiskey in Girard (the old name for Phenix City). Steve Suitts, *Hugo Black of Alabama: How His Roots and Early Career Shaped the Great Champion of the Constitution* (Montgomery: New South Books, 2005), 192–97.

35. Editorial, "Our Low Politics," *Montgomery Advertiser*, March 25, 1914.

36. Thomas W. Martin to Frank S. Washburn, September 1, 1914 [1.1.1.4.1].

37. Thomas W. Martin to Frank S. Washburn, February 3, 1914 [2.1.1.42.7]; Frank S. Washburn to F. H. Chamberlain, September 28, 1914 [3.1.1.29.9].

38. *Birmingham Age-Herald*, November 22, 1913.

39. Forney Johnston to Oscar W. Underwood, January 18, 1915, Underwood Papers, ADAH; R. B. Rosenburg, "Emmet O'Neal, 1911–1915," 160, and Lee N. Allen, "Charles Henderson, 1915–1919," 163–64, both in Samuel L. Webb and Margaret E. Armbrester, *Alabama Governors: A Political History of the State* (Tuscaloosa: University of Alabama Press, 2001); John W. Worthington to F. P. Glass, January 16, 1915, copy in Underwood Papers, ADAH.

40. Typescript of Washburn testimony, House of Representatives, Committee on Agriculture, February 9, 1916, 26, TVA Library, 43101, copy courtesy of Mary S. Miller; *Congressional Record*, Senate, March 30, 1916, 5552–58.

41. King, *Conservation Fight*, 59–60; Washburn, "Relation of Water Power to Crop Production," 59–62; Daniel, "Worthington," 201–02; Martin, *Electricity in Alabama*, 32.

42. *Montgomery Advertiser*, March 23, 1914.

43. Edgar told the *Wall Street Journal* that British investments in the United States over the preceding ten years totaled $1 billion and that Sperling was withdrawing from Brazil and Mexico because of "internal troubles and political unrest in those countries." *Wall Street Journal*, March 12, 1914.

44. W. E. Mitchell, "Remarkable Hydro-Electric Development in Alabama," *Montgomery Advertiser*, March 29, 1914; "History and Development of Alabama Power Company and Its Property," 22–28 [2.1.1.56.20].

45. James Mitchell to Carolyn Mitchell, December 4, 1914; James Mitchell to Carolyn Mitchell, December 18, 1914, in James Mitchell Personal Papers.

46. James Mitchell to Carolyn Mitchell, December 25, 1914, in ibid.

47. James Mitchell to Carolyn Mitchell, February 11, 1915; James Mitchell to Carolyn Mitchell, February 13, 1915, in ibid.

48. Minutes, Board of Directors, Alabama Power Company, February 19, 1915, 179. The companies were the Huntsville Railway Light & Power Company, the Decatur Light, Power & Fuel Company, the Etowah Light & Power Company, the Pell City Light & Power Company, and a few others. Martin, *Electricity in Alabama*, 85.

49. James Mitchell to Carolyn Mitchell, February 27, 1915, James Mitchell Personal Papers.

50. James Mitchell to Frank S. Washburn, December 12, 1913 [3.1.1.39.31].

51. Martin, *Electricity in Alabama*, 85–86.

52. Minutes, Board of Directors, Alabama Power Company, February 19, 1915, 178–79.

53. Ibid., March 1, 1915, 197–200; King, *Conservation Fight*, 59–60.

54. F. H. Chamberlain to James Mitchell, July 8, 1915 [3.1.1.29.8].

55. James Mitchell to Carolyn Mitchell, May 7, 1915, James Mitchell Personal Papers. Mitchell notes he heard the news of the *Lusitania* being torpedoed off the coast of Ireland. The *Huntsville Mercury Banner*, April 9, 1915, reported Tileston's death as falling, coming into contact with a live wire, and dying instantly [4.1.2.27.11].

56. Remarks of Carolyn Marion Mitchell Stancioff, "Unveiling of Plaques of William P. Lay, James Mitchell, Thomas W. Martin," Industry Room, Alabama Department of Archives and History, September 14, 1962, copy in ADAH.

57. Frank S. Washburn to Thomas W. Martin, February 9, 1914 [3.1.1.17.7].

58. The term "floating on the line" was commonly used in early correspondence, but in 2006 it was called "motoring."

59. Martin, *Electricity in Alabama*, 42–45.

60. *Birmingham News*, April 18, 1916; *Wall Street Journal*, April 21, 1916.

61. Murray, *Martin*, 45, 50–51. The Gorgas post office began operating April 18, 1918.

62. Thomas W. Martin to Frank S. Washburn, January 28, 1915, including copy of the governor's bill, and Frank Washburn to Thomas W. Martin, February 5, 1915 [2.11.70.60]. The state utilities group, called the Alabama Light & Traction Association, included power companies all over the state. F. H. Chamberlain attended the meeting to represent Alabama Power. He reported to Martin that the representatives of Henry L. Doherty's interests in Alabama, especially in Montgomery, "were opposed to utility legislation at this time," which seemed to be any regulation, while Mitchell and Washburn's position was that regulation was necessary and fair regulation acceptable.

63. Allen, "Henderson," in Webb and Armbrester, *Alabama Governors*, 163–64; Owen, *History of Alabama and Dictionary of Alabama Biography*, 2:1152–55.

64. James Mitchell to Carolyn Mitchell, October 21, 1915, James Mitchell Personal Papers.

65. Reuben A. Mitchell to F. H. Chamberlain, June 12, 1914, and Thomas W. Martin to Wiley Alford (treasurer), June 30, 1914 [3.1.1.17.7].

66. James Mitchell to Carolyn Mitchell, November 5, 1915, James Mitchell Personal Papers.

67. James Mitchell to J. W. Worthington (discussing 1915), May 15, 1916, Martin Library, SRI. Tom Martin's distrust of Worthington also increased in 1915. For instance, when Worthington planned a meeting for state and national leaders at Muscle Shoals for May 10, 1915, he wrote Martin and told him to stay away. Martin replied he had no plans to come anyway. J. W. Worthington to Thomas W. Martin, May 2, 1915, and Thomas W. Martin to J. W. Worthington, May 9, 1915, in ibid.

68. F. H. Chamberlain to James Mitchell, March 29, 1916 [2.1.1.18.9]. James Mitchell to J. W. Worthington, May 15, 1916, Martin Library, SRI. Daniel, "Worthington," 205, gives his needing more time for lobbying as the reason Worthington resigned from the Alabama Power Company board and as vice president.

69. Minutes, Alabama Power Company, November 2, 1915; Thomas W. Martin to James Mitchell, November 11, 1915 [3.1.1.17.8]; and James Mitchell to J. W. Worthington, May 15, 1916; Thomas W. Martin sent Worthington $2,500 for expenses and salary for December, January, and one-half of February; see Thomas W. Martin to J. W. Worthington, December 27, 1916, Martin Library, SRI.

70. John Temple Graves II, draft of manuscript, Black Zip Notebook, VII-1, Martin Library, SRI.

71. Thomas W. Martin to James Mitchell, March 8, 1915 [3.1.1.17.9]; James Mitchell to Thomas W. Martin, March 9, 1915; and other letters [3.11.17.18].

72. Memorandum: Organization Plan Anniston Steel Company, Anniston Ordnance Company, and Southern Munitions Company [3.1.1.49.2]; memorandum of interview with W. E. Mitchell, August 2, 1917 [3.1.1.49.1]. In July 1918 Tom Martin was serving as president of the Anniston Steel Company [3.1.1.49.3]; Powergrams, April 1921, 3.

73. Anniston Star, February 25, 1917 [4.1.2.27.10]. Griffith and Satterfield, Triumphs and Troubles, 32–33.

74. "James Mitchell Annistonian," Anniston Evening Star, December 2, 1915; "New Munitions Plant Officers Discuss Plant," Birmingham News, December 2, 1915; James Mitchell to Editor, Birmingham Ledger, December 2, 1915; Industrial Record, December 15, 1916 [4.1.2.27.10].

75. W. E. Mitchell wrote his brother James Mitchell on August 1, 1917, that neither Southern Munitions nor Southern Ordnance Company was highly thought of in Washington, D.C., and that "most of our troubles at present are very simple and are soluble by a simple application of common sense." See 3.1.1.49.1.

76. J. J. Willett, "Some Recollections of James Mitchell," Powergrams, September 1920, 13–14; Griffith and Satterfield, Triumphs and Troubles, 31–33. By war's end W. E. Mitchell was running Anniston Steel. H. S. Swan to U.S. Steel Corporation, August 12, 1918 [4.1.1.27.29].

77. L. P. Sweatt Jr., "James Mitchell, The Man," Powergrams, September 1920, 11.

78. The [Birmingham] State Sentinel, January 22, 1916, microfilm, Samford University. This newspaper was so insignificant that it was not listed or discussed by George N. Cruikshank in the Birmingham newspaper section in his 1920 study, A History of Birmingham and Its Environs, 2 vols. (Chicago: Lewis Publishing Co., 1920), 1:100.

79. Hornady, Soldiers of Progress, 86. The modern treatment of this issue is Richard Rudolph and Scott Ridley, Power Struggle: The Hundred-Year War Over Electricity (New York: Harper & Row, 1986), but there is no discussion of Alabama Power Company.

80. None of the books on the Muscle Shoals for this time period is complete. Daniel, Formative Period, gives the background and covers 1916 only briefly, 171–76. For the perspective of the anti-private power group see King, Conservation Fight, 59–92. Donald Davidson, The Tennessee, vol. 2, The New River, Civil War to TVA (New York: Rhinehart & Co., 1948), 176–85, emphasizes the river. Clopper Almon, "J. W. Worthington and His Role in the Development of Muscle Shoals and the Tennessee River," Journal of Muscle Shoals History 3 (1975): 49–57, is a very brief account. Preston J. Hubbard's dissertation and book detail the legislative history. Mary S. Miller has researched the Muscle Shoals, and synopses of her proposed chapters are in the Alabama Power Company Corporate Archives where she did some of her research. Her emphasis is upon J. W. Worthington, the chemical industry, Frank S. Washburn, the ambitions of national corporate interests to control the Shoals, and the financing of these interests and their conflicts.

81. Daniel, Formative Period, 172–73; Washburn testimony, House of Representatives, Committee on Agriculture, February 9, 1916.

82. All of this maneuvering was explained by Mitchell in a letter to Worthington. James Mitchell to J. W. Worthington, May 15, 1916, Martin Library, SRI; Minutes, Board of Directors, Alabama Power Company, March 10, 1916, 236.

83. James Mitchell to Carolyn Mitchell, March 3, 1916, James Mitchell Personal Papers. Mitchell consistently spelled cyanamide without the "e".

84. Digest of the Statements Made on Muscle Shoals Propositions at the Hearings before the Committee on Military Affairs of the House of Representatives, February 8, 1922–March 13, 1922 (Washington, D.C.: Government Printing Office, 1922), 16; Moody's Industrials, 1918, 47–48; Wall Street Journal, December 13, 1916. Robert F. Durden in his Electrifying the Piedmont Carolinas: The Duke Power Company, 1904-1997 (Durham, N.C.: Carolina Academic Press, 2001), 100, writes that J. B. Duke was operating an electric furnace by November 1914 in a plant at Mount Holly, North Carolina, and that "all these ventures would ultimately lead to J. B. Duke's having a controlling interest in the American Cyanamid Company."

85. Wall Street Journal, December 13, 1916; Johnson, Underwood, 344–45.

86. Although Underwood believed that cheap fertilizer would come from the nitrates produced by Muscle Shoals electricity, and this goal motivated him as well as organized farm groups, at this time period the technology was never able to match the pricing structure of fertilizers and make manufacture of fertilizer profitable.

87. In 1922 Alabama congressman William Bacon Oliver claimed that the provision was added to the bill to prevent Alabama Power Company from being involved. Preston J. Hubbard, "The Muscle Shoals Controversy, 1920–1932, Public Policy in the Making" (Ph.D. diss., Vanderbilt University, 1955), 2–3; Digest of the Statements Made on Muscle Shoals Propositions, 32.

88. Daniel Schaffer, "War Mobilization in Muscle Shoals, Alabama, 1917–1918," Alabama Review 39 (April 1986): 116–17.

89. Tom Martin's copy was leather bound with his name imprinted in gold on the cover. The book was produced under the name of Willis G. Waldo and the Nashville Section of the Engineering Association of the South. Waldo, who was the executive secretary of the Nashville group, was a close associate and at one time an employee of J. W. Worthington.

90. Johnson, Underwood, 346–47; Davidson, The Tennessee, 2:181; Daniel, "Worthington," 206.

91. Thomas W. Martin, The Muscle Shoals Situation: Statement of Alabama Power Company, series A, pamphlet no. 1, March 1922, 34. Bound in Muscle Shoals Pamphlets, 1922 [2.1.2.36.29]. The figure of half a million dollars is not inflated and is much closer to $1.5 million if the stock Mitchell swapped in Alabama Traction is included. Documents show that $400,000 worth of bonds of the Muscle Shoals Hyrdo-Electric Company were paid off by Alabama Traction, Light & Power Company, and this figure does not include engineering surveys that were commissioned later. Different evaluations of this asset are found in newspapers and in the files. See files in 3.1.1.41.8, especially Charles H. Baker to Frank S. Washburn, April 12, 1912, and Resolution of the Board of Directors, Alabama Interstate Power Co. Paul K. Conkin, "Intellectual and Political Roots," in Erwin C. Hargrove and Paul K. Conkin, eds., TVA: Fifty Years of Grass-roots Bureaucracy (Urbana: University of Illinois Press, 1983), 11. Although Conkin knows the dam was planned by Alabama Power Company working with the Corps of Engineers, he does not seem to know that until February 18, 1918, the dam site and flowage lands belonged to Alabama Power Company.

92. Thomas A. Bailey and David M. Kennedy, The American Pageant: A History of the Republic (Lexington, Mass.: D. C. Heath, 1983), 650–64; biographies of Fritz Haber and Carl Bosch in Nobel Lectures, Chemistry, 1901–1921 (Amsterdam: Elsevier Publishing Co., 1966), accessed at Nobelprize.org.

93. Schaffer, "War Mobilization in Muscle Shoals," 122.

94. Congressman W. B. Oliver to J. W. Worthington, March 6,

1930, Worthington Family Papers, BPL.

95. James Mitchell to Carolyn Mitchell, December 3, 1917, James Mitchell Personal Papers.

96. Digest of the Statements Made on Muscle Shoals Propositions, 40–41.

97. Contract No. T-69, Army No. 12835, December 1, 1917, and Supplementary Contract T-69, August 1, 1919, in bound Muscle Shoals Pamphlets, 1922 [2.1.2.36.29]. See Art. 22, 20–22. Also Thomas W. Martin, Forty Years of Alabama Power Company, 1911–1951 (Newcomen Society in North America, 1952), 24.

98. Martin, Muscle Shoals Situation, 9.

99. Martin, Electricity in Alabama, 99.

100. Thomas W. Martin, Power Development in Alabama (Birmingham: Alabama Power Co., August 1918), 33–34. Martin was including the government's Gorgas unit and the new 60,000-kilowatt steam plant at Sheffield, but in 2006 Jerry Stewart, executive vice president of generation, figured that "some 3,000 tons a day" was an excessive estimate since both units (20,000-kilowatts and 30,000-kilowatts) at Gorgas combined were only capable of burning 1,200 tons a day. E-mail, Cassandra Carter to Leah Atkins, February 27, 2006.

101. Schaffer, "War Mobilization in Muscle Shoals," 133–37.

102. See "last draft of deed to Muscle Shoals" [1.1.1.4.11].

103. Minutes, Board of Directors, Alabama Power Company, February 18, 1918, 91–92. The meeting of the Muscle Shoals company was scheduled for March 2, 1918. For the resolution itself and newspaper accounts, especially Sheffield Tri-Cities Daily clipping, see 1.1.1.4.11. James Mitchell to Thomas W. Martin, February 18, 1918, illustrates Mitchell's concern over Washburn's activities in Washington [4.1.1.27.31].

104. Almost the entire letter is included in chapter 10, "Water Power," in Owen, Story of Alabama, 5:326.

105. Murray, Martin, 50. The photograph appeared in "An Appreciation of Patriotism," Powergrams, May 1921, 12–13.

106. John H. Bankhead Sr. to J. W. Worthington, February 19, 1918, copy of telegram [1.1.1.4.11].

107. Griffith and Satterfield, Triumphs and Troubles, 36–37. Mitchell had backed Swann financially.

108. James Mitchell to Thomas W. Martin, Washington, D.C., February 18, 1918 [4.1.1.27.31]. This was the site where Wheeler Dam was eventually constructed as part of the Tennessee Valley Authority.

109. H. S. Swan to Thomas W. Martin, July 9, 1918 [3.1.1.17.11].

110. Thomas W. Martin to James Mitchell, July 24, 1918 [3.1.1.17.11]. Worthington was to be paid through July, but his salary was to cease on August 1, 1918.

111. Telegram, James Mitchell to W. N. Walmsley, September 1, 1916 [2.1.1.18.9].

112. Powergrams, June 1920, 3.

113. Digest of the Statements Made on Muscle Shoals Propositions, 1. The actual figures given by Secretary of War John W. Weeks were $12,887,941.42 for Plant No.1 and $69,674,000 for Plant No. 2. In various sources there are slight differences in the figures reported for these plants because of a difference in what items were included.

114. Hubbard, "Muscle Shoals Controversy," 3–5. It is interesting to note that Bernard M. Baruch, who was placed in charge of the War Industries Board by President Wilson in March 1918, wrote in his autobiography that the "most critical single problem of supply we faced in the whole war was with nitrates." He went on to explain how he solved the problem by convincing the Chilean government to commandeer 200,000 tons of nitrates that Germany owned in Chile. The United States agreed to pay the Chilean government for the nitrate, and Baruch sent ships to pick it up. Bernard M. Baruch, Baruch: My Own Story (New York: Henry Holt & Co., 1957), 312–14; Bernard M. Baruch, American Industry in the War: A Report of the War Industries Board, March 1921 (New York: Prentice-Hall, 1941), 165–66. The full story and the involvement of the British and of Winston Churchill is told in Margaret L. Coit, Mr. Baruch (Boston: Houghton Mifflin Co., 1957), 208–11. If Baruch's story is true, then everything the federal government did at Muscle Shoals during World War I was unnecessary.

115. Martin, Electricity in Alabama, 165; James Mitchell to Carolyn Mitchell, December 3, 1917, James Mitchell Personal Papers.

116. See correspondence in W. E Mitchell's files [4.1.1.27.33] and files of W. N. Walmsley [3.1.1.38.10]. Darlington was a talented and popular engineer. He was on the Alabama Power Company board of directors from August 20, 1913, to February 23, 1914. This was the second time influenza had ravaged the power company office. James Mitchell wrote his wife on January 14, 1916, that "our Alabama office has been very short handed as many of the employees are down with grippe and pneumonia." James Mitchell Personal Papers.

117. D. H. Cronheim to W. E. Mitchell, December 4, 1918 [4.1.1.27.32].

118. See 3.1.1.49.1; Tom Martin was president of Anniston Steel, and after the war he was in charge of trying to sell it. Thomas W. Martin to Robert I. Ingalls, January 26, 1920 [3.1.1.49.13].

119. Powergrams, June 1920, 13; W. E. Mitchell heard about his brother's stroke and telegraphed W. N. Walmsley, who was in New York: "Understand James Mitchell seriously ill. Please advise. Swan arrives N.Y. Mon. morning," June 28, 1919 [4.1.1.27.33].

120. He was suffering from lumbago when he wrote to her in March 1916. James Mitchell to Carolyn Mitchell, March 10, 1916, and other letters in James Mitchell Personal Papers.

121. Tom Martin once indicated that S. Z. Mitchell had nominated him to succeed James Mitchell. Murray, Martin, 55.

122. Powergrams, July 1922, 3; F. D. Mahoney to Howard Duryea, January 10, 1920 [4.1.1.27.17].

123. Howard Duryea to F. D. Mahoney, December 31, 1919 [4.1.1.27.17]; Birmingham Age-Herald, February 17, 1920, and Montgomery Journal, February 22, 1920, clippings, Scrapbook, Martin Library, SRI; Murray, Martin, 54–55.

124. Martin, Electricity in Alabama, 55.

125. Murray, Martin, 57.

126. Typed list of board of directors with identification and handwritten notes by Tom Martin in Thomas W. Martin correspondence file [3.1.1.17.14]; Martin, Electricity in Alabama, 162.

127. Stephen A. Dawley to Thomas W. Martin, May 12, 1920 [3.1.1.17.4]. James Mitchell obituary, New York Times, July 24, 1920 [4.1.1.27.33]; James Mitchell obituary, Electrical World, July 31, 1920 [3.1.1.19.2].

128. New York Times, July 29, 1920, clipping from Mitchell-Stancioff Family Papers, courtesy of Peter Stancioff; Last Will and Testament of James Mitchell, dated July 14, 1916, codicil dated January 17, 1920, James Mitchell Personal Papers. Mitchell left generous bequests to his brothers and life trusts for his sisters and his sister-in-law Lena of Gorgas, widow of his brother Robert, "as long as she refrains from marriage." He left one-third of his estate to his widow Carolyn Stevenson-Cook Mitchell, one-third to his son Charles Malcolm

Mitchell, and one-sixth to his daughter Carolyn Marion Mitchell, with the notation that he intended for his wife to "minimize the difference" in the bequests. Executors of the estate were Mitchell's brother Will and his two longtime associates, Frederick S. Ruth of Mountain Lake, Florida, and Harold S. Swan of Brooklyn. The official estate appraisal and distribution papers are in James Mitchell Personal Papers. The estate appraisal appeared in the *New York Times*, July 30, 1921. Mrs. Mitchell received $822,406, daughter Carolyn $208,274, and son Charles Malcolm $1,006,325. A claim was made against the estate by singer Kathryn Lee for $50,000, but it was denied by the executors. *New York Times*, December 30, 1923, and affidavit in James Mitchell Personal Papers. See also the audit of the estate from the accounting firm Marwick, Mitchell & Co. that was sent to executors on October 11, 1920, in James Mitchell Personal Papers.

129. List of pall bearers, James Mitchell's funeral, and Howard Duryea to W. N. Walmsley, August 10, 1920 [4.1.1.27.31].

130. Marwick, Mitchell & Co. (accounting and auditors) to W. E. Mitchell, Frederick S. Ruth, and H. S. Swan, executors of estate of James Mitchell, October 11, 1920, in James Mitchell Personal Papers.

131. Murray, *Martin*, 55.

132. Tindall, *Emergence of the New South*, 111–12.

133. Brian Kelly, *Race, Class, and Power in the Alabama Coalfields, 1908–1921* (Urbana: University of Illinois Press, 2001), 171–72.

134. Donald Comer to Alabama Power Company, December 31, 1920 [3.1.1.17.14].

135. Murray, *Martin*, 57.

136. *Powergrams*, June 1920, 23; August 1920, 19.

137. Martin, *Electricity in Alabama*, 86; Thomas W. Martin to Roy V. Happy, Southern California Edison Co., October 13, 1920; R. (Robert) M. MacLetchie (comptroller) to Thomas W. Martin, October 25, 29, 1920; Thomas W. Martin to R. M. MacLetchie, October 26, 1920; R. A. Mitchell to Thomas W. Martin in Washington, D.C., November 9, 1920 [3.1.1.17.14].

138. H. M. Addinsell (Harris, Forbes & Co.) to Thomas W. Martin, November 17, 26, 1920; Thomas W. Martin to Harris, Forbes & Co., December 2, 1920; H. M. Addinsell to Thomas W. Martin, December 9, 1920; Thomas W. Martin to Lawrence Macfarlane, December 2, 14, 1920; Lawrence Macfarlane to Thomas W. Martin, December 6, 15, 1920; Thomas W. Martin to Harris, Forbes & Co., December 10, 1920; Thomas W. Martin to S. Z. Mitchell, December 15, 1920 [3.1.1.17.14]. See the trust agreement with Irving National Bank, April 21, 1920 [2.1.1.44.1].

139. *Annual Report*, Alabama Power Company, 1921, 7.

140. Hubbard, "Muscle Shoals Controversy," 29–30.

141. See *Prunes, Did they bathe at Muscle Shoals?* and *Government by Inquisition*, flyers produced by the Press Service Company [1.1.2.20.21]. These compare Graham's report with Air Nitrates Corporation responses, documents, and testimony, and were printed by Air Nitrates.

142. Preston J. Hubbard, *Origins of the TVA: The Muscle Shoals Controversy, 1920–1932* (New York: W. W. Norton, 1961), 9; Hubbard, "Muscle Shoals Controversy," 6–15.

143. King, *Conservation Fight*, 80–81; Haynes, *Chemical Pioneers*, 256; Press Service Company releases [1.1.2.20.21]. Washburn died after an extended illness at his home in Rye, New York, on October 9, 1922. Irene Russell Washburn to Mr. Mangum at the Alabama Power Company, October 20, 1922 [2.1.1.56.17]. In many ways the Muscle Shoals killed two good men.

144. James Mitchell to J. W. Worthington, May 15, 1916, Martin Library, SRI.

145. Edward Eyre Hunt, ed., *The Power Industry and the Public Interest* (New York: Twentieth Century Fund, 1944), 23.

146. King, *Conservation Fight*, 46–47.

147. Thomas W. Martin to Senator John H. Bankhead Sr., January 17, 1920, Bankhead Papers, ADAH.

148. King, *Conservation Fight*, 59–74; Hubbard, "Muscle Shoals Controversy," 42–44; Johnson, *Underwood*, 298–99.

149. Charles G. Adsit, "Report on Muscle Shoals," May 20, 1921 [2.1.1.36.3].

150. Davidson, *The Tennessee*, 2:183; Johnson, *Underwood*, 348–51.

151. Hubbard, "Muscle Shoals Controversy," 20–23, 36. Alabama Power Company was accused of paying for literature distributed by the Muscle Shoals Association asking for the completion of the dam. The treasurer of the association denied the power company had financed the materials.

152. Thomas W. Martin to Major General Lansing H. Beach, May 28, 1921, printed in Martin, *Muscle Shoals Situation*, 68–72.

153. Major General Lansing H. Beach to Senator Lawrence Davis Tyson, October 15, 1926, Worthington Family Papers.

154. Ibid.; Harry E. Wilson, "History of the Shoals," an online history posted by the *Florence Times Daily*, February 25, 1999; Leslie S. Wright, "Henry Ford and Muscle Shoals," *Alabama Review* 14 (July 1961): 196–205.

155. Allan Nevins and Frank Ernest Hill, *Ford, Expansion and Challenge, 1915–1933* (New York: Charles Scribner's Sons, 1954), 306. The authors are in error in stating that it was former governor Edward A. O'Neal who was a leader of the American Farm Bureau in the 1920s because former governor E. A. O'Neal died in 1890. His son Emmet O'Neal was governor 1911–15, and he did support the Ford proposal. A relative of the governors, Edward Asbury O'Neal III, of Lauderdale County, was elected vice president of the American Farm Bureau and served from 1924 to 1931, when he was elected president of the farm organization. P. O. Davis, *One Man: Edward Asbury O'Neal III of Alabama* (Auburn: Alabama Polytechnic Institute, 1945), 10.

156. Hubbard, "Muscle Shoals Controversy," 51–52. A copy of Beach's letter to Ford dated July 8, 1921, is in 2.1.1.36.21.

157. J. W. Worthington to Oscar W. Underwood, June 21, 1921, Underwood Papers, ADAH.

158. "Preliminary Memorandum," attached to Worthington to Underwood, June 21, 1921, in ibid.

159. *Chicago Daily Tribune*, July 27, 28, 29, 30, 31, 1921. The letters also proved that the lobby efforts in Washington on behalf of the Muscle Shoals project by the Mississippi Valley Association were being funded by Worthington.

160. *Chicago Daily Tribune*, July 29, 1921.

161. J. W. Worthington to E. G. Liebold, July 28, August 14, 1921, Henry Ford's Benson Ford Research Center, Dearborn, Michigan.

162. Norman L. Zucker, *George W. Norris: Gentle Knight of American Democracy* (Urbana: University of Illinois Press, 1966), 74–77; Davidson, *The Tennessee*, 2:187; Martin, *Electricity in Alabama*, 100–102.

163. *Muscle Shoals: Facts Essential to an Understanding of the Controversy*

Over Offer of Henry Ford (New York: Institute of American Business, 1922). Ford was to acquire both dams, Nitrate Plants Nos. 1 and 2, the Waco Quarry of 420 acres, 4,200 acres of land, railroad tracks, locomotives, 350 residences, 500 temporary houses, and numerous other government assets, plus the Warrior Reserve Steam Plant at Gorgas, rights-of-way, and transmission lines to Muscle Shoals.

164. Nevins and Hill, Ford, 311–13; Hubbard, Origins of the TVA, 35–37.

165. William C. Richards, The Last Billionaire: Henry Ford (New York: Charles Scribner's Sons, 1949), 95; Hubbard, "Muscle Shoals Controversy," 62–65.

166. Hubbard, "Muscle Shoals Controversy," 59–61. Wall Street lawyer Samuel Untermyer attacked Ford's anti-Semitism, writing in the New York Times of December 5, 1921, that "The man is so densely ignorant on every subject except automobiles and so blinded by a depth of bigotry that belongs to the dark ages from which he has not emerged, that he is fool enough to publicly exploit this madhouse bug of his about the international bankers owning the gold of the world. He imagines that the great international bankers of the world are Jews, which is not true." Quoted in Hubbard, "Muscle Shoals Controversy," 60. Stories about Martin and Ford automobiles are anecdotal. Interview with Joe Farley, February 9, 2004.

167. Hubbard, "Muscle Shoals Controversy," 63–64.

168. Christian Science Monitor, February 21, 1922.

169. Martin, Electricity in Alabama, 100–101; Richard Lowitt, George W. Norris: The Persistence of a Progressive, 1913–1933 (Urbana: University of Illinois Press, 1971), 200–201. Lowitt writes that although there were several other proposals for the Shoals, the Ford proposal and the Alabama Power Company proposal were the most important ones.

170. Alabama Power Company, contract dated December 1, 1917, and signed November 7, 1918, "Muscle Shoals Proposition," Committee on Military Affairs, 67th Cong., 2d sess., Report 1084 [2.1.2.36.29]. The plant was officially the Warrior Reserve Steam Plant until it was dedicated to Gorgas in 1944, although it was called Gorgas in most company and public reports and files.

171. See pamphlets: The Muscle Shoals Situation and Its Interest to the Central Station Industry (ca. 1922) [1.1.2.20.21]; Comments by Government Officials on Contract Between United States Government and Alabama Power Company (June 3, 1922) [2.1.2.36.24]; Statement by Thomas W. Martin, President Alabama Power Company, in Answer to Statements Made before Military Affairs Committee of the House of Representatives on March 8, 1922 (no date) [2.1.2.36.24].

172. Williams, comp., "History of Balch & Bingham," 3–11.

173. Montgomery Advertiser, February 17, 18, 19, 20, 1922.

174. Cordova Courier, February 24, 1922 [4.1.2.22.5].

175. Montgomery Advertiser, February 20, 23, 27, 1922.

176. Davis, Edward Asbury O'Neal III, 124–25.

177. See "Speeches of W. L. Martin in Connection with the 'Muscle Shoals' Matter" [3.1.1.52.7]. Martin often debated with Congressman William Bacon Oliver. Once Logan Martin read earlier correspondence from Oliver to Tom Martin that showed the Tuscaloosa attorney supporting the mission of the power company. For the charge on Sections 231–36 of the Constitution of 1901, see 78–79.

178. Montgomery Advertiser, February 23, 1922; Hornady, Soldiers of Progress, 154–55.

179. Hornady, Soldiers of Progress, 155–62. There were two studies made in 1921–22 of the reproduction and original cost of the company's property. One was done for the Alabama Mining Institute and one was commissioned by the Alabama Public Service Commission. See Special Investigation of the Alabama Power Company, February 1922, Morris Knowles, Inc., Engineers, Pittsburgh, for Alabama Mining Institute, and Report on Alabama Power Company Made for the Alabama Public Service Commission, June 1922, Reproduction Cost and Original Cost Studies, I. F. McDonnell, Consulting Engineer, Birmingham.

180. General C. C. Williams, testimony before the House Military Affairs Committee, February 9, 1922, 69; Colonel J. W. Joyes, Nitrate Division, testimony, 1039, in Muscle Shoals Pamphlets, 1922 [2.1.2.36.29].

181. See the correspondence between Secretary of War John W. Weeks and Thomas W. Martin between August 19 and September 24, 1923, printed and bound in the back of Muscle Shoals Pamphlets, 1922 [2.1.2.36.29]; Martin, Electricity in Alabama, 100; Hubbard, "Muscle Shoals Controversy," 165–66. Hubbard gives an incorrect figure of $2,472,000 on page 166 of his dissertation, which was probably a typographical error. He fails to correct the error in his book, Origins of the TVA, 99. The power company first offered a lesser amount but agreed to the arbitration figure, which they paid. Birmingham-Age Herald, July 8, 1923.

182. New York Times, January 19, 1924; Wall Street Journal, January 5, 1924.

183. Hubbard, Origins of the TVA, 112–31; King, Conservation Fight, 102, 118; Davidson, The Tennessee, 2:184–85.

184. King, Conservation Fight, 118–21; telegram quoted in Hubbard, "Muscle Shoals Controversy," 213.

185. Johnson, Underwood, 254–57.

186. Hubbard, "Muscle Shoals Controversy," 289–90; Hubbard, Origins of TVA, 168. Such attacks were one reason General Electric divested itself of any interest in Electric Bond & Share the next year. In 1925 GE distributed EBASCO stock as a dividend to General Electric stockholders. In eighteen months the stock was widely distributed. See Forrest MacDonald, Let There Be Light: The Electric Utility Industry in Wisconsin, 1881–1955 (Madison, Wis.: American History Research Center, 1957), 312.

187. Quoted by William Logan Martin, "Speeches of W. L. Martin in Connection with the 'Muscle Shoals' Matter," 74 [3.1.1.52.7].

Chapter Four

1. Robert Sobel, The Great Bull Market: Wall Street in the 1920s (New York: W. W. Norton & Co., 1968), 107.

2. John Kenneth Galbraith, The Great Crash of 1929 (Boston: Houghton Mifflin Co., 1961), 8.

3. Oscar Theodore Barck Jr. and Nelson Manfred Blake, Since 1900: A History of the United States in Our Times (New York: Macmillan, 1959), 396–98; Tindall, Emergence of the New South, 104–95.

4. Henry J. Pierce was the EBASCO lobbyist. Alabama Power contributed $7,000 to the effort, and Pierce kept Martin informed of the progress and the wording of the bill. On June 8, 1920, Pierce sent Martin a telegram telling him that President Wilson had signed the waterpower bill. See correspondence, Henry J. Pierce to Thomas W. Martin [2.1.1.70.33], and correspondence and drafts of bills [2.1.1.70.68].

5. For instance, see the drafts of various waterpower bills and

amendments with Martin's comments [2.1.2.49.8–.13, and 1.1.1.4.7].

6. Emily Owen, *Thomas E. Kilby in Local and State Government* (Anniston: privately printed, 1948), 2–17. This is based on Owen's master's thesis at the University of Alabama. The total revenue from property taxes on the state's utilities, including power utilities, was $3,630,093, which was 13.9 percent of Alabama's total revenue for the period of Kilby's governorship. Owen, *Kilby*, 41.

7. James Mitchell to W. N. Walmsley, October 23, 1917 [2.1.1.18.9].

8. Owen, *Kilby*, 65.

9. *Powergrams*, January 1921, 3; Walter M. Hood to Thomas W. Martin, August 24, 1920 [3.1.1.17.14].

10. *General and Local Laws of the Legislature of Alabama, Special Session*, 1920, vii, 38–60.

11. Lamar Wiley, "Statutory History of Alabama Public Service Commission," October 1, 1938, 7–9, Public Commission Records, ADAH; Alabama Public Utility Act of 1920, No. 87, 38–59; Donald Comer to Alabama Power Company, December 31, 1920 [3.1.1.17.14]; interview with Eason Balch, August 4, 2003. The act went into effect October 1, 1920.

12. *Governor's Message, General Laws and Joint Resolutions of the Legislature of Alabama*, 1915, cxxxvi–cxxxvii.

13. *General and Local Laws of the Legislature of Alabama, Special Session*, 1920, vii, 38–60.

14. *Montgomery Advertiser*, December 20, 1921; *Chilton County News*, December 22, 1921 [4.1.2.22.5]. The tax figure given by the *Chilton County News* in December 1921 was slightly more than the figure reported for the company's tax payment for 1921 listed in the Alabama Power *Annual Report* for 1923, which was $70,174.33 (page 6). This discrepancy may be due to the fact that the amount was being adjudicated.

15. *Greenville Advocate*, quoted in Alabama Power Company advertisement giving state press opinions on tax exemptions, *Montgomery Advertiser*, February 5, 1923.

16. *Montgomery Advertiser*, February 2, 1923 [1.1.2.65.2].

17. Lee N. Allen, "William W. Brandon, 1923–1927," in Webb and Armbrester, *Alabama Governors*, 170–72; *General Laws and Joint Resolutions of the Legislature of Alabama, Session 1923* (Montgomery: Brown Printing, 1923), 160.

18. *Montgomery Advertiser*, February 6, 1923 [1.1.2.65.2].

19. *Annual Report*, Alabama Power Company, Year Ended December 31, 1923, 6.

20. Ibid., Year Ended December 31, 1924, 7.

21. *Powergrams*, April 1920, 8–9, 13.

22. Martin, *Electricity in Alabama*, 31.

23. James Mitchell, *Memorandum Relating to Water Power Development of Alabama Power Company*, May 4, 1914, 4 [1.1.2.15.10].

24. Martin, *Electricity in Alabama*, 90.

25. Testimony of Thomas W. Martin, probably before the Federal Power Commission, ca. 1942, 16 [5.1.1.98.239].

26. Murray, *Martin*, 59; Martin, *Electricity in Alabama*, 91; Baker, *Milestones in Marketing*, 3; *Powergrams*, June 1920, 15.

27. Manhattan Press Comment issued by the Southern Exposition Headquarters [1.1.2.65.2]; *New York Times*, October 25, 1925, clipping in Scrapbook No. 1, 11, Martin Library, SRI.

28. T. D. Johnson, "The New Industries Division: Its Purpose and Function," ca. 1941, 8 [5.1.1.98.237]; Murray, *Martin*, 59; Martin, *Electricity in Alabama*, 91. A number of different dates were given by Johnson and by Martin in various histories and sworn testimonies in the company's archives.

29. Johnson, "New Industries Division," 9, 13–14 [5.1.1.98.237]; *Alabama*, April 25, 1938, 14 [5.1.1.98.243]; interview with John V. Denson, April 27, 2004. Isham "Ike" J. Dorsey was later a state senator.

30. Alabama Power Company: New Industries Located in Service Area, 1925–1952, Inclusive [5.1.1.98.241]. The last sheets give a separate listing of war industries located in the state during World War II.

31. Plants Located in Service Territory of Alabama Power Company, 1925–1952, Inclusive [5.1.1.98.241]. Dates reflect the year when the power contract was signed.

32. *Montgomery Advertiser*, May 29, 1927; *Birmingham News*, June 20, 1927; *Textile World*, February 4, 1928 [5.1.1.98.244].

33. Alabama Power Company: New Industries Located in Service Area, 1925–1952, Inclusive [5.1.1.98.241].

34. Johnson, "New Industries Division," 16–18 [5.1.1.98.237].

35. "Alabama plans to tell world of advantages," clipping, n.d., n.p., in Thomas W. Martin Scrapbook, 1925–1954, Martin Library, SRI.

36. *Annual Report*, Alabama Power Company, Year Ended December 31, 1922, 6.

37. One of the interesting books in Sutherland's library was E. S. Lincoln, *The Electric Home: A Standard Ready Reference Book* (New York: Electric Home Publishing Co., 1934), which explained electricity and detailed how various electrical home appliances should be used.

38. Baker, *Milestones in Marketing*, 3, 7; *Powergrams*, September 1921, 20; March 1923, 8.

39. S. M. Kennedy, *Winning the Public* (New York: McGraw-Hill, 1920), is in the Alabama Power Company Corporate Archives. Other books are a 1921 edition of *The Electric Range Handbook* and *How to Sell Electrical Labor-Saving Appliances* (comp. Electrical Merchandising, New York: McGraw-Hill, 1918).

40. Ed Thompson to Leah Atkins, November 1, 2003.

41. *Powergrams*, December 1927, 12.

42. Martin, *Electricity in Alabama*, 83; *Powergrams*, June 1925, 13; April 1926, 1–2; Baker, *Milestones in Marketing*, 4. On April 3, 2004, e-Bay was offering sixteen Reddy Kilowatt items, including a "Chicago 1933 World Fair Hawaii Reddy Kilowatt Dime," which had an offer of $110. Collins eventually left Alabama Power to promote Reddy Kilowatt.

43. Marcus A. Dow, "History of the Safety Movement," *Powergrams*, November 1922, 1–2.

44. *Powergrams*, April 1920, 16; November 1920, 15, 24; January 1921, 23; March 1921, 3, 24; February 1921, 17; November 1922, 1–3. Loyd called accidents the "crime of carelessness."

45. S. R. Benedict, "Accident Instruction to Foremen and Employees," was one such list. *Powergrams*, April 1920, 12.

46. *Powergrams*, September 1922, 3; *Transactions of the Alabama Power Company's Surgeons, Sixth Annual Meeting, 1922* (New York: International Journal of Surgery, 1922–23) and program, Annual Meeting of Association of Surgeons of Alabama Power Company, Mitchell Dam, 1941. The Surgeons Association was inactive after 1935. See letter of Lucie M. Bouchelle, March 17, 1958 [1.1.2.74.15].

47. *Powergrams*, March 1924, 15.

48. Jackson, *Inside Alabama*, 162.

49. Nelda Steele, "Home Service Department," 1; Anita Sanders Bosley, "In the Kitchen with Grandma," *Powergrams*, clipping, n.d., copy from Nelda Steele.

50. Leah Rawls Atkins, *A Century of Women at Auburn: Blossoms Amid the Deep Verdure* (Auburn University, 1992), 16–18; *Powergrams*, March 1923, 12.

51. *Annual Report*, Alabama Power Company, 1925, 14.

52. See the estate papers in the James Mitchell Personal Papers.

53. H. S. Swan to Thomas W. Martin, September 5, 1920 [3.1.1.17.14]. See the estate papers in James Mitchell Personal Papers.

54. Thomas W. Martin to W. N. Walmsley, April 22, 1921; J. M. Gayle to Martin, Walmsley, W. E. Mitchell, and Duryea, May 10, 1921; W. N. Walmsley to J. M. Gayle, May 10, 1921; Howard Duryea to W. N. Walmsley, May 24, 1921 [2.1.1.18.21].

55. *Powergrams*, October 1922, 27; March 1923, 28.

56. Ibid., January 1923, 8.

57. Ibid., June 1920, 13; Royce Dean Northcutt Sr., *I Remember Gorgas* (n.p., n.d.), is a delightful account of growing up in Gorgas in the depression days of the 1930s.

58. State of Alabama, *Annual Report of Coal Mines*, 1918, 14, 31, 86; 1920, 20; 1921, 81. These safety reports noted there was good ventilation and safety at the mine.

59. Rogers et al., *Alabama: History of a Deep South State*, 418–20; Daniel Letwin, *The Challenge of Interracial Unionism: Alabama Coal Miners, 1878–1921* (Chapel Hill: University of North Carolina Press, 1998), 160. On his map on page 33, Letwin does not even locate Gorgas. Kelly, *Race, Class, and Power*, 172–74; Wayne Flynt, "Organized Labor, Reform, and Alabama Politics, 1920," *Alabama Review* 23 (July 1970):179; Jimmie Frank Gross, "Strikes in the Coal, Steel, and Railroad Industries in Birmingham from 1918 to 1922" (master's thesis, Auburn University, 1962), 75, 79–80. See also Edwin L. Brown and Colin J. Davis, eds., *It Is Union and Liberty: Alabama Coal Miners and the UMW* (Tuscaloosa: University of Alabama Press, 1999), 57–58.

60. *Settlement of Alabama Coal Miners Strike of 1920–1921*, 3–6, (no publication information, rare item from University of Alabama Library); Letwin, *Alabama Coal Miners, 1878–1921*, 33.

61. Drifton Coal Company, Special Meeting of Board of Directors, November 28, 1924; General Balance Sheets, Drifton Coal Company, and Union Coal Company, November 1924; Report of the Southeastern Fuel Company, September 30, 1925 [2.1.1.44.7].

62. Northcutt, *I Remember Gorgas*, 13–14.

63. Ibid., 5–6, 34–36.

64. *Powergrams*, September 1924, 1.

65. *Birmingham Age-Herald*, April 25, 1922.

66. *Powergrams*, July 1922, 10–11, 23; March 1923, 9–14.

67. Martin, *Electricity in Alabama*, 77–79; Minutes, Board of Trustees, Alabama Polytechnic Institute, February 23, 1925, 155, Auburn University Archives; *Powergrams*, February 1925, 22; History of WAPI, on Website.

68. For instance, see Oliver R. Hood to R. A. Mitchell, June 28, 1920; W. P. Lay to R. A. Mitchell, July 1, 1920 [3.1.1.17.14].

69. Martin, *Lightning Route*, 15.

70. Murray, *Martin*, 28, 36, 230; R. M. Hobbie, "Montgomery's

Welcome," *Powergrams*, April 1923, 1–3, 40. Several articles in this issue of *Powergrams* featured Montgomery and its electrical history.

71. *Montgomery Advertiser*, February 6, 1923 [1.1.2.65.2].

72. *Annual Report*, Alabama Power Company, 1923, 10–11, 26; Martin, *Lightning Route*, 15.

73. Harry Slattery, *Rural America Lights Up* (Washington, D.C.: National Home Library Foundation, 1940), 3; Deward Clayton Brown, "Rural Electrification in the South, 1920–1955" (Ph.D. diss., University of California, 1971), 15.

74. E. C. Easter, "Rural Electric Development in Alabama," CREA *Bulletin*, April 6, 1926, 2, 7 [1.1.2.62.16]; Baker, *Milestones in Marketing*, 5.

75. Slattery, *Rural America Lights Up*, 3–4.

76. Unidentified clipping, "Charleston's Growth Certain Says Martin, Southeast Power Head," January 28, 1927, Scrapbook, 1925–1954, Martin Library, SRI.

77. E. C. Easter, "Engineering Problems in Taking Electric Service to the Farm," *Powergrams*, September 1952, 35.

78. Agreement between Alabama Polytechnic Institute and Alabama Power Company, December 24, 1923 [2.1.1.65.71]. The board of trustees approved the document the next month. Minutes, Board of Trustees of the Alabama Polytechnic Institute, called meeting, January 2, 1924, 12, Auburn University Archives; *Powergrams*, February 1924, 1.

79. M. J. Funchess, "The Agricultural College and Rural Electrification," *Powergrams*, October 1926, 3–5; Walter L. Baker and M. B. Penn, "Alabama Power Company, Progress of Rural Electrification during 1946" [1.1.2.20.8].

80. Norwood Allen Kerr, *A History of the Alabama Agricultural Experiment Station, 1883–1983* (Auburn: Auburn University, 1985), 50; E. C. Easter, "Summary of Rural Electric Development as of August 31, 1947" [2.1.1.56.19]; agreement between the Alabama Polytechnic Institute and Alabama Power Company, December 24, 1923 [2.1.1.65.71]; Martin, *Electricity in Alabama*, 72–73; Agnes Ellen Harris, "What Electricity Means to the Farm," *Powergrams*, October 1926, 17–18.

81. Interview with Walter Baker, June 24, 2004.

82. H. M. Weathers, "The Part the Company Plays in Rural Electrification," *Powergrams*, October 1926, 8–9.

83. A. C. Polk to E. A. Yates, May 6, 1924 [2.1.1.31.4].

84. E. C. Easter to H. M. Weathers, Alabama Power Company, February 10, 1926, and Progress Report, attached [2.1.1.6.5.71]; Easter, "Rural Electric Development in Alabama," 3–9.

85. Alabama Farm Bureau, *Progress in Rural Electric Service in Alabama*, pamphlet, 1925, 1–3 [1.1.2.62.13].

86. E. A. O'Neal, "The Place of the Farmer in Rural Electric Developments," copy in *Powergrams*, October 1926, 1–2.

87. "Rural Line Statistics, December 31, 1929," located in unmarked box, not accessioned. On this form there was no analysis of the cost of these programs compared to income.

88. Tom Martin, "Rural Electric Service in Alabama," Developing Electric Service for the Farm, Report of the Rural Electric Service Committee, 1928–29, iv [2.1.1.24.5].

89. *Developing Electric Service for the Farm. As Exemplified by the Organizations and Methods of Alabama Power Company. Rural Electric Service Committee, 1928–29*, National Electric Light Association, New York, Publication No. 289-65 [2.1.1.24.5].

90. Seth P. Storrs, "Central Station from the Farmer's Standpoint," *Powergrams*, October 1926, 6–7; William J. Baldwin, *There Was a Man Named Martin*, pamphlet [1.1.2.44.13].

91. Richard A. Pence, ed., *The Next Greatest Thing* (Washington, D.C.: National Rural Electric Cooperative Association, 1984), 5.

92. Brown, "Rural Electrification in the South," 302.

93. H. M. Van Gelder, Dwight Robinson and Company, Inc., to W. E. Mitchell, August 13, 1920; W. E. Mitchell to H. M. Van Gelder, August 31, 1920 [4.1.1.27.33].

94. R. A. Mitchell to Thomas W. Martin, November 6, 1920 [3.1.1.1.7.14]; *Gadsden Evening Journal*, June 19, 1920.

95. Petition, Coosa County, January 1922. Property owners signed petitions that they were treated fairly by the power company in compensating them for their land. See 4.1.1.33.33. Jackson, "*Loafing Streams*," 64.

96. The *Alabama Sportsman* (August–September 1926), 9, copy in Martin Library, SRI; L. M. Smith, "Miscellaneous Notes Alabama Power Company History" [2.1.1.56.17]; Jackson, "*Loafing Streams*," 64.

97. *Powergrams*, February 1922, 3.

98. *Birmingham Age-Herald*, September 18, 1921 [4.1.2.22.5].

99. *Powergrams*, January 1922, 2–3, 12, 14; *Annual Report, Alabama Power Company for Year Ending December 31, 1921, 3–4*; *Birmingham Age-Herald*, December 20, 1921; *Chilton County News*, December 22, 1921 [4.1.2.22.5]; Jackson, "*Loafing Streams*," 198; Murray, *Martin*, 66–67.

100. *Powergrams*, November, December 1921, January, February, May 1922, reported stories about the hospital at Mitchell, floods, construction, and even the Halloween dance for Mitchell Dam employees.

101. *Powergrams*, May 1922, 12–13.

102. Ibid., December 1922, 15; February 1923, 12–13.

103. Ibid., March 1924, 1–3; October 1924, 7.

104. Winton M. "Red" Blount with Richard Blodgett, *Doing It My Way* (Lyme, Conn.: Greenwich Publishing Group, 1996), 10. William Blount was Red Blount's grandfather.

105. Martin Dam, History of Construction, 3:2–8 [1.1.1.87.4]; Michael J. Dunn III, "The Birmingham & Southern Railroad," *Alabama Historical Quarterly* 27 (Spring/Summer 1965): 65–66 (contents of this essay prove that there is a typographical error in the title; it should be Southeastern, not Southern); Wayne Cline, *Alabama Railroads* (Tuscaloosa: University of Alabama Press, 1997), 219–21; *Powergrams*, September 1924, 38–39.

106. Martin Dam, Annual Report of 1926, January 11, 1927 [1.1.2.86.8]; Jackson, "*Loafing Streams*," 131–34.

107. Martin, *Electricity in Alabama*, 66–67.

108. Laying the Cornerstone and Dedication of Martin Dam, 7–9 [1.1.2.20.4].

109. Jackson, "*Loafing Streams*," 117–36.

110. Martin Dam, History of Construction, 4:51–56 [1.1.1.87.4].

111. Minutes, Board of Directors, Alabama Power Company, June 16, 1926, 7:51–52.

112. Unidentified clipping, April 23, 1928, in Scrapbook No. 1, Martin Library, SRI.

113. Laying the Cornerstone and Dedication of Martin Dam, 16–39 [1.1.2.20.4]; Murray, *Martin*, 95–100; Jackson, "*Loafing Streams*," 150.

114. Major H. Burgess, Corps of Engineers, Report, House of Representatives, April 5, 1915, 64th Cong., 1st sess., Doc. No. 1261, 41 [2.1.2.36.14].

115. "Report of Power Market and Use of Central Station Power in Southern States" (n.d., ca. 1913). These statistics were based upon 1910 census data. Map of Transmission Systems of Power Companies in Southern States, 1913 [2.1.1.56.7].

116. Memorandum to the Directors of the Alabama Traction, Light & Power Co., Ltd., from James Mitchell, President, Alabama Power Company, marked "Private-Confidential," n.d., but ca. 1919 [2.1.1.26.6].

117. Map dated January 5, 1916, and James Mitchell to W. N. Walmsley, February 19, 1917 [2.1.1.18.26].

118. In all early documents and correspondence in the APC files, the writers refer to the Georgia Railway, Light & Power Company, while Wade H. Wright, *History of the Georgia Power Company, 1855–1956* (Atlanta: Georgia Power, 1957), uses the name Georgia Railway & Power Company. Oscar G. Thurlow to W. N. Walmsley, January 26, 1917; W. E. Mitchell to W. N. Walmsley, April 4, 1917 [2.1.1.18.26].

119. "The Power Situation During the War," report of the Chief of Engineers, United States Army, 1921, quoted at length in draft of a history of the Alabama Power Company with notes written by Tom Martin, 124–26 [2.1.1.56.17].

120. *Birmingham News*, October 31, 1921 [4.1.2.22.5].

121. Martin, *Electricity in Alabama*, 58; Carol Muse Evans, *The Complete Guide to Alabama Weather* (Birmingham: Seacoast Publishing, 1999), 96.

122. Martin, *Electricity in Alabama*, 58–59.

123. *Los Angeles Times*, November 12, 1923.

124. *Blue Book of Southern Progress*, Manufacturers Record, Baltimore, Maryland, 1924, 130–31 [3.1.2.52.8]. This book had much of the same material in it that came from an article Tom Martin wrote for *Manufacturers Record* the same year. See Thomas W. Martin, "Hydro-Electric Development in the South," *Manufacturers Record*, December 11, 1924, 241–52, copy in 1.1.2.20.16.

125. Thomas W. Martin, *Southern Power Development*, speech to the spring convention of the American Institute of Electrical Engineers, April 8, 1924 [1.1.2.20.16].

126. *Birmingham News*, December 18, 1921 [4.1.2.22.5].

127. *Christian Science Monitor*, March 22, 1922. The newspaper reported that 58 percent of the ownership was held in England, Scotland, the Netherlands, and Canada.

128. *Annual Report*, Alabama Power Company, Year Ended December 31, 1923, 4; Pynchon & Company advertisement, *Wall Street Journal*, June 22, 1923; *Birmingham Age-Herald*, December 15, 1921; *Powergrams*, January 1923, 18; March 1923, 8.

129. Lee N. Allen, "Twenty-Four Votes for Oscar W. Underwood," *Alabama Review* 48 (October 1995): 243–68; *New York Times*, July 6, 8, 10, 12, 14, 1924. The *New York Times* published a long list of some of the bar association members who sailed on July 12, but Martin's name is not on the list. Hotel receipt from Queen Anne's Mansions, St. James Park, shows the Martins arrived in London on July 18, so they probably sailed from New York about July 9, which incidentally was the day the Democratic convention adjourned after nominating Wall Street lawyer John W. Davis. Martin's biographer is incorrect in saying the Martins left New York on July 19, and he is also incorrect in spelling E. Mackay Edgar's name. See Murray, *Martin*, 71. Hotel receipt, programs,

and social invitations from the bar association meeting are in London Travel file, Martin Library, SRI. On July 9, the *Times* (London) published a report that Alabama Traction, Light & Power preferred stock would be receiving a 3 percent dividend on July 10.

130. *New York Times*, July 6, 1924. Martin certainly had worked closely with Edgar and Sperling in the months leading up to his trip to London, and they surely understood the reasons for his visit.

131. *Powergrams*, April 1920, 5.

132. *New York Times*, December 16, 1923; *Wall Street Journal*, December 17, 1923; *New York Times*, November 2, 1923. James Mitchell was involved in the Sperling deal with Doherty and Company, but this was initiated in July 1911 before he came to Alabama.

133. *Wall Street Journal*, October 15, 1924; *New York Times*, March 5, 1925.

134. Martin, *Electricity in Alabama*, 42–44, 58–59; Murray, *Martin*, 70–72.

135. London Travel file, Martin Library, SRI.

136. *New York Times*, January 6, 1926; obituaries of Sir Edward Mackay Edgar, *New York Times*, October 9, 1934; "Newsletter Number Five," Society of Edgar Families, from the *Argus*, Melbourne, Australia, November 10, 1934. Edgar had one son who predeceased him, so there was no heir for the baronetcy. No correspondence has been found between Edgar and Tom Martin after Edgar's bankruptcy, but it would be in Martin's character for him to have found quiet ways to see that funds reached Edgar in his years of distress. Martin did keep Sir Edgar on the board of directors of Southeastern Power & Light Company as long as he controlled that holding company.

137. *Wall Street Journal*, September 9, 1924; *Washington Post*, September 9, 1924.

138. Southeastern Power & Light Company, Articles of Agreement, Minutes of Meetings, Certificate of Organization and By-Laws [1.1.1.1.158].

139. Heys interview with Jack Bingham, March 25, 1999, 4; interviews with Betty Clark Brower, September 15, 22, 2004.

140. "Notice, To Shareholders, Alabama Traction, Light & Power Co., Ltd.," October 15, 1914 [3.1.1.17.15].

141. Martin, *Electricity in Alabama*, 59; *Wall Street Journal*, September 11, October 11, 1924; *Chicago Daily Tribune*, October 11, 1924; *New York Times*, October 11, 1924.

142. *Powergrams*, July 1926, 1, 6.

143. Information from W. J. Henderson's granddaughter, Joan Henderson Warbis, March 24, 2006; William J. Henderson, "An Overview of the Development of Alabama Traction, Light and Power Company, Ltd.," Montreal, January 21, 1924, Henderson file; flyer, Coffin & Burr; flyer, Harris, Forbes & Co. [3.1.1.17.15].

144. Martin, *Electricity in Alabama*, 57.

145. Joseph M. Farley, *Alabama Power Company: "Developed for the service of Alabama"* (New York: Newcomen Society of the United States, 1988), 13.

146. Joseph M. Farley, Eason Balch, and Chris Conway, "Alabama Power Company History Project: 'Good Name and Destiny,'" unpublished ms., copy in Alabama Power Corporate Archives, 26.

147. Copies of Southeastern Power & Light Company sample stock certificates and Voting Trust Agreement, W. H. Hassinger and Thomas W. Martin, Trustees, October 15, 1924 [1.1.1.1.158].

148. W. E. Mitchell to Thomas Bragg, January 13, 1924 [4.1.1.27.12], and Voting Trust Agreement [1.1.1.1.158].

149. Howard Duryea to W. E. Mitchell, July 10, 1923 [4.1.1.27.12].

150. "Holders of 10,000 Shares or More of Southeastern Power & Light Company, Common Stock, As At June 21, 1927" [3.1.1.17.15]. There were only three listings of non-USA holders: Sir Edward Baulet Stracey (London), 20,350 (.961 percent); Kleinwort Sons & Company (London), 34,000 (1.608 percent); and W. W. Thompson and V. H. Crouch (Montreal), 52,635 (2.486 percent).

151. Marwick, Mitchell & Company, Accountants and Auditors, to W. E. Mitchell, Frederick S. Ruth, and H. S. Swan, October 11, 1920, audited books and records of James Mitchell, January 1 to July 22, 1920. The estate accounting shows that Mitchell held only 18,383 shares of common stock and 100 shares of preferred in Alabama Traction. See James Mitchell Personal Papers. The corporate minute books for Alabama Traction, Light & Power Company and Southeastern Power & Light have not been located.

152. *Mobile Register*, July 22, 1929. During the 1920s the Mobile newspaper was extremely hostile to the Alabama Power Company but was probably correct on the stock sale because it fits with information in APC files [1.1.2.65.7 and 3.1.1.17.15].

153. "Holders of 10,000 Shares or More of Southeastern Power & Light Company, Common Stock, As At June 21, 1927" [3.1.1.17.15].

154. Norman Sharpe Buchanan, "The Electric Bond and Share Company: A Case Study of a Public Utility Holding Company" (Ph.D. diss., Cornell University, 1931), 182. It is also interesting that Buchanan explains the voting trust that EBASCO had in place to protect itself, and the trustee of this trust was S. Z. Mitchell; see page 129.

155. Lewis, *Sloss Furnaces*, 180–81; Bernice Shield Hassinger, *Henderson Steel: Birmingham's First Steel* (Birmingham: Gray Printing/Birmingham Jefferson County Historical Commission, 1978), vii, 1, 49; Armes, *Story of Coal and Iron*, 256–57; James Bowron gives a different view of Hassinger; see Robert J. Norrell, ed., *James Bowron: The Autobiography of a New South Industrialist* (Chapel Hill: University of North Carolina Press, 1991), 196–200.

156. Farley, Balch, and Conway, "'Good Name and Destiny,'" 26.

157. *Wall Street Journal*, July 31, August 13, 1925; *Washington Post*, August 13, 1925.

158. *Los Angeles Times*, August 19, 1925; *Wall Street Journal*, August 21, 1925; *New York Times*, August 21, 1925.

159. *Wall Street Journal*, August 26, 1925.

160. Ibid., December 3, 1925.

161. F. S. Keeler, "Talk for Lions and Engineers Clubs of Mobile," reprinted, *Powergrams*, July 1943, 6–8.

162. W. Hubert Joiner, *Let Us Reason Together: A History of Labor Relations of the Georgia Power Company* (Atlanta: Georgia Power Co., 1979), 29.

163. Wright, *History of Georgia Power*, 214–15.

164. To Stockholders of Georgia Railway & Power Company, January 18, 1926, and H. M. Atkinson to Thomas W. Martin, February 20, 1926 [3.1.1.18.7]; "History of the Southeastern Power & Light Company" (no author, but typescript has editing in Tom Martin's handwriting; n.d., but ca. 1927), 6 [1.1.1.4.19]; *Annual Report*, Southeastern Power & Light Company, 1926, 3 [1.1.1.43.6].

165. Eugene A. Yates to W. J. Henderson, April 1, 1926 [3.1.1.17.15].

166. W. E. Mitchell to Eugene A. Yates, June 24, 1926

[3.1.1.18.7]; Southeastern Engineering Company, incorporation records [3.1.1.29.62].

167. *Atlanta Constitution*, June 14, 1926 [3.1.1.18.7].

168. Eugene A. Yates to Preston S. Arkwright, June 15, 1926 [3.1.1.18.7]; *Annual Report*, Southeastern Power & Light Company, 1926, 3; *Snap Shots*, March 1927, 4 [1.1.2.65.3]; Wright, *History of Georgia Power*, 213–18; A. W. Dahlberg, *Georgia Power Company: A Story of Georgia's Growth and Georgia's Future* (New York: Newcomen Society of the United States, 1994), 9–12. Dahlberg, a former president of Georgia Power and in 1994 president of the Southern Company, failed to mention the part Thomas W. Martin and Southeastern Power & Light played in the creation of Georgia Power. This is not unusual for Newcomen papers. For instance, William T. McCormick Jr., CEO of CMS Energy Corporation, stated in his history of CMS Energy that Michigan's Consumers Power Company was "the strongest, biggest part of one of the largest holding company groups—The Commonwealth & Southern Corporation." McCormick, *EMS Energy Corporation* (New York: Newcomen Society of the United States, 1995), 13. James C. Bonbright and Gardiner C. Means, *The Holding Company: Its Public Significance and Its Regulation* (1932; reprint, New York: Augustus M. Kelley, 1969), 129, gives the Georgia Power Company and its six subsidiaries alone assets of $274 million that equal Consumers Power's $274 million. Alabama Power Company assets were listed as $190 million. The Commonwealth & Southern annual report for 1932 does not list assets by companies.

169. Harllee Branch Jr., *Alabama Power Company and The Southern Company* (New York: Newcomen Society of the United States, 1966), 13–14.

170. Tindall, *Emergence of the New South*, 24.

171. Chester Morgan and Donald M. Dana Jr., *A Priceless Heritage: The Story of Mississippi Power Company* (Gulfport: Mississippi Power Co., 1993), 1–5; A. J. Watson Jr., *Electric Power and People Power: The Story of the Mississippi Power Company* (New York: Newcomen Society in North America, 1960), 9.

172. J. M. Barry, "Report to Mr. T. W. Martin on Mississippi Situation," January 5, 1925 [1.1.1.4.20]. Barry gave a town-by-town analysis of the Mississippi electrical situation.

173. Morgan and Dana, *Priceless Heritage*, 1–11. This was actually the second Mississippi Power Company. An earlier organizational attempt was folded into this company.

174. *A Tradition of Service: Gulf Power Company, 1926–2001* (Pensacola: Gulf Power Co., 2001), 2.

175. *Annual Report*, Southeastern Power & Light Company and Subsidiary Companies, Including Alabama Traction, Light & Power Company, Ltd., 1924, 5; 1926, 6 [1.1.1.42.6]; *Tradition of Service: Gulf Power*, 1–2.

176. Wells M. Stanley to Eugene A. Yates, February 9, 1925 [3.1.1.18.16]; Crist, *They Electrified the South*, 135.

177. *Powergrams*, June 1921, 3; Alabama Power Company, Exhibits, Biographical Sketch of Wells M. Stanley [3.1.1.19.12].

178. *Annual Report*, Southeastern Power & Light Company, 1927, 4; 1928, 3 [1.1.1.43.6]; Farley, *Alabama Power Company*, 12.

179. *Tradition of Service: Gulf Power*, 1–4.

180. *Annual Report*, Southeastern Power & Light Company, 1925, 3 [1.1.2.113.2].

181. Nell C. Pogue, *South Carolina Electric & Gas Company, 1846–1964* (Columbia, S.C.: State Printing Co., 1964), 23–25, 27–29.

182. *Forbes*, June 15, 1925, 323–25 [1.1.2.65.2]; B. C. Forbes, "Forbes Public Service Club," *San Francisco Examiner* (n.d., but 1924), clipping in Scrapbook No.1, Martin Library, SRI.

183. Marjorie Longnecker White, *Downtown Birmingham: Architectural and Historical Walking Tour Guide* (Birmingham: Birmingham Historical Society, 1980), 34–35, 118–19; typed sheet, no author, n.d., in folder, Electra/1925 Building.

184. *In Celebration of the Restoration of Alabama Power Company's 1925 Tower*, Alabama Power Company brochure (written by James Alexander with research by Marjorie White), ca. 1988, in folder, Electra/1925 Building.

185. *Powergrams*, December 1924, 18. For the association of Nesselroth and Warren, Knight & Davis and a feature on the building, see *Birmingham News*, November 1, 1925, gravure section. Copy in Thomas W. Martin, Scrapbook No. 1, front pocket, Martin Library, SRI.

186. John M. Schnorrenberg, *Remembered Past, Discovered Future: The Alabama Architecture of Warren, Knight & Davis, 1906–1961* (Birmingham: Birmingham Museum of Art, 1999), 69, 134, note 182.

187. William T. Warren to Thomas W. Martin, August 9, 1926, in Nesselroth file.

188. *Annual Report*, Alabama Power Company for Year Ended December 31, 1924, 27; Marjorie White, "The Birmingham District: A Survey of Cultural Resources," Birmingham Historical Society Study for National Park Service, 1993, 224–26; *In Celebration of Restoration: Remembered Past, Discovered Future: The Alabama Architecture of Warren, Knight & Davis, 1901–1961: A Self-Guided Walking Tour*, Birmingham Museum of Art brochure, folder, Electra/1925 Building; Robert Gamble, *The Alabama Catalog: Historical American Building Survey* (Tuscaloosa: University of Alabama Press, 1987), 158–59; White, *Downtown Birmingham*, 4; *Powergrams*, March 1925, 7, 14.

189. *Annual Report*, Alabama Power Company, 1925, 14.

190. *Electra: Symbol of Alabama Electrified*, APC brochure; Sigmund Nesselroth, "Statue to Surmount Building," *Powergrams*, May 1925, 1; "Interview with Edward Field Sanford, Jr.," *Powergrams*, July 1925, 10; R. K. Jeffries, "Raising the Statue," *Powergrams*, July 1926, 6.

191. See the collected chapters of "The Love Story of Vulcan and Electra," reprinted in July 1926, as they appeared in the *Birmingham Post*. The nom de plume of the columnist had something to do with a nickname given to a twenty-nine-year-old, who at the time was calling Birmingham Barons baseball games from a ticker tape at the local radio station. Filling in gaps on the tape by "shooting the bull," Eugene Connor's booming voice was gaining popularity in the city, and he was soon called "Bull." William A. Nunnelley, *Bull Connor* (Tuscaloosa: University of Alabama Press, 1991), 12.

192. H. C. Nixon, *Lower Piedmont Country: The Uplands of the Deep South* (New York: Duell, Sloan & Pierce, 1946; reprint, Tuscaloosa: University of Alabama Press, 1984), 22. Andrew Lytle's novel, *The Long Night* (1936; reprint, Tuscaloosa: University of Alabama Press, 1988), is set in the Wetumpka–Devil's Staircase area of the Coosa River where in the dark one could "get his bearings by the sound of the Staircase" (139).

193. Jackson, "Loafing Streams," 157–59.

194. Thomas W. Martin, Notes for Jordan Dam Dedication, Jordan Dam file, Martin Library, SRI.

195. Jordan Dam Dedication Program, November 21, 1927, 9.

196. Minutes, Board of Trustees, University of Alabama, September 1, 1927, Hoole Library, UA.

197. *Powergrams*, October 1927, 1–2; December 1927, 16–20.

198. *Annual Report*, Alabama Power Company for the Year Ending December 31, 1929.

199. *Powergrams*, December 1925, 13–16.

200. Golden, *History of Tallassee*, 64; Martin, *Electricity in Alabama*, 16, 38; Jackson, "Loafing Streams," 203–04.

201. Unidentified clipping, April 23, 1928, in Scrapbook No. 1, Martin Library, SRI; Thurlow Dam Dedication Program [1.1.2.88.4]; Jackson, "Loafing Streams," 204–06.

202. *Powergrams*, November 1939, 3; Thurlow Dam Dedication Program [1.1.2.88.4].

203. *Florence News*, September 25, 1928; *Alabama Journal*, September 25, 1928; *Mobile Register*, September 29, 1928 [1.1.2.65.6].

204. See photograph of the lobby directory, *Powergrams*, April 1927, 15.

205. *Birmingham News*, September 29, 1928.

206. James B. Sellers, "History of the University of Alabama, 1902–1957," ms., 36, and George H. Denny to the Board of Trustees, October 16, 1928, attached to the Minutes of the Board of Trustees, October 20, 1928, 564–70, Hoole Library, UA. Thomas left the power company after the controversy broke and for several months worked under the auspices of the State Industrial Commission pushing his industrial diversification campaign; however, some months later he left the university and was employed full time by Alabama Power Company.

207. Ralph E. Poore Jr., "Alabama's Enterprising Newspaper: The *Mobile Press-Register* and Its Forebears, 1813–1991," 193, ms. available at the Mobile City Archives and the University of South Alabama; *The Telegraph* (Macon, Georgia), clipping, n.d.; *Mobile Register*, July 7, 14, 1929 [1.1.2.65.7].

208. Victor Hanson acquired a controlling interest in the *Birmingham Age-Herald* on March 1, 1927, and all stock on June 1, 1927. Leah Rawls Atkins, "A Sense of Mission: The 1920s," in *The Birmingham News: Our First 100 Years*, ed. Emily Jones (Birmingham: Birmingham News, 1988), 75.

209. Judith Sheppard, "Mobile's Own Ozymandias: Ralph B. Chandler and His Newspapers," *Alabama Heritage* 51 (Winter 1999): 26–27; King E. Williams Jr., *The Press of Alabama: A History of the Alabama Press Association* (Birmingham: Alabama Press Association, 1997), 67.

210. Some investors in the *Mobile Press* were J. L. Bedsole, W. D. Bellingrath, D. P. Bestor Jr., John T. Cochrane, Francis Inge, F. Marion Inge, J. F. and J. G. McGowin, T. M. Stevens, Jasper Van Antwerp, and G. M. Luce. List of names and biographical data published in *Mobile Press*, July 1, 1929. John M. Collier, *Earl McGowin of Alabama: A Portrait* (New Orleans: Faust Publishing Co., 1986), 10–20.

211. Sheppard, "Mobile's Own," 28. Sheppard gives the name as U.S. Senator Frank Norris, but there was no such person. It was George Norris.

212. Walter C. Johnson and Arthur T. Robb, *The South and Its Newspapers*, 1903–1953 (Chattanooga, Tenn.: Southern Newspaper Publishers Association, 1954; reprint, Westport, Conn.: Greenwood Press, 1974), 141–42.

213. *New York Times*, May 27, 1929.

214. *Mobile Press*, July 5; *Alabama Journal*, July 3, 5; *Birmingham Age-Herald*, June 20; *Washington Herald*, June 20; *Mobile Register*, June 19, 24, 25, 28, 30, July 1, 7, 1929 [1.1.2.65.7]. The national newspapers were filled with information about this testimony in Washington.

Note that it was at the same time that the Commonwealth & Southern Corporation was getting off the ground and Southeastern Power & Light stock was being transferred to C&S stock. See *Washington Post*, June 11, 12, 1929; *New York Times*, June 15, 20, 21, 1929; *Los Angeles Times*, June 20, 1929; *Wall Street Journal*, June 13, 1929.

215. Poore, "Mobile Press-Register," 194, 198–99; Sheppard, "Mobile's Own," 28–30. The interesting thing about this testimony is the pitting of the legal brains of the FTC attorney, who was questioning, and Tom and Logan Martin, who were answering, and while not about to lie neither would they volunteer anything [1.1.2.65.7].

216. Poore, "Mobile Press-Register," 199.

217. See Ernest Gruening, *The Public Pays: A Study of Power Propaganda* (1931; reprint, New York: Vanguard Press, 1964).

218. George Bush, *Future Builders: The Story of Michigan's Consumers Power Company* (New York: McGraw-Hill, 1973), 167–68.

219. Forrest McDonald, *Insull* (Chicago: University of Chicago Press, 1962), 249.

220. *New York Times*, May 7, September 5, 1928.

221. Ibid., August 1, 1925, May 1, 1926.

222. *Los Angeles Times*, March 12, 1927.

223. *Wall Street Journal*, May 24, 1928, clipping in Scrapbook No. 1, Martin Library, SRI.

224. *New York Times*, August 21, 1927, December 11, 1928, January 13, 1929.

225. Southeastern Power & Light's *Annual Report* for 1927 showed a new income of $6.1 million, an increase of $1.3 million over the previous year. *New York Times*, June 28, 1928.

226. *New York Times*, January 11, 1929; Bonbright and Means, *Holding Company*, 39, 127–37.

227. Jennet Conant, *Tuxedo Park: A Wall Street Tycoon and the Secret Palace of Science That Changed the Course of World War II* (New York: Simon & Schuster, 2002), 39–41.

228. In December 1929 the *Wall Street Journal* gave a review of the mergers and developments in utilities over the year, noting that "no other year has witnessed merger operations of the same size." *Wall Street Journal*, December 25, 1929.

229. *New York Times*, April 5, May 5, 1929.

230. Report on Property and Operations of the Southeastern Power & Light Company, Coverdale & Colpitts, November 28, 1927 [1.1.1.70.3].

231. *New York Times*, September 5, 1928; Hearing before the Securities and Exchange Commission, Answer, The Commonwealth & Southern Corporation, 58–59, filed April 30, 1940, 5.

232. Bush, *Future Builders*, 245–46, 503.

233. Oral history interview with Lyman Robinson, ca. 1970s, 29–30, courtesy of Consumers Power Company/Consumers Energy, Jackson, Michigan.

234. Bush, *Future Builders*, 245–46, 503.

235. Conant, *Tuxedo Park*, 41; *Annual Report*, Commonwealth & Southern, 1929–30.

236. Certificate of Incorporation, C&S Corporation, May 23, 1929, Martin Library, SRI. *Christian Science Monitor*, May 24, 1929.

237. Testimony of W. Logan Martin before the Federal Trade Commission, Wednesday, June 26, 1929, reprinted in *Mobile Register*, June 26, 1929. The attorney who was questioning Logan

Martin regrettably changed his line of questions without asking for details on the organization of Commonwealth & Southern.

238. *Wall Street Journal*, May 30, 1929. Southeastern Power & Light option warrants were offered two shares of Commonwealth & Southern and one option warrant.

239. *New York Times*, June 1, 7, 1929. Southeastern Power & Light stock, which was being sold on the Curb Market, was up. Everyone anticipated it would eventually be folded into C&S. *Wall Street Journal*, June 7, 8, 11, 1929.

240. *New York Times*, June 13, 1929; *Wall Street Journal*, June 13, 1929; *Washington Post*, June 14, 1929. On June 22 the *Wall Street Journal* reported that the demand for transferring stock to Commonwealth & Southern stock was so overwhelming that the company was not able to do it "in the usual time." *Los Angeles Times*, July 11, 1929. The *Wall Street Journal* reported on July 14 that Southeastern Power would be moving into offices at 20 Pine Street and that C&S owned 90 percent of its common stock.

241. Bonbright and Means, *Holding Company*, 128–29. United Gas Improvement Company held control of 26.2 percent of the market and Niagara Hudson Power Corporation held 22.3 percent.

242. Report to the Stockholders, the Commonwealth & Southern Corporation, June 23, 1930; Martin, *Electricity in Alabama*, 140.

243. For instance, see *Carrollton Herald*, June 13, 1929, *Bessemer Advocate*, June 13, 1929, and *Atlanta Constitution*, May 31, 1929, clippings in C&S file, and Hobert A. McWhorter to Thomas W. Martin, June 6, 1929, all in Martin Library, SRI.

244. Crist, *They Electrified the South*, 54.

245. Lyman Robinson interview, 11, 14.

246. Murray, *Martin*, 93.

247. Program, Dedication of Thurlow Dam, 45–46 [1.1.2.88.4].

248. Robert Sobel, *The Big Board: A History of the New York Stock Market* (New York: Free Press, 1965), 259.

249. Edwin P. Hoyt Jr., *The House of Morgan* (New York: Dodd, Mead & Co., 1966), 374–76.

250. Galbraith, *Great Crash of 1929*, 5–6.

251. Sobel, *Big Board*, 259.

252. Robert Sobel, *Panic on Wall Street: A History of America's Financial Disasters* (New York: Macmillan, 1968), 350–56.

253. Murray, *Martin*, 52–53, 83, 88.

254. *New York Times*, October 20, 1929; Galbraith, *Great Crash of 1929*, 100.

255. Martin, *Electricity in Alabama*, 101, 175; Murray, *Martin*, 83–84, 88.

256. *New York Times*, October 27, 1929.

257. Galbraith, *Great Crash of 1929*, 101–23.

258. Minutes, Board of Directors, Alabama Power Company, October 29, 1929, 9:1–2. There are no cumulative pages in this volume.

259. Dedication of the Lock 12 Development of Alabama Power Company, Designated as Lay Dam [4.1.2.22.5]. See also file 1.1.1.4.25 for details of the event.

260. *New York Times*, October 30, 1929.

261. McDonald, *Let There Be Light*, 299–300.

262. The official cause of death for Searle, who was sixty years old, was "suicide during temporary mental derangement." A gas jet in a wall was found open. He was president of the Rochester Gas and Electric Corporation. *New York Times*, November 14, 1929.

263. Murray, *Martin*, 88.

Chapter Five

1. Anthony J. Badger, *The New Deal: The Depression Years, 1933–1940* (New York: Hill & Wang, 1989), 1–38.

2. *New York Times*, August 31, 1930.

3. On May 13, 1930, C&S warrants sold for a high of $6\frac{1}{4}$ and a low of $3\frac{1}{2}$, and the next day stock was selling at a low of $17\frac{1}{8}$ and a high of $17\frac{1}{4}$. Two years later C&S stock was selling at a high of $10\frac{1}{2}$ and low of 2. *New York Times*, May 13, 14, 15, 1930, April 12, 1932. Ellsworth Barnard, *Wendell Willkie: Fighter for Freedom* (Marquette: Northern Michigan University Press, 1966), 79.

4. There are many personal reminiscences of the Great Depression in Alabama. Perhaps the strongest may be found in James Seay Brown Jr., ed., *Up before Daylight: Life Histories from the Alabama Writers' Project, 1938–1939* (Tuscaloosa: University of Alabama Press, 1982). From the power company's standpoint the most interesting essay is by Jack Kytle, "I'm Allus Hongry," 118–27.

5. *Annual Report*, Alabama Power Company, 1930, 4–5.

6. Ed Thompson to Leah Atkins, November 1, 2003.

7. Typed Notes, December 19, 1929 [3.1.1.27.56].

8. *New York Times*, January 8, 1930; *Wall Street Journal*, January 8, 1930; *New York Times*, February 15, 1930.

9. *Christian Science Monitor*, February 15, May 24, 1930; *New York Times*, May 21, 1930.

10. *Christian Science Monitor*, January 11, 1930; *Wall Street Journal*, January 16, 30, 1930; *New York Times*, January 8, February 15, 1930. Intermediate holding companies, including Southeastern Power & Light Company, were abolished in July.

11. *Wall Street Journal*, January 16, 30, April 4, 1930; *New York Times*, April 4, May 25, 1930.

12. *Wall Street Journal*, July 3, 1930.

13. Ibid., November 13, 1930.

14. *Annual Report*, Commonwealth & Southern Corporation, 1930, 5; *Annual Report*, Commonwealth & Southern Corporation, 1932, 10; Barnard, *Willkie*, 83.

15. Salary sheet with B. C. Cobb correspondence in the Wendell L. Willkie Papers, courtesy of the Lilly Library, Indiana University, Bloomington, Indiana.

16. Howard Duryea to Thomas W. Martin, November 26, 1929 [3.1.1.27.60]; Robert M. MacLetchie to Eugene A. Yates, February 8, 1930 [3.1.2.27.55].

17. Crist, *They Electrified the South*, 54. Although the companies in Commonwealth & Southern were more midwestern than northern, the word northern is used by company employees and in company records.

18. Lyman Robinson interview, 30–31.

19. Barnard, *Willkie*, 80.

20. Smith asked Roosevelt, but his first choice was Owen Young, head of General Electric. Christopher M. Finan, *Alfred E. Smith: The Happy Warrior* (New York: Hill & Wang, 2002), 236.

21. Frank Freidel, *Franklin D. Roosevelt: A Rendezvous with Destiny* (Boston: Little, Brown & Co., 1990), 40. Antony C. Sutton, in his book, *Wall Street and FDR* (New Rochelle, N.Y.: Arlington House Publishers, 1975), gives interesting information and interpretations on the connections among various businesses housed at 120 Broadway and the men who worked in that building, particularly in his chapter, "The Corporate Socialists at 120 Broadway." It is difficult to believe that Martin would have been ignorant of the political connections and philosophical leanings of some of these powerful groups. Owen D. Young and General Electric, as well as Bernard Baruch, Stone & Webster, and the Federal Reserve Bank of New York were located there in the 1920s. In the 1930s, the New York offices of Commonwealth & Southern were located at 20 Pine Street, which was just around the corner from 120 Broadway.

22. Willkie's entire speech, including the full letter, is included in *Government and the Public Utilities*, an Address of Wendell L. Willkie, January 21, 1935, Rare Books, Hoole Library, UA, 25–26. Willkie quoted part of the letter in his testimony against the Wheeler-Rayburn bill (which became the Public Utility Holding Company Act) in the spring of 1935. See *Hearings, House Committee on Interstate and Foreign Commerce*, Public Utility Holding Companies, Parts 1, 2, and 3, 74th Cong. (Washington, D.C.: Government Printing Office, 1935), Part 2: 604, 645; Barnard, *Willkie*, 91. Roosevelt's version is different as it appears in an excerpt of a Barnesville, Georgia, speech that he made on August 11, 1938, to dedicate a municipal power corporation. It is included in Wright, *History of Georgia Power*, 284–93. On page 6 of the *Annual Report*, Southeastern Power & Light, 1926, the company notes that by constructing "480 miles of transmission lines several of the isolated steam electric power plants and local distribution systems obtained through the Georgia acquisition have been interconnected with the power system of the Georgia Power Company and their operations coordinated and directed by that Company." See also the map attached to the report.

23. Quoted in "Alabama Industrial Program," address of Thomas W. Martin, September 16, 1936, 5 [1.1.2.20.16].

24. Frank Freidel, *Franklin D. Roosevelt: Launching the New Deal* (Boston: Little, Brown & Co., 1973), 27–28, 63–64.

25. Daniel R. Fusfeld, *The Economic Thought of Franklin D. Roosevelt and the Origins of the New Deal* (New York: AMS Press, 1970), 135–36; James MacGregor Burns, *Roosevelt: The Lion and the Fox* (New York: Harcourt, Brace & World, 1956), 114–15.

26. Bernard Bellush, *Franklin D. Roosevelt as Governor of New York* (New York: Columbia University Press, 1955; reprint, New York: AMS Press, 1968), 208–09, 212–18, 220–21.

27. On April 15, 1931, Senator Thomas J. Walsh of Montana wrote Roosevelt that his victory in the St. Lawrence dispute would affect the Muscle Shoals controversy. Bellush, *Roosevelt as Governor*, 237–38.

28. The book was published in New York by McGraw-Hill and was reprinted in 1969 by Augustus M. Kelley.

29. *New York Times*, August 30, 1929; Burns, *Roosevelt*, 117.

30. Carl D. Thompson, *Confessions of the Power Trust* (New York: E. P. Dutton & Co., 1932), 574–95, denies any connections between the National Popular Government League, the People's Legislative Service, and the Public Ownership League and the Socialist Party, yet Thompson was the Social Democratic candidate for governor of Wisconsin in 1912 and was associated in the 1920s with progressives who advocated government ownership; King, *Conservation Fight*, 88; Rudolph and Ridley, *Power Struggle*, 45–46; Edwin Vennard, *Government in the Power Business* (New York: McGraw-Hill, 1968), 35–36; and Frederick L. Collins, *Uncle Sam's Billion-Dollar Baby: A Taxpayer*

Looks at the TVA (New York: G. P. Putnam's Sons, 1945), 80–81. One thought to keep in mind is that the perception of the differences between "progressivism" and "socialism" has changed over the years and needs to be understood here in the context of the 1920s and 1930s.

31. Rudolph and Ridley, *Power Struggle*, 47.

32. Davidson, *The Tennessee*, 2:187; Hubbard, *Origins of the TVA*, 147.

33. Johnson, *Underwood*, 360–61. Stephen Raushenbush, *The Power Fight* (New York: New Republic, 1932), 185, makes the same charge, which was commonly found in the print media of the period. All internal documents show that despite EBASCO being the agent for some bond sales, owning some common stock, holding securities, and one or two men associated with EBASCO on the board of directors of Alabama Power Company or Southeastern Power & Light Company, neither company was "owned" or "controlled" by EBASCO; actually preventing such EBASCO control was a continuing thread in the company's history.

34. Even a Federal Trade Commission staff investigator testified in January 1931 that there appeared to be a "connection or community of interest" between Alabama Power Company and the Birmingham Electric Company because C. E. Groesbeck and Sidney Z. Mitchell served on the Alabama Power and Commonwealth & Southern boards and also on the Electric Bond & Share board that owned Birmingham Electric Company, a wholesale customer of Alabama Power. See *Utility Corporations, Federal Trade Commission, Alabama Power Co.*, 70th Cong., 1st sess., Doc. 92, Part 30 (Washington, D.C.: Government Printing Office, 1931), 5; Buchanan, "Electric Bond and Share," 85.

35. Thomas W. Martin to W. J. Henderson, December 22, 1932, Henderson file. A minority interest might exert control over a company because other stock ownership was scattered and widespread; however, James Mitchell personally held a large block of stock in Alabama Traction. This was the stock (noted in the last chapter) that went into the holding trust that W. H. Hassinger helped create and Tom Martin controlled. See Bonbright and Means, *Holding Company*, 6–9.

36. "The Reference to a Commission and Joint Committee: Climax of the Effort for Private Power Development," chap. 7 in Hubbard, "Muscle Shoals Controversy," 291–329.

37. Robert Sobel, *Coolidge: An American Enigma* (Washington, D.C.: Regnery Publishing, 1998), 274.

38. William Allen White, *A Puritan in Babylon: The Story of Calvin Coolidge* (New York: Macmillan, 1940), 261–62.

39. Martin, *Electricity in Alabama*, 102–04; *Annual Report*, Alabama Power Company, 1926, 14–15; 1927, 14.

40. "Joint Proposal, Muscle Shoals Fertilizer Co. and Muscle Shoals Power Distribution Co., as Reported to Congress by Joint Committee on Muscle Shoals, April 26, 1926," compares the power company bid with that of Air Nitrates, the subsidiary of the American Cyanamid Company [1.1.2.20.2].

41. "Proposal Relating to Muscle Shoals," submitted by Air Nitrates Corporation and American Cyanamid Company, April 9, 1926, in Lister Hill Papers, Hoole Library, UA; Johnson, *Underwood*, 367–68.

42. *Montgomery Journal*, April 14, 1926, clipping in Lister Hill Papers, Hoole Library, UA.

43. Hubbard, *Origins of the TVA*, 183–203, 222; Virginia Van der Veer Hamilton, *Hugo Black: The Alabama Years* (Baton Rouge: Louisiana State University Press, 1972), 125–26; Johnson, *Underwood*, 364–69.

44. New York Times, June 29, July 1, 1930.

45. Anne O'Hare McCormick, "The Great Dam Controversy," New York Times, April 20, 1930.

46. McDonald, Insull, 265–67; Richard Cudahy, "Insull and Enron: Is There a Parallel?" Infrastructure 42–43 (Spring, Summer, Fall 2003): Part 3, 7–8 .

47. McDonald, Insull, 267–70.

48. See an interview with Walsh, clipping, New York Times, October 13, 1929, in Scrapbook No. 1, 3, Martin Library, SRI.

49. Hubbard, Origins of the TVA, 219–21.

50. Thomas W. Martin to Hon. J. Thomas Heflin, February 25, 1928, printed pamphlet, 2–3 [2.12.66.3]; Congressional Record, 70th Cong., 1st sess., 69:4403–04.

51. King, Conservation Fight, 176; Thompson, Confessions of the Power Trust, 225. King's footnotes do not provide corroborating evidence for his charge.

52. Utility Corporations, Federal Trade Commission, Alabama Power Co., 70th Cong., 1st sess., Doc. 92, Part 30, 5–19; Powergrams, January 1931, 1.

53. Alabama Journal, February 18, 1932 [1.1.2.65.11].

54. Ibid., February 26, 1931; Alabama Official and Statistical Register, 1931, 194, 204, 222–23. See the notebook of clippings from the Montgomery Journal, Mobile Register, and Birmingham Age-Herald, which cover the period from February 18 to May 14, 1931 [1.1.2.65.11].

55. Kelly introduced two resolutions, H.J.R. 51 and H.J.R. 80, the latter of which was approved by both the house and senate. Journal of the House of Representatives of the State of Alabama, 1931, 1:478, 732–33, 767, 785, 815–16.

56. Alabama Journal, March 31, 1931 [1.1.2.65.11].

57. Alabama Official and Statistical Register, 1931, 159, 169–70, 164–65, 192–97, 221, 210–11, 217–18, 215. Richard Kelly Jr., known as Dick, was the brother of Alabama's first woman attorney, Maud McLure Kelly, who was also a genealogist and who wrote her brother's biographical sketch, the longest in the Official and Statistical Register. Maud Kelly's biography gives no clue to explain Dick Kelly's attack on Alabama Power. His war injuries did prevent him from working in the 1920s. Cynthia Newman, Maud McLure Kelly: Alabama's First Woman Lawyer (Birmingham: Samford University Library Research Series, Paper No. 6, 1984), 23–24.

58. "Legislative Investigation of Public Utilities in Alabama, by Joint Committee of the Senate and House of Representatives of the Alabama Legislature of 1931, Created Under House Joint Resolution, No. 51," complete transcribed testimony, 1 [1.1.2.50.7].

59. "Report of Joint Committee," Journal of the House, 1931, 2:2919.

60. "Statement of Thomas W. Martin, President of Alabama Power Company Before Alabama Legislative Joint Committee Investigating Public Utility Companies, H.J.R. 80," May 20, 1931 [2.1.2.66.3]; Powergrams, May 1931, 1.

61. "The Kelly Resolution" and "Reply from the Public Service Commission to Joint Commission Senate and House of Representatives of Alabama Legislature of 1931, created under House Joint Resolution No. 51," 80–82, Public Service Commission files, ADAH; "Report of the Legislative Investigating Committee on Public Utilities in Alabama under House Joint Resolution No. 80," July 25, 1931, 15 [2.12.66.3]; Summary of the Inception, Growth and Development of Alabama Power Company, ca. 1930 [1.1.2.20.16].

62. Journal of the House, 1931, 2:2936–39.

63. Johnson, Underwood, 365; Thomas K. McCraw, TVA and the Power Fight, 1933–1939 (Philadelphia: J. B. Lippincott, 1971), 23–24; Hubbard, Origins of the TVA, 217–40.

64. Herbert Hoover, The Memoirs of Herbert Hoover, vol. 2, The Cabinet and the Presidency, 1920–1930 (New York: Macmillan, 1952), 302.

65. Robert Birley, Speeches and Documents in American History, 1914–1939, vol. 4 (1942; reprint, London: Oxford University Press, 1951), 107; Hoover, Memoirs, 2:305; Powergrams, April 1931, 4; Hubbard, Origins of the TVA, 242–86.

66. Huet Massue, Factual Analysis of the Tennessee Valley Authority (New York: Edison Electric Institute, 1946), iii.

67. The Wheeler Project, Technical Report No. 2 (Washington, D.C.: U.S. Government Printing Office, 1940), 5, 215.

68. Davidson, The Tennessee, 2:188–91. For a detailed account of these bills and congressional fights, see Hubbard, Origins of the TVA, 163, 190–286.

69. Annual Report, Commonwealth & Southern, 1931, Thomas W. Martin's copy [1.1.1.24.8].

70. Martin's successor, Wendell Willkie, the next year had the C&S board write off $563,123, 255.37 "to reduce the book value of investments in subsidiary companies." It is reasonable to assume that Martin was concerned about this book value in 1932. Martin would have been alarmed under any circumstances, but he was especially mindful of the campaign against "the power trusts" based in part on "stock watering." See Barnard, Willkie, 94, and compare Annual Reports, Commonwealth & Southern, for 1930, 1931, 1932. The issue will be explained later in this chapter.

71. Bonbright and Means, Holding Company, 186–87.

72. Murray, Martin, 88.

73. Thomas W. Martin, "Address Presented at Joint Session of Alabama Legislature, August 11, 1961, Pursuant to Invitation Extended by Resolution of the Legislature," Montgomery, Alabama, 30, copy in Thomas W. Martin Collection, Archives, Draughon Library, Auburn University.

74. The ellipsis is in the typescript. "History of the APCO," typed manuscript, Black Zip Notebook No. 2, 121. In one page of a proof galley of a book to be entitled "Dynamos of the New South: The Development of Electricity and the Role of Thomas W. Martin" (to be published, but it was never published by Alabama Power Company), Martin had edited the copy and marked out one phrase that Cobb's attitude was that a holding company "might be manipulated financially for profits through inside knowledge of security flotations, loans without competitive bids." These were drafts that eventually evolved into the biography that Murray compiled after Martin's death. Thomas W. Martin Library, SRI. Ellsworth Barnard, whose biography of Willkie was published in 1966, quotes a letter he received from Joseph Barnes about a book on Willkie published in 1952. Barnes wrote: "I have often heard WLW say that his own housecleaning in C&S had turned up and eliminated more corruption than Washington had ever heard of, and that it was the reason why the right wing utility interests always feared and hated him." But Barnard says that Willkie never gave Barnes any specifics. Barnard placed this information in his notes. (See Barnard, Willkie, 527–28, note 66.) Joe Farley recalls Tom Martin saying that when he arrived in New York to work with Cobb, he was shocked to find out that when securities were issued, they were not put out for bids as Southeastern Power & Light had always done. Martin was told in essence, "We don't do that. We

deal with our friends." Interview with Joe Farley, January 5, 2004.

75. *Alabama Official and Statistical Register*, 1931, 91–94.

76. Thomas W. Martin and Perry W. Turner, memo to the files, May 11, 1932 [1.1.1.24.8].

77. *Birmingham News*, June 28, 29, 1932; *Birmingham Age-Herald*, June 29, 1932; *New York Times*, June 29, 1932; *Powergrams*, June 1932, printed a press release from New York.

78. *Birmingham News*, June 29, 1933.

79. Hubbard, *Origins of the TVA*, 312; Eugene H. Roseboom, *A Short History of Presidential Elections* (New York: Collier Books, 1967), 186–88; *Birmingham News*, June 29, 1932.

80. David M. Kennedy, *Freedom from Fear: The American People in Depression and War, 1929–1945* (New York: Oxford University Press, 1999), 99; Hubbard, *Origins of the TVA*, 312; Burns, *Roosevelt*, 139–40.

81. *Powergrams*, June 1932, 1.

82. Interview with Joe Farley, January 26, 2004.

83. Heys interview with Jack Bingham, March 25, 1999, 7–9.

84. Hubbard, "Muscle Shoals Controversy," 528–29.

85. McDonald, *Insull*, 301.

86. Ibid., 294–97; Rudolph and Ridley, *Power Struggle*, 66–67.

87. Burns, *Roosevelt*, 142; Rudolph and Ridley, *Power Struggle*, 67.

88. Herbert Hoover, *The Memoirs of Herbert Hoover*, vol. 3, *The Great Depression, 1929–1941* (New York: Macmillan, 1952), 324.

89. Thomas W. Martin to Lister Hill, August 20, 1931; Lister Hill to Thomas W. Martin, August 26, 1931; Lister Hill to Governor Franklin D. Roosevelt, November 30, 1931; Lister Hill to W. M. Richardson, November 30, 1932. In a December letter, Richardson warned Hill that FDR is "a very charming and agreeable gentleman. He is just the kind of fellow who will ask you for information, listen to your ideas with delight, ask and get your advice, then do as he pleases." He also commented that "we are fearful of the Norris influence on Mr. Roosevelt." W. M. Richardson to Lister Hill, December 2, 1932, Lister Hill Papers, Hoole Library, UA.

90. *Birmingham News*, January 2, 1933; Lowitt, *Norris: Persistence of a Progressive*, 567–68.

91. W. M. Richardson to Lister Hill, January 7, 1933, Lister Hill Papers, Hoole Library, UA.

92. J. W. Worthington to Lister Hill, January 15, 1933, in ibid.

93. Sallie Bolling Powell to Lister Hill, February 12, 1933; Lister Hill to Sallie Bolling Powell, February 18, 1933, in ibid.

94. Kennedy, *Freedom from Fear*, 147.

95. *Birmingham News*, January 10, 21, 1933.

96. Kennedy, *Freedom from Fear*, 148; Arthur M. Schlesinger Jr., *The Age of Roosevelt: The Coming of the New Deal* (Boston: Houghton Mifflin Co., 1959), 324; *Birmingham News*, January 23, 1933; Frank Freidel, *F.D.R. and the South* (Baton Rouge: Louisiana State University Press, 1965), 17–18, 22.

97. Bush, *Future Builders*, 261–63.

98. Steve Neal, *Dark Horse: A Biography of Wendell Willkie* (Lawrence: University Press of Kansas, 1989), 23–24. See Willkie's testimony before the House committee hearings on the Wheeler-Rayburn (Public Utility Holding Company) bill in March 1935, *Hearings before the Committee on Interstate and Foreign Commerce, House of Representatives*,

74th Cong., 1st sess., March 14, 1935, 588.

99. Conant, *Tuxedo Park*, 18.

100. Barnard, *Willkie*, 80.

101. Neal, *Dark Horse: Wendell Willkie*, 28; Willkie's 1940 campaign biography does the same thing. See Joe Mitchell Chapple, *Willkie and American Unity* (New York: Joe Mitchell Chapple, Inc., 1940), 47–48. There are numerous errors included in this rather simple treatment of Willkie, B. C. Cobb, and Commonwealth & Southern.

102. *Powergrams*, 1941, 3–5; Neal, *Dark Horse: Wendell Willkie*, writes that Willkie "introduced" the objective rate plan, 28. Barnard, *Willkie*, admits that "it was C&S engineers who . . . developed the so-called 'objective rate,' of which Willkie was properly proud," 95.

103. W. R. Waggoner, "Significant Dates in the Development of C&S Objective Rate Plan in Alabama, Georgia and Tennessee" [3.1.2.11.28]; "Testimony of W. R. Waggoner with Respect to the Objective Rate Plan," Exhibit W-77, 1–3 [3.1.1.20.27]; Bush, *Future Builders*, 204, 213; Martin, *Electricity in Alabama*, 71.

104. Waggoner, "Significant Dates in the Development of C&S Objective Rate Plan" [3.1.2.11.28]. McCraw, *TVA and the Power Fight*, 75, also does not tell the full story of Alabama Power Company's role.

105. Gregory Blaise Field, "Political Currents: David E. Lilienthal and the Modern American State" (Ph.D. diss., University of Massachusetts, 1994), 153–57, discusses the TVA rate-making decision and Lilienthal's philosophy and Llewellyn Evans's role.

106. McCraw, *TVA and the Power Fight*, 75.

107. Thomas W. Martin to Frank A. Newton, March 28, 1935 [3.1.2.11.28].

108. Morgan and Dana, *Priceless Heritage*, 62.

109. Martin, *Electricity in Alabama*, 71.

110. McDonald, *Insull*, 313.

111. Ibid., 323–33; Cudahy, "Insull," Part 3, 9.

112. *Annual Report*, Commonwealth & Southern, 1930, 11.

113. Neal, *Dark Horse: Wendell Willkie*, 29; Barnard, *Willkie*, 85.

114. Virginia Van der Veer Hamilton, *Lister Hill: Statesman from the South* (Chapel Hill: University of North Carolina Press, 1987), 70; King, *Conservation Fight*, 271.

115. This is a very abbreviated version of the legislative maneuvering. More should be said about Lister Hill's position. Although Hill seemed to be following the president's wishes, his bill was more favorable to the private utilities. He and Bankhead wanted some restrictions on transmission by the government and were probably working together to rein in the government power included in Norris's bill. The Alabama congressmen were also concerned that the federal government was not forced to manufacture fertilizer but only *could* do so, which TVA only did experimentally. Neal, *Dark Horse: Wendell Willkie*, 29; King, *Conservation Fight*, 269, 274–75; Hamilton, *Lister Hill*, 70–71; Freidel, *Roosevelt: Launching the New Deal*, 351–52.

116. Freidel, *Roosevelt: Launching the New Deal*, 354.

117. Barnard, *Willkie*, 86.

118. Birley, *Speeches and Documents*, "The Tennessee Valley Act," 107, 108–13.

119. Arthur A. Ekirch Jr., *Ideologies and Utopias: The Impact of the New Deal on American Thought* (Chicago: Quadrangle, 1969), 120; Bailey and Kennedy, *American Pageant*, 762.

120. Dr. Arthur E. Morgan, a famous engineer, idealist, and president of Antioch College, was chairman. David Lilienthal was a Harvard-educated lawyer and protégé of Felix Frankfurter who as the public service commissioner of Wisconsin was the author of utilities laws copied by many states. Canadian-born Dr. Harcourt A. Morgan was president of the University of Tennessee and was a longtime resident of Tennessee who was well acquainted with the problems of the region. Willson Whitman, *David Lilienthal: Public Servant in a Power Age* (New York: Henry Holt & Co., 1948), 32–37.

121. Barnard, *Willkie*, 89; Neal, *Dark Horse: Wendell Willkie*, 29–30; Joseph Barnes, *Willkie: The Events He Was Part of—The Ideals He Fought For* (New York: Simon & Schuster, 1952), 65–66.

122. This conclusion is based on correspondence between the two after 1940. Although two filing cabinet drawers of Willkie's Commonwealth & Southern correspondence are listed on the inventory of Willkie papers compiled following his death, the drawers were empty when Ellsworth Barnard began research for his biography published in 1966, and neither Willkie's wife nor son Philip had knowledge of what happened to them. Barnard, *Willkie*, 506.

123. David E. Lilienthal, *The Journals of David E. Lilienthal: The TVA Years, 1939–1945, Including a Selection of Journal Entries from the 1917–1939 Period*, vol. 1 (New York: Harper & Row, 1964), 38–39, 711–13; Barnard, *Willkie*, 88–89.

124. See the list of market quotations on securities from 1928 to 1934 in *Annual Report*, Alabama Power Company, 1934, 7.

125. Martin, *Electricity in Alabama*, 106–07.

126. Thomas W. Martin to R. H. Woodrow, August 11, 1934, in "Demands of Preferred Stockholders of Alabama Power Company . . . *Ashwander, et al. vs. Tennessee Valley Authority, et al.*," 3, Hoole Library, UA.

127. Some have suggested that the stockholders were encouraged to file suit against TVA because the Supreme Court had recently ruled key New Deal programs invalid, but the *Schechter* decision invalidating a portion of the National Industrial Recovery Act (which delegated lawmaking authority to the NRA, the National Recovery Administration) was not decided until 1935, and a decision on the *Butler* case that held portions of the Agricultural Adjustment Act unconstitutional was not rendered until 1936. The first TVA suit was filed in 1934. Joseph C. Swidler, "Legal Foundations," in TVA: *The First Twenty Years, A Staff Report*, ed. Roscoe C. Martin (University: University of Alabama Press and Knoxville: University of Tennessee Press, 1956), 29–33.

128. Pat Boyd Rumore, *Lawyers in a New South City: A History of the Legal Profession in Birmingham* (Birmingham: Association Publishing Co., 2000), 84–85, 205.

129. Brief, in Circuit Court for the Eighth Judicial Circuit of Alabama, Complainants v. TVA, Ashwander files, Cabaniss and Johnston. The only remaining Ashwander records at the firm available to me were all printed public documents.

130. Neal, *Dark Horse: Wendell Willkie*, 30; Barnard, *Willkie*, 88–89, 527, note 46.

131. Rumore, *Lawyers in a New South City*, 85.

132. Davidson, *The Tennessee*, 2:307.

133. Alabama Power Company's construction of dams and the flooding of lands in the lower Coosa and Tallapoosa Valleys were not met with the passion that followed the government's flooding of lands in the Tennessee Valley. Perhaps the power company paid a fairer price for the land, perhaps the land was more isolated, not as fertile, and less people were involved. Certainly, the Tennessee Valley had a longer history of settlement, but most likely it was the Tennessee Valley's Ap-

palachian mountain and hill country culture that caused the people to resent intrusion into their world, inspiring novelists to write about it. The TVA dams have often been the subject of novels, for instance, T. S. Stribling's *Unfinished Cathedral*, Robert Penn Warren's *The Flood*, Madison Jones's *A Buried Land*, Borden Deal's *Dunbar's Cove*, and William Bradford Huie's *Mud on the Stars*.

134. Barnes, *Willkie*, 105–06; Lilienthal, *Journals: TVA Years*, 53–54.

135. Crist, *They Electrified the South*, 83–84. This quotation, not identified in Crist's book, is taken from a Scrapbook with only the introductory sentence added. See 15.21.45.1, Scrapbook of photographs, taken May 1940 by an unnamed Alabama Power Company line foreman.

136. Heys interview with Bill Whitt, June 13, 1999, 15–16.

137. Farley, Balch, and Conway, "'Good Name and Destiny,'" 52–53; Heys interview with Bill Whitt, June 13, 1999, 16.

138. See particularly the letters from city comptroller C. E. Armstrong to commission president James M. Jones Jr., 1933, Jones Papers, ADAH.

139. Glenn Feldman, *From Demagogue to Dixiecrat: Horace Wilkinson and the Politics of Race* (New York: University Press of America, 1995), 102–05; *Alabama Herald*, March 19, 1935.

140. Leah Rawls Atkins, "Feuds, Factions, and Reform: Politics in Early Birmingham," *Alabama Heritage* 1 (Summer 1986): 30–31.

141. *Birmingham News*, October 1, 1933. A large section of the editorial page was given over to letters to the editor on the issue. Most opposed city ownership.

142. Ibid., October 8, 1933.

143. *Birmingham Municipal Ownership Election*, flyer [3.1.1.56.9].

144. "Shall Birmingham Go Into The Utility Business?" Citizens Protective Committee, Holt McDowell, Secretary [1.1.2.74.26]. Also, Citizens Protective Committee flyer [3.1.2.11.28].

145. *Birmingham News*, October 2, 1933; *Birmingham Age-Herald*, October 3, 9, 1933.

146. "Excerpts from Address of M. H. Sterne," October 3, 1933 [1.1.2.74.23].

147. *Birmingham News*, October 10, 1933; *Birmingham Age-Herald*, October 10, 11, 1933; *Powergrams*, September 1933, 1.

148. Barbara Connell Bailey, "The Trying Years: A History of Bessemer, Alabama, 1929–1939" (master's thesis, Samford University, 1977), 125–31. TVA crews began work on June 9, 1938, and the first year of TVA power for Bessemer was 1940–41.

149. This is phrased rather politely. See Forney Johnston to Oscar W. Underwood, January 12, 1915; Oscar W. Underwood to Forney Johnston, January 16, 1915, Underwood Papers, ADAH. Johnston's specific anger is directed at the company and at J. W. Worthington. Interview with Eason Balch, January 11, 2004.

150. While these are my words and conclusions, I discussed this issue with Jack Bingham and Eason Balch and both believe that Tom Martin knew something about the Ashwander suit before it was filed. See Heys interview with Jack Bingham, March 25, 1999, 9–10.

151. Martin, *Electricity in Alabama*, 106–07; Barnes, *Willkie*, 101–02; Davidson, *The Tennessee*, 2:307–09. Eason Balch noted "the court held that the electric power generated at the multipurpose dams and the steam plant at Muscle Shoals, which was surplus to its needs, was property which the government, in accordance with the contract, was authorized to dispose of and that the electric

power facilities which TVA would acquire under contract enabled it to dispose of its surplus power." Alabama Power also transferred its transmission lines in the Northern Division. Interview with Eason Balch, May 21, 2006.

152. Martin, *Electricity in Alabama*, 107.

153. Branch, *Alabama Power Company*, 17; McCraw, *TVA and the Power Fight*, 119. The Supreme Court held that the utility companies had no standing to maintain the suit. Interview with Eason Balch, May 31, 2006.

154. Franklin D. Roosevelt, *"Nothing to Fear": The Selected Addresses of Franklin Delano Roosevelt*, ed. B. D. Zevin (Boston: Houghton Mifflin, 1946), 52.

155. Jim Powell, *FDR's Folly: How Roosevelt and His New Deal Prolonged the Great Depression* (New York: Crown Forum, 2003), 23.

156. Burton Kendall Wheeler, *Yankee from the West: The Candid, Turbulent Life Story of the Yankee-born U.S. Senator from Montana* (New York: Doubleday, 1962), 306–07. Eason Balch points out that the Public Utility Holding Company provision was only part of the Wheeler-Rayburn bill. Other parts increased the authority of the Federal Power Commission to regulate public utilities that operated interstate transmission for the sale of electric power for resale. Interview with Eason Balch, May 31, 2006.

157. Barnard, *Willkie*, 94, is in error on the date. The annual C&S report signed by both Willkie and Cobb was signed in 1934 but was for the year 1933.

158. *Hearings before the Committee on Interstate and Foreign Commerce*, House of Representatives, 74th Cong., 1st sess., Part 2, March 14, 1935, 604.

159. Willkie's opening statement to the House Interstate and Foreign Commerce Committee was printed in *Powergrams*, April 15, 1935, 1–2, 5; April 22, 1935, 2–5. *Powergrams* was usually published only once a month, but in 1935 it occasionally appeared more than once a month and the publication carries a full date.

160. United Corporation had a 5.3 percent ownership in C&S, EBASCO a 6.1 percent interest, and American Superpower Corporation, incorporated in 1923 by Bonbright & Company, held 13.2 percent interest according to Buchanan, "Electric Bond and Share," 316. Buchanan also noted that Bonbright was closely connected to J. P. Morgan & Company and that in 1931 S. Z. Mitchell's son was a vice president at Bonbright; see page 315.

161. Willkie's long testimony on March 14, 1935, before the House committee gave him an opportunity to educate the congressmen on the operations of utility holding companies. It provides an excellent view of the operation of Commonwealth & Southern and its history. See *Hearings before the Committee on Interstate and Foreign Commerce*, House of Representatives, 74th Cong., 1st sess., 577–656. Also in Wendell L. Willkie, *Argument Presented to Interstate & Foreign Commerce Committee of United States House of Representatives, March 14, 1935. In Opposition to Wheeler-Rayburn Holding and Operating Company Bill* (Commonwealth & Southern Corporation). Willkie's opposition to the Wheeler-Rayburn bill is best summarized in Willkie's essay, *The Public Utility Problem: Its Recent History and Possible Solution* (New York, 1935), copy in Alabama Power Company, Research Services Library.

162. Wheeler, *Yankee from the West*, 310–13. In the next six decades, millions of dollars were spent by the federal government and by utilities trying to find agreement on what the act meant.

163. *Hearings, the Committee on Interstate Commerce, United States Senate*, 74th Cong., 1st sess., 533–52. Willkie does not name his "predecessor" and in context it is impossible to determine whether he means B. C. Cobb or Tom Martin. Eason Balch believes it was Martin about whom Willkie was speaking. Both Cobb and Martin were known for their honesty and were still living, but Willkie's description fits Martin much better than it does Cobb. At this time Cobb was retired and in very poor health. Martin was active and the relationship between Martin and Willkie had grown close especially since the TVA crisis began. See the Martin-Willkie correspondence in the Willkie Papers, Lilly Library, Indiana University, Bloomington, Indiana. See also W. R. Waggoner's time line of the development of the objective rate at Alabama Power in relation to TVA [3.1.2.11.28]. Cobb retired "early in the year [1934] on account of ill health, and at the meeting of the stockholders on June 20, 1934, the by-laws were amended and the office of chairman eliminated." *Annual Report*, Commonwealth & Southern, 1934, 7. Before leaving Wendell Willkie, a story of interest, but not part of the story of Alabama Power Company, should be told. Willkie began a long and intimate relationship in 1935 with Irita Van Doren, who had been born in Birmingham in 1891. She was the literary editor of the *New York Herald Tribune*, a radiant, articulate woman with "impeccable southern manners." She was the former wife of Carl Van Doren, Pulitzer Prize–winning historian, and she had great influence in the New York publishing world. Mrs. Van Doren and Willkie were both interested in southern history, a subject that had drawn them together. In 1935 Willkie sent Mrs. Van Doren galleys sent to him by John Marsh, the manager of the public relations department (later the advertising department) of the Georgia Power Company. The galleys were of the novel, set in antebellum and Civil War north Georgia and Atlanta, written by Marsh's wife, Margaret "Peggy" Mitchell. It was published in 1936 as *Gone With The Wind*. See Neal, *Dark Horse: Wendell Willkie*, 39–40; Wright, *History of Georgia Power*, 364. In her biography of Mitchell and Marsh, Marianne Walker tells the story of Willkie writing Georgia Power president Preston S. Arkwright requesting he ask John to have Peggy autograph his personal copy of *Gone With The Wind*. By this time Peggy Mitchell was refusing to autograph books, and Marsh declined. The book was returned to Willkie. The story was told to Walker by Joe Kling, who worked with John at Georgia Power. Marianne Walker, *Margaret Mitchell & John Marsh: The Love Story Behind Gone With The Wind* (Atlanta: Peachtree Publishers, 1993), xiii, 343, 539.

164. Wheeler, *Yankee from the West*, 312–13; Hamilton, *Black*, 250, 258; William E. Leuchtenburg, *Franklin D. Roosevelt and the New Deal, 1932–1940* (New York: Harper & Row, 1963), 156; Rudolph and Ridley, *Power Struggle*, 76–77; Wendell Willkie, *The Public Utility Problem*, 8–9.

165. Martin, *Electricity in Alabama*, 69.

166. *Annual Report*, Alabama Power Company, 1935, 11; 1936, 6.

167. Ibid., 1936, 16–17.

168. Bureau of Business Research, University of Alabama, 1936, quoted in ibid., 1935, 13.

169. Barnard, *Willkie*, 96.

170. Tindall, *Emergence of the New South*, 455; Lilienthal, *Journals: TVA Years*, 713–14.

171. Gregory B. Field, "'Electricity for all': The Electric Home and Farm Authority and the Politics of Mass Consumption, 1932–1935," *Business History Review* 64 (Spring 1990); and Joseph D. Coppock, "Government as Enterpriser-Competitor: The Case of the Electric Home and Farm Authority," *Explorations in Entrepreneurial History* 1 (1964): 187, 191–99.

172. Audra J. Wolfe, "'How Not to Electrocute the Farmer': Assessing Attitudes to Electrification on American Farms, 1920–1940," *Agricultural History* 74 (Spring 2000). Also see Ronald C.

Tobey, *Technology as Freedom: The New Deal and the Electrical Modernization of the American Home* (Berkeley and Los Angeles: University of California Press, 1996), but note that Tobey's test case of Riverside, California, is different from the Alabama experience where Alabama Power pushed for middle-class and working-class customers.

173. Company Appliance Sales, chart, *Annual Report*, Alabama Power Company, 1936, 7.

174. *Powergrams*, May 1935, 2; June 3, 1935, 1; July 8, 1935, 4, 6; July 15, 1935, 1, 3; January 6, 1936, 1; February 10, 1936, 1; *Annual Report*, Alabama Power Company, 1936, 7.

175. *Powergrams*, November 1931, 5; July 29, 1935, 2; December 16, 1935, 1–2.

176. Ibid., July 15, 1935, 3.

177. Ibid., August 26, 1935, 3.

178. Ibid., September 2, 1935, 2.

179. Ibid., November 1933, 6.

180. Pence, *The Next Greatest Thing*, 63–66; *Powergrams*, October 14, 1935, 7.

181. *Powergrams*, October 14, 1935, 1; S. Jonathan Bass, "Gordon Persons, 1951–1955," in Webb and Armbrester, *Alabama Governors*, 206–07.

182. Martin, *Electricity in Alabama*, 75; chart, Alabama Power, Rural Line Construction, 1923–1968 [1.1.2.19.28]; Fifty Years of Rural Electrification in Alabama, notebook compiled by Carmichael Library of the University of Montevallo. (The spine lists Martin as the author. There is no date.)

183. Bailey and Kennedy, *American Pageant*, 766–67.

184. *Annual Report*, Alabama Power Company, 1939, 1, 13–14.

185. *Powergrams*, April 8, 1935, 3.

186. Sidney Z. Mitchell to Thomas W. Martin, January 27, 1937, Martin Library, SRI.

187. Durden, *Electrifying the Piedmont Carolinas*, 104, 106. This was Lee's last major address. He died the next year.

188. Clipping from *Montgomery Advertiser*, November 5, 1935, in Scrapbook No. 3, Martin Library, SRI.

189. Clipping, n.d., n.p., Scrapbook, 1925–1954, Martin Library, SRI.

190. Louis Johnson to Lister Hill, November 4, 1938; Secret Document, copy No. 22, "Confidential Memorandum on Shortages of Electric Generating Capacity for Wartime Needs," Federal Power Commission, July 1, 1938, Lister Hill Papers, Hoole Library, UA.

191. Report of the Public Utilities Division to the Securities and Exchange Commission with Respect to the Holding Company System of the Commonwealth & Southern Corporation and Its Subsidiary Companies, March 10, 1941, 198 [3.1.1.19.22].

192. *Powergrams*, October 1938, 6, 12.

193. Ibid., November 1935, 4.

194. *Annual Report*, Alabama Power Company, 1940, 8.

195. Interview with Mrs. Bill Brownlee, February 9, 2004.

196. Interview with Joe Farley, February 9, 2004.

197. Ibid., January 5, 2004.

Chapter Six

1. *Alabama: News Magazine of the Deep South*, February 7, 1938, 15.

2. Ibid., April 11, 1938, 7; Leah Rawls Atkins, "Senator James A. Simpson and Birmingham Politics of the 1930s: His Fight Against the Spoilsmen and the Pie-Men," *Alabama Review* 41 (January 1988): 3–39.

3. *Alabama: News Magazine of the Deep South*, February 7, 1938, 15.

4. Ibid., February 14, 1938, 10.

5. Glenn A. Feldman, "Frank M. Dixon, 1939–1943," in Webb and Armbrester, *Alabama Governors*, 185–88; *Annual Report*, Alabama Power Company, 1938, 3.

6. *Alabama Official and Statistical Register*, 1939, 244; *Montgomery Advertiser*, September 3, 1939; *Journal of the Senate*, 1939, 1802–03; *General Laws and Joint Resolutions of the Legislature of Alabama*, 1939, 405–08.

7. John M. Carmody to Governor Frank Dixon, February 1, 24, March 28, 1939, Governor Frank Dixon Papers, SG12240, folder 6, ADAH.

8. *Birmingham News*, September 2, 1939; *Montgomery Advertiser*, September 2, 3, 1939.

9. *Montgomery Advertiser*, September 5, 6, 7, 1939.

10. Ibid., September 1, 1939.

11. Daniel Webster Hollis, *An Alabama Newspaper Tradition: Grover C. Hall and the Hall Family* (Tuscaloosa: University of Alabama Press, 1983), 64–65; *Alabama: News Magazine of the Deep South*, September 4, 11, 18, 1939.

12. *Birmingham News*, September 6, 1939; Secretary of State, Bills & Resolutions, 1939, SB495, ADAH. The amended bill passed the senate on September 9 and the house on September 12, just three days before the end of the session.

13. Farley, Balch, and Conway, "'Good Name and Destiny,'" 55; *Powergrams*, September 1939, 3.

14. *Birmingham News*, September 7, 8, 10, 1939.

15. *Journal of Commerce and Commercial* (New York), May 20, 1940, 36 [3.1.2.19.8].

16. Morton Sosna, "Introduction," in Neil R. McMillen, ed., *Remaking Dixie: The Impact of World War II on the American South* (Jackson: University of Mississippi Press, 1997). Gavin Wright dates the beginning of a new southern economy from World War II in *Old South, New South* (Baton Rouge: Louisiana State University Press, 1986), 80, 239.

17. *Fortune*, March 1952, 93 [1.1.2.20.16].

18. Allen Cronenberg, *Forth to the Mighty Conflict: Alabama and World War II* (Tuscaloosa: University of Alabama Press, 1995), 2; Peter Fearson, *War, Prosperity and Depression: The U. S. Economy, 1917–1945* (Lawrence: University Press of Kansas, 1987), 261.

19. T. D. Johnson, "Why Not Build Some of Those Defense Industrial Plants in Alabama?" *Powergrams*, July 1940, 2.

20. Alabama Power Company, New Industries Located in Service Area, 1925–1952 [5.1.1.98.241]; State Distribution of Contract Awards, June 1940–September 1941, Office of Production Management, October 20, 1941, Dixon Papers, SG12274, folder 16, ADAH.

21. The sale of Alabama Power Company's Northern Division to TVA was not concluded until July 18, 1940.

22. Alabama Power Company, New Industries Located in Service Area, 1925–1952 [5.1.1.98.241].

23. *Alabama: News Magazine of the Deep South*, April 25, 1938, 12–16.

24. Frank W. Boykin to Edward J. Harding, July 3, 1940, signed copy with note to Dixon in Dixon Papers, SG12252, folder 4, ADAH. To understand Congressman Boykin see Edward Boykin, *Everything's Made For Love In This Man's World: Vignettes From the Life of Frank Boykin* (Mobile: Privately printed, 1973).

25. E. W. Robinson to C. Paul Barker, November 22, 1937; E. W. Robinson to Department Heads and Principal Supervisors, November 22, 1937, File 8, NLRB Case No. XVR 125, 1937, files, Labor Relations Department.

26. Charles H. Logan, Regional Director, to APC with copy to Hobart McWhorter, Case No. XVR 125, December 8, 1937 (copy), in ibid.

27. O. A. Walker, International Brotherhood of Electrical Workers, E. W. Robinson, Alabama Power Company, C. Paul Barker, National Labor Relations Board, December 7, 1937. Official results of ballots among Alabama Power Company employees under supervision of the National Labor Relations Board, November 29, 30, and December 1, 8, 1937. Total votes, 1,191; ballots spoiled, 5; votes counted, 1,186; Yes, 551; No, 635; challenged ballots unopened and uncounted, 83. File 8, NLRB Case No. XVR 125, 1937, in ibid.

28. E. W. Robinson to Superintendents of All Generating Plants, September 30, 1940; E. W. Robinson to C. Paul Barker, October 11, 1940; James M. Barry to All Employees, December 26, 1940, File, NLRB Case No. XVR 489, 1940, in ibid.

29. Transcript of meetings beginning October 23, 1940, especially pages 5, 31; Contract and Proposals, 1940 file; *Memorandum of Agreement Between Alabama Power Company and International Brotherhood of Electrical Workers*, October 16, 1940, in ibid. One sticky point was that the company insisted that promotions be based upon "competency" to fill the position and the working definition of competent.

30. Joiner, *Let Us Reason Together*, 66–73, 85–96.

31. *Huntsville Mercury Banner*, April 9, 1915; Mitchell Family Genealogy, courtesy of Peter Stancioff. The family genealogy notes that Nathaniel's death was from drowning while he was working on a dam, but it is more likely that he was electrocuted, according to the 1915 newspaper account that came from Gadsden to the Huntsville newspaper. There was no Alabama Power Company dam in Gadsden. Perhaps it was a death so terrible that Mitchell never told his family the full story.

32. Kennedy, *Freedom from Fear*, 289–92; interview with Eason Balch, July 21, 2004.

33. Compare *Memorandum of Agreement Between Alabama Power Company and International Brotherhood of Electrical Workers*, October 16, 1940, with the agreement dated January 29, 1942.

34. E. C. Boswell to Governor Frank Dixon, September 30, 1939; M. M. Woodham to Hon. E. C. Boswell, September 29, 1939; Madison Jones to Governor Dixon, August 23, 1939, Governor Frank Dixon Papers, Public Service Commission file, SG12240, folder 6, ADAH.

35. Public Service Commission, Docket 6483, August 29, 1933, Cotton Gin Power, and a History of Rates and Rate Structures, no page numbers, but last page of document, in files of Rate Department, and Docket 908, July 23, 1934.

36. *Annual Report*, Commonwealth & Southern, 1940, 7.

37. Farley, *Alabama Power Company*, 15.

38. Kennedy, *Freedom from Fear*, 454–55; Neal, *Dark Horse: Wendell Willkie*, 46–109. Mencken wrote *New York Daily News* reporter Doris Fleeson a few days after the convention that "I am thoroughly convinced that the nomination of Willkie was managed by the Holy Ghost in person." Neal, *Dark Horse: Wendell Willkie*, 116.

39. Press Release, Commonwealth & Southern, Wilmington, Delaware, July 17, 1940 [1.1.2.62.30].

40. Kennedy, *Freedom from Fear*, 456–57; Neal, *Dark Horse: Wendell Willkie*, 125; Bush, *Future Builders*, 347–50.

41. Neal, *Dark Horse: Wendell Willkie*, 176.

42. Thomas W. Martin to Wendell L. Willkie, April 7, 1944, and Wendell Willkie to Thomas W. Martin, April 17, 1944, (copy) in Willkie Papers, courtesy of Lilly Library, Indiana University, Bloomington, Indiana. Martin's earlier correspondence and Willkie's C&S papers are not part of the collection.

43. Wendell Willkie to Thomas W. Martin, April 17, 1944, Martin Library, SRI.

44. Thomas W. Martin to Wendell L. Willkie, September 25, 1944; Secretary to Thomas W. Martin, October 2, 1944, (copy) Willkie Papers. Courtesy of Lilly Library, Indiana University, Bloomington, Indiana; Neal, *Dark Horse: Wendell Willkie*, 323.

45. Bush, *Future Builders*, 347.

46. *Electric Bond & Share Company v. S.E.C.*, 303 U.S. 419 (1938).

47. Rudolph and Ridley, *Power Struggle*, 86; Bush, *Future Builders*, 353–56.

48. Before the Federal Power Commission, Alabama Power Company Project No. 82, Mitchell Dam, December 11, 1939, Washington, D.C., 21, 24, 28–30 [3.1.2.11.14].

49. *Alabama Power v. McNinch*, 68 App. D.C. 132, 94 F2d 601; Federal Power Commission, *Opinions and Decisions of the Federal Power Commission*, 1: January 1, 1931–June 30, 1930 (Washington, D.C.: U.S. Government Printing Office, 1940), 25; Federal Power Commission, 2: July 1, 1939–December 31, 1941; Exhibit "A," Part 8a, in Exhibits of Alabama Power Company before the Atomic Energy Commission, Docket Nos. 50-348A., 50-364A., vol. 2.

50. William L. O'Neill, *A Democracy at War: America's Fight at Home and Abroad in World War II* (New York: Free Press, 1993), 24–25; Rogers et al., *Alabama: History of a Deep South State*, 512–13.

51. *Annual Report*, Alabama Power Company, 1941, 3–4; Thomas W. Martin testimony, March 11, 1940, *Proceedings before the Securities and Exchange Commission*, 446–48.

52. Interview with Leonard Bill Crouch, September 7, 2004.

53. Alabama Power Company memo, October 4, 1941 [3.1.1.19.26].

54. *Annual Report*, Alabama Power Company, 1940, 3; 1941, 5 [1.1.2.96.32].

55. Lister Hill to Colonel Richard Park, August 22, 1939, Lister Hill Papers, Hoole Library, UA.

56. Clipping, *Alabama Journal*, February 6, 1941, in ibid.

57. J. W. Worthington to Lister Hill, April 30, 1941; clipping, *Knoxville Journal*, May 15, 1941, attached to J. W. Worthington to Senator Lister Hill, May 15, 1941, in ibid.

58. Telegram, Lister Hill to David E. Lilienthal, May 23, 1941; telegram, David E. Lilienthal to Lister Hill, May 28, 1941, in ibid. Davidson, *The Tennessee* 2:332–33, discusses the growing opposition to TVA in the Cumberland River region.

59. Lister Hill to J. R. Hornaday, May 29, 1941, Lister Hill Papers, Hoole Library, UA.

60. J. W. Worthington to Lister Hill and Memorandum, May 2, 19, 24, 1941; Lister Hill to J. W. Worthington, May 22, 1941; Leland Olds, chairman of Federal Power Commission, to Lister Hill, May 22, 1941; Captain O. B. Beasley, War Department, to J. W. Worthington, May 27, 1941, all in ibid. Worthington, as he was in the past, was hostile to Alabama Power Company in this correspondence.

61. J. W. Worthington to Lister Hill, May 27, 1941, in ibid.

62. J. W. Worthington to Lister Hill, May 29, 1941, in ibid.

63. J. W. Worthington to Lister Hill, May 30, June 1, June 6, 1941; Lister Hill to J. W. Worthington, June 7, 1941, in ibid.

64. *Montgomery Advertiser*, March 3, 1945.

65. J. Herbert Meighan to Gov. Frank Dixon, November 17, 1941; Frank Dixon to J. Herbert Meighan, November 27, 1941; *Gadsden Times*, November 16, 1941, Dixon Papers, ADAH.

66. John Temple Graves, Black Zip Notebook, VII–1, Martin Library, SRI; Daniel, "Worthington," 208; William H. Mitchell, "J. W. Worthington," in letter, William H. Mitchell to Hill Ferguson, May 18, 1953, Hill Ferguson Collection, BPL.

67. E. A. de Funiak to Sid B. Jones, April 9, 1942, in Worthington Family Papers, BPL.

68. *Powergrams*, December 1940, 3.

69. *Annual Report*, Alabama Power Company, 1940, 11; 1941, 15; *Powergrams*, January 1941, 13.

70. *Powergrams*, November 1943, 4; *Annual Report*, Alabama Power Company, 1943, 10.

71. *Powergrams*, July 1946, 2.

72. Jacob Hekma to Thomas W. Martin, June 14, 1940 [3.1.2.11.28].

73. Interview with Joe Farley, February 15, 2004; interview with Walter McFarland "Mac" Beale, January 28, 2004; clipping, Scrapbook, 1925–1954, Martin Library, SRI.

74. Testimony of Joe Farley before the Atomic Energy Safety and Licensing Board, Antitrust Suit, 207; interview with Walter McFarland "Mac" Beale, February 16, 2004. This trust agreement was in place in 2004.

75. "Something About Our Refinancing Program," *Powergrams*, February 1942, 3–4; *Annual Report*, Alabama Power Company, 1941, 11.

76. Draft of letter, Thomas W. Martin to Preferred Stockholders, August 25, 1942, as part of SEC exhibits [3.1.1.19.25]. The company could pay such dividends only when there was sufficient surplus to cover preferred dividends for a period of two years on the outstanding preferred stock. Martin was particularly concerned about the impact of the proposed congressional tax bill of 1942, which would increase the company's already heavy federal tax burdens.

77. Eugene A. Yates, "Address on the Dedication of Yates Dam," June 28, 1947, 35 [1.1.2.23.11].

78. Testimony of Joe Farley before the Atomic Energy Safety and Licensing Board, Antitrust Suit, 208–09.

79. Allen Cronenberg, "Mobile and World War II, 1940–1945," in *Mobile: The New History of Alabama's First City*, ed. Michael V. R. Thomason (Tuscaloosa: University of Alabama Press, 2001), 215, 217; *Powergrams*, May 1941, 3–4; F. S. Keeler, "Growth of Electric Service in Mobile," July 1943, 6, 8.

80. Mary Martha Thomas, *Riveting and Rationing in Dixie: Alabama Women and the Second World War* (Tuscaloosa: University of Alabama Press, 1987), 8–9.

81. Cronenberg, *Forth to the Mighty Conflict*, 5, 15, 51–52.

82. Northcutt, *I Remember Gorgas*, 156; *Powergrams*, September 1944, 7; October 1944, 1–10.

83. *Annual Report*, Commonwealth & Southern, 1942, 5; 1943, 4; 1944, 7; Justin Whiting, "Power in the South," *Powergrams*, November 1942, 6, reprinted from *Southern Agriculture*.

84. Preliminary Statement of Income, Alabama Power Company, 1944 [1.1.1.18.6].

85. *Powergrams*, December 1944, 3–4.

86. Ibid., March 1944, 7.

87. Ibid., 5.

88. Ibid., April 1941, 6; February 1942, 16; September 1942, 1; October 1942, 1; December 1944, 10; February 1944, 5; April 1944, 3.

89. Ibid., May 1942, 10.

90. Ibid., January 1944, 2; February 1944, 11; June 1944, 5; September 1944, 18. Additional information about the Martin family of Mobile courtesy of Carol C. Mitchell.

91. The August 1985 issue of *Powergrams* featured the World War II recollections of Alabama Power Company employees; however, many of them joined the company after the war. Included in this feature were war stories by Ward Dockery, Jim Beckham, Gerald Davidson, Ed Thompson (pages 8–10), Ralph McCullers, Grady Sivley, Laslie M. Stewart, James Gibson Lanier, Sr. (father of Gibson and Randolph Lanier), Lucy Wright, Primus Ridgeway, Jack Swift, Plemer East, Henry Sledge, Clayton Nordan, Dee Miller, John Kyser, Max Alexander, Bill Mobley, and Kenneth Lemley.

92. *Powergrams*, July 1944, 4, 5; February 1944, 8; October 1944, 20–21.

93. Ibid., April 1945, 15; August 1945, 13, 17.

94. Interview with Jackie Darnell, September 7, 2004, and newspaper clipping, courtesy of Jackie Darnell.

95. *Powergrams*, August 1985, 1.

96. Executive Department, General Orders, No. 25-A, Birmingham, April 30, 1941 [3.1.1.19.10].

97. Interview with Jack Minor, February 26, 2004.

98. Executive Department, General Orders, No. 25, Birmingham, July 12, 1940 [3.1.1.19.10]; *Powergrams*, March 1942, 3; April 1942, 15.

99. *Powergrams*, January 1942, 4, 9; February 1942, 3, 17; April 1942, 10, 15; May 1942, 19; June 1942, 9; November 1942, 17; May 1943, 14; February 1945, 10.

100. Ibid., June 1942, 19.

101. Ibid., January 1942, 11, 17.

102. Ibid., October 1945, 12.

103. Ibid., see issues of May 1942 and May 1943; March 1944, 15.

104. Ibid., April 1945, 7.

105. Ibid., February 1944, 1; Farley, Balch, and Conway, "'Good Name and Destiny,'" 135.

106. Thomas W. Martin, "Planning for Post-War Jobs," speech to the Birmingham Kiwanis Club, November 9, 1943 [1.1.2.20.16]. Clippings, *Birmingham Age-Herald*, September 1, November 10, 1943, *Alabama: The News Magazine of the Deep South*, November 1943, in Scrapbook, 1925–1954, Martin Library, SRI.

107. *Powergrams*, October 1943, 13; November 1943, 1.

108. Ibid., September 1943, 3. Lester had first joined the company in 1919 but left after a year to go into the electrical business. He returned to the company in 1921.

109. Ibid., May 1945, 16.

110. Ibid., February 1945, 3.

111. Pension Plan, Employee Group Life Insurance, A Financial History of the Alabama Power Company, January 1, 1948, sec. 1, typed manuscript courtesy of Jack Minor. No page numbers.

112. *Powergrams*, December 1944, 2.

113. Ibid., January 1945, 7; February 1945, 3, 4.

114. Ibid., May 1942, 16.

115. Farley, Balch, and Conway, "'Good Name and Destiny,'" 56; biographical information from Walter Baker; *Powergrams*, November 1957, 10; November 1962, 6; interview with Bill Cochran, August 26, 2004.

116. Martin, *Electricity in Alabama*, 75.

117. Walter Baker and M. B. Penn, "Progress of Rural Electrification during 1946," submitted to Prize Committee of the Edison Electric Institute for the Thomas W. Martin Farm Electrification Award [1.1.2.20.8]; Walter L. Baker Jr. to Leah Atkins, February 25, 2004; Baker, *Milestones in Marketing*, 11–12.

118. Martin, *Electricity in Alabama*, 75; Baker, *Milestones in Marketing*, 5.

119. Interview with Bill Cochran, August 26, 2004.

120. Baker, *Milestones in Marketing*, 12.

121. Baker and Penn, "Progress of Rural Electrification during 1946" [1.1.2.20.8].

122. Extended Remarks of Frank Boykin, *Congressional Record*, April 14 and 24, 1947 [1.1.2.11.21].

123. *Birmingham Post*, August 6, 1947; E. C. Easter, Alabama Power Company: Survey of Rural Electric Development as of August 31, 1947, September 8, 1947, 3 [2.1.1.56.19].

124. *Powergrams*, August 1945, 6.

125. Interview with Walter Baker, April 21, 2004.

126. *Triumph of Community Enterprise: A Brief History of the Talladega County War Plants Conversion Committee, 1944–1948* (n.p., n.d.), 3–1, copy in Thomas W. Martin Collection, Archives, Draughon Library, Auburn University; biographical essay on Thomas Wesley Martin, June 1951 (no author), Martin folder.

127. *Triumph of Community Enterprise*, 20–23.

128. *Forward March* (Alabama Power Company, 1950). The author's personal copy, according to the cover, was distributed by the Alabama Historical Association. Thomas W. Martin was a charter member of the association, which was organized in Montevallo on April 19, 1947.

129. C. A. Basore to Ben Russell, October 13, 1941, Martin Library, SRI. Professor Cleburne Basore was head of the Department of Chemical Engineering at Alabama Polytechnic Institute.

130. John Temple Graves, *History of Southern Research Institute* (Birmingham: Birmingham Publishing Co., 1955), 20–55, 180–84; information from Mary Jo Funderburk, SRI, April 21, 2004.

131. *Powergrams*, December 1946, 8–11.

132. Milton H. Fies, "Alabama Industry and the Post War," a paper delivered at the Faculty Forum of the Alabama Polytechnic Institute at Auburn, March 26, 1945 [2.1.2.55.6].

133. Baker, *Milestones in Marketing*, 13.

134. Rogers et al., *Alabama: History of a Deep South State*, 520–21.

135. See S. L. Papas and F. R. O'Brien, "Availability of Ground Water in the Area Served by the Alabama Power Company for Southern Services, Inc.," Southern Research Institute, June 2, 1953, Special Collections, Samford University.

136. *Powergrams*, April 1946, 2–3; IEA Heat Pump Centre Newsletter, March 2001, 13.

137. Baker, *Milestones in Marketing*, 13; Annual Report, Alabama Power Company, 1946, 6–7; *Powergrams*, April 1946, 2; July 1946, 5.

138. *Powergrams*, April 1950, 2; May 1950, 5–6; notes from Walter Baker, August 24, 2004.

139. *Powergrams*, April 1949, 11.

140. Ibid., April 1949, 11; June 1949, 1, 26; "Some High Spots of 1948," 1 [2.1.1.56.16].

141. Heys interview with Eason Balch, February 25, 1999, 8.

142. Securities and Exchange Commission, Public Utilities Division Report, Commonwealth & Southern Corporation and Its Subsidiary Companies, March 10, 1941, 3–5 [3.1.1.19.22]. Other large owners of C&S stock were the United Corporation (5.12 percent), United Gas Improvement Company (2.6 percent), Electric Bond & Share (4.62 percent). Other stockholders owned 77.63 percent.

143. Annual Report, Commonwealth & Southern Corporation, 1940, 9–10; 1941, 16; Martin, *Electricity in Alabama*, 141; Bush, *Future Builders*, 353–54.

144. Narrative Testimony to be Given and Exhibits to be Introduced by Thomas W. Martin before Securities and Exchange Commission, November 18, 1941 [3.1.1.11.8]. Included is a detailed assessment of the cost of properties beginning in 1912.

145. Annual Report, Alabama Power Company, 1941, 13–14; Bush, *Future Builders*, 352–54.

146. *New York Times*, June 8, 1943 [3.1.1.19.27].

147. Testimony of H. J. Scholz, Report of System Studies before the SEC, n.d., ca. 1942 [3.1.1.20.16].

148. Crist, *They Electrified the South*, 92.

149. Hayden N. Smith to Thomas W. Martin, June 13, 1942. Smith was with Winthrop, Stimson, Putnam & Roberts, a firm in New York City [3.1.1.11.30].

150. Martin, *Electricity in Alabama*, 140.

151. John Temple Graves manuscript, typeset version, chapter one, Epochal Decision, 1–3–1–4, Martin Library, SRI.

152. John Temple Graves manuscript, draft (January 2, 1963), 134, Martin Library, SRI; Record Files for Southern Company Minutes, documents No. 1 and No. 2, Southern Company, Southern Company Library, Atlanta.

153. Minutes, Southern Company board of directors, February 15, 1946, 1:10, Southern Company Library.

154. Notation in Martin's handwriting on collection called "Certain Reference Material and Suggested Changes," no page number, Graves manuscripts, Martin Library, SRI.

155. Murray, Martin, 143. Graves wanted Martin to be candid and allow him to tell the entire story of Martin's "foresight in making sure the Southern Company would be really Southern" and "let the inside story of your letter be included." Graves also urged Martin to allow "a frank discussion of what was wrong from the beginning." John Temple Graves to Thomas W. Martin, August 4, 1958 [2.1.1.66.1].

156. William H. Brantley Jr., Biographical Essay, Alabama Review 50 (January 1997): 41–42; Branch, Alabama Power and Southern Company, 9. Bill Brantley III commented that "a fight for a southern company and beating Yankees was a fight my Daddy would have enjoyed." Interview with W. H. Brantley III, March 30, 2004.

157. W. H. Brantley Jr. to John Temple Graves, January 13, 1959, Martin Library, SRI; Wright, History of Georgia Power, 350–51, 352–54. The Brantley letter is particularly significant because whereas Tom Martin, especially in his later years, was not above emphasizing his own role in events of history, Brantley, while supporting Martin, was not intimidated by him and as a historian would have been unlikely to have altered his memory of events to fit Martin's view of his own role. To understand Brantley's personal and not complimentary but honest feelings about Martin, see his private diary, especially entries for August 13 and September 21, 1956, Diary, William H. Brantley Collection, Special Collections Library, Samford University.

158. W. H. Brantley Jr. to John Temple Graves, January 13, 1959, Martin Library, SRI.

159. Bush, Future Builders, 530. Typeset page proofs of unpublished manuscript, John Temple Graves, "Dynamos of the New South: The Development of Electricity and the Role of Thomas W. Martin," 1964, I-4, Martin Library, SRI. During the writing process Martin wanted a book focusing more on electricity in Alabama, while Graves wanted to write a biography of Martin. This book was never published because Graves died unexpectedly in 1961 before the final writing and editing were completed. Martin died in 1964. William M. Murray Jr. used this material as well as other information to compile his biography of Tom Martin, which was published by Southern Research Institute in 1978. See Murray, Martin, v.

160. Minutes, Southern Company board of directors, October 9, 1946, 1:19–20, 31, 33, 35, 42, Southern Company Library.

161. Thomas W. Martin to Justin Whiting, February 22, 1947 (photostatic copy); Graves, "Dynamos of the New South," I-5. In his manuscript Graves writes that Martin later found out that Whiting had read his confidential letter "to his group at C&S," probably including Bourne, a betrayal of trust that did nothing to improve the relationship between Martin and Whiting. Whiting did not reply to Martin's letter for almost a month, noting that the letter had been forwarded to him in Florida. Justin Whiting to Thomas W. Martin, March 17, 1947. All in Martin Library, SRI.

162. Annual Report, Commonwealth & Southern, 1946, 7.

163. Graves, draft of manuscript (January 2, 1963), 133; Alabama: News Magazine of the Deep South, November 11, 1949, 8.

164. New York Times, January 16, 1941, November 6, 1942, clippings in Robert W. Woodruff Papers, Woodruff Library, Emory University.

165. Program for dinner at the Roebuck Country Club, Birmingham, November 13, 1926, copy in William J. Henderson file. Atlanta Constitution, July 21, 1959, clipping in Robert W. Woodruff Papers, Emory University; Adrienne Moore Bond, Eugene W. Stetson (Macon, Ga.: Mercer University Press, 1983), 58–63, 97–103; "Eugene William Stetson," National Cyclopaedia of American Biography, vol. 44 (New York: James T. White & Co., 1962), 422–23; Graves, draft of manuscript, several versions with various editing, page numbers vary, Martin Library, SRI; Mercer University, Macon, Georgia, Stetson School of Business & Economics, biographical sketch of Eugene W. Stetson, www.2.mercer.edu/Business/About/About-Stetson.htm, accessed February 24, 2004. Stetson was also chairman of the executive committee of the Illinois Central Railroad Company, which he shepherded through the depression years without bankruptcy, restructuring its debt without compromising the securities of investors. James L. Hunt, a law professor at Mercer University, is writing a new biographical study of Eugene Stetson, which should be published sometime in 2007. He details the working relationships of Stetson, John A. Sibley, and Robert W. Woodruff, and the organization of the Southern Company.

166. Graves, draft of manuscript. Stetson could not accept a position on the Southern Company board because of his position on the board of Guaranty Trust, but "he was given credit for having been of substantial assistance in integrating the financial strength of the four operating members of Southern Company, which was organized on the basis of his advice as financial consultant." National Cyclopaedia of American Biography, 44:422.

167. The position of chairman of the board was eliminated at a board meeting on August 21, 1947. Yates was elected president and Bourne vice president; however, the chairman position was reestablished, and on January 23, 1950, Yates again became chairman of the Southern board when Clifford B. McManus became president of Southern Company. Minutes board of directors Southern Company, June 29, 1949, 1:156; Southern Company, Chronological Listing of Officers, 3.3, Southern Company Library; Crist, They Electrified the South, 111–16.

168. Branch, Alabama Power and Southern Company, 19.

169. Tallassee Tribune, June 26, 1947 [1.1.2.23.11].

170. John Temple Graves in his column "This Afternoon," Birmingham Post, June 30, 1947. Graves noted that Martin was not "a stuffed shirt."

171. Yates, "Address on the Dedication of Yates Dam," 38, 40 [1.1.2.23.11]; Murray, Martin, 144–45; Powergrams, July 1947, 6.

172. Branch, Alabama Power and Southern Company, 19.

173. Eugene W. Stetson to John A. Sibley, February 2, 1948, in John A. Sibley Papers, Woodruff Library, Emory University.

174. Brantley Diary, vol. 1, May 11, 12, 1948, Special Collections, SU. Some portions of Brantley's diary were lost, and there are long gaps between dates when he did record events. Bill Brantley III recalled that "The legal proceedings of the Southern Company damn near killed my father and did bring on his first heart attack." Interview with W. H. Brantley III, March 30, 2004.

175. Brantley Diary, vol. 1, May 20, June 28, July 10, 1948. On July 16 there was "strong pressure" for Brantley to pull his stock from Al Snyder's representation.

176. Southern Company, Chronological Listing of Officers, 3.3.

177. Eugene W. Stetson to John A. Sibley, June 1, 1949, Sibley Papers, Woodruff Library, Emory University.

178. Alabama Journal, July 23, 1949; Birmingham News editorial, July 24, 1949; Birmingham Age-Herald, July 24, 1949; clippings

in Martin Scrapbook, 1925–1954, Martin Library, SRI; typed carbon of press release, no date, Sibley Papers, Woodruff Library, Emory University.

179. In the Matter of Commonwealth & Southern Corporation (Delaware), the Commonwealth & Southern Corporation (New York), and The Southern Company, et al., September 23, 1949, 315–18, 320.

180. Bush, Future Builders, 358.

181. Martin gathered "30 to 50 Birmingham men" at the Mountain Brook Club to listen to Sibley. Thomas W. Martin to John A. Sibley, December 9, 1948, Sibley Papers, Woodruff Library, Emory University. Martin also pressed southern insurance companies to invest more of their funds in the bonds of the operating companies of Southern Company. His statistics showed that insurance companies in the South owned 1.63 percent of the bonds of the operating companies while insurance companies in the rest of the nation owned 98.37 percent of the bonds. Thomas W. Martin to John A. Sibley, April 25, 1949, in ibid.

182. Brief, Before the SEC, March 1948 [1.1.2.39.15]. Martin, Electricity in Alabama, 141. Crist has a long story about the sale of South Carolina Power Company for $10.2 million. Crist, They Electrified the South, 92–95.

183. Crist, They Electrified the South, 151–52. This would have been the 1914 Tutwiler Hotel on the southeast corner of Twentieth Street and Fifth Avenue.

184. Martin, Electricity in Alabama, 141; Branch, Alabama Power and Southern Company, 21; Annual Report, Southern Company, 1949, 4.

185. Birmingham News, September 28, 1949; Birmingham Age-Herald, September 28, 1949 [1.1.2.67.1]; Crist, They Electrified the South, 152.

186. Murray, Martin, 142–45.

187. Crist, They Electrified the South, 96–97.

188. Annual Report, Southern Company, 1959, 3.

189. It is interesting to note that when Granville Bourne resigned as controller of Consumers Power on July 22, 1947, he was succeeded by H. B. Hardwick, who served Consumers Power until his death on December 28, 1950. Hardwick began his career with Alabama Power Company in 1918, went with Southeastern Power & Light in 1925, then with C&S. Hardwick moved to Consumers Power before C&S was dissolved. Bush, Future Builders, 530, 562.

190. Birmingham Age-Herald, October 29, 1949; Alabama: The News Magazine of the Deep South, November 4, 1949, 12. This issue of Alabama also reported that Tom Martin was recovering from a broken arm, the result of an accident while horseback riding. See also Martin, Electricity in Alabama, 145.

191. Crist, They Electrified the South, 119–20.

192. Interview with Jack Bingham, February 25, 2004.

193. Birmingham News, June 22, 23, 1950; New York Times, June 23, 1950 [1.1.2.67.10]; Powergrams, June 1950, 36.

194. Thomas W. Martin et al. to G. S. Thorn and Birmingham Electric Employees, September 14, 1950, copy in Powergrams, September 1950, 3.

195. Annual Report, Alabama Power Company, 1951, 21; 1952, 14; Martin, Electricity in Alabama, 153; Crist, They Electrified the South, 121–22; Powergrams, December 1952, 4. The SEC case against C&S was far ahead of hearings on EBASCO, BECO, and National Power & Light, which sold BECO before being ordered to divest itself of the transportation system in Birmingham.

196. Annual Report, Alabama Power Company, 1941, 8; Annual Report, Southeastern Power & Light Company, 1925, 9; Manuscript History of the Alabama Power Company, sec. 6, Capital Assets (no author, no page numbers), courtesy of Jack Minor. This land was probably part of the 16,000 acres acquired by Joseph F. Johnston when he was president of Sloss. Lewis, Sloss Furnaces, 167. There were mineral rights to 9,400 acres and 8,800 acres in fee simple with titles resting in the company. History and Development of Alabama Power Company and Its Property, ca. 1950, 125 [2.1.1.56.20]. Interview with Joe Farley, March 1, 2004.

197. History and Development of Alabama Power Company and Its Property, 125–26 [2.1.1.56.20]; Powergrams, October 1941, 3.

198. Powergrams, January 1950, 20; December 1955, 17.

199. Ibid., October 1942, 7; January 1943, 9, 17; April 1944, 4; July 1944, 6.

200. Ibid., April 1945, 16; October 1945, 2–3; Manuscript History of Alabama Power Company, sec. 6.

201. Manuscript of talk by W. H. Parker given over Alabama Educational Television, March 1, 1960, Agee Collection, Hoole Library, UA.

202. Milton H. Fies and W. C. Schroeder, "Underground Gasification: An Account of Experiments on Coal Conducted at Gorgas, Alabama," Mechanical Engineering (February 1948), 127–35; Powergrams, April 1949, 2; October 1950, 23.

203. Interview with Ray Olive, June 24, 2003.

204. Interview with Joe Farley, February 13, 2004.

205. Comments on Legal Work of Mr. Hobart A. McWhorter with the Firm of Martin, Turner & McWhorter and Predecessor Firms, copy courtesy of Joseph M. Farley.

206. Williams, comp., "History of Balch & Bingham," 11–13; telephone conversation with Hobart A. McWhorter Jr., April 18, 2004; telephone conversation with Gail McWhorter Rummel, April 25, 2004; e-mail from Gail McWhorter Rummel, April 27, 2004; Powergrams, January 1951, 19; interview with Joe Farley, February 2, 2004; Diane McWhorter, Carry Me Home: The Climactic Battle of the Civil Rights Revolution (New York: Simon & Schuster, 2001), 79–80.

207. Compare Annual Reports, Alabama Power Company, for years 1940 (5, 14, 17) and 1950 (5, 30–32).

208. Alabama Magazine, June 30, 1950 [1.1.2.67.10]; Powergrams, February 1950, 6.

209. Lewis M. Smith, "What Are Our Goals?" Powergrams, May 1950, 2–3. Smith gives the number of Alabama Power customers as 335,000 in March, but the Annual Report for 1950, which covers figures to the end of the year, gives the number as 355,282.

Chapter Seven

1. Powergrams, March 1952, 17.

2. Harding College was then a small Christian school in Searcy, Arkansas, associated with the Church of Christ. Powergrams included many articles about Freedom Forum; for one, see May 1955, 12. The forum also had sessions on understanding and respecting each other in employer-employee relationships.

3. Selma Times-Journal, January 22, 1950 [1.1.2.67.1].

4. Clipping [1.1.2.67.10]; Martin, *Forty Years of Alabama Power Company*, 43. Barry Steam Plant began operating July 11, 1954, and was dedicated April 16, 1956. *Powergrams*, September 1956, 5.

5. *Powergrams*, March 1952, 19; January 1951, 35; May 1952, 5.

6. Ibid., February 1951, 12, 22; November 1950, 11; July 1951, 8.

7. *Alabama Power Company, Golden Anniversary*, December 4, 1956, 36.

8. Arthur Krock, *Memoirs: Sixty Years on the Firing Line* (New York: Funk & Wagnalls, 1968), 278–79.

9. Barck and Blake, *Since 1900*, 770–71; Numan V. Bartley, *The New South, 1945–1980*, vol. 11 in Stephenson and Coulter, *History of the South*, 101–02; Rogers et al., *Alabama: History of a Deep South State*, 537.

10. Robert A. Diamond, ed., *National Party Conventions, 1831–1972* (Washington, D.C.: Congressional Quarterly, 1976), 93–94.

11. Richard H. Rovere, *Affairs of State: The Eisenhower Years* (New York: Farrar, Straus & Cuddy, 1956), 358.

12. Heys interview with Eason Balch, February 25, 1999, 24.

13. Interview with Joe Farley, June 6, 2003; interview with Eason Balch, October 21, 2003.

14. Interview with Harold Williams, January 22, 2004.

15. Interview with Joe Farley, June 6, 2003.

16. Dwight David Eisenhower to Robert Lily Spragins, October 21, 1951, in Louis Galambos, ed., *NATO and the Campaign of 1952*, vol. 8 of *The Papers of Dwight David Eisenhower* (Baltimore: Johns Hopkins University Press, 1989), 1394.

17. Rogers et al., *Alabama: History of a Deep South State*, 537.

18. Interview with Jack Bingham, February 25, 2004.

19. *Annual Report*, Southern Company, 1952, 13.

20. "Tributes in Memory of Lewis M. Smith Given at the Dedication of Lewis Smith Dam," May 23, 1961, 6–7, 12–13; Murray, *Martin*, 179–80; interview with Joe Farley, June 6, 2003; interview with Walter Johnsey, April 1, 2003; interview with Walter Baker, July 14, 2004.

21. "Tributes in Memory of Lewis M. Smith," 17.

22. D. D. Wendel, employee clipping files.

23. Interview with Lee J. Styslinger Jr., August 16, 2004.

24. Interview with Walter Johnsey, April 1, 2003.

25. Interviews with Walter Johnsey, February, 26, 2003, June 18, 2004; Heys interview with Bill Whitt, June 13, 1999, 1; Chris Conway interview with Bill Whitt, no date, typed transcript, Conway files.

26. Heys interview with Bill Whitt, June 13, 1999, 2.

27. During an August 23, 2005, meeting where Birmingham Division employees and retirees were interviewed for this book, Eddie Crotwell, a retiree from the Gardendale district office, took issue with this statement. Crotwell, a former employee of Birmingham Electric Company, insisted that BECO paid more than Alabama Power. He remembered taking a pay cut after Alabama Power took over Birmingham Electric. On November 14, 2005, I returned to the Labor Relations office and had Tom Killian go back over the files and labor contracts with me. Killian agreed that although there were some differences in job titles, when we compared the same jobs, the range of hourly pay was higher at Alabama Power except for the lowest paying jobs, where BECO was a few cents per hour higher. For instance, BECO paid a meter reader $1.83 to $2.84 per hour, while Alabama Power paid $2.04 to $2.89 per hour. Compare the two contracts with IBEW, Birmingham Electric (amended December 28, 1950), and Alabama Power (amended July 17, 1950), files, Labor Relations Department.

28. Negotiations, 1953, Information Bulletins; J. O. Henkel Jr., March 23, 1952, to J. M. Barry et al., Birmingham Electric Studies, IBEW, 1953; Agreement between Birmingham Electric Company and Local Union 1322, International Brotherhood of Electrical Workers, March 1, 1947, amended December 28, 1950, files, Labor Relations Department.

29. Neely Henry to Executive Officers, August 18, 1953, in Negotiations, 1953, Information Bulletins, and Memorandum of Agreement between Alabama Power Company and the Following Local Unions to International Brotherhood of Electrical Workers . . . October 19, 1953, files, Labor Relations Department.

30. *Powergrams*, August 1953, 6.

31. Baker, *Milestones in Marketing*, 15.

32. Stephen E. Ambrose, *Eisenhower: The President*, 2 vols. (New York: Simon & Schuster, 1984), 2:116.

33. Emmet John Hughes, *The Ordeal of Power: A Political Memoir of the Eisenhower Years* (New York: Atheneum, 1963), 152; Bailey and Kennedy, *American Pageant*, 839.

34. Eugene A. Yates, Preliminary Report on Coosa and Tallapoosa Development, July 2, 1912, James Mitchell copy [2.1.1.56.5].

35. See the correspondence in the Lister Hill Papers, Hoole Library, UA. It is unclear if the sentence in the bill was included without Martin being aware of it or if he was not able to prevent its inclusion.

36. The contract was signed on November 11, 1954, but throughout 1954 the issue was before the public and was injected into the 1954 fall congressional elections. Eisenhower signed the Coosa legislation on June 28, 1954. *Annual Report*, Southern Company, 1954, 1; Alabama Power Company, "The Coosa and Warrior River Developments of Alabama Power Company" [6.1.1.9.1].

37. Dwight David Eisenhower, *The White House Years: Mandate for Change, 1953–1956* (New York: Doubleday, 1963), 377.

38. In his memoir Eisenhower quotes figures for one year of his administration when federal agencies invested approximately $288 million in power facility construction, public nonfederal organizations invested about $468 million, and "investor-owned utilities nearly $3 billion." He wrote that if the federal government assumed the guarante of power across the nation, it would have to spend "$5 billion every year for the next twenty years—an annual amount ten times the entire fiscal year 1956 budget for all river-based development projects of the Bureau of Reclamation and the Corps of Engineers." Eisenhower, *Mandate for Change*, 379.

39. Copies of E. A. Yates to Gordon R. Clapp, February 9, 1954, and Gordon R. Clapp to E. A. Yates, March 1, 1954, Governor Gordon Persons Papers, ADAH. See reference to this correspondence in Aaron Wildavsky, *Dixon-Yates: A Study in Power Politics* (New Haven: Yale University Press, 1962), 53–54.

40. A. J. G. Priest, "Dixon-Yates and the Public Interest," *Virginia Law Review* 41 (April 1955): 289–93. Priest, a utilities lawyer, points to the contradictions of those opposed to the contract.

41. Wildavsky, *Dixon-Yates*, vii, 1–30; Eisenhower, *Mandate for Change*, 378. Wildavsky's book is the best overall treatment but is written from the government policy view and is somewhat hostile to the Dixon-Yates position.

42. Brantley Diary, vol. 1, October 14, 1954, Brantley Collection,

Special Collections Library, Samford University. Five days later, October 19, Brantley wrote that "we are going to fight with or without the help of Mid-South—and I take it also without help from the Atomic Energy Commission or the Republican National Committee."

43. Priest, "Dixon-Yates," 289, 296.

44. Hamilton, *Lister Hill*, 200–201.

45. Wildavsky, *Dixon-Yates*, 123–24. The intricacy of this controversy, its timetable, and the people who were involved cannot be discussed fully here. See also "Summary of Salient Dixon-Yates Facts, December 1955," and clipping, Ralph Henderson, "Dixon-Yates Deal," *New York World-Telegram and Sun*, December 29, 1955, Brantley Collection, SU.

46. *Wall Street Journal*, December 15, 1955, clipping sent to Bill Brantley by E. A Yates, Brantley Collection, SU.

47. Harllee Branch Jr., *The Crowd and the Commonplace* (Atlanta: Southern Services, Inc., 1971), 174–75.

48. Obituary, Eugene A. Yates, *Birmingham News*, October 6, 1957; *Powergrams*, October 1957, 18.

49. *Knoxville Journal*, December 19, 1959, Brantley Collection, SU.

50. Harllee Branch Jr. to Company Directors, Southern Company, December 29, 1959, with copies of articles from various newspapers; *Chattanooga News-Free Press*, December 19, 1959, in ibid. Bill Brantley collected Dixon-Yates political cartoons from all over the world and bound them in a book.

51. Remarks of Fernand C. Weiss, groundbreaking, April 26, 1958.

52. *Powergrams*, November 1953, 3.

53. *Annual Report*, Alabama Power Company, 1953, 8–9; *Birmingham Post-Herald*, May 24, 1954.

54. Fernand C. Weiss, "Coosa and Warrior River Hydro Program of the Alabama Power Company," speech before the Engineering and Operation Section Conference of the Southeastern Electric Exchange, New Orleans, April 7–8, 1955 [2.1.2.55.6].

55. Joe Farley, "Introduction of Mr. Bouldin," dedication of Walter Bouldin Dam, September 19, 1969, 6.

56. John Temple Graves, unpublished manuscript, chapter ten, Martin Library, SRI.

57. Crist, *They Electrified the South*, 125.

58. E-mail, Walter Bouldin Jr. to Leah Atkins, June 4, 2004.

59. Farley, "Introduction of Mr. Bouldin," 6; *Annual Report*, Alabama Power Company, 1952, 12.

60. Williams, comp., "History of Balch & Bingham," 37; interview with Ollie Smith, May 25, 2004.

61. Vogtle made five escape attempts; the last one was successful. Steve McQueen had the starring role in the movie. Interview with Harold Williams, November 7, 2005.

62. *Powergrams*, June 1963, 3; Heys interview with Eason Balch, February 25, 1999, 22–23; interview with Eason Balch, July 13, 2004.

63. Interview with Joe Farley, June 6, 2003.

64. See this form letter and the large collection of letters supporting Alabama Power's Coosa development in the Lister Hill Papers, Hoole Library, UA.

65. Farley, *Alabama Power Company*, 17; interview with Joe Farley, June 6, 2003. See correspondence in Lister Hill Papers, Hoole Library, UA. Albert Rains was joined by Frank Boykin of Mobile,

George M. Grant of Troy, George W. Andrews of Union Springs, Kenneth A. Roberts of Piedmont, Armistead I. Selden Jr. of Greensboro, Carl A. Elliott of Jasper, and Laurie C. Battle of Birmingham. For Persons's attitude see his administrative file on the Coosa development, Governor Gordon Persons Papers, ADAH.

66. See Memorandum to the Alabama Congressional Delegation from Alabama Rural Electric Association of Cooperatives, March 26, 1954; Maury A. McWilliams to Everett Lay, March 27, 1954; and the copy of J. C. Blakey's March 31, 1954, legal opinion, "Jurisdiction of the Federal Power Commission to Grant to Alabama Power Company a License to Construct Dams on the Coosa River Between Wetumpka and Rome," sent to Thomas W. Martin, copies in Governor Gordon Persons Papers, ADAH; J. C. Blakey to Thomas W. Martin, March 30, 1953, Legal Memoranda and Opinion, Balch & Bingham [2146-18].

67. Williams, comp., "History of Balch & Bingham," 18; interview with Harold Williams, January 22, 2004.

68. Farley, *Alabama Power Company*, 17–18.

69. *Standard and Times*, April 2, 1954, clipping, Governor Gordon Persons Papers, ADAH.

70. Thomas W. Martin to Gordon Persons, April 8, 1954, in ibid. Note that Martin wrote and signed the letter as chairman of the board. Lewis M. Smith, who was president of the company, seemed to play no role in these discussions or the decisions.

71. Interview with Joe Farley, June 6, 2003.

72. Charles R. Lowman, *Power Pioneers: AEC's First Fifty Years, A History of Alabama Electric Cooperative* (Andalusia: Alabama Electric Cooperative, 1991), 40–41.

73. A. M. Redd to Gordon Persons, April 9, 1964, and Gordon Persons to A. M. Redd, April 14, 1954, Governor Gordon Persons Papers, ADAH.

74. Gordon Persons to George A. Dondero (chairman of the House Committee on Public Works), May 7, 1954; Lister Hill to Gordon Persons, June 3, 1954, in ibid.

75. *Birmingham News*, May 23, 1954. The Brown decision ruled that "separate but equal" schools for black and white students were unconstitutional, and the U.S. Supreme Court ordered the integration of the nation's educational systems with "all deliberate speed." Eason Balch recalls that Senator John Sparkman, whose Huntsville law firm represented Alabama Power before TVA, gave the speech in the Senate arguing for private development of the Coosa and made a compelling case for Alabama Power. Interview with Eason Balch, May 31, 2006.

76. See file 2146-18, Balch & Bingham, Legal Memoranda and Opinions, Martin, Vogtle, Balch & Bingham. This file has a number of opinions involving the Coosa projects on a variety of legal issues written mostly by J. C. Blakey and Joe Farley.

77. Interview with Joe Farley, July 6, 2004; *Powergrams*, November 1953, 3. It might be noted that company engineers also discussed rebuilding Mitchell Dam. Because of its placement between high mountains, the site could take a much higher dam, one that would flood Lay Dam and inundate lands north of Childersburg creating a huge reservoir. This proposal was known as "High Mitchell" but was discarded because it was not economical and construction would involve a number of problems.

78. Yates sent a copy of this memorandum to Bill Brantley and hand-wrote on the bottom: "Bill—This is quite a problem. EAY." Yates Memorandum, September 13, 1957, Brantley Collection, SU.

79. Crist, *They Electrified the South*, 166–67.

80. Interview with Joe Farley, July 6, 2004.

81. Crist, *They Electrified the South*, 167.

82. Lister Hill stressed this point and Martin quoted him in his June 7, 1956, article for *Public Utilities Fortnightly*. Reprinted as Thomas W. Martin, *Coosa River Development—Past and Proposed*, 5, Thomas W. Martin Collection, Auburn University.

83. *Powergrams*, November 1944, 23; interview with Mary Cochran, June 25, 2004; Martin, *Electricity in Alabama*, 2ᵈ ed., 51.

84. *Powergrams*, April 1959, 5–6.

85. Interview with Douglas McCrary, November 14, 2003.

86. *Annual Report*, Alabama Power Company, 1954, 6; interview with Joe Farley, July 6, 2004; Atkins, *The Warrior and the Tombigbee*, 11.

87. *Powergrams*, July 1927, 9.

88. Neal G. Lineback and Charles T. Traylor, *Atlas of Alabama* (Tuscaloosa: University of Alabama Press, 1973), 5–7; Corps of Engineers, Navigation Charts of Tombigbee, Warrior, and Black Warrior Canalized System (Mobile: United States Engineer Office, ca. 1943), charts 20 and 21. See also Kenneth D. Willis, *The Harnessing of the Black Warrior River* (Tuscaloosa: City of Tuscaloosa, 1989).

89. Alabama Planning Board, Pertinent Facts about the Warrior-Tombigbee River System, April 3, 1950, 4, in Governor Gordon Persons Papers, ADAH.

90. *Annual Report*, Alabama Power Company, 1952, 6–7; *Alabama Power Company's Coosa and Warrior Rivers Projects*, 16 [1.1.2.003.026].

91. *Birmingham Post-Herald*, July 27, 1954, Scrapbook, Martin Library, SRI.

92. Carl Elliott to Gordon Persons, August 27, 1954, Governor Gordon Persons Papers, ADAH.

93. *Alabama Power Company's Coosa and Warrior Rivers Projects*, 16 [1.1.2.003.026]; *Powergrams*, December 1957, 3.

94. *Powergrams*, December 1955, 2; December 1956, 16–17.

95. No. 6–9, Lewis Smith Dam; Lewis Smith Dam, statistical sheet, Smith Dam file; *Alabama Power Company's Coosa and Warrior Rivers Projects*, 14 [1.1.2.003.026]; Weiss, "Coosa and Warrior River Hydro Program" [2.1.2.55.6].

96. *Powergrams*, September 1961, 2; August 1963, 2.

97. Ibid., January 1963, 14–15.

98. Chris Conway interview with Harold Williams, no date, typed transcript in Conway files.

99. Interviews with Ollie Smith, May 25, 2004, June 12, 2004; interview with Harold Williams, January 22, 2004.

100. Rumore, *Lawyers in a New South City*, 105–06, 196; interview with Harold Williams, January 22, 2004.

101. Interview with C. J. Coley Jr., October 23, 2003.

102. Interview with Douglas McCrary, November 14, 2003; Douglas McCrary, "Daisye's Child," 13, 55, 80. This is an excellent unpublished autobiography, copy courtesy of Douglas McCrary.

103. McCrary, "Daisye's Child," 80–82.

104. Chris Conway interviews with Harold Williams and with Douglas McCrary, no dates, typed transcript in Conway files.

105. Interview with Harold Williams, January 22, 2004.

106. Ibid.

107. Graves, unpublished manuscript, chapter six, page 5, Martin Library, SRI.

108. "Coosa and Warrior Rivers Developments of Alabama Power Company" [6.1.1.9.1].

109. Zipp Newman, "Dusting 'em Off," *Birmingham News*, April 21, 1968.

110. Dedication of Logan Martin Dam, June 24, 1967, program, 8.

111. Zipp Newman, "Dusting 'em Off," *Birmingham News*, April 28, 1968.

112. Interview with David Holland, David Fring, Ron Robinson, and Charles E. Shirah, September 8, 2004; McCrary, "Daisye's Child," 91–93; John D. Jones, "Presentation to the Alabama Power Company Board of Directors," May 16, 1980, files, Logan Martin Dam.

113. Zipp Newman, "Dusting 'em Off," *Birmingham News*, May 12, 1968.

114. Interview with John Farley, June 15, 2004; John Farley, "The Environmental Movement and Alabama Power Company," 1971, 1–3, copy courtesy of Willard Bowers.

115. Interview with John Farley, June 15, 2004.

116. William Voigt Jr. (executive director, Izaak Walton League of America) to Gordon Persons, May 14, 1954; Thomas W. Martin to Gordon Persons, May 26, 1954, Governor Gordon Persons Papers, ADAH.

117. H. Neely Henry, employee clipping files. Graves, unpublished manuscript, chapter eleven, Martin Library, SRI; interview with Walter Johnsey, April 1, 2003.

118. McCrary, "Daisye's Child," 94.

119. Farley, Balch, and Conway, "Good Name and Destiny,'" 79.

120. Interview with Elmer Harris, January 18, 2005.

121. Ibid.

122. Interview with Joe Farley, August 30, 2004.

123. R. L. Harris, employee clipping files. *Powergrams*, June 1956, 8; interviews with Walter Johnsey, April 1, 2003, September 2, 2004.

124. Robert W. Deutsch, *Nuclear Power: A Rational Approach* (Columbia, Md.: GP Courseware, 1987), 6; James M. Barry, "The Story of Electric Power Is the Story of Progress," *Alabama Purchaser*, September 1952, 9 [2.1.2.55.6]; Joseph A. Camilleri, *The State and Nuclear Power: Conflict and Control in the Western World* (Seattle: University of Washington Press, 1984), 12. Rudolph and Ridley, *Power Struggle*, 87–103. The account is decidedly hostile to private power.

125. Chester J. Pach Jr. and Elmo Richardson, *The Presidency of Dwight D. Eisenhower*, rev. ed. (Lawrence: University Press of Kansas, 1991), 56; Argonne National Laboratory, official Website, accessed June 18, 2004; *Annual Report*, Alabama Power Company, 1952, 8–9; Rudolph and Ridley, *Power Struggle*, 104–09.

126. Walter C. Patterson, *Nuclear Power* (New York: Penguin Books, 1983), 68, 128–29, 134; Camilleri, *The State and Nuclear Power*, 36; H. J. Scholz, "Atomic Energy in Industry," speech before the Birmingham Rotary Club, February 4, 1953, *Powergrams*, February 1953, 29–31; *Powergrams*, April 1954, 28; February 1956, 8.

127. *Annual Report*, Alabama Power Company, 1955, 4; Rudolph and Ridley, *Power Struggle*, 110; Thomas W. Martin, *Address to the*

Joint Session of the Alabama Legislature, August 11, 1961, 21, Martin Collection, Auburn University Archives.

128. *Powergrams*, May 1956, 8. Construction on the Enrico Fermi Plant of the Power Reactor Development Company began outside Detroit in the summer of 1956. *Powergrams*, January 1957, 3. In the fall of 1958 H. J. Scholz and Harllee Branch attended the Geneva conference on peaceful uses of atomic energy. *Powergrams*, January 1959, 19.

129. Farley, Balch, and Conway, "'Good Name and Destiny,'" 104–05.

130. Thomas W. Martin to Gordon Persons, February 28, 1951, Governor Gordon Persons Papers, ADAH.

131. Frank W. Boykin to Gordon Persons, July 24, 1951, in ibid.; Martin, *Forty Years of Alabama Power*, 37; *Birmingham News*, August 17, 1951.

132. Baker, *Milestones in Marketing*, 14.

133. *Powergrams*, January 1953, 2–3, 7.

134. Ibid., April 1953, 7; March 1956, 15; interview with Joe Farley, August 30, 2004.

135. Baker, *Milestones in Marketing*, 16–17.

136. *Powergrams*, December 1956, 6.

137. Baker, *Milestones in Marketing*, 17. The home service department stayed in the general offices until 1972.

138. *Powergrams*, April 1957, 8; July 1957, 11; January 1959, 12–13; interview with Joe Farley, August 30, 2004. Farley noted that the tight budget was to blame for the steel exterior selection.

139. *Powergrams*, February 1956, 3; January 1956, 25.

140. Interview with Alan Martin, February 24, 2005.

141. *Powergrams*, March, 1961, 21; July 1961, 35.

142. Ibid., April 1954, 26–27, 32; May 1954, 23; June 1954, 40; January 1955, 25; February 1955, 31.

143. Ibid., September 1959, 2; October 1959, 5; April 1960, 7.

144. Ibid., October 1960, 15.

145. Crist, *They Electrified the South*, 165–67; interview with Joe Farley, March 1, 2004.

146. *Annual Report*, Alabama Power Company, 1956, 7; *Powergrams* April 1957, 12–13.

147. Farley, Balch, and Conway, "'Good Name and Destiny,'" 77; interview with Joe Farley, August 30, 2004.

148. *Powergrams*, December 1957, 4.

149. *Alabama Power Company, Golden Anniversary*, December 4, 1956.

150. *Annual Report*, Alabama Power Company, 1956, 3, 7.

151. Baker, *Milestones in Marketing*, 5; *Powergrams*, June 1956, 14.

152. *Powergrams*, August 1956, 26; November 1963, 16.

153. Ibid., August 1954, 7–8; October 1953, 31; January 1954, 5; December 1958, 13; March 1963, 9.

154. Ibid., August 1960, 4.

155. Ibid., January 1964, 5.

156. Interview with Lee Styslinger Jr., August 16, 2004; Lee Styslinger Jr., "Altec, Inc., 60th Anniversary Speech to Rotary Club," April 5, 1987, courtesy of Lee Styslinger; Wayne Flynt, *Mine, Mill & Microchip: A Chronicle of Alabama Enterprise* (North-

ridge, Calif.: Windsor Publications for Business Council of Alabama, 1987), 276. There are a number of stories told by Alabama Power old-timers about the relationship between Altec and Alabama Power Company.

157. *Powergrams*, May 1954, 16; January 1955, 4; March 1960, 4–5; March 1963, 2–3.

158. Ibid., May 1953, 5.

159. Ibid., October 1964, 8; November 1953, 30–32.

160. Ibid., February 1956, 4; March 1957, 10; May 1957, 8–9; July 1963, 12.

161. Ibid., March 1957, 5–7; April 1962, 21; telephone interview with Mary Martin, September 1, 2004. Although Mrs. Martin retired in 1985, her son Alan Martin relates that, to those Alabama Power people who remember his mother so fondly, he will always be Mary Martin's son. Interview with Alan Martin, August 30, 2004.

162. *Annual Report*, Alabama Power Company, 1957, 19.

163. *Powergrams*, September 1955, 20; October 1960, 4; August 1962, 4.

164. Ibid., September 1950, 6; October 1950, 2–17; December 1951, 5–9; October 1955, 2–5.

165. Ibid., August 1956, 26; November 1962, 9.

166. Ibid., November 1956.

167. Ibid., August 1953, 19; August 1955, 7.

168. Interview with Joe Farley, July 6, 2004.

169. Murray, *Martin*, 209–11.

170. *Powergrams*, August 1956, 6; Martin, *Address to the Alabama Legislature*, August 11, 1961, 15; Murray, *Martin*, 246–48.

171. *Powergrams*, April 1964, 2.

172. History of Rates and Rate Structure, files, Rate Department.

173. *Powergrams*, August 1958, 6; E. A. Wilson, "The How and Why of Electricity Utility Rates," August 18, 1959 [2.1.2.55.6].

174. *Powergrams*, April 1964, 28; *Annual Report*, Alabama Power Company, 1964, 17.

175. Interview with William J. Ward, July 8, 2004.

176. *Powergrams*, December 1964, 16.

177. Murray, *Martin*, 207–09, 224–28, 236–38; *Powergrams*, October 1962, 6–7.

178. On April 10, 2006, this auditorium was dedicated to honor Joseph M. Farley, Alabama Power president 1969–1989. A new bronze plaque with Farley's image joins the plaques of Lay, Mitchell, and Martin in the foyer of the auditorium.

179. *Powergrams*, December 1964, 4; Richard A. Peacock to Al Stanton, December 7, 1964, letter in News Release Index [677-036].

180. Murray, *Martin*, 239–41; interview with Joe Farley, July 6, 2004; interview with William J. Ward, July 8, 2004.

181. Interview with Ollie Smith, June 12, 2004.

182. Record of Tribute to Thomas W. Martin, 75th Birthday, August 13, 1956, Martin Library, SRI.

183. Lewis M. Smith, "Thomas W. Martin, Our Colleague, Associate and Friend," *Powergrams*, August 1956, 31.

184. Brantley Diary, Monday, August 13, 1956, Brantley Collection, SU. See the complete remarks in Lewis M. Smith, "Thomas W. Martin," and "Remarks of John Temple Graves," in Record of a Tribute to Thomas W. Martin, Martin Library, SRI. Graves's trib-

ute was not republished in *Powergrams*. Graves compared Martin to his father, who was also a little man, but he always thought a man small of stature was very big.

185. Murray, *Martin*, 208–09; Brantley Diary, Monday, August 13, 1956, Brantley Collection, SU.

186. Murray, *Martin*, 246.

187. *Birmingham News*, November 14, 1951; *Birmingham Post-Herald*, August 13, 1955, in clipping files, Thomas W. Martin, BPL.

188. Interviews with John Patterson, June 4, August 17, 2005; *Powergrams*, June 1990, 8.

Chapter Eight

1. The epigraph quote is from Joseph M. Farley, Letter to Stockholders, March 29, 1976, *Annual Report*, Alabama Power Company, 1975, 2.

2. Frye Gaillard, *Cradle of Freedom: Alabama and the Movement that Changed America* (Tuscaloosa: University of Alabama Press, 2004), 6, 226–28.

3. Rogers et al., *Alabama: History of a Deep South State*, 255–56, 260–61.

4. Jackson, "Loafing Streams," 25–26.

5. Ibid., 22–23.

6. *Birmingham News*, June 14, 1921; *Birmingham Age-Herald*, May 12, 31, 1922; Glenn Feldman, *Politics, Society, and the Klan in Alabama, 1915–1949* (Tuscaloosa: University of Alabama Press, 1999), 53; David M. Chalmers, *Hooded Americanism: The History of the Ku Klux Klan* (Durham: Duke University Press, 1987), 79, 83; William R. Snell, "Masked Men in the Magic City: Activities of the Revisited Klan in Birmingham, 1916–1940," *Alabama Historical Quarterly* 34 (Fall–Winter 1972): 206–27; William R. Snell, "The Ku Klux Klan in Jefferson County, Alabama, 1916–1930," (master's thesis, Samford University, 1967), 64–65.

7. Interview with John Thomas Porter, August 31, 2004; interview with William J. Ward, July 8, 2004; interview with Joe Farley, August 27, 2004. Reverend John Thomas Porter called Martin "a typical white bigot" in his Oral History Interview conducted by Dr. Horace Huntley, March 26, 1997, typed transcript, page 2, Archives, Birmingham Civil Rights Institute.

8. Glenn T. Eskew, *But for Birmingham: The Local and National Movements in the Civil Rights Struggle* (Chapel Hill: University of North Carolina Press, 1997), 223–24, 246; *Annual Report*, Alabama Power Company, 1993, 20–21; interview with John Thomas Porter, August 31, 2004. Louis J. Willie, who joined the board on March 23, 1984, was the first African American to serve on the company's board of directors.

9. Feldman, *Politics, Society, and the Klan in Alabama*, 310.

10. Robert Gaines Corley, "The Quest for Racial Harmony: Race Relations in Birmingham, Alabama, 1947–1963" (Ph.D. diss., University of Virginia, 1979), 21, 53, 64, 287.

11. Ibid., 53.

12. There are differences between the two acts. For specific details of each, see promotional material by State of Alabama, Planning and Industrial Development Board, "Alabama: An Ideal Location for Industry," Governor George C. Wallace Papers [SG-22379], ADAH.

13. J. Mills Thornton III, *Dividing Lines: Municipal Politics and the Struggle for Civil Rights in Montgomery, Birmingham, and Selma* (Tuscaloosa: University of Alabama Press, 2002), 164–65.

14. Interview with Joe Farley, September 1, 2004.

15. John E. Steger [executive vice president of the chamber] to W. Cooper Green, September 25, 1963, copy, Senior Citizens Committee files, Birmingham Chamber of Commerce Papers, Department of Archives and Manuscripts, BPL; Eskew, *But for Birmingham*, 278, 205, 373n. Before the files were released, Mills Thornton determined from his research that a high-ranking executive at Alabama Power Company chaired the committee. He assumed it was Tom Martin. See Thornton, *Dividing Lines*, 648n, 128; Anthony Paul Underwood, "A Progressive History of the Young Men's Business Club of Birmingham, Alabama, 1946–1970" (master's thesis, Samford University, 1980), 110. The *Montgomery Advertiser* published a feature article on Cooper Green on March 20, 1945, including the information that Green, then mayor, had once served as the secretary of the Tarrant City Ku Klux Klan. For Green's 1960s industrial development views, see article by Brandy Ayers, *Anniston Star*, October 28, 1962, and *Birmingham News*, November 4, 1962. Jim Miller Jr. recalls Walter Bouldin asking him to attend a meeting in Birmingham where a group of Atlanta businessmen were going to discuss how Atlanta had moved through the civil rights movement. The group advised Birmingham businessmen: "Don't be against it. Sit and let it happen." Interview with Jim Miller Jr., November 11, 2004. Sid Smyer deserves much credit for enduring the crisis.

16. Rogers et al., *Alabama: History of a Deep South State*, 570–71. Marshall Frady, *Wallace* (1968; reprint, New York: Meridian Books, 1970), 132–35; Dan T. Carter, *The Politics of Rage: George Wallace, the Origins of the New Conservatism, and the Transformation of American Politics* (New York: Simon & Schuster, 1995), 104–09. The Wallace and Cater Acts were a successful part of economic development. Stephan Lesher, *George Wallace: American Populist* (Reading, Mass.: Addison-Wesley Publishing Co., 1994), 86–87. Lesher writes that Wallace considered the Wallace and Cater Acts among his most significant contributions to Alabama.

17. Thornton, *Dividing Lines*, 277.

18. *Powergrams*, October 1962, 9. R. A. Puryear Jr. to Member[s], Birmingham Chamber of Commerce, September 19, 1962, Senior Citizens Committee, Chamber of Commerce Papers, BPL. Diane McWhorter interprets this statement as "one of Birmingham's invisible turning points" where "the power structure implicitly acknowledged that it had control over the actions of the Ku Klux Klan." McWhorter has a different interpretation of this document from historians. She writes that while the statement was "cleverly worded to apply most obviously to would-be black demonstrators, it was really aimed at whites who might be involved in the Klan's welcome for SCLC." McWhorter, *Carry Me Home*, 293–94.

19. Pepperell representatives first visited Alabama in 1922, according to *Electricity in Alabama* (page 92), agreed to build in Opelika in 1924, and signed the contract for electricity in 1925. Alabama Power Company, New Industries Located in Service Area, 1925–1952, inclusive [5.1.1.98.241]. Jeff Frederick, "Command and Control: George Wallace, Governor of Alabama 1963–1972" (Ph.D. diss., Auburn University, 2003), 129–30.

20. Frederick, "Command and Control: George Wallace," 130.

21. *Annual Report*, Alabama Power Company, 1963, 5; Thornton, *Dividing Lines*, 165, 235, 255, 257–59, 652, n.140; Underwood, "Young Men's Business Club," 100–106.

22. Andrew M. Manis, *A Fire You Can't Put Out: The Civil Rights Life*

of *Birmingham's Reverend Fred Shuttlesworth* (Tuscaloosa: University of Alabama Press, 1999), 328; interview with Banks Farris, November 10, 2004; interview with Charles McCrary, November 8, 2004.

23. E. Culpepper Clark, *The Schoolhouse Door: Segregation's Last Stand at the University of Alabama* (New York: Oxford University Press, 1993), 208–37.

24. Thornton, *Dividing Lines*, 452.

25. Interview with Walter Baker, August 24, 2004.

26. Frye Gaillard, *Southern Voices: Profiles and Other Stories* (Asheboro, N.C.: Down Home Press, 1991), 58; Frank Sikora, *Until Justice Rolls Down: The Birmingham Church Bombing Case* (Tuscaloosa: University of Alabama Press, 1991), 16.

27. Interview with Joe Farley, November 1, 2004.

28. *Birmingham News*, January 20, 1974, February 6, 1976. Governor Wallace appointed Green to a vacancy, and he became president of the Jefferson County Commission.

29. *Annual Report*, Alabama Power Company, 1965, 4; Heys interview with Joe Farley, February 26, 1999, 37.

30. Interview with Joe Farley, February 2, 2005; Lowman, *Power Pioneers*, 56.

31. Press Release, September 25, 1964, News Releases Index, 1964 [677-036].

32. Ibid., September 25, 28, October 13, 19, 20, 26, 1964, News Releases Index, 1964 [677-036].

33. Interview with Jim Miller Jr., November 11, 2004; interview with Jack Bingham, February 25, 2004.

34. Heys interview with Eason Balch, February 25, 1999, 44–45; interview with Eason Balch, June 13, 2004; A. M. Rosenthal, ed., *The Night the Lights Went Out* (New York: New American Library, 1965), 5–10.

35. Press Releases, November 21, 23, 27, 1964, News Releases Index, 1964 [677-036]; *Annual Report*, Alabama Power Company, 1967, 3; Lowman, *Power Pioneers*, 56; *Powergrams*, December 1967, 7.

36. Lowman, *Power Pioneers*, 154.

37. The amount given in Lowman's book is $20,526,611, which is slightly more than the loan amount in Alabama Power records. Lowman, *Power Pioneers*, 51–52.

38. Alvin W. Vogtle Jr. to Edison Electric Institute, February 23, 1962. See specifically Exhibits 1, 81, and 82, and Balch & Bingham files [588-007]. Eason Balch recalls that Walter Bouldin discussed the matter with David Hamil, the REA administrator under the Eisenhower administration, and pointed out that the only basis for the alleged economic advantage to the AEC was that AEC could borrow money from REA at a subsidized rate and avoid taxes that Alabama Power Company paid. Hamil did not approve the AEC loan application. Interview with Eason Balch, May 31, 2006.

39. Kenneth O. Gilmore and Eugene H. Methvin, "The REA—A Case Study of Bureaucracy Run Wild," *Reader's Digest*, reprint from December 1963 issue, 7, copy in history files of Eason Balch.

40. Harllee Branch Jr., Before the New York Society of Security Analysts, New York, September 26, 1962, copy in Brantley Collection, SU.

41. Document of Approval, signed by Maurice Patterson, Director of Finance, State of Alabama, December 9, 1962, Balch & Bingham files [595-012]. The finance order was dated December 9 but was not announced until January 9, 1963. Patterson was a lame duck director. His brother, Governor John Patterson, had been

defeated by George C. Wallace and Patterson's term of office was drawing to a close.

42. The Alabama Power exhibits and testimony in Balch & Bingham files [588-007 and 616-006B] contradict the charges of inadequate power supply in the Southeast and that the "low-voltage conditions experienced on the AEC system were the result of APSCo's poor service," in Lowman, *Power Pioneers*, 33. The issue involving the small Gantt steam plant caused a dispute between editor Charles G. Dobbins of the *Montgomery Advertiser* and his publisher, R. F. Hudson, as well as his son, R. F. Hudson Jr. Dobbins refused to run an editorial against the REA proposal without it being attributed to Hudson. When Hudson refused, Dobbins resigned. See Charles G. Dobbins, "Alabama Governors and Editors, 1930–1955: A Memoir," *Alabama Review* 29 (April 1976): 147–48. *Alabama Electric Cooperative, Inc., et al. v. Alabama Power Co.*, 251 Ala. 190, 36 So.2d 523.

43. Heys interview with Eason Balch, February 25, 1999, 27. *Alabama Electric Cooperative, Inc. et al. v. Alabama Power Company et al.*, 278 Ala. 123, 176 So.2d 483.

44. *Alabama Power Company, Appellant, v. Alabama Electric Cooperative, Inc., Appellees, et al.*, United States Court of Appeals Fifth Circuit, No. 23016, April 2, 1968, Westlaw, 394 F.2d 672. Interview with Joe Farley, January 12, 2004; interview with Eason Balch, June 13, 2004; S. Eason Balch to W. H. Skinner, July 22, 1965, Balch & Bingham files [595-012]; interview with Eason Balch, May 31, 2006. The federal court case was directed by Balch, Jack Bingham, Frank H. Hawthorne, and James H. Hancock.

45. *Annual Report*, Alabama Power Company, 1966, 5.

46. Walter Bouldin to Gentlemen, August 12, 1966 [4.1.1.82.6].

47. Heys interview with Bill Whitt, June 13, 1999, 3–6.

48. W. O. Whitt to All Division Employees [January 15, 1967], in 1966 files, Labor Relations Department.

49. Interview with Brad Sandlin, September 30, 2004.

50. McCrary, "Daisye's Child," 95–96.

51. "White Collar Men Keep Alabama Power Going," *Electric World*, October 10, 1966, 17–18; interview with Joe Farley, August 1, 2003; interview with Jim Clements, September 14, 2004; interview with Jim Miller Jr., November 11, 2004; interview with John Farley, June 15, 2004; interview with Walter Johnsey, February 26, 2003; Heys interview with Joe Farley, June 25, 1999, 19.

52. Interview with Jabo Waggoner Jr., September 21, 2004; interview with Jimmy Long, February 7, 2005.

53. Interview with Jack Bingham, January 31, 2006.

54. Interview with Steve Spencer, January 30, 2006.

55. Clipping, *Mobile Register*, October 31, 1966, in 1966 files, Labor Relations Department; *Montgomery Advertiser*, December 8, 1966.

56. Interviews with Brad Sandlin and David Shaw, September 30, 2004.

57. Frederick, "Command and Control: George Wallace," 220; Heys interview with Bill Whitt, June 13, 1999, 8.

58. Robert J. Norrell, "George Wallace and Union Politics in Alabama," in Robert H. Zieger, ed., *Organized Labor in the Twentieth-Century South* (Knoxville: University of Tennessee Press, 1991), 264. This poll showed that in a race between Wallace and Senator John Sparkman, Wallace was preferred two to one. In this study, Norrell does not cover the politics of the IBEW.

59. Interview with Joe Farley, January 22, 2003.

60. *Birmingham News*, January 6, 1967. Negotiating for the governor were Arliss Fant, state labor director; Seymore Trammel, state finance director; Cecil Jackson, executive secretary; and state senator-elect O. J. Goodwyn of Montgomery, who had been Wallace's floor leader in the house.

61. Interview with Joe Farley, August 1, 2003; interview with Jeff Frederick, January 22, 2003; Governor George C. Wallace to Walter Bouldin, January 13, 1967, in 1966 files, Labor Relations Department.

62. *Birmingham News*, January 6, 13, 1967. Charles T. Brasfield Jr. and E. Davis Long, Information Bulletin No. 21, January 13, 1967, and Walter Bouldin to All Employees, September 16, 1966, in 1966 files, Labor Relations Department; *Powergrams*, January 1967, inside front cover.

63. Harllee Branch to Walter Bouldin, January 13, 1967, in 1966 files, Labor Relations Department.

64. Heys interview with Bill Whitt, June 13, 1999, 9.

65. Interview with Joe Farley, August 1, 2003; McCrary, "Daisye's Child," 95–97; interview with Jim Miller Jr., November 11, 2004.

66. Crist, *They Electrified the South*, 155–56; *Powergrams*, December 1967, 19.

67. Harbert Corporation Newsletter, June 1966, 9–10.

68. *Powergrams*, October 1967, 1; *Annual Report*, Alabama Power Company, 1967, 11–12; 1969, 12; 1970, 10.

69. *Powergrams*, September 1968, 5–6, 24–25; October 1968, 1–6.

70. *Powergrams*, September 1967, 1; October 1969, 1–10; personal memorabilia and program, Dedication of Walter Bouldin Dam, September 19, 1969, courtesy of Dr. Walter Bouldin Jr.; *Annual Report*, Alabama Power Company, 1969, 14–15.

71. Telegrams, Dwight Eisenhower to Walter Bouldin, April 21, 1960; President Lyndon Johnson to Walter Bouldin, January 24, 1964; and Richard Nixon to Walter Bouldin, March 1, 1971, copies courtesy of Dr. Walter Bouldin Jr.

72. Frederick, "Command and Control: George Wallace," 292–93.

73. Holt License, 6–7, Holt Project (No. 2203), in Holt Project, No. 2203, Notebook, files, Balch & Bingham.

74. History and Development of Alabama Power Company and Its Property, 29 [2.1.1.56.20]. *Powergrams*, October 1967, 1.

75. *Birmingham News*, March 24, 1968. These articles were reprinted by Alabama Power Company, with permission of the *Birmingham News* and Newman, into a book entitled *Alabama Power Company Lakes Create 145,000 Acres of Fun* (1968).

76. Bailey and Kennedy, *American Pageant*, 871–77.

77. Heys interview with Joseph M. Farley, February 26, 1999, 37.

78. Walter Bouldin to Stockholders, March 29, 1968, in *Annual Report*, Alabama Power Company, 1967, 2.

79. *Powergrams*, August 1982, 10–11.

80. *Annual Report*, Alabama Power Company, 1964, 7.

81. Heys interview with Jack Bingham, March 25, 1999, 26; Farley, Balch, and Conway, "'Good Name and Destiny,'" 85.

82. Interview with Jack Bingham, February 25, 2004; Heys interview with Jack Bingham, March 25, 1999, 27; interview with Eason Balch, July 20, 2004.

83. *Alabama Official and Statistical Register*, 1951, 158; Howell

Raines, *My Soul Is Rested: The Story of the Civil Rights Movement in the Deep South* (1977; reprint, New York: Penguin Books, 1983), 166.

84. Interview with Joe Farley, February 7, 2005.

85. Nunnelley, *Bull Connor*, 167–68.

86. *Birmingham News*, February 8, 9, 1967; *Birmingham Post-Herald*, February 8, 9, 1967; *Birmingham News*, March 2, 1960. Twenty-six people died in the fire. Pepper was accused of four incidents from three trucking lines and one water system.

87. Raines, *My Soul Is Rested*, 166. Raines comments that Connor "consistently" voted for higher electrical rates, which is not correct. Connor voted against Alabama Power's 1968 rate request. Nunnelley, *Bull Connor*, 167–68.

88. *Alabama Official and Statistical Register*, 1967, 235.

89. Sibyl Murphree Pool (1901–73), Biographical Essay, Alabama Women's Hall of Fame; *Alabama Official and Statistical Register*, 1967, 234–35. *Alabama News Magazine* called her a "pretty pioneer in Alabama politics," November 1973, 6. (This magazine changed its name several times.)

90. *Energy Information Administration, Annual Energy Review*, 2003, 214–15, copy courtesy of Walter Johnsey, Drummond Company; interview with Eason Balch, July 20, 2004; interview with Joe Farley, November 1, 2004.

91. Hearings Before Alabama Public Service Commission, June 14, 1968, Docket 16044, vol. 8–9, 2933, files, Balch & Bingham.

92. The minutes of the hearing recorded that Connor said: "I vote with you, Miss Pool," but those attending insist that what he really said was, "I vote with the lady." The transcriber probably made certain the record showed Connor voted with Sibyl Pool. Hearings Before Alabama Public Service Commission, June 14, 1968, Docket 16044, vol. 8–9, 2933, 2949–52, 2954, files, Balch & Bingham; interview with Eason Balch, July 20, 2004; interview with Jack Bingham, February 25, 2003; Heys interview with Joe Farley, February 26, 1999, 38; Farley, Balch, and Conway, "Good Name and Destiny,'" 86. Henry Simpson believed that Connor was "such a populist" that he opposed the power company and that he knew exactly what he was doing. Interview with Henry Simpson, November 12, 2004.

93. Minutes, Alabama Public Service Commission, June 24, 1968, 5–32 [SG-5534], ADAH.

94. *Annual Report*, Alabama Power Company, 1968, 3; 1969, 3; Farley, Balch, and Conway, "'Good Name and Destiny,'" 86–87.

95. *Annual Report*, Alabama Power Company, 1967, 2.

96. Wayne Flynt, "Bibb Graves," in Webb and Armbrester, *Alabama Governors*, 177; Flynt, *Alabama in the Twentieth Century*, 8.

97. Flynt, *Alabama in the Twentieth Century*, 78.

98. *Annual Report*, Alabama Power Company, 1968, 4; Farley, Balch, and Conway, "'Good Name and Destiny,'" 80–81; *Powergrams*, December 1968, 1, 9.

99. Interview with Jim Miller Jr., November 11, 2004.

100. *Annual Report*, Southern Company, 1968, 31.

101. Interview with Eason Balch, July 20, 2004; Heys interview with Eason Balch, February 25, 1999, 36.

102. Baker, *Milestones in Marketing*, 28; interview with Jack Minor, February 26, 2004.

103. In a June 1974 interview with *Alabama News Magazine*, Farley is quoted as saying, "I guess I am sorta shy . . . by nature and by design. I feel that in the position I'm in I should be rather low key,"

but the magazine concluded there was nothing shy about Farley's leadership of Alabama Power (page 5).

104. Interview with Walter Johnsey, September 29, 2004.

105. Heys interview with Eason Balch, February 25, 1999, 39.

106. *Annual Report*, Alabama Power Company, 1969, 37.

107. *Powergrams*, June 1969, 1, 6; July 1969, 36; August 1969, 1.

108. *Annual Report*, Alabama Power Company, 1969, 3; *Powergrams*, September 1969, 8; October 1969,1; November 1969, 1.

109. Typed but undated interview with Don Thornburgh, probably by Chris Conway, found in Conway files, 4; interview with Charles McCrary, August 22, 2003.

110. *Powergrams*, October 1969, 11; November 1969, 7.

111. McCrary, "Daisye's Child," 110; interview with Joe Farley, August 27, 2004; C. R. "Red" Canup and W. D. Workman Jr., *Charles E. Daniel: His Philosophy and Legacy* (Columbia, S. C.: R. L. Bryan Co., 1981), 17–18, 70–71.

112. *Annual Report*, Alabama Power Company, 1970, 12; 1972, 15; *Powergrams*, September 1973, 22–23; Farley, Balch, and Conway, "'Good Name and Destiny,'" 107.

113. Farley, Balch, and Conway, "'Good Name and Destiny,'" 107–08.

114. Memo, by R. L. McDonald, September 11, 1990; Robert R. Todd to Selection Committee, State of Alabama Engineering Hall of Fame, September 12, 1990, copies in Conway files.

115. McCrary, "Daisye's Child," 110.

116. Ibid., 110–11; *Powergrams*, January 1974, 1, 4.

117. *Powergrams*, August 1977, 2.

118. Farley, Balch, and Conway, "'Good Name and Destiny,'" 108–09.

119. Interview with Terry Waters, October 11, 2004; Walter Baker to Leah Atkins, October 11, 2004, in files of Leah Atkins.

120. Baker, *Milestones in Marketing*, 23, 27–28, 30–31.

121. Ibid., 31.

122. For instance, see Bill Beck, *Northern Lights: An Illustrated History of Minnesota Power* (Duluth: Minnesota Power, 1985), 427; Morgan and Dana, *Priceless Heritage*, 178–81. See also Durden, *Electrifying the Piedmont Carolinas*, chapter 5, "A Troubled Time for Duke Power, 1969–1975," and chapter 6, "Climbing Out of a Financial Hole, 1975–1985."

123. Rogers et al., *Alabama: History of a Deep South State*, 575–76; Carter, *Politics of Rage*, 367–69; Lesher, *Wallace: American Populist*, 430.

124. *Annual Report*, Alabama Power Company, 1970, 2.

125. Ibid., 2, 11–12.

126. Minutes, Public Service Commission, vol. 30, Docket 16359, 287; Rogers et al., *Alabama: History of a Deep South State*, 576; Bob Ingram, *That's the Way I Saw It* (Montgomery: B&E Press, 1986), 57; Harnett T. Kane, *Louisiana Hayride: The Rehearsal for Dictatorship, 1928–1940* (New York: William Morrow & Co., 1941), 48–49; T. Harry Williams, *Huey Long* (New York: Alfred A. Knopf, 1969), 154–55, 244–47, 263; James Coltfelter and William R. Hamilton, "Beyond Race Politics: Electing Southern Populists in the 1970s," in H. Brandt Ayers and Thomas H. Naylor, eds., *You Can't Eat Magnolias* (New York: McGraw-Hill, 1972), 142–43; Website, Old Dominion University Libraries, The Papers of Henry Evans Howell Jr., Biographical Sketch; Paul G. Edwards, "Henry Howell Running in 'Henry Style,'" *Washington Post*, April 7, 1977; Bill McAllister, "The Great No-Compromiser: Henry Howell, the Independent Thinker of Virginia Politics," *Washington Post*, July 9, 1997; Farley, Balch, and Conway, "Good Name and Destiny,'" 82.

127. Stewart Alsop, "Wallace and the Shape of Politics," *Newsweek*, May 4, 1970, 108.

128. Hollis, *Alabama Newspaper Tradition*, 128–31; interview with Joe Farley, November 1, 2004; interview with Eason Balch, November 7, 2004; Rogers et al., *Alabama: History of a Deep South State*, 576.

129. Interview with Eason Balch, January 14, 2003; Heys interview with Eason Balch, February 25, 1999, 39–40; Williams, comp., "History of Balch & Bingham," 63; Farley, Balch, and Conway, "'Good Name and Destiny,'" 88.

130. Heys interview with Joe Farley, February 26, 1999, 40.

131. Farley, Balch, and Conway, "'Good Name and Destiny,'" 89; Frederick, "Command and Control: George Wallace," 564.

132. *Birmingham News*, March 23, 24, 31, 1971.

133. Ibid., April 9, 13, 1971.

134. Interviews with John Burks, May 8, 2005, September 2, 2004.

135. Ibid., September 2, 2004; interview with Walter Johnsey, September 29, 2004.

136. Interview with Jack Minor, February 26, 2004.

137. *Powergrams*, September 1969, 9; interview with Rolland Casey, July 9, 2004.

138. Interviews with Jack Minor, February 26, October 24, 2004; interview with Jim Elliott by Chris Conway, no date, typescript, Conway files; *Powergrams*, September 1969, 9.

139. Interview with Jack Minor, October 24, 2004; interview with Bruce Hutchins, August 19, 2003.

140. Interview with Gibson Lanier, April 28, 2005.

141. William J. Baxley to Butler & Potter, January 29, 1971, Governor George C. Wallace Papers [SG-22668-08], ADAH; *Birmingham News*, April 1, 7, 9, 1971.

142. Arthur A. Thompson Jr. and A. J. Strickland III, *Strategy and Policy: Concepts and Cases* (Dallas, Tex.: Business Publications, 1978), 827; *Powergrams*, April 1971, 20; October 1972, 1, 20–22; December 1972, 1, 20.

143. Maurice F. Bishop to Governor George C. Wallace, April 24, 1971, Governor George C. Wallace Papers [SG-22668-08], ADAH; Minutes, Public Service Commission, vol. 30, Docket 16359, 290, ADAH.

144. Minutes, Public Service Commission, vol. 30, Docket 16359, 287–96, ADAH; *Annual Report*, Alabama Power Company, 1971, 1; Farley, Balch, and Conway, "'Good Name and Destiny,'" 89; Heys interview with Jack Bingham, June 15, 1999, 1–2; Thompson and Strickland, *Strategy and Policy*, 819.

145. Farley, Balch, and Conway, "'Good Name and Destiny,'" 89.

146. Frederick, "Command and Control: George Wallace," 568–69.

147. Farley, Balch, and Conway, "'Good Name and Destiny,'" 83.

148. Interview with Charles L. "Buddy" Eiland, July 8, 2003.

149. Lesher, *Wallace: American Populist*, 479–82.

150. *Powergrams*, September 1972, 2–5; Farley, Balch, and Conway, "'Good Name and Destiny,'" 89.

151. *Powergrams*, July 1972, 1–7.

152. "Farley Answers Questions on Rate Issue," *Powergrams*, July 1972, 1–7; Proposed Remarks of Joseph M. Farley to the Governor's Advisory Committee on Public Utilities, July 19, 1972. Copy courtesy of Joe Farley.

153. Reprinted in *Powergrams*, September 1972, 28. See also letters in *Powergrams*, October 1972, 24.

154. *Powergrams*, January 1973, 1, gives the rate figure as a $29.9 million increase. Heys interview with Jack Bingham, June 15, 1999, 2–3; Farley, Balch, and Conway, "'Good Name and Destiny,'" 89–90; Nunnelley, *Bull Connor*, 179–80.

155. *Annual Report*, Alabama Power Company, 1972, 2.

156. See George C. Wallace to Mike Brooks, January 3, 1973, Governor George C. Wallace Papers [SG-22719], ADAH. Cecil Bauer, who became the first president of South Central Bell when Southern Bell was divided in 1968, was interviewed in February 1973 about the impact of inflation on his company. He noted that although the consumer price index had risen 58 percent since 1954, telephone service had risen only 7 percent. He had 9,000 people in Alabama who wanted telephone service, but he could not provide it because he had no funds to cover the cost of planning and building the facilities to deliver that service. *Alabama News Magazine*, February 1973, 8–9.

157. *Annual Report*, Alabama Power Company, 1973, 3.

158. Interview with Rod Mundy, January 21, 2004; interview with Eason Balch, July 20, 2004.

159. *Powergrams*, August 1972, 1, 33; January 1973, 6; August 1973, 25; September 1973, 1.

160. Erwin C. Hargrove, "The Task of Leadership: The Board Chairmen," in Hargrove and Conkin, *TVA: Fifty Years*, 107–08; Heys interview with Eason Balch, February 25, 1999, 14; *Birmingham News*, August 3, 1958; interview with Joe Farley, February 7, 2005. Harllee Branch worked hard for this legislation's approval and was aided by the Democratic senator from West Virginia, Jennings Randolph, who was concerned about TVA intruding into his state.

161. *Birmingham News*, March 2, 1960; *Powergrams*, March 1960, 4–8; *Alabama Power Company v. City of Bessemer, et al.*, files, Balch & Bingham [10004272]; interview with Joe Farley, October 13, 2004; interviews with J. L. Vick, April 12, 23, 2006.

162. Walter Bouldin to Mayor Jess Lanier, March 16, 1966, in *Alabama Power Company v. City of Bessemer, et al.*, files, Balch & Bingham [10004272].

163. Agreement Among City of Bessemer, Alabama, Alabama Power Company, and Tennessee Valley Authority, August 12, 1971, files, Balch & Bingham [10014754]; Exhibit 1, Map of Area per Agreement, files, Balch & Bingham [10004272]; interview with Harold Williams, January 22, 2004; interview with Joe Farley, February 7, 2005.

164. Wilmon H. Droze, "The TVA, 1945–80: The Power Company," in Hargrove and Conkin, *TVA: Fifty Years*, 78–82.

165. *Mitchell Dam Project No. 82, Report to the Federal Power Commission* (Birmingham: Alabama Power Co., 1967), 5–11 [1.1.1.23.7].

166. Farley, Balch, and Conway, "'Good Name and Destiny,'" 72–73.

167. Ibid., 73–74; interview with Joe Farley, November 12, 2004.

168. *Alabama Power v. Federal Power Commission*, 482 F.2d 1208.

169. Richard H. K. Vietor, *Energy Policy in America since 1945: A Study of Business-Government Relations* (Cambridge: Cambridge University Press, 1984), 193–94.

170. Minutes of the First Alabama Energy Advisory Council, March 22, 1973; John M. Harbert III to Governor George C. Wallace, May 31, 1973, Governor George C. Wallace Papers [SG-22684], ADAH. Garry Neil Drummond and Barney Champion were the other two original members of the council.

171. David Burner et al., *An American Portrait: A History of the United States*, vol. 2 (New York: Charles Scribner's Sons, 1985), 806; Baker, *Milestones in Marketing*, 33.

172. Thompson and Strickland, *Strategy and Policy*, 828–29.

173. Joseph F. Paquette Jr., *PECO Energy: Electricity—Back to the Future?* (New York: Newcomen Society of the United States, 1996), 16.

174. Interview with Joe Farley, October 20, 2004.

175. *Annual Report*, Alabama Power Company, 1973, 11; Farley, Balch, and Conway, "'Good Name and Destiny,'" 90.

176. *Powergrams*, November 1968, 1; *Annual Report*, Alabama Power Company, 1973, 3; 1974, 13; *Powergrams*, January 1974, 17. The initial request to the Federal Power Commission was made on November 7, 1968, but financial problems delayed construction. The generating facilities at the Harris Dam were not in service until 1983.

177. Glenn T. Eskew, "George C. Wallace," in Webb and Armbrester, *Alabama Governors*, 226.

178. *Powergrams*, June 1974, 4–6; July 1974, 22–23; September 1974, 20.

179. Langum information from biographical sketch in program for Colorado College Awards Ceremony, October 15, 1994, in Conway files; *Powergrams*, September 1974, 22–23.

180. *Powergrams*, January 1975, 30; *Annual Report*, Alabama Power Company, 1974, 2–3.

181. Bob Ingram, "The Alabama Scene," *Alabama News Magazine*, November 1974, 3.

182. *Alabama News Magazine*, July 1975, 30; Farley, Balch, and Conway, "'Good Name and Destiny,'" 90; Heys interview with Jack Bingham, June 15, 1999, 3–4.

183. *Atlanta Constitution*, March 6, 1975, copy of clipping in Conway files.

184. *Alabama News Magazine*, February 1975, 6.

185. McCrary, "Daisye's Child," 114.

186. Interview with Joe Farley, November 13, 2004.

187. Walter W. Tidwell to the Honorable Bill Baxley, Attorney General, February 21, 1975, copy in Governor George C. Wallace Papers [SG-23366], ADAH.

188. Maurice Bishop to Jeff Davis, December 7, 1975, and T. Jeff Davis to Maurice F. Bishop, December 11, 1975, Governor George C. Wallace Papers [SG-23392], ADAH.

189. Heys interviews with Jack Bingham, June 15, 1999, 5; March 25, 1999, 40; interview with Joe Farley, November 12, 2004.

190. *Birmingham News*, March 7, 1975.

191. McCrary, "Daisye's Child," 115. McCrary's close working relationship with labor unions developed during his years in construction. He was admitted as a journeyman pipefitter to the Montgomery local of the Plumbers and Steamfitters Union and

carried his union card with pride.

192. Interview with Joe Farley, November 1, 2004.

193. *Birmingham News*, March 8, 1975. In 1977 United States Attorney Douglas Broward Segrest successfully prosecuted Foshee for his involvement in a check kiting scheme. Farley, Balch, and Conway, "'Good Name and Destiny,'" 92.

194. *Birmingham Post-Herald*, March 8, 1975; *Birmingham News*, March 8, 1975. The committee also asked for a list of companies with whom Alabama Power did more than $50,000 in business. Farley, Balch, and Conway, "'Good Name and Destiny,'" 92; interview with Joe Farley, November 12, 2004.

195. *Birmingham News*, March 8, 1975.

196. Interview with Joe Farley, November 12, 2004; Farley, Balch, and Conway, "'Good Name and Destiny,'" 92.

197. *Birmingham News*, March 5, 6, 1975; *Montgomery Advertiser*, March 4, 1975.

198. *Montgomery Advertiser*, March 6, 7, 1975.

199. *Alabama News Magazine*, March 1975, 7. Wallace warned the legislators that the utility issue would be "one of the most serious matters you will face in your legislative career." *Journal of the House of Representatives of the State of Alabama*, Third Extraordinary Session of 1975, 3–4, 7–8; *Birmingham News*, March 18, 19, 1975; *Montgomery Advertiser*, March 7, 1975.

200. *Journal of the House of Representatives of the State of Alabama*, Third Extraordinary Session of 1975, 9.

201. *Alabama News Magazine*, April 1975, 26.

202. *Birmingham News*, March 20, 1975.

203. *Montgomery Advertiser*, March 8, 1975; News Releases, Alabama Power Company, March 17, 1975, News Releases Index [677-037].

204. *Birmingham News*, March 20, 21, 22, 1975. Copies courtesy of Jim Noles.

205. Ibid., March 25, 1975.

206. Ibid., March 26, 1975.

207. Ibid., March 21, 1975.

208. Bob Ingram, "The Alabama Scene," *Alabama News Magazine*, May 1975, 3; also articles on pages 4–5, 10.

209. Ibid., September 1975, 3.

210. *Powergrams*, October 1975, 1–7; December 1975, 3–4. Damage from Eloise was greatest in Auburn, Union Springs, Ozark, Enterprise, Florala, Roanoke, Headland, Geneva, and Phenix City, and 135,000 customers suffered interruptions in service.

211. The case involved kickbacks on vending machines installed by a vending company in South Central Bell buildings. Hammond had asked the telephone company to install the vending machines, then the vending machine company refused to pay Hammond and reported the kickback request. Hammond was sentenced and removed from the Public Service Commission in December 1975 but appealed his case until the U.S. Supreme Court refused to review. He began a three-year prison sentence in December 1978. *Montgomery Advertiser*, November 22, 1978.

212. Interview with Tom Sanford, December 2, 2004; interview with J. E. (Jimmy) Snow, December 11, 2004.

213. *Montgomery Advertiser*, February 11, 1975.

214. Interview with Ron Parsons, November 19, 2004.

215. Interview with Rod Mundy, November 18, 2004; interview with Tom Sanford, December 2, 2004; interview with Ron Parsons, November 19, 2004. Jordan Lake was maintained at 247 feet after February 16 to allow construction of the temporary dam across the inlet canal into Bouldin. Jordan Lake began refilling on March 12, 1975, which was accomplished rapidly because of heavy rains between March 18 and 24, 1975. Alabama Power Company, News Releases, March 7, April 18, 1975, News Releases Index [677-037].

216. *Montgomery Advertiser*, February 11, 12, 1975; *Powergrams*, March 1975, 28; *Annual Report*, Alabama Power Company, 1975, 33.

217. Alabama Power Company, News Releases, April 29, 1975, New Releases Index [677-037]. Dispersive clays had been known to cause earth dikes to fail, but the west and east dikes were built at the same time, and investigation and testing of soil samples showed there was no use of these clays in the dam.

218. Suit was filed in Jefferson County, February 6, 1976, Alabama Power Company, News Releases, February 6, 1976, News Releases Index [677-037]. Lange Simpson had been on retainer and had done legal work for Alabama Power since its client Birmingham Electric Company was folded into Alabama Power. The firm was used for land title research and condemnation, especially on Logan Martin Lake, labor work, and rate cases. Interview with Robert McDavid Smith, December 14, 2004.

219. Interview with Robert McDavid Smith, November 21, 2004.

220. Interview with Joe Farley, December 8, 2004; interview with Robert McDavid Smith, December 14, 2004; Dave Gillette, "Breach Formation in Piping and Seismic Failures of Embankment Dams," U.S. Bureau of Reclamation, Denver; interview with Bill Reed, February 12, 2005.

221. Federal Power Commission, Opinion No. 795, Alabama Power Company, Project No. 2146, 409–11, 439, 443, 447–50.

222. *Powergrams*, September 1974, 4–5; *Annual Report*, Alabama Power Company, 1974, 4.

223. The announcements were made by Joe Farley on May 16, 1975. *Powergrams*, June 1975, 7–8; Alabama Power Company, News Releases, May 16, 1975, News Releases Index [677-037].

224. Interview with Robert Holmes, July 13, 1970.

225. *Powergrams*, September 1972, 32–33.

226. Baker, *Milestones in Marketing*, 33–35.

227. Nelda H. Steele, Home Economists in Business Hall of Fame Form, courtesy of Nelda Steele; Baker, *Milestones in Marketing*, 33–34.

228. Baker, *Milestones in Marketing*, 34–36; interview with John Burks, September 2, 2004.

229. Thompson and Strickland, *Strategy and Policy*, 826.

230. Richard Munson, *The Power Makers* (Emmaus, Pa.: Rodale Press, 1985), 185.

Chapter Nine

1. Rudolph and Ridley, *Power Struggle*, 199.

2. Peter G. Bourne, *Jimmy Carter: A Comprehensive Biography from Plains to Post-Presidency* (New York: Scribner, 1997), 252, 257.

3. Vietor, *Energy Policy in America*, 3, 193–95.

4. Bailey and Kennedy, *American Pageant*, 898–907; Rudolph and Ridley, *Power Struggle*, 199–201.

5. *Powergrams*, January 1976, 1.

6. *Annual Report*, Alabama Power Company, 1976, 3.

7. Interview with Willard Bowers, May 3, 2005.

8. Ibid.

9. Interview with Rod Mundy, January 21, 2004; *Annual Report*, Alabama Power Company, 1973, 15; 1976, 33; 1977, 11; News Releases, Alabama Power Company, January 22, 1976, November 18, December 29, 1977, News Releases Index [667-037].

10. See the many copies of these surveys in News Releases Index [677-037]; for instance, the April 28, 1976, survey showed Alabama Power sixth from the bottom with a $10.57 cost for 250 kWh compared to the $20.84 cost of 250 kWh in New York City.

11. Interview with Joe Farley, February 28, 2005.

12. News Releases, Alabama Power Company, February 9, 1976, News Releases Index [667-037].

13. Joseph M. Farley, Testimony before the Alabama Public Service Commission, February 1976, quoted in Thompson and Strickland, *Strategy and Policy*, 836–37. The testimony of people can be followed in the News Releases from February 1976, News Releases Index [667-037].

14. Interviews with Joe Farley, February 4, 7, 2005; interview with Walter Johnsey, February 7, 2005; *Powergrams*, February 1973, 1; *Annual Report*, Alabama Power Company, 1973, 15.

15. *Powergrams*, September 1979, 2–5; interview with Steve Payne, Mike Little, Bud McClendon, Roy Jones, February 16, 2005; Alabama Power, *Alabama Power's General Services Complex*, brochure.

16. "Summary of Key Employees Who Were Vital to the Company's Financial and Accounting Management during the Period 1968–1982," 4, no author, Conway files.

17. Interview with Jack Minor, February 26, 2004.

18. Interview with Elmer Harris, December 7, 2004.

19. *Montgomery Advertiser*, May 10, 1965; interview with Jim Miller Jr., November 11, 2004; interviews with Banks Farris, November 12, 2004, June 28, 2005; interview with Elmer Harris, December 7, 2004. *Powergrams*, June 19, 1995, 2, states that the farm belonged to H. C. Blackwell and was located in Seman in Elmore County. Warren Trest and Don Dodd, *Wings of Denial: The Alabama Air National Guard's Covert Role at the Bay of Pigs* (Montgomery: New South Books, 2001), 16. Doster was involved in the Bay of Pigs disaster some years before Harris joined the Air National Guard and learned to fly.

20. Interview with Jim Miller Jr., November 11, 2004; Elmer Harris, employee file and biographical information sheet; interview with Elmer Harris, January 29, 2003; *Powergrams*, June 1973, 3; July 1973, 3.

21. Interview with Banks Farris, November 12, 2004.

22. News Releases, Alabama Power Company, March 24, 1976, News Releases Index [677-037]; *Annual Report*, Alabama Power Company, 1976, 26.

23. News Releases, Alabama Power Company, March 15, 24, June 25, 1976, News Releases Index [677-037]. Interview with Banks Farris, June 28, 2005.

24. Thompson and Strickland, *Strategy and Policy*, 845–47; Alabama Power Company Return on Common Equity, chart, Corporate Finance and Planning; *Annual Report*, Alabama Power

Company, 1976, 3; Farley, Balch, and Conway, "'Good Name and Destiny,'" 93.

25. *Annual Report*, Alabama Power Company, 1976, 33. The day before the PSC had granted South Central Bell's full $52 million emergency rate increase. *Montgomery Advertiser*, September 17, 1977.

26. Thompson and Strickland, *Strategy and Policy*, 827–28.

27. News Releases, Alabama Power Company, May 5, 1976, News Releases Index [677-037].

28. Ibid., October 15, 1976 [677-037].

29. See letters in Governor George C. Wallace Papers [SG-23392], ADAH.

30. Notice of Further Hearing, Alabama Power Company, Petitioner, Wallace Tidmore, secretary, Alabama Public Service Commission, copy in files of Gibson Lanier.

31. Heys interview with Joe Farley, February 26, 1999, 48.

32. Interview with Jack Bingham, February 6, 2006.

33. Ibid.

34. *Montgomery Advertiser*, January 5, 6, 1977. The crowd was estimated from different sources as 500 to as many as 2,000. News Releases, Alabama Power Company, December 6, 1976, News Releases Index [677-037]; interview with Joe Farley, November 12, 2004.

35. *Montgomery Advertiser*, January 4, 1977.

36. Ibid., January 6, 1977.

37. Docket No. 17261, analysis in files of Gibson Lanier. Juanita McDaniel and Jim Zeigler voted for the emergency increase; Chris Whatley voted against.

38. *Montgomery Advertiser*, January 22, 1977. Clipping from Senate Special File, Alabama Power Company, courtesy of McDowell Lee.

39. Joseph M. Farley to Governor George C. Wallace, April 26, 1977. Copy in Conway files.

40. Glenn Eskew, "George C. Wallace," in Webb and Armbrester, *Alabama Governors*, 216–21; Heys interview with Joe Farley, February 26, 1999, 40; interview with Joe Farley, July 6, 2004; interview with George Wallace Jr., July 9, 2004.

41. *Montgomery Advertiser*, April 27, 28, 1977.

42. Ibid., May 6, 1977. Clipping from Senate Special File, Alabama Power Company, courtesy of McDowell Lee.

43. Ibid., April 28, 1977. After rejecting the governor's utility legislation, the senate passed the roll-back bill twenty-six to zero. There was a strong feeling that the bill was unconstitutional and could not be implemented. *Montgomery Advertiser*, April 30, 1977.

44. Joseph M. Farley to Honorable George C. Wallace, April 26, 1977, copy in Conway files.

45. *Birmingham Post-Herald*, May 6, 1977.

46. Ibid., May 12, 1977.

47. See Governor Wallace's Address to the Special Session of Alabama Legislature, May 17, 1977, in *Acts of Alabama*, 1977, vol. 1, 1403–04, and compare with News Releases, Alabama Power Company, May 24, 1977, News Releases Index [677-037].

48. News Releases, Alabama Power Company, May 23, 1977, copy in notebook, "Outside Pressures on Alabama Power Company," October 3, 1977. Joe Farley's letter to Governor Wallace is

printed in *Powergrams*, August 1977, 10–11.

49. Act No. 22, First Special Session, 1977, copy in Governor George C. Wallace Papers [SG-4708], ADAH. The senate committee on commerce, transportation, and utilities was composed of Eddie H. Gilmore, chair, Bessemer; George McMillan, vice chair, Birmingham; Bingham Edwards, Decatur; Joe Fine, Russellville; Obie J. Littleton, Clanton; Sid McDonald, Arab; Mason Mims, Uriah; J. Richmond Pearson, Birmingham; and John Teague, Childersburg. Teague introduced two bills that would have been devastating to Alabama Power. Bill S 81 would have prevented a utility from filing an application for a rate increase if a previous application was pending before the PSC or any court. Bill S 83 would have prohibited any electric utility from charging higher rates from May 1 through October 31 of each year than it charged during other months of the year. These bills went nowhere. *Journal of the Senate, State of Alabama, First Extraordinary Session*, 1977, 33. Alabama Power had six registered lobbyists for this session: S. Eason Balch Jr., John (Jack) Bingham, Sam Engelhardt, Walter F. Johnsey, E. Clark Richardson, and Jesse S. Vogtle. *Journal of the Senate, First Extraordinary Session*, 1977, 272.

50. *Montgomery Advertiser*, June 17, 1977.

51. *Annual Report*, Alabama Power Company, 1977, 30. Compare News Releases, Alabama Power Company, July 18, 1977, News Releases Index [677-037], with articles in *Montgomery Advertiser*, July 19, 1977, *Alabama Journal*, July 19, 1977, *Birmingham Post-Herald*, July 20, 1977, *Gadsden Times*, July 20, 1977, *Anniston Star*, July 20, 1977, *Tuscaloosa News*, July 20, 1977, *Jasper Daily Mountain Eagle*, July 20, 1977, *Selma Times-Journal*, July 20, 1977, and the *Opelika-Auburn News*, July 20, 1977.

52. *Alabama Journal*, July 21, 1977.

53. Ibid.

54. Ibid.

55. Interview with Bob Andrews, March 30, 2005.

56. Interview with Mary Lynne Farley Morris, February 26, 2005; interview with Joe Farley, February 27, 2005.

57. *Powergrams*, December 1968, 5.

58. Ibid., March 1979, 17.

59. McCrary, "Daisye's Child," 120; interview with Bill Reed, June 30, 2004; *Powergrams*, March 1979, 17.

60. Interview with Joe Farley, February 26, 2004; interview with Mac Beale, April 19, 2005; memorandum to the files from W. T. Baker Jr., September 9, 1977, and memorandum to files from W. T. Baker Jr., September 14, 1977, copies courtesy of Thelen Reid & Priest. Farley, Balch, and Conway, "'Good Name and Destiny,'" 93. The Wall Street law firm then called Reid & Priest issued an opinion that by using only the wholesale rate case coverage the stock could be sold. Information courtesy of Mac Beale.

61. The law firm in 1970 was named Martin, Balch, Bingham, Hawthorne & Williams and became Balch & Bingham in 1985; interview with Mac Beale, January 28, 2004.

62. *Montgomery Advertiser*, October 21, 1977. See also *Annual Report*, Alabama Power Company, 1977, 28.

63. News Releases, Alabama Power Company, January 6, 1978, News Releases Index [677-038].

64. Ibid., January 18, 25, 1978.

65. Ibid., February 15, 17, March 17, 24, 28, 1978.

66. Price Waterhouse & Company, Report on the Financial Audit and Management Study of the Alabama Power Company and Southern Company Services, Inc., April 28, 1978. Copy in Alabama Power Company Corporate Archives. News Releases, Alabama Power Company, May 18, 1978, News Releases Index [677-038].

67. Interview with Joe Farley, March 9, 2005.

68. Price Waterhouse Report, section 1, 7, 15.

69. News Releases, Alabama Power Company, May 14, 1976, News Releases Index [677-037]; *Annual Report*, Alabama Power Company, 1976, 19–20.

70. *Alabama Reporter, Alabama Power Company v. Public Service Commission, et al.*, 358 So.2d 424, 776–80.

71. *Annual Report*, Alabama Power Company, 1978, 5; News Releases, Alabama Power Company, April 7, 1979, News Releases Index [677-038].

72. Baker, *Milestones in Marketing*, 35.

73. *Annual Report*, Alabama Power Company, 1978, 7; Baker, *Milestones in Marketing*, 36.

74. James S. Brown Jr., professor of history at Samford University, has lectured about the "Paradigm of the Development of Modern Nations" in which an identifiable cultural group is impacted by a negative force thus bringing about cultural nationalism. The next step in Brown's model is political nationalism, which is then followed by the creation of an independent country. On those occasions in Alabama Power Company's history when the company was attacked, unfairly in the opinion of its employees, the result was a coming together, a bonding, the creation of a strong loyalty and defense of the company. This bonding occurred especially in three time periods—in the 1920s over the Muscle Shoals—Henry Ford fight; in the 1930s after the creation of TVA; and in the 1970s when the company was under attack by Governor George Wallace.

75. Interview with Joe Farley Jr., December 22, 2004. Sheila Farley died from a massive infection that ravaged her body after she received a kidney transplant.

76. Heys interview with Jack Bingham, March 25, 1999, 39; Heys interview with Eason Balch, February 25, 1999, 38–39; interview with Alan Martin, August 30, 2004.

77. Interview with Alan Martin, August 30, 2004.

78. *Annual Report*, Alabama Power Company, 1978, 3.

79. Interview with Steve Bradley, January 28, 2004; *Powergrams*, September 1979, 7.

80. Interview with Jesse S. Vogtle, April 28, 2006; Heys interview with Joe Farley, February 26, 1999, 42.

81. Interview with Steve Bradley, January 28, 2004.

82. Interview with Neal Wade, June 1, 2005.

83. Interview with Elmer Harris, March 23, 2005; interview with Steve Bradley, March 22, 2005; *Powergrams*, April 1983, 12–16.

84. *Powergrams*, April 1980, 6–7.

85. Interview with Steve Bradley, January 28, 2004.

86. Interview with Chris Conway, June 2, 2005.

87. Interview with Steve Bradley, March 22, 2005.

88. Ibid.

89. Interview with Joe Farley, February 2, 2005.

90. Title 10, 7A, *Alabama Code* (1979), Sec. 10-1-2.

91. *Powergrams*, August 1986, 12–14.

92. Interview with Eason Balch Jr. and Ann Skipper, July 8, 2005.

93. Bailey and Kennedy, *American Pageant*, 908.

94. *Annual Report*, Alabama Power Company, 1978, 7.

95. Clippings, *Montgomery Advertiser*, December 13, 22, 1978, in Alabama Power Company, special files, Alabama Senate, courtesy of McDowell Lee; Public Service Commission Order, Docket No. 17437, November 22, 1978, 18, in files of Gibson Lanier; interview with Gibson Lanier, February 9, 2006.

96. Alabama Power Company, Retail Rate Increase Summary, Rate Case No. 7, Docket No. 17667, and Rate Case No. 7, Docket No. 17667, files of Gibson Lanier; interview with Joe Farley, January 4, 2006; Farley, Balch, and Conway, "'Good Name and Destiny,'" 97–98.

97. See unpublished court order, 78-164, January 4, 1979, October Term, 1978–79, Alabama Supreme Court, copy in files of Gibson Lanier.

98. *Annual Report*, Alabama Power Company, 25; extract of *Birmingham News* article printed in *Powergrams*, March 1979, 14.

99. Interview with Bill Baxley, March 29, 2003.

100. Alabama Public Service Commission, Dockets No. 17439 and No. 17451, November 22, 1978; 78-164, January 18, 1979, October Term, 1978–79; 78-164, January 18, 1979; court order 78-122, January 18, 1979; 78-120, 78-120A; 78-120B; 78-120C, Alabama Supreme Court. Copy of 78-164, an unpublished order in files of Gibson Lanier. There are two separate court orders numbered 78-164, one dated January 4 and the other January 18, 1978.

101. *Southern Highlights*, March 1979, 13.

102. *Powergrams*, January 1979, 26.

103. News Releases, Alabama Power Company, December 29, 1978, News Releases Index [677-038].

104. Farley, Balch, and Conway, "'Good Name and Destiny,'" 98.

105. Interview with Mac Beale, January 28, 2004; interview with Jack Minor, February 26, 2004; interview with Elmer Harris, January 29, 2003.

106. *Southern Highlights*, March 1979, 1–3.

107. Mrs. Phillip A. Sellers to Old Grandma [a letter to the editor column], *Montgomery Advertiser*, July 9, 1980.

108. *Birmingham News*, January 26, 1979.

109. William H. Stewart, "James E. Folsom Jr.," in Webb and Armbrester, *Alabama Governors*, 254–55; interview with Jim Folsom Jr., January 6, 2005.

110. Interview with Jim Folsom Jr., January 6, 2005; biographical sketch of Pete Mathews, courtesy of Alabama Retail Association. For many years Mathews served as the legislative liaison for the retail association. William J. "Jimmy" Samford Jr., who was appointed to the Public Service Commission by Governor Fob James after Juanita McDaniel resigned in February 1980, often told the story about Mathews's response to a constituent who wrote to complain that her power bill was higher than her mortgage payment. Mathews responded and asked her, "Madam, have you ever considered buying a better house?" Interview with Charles McDonald, February 1, 2005.

111. Interview with Joe Farley, November 1, 2004; interview with Elmer Harris, March 16, 2005. Joe Farley's pocket date book for February 9, 1979, has written in his handwriting "Governor's office, 8:00 A.M."

112. Joseph M. Farley to Stockholders, *Annual Report*, Alabama Power Company, 1979, 2.

113. *Powergrams*, February 1979, 2–6.

114. This increase was implemented on March 9. *Powergrams*, June 1979, 8.

115. Farley, Balch, and Conway, "'Good Name and Destiny,'" 98; Alabama Power Company Return on Common Equity, chart, and Rate Case No. 7, Docket No. 17667, in files of Gibson Lanier.

116. *Powergrams*, October 1978, 2–6.

117. Ibid., August 1981, 1.

118. Ibid., September 1979, 7; *Annual Report*, Alabama Power Company, 1979, 7–8; *Powergrams*, August 1981, 3.

119. *Powergrams*, January 1979, 8–10; May 1979, 2–4.

120. Ibid., April 1979, 9.

121. Interview with Bob Haubein, April 3, 2005; interview with Robin Hurst, August 20, 2004.

122. Interview with Bill McDonough, April 2, 2005; Mobile Division meeting, June 15, 2005.

123. This account of the Mobile Division's reaction to Hurricane Frederic was taken from a series of typed transcripts in the company archives. There are no dates, no page numbers, and no titles to the interviews, which are separated only by gem clips. Unfortunately, the transcriber did not identify the names of the voices on the tape, and no effort was made later to identify who is speaking. At one point, it is evident that divisional vice president William L. "Bill" McDonough is answering the questions. These tapes were the result of an effort to update the Mobile Division's hurricane or storm procedures, which had been written in 1969 by Ben Hutson after the shock wore off from the devastation of Hurricane Camille. Hutson was then the division manager in Mobile. When the Mobile Division recovered from Hurricane Frederic, there was a concerted effort to document what had taken place, what the company's response had been, what the problems were, and the outcomes of those decisions in order to determine what improvements could be made in the storm plan. See file 4.1.1.82.15. Interview with Roy Jones, February 16, 2005.

124. *Powergrams*, September 1980, 3; January 1989, 5; interviews at Mobile Division meeting, June 15, 2005.

125. Sandra Baxley Taylor, *Governor Fob James: His 1994 Victory, His Incredible Story* (Mobile: Greenbury Publishing Co., 1995), 140; interview with Bob Haubein, April 3, 2005.

126. Interview with Bill McDonough, April 2, 2005; *Annual Report*, Alabama Power Company, 1979, 13.

127. *Powergrams*, January 1989, 4.

128. Interview with Bob Haubein, April 3, 2005.

129. *Powergrams*, October 1979, 2–5; interview with Jerry Stewart, February 24, 2005.

130. *Powergrams*, September 1980, 4.

131. Interview with Robin Hurst, February 24, 2005.

132. Interview with Bill McDonough, April 2, 2005; interview with Robin Hurst, February 24, 2005; interview with Bob Haubein, April 3, 2005. Also file 4.1.1.82.15.

133. *Powergrams*, October 1979, 5; Taylor, *Governor Fob James*, 142; Mobile Division meeting, June 15, 2005.

134. Hurricane Frederic file [4.1.1.82.17]; Mobile Division meeting, June 15, 2005.

135. Hurricane Frederic file [4.1.1.82.17]; interview with Robin

Hurst, February 24, 2005; *Powergrams*, January 1989, 4.

136. Interviews with Robin Hurst, August 20, 2004, April 5, 2005; *Powergrams*, April 1990, 2–5; Mobile Division meeting, June 15, 2005.

137. *Annual Report*, Alabama Power Company, 1979, 2.

138. Interview with Robin Hurst, February 24, 2005.

139. *Annual Report*, Alabama Power Company, 1979, 13.

140. Interview with Joe Farley, March 1, 2004; interview with Mike Little and Steve Payne, February 16, 2005.

141. Mobile Division meeting, June 15, 2005; *Powergrams*, October 1979, 5.

142. See the "Chronological Highlights of Hurricane Frederic" for details of the company's fight to restore electricity [4.1.1.82.14]; *Powergrams*, November 1979, 9.

143. *Powergrams*, January 1980, 4.

144. Rate Case No. 8, Docket No.17859, in files of Gibson Lanier.

145. Interviews with Jerry Stewart, July 10, 2003, February 24, 2005.

146. Southern Division meeting, June 13, 2005; interview with Jone Davis and Rayford Davis, June 17, 2003.

147. Interview with Jerry Stewart, Alan Martin, and Robin Hurst, February 24, 2005.

148. Joseph M. Farley to Stockholders, March 12, 1981, in *Annual Report*, Alabama Power Company, 1980, 1.

149. Rudolph and Ridley, *Power Struggle*, 199–202.

150. Carter, *Politics of Rage*, 458; Bartley, *The New South*, 414–15; Montgomery Advertiser/Alabama Journal Sunday joint edition, January 2, 1977; *Birmingham Post-Herald*, March 23, 1979; April 16, 1979; May 30, 1979.

151. See newspaper coverage, especially *Birmingham Post-Herald*, May 13–20, 1980.

152. *Birmingham Post-Herald*, July 16, 1980.

153. Ibid., April 21, May 30, 1979; interview with Walter Johnsey, September 29, 2004.

154. *Birmingham Post-Herald*, August 3, 1979, May 2, 1980.

155. Ibid., June 5, 1980.

156. Ibid., July 11, 1980.

157. Ibid., May 13–17, 1980.

158. Ibid., June 7, 10, 11, 12, 17, 19, 20, 21, 24, 25, 27, July 1, 2, 3, 1980.

159. Interview with Walter Johnsey, February 7, 2005; interview with Eddie Gilmore, April 1, 2005; interview with Joe Farley, May 31, 2005; *Birmingham Post-Herald*, July 3, 9, 10, 11, 15, 16, 1980; *Birmingham News*, July 15, 1980; *Montgomery Advertiser*, July 9, 1980. Eddie Gilmore recalled that as the court took its lunch break, his wife saw a prosecutor drawing a seating chart for two women, and Gilmore alerted his attorney David Byrne, who made certain that everyone changed places.

160. "Before the New Mexico Public Service Commission," Case No. 1196, and "A New Rate Making Concept and Public Service Company of New Mexico," Southwest Regional Utility Studies, in files of Corporate Finance and Planning.

161. Interview with Gibson Lanier, February 1, 2005.

162. Tom Gordon and John Mangels et al., *Wallace: A Portrait of Power* (Birmingham: Birmingham News, 1998), 84–85.

163. Lesher, *Wallace: American Populist*, 496–97; interview with Elmer Harris, January 29, 2003.

164. Interviews with Billy Joe Camp, June 30, 2004, March 16, 2005; interview with Elmer Harris, March 16, 2005; interview with Bruce Hutchins, November 23, 2004; *Alabama News Magazine*, October 1981, 6–9.

165. Interview with Gibson Lanier, March 15, 2005.

166. Interview with Billy Joe Camp, March 14, 2005.

167. Interview with Gibson Lanier, March 15, 2005.

168. *Montgomery Advertiser*, March 20, 1981.

169. Interview with Charles McDonald, February 1, 2005.

170. *Birmingham News*, June 13, 1982; Farley, Balch, and Conway, "'Good Name and Destiny,'" 100; *Alabama News Magazine*, February 1982, 7.

171. Rate Case No. 9, Docket No. 18117, in files of Gibson Lanier.

172. Order, Docket No. 18004, October 16, 1981, Alabama Public Service Commission, 2–4, 7.

173. State of Alabama in the Supreme Court of Alabama, 1981–82 Term, 81-48, *Alabama Power Company v. Alabama Public Service Commission*, Docket No. 18117, unpublished decision rendered February 12, 1982, in files of Gibson Lanier.

174. Ibid.; Rate Case No. 9, Docket No.18117, in files of Gibson Lanier.

175. Interview with Bruce Hutchins, March 22, 2005; interview with Elmer Harris, March 16, 2005; *Powergrams*, January 1989, 9.

176. *Update*, October 1, 1982, 2.

177. *Alabama Power Company v. Alabama Public Service Commission*, and R. S. *Crowder v. Alabama Public Service Commission*, Supreme Court of Alabama, November 5, 1982, in 422 *Alabama Reporter*, 767; Rate Case No. 9, Docket No. 18117, in files of Gibson Lanier.

178. State of Alabama Judicial Department, Supreme Court of Alabama, October Term, 1982–83, *Alabama Power Company, a Corporation v. Alabama Public Service Commission* [81-48], and R. S. *Crowder v. Alabama Public Service Commission* [81-117], Appeals from Alabama Public Service Commission, November 5, 1982. Robert Crowder was an individual who frequently was an intervenor taking the side of Alabama Power.

179. Interview with Ron Mundy, March 18, 2005; interview with Billy Joe Camp, March 16, 2005.

180. *Montgomery Advertiser*, November 12, 13, 1982; *Birmingham News*, November 12, 1982. At the beginning of discussions, Elmer Harris wanted a rate of return between 15.5 percent and 16.9 percent, then revised that request to 14 percent to 15.5 percent. Camp and Folsom would not budge from 13.5 percent to 15 percent. Lynn Greer offered a compromise of 13.75 percent to 15.25 percent. Harris said that at 15 percent the company would have to cut expenses and that was "not in the best interest of the customers of the company, but with that notice served, the company will accept the proposal."

181. *Montgomery Advertiser*, November 13, 1982; Rate Case No. 10, Docket No. 18416, in files of Gibson Lanier; *Powergrams*, January 1989, 9. The decision was actually made at the PSC meeting on Friday, November 12, but the order was signed on November 17, 1982. See *Montgomery Advertiser*, November 13, 1982, and Opinion and Order, Alabama Public Service Commission, Docket No. 18117 and Docket No. 18416, November 17, 1982, and also Order Approving Filed Rate Schedules, Alabama Public Service Commission, November 22, 1982, both signed by Billy Joe Camp, Lynn Greer, and Jim Folsom Jr.

182. For two different criticisms of the PSC see *Alabama News Magazine*, February 1982, 7, and April 1982, 3.

183. The appointment presented a problem because if the son accepted the PSC appointment, the father had to resign his position in the Wallace cabinet, but this problem was worked out, and Charles Sullivan resigned.

184. Interview with Billy Joe Camp, June 30, 2004; interview with Jim Sullivan, June 1, 2004. *Alabama News Magazine* announced Sullivan's appointment in its February 1983 issue (page 6). In one of his first interviews after becoming president of the commission, Jim Sullivan told *Alabama News Magazine* (March 1983, 7) that Camp first called him, which was probably correct since Sullivan had been Covington County coordinator for Camp's recent congressional race.

185. *Alabama News Magazine*, March 1983, 6, commented that this was like "trying to serve two masters, and the Good Book."

186. Interview with Jim Sullivan, June 1, 2004.

187. *Annual Report*, Alabama Public Service Commission, 2002, 12.

188. Ibid., 12–13.

189. *Birmingham News*, July 13, 1982; interview with Bill Baxley, March 29, 2005.

190. *Alabama Metallurgical v. Alabama Public Service Commission*, Supreme Court of Alabama, September 16, 1983, 441 So.2d 565 (Ala. 1983).

191. *Birmingham News*, September 5, 1982, clipping in 4.1.2.82.7.

192. *Powergrams*, October 1982, 30–31; interview with Rayford Davis, June 17, 2003.

193. *Birmingham Post-Herald*, October 1, 4, 1982, and *Birmingham News*, October 5, 14, 1982, clippings in 4.1.2.82.7.

194. *Birmingham Post-Herald*, September 2, 1982, clipping in 4.1.2.82.7.

195. Interview with Jack Bingham, February 2, 2006; interview with Harold Bowron Jr., February 3, 2006.

196. Interview with Alan Martin, August 20, 2004; *Birmingham News*, October 14, 1982; *Powergrams*, October 1982, 30–33.

197. Interview with Buddy Eiland, October 4, 2004.

198. Interview with Bill Frederick and Philip Hamilton, October 20, 2004; interview with Don Dawson, April 19, 2005.

199. Interview with David Cooper, July 16, 2004; *Powergrams*, November 1982, 6–9; *Update*, October 1, 1982, 1–3.

200. Interview with Robert Collins, March 29, 2005.

201. Amy Thompson McCandless, *The Past in the Present: Women's Higher Education in the Twentieth-Century American South* (Tuscaloosa: University of Alabama Press, 1999), 152–58; Robert J. Norrell, *A Promising Field: Engineering at Alabama, 1837–1987* (Tuscaloosa: University of Alabama Press, 1990), 205–07; Atkins, *Century of Women at Auburn*, 18–19, 36.

202. Interview with Bill McDonough, April 2, 2005.

203. Bernard E. Anderson, *Negro Employment in Public Utilities: A Study in Racial Policies in the Electric Power, Gas, and Telephone Industries* (Philadelphia: University of Pennsylvania Wharton School of Finance and Commerce, 1970), 213.

204. Interview with Gary D. Grooms, December 15, 2004; interview with Bob Andrews, March 30, 2005; interview with Paula Bryan, March 30, 2005; *Annual Report*, Alabama Power Company, 1975, 17; 1976, 11, 38.

205. Interview with Robert Collins, March 29, 2005; interview with Walter Graham, April 6, 2005.

206. Consent Decree, *Equal Employment Opportunity Commission v. Alabama Power Company and International Brotherhood of Electrical Workers*, CV 81-HM-0485-S, copy courtesy of Walter Graham; interview with Gary Grooms, December 15, 2004.

207. Interview with Brenda Faush, February 2, 2006.

208. Interview with Robert Holmes, July 13, 2004; *Powergrams*, December 1987, 14; interview with Bobbie Knight, October 30, 2003.

209. Interview with Audrey Vaughan, September 9, 2004; interview with Sheila Ash Garrett, July 22, 2004.

210. Interview with Marsha Johnson, November 10, 2003.

211. Résumé of Christopher C. Womack, courtesy of Chris Womack.

212. Interview with Donna Smith, November 5, 2004; interview with Paula Bryan, March 30, 2005.

213. Interview with Susan N. Story, August 26, 2004; biographical sketch dated 6/23/04; Susan Story, biographical clipping files compiled by Jim Clements, corporate archives; Susan Story's résumé, August 26, 2004.

214. Interview with Bob Andrews, March 30, 2005.

215. *Powergrams*, April 1987, 14–15.

216. Interview with Paula Bryan, March 30, 2004.

217. Interview with Walter Graham, April 6, 2005.

218. Southern Division meeting, June 13, 2005.

219. *Powergrams*, March 1978, 9.

220. *Annual Report*, Alabama Power Company, 1974, 3; 1983, 2; *Alabama News Magazine*, January 1974, 21; News Releases, Alabama Power Company, October 1982, News Releases Index [677-038].

221. *Powergrams*, March 1983, 6–8.

222. *Powergrams*, January 1989, 16–17; Baker, *Milestones in Marketing*, 38; Nelda Steele to Leah Atkins, May 10, 2004, and Steele, "Home Service Department."

223. *Annual Report*, Alabama Power Company, 1988, 7; *Powergrams*, January 1989, 18.

224. Walter L. Baker Jr. to Leah Atkins, March 16, 2004; interview with Alan Martin, August 30, 2004; interview with Walter Baker, February 10, 2004; Baker, *Milestones in Marketing*, 42–45.

225. *Update*, October 29, November 5, December 28, 1982; *Powergrams*, December 1982, 2–3; April 1983, 21; *Enterprise Ledger*, December 12, 1982; *Birmingham News*, December 17, 1982; *Eufaula Tribune*, January 28, 1986.

226. Farley, Balch, and Conway, "Good Name and Destiny,'" 75–76.

227. See the statistics on U.S. dams in Edison Electric Institute, *The Fair and Equitable Relicensing of Hydroelectric Projects* (1985), 17–70; interview with Joe Farley, March 30, 2005; Farley, Balch, and Conway, "Good Name and Destiny,'" 75.

228. Edison Electric Institute, *The Benefits to Consumers from Hydroelectric Projects Operated by Investor-Owned Utilities, Now and in the Future* (1983), 9–10; Scott Ridley, "The Fight Over the Private Dams," *Nation*, March 17, 1984, 321–23.

229. Interview with Julian Smith, September 29, 2004.

230. The House bill was HR 44 and the bill in the Senate was S 426. Edison Electric Institute, *Fair and Equitable Relicensing*, 7–9; *Powergrams*, October 1985, 17–18; Farley, Balch, and Conway, "'Good Name and Destiny,'" 75; interview with Julian Smith, September 29, 2004.

231. *Powergrams*, June 1982, 1; *Annual Report*, Alabama Power Company, 1986, 1, 11; *Birmingham News*, September 28, 1988, copy of clipping in Conway files.

232. *Powergrams*, May 1983, 2–4.

233. Ibid., April, 1986, 4–7.

234. Interview with Eason Balch, July 20, 2004; typescript of interview with Rod Mundy (interviewer unknown), October 28, 1997, 3.

235. Interview with Rod Mundy, January 21, 2004. The fire was in the hotel kitchen and was quickly extinguished.

236. Ibid., April 1, 2005.

237. Typescript of interview with Rod Mundy (interviewer unknown), October 28, 1997, 3.

238. Interview with Eason Balch, January 14, 2003; interview with Rod Mundy, January 21, 2004; Lowman, *Power Pioneers*, 89.

239. Farley, *Alabama Power Company*, 18.

240. Heys interview with Joe Farley, March 24, 1999, 1; Farley, *Alabama Power Company*, 18.

241. Heys interview with Joe Farley, March 24, 1999, 1–2; *Annual Report*, Alabama Power Company, 1988, 3, 13; Lowman, *Power Pioneers*, 113–14, 141, 154; interview with Rod Mundy, January 21, 2004; *Annual Report*, Alabama Power Company, 1983, 9; Farley, Balch, and Conway, "'Good Name and Destiny,'" 122–23.

242. *Powergrams*, August 1988, 2–3; interview with Griffin Lassiter, April 18, 2005.

243. *Annual Report*, Alabama Power Company, 1987, 35; *Powergrams*, April 1988, 2; interview with Bill Guthrie, March 8, 2005.

244. *Powergrams*, February 1987, 1–3.

245. Interview with Joe Farley, June 2, 2005.

246. Interview with Walter Johnsey, October 22, 2004.

Chapter Ten

1. *Annual Report*, Alabama Power Company, 1985, 2, 4; 1988, 1, 3, 5; *Opelika-Auburn News*, June 8, 1985, clipping from Jim Sullivan's Notebook, vol. 1, 1983–85.

2. *Powergrams*, June 1989, 3; *Annual Report*, Alabama Power Company, 1985, 34.

3. Interview with Joe Farley, March 1, 2004; Heys interview with Joe Farley, March 24, 1999, 15–16; interview with Jim Miller Jr., November 11, 2004.

4. Heys interview with Joe Farley, March 24, 1999, 16; interview with Joe Farley, March 1, 2004.

5. Task Force Leadership List, Task Force Report to the Southern Company Board, and Southern Company Press Release, May 18, 1988, in Conway files.

6. A. W. Dahlberg, Southern Nuclear, December 14, 1988, copy in Conway files.

7. Ibid.

8. Heys interview with Joe Farley, March 24, 1999, 17.

9. Interview with Charles McCrary, August 22, 2003.

10. Interview with Joe Farley, August 19, 2005.

11. Interview with Charles McCrary, June 21, 2005.

12. Interview with Joe Farley, May 12, 2005.

13. News Release, Alabama Power Company, February 24, 1989, copy in Conway files; *Birmingham News*, undated clipping in Elmer Harris files.

14. *Powergrams*, May 1989, 1–6.

15. Interview with Elmer Harris, March 16, 2002; interview with Joe Farley, April 19, 2005.

16. Interview with Rod Mundy, May 10, 2005.

17. *Powergrams*, June 1989, 3–5. Interview with Elmer Harris, December 8, 2004. Harris has several filing cabinets of letters he received as president of Alabama Power Company and some copies of his own letters, but these do not deal with substantive company issues.

18. Interviews with Doris Ingram, March 23, May 10, 2005; interview with Elmer Harris, January 29, 2003; *Powergrams*, January 14, 2002, 2.

19. Interview with Elmer Harris, July 6, 2005; interview with Banks Farris, June 28, 2005; Banks Farris, biographical file.

20. *Annual Report*, Alabama Power Company, 1991, 36; interview with Elmer Harris, July 6, 2005.

21. Banks Farris, Travis Bowden, Bill Guthrie, Pat McDonald, biographical files; interview with Banks Farris, November 12, 2004; interviews with Elmer Harris, July 6, November 23, 2005; *Annual Report*, Alabama Power Company, 1989, 34; 1990, 35; 1991, 36.

22. Interview with Elmer Harris, December 8, 2004; interview with Banks Farris, June 28, 2005.

23. Interview with Elmer Harris, January 29, 2003; *Jefferson Advertiser News Magazine*, December 1, 1991, 28. Harris was speaking at Jefferson State Community College on November 19.

24. Interview with Art Beattie, May 11, 2005.

25. Interview with Elmer Harris, November 23, 2005.

26. *Annual Report*, Alabama Power Company, 1997, 27; 2000, 34.

27. Ibid.,1989, 17; 2000, 34; information from Donna Smith, June 2005.

28. Memo, Elmer Harris to Leah Atkins, March 31, 2005.

29. Interview with Carla Roberson, May 12, 2005.

30. Interview with Elmer Harris, January 29, 2003; *Powergrams*, September 4, 1995, 3.

31. Interview with Elmer Harris, January 29, 2003; memo, Elmer Harris to Leah Atkins, March 31, 2005; interviews with Jack Minor, May 12, November 24, 2005.

32. Interview with Elmer Harris, November 23, 2005.

33. Interviews with Art Beattie, May 4, 11, 2005.

34. Interview with Elmer Harris, December 8, 2004.

35. Joe Webb, "Thoughts About Alabama Power Company," June 15, 2005, in Leah Atkins's files.

36. Bruce Jones, interview during Mobile Division meeting, June 15, 2005; interview with Curtis Jones, June 30, 2005.

37. Ben Hutson, Bruce Jones, interviews during Mobile Division meeting, June 15, 2005; interview with Jerry W. Johnson, July 8, 2005; interview with Bill Johnson, June 1, 2005.

38. Interview with Bill Johnson, June 1, 2005; Banks Farris, biographical file; Bruce Jones, interview at Mobile Division meeting, June 15, 2005; interview with Banks Farris, June 23, 2005.

39. Interview with Bill Zales, July 1, 2005; interview with Banks Farris, June 23, 2005.

40. Interview with Banks Farris, June 28, 2005; interview with Bill Johnson, June 1, 2005; interviews at Mobile Division meeting, June 15, 2005.

41. Interview with Banks Farris, June 28, 2005; Bruce Jones, interview at Mobile Division meeting, June 15, 2005; interviews at Southern Division meeting, Montgomery, June 13, 2005; interview with Jerry W. Johnson, June 30, 2005.

42. Interviews at Southern Division meeting, Montgomery, June 13, 2005; interview with Elmer Harris, November 23, 2005.

43. Interview with Elmer Harris, July 6, 2005.

44. Interview with Banks Farris, June 28, 2005.

45. Interview with Bill Johnson, June 1, 2005; interviews at Southern Division meeting, Montgomery, June 13, 2005; interview with Curtis Jones, June 29, 2005.

46. Powergrams, May 23, 1994, 1, 4; Annual Report, Alabama Power Company, 1993, 22.

47. Powergrams, March 13, 1995, 1, 3; January 15, 1996, 1–2.

48. Ibid., May 1995, 1.

49. Interview with Elmer Harris, November 23, 2005.

50. Interview with Banks Farris, June 28, 2005; Powergrams, March 1988, 6–7; May 1989, 11–13; January 1990, 16; March 1990, 5; interview with Art Beattie, May 11, 2005.

51. Powergrams, September 13, 1993.

52. Interview with Elmer Harris, December 8, 2004.

53. Interview with Robert Holmes, July 13, 2004; interview with Elmer Harris, March 16, 2005; Annual Report, Alabama Power Company, 1991, 36.

54. Résumé, Christopher C. Womack; Annual Report, Alabama Power Company, 1993, 22; Powergrams, February 13, 1995.

55. Interview with Susan Story, August 26, 2004.

56. Interview with Brenda C. Faush, February 2, 2006; interview with Walter Heglar Jr., October 4, 2005; résumé, Walter Heglar Jr.

57. Powergrams, April 6, 1998, 3; Mobile Register, April 26, 1998; interview with Cheryl Thompson, November 15, 2004; interview with Banks Farris, June 28, 2005.

58. Interviews with Donna Smith, November 5, 2003, December 13, 2005; Powergrams, March 1988, 12–13; e-mail, Penny Morris Manuel to Leah Atkins, March 1, 2006; Annual Report, Alabama Power Company, 1998, 19.

59. Interview with Walter Graham, July 13, 2005.

60. Interviews with Marsha S. Johnson, November 10, 2003, July 13, 2005; Annual Report, Alabama Power Company, 2000, 36.

61. Powergrams, May 30, 1994, 2.

62. E-mail, Paula Martese Marino to Leah Atkins, April 4, 2006.

63. Interview with Doris Ingram, March 23, 2005.

64. E-mail, Carla Davis to Leah Atkins, February 28, 2006.

65. Interview with Joe Farley, August 19, 2005; Annual Report, Alabama Power Company, 1989, 2; Articles of Incorporation, filed October 31, 1989, copy in corporate archives. The articles were amended in 1991 to fit with the Internal Revenue Code of 1989 and to allow scholarships to eligible children of Alabama Power Company employees. See amendment to Article III, filed March 11, 1991, in Alabama Power Foundation file. Interview with Bill Zales, July 1, 2005.

66. Interview with Elmer Harris, January 29, 2003.

67. Annual Report, Alabama Power Foundation, 1992, 5.

68. "Outline of Growth and Development of Electric Properties" [2.1.2.66.5]; interview with Elmer Harris, January 29, 2003; Martin, Electricity in Alabama, 32. Powergrams reported on May 1, 1995 (page 3), that the canyon became an Alabama Power Company property in 1917 when Alabama Power absorbed Little River Power Company, but Alabama Traction, Light & Power acquired it much earlier. There is correspondence between James Mitchell and his Birmingham manager W. W. Freeman during 1913 involving certain pending claims against the Little River Canyon operation that Electric Bond & Share was to have settled before transferring the property to Alabama Traction. Mitchell evidently accomplished this transaction in the summer and fall of 1912. See W. W. Freeman to James Mitchell, July 16, 1913 [3.1.1.41.9].

69. Interview with Elmer Harris, January 29, 2003; interview with Bill Johnson, June 1, 2005.

70. Elmer Harris insert for Powergrams on Little River Canyon National Preserve, no date but after April 19, 1995.

71. Powergrams, May 1, 1995, 1, 3. There was not a ground survey made of the land conveyed to the United States Department of Interior, National Park Service, but the best estimate was about 8,580 acres, which is probably why the figure is sometimes given as 8,500 acres to round it off. Jerry D. Roberson to James L. Scott and Leah R. Atkins, e-mail, June 22, 2005.

72. Interview with Bill Johnson, June 1, 2005.

73. Inspiring Investments: Goals and Strategies for the Alabama Power Foundation (1992), 15–22, 36.

74. Annual Report, Alabama Power Foundation, 1993, 3.

75. Ibid., 1994, 5.

76. Interview with Bill Johnson, June 1, 2005; interview with Elmer Harris, January 29, 2003.

77. Annual Report, Alabama Power Foundation, 1997, 3; interview with Bill Johnson, June 1, 2005.

78. Interview with Elmer Harris, December 8, 2004; information from minutes of Alabama Power Service Organization, courtesy of Don Franklin and Carla Roberson, and Powergrams, March 27, 2000, 2; e-mail, Patsy Topazi to Leah Atkins, March 1, 2006.

79. Interviews with Glenda Harris, March 23, May 12, 2003; Farley, Balch, and Conway, "'Good Name and Destiny,'" 159.

80. Walter Baker, Energizers History (Birmingham: Alabama Power Foundation, 2000), 1–4.

81. Interview with Walter Baker, February 10, 2004; Baker, Energizers, 6–14.

82. Jefferson Advertiser News Magazine, December 1, 1991, 28.

83. Flynt, Alabama in the Twentieth Century, 165, 233.

84. Powergrams, March 21, 1994, 3.

85. Ibid., June 20, 1994, 3.

86. Ibid., May 1, 1995, 2; interview with Elmer Harris, November 23, 2005; and interview with Robbie Roberts, August 4, 2006.

87. Powergrams, December 1990, 10–11.

88. Program, Plant Miller Dedication, October 18, 1991.

89. Powergrams, January 24, 1994, 2; July 4, 1994, 1; January 9, 1995, 1.

90. Information from Bob Waters.

91. Powergrams, December 1989, 1–6; January 1990, 18.

92. David Lewis, "Andrew: A Rambling Account," copy courtesy of M. Stephen Daniel, Alabama Power engineer, who was co-director of the storm team with Lewis in restoration work after Hurricane Andrew.

93. Powergrams, May 1993, 1–5.

94. Ibid., 14–20.

95. Annual Report, Alabama Public Service Commission, 2002, 12; interview with Judy McLean, June 1, 2004.

96. Powergrams, August 14, 1995, 1.

97. Ibid., September 6, 1995, 1; October 16, 1995 1–2.

98. Ibid., April 1990, 8–10; November 20, 1995, 2.

99. Interview with Elmer Harris, March 23, 2005.

100. Ibid.; interview with Neal Wade, June 1, 2005.

101. Charlotte Hood, "Ten Islands Historic Park Dedication, Neely Henry Dam, May 18, 1993"; clippings, [Talladega-Sylacauga-Pell City] The Daily Home, May 19, 1993; Birmingham News, May 24, 1993; St. Clair News-Aegis, June 3, 1993, all in corporate archives.

102. Interview with Don Erwin, May 6, 2005; International Herald Tribune, January 28, 1993, copy courtesy of Don Erwin.

103. Stewart, "James E. Folsom Jr.," in Webb and Armbrester, Alabama Governors, 255–56; interview with James E. Folsom Jr., January 6, 2005.

104. Interview with Elmer Harris, May 6, 2005.

105. Interview with Neal Wade, June 1, 2005.

106. Elmer Harris to Garry Neil Drummond, July 31, 1991, in Elmer Harris files.

107. Interview with Elmer Harris, May 5, 2005; interview with James E. Folsom Jr., January 6, 2005.

108. Interview with Anthony Topazi, January 10, 2006; typed notes courtesy of Anthony Topazi.

109. Interview with Derry Bunting, May 8, 2005; interview with Don Erwin, May 6, 2005.

110. Typed notes courtesy of Anthony Topazi.

111. Interview with Elmer Harris, November 23, 2005; Powergrams, October 11, 1993, 1.

112. Interview with James E. Folsom Jr., January 6, 2005; interview with Anthony Topazi, January 10, 2006; typed notes courtesy of Anthony Topazi.

113. Interviews with Elmer Harris, May 5, November 23, 2005.

114. Interview with James F. Hughey, February 6, 2006.

115. Interview with James E. Folsom Jr., January 6, 2005.

116. Ibid.

117. Powergrams, October 11, 1993, 2; interview with Anthony Topazi, January 10, 2006.

118. Powergrams, October 11, 1993, 1.

119. Ibid.

120. Ibid., May 16, 1994, 1–2.

121. Ibid., February 14, 1994, 2.

122. Ibid., February 21, 1994, 1; July 24, 1995, 1. Using discretionary powers, FERC granted a forty-year license instead of a fifty-year license.

123. Ibid., September 15, 2000, 1.

124. David E. Miller and Charles M. Stover, "Computer Forecasting: The Future of Hydro Management," Hydro Review, June 1994, 40–44.

125. Environmental Quick Reference Guide, Alabama Power, 2000; interview with Willard Bowers, May 3, 2005; Earth Day, 1990: Alabama Power Company Protecting Our Environment; interview with Willard Bowers, August 29, 2005.

126. Environmental Overview, Alabama Power, 2000.

127. Prudence Review 1990, Clean Air Act Amendments, 1–4, copy courtesy of Karl R. Moor.

128. The Southern Company Strategic Plan, 1991, 11.

129. Prudence Review 1990, Clean Air Act Amendments, 17, copy courtesy of Karl R. Moor.

130. Our Environmental Commitment, Southern Company, 2000; Annual Report, Alabama Power Company, 1991, 22; 1992, 30; 2000, 12; 2001, 12.

131. Corporate Policy, Compliance with Laws and Regulations, No. I-8, January 31, 1992.

132. Corporate Policy, Environmental Policy, No.1–10, September 16, 1992,10.

133. Annual Report, Alabama Power Company, 2001, 12.

134. Environmental Overview, Alabama Power, 2000.

135. Annual Report, Alabama Power Company, 2000, 12; 2001, 12; Corporate Policy, Environmental Policy, No.1–10, September 16, 1992.

136. Environmental Quick Reference Guide, Alabama Power, 2000.

137. Powergrams, January 3, 1994, 3.

138. William H. Stewart, "Fob James Jr.," in Webb and Armbrester, Alabama Governors, 246–47; Powergrams, January 2, 1995, 3.

139. Powergrams, May 5, 1997, 1–2; interview with Gordon G. Martin, November 9, 2004.

140. Powergrams, February 13, 1995, 1; September 18, 1995, 1–2.

141. Alabama Power Company et al. vs. Tennessee Valley Authority et al., January 12, 1996; Jay Reeves, "Southern Company Divisions Sue TVA Over Power Sales," Associated Press News Release, January 12, 1996, and draft of letter from Gordon G. Martin to various parties, January 12, 1996, copies in Conway files.

142. Powergrams, September 23, 1996, 1–3.

143. Ibid., May 5, 1997, 1–2.

144. Montgomery Advertiser, December 14; Mobile Register, December 15; Birmingham Post-Herald, December 15, 1992.

145. Powergrams, August 22, 1994, 1–2.

146. Ibid., September 1990, 2; interview with Rod Mundy, August 5, 2005.

147. Powergrams, January 1993, 9; November 1993, 1. Leonard

S. Hyman, Andrew S. Hyman, and Robert C. Hyman, *America's Electric Utilities: Past, Present and Future* (Vienna, Va.: Public Utilities Reports, 2000), 184–85. The act is also referred to as National Energy Act. A good discussion of stranded costs and these issues, although it is from an advocate of deregulation and competition, may be found in the book by a consultant on competition in the electrical industry, Sally Hunt, *Making Competition Work in Electricity* (New York: John Wiley & Sons, 2002), 39–40, 262–63.

148. *Powergrams*, January 2, 1995, 1, 3.

149. Interview with Donald W. Reese, July 13, 2005.

150. *Powergrams*, May 20, 1996, 1; April 28, 1997, 1; interview with Elmer Harris, November 23, 2005.

151. Bill Guthrie biographical file; interviews with Charles D. McCrary, August 19, 2004, June 21, 2005; Hunt, *Making Competition Work*, 65–66; Loren Fox, *Enron: The Rise and Fall* (New York: John Wiley & Sons, 2003), 111–13.

152. Charles McCrary's Video & Speech, Southern Company Generation, September 14, 1998; interview with Charles McCrary, August 22, 2003.

153. Interview with Elmer Harris, March 23, 2005; *Powergrams*, May 20, 1996, 1; Fox, *Enron*, 67–68, 196–200.

154. Interview with Charles D. McCrary, June 21, 2005; interview with Jerry L. Stewart, September 7, 2004; *Annual Report*, Alabama Power Company, 2000, 10.

155. *Powergrams*, September 11, 1995.

156. Technology information provided by Bob Waters.

157. Ibid.

158. *Powergrams*, January 16, 1995, 1; January 5, 1998, 1; interview with Elmer Harris, December 8, 2004.

159. *Annual Report*, Alabama Power Company, 2000, 1–3, 6–9.

160. *Powergrams*, February 28, 2000, 4–5.

161. Interview with Elmer Harris, July 6, 2005.

162. Interview with John Young, August 1, 2005.

163. Interview with Joe Farley, August 15, 2005; interview with Allen Franklin, July 26, 2005.

164. Interview with Walter Johnsey, October 22, 2004.

165. Interview with Bill Johnson, June 1, 2005.

Chapter Eleven

1. Minutes, Board of Directors, Alabama Power Company, April 26, 2001. The evening meeting was held in Prattville before the regular board meeting scheduled for the following day. This was Rev. John Porter's last board meeting after announcing his retirement, and there was a dinner that night in his honor at the Legends Hotel at Capitol Hill in Prattville.

2. Memorandum, Bill Dahlberg to Southern Company Executives, May 19, 1999. Franklin's appointment was to become effective on June 1, 1999. He became CEO on March 1, 2001, and chairman of the board effective April 2, 2001.

3. *Powergrams*, February 21, 2001, 3; special issue, April 30, 2001, 1.

4. Interview with Joe Farley, May 12, 2005.

5. Ibid., July 12, 2005.

6. *Birmingham News*, October 26, 2001. Harris planned to work with the nonprofit think tank, Public Policy Group of Alabama, which he founded with two former Alabama governors, Albert Brewer and Jim Folsom Jr.

7. Interview with Joe Farley, January 5, 2005.

8. Interview with Allen Franklin, July 26, 2005; interview with Charles D. McCrary, August 19, 2003; interview with Douglas McCrary, November 14, 2003.

9. *Birmingham News*, July 16, 2002, has an article about McCrary's jukeboxes and hobbies of taking things apart and restoring them. Interview with Bill Frederick, October 20, 2004.

10. Interview with Charles D. McCrary, June 21, 2005.

11. Interview with Jim Turner, July 14, 2004.

12. *Annual Report*, Alabama Public Service Commission, 2002, 4, 24; interview with Zeke Smith, October 27, 2005.

13. *Powergrams*, March 1992, 6.

14. Ibid., October 18, 1993.

15. Interview with Steve Spencer, August 25, 2005.

16. Interview with John Young, August 1, 2005.

17. Interview with C. Alan Martin, August 30, 2004; Power Notice, memo from Charles D. McCrary, April 30, 2001; *Powergrams*, May 7, 2001; interview with Mike Scott, September 27, 2005.

18. Interview with Steve R. Spencer, September 13, 2004; *Birmingham News*, March 16, 2003.

19. Power Notice, memo from Charles D. McCrary, April 30, 2001; *Powergrams*, May 7, 2001.

20. Interview with John O. Hudson III, February 7, 2006.

21. Interview with Elaine Kwarcinski, March 27, 2006.

22. Charles D. McCrary to My Fellow Employees, August 16, 2002.

23. *Birmingham News*, May 20, 2001.

24. *Birmingham Business Journal*, December 28, 2001.

25. Charles D. McCrary to all Alabama Power officers, managers, supervisors, and budget coordinators, August 15, 2001; interview with John O. Hudson III, February 7, 2006.

26. Charles D. McCrary, "Electric utilities are an unpredictable business," *Birmingham Business Journal*, January 4, 2002.

27. Charles D. McCrary to My Fellow Employees, September 11, 2001.

28. *Birmingham News*, September 20, October 26, December 4, 2001.

29. Interview with Randy Mayfield, June 29, 2005; Charles D. McCrary to My Fellow Employees, October 5, 2001.

30. Interview with Randy Mayfield, June 29, 2005; interview with Lyle Mitchell, December 16, 2005.

31. Memo from Charles D. McCrary, April 30, 2001; Elmer Harris, Biographical Sketch, November 2001, courtesy of Elmer Harris; interview with Steve R. Spencer, August 25, 2005.

32. Interview with Steve Fant, September 13, 2005.

33. Interview with Charles D. McCrary, August 30, 2005.

34. *Powergrams*, December 30, 2002, 1, 3; interview with Charles D. McCrary, August 30, 2005.

35. Interview with Chris Bell, August 24, 2004; interview with Steve R. Spencer, August 25, 2005.

36. Alabama Power Company, Economic Development Strategic Plan, 2002–2007. All economic development materials are from the economic development files.

37. Christopher T. Bell to various company leaders, May 20, 2002.

38. *Powergrams*, May 20, 2002, 1–2, 7–8.

39. Steve R. Spencer to Alabama Power Management Council and Department Heads, May 31, 2002.

40. Chris Bell, Economic Development, Presentation, July 2002.

41. Chris Bell to Leah Atkins, August 8, 2005; Chris Bell to targeted participants in Economic and Community Development Forums, December 3, Prattville, and December 5, 2002, Birmingham.

42. Interview with Jerry Stewart, September 7, 2004.

43. Christopher T. Bell to Charles D. McCrary, February 4, 2004.

44. *Powergrams*, May 5, 2003, 1, 3.

45. Christopher T. Bell to William B. Hutchins, May 27, 2004.

46. Interviews with Chris Bell and Steve Spencer, March 7, 2006; Impact of Economic Development Projects, Alabama Power Company, 2005.

47. Interview with Charles D. McCrary, May 4, 2005; interview with Willard Bowers, November 23, 2005.

48. U.S. Environmental Protection Agency, *Acid Rain Program*, 2003 *Progress Report*, September 2004, 1, 3, 7; interview with Willard Bowers, November 23, 2005; Alabama Power Company 2004 Strategic Issues Survey, December 8–20, 2004, 22.

49. Interview with Willard Bowers, May 3, 2005; *The Environment Counts at Alabama Power*, brochure.

50. Carl Carmer, *Stars Fell on Alabama* (1934; reprint, Tuscaloosa: University of Alabama Press, 1985), 81.

51. *Birmingham Post-Herald*, December 19, 2003.

52. U.S. Environmental Protection Agency, *National Air Quality and Emissions Trends Report*, 2003, 59–60. The Birmingham metropolitan district was a nonattainment area in ozone and was classified as moderate.

53. Charts, Alabama Power Company, Environmental Department.

54. *Powergrams*, June 17, 2002, 1–4; July 1, 2002, 1.

55. Ibid., April 8, 2002, 1–2; June 17, 2002, 1–4; July 1, 2002, 1.

56. Interview with Willard Bowers, November 23, 2005; *Birmingham News*, May 30, 2003.

57. The Particle Pollution Report, Environmental Protection Agency, 2003, 1; Annual Fossil Generation and Emission Rate Reductions, 1990–2004.

58. Willard Bowers to *Anniston Star*, May 13, 2005.

59. *Annual Report*, Alabama Power Company, 2001, 13; 2002, 13–15; 2003, 9–11; 2004, 9; *Birmingham News*, June 7, 2005. U.S. district judge Virginia Hopkins took issue with the EPA on a number of key points, including that the EPA had been too inconsistent in interpreting the New Source Review.

60. See filings April 24, 2006, in U.S. District Court, Northern District of Alabama, Southern Division, Case No. 2:01-cv-000152-VEH; *Birmingham News*, April 25, 2006; *United States v. Alabama Power Co.*, No. 01-0152 (N.D. Ala. Aug. 14, 2006).

61. *Powergrams*, March 24, 2003, 1.

62. Ibid., December 16, 2002, 1, 3; March 24, 2003, 1; July 14, 2003, 1; October 10, 2005.

63. Southern Company, *Environmental Progress Report*, 2003, 17.

64. Interview with Willard Bowers, September 26, 2005; Southern Company also offered solar. See Our Environmental Commitment, *EarthCents Solar*, Southern Company, flyer, 2005.

65. Information from Willard Bowers, November 30, 2005.

66. See packet of material on Operation Enduring Family, revised March 28, 2003, in Operation Enduring Family file, in files of Betsy Shearron.

67. Charles D. McCrary, Family Counts Day; Wrap-Up Report, Family Counts; Power Notice, March 6, 2003, files of Betsy Shearron.

68. *Powergrams*, October 20, 2003.

69. *Highlights*, Southern Company, September 20, 2004, 1.

70. Interview with Robin Hurst, September 13, 2005.

71. *Highlights*, October 11, 2004, 1, 6; *Birmingham News*, September 19, 24, 2004.

72. Interview with Vicki Grimsley, September 17, 2004; interviews with Carrie Kurlander, September 16, 19, 2005; press release, Alabama Power Company, September 18, 2004; *Birmingham News*, September 19, 2004.

73. Donald Boyd, "High Level Talking Points on Mutual Assistance."

74. *Birmingham Post-Herald*, September 21, 2004; *Birmingham News*, September 21, 2004; Charles D. McCrary to My Fellow Employees, September 20, 2004; *Powergrams*, special edition, September 23, 2004, 1–4.

75. *Mobile Register*, September 11, 2005.

76. *Powergrams*, September 19, 2005.

77. Power Delivery Update, Tuesday, August 30, 2005, 7:30 A.M., gives totals as 634,654. The additional outages came later as the storm moved into the Western and Birmingham Divisions. Mark Williams, "Transmission system takes hit," *Highlights*, Southern Company, September 26, 2005.

78. E-mail, Daniel K. Glover to Leah Atkins, January 17, 2006.

79. *Wall Street Journal*, September 8, 2005.

80. E-mail and notes, Bob Waters to Leah Atkins, November 7, 8, 12, 2005.

81. Anthony Topazi to Mississippi Power employees, *Today's Dialogue*, Mississippi Power Company, September 12, 2005; interview with Robin Hurst, October 7, 2005; interview with Anthony Topazi, January 10, 2006.

82. Carrie Kurlander, notes from telephone conversation between Rebecca Smith of the *Wall Street Journal* and Robin Hurst, September 1, 2005.

83. Interview with Scott Bishop, September 22, 2005; *Powergrams*, September 9, 2005, 1.

84. E-mail, Marshall Ramsey to Leah Atkins, March 22, 2006.

85. Interview with Scott Bishop, September 22, 2005.

86. *Powergrams*, April 4, 2005, 3, 4.

87. E-mail, Ron Campbell to Leah Atkins, November 12, 2005.

88. E-mail, Randy Plyler to Leah Atkins, November 7, 2005.

89. Ibid.

90. E-mail, Richard H. Greene to Leah Atkins, October 31, 2005.

91. Ronald Glenn Parsons to Leah Atkins, November 1, 2005. See Alabama Control Center Strategic Plan, and also brochure, *Alabama Power's Alabama Control Center*.

92. Information from Bob Waters, November 1, 2005.

93. Interview with Julia Segars, August 31, 2004; e-mail, Julia Segars to Leah Atkins, May 1, 2006.

94. Interviews with Carla Roberson, May 12, 2005, January 30, 2006; interview with Steve Spencer, January 30, 2006.

95. Charles D. McCrary, Tuskegee Airmen Convention, August 4, 2004, CR-Rom.

96. Interview with Carla Roberson, October 6, 2005.

97. Interview with Bill Johnson, June 1, 2005.

98. See charts, Alabama Power Company: Total Retail Revenue; Residential, Commercial & Industrial Revenue; Total Retail Energy Sales, from Mike Scott.

99. Interview with Mike Scott, August 3, 2005; brochure, *Alabama Power Retail Marketing Strategy*.

100. Interviews with Mike Scott, August 3, September 29, December 1, 2005.

101. *Powergrams*, August 22, 2005, 1.

102. List of Exhibits, No. 91, General Manager's Report for 1919 [3.1.1.19.12].

103. The property was sold by Alabama Power Development Company (the EBASCO holding company) to Mitchell through Alabama Traction on July 22, 1912, and was ratified by all the boards of directors of these small companies on July 28, 1912. Alabama Traction became an operating company on that date. However, these assets were not folded into Alabama Power Company until July 28, 1913. Tom Martin gives this date as the date when Alabama Power became an operating company. This explains why he says the Gadsden Steam Plant was completed only a few days after Alabama Power acquired it, because when Mitchell purchased it the previous year, the steam plant at Gadsden was described as being under construction. See Martin, *Electricity in Alabama*, 31–36; History and Development of Alabama Power Company and Its Properties, ca. 1948, 26–28 [2.1.1.56.20]; Annual Report, Alabama Traction, Light & Power Company, 1913, 5.

104. History and Development of Alabama Power Company and Its Properties, ca. 1948, 22–27 [2.1.1.56.20]; Grace Hooten Gates, *The Model City of the New South: Anniston, Alabama, 1872–1900* (1978; reprint with new preface, Tuscaloosa: University of Alabama Press, 1996), 3–4, 40–41; *Powergrams*, May 1982, 22–23.

105. *Powergrams*, May 1982, 3–4.

106. Ibid., September 1987, 12–14.

107. Interviews at Eastern Division meeting, September 21, 2005.

108. Ibid.

109. *Powergrams*, July 20, 2005, 1, 4; *Birmingham News*, July 25, 2005.

110. Interview with William R. "Ronnie" Smith and Buddy Eiland, September 21, 2005.

111. Ronnie Smith to Leah Atkins, October 5, 2005.

112. Interview with Ronnie Smith and comments of others at Eastern Division meeting, September 21, 2005.

113. Statistics courtesy of Larry Kikker, accounting.

114. E-mail, Julia H. Segars to Leah Atkins, April 24, 2006.

115. Interview with Roy Lamon and comments of others at Western Division meeting, July 20, 2005.

116. *Powergrams*, September 1982, 1.

117. Ibid., 2; interview with Lucy Wallace and comments of others at Southern Division meeting, June 13, 2005; *Powergrams*, June 1990, 6–7.

118. Interview with Dot Scott, Gordon G. Martin, and Elaine Lassiter at Southern Division meeting, June 13, 2005.

119. Wayne Greenhaw, *Montgomery: The River City* (Montgomery: River City Publishing, 2002), 120–22; Jerome A. Ennels and Wesley Phillip Newton, *The Wisdom of Eagles: A History of Maxwell Air Force Base* (Montgomery: River City Publishing, 2002), 14–17; interview with Gordon G. Martin, October 18, 2005.

120. Interview with Curtis Jones, Gordon G. Martin, Steve Sprayberry, and Charlie Britton at Southern Division meeting, June 13, 2005.

121. Interview with Gordon G. Martin, November 9, 2004; Biographical Sketch, Gordon G. Martin.

122. Statistics courtesy of Larry Kikker, accounting.

123. E-mail, Gordon G. Martin to Leah Atkins, October 5, 2005.

124. Interviews at Southern Division meeting, June 13, 2005; e-mail, Gordon G. Martin to Leah Atkins, October 18, 2005.

125. *Annual Report*, Alabama Power Company, 1923, 10–11; Roy Lamon, questionnaire and interview at Western Division meeting, July 20, 2005; *Powergrams*, October 1982, 1–3.

126. *Powergrams*, October 1982, 1–2.

127. Interview with Terry Waters, October 11, 2004.

128. *Powergrams*, October 1982, 4–27.

129. Questionnaires from Brenda Randall, Emily Rogers, and Elaine Acker, comments by J. G. Brazil, and interviews at Western Division meeting, July 20, 2005.

130. Questionnaires from Brenda Randall and Michael R. Burroughs and interviews at Western Division meeting, July 20, 2005.

131. Questionnaire from Roy Lamon and interview with Terry Waters at Western Division meeting, July 20, 2005.

132. Interview with Terry Waters, October 11, 2004; biographical information, Terry H. Waters; Financial Update, speech by Terry Waters, May 5, 2005; interview with Roy Lamon, October 2, 2005.

133. Interview with Foots Mathews and Mildred Hutchins and interviews at Western Division meeting, July 20, 2005; statistics courtesy of Larry Kikker, accounting.

134. Frank S. Keeler, "Talk Before the Mobile Traffic & Transportation Club," February 14, 1950, 1; *Mobile Register*, February 22, 1919.

135. Questionnaires from Chuck Hrabe and Mary Jo Hrabe and comments at Mobile Division meeting, June 15, 2005.

136. Ibid.

137. *Powergrams*, March 1982, 1–2.

138. *Annual Report*, Alabama Power Company, 1942, 5; Cronenberg, "Mobile and World War II," in Thomason, *Mobile*, 217.

139. *Powergrams*, March 1982, 7; Bill McDonough, comments at Mobile Division meeting, June 15, 2005.

140. *Powergrams*, March 1982, 1–2; statistics courtesy of Larry

Kikker, accounting.

141. Bruce Jones, comments at Mobile Division meeting, June 15, 2005; *Powergrams*, March 1982, 19–21.

142. Sam Covert interview with John H. Finklea, April 30, 2004; John H. Finklea, historical essay, in Finklea file.

143. *Mobile Register*, April 26, 1998; interview with Cheryl Thompson, November 15, 2004; *Partners for Growth*, pamphlet, Mobile Area Chamber of Commerce.

144. The Courtaulds Fibers plant was on the site of Old Mobile, the 1702 French town on the Mobile River. Alabama Power also owned land that was part of this site. See Gregory A. Waselkov, *Old Mobile Archaeology* (Tuscaloosa: University of Alabama Press, 2005), 62.

145. Interview with Ben Hutson, June 22, 2005; comments at Mobile Division meeting, June 15, 2005.

146. E-mail, Cheryl G. Thompson to Leah Atkins, September 28, 2005.

147. Interview with Charles D. McCrary, October 12, 2005.

148. Interviews at Southeast Division meeting, July 26, 2005; *Powergrams*, January 1983, 6–7; Robert H. Flewellen, *Along Broad Street: A History of Eufaula, Alabama, 1823–1984* (Eufaula, 1991), 302.

149. Flewellen, *Along Broad Street*, 264.

150. *Powergrams*, January 1983, 23–33.

151. Val L. McGee, *The Origins of Fort Rucker* (Ozark: Dale County Historical Society, 1987), 105–19; *Powergrams*, January 1983, 26; statistics courtesy of Larry Kikker, accounting.

152. John Grimes, comments and interviews at Southeast Division meeting, July 26, 2005.

153. *Powergrams*, January 1983, 9.

154. Margaret Slade, comments and interviews at Southeast Division meeting, July 26, 2005.

155. John R. Mills and George Simpkins, comments and interviews at Southeast Division meeting, July 26, 2005.

156. E-mail, R. Michael Saxon to Leah Atkins, September 19, 2005.

157. *Annual Report*, Alabama Power Company, 1952, 13, 17; statistics courtesy of Larry Kikker, accounting.

158. Information from Gerald Johnson, October 4, 2005; interview with Gerald Johnson, November 17, 2005.

159. E-mail, Gerald Johnson to Leah Atkins, November 23, 2005.

160. Interview with Bruce Jones, September 12, 2005; interview with Homer Turner, October 3, 2005.

161. E-mail, Gerald Johnson to Leah Atkins, November 23, 2005.

162. Interview with Homer Turner, October 3, 2005.

163. Interview with Bruce Jones, September 12, 2005.

164. *Birmingham Business Journal*, June 13, 2003.

165. Video of Business Forum; Special 2003 insert in *Powergrams*, April 2003.

166. *Annual Report*, Alabama Power Company, 2004, 4.

167. Jerry L. Stewart, 2006 Business Forum presentation; *Powergrams*, January 23, 2006, 1, 3; *Powergrams* 2006 insert; Alan Martin, 2006 Business Forum presentation; information from Charlie Shaw, March 2, 2006.

168. *Birmingham News*, February 15, 2002.

169. Ibid., May 19, 2002.

170. E-mail, John Ashford to Leah Atkins, November 16, 2005.

171. Charles D. McCrary's talking points on the Black Belt, n.d.; statistics from Alabama Development Office, May 1, 2006.

172. *Birmingham News*, March 15, 16, 17, 2006.

173. Christopher T. Bell, "Thoughts on Economic and Community Development," September 25, 2005.

174. Charles D. McCrary, Economic Development Stump Speech, 2005.

175. Interview with Willard Bowers, May 3, 2005.

Construction crew erecting
a four-pole wood and steel
transmission tower on the
Bessemer-Warrior line,
December 16, 1918.

Index

Henry, H. Neely, 236, 268, 292, 333–43, 575

Henslee, R. Kent, 577

Herring, Clyde, 530

Hess, Emil, 576

Heys, Samuel, xix

Hicks, Joyce, xxiii

Hickson, Joe, 545

Hight, Sandra, xx

Hildreth, Emmett F., 179

Hill, Lister, 187–89, 193, 228–29, 244, 270, 272, 276, 278, 448

Hilliard, Georgia, 237

Hillman Hospital, 118

Hines, Anita, xxii

Hinman, David, 368, 511

History of the Southern Research Institute, 251

Hitchcock, Edith, 241

Hiwassee Dam, 229

Hixon, J. F., 237

Hobbie, Richard Martin, 89, 230, 574

Hocutt, Owen W. "Woody", 236

Hodnette, Toppy, xxvi

Hohenberg, Adolphe, 26

Holland, David, 290

Holland, J. W., 245

Holley, J. M., 26

Holley, Robert W., 586

Hollingsworth and Whitney, 219

Hollingsworth, John F., 401

Holmes, Judge Oliver Wendell, 55

Holmes, Robert, xxiii, 376–77, 436, 467, 495, 509

Holt Lock and Dam, 285, 333, 335

Holt, Henry, 586

home demonstration agents, 119, 127

home service department, 119, 208, 631 (n.137)

Honda, 515, 539

Honda plant, 495, 538–39

Hood, Charlotte, 483

Hood, James, 321

Hood, O. R., 28, 41, 244, 573

Hood, Walter M., 89, 109, 212, 237, 574

Hooper, William L., Jr., 327

Hoover, President Herbert, 164, 171–72, 181–82

Hopper, Bill, 331

Hopper, Clara, xx

Hornady, John R., 102, 228

Horne Alabama Railway Power Company, 34

Horne, Henry, 19, 26

Horseshoe Bend National Military Park, 308

Horseshoe Bend, 3, 307–08

Houston County, 345

Howard, Bob, 515, 558

Howard, George Leland, 377

Howard, Harold, 207

Howard, R. E., Jr., 226

Howard University, 36

Howell Mills Shoals, 273

Howell, Henry E., Jr., 352

Hrabe, Chuck, 547

Hrabe, Mary Jo, 547

Hubbard, Preston J., 92

Hudson, John O., III, 509–10

Huffman, Robert E., 421, 459

Hughey, James F., Jr., 487

Huguley, Norma, 481

Hume, Richard R., 391

Hundred Days Congress, 192

Hunt Refining, 545

Hunt, Governor Guy, 449, 484

Hunter, Charles T., 269, 361, 552–53, 587

Hunter, J. T., 52

Hunter, Marshall K., 576

Huntly, Scotland, 17

Huntsville Railway, Light and Power Company, 40, 605 (n.48)

Huntsville, 16, 69–70, 124–25, 147, 212–13

Hurricane Andrew, 478–79

Hurricane Camille, 414, 525

Hurricane Dennis, 521, 524, 567

Hurricane Elena, 418

Hurricane Eloise, 373, 637 (n.210)

Hurricane Erin, 481

Hurricane Frederick, 413–20

Hurricane Hugo, 478–79

Hurricane Isabel, 521

Hurricane Ivan, 521, 524, 526, 567

Hurricane Katrina, 521, 524, 526–28, 550, 567

Hurricane Opal, 481–82, 522, 528

Hurst, Linda, 474

Hurst, Robin, xxi, 414–17, 459, 522–23, 526–27, 531

Huston, Claudius H., 96–97

Hutchins, Mildred, 545–46

Hutchins, Priscilla, 474

Hutchins, William B. "Bruce", xxi, 354–55, 396, 424–26, 447, 450, 459, 473–74

Hutson, Ben W., 414, 463, 549, 586

hydro relicensing, 442

Hyundai, 515, 543

IBEW *see* International Brotherhood of Electrical Workers

Ickes, Harold L., 193, 223

Independent Union of Alabama Power Employees, 221

industrial development, 9, 293

Industries Light & Power Company, 32

Ingalls, R. I., 574

Ingram, Bob, 367

Ingram, Doris, xviii, 458–59, 467

Insull, Samuel, 57, 159–60, 176, 186, 191

interconnection, 135

International Brotherhood of Electrical Workers, 122, 220–22, 268, 326–32, 368, 432, 434, 436, 438

International Life Insurance Company of St. Louis, 22

Inzer, J. Clarence, 276, 289, 576

I Remember Gorgas, 122

Ivy, James Roland, 554

Izaak Walton League, 291

Jackson County, 5, 178

Jackson Shoals, 47, 57, 69, 72, 535

Jackson, Andrew, 3, 153, 307, 483

Jackson, Cecil, 335

Jackson, Charles P., 345, 376

Jackson, Ervin, 575

Jackson, Harvey H., III, 4–5, 43, 51, 54, 118, 133

Jackson, John, 238

Jackson, L. W., 585

Jackson, Philip C., Jr., 576

Jackson, S. W., 26

Jackson, T. K., 547, 574

Jackson, Mississippi, 135

Jackson's Gap, 37

Jacksonville (Florida) Electric Authority, 384, 427

James, Carl, 155, 254, 574

James, Governor Forrest, Jr., 405, 407, 410, 419, 424, 493, 498

Jasper, 418

Jefferson County, 6, 179

Jelks, Governor William D., 23

J. M. Starke's University School, 23

Jenkins, Ellen, xx

Jent, Billy Eugene, 565

Johns, John D., 578

Johnsey, Walter, xxi, 267–68, 292–93, 339, 344–46, 354, 367, 370, 383, 385, 388–89, 421, 423–24, 503, 576

Johnson, Bill, xxi, 463, 473, 532

Johnson, Crawford T., III, 576

Johnson, Crawford, Jr. 575

Johnson, Evans C., 64, 79

Johnson, Gerald xxi, 553–54, 587

Johnson, Jerry W., 464

Johnson, Lyndon B., 322, 337

Johnson, Marsha S., xxi, 437, 469, 553, 587

Johnson, Milton Jerrell "Jerry", 487

Johnson, Thomas D., 113–14, 220, 238

Johnson, Tom, 114

Johnson, William B., 586

Johnson, Wylie, 318, 323

Johnston, Forney, 195

Johnston Governor Joseph F., 7, 23

Johnston, Margaret F., 237

Johnstone, Douglas, 370

Johnstone, Harry M., 258

Johnstown tragedy, 28–29

Joiner, W. Hubert, 145

Jones, Bob, 272, 276–77, 289

Jones, Carl E., Jr., 577

Jones, Curtis, 374, 542

Jones, Henry C., 20, 22, 26, 154

Jones, J. Bruce, xxi, 414, 417, 460, 463, 468–69, 548, 553–54, 586

Jones, Jimmie, 199

Jones, John D., 376

Jones, Julius, 52

Jones, Linda E., 474

Jones, Macie, 238

Jones, Madison, 222

Jones, Thomas G., 603 (n.179)

Jordan Dam, 26, 41, 68, 144, 152, 205, 222, 226, 233, 264, 279, 281, 305, 307, 333–34, 373–75, 547, 562

Jordan No. 2 Development, see Bouldin Dam

Jordan, Ann Spivey, 14, 153, 597 (n. 7)

Jordan, Elmira Sophia, 153, 596 (n.1)

Jordan, Reuben, 153

Jowers, J. O. "Buddy", 212

Joyes, J. W., 82, 85, 103

J. P. Morgan & Company, 169

Junior Achievement, 305

Karst, Keith, 525

KDKA, 123

Keahey, Tabby, xx

Kearns, Raphael Elmore, 236

Keeler, Frank S., 233, 296, 547, 586

Keep Alabama Beautiful, 490, 516

Kelly Creek, 289

Kelly Ingram Park, 316, 320

Kelly, Richard Bledsole, Jr., 178–180, 618 (n.57)

Kellyton, 154

Kennedy, John F., 322, 326, 337

Kennedy, Robert, 322

Kennedy, Sam, 109

Kennedy, Ted, 476

Kennedy, Walter, 576

Kent, 133

Kenyon, A. L., 585